Queen Elizabeth II

Queen Elizabeth II

AN ORAL HISTORY

Deborah Hart Strober
& Gerald Strober

PEGASUS BOOKS

NEW YORK LONDON

QUEEN ELIZABETH II

Pegasus Books, Ltd.
148 West 37th Street, 13th Floor
New York, NY 10018

Printed in the United States of America
Distributed by Simon & Schuster
www.pegasusbooks.com

In loving memory of Judith Civan, Bryan Sterling,
Jonathan Strober, and Muriel and Myron Strober

Contents

Foreword   ix

Part One: The House of Windsor

1. The Accession of Queen Elizabeth II   2
2. A Family Nightmare: The Abdication   23
3. The War and the Royal Family   47
4. The Marriage of Princess Elizabeth to Prince Philip   56
5. The Coronation of Queen Elizabeth II   69
6. The Consort   87

Part Two: The Institution of the Monarchy

7. Who Is the Queen?   104
8. What Does the Monarchy Mean to British Subjects
   and Others?   143
9. The Queen and the Institution of the Monarchy   165
10. The Queen and her Prime Ministers   180
11. The Monarch as Defender of the Faith   211
12. The Queen's Travels Abroad   225
13. Life at Court   238
14. Visiting a Royal Residence at the Queen's Invitation   254

Part Three: The Queen and the Commonwealth

15. The Commonwealth   278
16. Canada   306
17. Australia   322
18. Africa   345
19. The Future of the Commonwealth   356

Part Four: Major Issues of the Reign

20. Northern Ireland   364
21. Suez and Hong Kong   383
22. The Falkland Islands War   394

Part Five: The Evolution of the Monarchy

23. Pandora's Box   410
24. Prince Charles and Princess Diana   428
25. The Death of Princess Diana   447
26. Lords Reform and Scottish Devolution   467

Part Six: The Future of the Monarchy

27. The Heir Apparent: Who *Is* He?   482
28. Queen Elizabeth II's Legacy and the Future of
    the Monarchy   498

Afterword   521
References   525
List of Interviewees   537
Abbreviations of Titles   541
Bibliographical Note   543
Photograph Permissions   545
Acknowledgments   547

Foreword

WE WERE YOUNG children living in the United States at the outbreak of World War Two. Our memories of that era are replete with images of the British Royal Family, as well as the British nation, enduring the dangers and hardships of war, and of King George VI, Queen Elizabeth, later the Queen Mother, and the Princesses, Elizabeth and Margaret Rose, inspecting damage and comforting the injured in bombed-out London.

As young adults, prior to meeting and marrying, each of us had lived in Britain for short periods of time, in the 1960s and 1970s respectively, and so we became increasingly aware of the Queen's substance beyond the pomp and ceremony of her constitutional role.

In 1998, after having written oral histories of the administrations of three of the major American presidents of the latter part of the twentieth century—John F. Kennedy, Richard M. Nixon, and Ronald W. Reagan—we sought as our next subject a personality of like stature. Queen Elizabeth II, with the historical sweep of her reign, coupled with the fascination of many Americans with the institution of the British monarchy, provided us with a most worthy subject.

Embarking on this project, we spent a considerable amount of time in the United Kingdom from 1998 to 2000, as well as traveling to the Commonwealth, and elsewhere, to gather information and perspective about the institution of the British monarchy.

When we returned to this book in 2020 for this revised edition, we realized just what a fascinating collection of insights about the first fifty years of the Queen's reign we had. Many of the contributors have now sadly died, and we feel extremely grateful to have been able to interview them and hear their experiences.

We had intended to travel again to the U.K. to interview more people on the last twenty years of Queen Elizabeth II's reign, but the global COVID-19 pandemic of course made that difficult. We have been fortunate to be able to connect with a number of new interviewees as well as to have renewed contact with some of our original ones. We have made clear in the interviewees' biographies if they were interviewed for this second edition.

Any edits made to the original material are indicated with square brackets.

As we have closely followed the Queen's activities over the past two decades, it has been our pleasure to revisit her extraordinary reign.

Deborah Hart Strober and Gerald S. Strober
New York

PART ONE

The House of Windsor

CHAPTER 1

The Accession of Queen Elizabeth II

I N THE EARLY morning hours of February 6, 1952, the Princess Elizabeth Alexandra Mary of Windsor, twenty-five, heiress presumptive[1] to the British Throne, became Queen Elizabeth II, by the Grace of God, Queen of the United Kingdom of Great Britain and Northern Ireland and of her other Realms and Territories, Head of the Commonwealth, Defender of the Faith.

King George VI had died in his sleep of a heart attack during the night. The King's body was discovered at 7:30 that morning by his valet.

Only a day earlier, the King had been out in an unusually brilliant winter sunshine, enjoying his favorite sport, shooting. He had bagged nine hares and one pigeon. His last words to his companions were: "Well, it's been a very good day's sport, gentlemen!"

At 11:45 A.M., London time, on the day of the King's death, the heiress presumptive was at Sagana Lodge, a farm she and her husband, Prince Philip, the Duke of Edinburgh, had been given as a wedding gift by the colonial government of Kenya. It was the first leg of a Commonwealth tour she had begun only days earlier, standing in for her ailing father.

Confusion reigned in the immediate hours after the King's death. Purportedly, a telegram was sent from Buckingham Palace to Kenya, informing the royal party of the King's death.

The heiress to the Throne actually learned that she had become Queen, however, after Martin Charteris, then attached to her Household and traveling with the royal couple in Kenya, heard a report on the radio and relayed the news to Michael Parker, a close friend of Prince Philip's who was in the royal entourage. Parker informed Prince Philip of the King's death, and he in turn broke the news to his wife.

* * *

Lieutenant Commander John Michael Avison Parker (1920–2001), CVO, AM, equerry-in-waiting to Princess Elizabeth and the Duke of Edinburgh, 1947–52; private secretary to the Duke of Edinburgh, 1947–57 We'd been up the tree, and we'd seen a great herd of elephants and a lot of animals. At the dawn, I discovered a ladder going up to the top of the tree, where you could look over the jungle at Mount Kenya.

Prince Philip was asleep and she was looking out there, and I said: "Ma'am, would you like to come and look at the view?" So up she came with me and we had a look at the dawn of that terrible day, out there in Africa. But what a beautiful dawn it was; it was a fantastic sight!

We went down, and we all went on to Sagana Lodge, which was where we were staying. We had a day or so to adjust, and rest, and do things, before we went on to Mombasa, where we were going aboard a ship and on to Australia.

Well, Prince Philip went to sleep in his little room that was off to one side. The Princess was at her desk, writing thank-you letters, and some family letters—and to the King, I suppose—because we were going to be out of reach for a while and this was the last mail to go.

Then the phone rang. And Martin Charteris, the Princess's private secretary, said: "Mike, there's a ghastly rumor going round that the King has died." He was at a hotel in Nyeri, amongst all the press people there, and they were saying that they had heard.

So I said: "Well, Martin, that's frightening, but I cannot do a thing on a rumor like that. I just won't do anything." And he said: "That's just as well, but stand by."

Down went the phone. I saw a radio on the shelf above me. There was a door open to where the Princess was sitting, so I shut the door and switched on the radio and hunted about for the BBC, and then I could hear the bells of Big Ben ringing, very slowly.

I thought: Ye gods. And my hair stood up a little bit more. Then I heard the announcement. And that was that. I whizzed round the outside of the house, to the veranda, and in to where Prince Philip was sleeping, and told him.

He had just woken up from a heavy sleep and an Australian bloke comes in and tells him that his wife's father, the King, has just died, and she's become Queen. Can you imagine the impact?

First of all, there was his complete concern, his consideration for *her* as a human being, and secondly, the implications of the fact that she was becoming the Queen and he is her husband. So a whole myriad of thoughts must have gone roaring through his brain.

His first reaction was almost as though a huge wave had hit him. And he just stood there, silently, and thought. It wasn't a moment when I should talk, so I just stood there too. Both of us were thinking the same thoughts, separately.

And then he straightened himself up and went in to tell the Queen. She was sitting at her desk, and he told her there. And then she got up and he put his arm around her and took her out onto the lawn. And they walked up and down the lawn together, very close, and she was weeping desperately for the loss of her father.

She did a bit of grieving like that, which was a good thing too. And then she straightened up and she went in, to the desk she had been working at, and started to send all these telegrams off, round the Commonwealth and to other countries, like the United States.

And Philip was right behind her, sitting there. His presence was a huge, huge piece of confidence for her. And he never left her; while she was working with Charteris and everybody else, he was there. One of the remarkable things was that he didn't interfere with me making all the arrangements. Some people would like to get their hands on. But he knew we would do the job of getting them home, so he didn't bother.

Lady Pamela Hicks, daughter to Edwina, Countess Mountbatten of Burma and Lord Louis Mountbatten, 1st Earl of Burma, cousin to the Duke of Edinburgh It was the most appalling shock to them. She was only twenty-five and he was only barely thirty. This really devastated their lives, actually, for a married couple at that moment.

When you think that she went up that ladder onto that platform as a Princess, and she came down as the Queen. They had had a marvelous night, she with her camera, filming all the animals, and looking—just the kind of thing they loved doing—and then to come down again into the little fishing lodge, to be told the news. It was the most appalling shock.

When Mike Parker received the telephone call from Martin Charteris and told Prince Philip, he just covered his face with his newspaper and remained in shock for about five minutes or so, taking in the full extent of what it meant—that his whole career in the Navy would go.

It was very much a conventional British household to the extent that he was very much the man of the family: he took the decisions; she looked after him in their private life. Obviously, as Princess, she had a lot of official things to do. But they were still able, with those two small children, to have a family group where he could be the *pater familias* and have authority. He was very, very accepting. But she was very careful to let him take part in things and relied on him enormously.

But think of this extremely active and enthusiastic young man who suddenly finds his whole life is going to be taken away from him—he'll be walking two steps behind his wife—and probably thinking he will have to become a yes man for the rest of his life.

She came back into this tiny little house and—it was a very typical reaction actually—she said: "Oh, I'm so sorry, it means we've all got to go home, I'm afraid."

And one was so overcome with sorrow for her that the only thing one could think of was giving her a kiss and a hug. And then I remember thinking: My God! Of course it means she's the *Queen*!

There was no time then, actually, for her, if she had wanted to, to grieve, which, perhaps, was a good thing. She was so busy because Martin Charteris arrived and they had to let all the prime ministers, and governors general of Australia, New Zealand, and all the rest of the Commonwealth know that the tour was canceled because, of course, we'd been right at the beginning of it. So all these telegrams had to go off. Martin Charteris didn't even know what name she was going to call herself as Queen—things like that. There was so much that she had to do.

* * *

To this day, there is confusion about whether the telegram breaking the news was ever sent from England.

* * *

Sir Edward Ford, GCVO, KCB, ERD, DL (1910–2006), assistant private secretary to King George VI, 1946–52; assistant private secretary to Queen Elizabeth II, 1952–67 It's a mystery. I can only tell you my side of it because I was in London and the King died at Sandringham. The private secretary there was the principal private secretary, Sir Alan Lascelles.

We had a code for various contingencies, and one was the death of the King. And at a quarter to nine one morning, I got a telephone call from Lascelles at Sandringham, saying "Hyde Park Corner," because that was the code. He simply said: "Hyde Park Corner. Go and tell Mr. Churchill, and the Queen Mary," and he rang off.

I had no further instructions. All I knew was that the King had died and that I had to go and tell his mother and the prime minister before the news could get out in any other way.

At the same time, I assumed—if I didn't know—that he'd sent that coded message to Sir Michael Adeane,[2] who was in Kenya with the Princess. But, in fact, the news of the King's death got there by other means.

And when I asked whether this telegram from Lascelles had ever been received nobody had any knowledge of it.

Was it sent? I can't tell you. I think it must have been. It was perfectly clear that the important thing was to tell them before anybody else, obviously, although that was not the way that the message was received in Kenya.

My theory is that the code was a very bad code. Actually, we had about four different codes for these various events and they all had London geographical names—Trafalgar Square, and Knightsbridge, or something like that.

To be quite honest, I had forgotten about them and only that night, seeing that my wallet was rather thick, I thought I'd just see if I couldn't off-load things, and I came across these codes, tucked away in my wallet. I was very lucky. I had forgotten almost that I had them. So I knew immediately what it meant. It might have taken me a little bit of time, otherwise, to find out.

So what is one to conclude? A possible explanation is that the Post Office getting a telegram saying: "Hyde Park Corner" thought this is just an address, and that was that. They didn't send it.

But it's interesting that it didn't affect the issue in any way. In fact, they got it on a local radio message; it wasn't through a telegram from Sandringham.

BREAKING THE NEWS AT HOME

In London, meanwhile, plans were being made to inform the British public, the Commonwealth, and the world of the King's death. First, however, members of the Royal Family and the government had to be notified.

Queen Elizabeth, née Lady Elizabeth Bowes-Lyon, the King's devoted wife of nearly twenty-nine years, and now by virtue of his death a widow at the age of fifty-one, was the first to be informed. Then Sir Alan Lascelles instructed Edward Ford to break the news to the prime minister, Winston Churchill.

* * *

Sir Edward Ford I wasn't worried about how to because I had no details. Therefore, I couldn't enlarge on the fact. And the point was really to be a sort of human telegram to him.

It's a commentary on the changes in affairs, but I drove my little car straight up to the door of Number 10 Downing Street; I wasn't stopped by anybody. I got out and rang the bell, and said: "I want to speak to the prime minister. I have a message to deliver to him."

The private secretary came down and took me up. And there he was, lying in the bed, a little sputtery green candle at the side of the bed. He always kept a light there because he was a bad cigar smoker: he chewed them up and they used to go out, and then he had to relight them. And he had lots of papers in front of him, all over the place—he was composing a speech for a foreign affairs debate on the next day.

I said to him: "Prime Minister, I've got bad news for you. The King has died in the night." He was absolutely stunned by this news, and he said: "Bad news? The *worst*!" Then he threw these papers aside and said: "How unimportant these various matters seem now."

Then he thought what to do. And I sat there in silence. And then he got onto his telephone and asked to speak to Anthony Eden, who was his deputy prime minister. And, curiously, they went on as they had in the war, thinking that you had to disguise what you said for security reasons. Instead of just saying: "The King is dead," he said to Anthony Eden: "Scramble. Ah, ah, we must have a cabinet." They couldn't scramble. I can't remember the exact paraphrase he used, but he didn't say: "The King is dead," which struck me as curious.

Then I said: "Well, I must go and tell the Queen Mary." So I left and went off to her. That was more difficult. I found her staff at breakfast at Marlborough House where she lived, and I said: "The King has died, and I've been asked to inform Queen Mary."

Their faces fell and Lady Cynthia Colville, who was her main lady-in-waiting, said: "I don't think you can do that. I think you'll have to tell her that he's very ill."

And I said: "I couldn't possibly do that! In half an hour the world will know this!" And she said: "Well, she's never forgiven me for the way in which I told her that the Duke of Kent[3] had been killed in the war."

However, she said: "I think I'll just go up and see her and tell her you're here." And she did. Then she came down and said: "Well, I have actually told her, and she'd like to see you."

So I went up. And there she was, sitting very upright in a chair, and she was in shock. Unfortunately, I had no information about the details, so I could only say: "He was found dead early this morning."

And so I went off, back to Buckingham Palace to arrange the public announcement, which was made very soon afterward.

The people who were utterly unprepared for it were the BBC, oddly enough. You would have thought that they would have been. But not a bit. They took nearly half an hour after the deadline.

It was supposed to be arranged when I got back to the Palace that the news should be promulgated at a quarter to eleven. And we had means of getting through to the Press Association and Reuters, and so on. So they were all told to release at a quarter to eleven, and they were given a few minutes or so.

And the BBC were still putting it out at a quarter to eleven. They went into conference as to how they should deal with it. One of the things they decided was that this news was of such importance that it had to be given to the world by someone called John Snagge,[4] who was the man who had established a considerable reputation in broadcasting the university boat races. And everybody was running round the BBC trying to find John Snagge because nobody else could make the announcement. And it wasn't till about ten past eleven that the BBC announced it.

Meantime, the Duke of Norfolk, the Earl Marshal, under whom all the business of a new reign comes—he is the one responsible for the royal funeral and the Coronation later—was traveling up from Arundel,[5] in Sussex, to London, and arrived at Victoria, to see a poster: "King Dead." He drove straight to Buckingham Palace and was there within twenty minutes, by about half past eleven. It was an astonishing coincidence.

HIS SUBJECTS' RESPONSE TO THE KING'S DEATH

Lady Angela Oswald, CVO, woman of the bedchamber to Queen Elizabeth the Queen Mother The King's death was one of my earliest memories. Everybody was shocked and horrified. The whole nation was really plunged into grief when the King died. Everybody was terribly, terribly shocked.

Robert Lacey, historian and royal biographer My first recollection—I was eight years old at the time—is of the death of King George VI and the sense of national gloom and mourning all over the country. And I can remember, in particular, the famous newspaper photograph of the three

Queens—Queen Mary, Queen Elizabeth, and the new Queen—all in black and in veils.

That was also the first time that the tabloid newspapers hit my consciousness because I remember seeing the tabloid front page—entirely a photograph—and I had been brought up in a respectable lower-middle-class home with the *Daily Telegraph*, which didn't do that sort of thing.

Baroness Young, Janet Mary, PC, DL (1926–2002), life peer, cr. 1971; Chancellor of Duchy of Lancaster, 1981–82; leader, Conservative Party in the House of Lords, 1981–83; Lord Privy Seal, 1982–83; minister of state, Foreign and Commonwealth Office, 1983–87 All of us in those days took the death of King George VI very seriously. I recall we were going out, my husband and I, to a party, and it was canceled because of the death of the King, as a mark of respect.

Sir Shridath "Sonny" Surendranath Ramphal, GCMG, AC, ONZ, OE, OCC, QC, born in British Guiana, now Guyana, Secretary-General of the Commonwealth, 1975–90; co-chair Commission on Global Governance, 1992 My own feeling was that another element of the old order was passing and the newness of the succession was welcomed.

Rev. Canon Paul Oestreicher, canon residentiary and director of the International Centre for Reconciliation at Coventry Cathedral, 1985–97 I wasn't a typical New Zealander. Frankly, I don't remember my immediate thoughts. It didn't impact on me—okay, we've got a young Queen now—because I didn't have that background. I had a German-Jewish background.[6] I wouldn't have dreamed of calling England home; it would be absurd.

To me, it was a constitutional event. I happen to be extremely interested in politics, and I went on to study politics—it became my obsession, if you like—so to me it was a political event of no great significance because nothing was going to change as a result: it was a tradition that was going to live on. And she [the new Queen] was a nice person.

Countess of Longford, Elizabeth, CBE (1906–2002), royal biographer I'm afraid I have to admit I was rather absorbed with my own family affairs. We knew he'd had an operation, and all the rest of it. You couldn't fail to know, because there were bulletins. But I don't think anybody expected him to die.

Neville Kenneth Wran, AC, CNZM, QC (1926–2014), premier New South Wales, 1976–86; a founder, Australian Republican Movement It's fair to say that we took it very seriously. And because the King had during the Second World War been the very visible figure in Great Britain, that translated itself into our imagery of what was going on. And the King was the *King*.

My only recollection of it, because I was only a teenager then, is that the shops in the whole city were draped in black and purple, and there was a genuine period of mourning. We regarded it as a very important occasion.

England had absolutely no effect or impact materially upon us at all. But when England went to war with Germany, we automatically regarded ourselves at war. We didn't have to make a separate declaration, such was the homogeneity of our relationship: when England went to war, the Empire were there. So it was a period of genuine mourning when George VI died.

Sir Michael Oswald, GCVO (1934–2021), manager of the Royal Studs, 1969–99 The first big military parade I took part in was the King's funeral at Windsor when I was seventeen. That I remember vividly because I was in the school Officers' Training Corps, and we marched up over Windsor Bridge and up past the Castle.

There were huge crowds and there was a deathly silence, which is quite unusual when you see large crowds of people—my impression was that there was a total hush. And then we were marched into the Castle and lined part of the route. It made a great impression on me really.

Dr. Vivien Noakes (1937–2011), biographer, co-author *The Daily Life of the Queen: An Artist's Diary* (2000) As a teenager, I went with my family [to watch the funeral procession pass]. My father was a member of something called the Royal Aero Club. Some of the members were given seats in windows.

I remember the music, particularly, the solemnity of it; I remember the whole thing was profoundly moving. I remember wearing a black armband, which we did in those days.

I wrote to the Palace and I said: "My Girl Guide patrol and I want to say how sorry they are." And a letter came back. I've got the letter still from them.

Ian Adams, former Foreign Office official We all sensed that we had lost a King who had done a really splendid job which he never wanted to do.

He was a very reluctant King, after all, and the Queen at the time was very reluctant that he should have to become King. If she could have put a stop to it, certainly she would have done.

We all sensed we'd lost somebody who had really shown the greatest possible sense of duty, and somebody for whom there was tremendous sympathy over his speech defect,[7] realizing what agony that was for him, to have to speak as he did, reasonably awkwardly, in public. There was a real affection there.

Philip Ziegler, CVO, FRS, former diplomat, historian and royal biographer I queued when he was lying in state in Westminster Hall.[8] It was immensely impressive, and very moving. But I couldn't at all honestly say that I felt any *personal* grief.

My first thoughts about his death were absolutely pitiful: should I, or should I not, put on a black tie? It was a kind of social status symbol: if you are of a certain level in society, or of a certain degree of conservatism, you put on a black tie.

I say this with shame *now*, but I remember myself putting on a black tie and then going to one kind of party, and then taking it off again and going to another kind of party. And I suspect there were quite a lot of people like that.

Baron Wright of Richmond, Patrick Richard Henry, GCMG (1931–2020), life peer, cr. 1994; private secretary (overseas affairs) to the prime minister, 1974–77; permanent under secretary of state and head of the Diplomatic Service, 1986–91 I was shocked by the news of the King's death because George VI was actually a rather popular figure, much more so than George V. But then those were more formal days.

Baron Healey, Denis Winston, CH, MBE, PC, life peer, cr. 1992; secretary of state for defense, 1964–70; Chancellor of the Exchequer, 1974–79; deputy leader, Labour Party, 1980–83 I remember very well, because I was a student when he took over from George V. I wouldn't say I had very *strong* emotions about it. He'd been ill for some time; his death wasn't unexpected.

Tim Heald, FRSL (1944–2016), author of, among other books, *The Duke: A Portrait of Prince Philip* (1991) My father was in the Army, stationed in Vienna, but when the King died we were all on a family holiday down on a lake in Austria. And I can see my father, wearing his

British Army overcoat—I was very small—taking me out onto the frozen lake, and saying, basically: "The King has died."

I didn't know much of what was going on, but for him it was very, very important—in an almost tribal way. I don't think it would be true of many people today, but I think that was a fairly normal reaction that you would have got from a serving British Army officer in those days. That was the first moment that I really was aware that the Royal Family meant something.

Sir Kenneth Percy Bloomfield, KCB, head of the Northern Ireland Civil Service and second permanent under secretary of state, Northern Ireland Office, 1984–91 I was at Oxford University, actually, when the King died, and I remember going to a terrific memorial service for him in St. Mary's, the university church, and the vice-chancellor parading in with the university mace, and all that stuff. It was very touching.

The King, I suspect, had become a more familiar figure to the people than would have normally been the case because of the war, in that he fairly regularly broadcast at a time when radio was the only thing—the television service had been suspended during the war, so radio was terribly important—and we all remembered this very conscientious kind of voice, trying to master an awful speech impediment. He really did have quite some difficulty in uttering speeches, and it was a marvelous thing to have overcome it as well as he did.

Venerable George Bernard Austin (1931–2019), archdeacon of York, 1988–99 I was at university in Wales when he died—I was in the second year of my degree—and I can remember going to Evensong that night in the chapel and hearing us pray for, instead of "George, our King," "Elizabeth, our Queen." And we had to change all the he's and his's into hers's.

We were all very sad. The monarchy then meant more to the nation, not least because we were conscious that George VI had stayed in London during the bombing. We never really believed that they suffered the same rationing we did. But they suffered the bombing—Buckingham Palace was bombed—whereas they could have fled to Canada, or Australia, and they didn't. They stayed in London with their people and they were very much loved.

I believe it's hard for people today to understand the affection in which they were held: they were completely separated; it's another role. I wouldn't say it was almost like the Japanese Emperor, but it wasn't far from it.

Sir Gordon Wesley Jewkes, KCMG, commercial consul to the Midwestern region of the United States (Chicago), 1969–72; deputy high commissioner, Trinidad and Tobago, 1972–75; head of the finance department, Foreign Office; governor, the Falkland Islands, 1985–88 There was genuine grief in the country—there's no question of it. And court mourning was ordained, which lasted for, I believe, six months: we wore black armbands; we did not go out; we had no parties.

I have to say that the end of court mourning did coincide with the week of my discharge from the military. I shall draw a veil over those celebrations, but that was a big relief.

But, of course, in between times, we became conscious of the very young Queen and her court—her mother, obviously, and Prince Philip at her side.

Michael Parker My first reaction was purely for *her*, then him: what in the name of heaven could I do now to help them? Obviously, the first thing I must do is get them back to London.

WAS THE KING'S DEATH UNEXPECTED?

While the King had been suffering from a variety of ailments and had been operated on the previous September for lung cancer, his death came as a surprise to his subjects, as well as to some members of the Royal Family.

* * *

Baron Armstrong of Ilminster, Robert Temple, GCB, CVO (1927–2020), life peer, cr. 1988; personal private secretary to Prime Ministers Edward Heath and Harold Wilson, 1970–75; secretary of the cabinet, 1979–87; head of the Civil Service, 1983–87 We had all seen pictures of him—when the Princess Elizabeth went off to Kenya, there were photographs taken of the King waving goodbye to her—and he looked a very ill man.

I believe that people were ready to acknowledge that he was an ill man—they must have known that he was an ill man—but his death, when it came, was not directly due to the illness; it was a heart attack, and so it was, in that sense, unexpected.

We all woke up in the morning on February 6, 1952, to learn that he had died in the night. It was a very great, sudden shock, compounded, of course, by the fact that we now had a young and attractive Queen.

Admiral of the Fleet Sir Henry Conyers Leach, GCB, DL (1923–2011), naval chief-of-staff and First Sea Lord, 1979–82; First and Principal Naval ADC to the Queen, 1979–82 I was in my office at the Gunnery School on Whale Island, Portsmouth, and, as I recall, this news flash came through something like eleven o'clock, in the forenoon—it was outside a normal news broadcast—and it just said that His Majesty had died quietly in his sleep the previous night.

It came as a great shock. I was completely surprised: I had no idea that the King had been unwell. I knew he had had an operation to remove one lung, but not much was said in public about that and I wasn't thinking in terms of cancer, and smoking, and all that sort of stuff. I smoked myself.

Admiral Sir J. F. "Sandy" Woodward, GBE, KCB (1932–2013), senior task group commander, South Atlantic, during the Falklands campaign, April–July 1982; commander-in-chief, Naval Home Command, 1987–89; flag aide de camp to the Queen, 1987–89 Just before King George died he was due to go to Northern Ireland in the cruiser *Sheffield*. I happened to be the senior midshipman and I would have been his runner. But the visit got canceled because he had entered the last few months of his life.

Sir Edward Ford He'd had two absolutely major illnesses: the first was the blood vessels in his leg, for which he was operated on by a Scottish surgeon who cut the nerve and he got back some of his control—the thermostatic flow of blood to his leg; and then, of course, he had the lung out.

And he'd not looked well. It was a very cold January—it was a raw day when he saw the Princess off. And people remarked then that he didn't look at all well. He was having to go out into the cold at Sandringham— he still was shooting and that sort of thing—but he had some electrically warmed gloves that he was wearing; he was well rugged-up.

It was known that he was at risk, but he might have lived; I don't think anybody expected him to die like that, *then*. He died in the beginning of February, but there were plans, of course, for him to go himself on a tour, perhaps of South Africa again.

General Andrew J. Goodpaster (1915–2005), staff secretary to President Eisenhower,[9] 1954–61 I don't think General Eisenhower was aware of the seriousness, of the probability that it could be fatal. I believe he was caught by surprise, although he knew the King was gravely ill.

I think we all had general knowledge of that. The knowledge that he was gravely ill still came as a surprise, and certainly a shock, to us—that this hero of British strength and the regard of the people had passed away.

Michael Parker He'd *been* ill—and he'd been very ill—we were right at his side all the time, so we'd seen the various ups and downs that had been going on, and we could see when he was better one day, and perhaps not so well on the other day—and he was extremely clever in hiding his feelings about how ill he was, to the point where we were leaving on that trip.

He put on a terrific front, a huge front, and up to that point he had built it up beforehand into making us think that it was safe to go away. The Princess would never have left, for one second, if she didn't think he was going to be pretty much okay for quite a while.

I remember seeing him at London Airport as we left. The photographs of him make him look as though he's about to step into the grave. In actual fact, he looked a hell of a lot better than that. Otherwise we wouldn't have gone.

He took me off to one corner as we were standing in the airport and he said: "Are you all set for this trip?" I said: "Yes, Sir, as much as we possibly can be." We chatted about things and he was vitally interested in everything we were doing. He asked me if I'd got all the necessary things to take with me. And I said yes.

And then, of course, he went to talk to somebody else, and I thought: What a marvelous man! Here he is, he has time as a King, seeing his daughter and everybody else off, to stop and see that bloke who's just a factotum making the arrangements. He impressed me enormously.

WAS THE ROYAL FAMILY IN A STATE OF DENIAL AS TO THE SERIOUSNESS OF THE KING'S ILLNESS?

Princess Margaret said publicly that her father at the time of his death had been "about to recover."

* * *

Sir Edward Ford I don't believe, medically, that any doctor would say that he was about to recover. But, at the same time, I don't believe any of them would have said: "You can't expect him to live till the end of the week."

Everybody knew he was a frail man. And, of course, February in England is not a very good month to be about. And he wouldn't have liked to be kept indoors, I don't think.

I believe it was totally unexpected as it came, though I've no doubt that a surgeon might tell one that his life was at total risk from the time he had the lung operation—that it might have killed him at any moment, really.

Seventh Earl of Harewood, George Henry Hubert Lascelles, KBE, AM (1923–2011), first cousin to the Queen I was pretty young, twenty-nine. It was, first of all, a reaction of shock because he was quite young, but, of course, not one of total shock because he had been very ill: he had had a lung out—it was a long time ago; the surgeons were perhaps less good at it then than now—and though he was recovering, he was very weak.

Philip Ziegler I don't believe that they knew he had cancer. The King certainly didn't. Presumably the Queen did. I've no reason to believe that Princess Elizabeth did.

It may have been wishful thinking; they would have told themselves: "At least we've got about ten years." At least they really believed that, so it was a terrible shock to them when the King died. It was so important to them that he should stay alive, so they may have told themselves that he was going to.

Michael Parker I'm sure he knew. I don't think if you're a doctor you would hide anything from a King, would you?

Maybe the possibility occurred to him that this was the last time he would be seeing his daughter. But he would have behaved the same in each case, so there's no way of telling.

And we, of course, were very sensitive—I was particularly sensitive, being responsible for their movements and everything else, which a chap should be if he was in charge of all the arrangements. So in the back of my head was the need to be prepared if something went wrong.

But it wasn't very heavily at the back of my head; it was just a glimmer. I was very happy because he looked so well, and was behaving so brilliantly.

Sir Michael Oswald The people quite close to King George must have realized how very ill he was. They may not have realized quite how quickly, how soon, he would die.

Now you might say that if people close to the King knew how ill he was, why didn't they keep the then-Princess Elizabeth back? Well, the

King would have been horrified; he would have wanted to know why she wasn't going as planned on that visit to Africa.

And there was then an idea—the great tradition—that you must carry on. And I'm not at all surprised that she did go on that tour.

Tim Heald I don't think for a moment that Prince Philip expected it to happen as early as it did.

Sir Edward Ford I think if [the possibility of the King's death] had really been anticipated by them, possibly even the whole of the Princess's visit to the Commonwealth would have been out. After all, she might have been in Australia, which is halfway across the world. She was going to do a tour which he'd planned.

Lady Pamela Hicks The King and she were very close—they were "we four" with the Queen Mother and the Princess Margaret. But in a way, perhaps, the now-Queen Elizabeth and her father were particularly close—and so to the Queen it was a great shock.

All those years they were always prepared for the King to die, but I don't believe they realized how ill he was. I'm sure she wouldn't have gone if they had thought that seriously there was a danger that within six months he'd be dead.

I think they thought: how sad; maybe in a year or two something dreadful might happen. But I'm sure not within six months of the tour.

* * *

Prime Minister Churchill reportedly told his then-private secretary Jock Colville, the son of Queen Mary's lady-in-waiting Lady Cynthia Colville, that he did not really know the new Queen and that to him, "she was only a child."

* * *

Sir Edward Ford I don't think he would have done. He would have recognized her but he wouldn't really have come across her; she hadn't fulfilled, in any sense, duties in which he'd have been involved. He knew her as the King's daughter, but I doubt that they'd really ever had a serious conversation together.

FIRST THOUGHTS ABOUT THE NEW QUEEN

Eighth Baron Thurlow, Francis Edward Hovell-Thurlow-Cumming-Bruce, KCMG (1912–2013), high commissioner in New Zealand, 1959–63; in Nigeria, 1964–67; governor and commander-in-chief of the Bahamas, 1968–72 People like myself felt it was a bit tough on the Princess to have to have been precipitated into this position at such an early age and unable to have a reasonable, semi-free life with her handsome young husband, and to be shackled with all the responsibilities of the monarchy.

But, of course, she shouldered it very gladly. And, of course, there was for the public at large something rather romantic about having a lovely young Princess as Queen.

Adm. Sir Henry Leach I had never met her then. She was a very charming-looking, natural person and it could fairly be said that she was popular with the general public—to the extent that the general public knew her, which was not to a great extent then.

And this handsome, sailor husband—Prince Philip, of course—was very good looking too. There was very much less scurrilous stuff floating round the media of the day, much less.

Lord Wright The concept of a lady Sovereign taking over is well-ingrained in us: we'd recently had the longest-reigning Sovereign, Queen Victoria. And Queen Elizabeth I is generally regarded as the greatest of the British Monarchs. So I think the fact that the Crown was changing gender didn't impact at all.

Sir David Aubrey Scott, GCMG (1919–2010), high commissioner to Uganda, 1967–70; high commissioner to New Zealand and governor of the Pitcairn Islands, 1973–75; ambassador to the Republic of South Africa, 1976–79 One of the things that interested me very much was the fact that she was in Kenya when it happened. That, in a way, defined her attitude to the Commonwealth.[10] I believe that it left her extraordinarily keen on the idea that the Commonwealth is something which has some meaning, that does hang together—although, obviously, there are problems.

Lord Armstrong Great sadness, from the King's point of view, and the Queen Mother's point of view, but a certain looking forward to the fact that somebody of my own generation was going to be on the Throne now who was likely to be the Sovereign for as long as I was around.

THE NEW QUEEN'S RETURN TO LONDON

Upon learning of the King's death, the new Queen and her entourage began immediately to make plans for their return to London.

Shortly before five o'clock in the afternoon, local time, the royal party departed Sagana Lodge, the Queen still wearing blue jeans. Local press photographers, respecting the Queen's privacy, did not take any pictures of the royal departure.

* * *

Michael Parker I got hold of the staff. I said: "We're going to break all records; we're going to pack up and you lot have got to do the whole of the packing while I arrange the aircraft and route the main aircraft."

The new Queen did not have an opportunity to speak with her mother before we left. We didn't have those communications. I doubt if they had ever been in such an isolated situation. In a kind of a way, it was a bit of a help: we could get on with things.

But in another way, we felt so alone, and so out of touch—there was all that big miasma of government over there in England and we had to tell the other countries we weren't coming, and had to change all the arrangements. It was big business.

We were in the middle of the jungle, Mount Kenya, roughly. We were not going for a couple of days, so we hadn't got an aircraft standing by. Our main aircraft was in Mombasa, fortunately, waiting to take a lot of stuff back that wasn't needed for the further voyage.

So I quickly got in touch with them, and I was only able to get through to them by the Army frequency. The governor was in a train—that's why *he* didn't tell us about the King's death—and various other people were all going to Mombasa to see the Princess off. So everybody was gone away somewhere and we were very, very much alone.

I thought: Well, okay. I got through to Mombasa and I spoke to the captain of the Queen's flight and I said: "We'd better get that old Argonaut over to Entebbe, which is near us, which is an international airstrip, and I'll find some way of getting the Princess and Prince Philip both to Entebbe, if you'd stand by there. And then we'll go straight to London."

So then at that point, I rang up East African Airlines and I said: "Queen's emergency. I want an aircraft to go from Nanyuki, the nearest airstrip to us, over the Aberdare Mountains to Entebbe."

He said: "Well, there's one going over in an hour. It's going to take all those gifts and things that the Queen was given out to the Argonaut, to go back to London."

I said: "Hold it. Get everything off it because we're coming. You've heard the news?" And he said: "Yes." And I said: "Well, get that aircraft ready." He said: "But there's quite a problem." I said: "What's that?" He said: "The weather report says there's a cloud bank closing in on two sides on the Aberdare Mountains. If it closes together, you won't be able to go because this cabin is unpressurized. How soon can you get to Nanyuki?"

I said: "In an hour." He said: "Well, in that case, you'll just make it, fingers crossed."

[...]

We get to Nanyuki, pile into the airplane—the Queen—you can imagine—the daughter, losing her father, and all of us clucking around, to do what we could for her, eminently brave, absolutely magnificent, the Queen now.

It was just us and the Queen. And she was sitting up there with Prince Philip, and we were getting on with whatever we were doing.

How can I describe it? You can imagine! And there she was, sitting there, and we were trying to divert her, or do something, but not too pushy about it, just *a* little bit every now and again.

Lady Pamela Hicks The Queen had a nice cabin. They kept to that a lot. It was not an easy trip—we got stuck at Entebbe, in Uganda, because of a storm. We had to wait out the storm and the governor and his wife, and various officials were there. And so, out of politeness, light conversation had to be made for rather a long time. It must have been quite an ordeal.

Michael Parker It took us about forty-five minutes to get to Nanyuki Airport, onto the airplane, a Dakota DC3. It must have been an hour-and-a-half to Entebbe Airport, then a wait for the Argonaut, the main aircraft, to come from Mombasa, and then board the Argonaut, and then on to London, quite a big flight.

That bank of cloud closed behind us as we went over. Somebody up *there* was helping, I think, and we flew into Entebbe. When we landed in the airport, there was nowhere really private that we could take her. The governor of Uganda turned up, and he was very helpful as a diversion.

She had to sit quite a while in this sort of public area, but we managed to get people away at least to give her a bit of privacy. But when you have to sit still, and you've had a shock of that kind, it must be a little bit harder to deal with. It brings tears to my eyes now to think of it and to talk of it.

Then we were able to join up with the Argonaut, and we landed in London at four o'clock in the afternoon, exactly as we planned in Kenya.[11]

I was getting all the information as to who was going to be there, and what was expected of us, according to them, because the Queen was going to decide what was going to happen.

She would have it presented to her and then she would say: "Yes, this is fine," or "What about so-and-so?" Advise and discuss—monarchs don't do anything more but advise, caution, discuss, or say: "Well done."

Those people in London must have been feeling much as we did, except that it wasn't as personal for them as it was for the Queen. But imagine Churchill, who had been close to the King, and all those ministers, who all knew him very, very well, they all must have been in a state of shock too. We appreciated that.

And I believe the whole country was rocked to the soles of its feet. After all, he took them through the war—he and the Queen Mum suffered in the war—so there had built up a huge affection for him, and it was solid right the way through the country, and throughout all the Commonwealth countries.

Lady Pamela Hicks As the plane was about to touch down in London Airport, and the prime minister, Winston Churchill, and my parents, and the Duke and Duchess of Gloucester, and all the receiving line of the cabinet were drawn up there, in their black clothes, the Queen leans across and looks out of the window of the aircraft and says: "Oh, God! They've sent the hearses!"—meaning that instead of her car, one of the big black Palace cars was there.

And in the way she said it, this twenty-five-year-old realized that the end of her private life had come—that for the rest of her life, she would be a public figure, until the day she died. And as she is by nature rather a private person, it was quite a blow.

* * *

The young woman who had departed London six days earlier as the heiress presumptive, now clad in black mourning clothes, emerged from the aircraft as Queen Elizabeth II. She descended the stairs to the tarmac, and walked solemnly toward Prime Minister Winston Churchill, the leader of the opposition, and other high government officials.

* * *

Sir Edward Ford One of the practical difficulties of her coming back was that she was out there in the sort of dress you'd wear for a safari in Kenya. And then you have to hop on an airplane and come back, and step down the airplane steps in London in a black hat, and coat, and skirt, dressed for mourning in London in winter.

Michael Parker The Queen had her black dress with her. Wherever we went, we took our black clothes, the Royal Standard, black armbands, black ties, all those things. I always had that box—a heavily disguised box—with me. To me it was always standard procedure.

The Queen was really bowled over. Forlorn. Fully conscious of the fact that she was Queen, and that she must tend to affairs immediately, but at the same time carrying the load of this new, awful news.

A brave person. Gosh! If I loved her before, boy did I love her after that!

Lady Longford I don't think it was easy, but she's a person who grapples with things that aren't easy.

And she did have the enormous advantage—for all too short a time, but still she had it—of being trained by her own father. They made a great point of that and he really, really wanted to train her much further, but death snatched him away.

She must have enjoyed those training sessions with Papa tremendously, because it was something so special between those two. Nobody else had it.

Peter Jay, ambassador to the United States, 1977–79; economics editor, BBC, 1990–2001, director Bank of England, 2003–09 As a child growing up during the war, I thought of Winston Churchill with awe. He was a great war leader. When she came back to Heathrow for King George VI's funeral and was received on the tarmac, it must to her have been an extraordinary moment: there was the Great Man, asking her permission to carry on with her government.

CHAPTER 2

A Family Nightmare:
The Abdication

T HE FUTURE QUEEN was born by Caesarean section—euphemisti-
cally referred to at the time as "a certain line of treatment"—at
2:40 in the morning on April 21, 1926, at 17 Bruton Street, the
London residence of her maternal grandparents, the Earl and Countess
of Strathmore.

It was customary at that time for the birth of a member of the Royal
Family to be officially witnessed, even if the infant was only third in line
in succession to the Throne, as was the case with Princess Elizabeth. She
was behind her uncle, Edward, then the Prince of Wales, and his younger
brother, her father, Albert, the Duke of York.

And so, despite the fact that Britain was on the eve of a crippling coal
strike that would begin only days later, Sir William Joynson-Hicks, the
Home Secretary in the government of Prime Minister Baldwin,[1] was sent
to the bedside of the then-Elizabeth, Duchess of York.

The newly born Princess Elizabeth would one day inherit a Throne
established by the Saxon monarchs who united England in the ninth
century, as well as the Norman King, William the Conqueror, who
vanquished the Saxon King Harold at the battle of Hastings in 1066.

From William the Conqueror and his descendants, the line passed to
the Plantagenet, Lancaster, York, Tudor, and Stuart houses. The Throne
line was broken only once, in the Stuart period, when in 1649 Charles I
was defeated by the troops of Oliver Cromwell's parliamentary Army.
He was beheaded and a Commonwealth was established which lasted for
eleven years, until 1660, when Charles's son, Charles II, was restored to
the Throne.

In 1714 the Throne passed to the House of Hanover when George Ludwig, Elector of Hanover, landed at Greenwich, making his claim through his maternal grandmother, Elizabeth of Bohemia, a daughter of King James I.

After George I came his son and great-grandson, both named George. George III and his wife, Sophia Charlotte of Mecklenburg-Strelitz, were the parents of nine sons and six daughters. Two of George's sons would reign: George IV would become Regent for his ailing father before assuming the Throne in his own right in 1820; ten years later, his younger brother would reign as William IV.

Upon William IV's death on June 20, 1837, he was succeeded by his eighteen-year-old niece, Victoria, born on May 24, 1819, in Kensington Palace. She was the daughter of Victoria of Saxe-Coburg and William's younger brother, Edward Duke of Kent, who had died in 1820. Victoria would reign for more than sixty-three years until her death on January 22, 1901.

The Princess whose birth was witnessed by Prime Minister Baldwin's Home Secretary on that April morning in 1926 is a great-great-granddaughter of Queen Victoria and the German-born Prince Albert; a great-granddaughter of Victoria's son King Edward VII and his Danish-born Queen, Alexandra; and the granddaughter of King Edward and Queen Alexandra's son King George V and his Queen, Mary of Teck.

* * *

Canon Paul Oestreicher The family is not just British, but thoroughly European. Queen Adelaide,[2] the wife of the King [William IV] before Queen Victoria, was a local Princess from the small, provincial German town in which I was born and grew up—royalty deeply imbued with a European and German tradition.

The British Royal Family is eighty-five percent German. They speak German. Until the First World War they spoke German naturally. All their relatives came to see them and the languages that were almost universally used were German and English.

* * *

A different style was adopted in 1917, during the First World War, when King George V, responding to anti-German feeling on the homefront and seeking to identify the monarchy more with Britain, changed the name of the Royal House from Saxe-Coburg-Gotha to the historically symbolic Windsor.

A MEMBER OF THE HOUSE OF WINDSOR
EVALUATES SOME OF HIS FOREBEARS

Earl of Harewood It [the House of Hanover/Saxe-Coburg-Gotha/ Windsor] has been through very difficult times, more often than one lately tends to remember. We had very difficult times when George III was thought to be mad. Of course, the media was much smaller; only a few people thought he was mad—he kept on recovering. He actually had a disease[3] which made him forget, or made him behave irrationally.

George IV was irresponsible, certainly when he was Prince Regent. He was very unpopular; people were very hostile.

But after that, there was a period of permanency—they found the new King highly accepted. William IV, who, obviously, was a very agreeable man, was made to marry: he had something like twelve children by an actress, but they decided she was an unsuitable person for him to marry, so the twelve children couldn't inherit the Throne.

But he never produced a [legitimate] child, so his niece became Queen Victoria—at seventeen. After the death of her husband she was tremendously unpopular; she didn't appear for a number of years—fifteen or twenty—just never appeared in public. That was unsatisfactory.

And then she did, which, probably because the newspapers were very supportive, produced a reaction in her favor, and her Golden Jubilee in 1887 was a tremendous celebration. Her Diamond Jubilee ten years later was even greater. She was only about eighty-one when she died. But, by then, the whole thing was a popular institution.

King Edward VII was a very skilled, and very unlucky, and very much put-upon Monarch. He was very good at the big diplomacy side of the monarchy, and in that short ten years was much liked.

His son [George V] was much more reclusive, and at the time of his Silver Jubilee in 1935, at which time I was twelve, he was apparently astounded at the huge reception he got at the big celebration: he just never guessed it would be like that, because he was a much less public figure than Kings and Queens have become since.

KING GEORGE V AND QUEEN MARY

King George V, born in 1865, the second son of Edward VII and Alexandra, did not become the heir apparent until the death of his elder brother by one year, Albert Victor ("Eddy"), Duke of Clarence, then twenty-eight, who had contracted influenza in January 1892 which turned into pneumonia, killing him within weeks.

In addition to becoming first in line to the Throne at that time, the then Prince George also inherited his late brother's fiancée, Princess Mary of Teck, two years George's junior and the daughter of the impoverished Duke and Duchess of Teck. The Duchess, Mary Adelaide, was not only a granddaughter of King George III but obese, and known in royal circles as "Fat Mary." The Duke himself was the product of a morganatic marriage, a circumstance that had deprived his father of his claim to the Throne of Würtemmburg, ensuring the family's relative poverty.

Princess Mary of Teck and Prince George were well-suited: he was a naval officer, gruff, anti-intellectual, and imbued with a strong sense of duty, finding pleasure mainly in his stamp collection. And while the Princess, having spent some of her formative years in exile with her parents in Florence, Italy, was a connoisseur of fine things, she was also austere, formal of manner and bearing, conscientious, and reverent of royalty.

* * *

Jeremy Thorpe, PC (1929–2014), Liberal M.P., 1959–79; leader, Liberal Party, 1967–76 I remember the Chinese Exhibition in 1935, at the Royal Academy. There was a tall, ramrod of a woman there and I said to my mother: "Now who is *that* lady?" And she said: "That is Queen Mary."

Garret Fitzgerald, Ph.D. (1926–2011), minister of foreign affairs of Ireland, 1973–77; leader and president, Fine Gael Party, 1977–87; taoiseach (prime minister) of Ireland, 1981–82 and 1982–87 My father[4] was our first minister of external affairs and he, therefore, had to attend functions at Buckingham Palace. My mother[5] didn't attend any of these occasions because my mother was a republican.

When the treaty was signed for our independence, she couldn't accept the treaty, and my father was a minister of the government that signed it, so there was a divergence of view. My mother did not accompany my father on this occasion. Queen Mary asked my father where was she. And my father had to make an excuse because she wasn't there. She wouldn't go to Buckingham Palace.

Seventeenth Earl of Perth, John David Drummond, PC, FSA Scot (1907–2002); minister of state for colonial affairs, 1957–62; first Crown Estate commissioner, 1962–77 She was a very forceful character, and when she wanted to do something, she did something. When she was visiting a grand house, she would like to see various things. And there was always a risk if she said: "Oh, I like that; that's really something very nice." It had almost reached the point that the host, whoever he or she was, felt impelled to send it on to her later.

Ian Adams None of that family, probably, had a particularly happy upbringing; I don't imagine that King George V and Queen Mary were ever very ideal parents. Probably there was affection, to an extent. But they were really such old-fashioned royalty.

It's not fair to tax anybody with not realizing what the changes were going to be. One has to live through these things and it's a very enlightened person who really sees what is actually happening, because you don't realize how seriously things have changed until years after the event. But they probably weren't the ideal parents for bringing up a new generation of royalty to face the changes of the post-war period.

Philip Ziegler Queen Mary was almost incapable of expressing physically the affection she felt for her children. I suspect that one tends to overdramatize this slightly. Edward VIII grossly over-dramatized his relationship with *his* parents—he made it out to be far colder and chillier than it was.

* * *

The children of King George and Queen Mary, especially the five bothers—David (Edward VIII), Albert (King George VI), Henry (Duke of Gloucester), George (Duke of Kent), and John, the youngest, who was epileptic and was shut away from the family until his death at the age of twelve—would all pay emotionally for the coldness of their parents. Their sister, Mary, the Princess Royal and the mother of the Earl of Harewood, was not treated as harshly as were her brothers.

WAS EDWARD VIII SUITED TO BE KING?

Edward Albert Christian George Andrew Patrick David—David to his family—was born on June 23, 1894. Upon the death of King George V at Sandringham, the royal estate in Norfolk, at five minutes before midnight on January 20, 1936, David became King Edward VIII. According to one account of the deathbed scene: "The Prince became hysterical, cried loudly, and kept on embracing the [now] Queen [Mother]."

* * *

Adm. Sir Henry Leach Edward VIII was, and not least for those days, a very good, very energetic, very effective Prince of Wales because everything at that time was protocol and all the general conduct of normal behavior was much stiffer, much more formal, and he broke from that and behaved generally, and publicly, in a much less formal fashion, which was a good thing for the Prince of Wales of the day to do because it brought the people closer to the Throne, so to speak.

But, on the other hand, he did not have the necessary natural dignity—if that's not too stuffy a word—to command respect as the Monarch himself. Now what he would have done if he'd gone on being King I don't know.

It's probably easier for an individual if you have the dignity but you're prepared to break it down and talk to very ordinary people in a very genuine and friendly fashion than to be rather yo-heave-ho-I'm-one-of-the-boys, and then try to be dignified. That way round is more difficult.

Imogen Campbell-Johnson, wife of Alan Campbell-Johnson, CIE, OBE, who was press secretary to Lord Louis Mountbatten He had been lacking duty along with character. I remember, as a schoolgirl, going to an enormous, great fête near Maidstone that he as Prince of Wales was supposed to be opening.

The afternoon went on, and on, and on, and he was about two hours late for the opening. And then he was terribly grumpy—he could be seen to be grumpy—and very unpleasant. Of course, that went right through the crowd there—an enormous number of people were there—and this was well before Mrs. Simpson.

EDWARD VIII SHOCKS THE NATION BY ANNOUNCING
HIS ABDICATION FOR "THE WOMAN I LOVE"

On the evening of December 11, 1936, King Edward VIII, in a radio address broadcast from Windsor Castle, stunned the British nation and the Empire when he informed his subjects: "At long last, I am able to say a few words of my own."

The King then went on to plead for their compassion and forgiveness for what he knew was a decision that flew in the face of British royal tradition, that would alter forever the lives of his diffident younger brother Bertie and his family. He said:

I want you to understand that in making up my mind I did not forget the country or the Empire which as Prince of Wales, and lately as King, I have for twenty-five years tried to serve. But you must believe me when I tell you that I have found it impossible to carry the heavy burden of responsibility and to discharge my duties as King as I would wish to do without the help and support of the woman I love ... God bless you all. God save the King.

* * *

Earl of Perth I happened, curiously enough, to be in America when the abdication speech was made. I was in downtown New York and one of the big American firms had arranged to relay his abdication speech over to their offices.

He came on at about seven o'clock at night. And I remember it very well, because I went to listen, naturally enough, and virtually the whole of Wall Street turned out to listen—they hadn't gone uptown, or anything else. That showed the interest from abroad.

Of course, one felt rather out of it, as I wasn't literally there at the moment of it happening, but one was, up to a point, nervous about what was happening, or could happen. It was well-handled. It was a very, very difficult issue, and in a sense, took everybody by surprise.

* * *

The "woman I love" was Wallis Warfield Spencer Simpson, a forty-year-old native of Baltimore, Maryland. She was known as "Mrs. Simpson," the name of her second husband.

Born Wallis Warfield on June 19, 1896, she was of a genteel background but spent most of her youth in an impoverished state due to the death of her father, Teakle Warfield, when she was only five months old. Her widowed mother then made ends meet by letting rooms to boarders.

Wallis Warfield was eventually befriended by an aunt, Bessy Merryman, who would serve as her confidante during Wallis's long courtship by the future King of England.

When she met Edward, then Prince of Wales, on January 10, 1931, at a weekend house party at Burrough Court, the home of Thelma, Lady Furness, one of Edward's married lovers, Wallis had parted from her first husband, Earl Winfield Spencer, whom she had married in 1916 and divorced in 1927, but was still very much married to mate number two, Ernest Simpson, whom she married in 1928.

Wallis Simpson and the Prince of Wales soon became lovers themselves. The coast cleared for Wallis when Lady Furness departed Britain for a long visit to the U.S. and asked her friend to "look after the little man."

OBJECTIONS TO WALLIS WARFIELD SIMPSON

Lord Armstrong She was twice divorced, and the question was whether it was appropriate for the King of England, who is the head of the Church of England—a church which didn't sanction divorce and even now has more than frowned on divorce—to be married to a divorcee.

Public opinion in those days made this a very real issue, not just in the country but in the countries of the Commonwealth—what was then called the Empire.

Earl of Perth I don't think the fact that she was American entered into it. It was mixture of other issues, particularly being a divorced woman. And she was a rather forceful character. I remember her before she got married, as well as after. But I never heard anybody say: "Oh, she's an American." Mind you, I might not care because I'm married to an American!

Earl of Harewood I'm sure it had nothing to do with her being an American. The divorce was the big thing. And now—I'm a divorced person[6]—that seems very old-fashioned. It wasn't old-fashioned *then*. There was rather a divide in the country: there was a minority of people who thought it was an exaggerated point of view—I'm not saying it was right; I'm just saying it was a minority.

After the war, I remember having a heated argument, as part of the minority, with a much older person, someone of my parents' age, just after my father died—I was twenty-three when my father died. It was his doctor I was talking to, and I took the view strongly that the Duke of Windsor ought to be forgiven for this breach of etiquette.

I don't know what people either knew, or thought they knew, about her. She was quite a lot liked in London; she had a lot of friends, English friends.

Seventeenth Duke of Norfolk, Miles Francis Stapleton Fitzalan-Howard, KG, GCVO, CB, CBE, MC, DL (1915–2002), premier duke of England and Earl Marshal Mrs. Simpson, from Baltimore, was so ambitious, and she got hold of Edward VIII and really dominated him. And the Royal Family weren't very proud of this.

The Royal Family loathed her, and the Queen Mother absolutely *hated* her. And they never made her into "Her Royal Highness"—she was "Duchess"; it was not "Her Royal Highness" that she went by.

Ian Adams There was a lot of that really. We were in a very curious situation at the time because, of course, some of the popular press were very much in favor of Edward VIII and would have willingly seen him marry Mrs. Simpson.

But, in fact, in the end, one has to admit that the opinion changed completely, and hardened. And I believe it hardened perhaps even more strongly against her than it did against him, because she was regarded as somebody who probably had him *there*, and probably did, and there was a feeling of reluctance to accept her as nice personality. I don't believe she ever conveyed to the public any degree of warmth, or softness. She was a hard-edged, hard figure.

Lady Longford She was maligned in the sense that, personally, she was not the evil genius, or wicked woman, or any of the things that some people liked to think.

I've heard so much the other side because I'm great friends with Diana Mitford, who finally landed up as Diana Mosley,[7] and she always stoutly defends the Duchess Windsor: she says it's laughable to suggest that this woman ever was the serpent in the garden, and really was far from a malign influence. I believe Diana was far nearer to the truth than people think she was.

I met her once or twice, she had very good manners and was very easy to talk to. And in that way, she would have fitted her new role and been a very good Queen.

But this doesn't mean that I'm not glad it didn't happen as it did. I am: it has been far better for the country to have the younger branch and all its descendants because I don't think they would have had any children, in any case.

Most people didn't think well of him for doing it; they thought it was his duty to be King because of his birth.

But at the time, it [the abdication] was very well done and the abdication speech which he made, which, incidentally, Winston Churchill had vetted, and improved—he put in the phrase "the woman I love"—made a great impression. And, therefore, nobody thought it was not serious. It was a real dilemma, and a real crisis, and a real tragedy; it wasn't some trumped-up thing.

Adm. Sir Henry Leach I never met the Duchess of Windsor—I didn't particularly want to. But I don't believe she would have filled the role, had she been the King's consort.

I don't think she would have endeared herself, in genuine terms of endearment, to the public—as the Queen Mum certainly has done. She was an enormous support to King George VI, especially in public, where he hated some of the public things he had to do because of his stammer. They were a marvelous pair.

Lord Thurlow When King Edward VIII abdicated, there was, on the whole, a great sense of regret. I believe that it was *misplaced* regret because I don't think that he would have been at all a good King: he didn't have at all a good attachment [to his duties as King].

Still, he had been an immensely popular figure as Prince of Wales throughout the whole Empire and, on the whole, worked pretty hard at it. He'd only been there [on the Throne] for less than a year, and so it was a rather somber affair, and quite moving in the final stages—the famous broadcast.

Duke of Norfolk It was what the prime minister wanted. The Royal Family does work a bit with the prime minister. Baldwin consulted the Commonwealth prime ministers, the American ambassador, the Church of England, and the Queen. The prime minister, and the executive in the cabinet, is in control.

He wasn't much of a chap, really. He let the side down, very much. I met him a bit. He was besotted with Mrs. Simpson. Churchill was the one who said: "Well, we've got to give him something; we'll get him out of harm's way."

Eric Moonman, OBE (1929–2017), Labour M.P., 1966–70, 1974–79; chair, British Zionist Federation, 1975–80 There was the whole manner of the abdication of the Duke of Windsor—the fact that there was a greater role to be played, that he abdicated for the love of a woman, which was quite romantic.

The politicians interfered in that, just as the politicians do now, but there was much less debate about it. It was done beyond the public view: the prime minister of the day and the editor of *The Times* each had a very distinctive role, which was to say that he could not, in fact, marry and have on the Throne a divorced woman. And that, again, highlighted the royal responsibility. But it worked [the abdication process].

Lord Thurlow I and my twin brother were staying down in Windsor Castle with a cousin of mine, the dean of Windsor, for the weekend, while the abdication crisis was going on. We were sitting in the library and the butler came in—in those days, deans of Windsor lived in great style—and said: "The King wishes you to come up"—we'd just arrived—and so we were bundled out of the room and Edward VIII came into the library because my cousin was one of his confidantes—he liked and respected him.

But it was a sad affair, the whole thing, and I don't think—with great respect to Americans—that Mrs. Simpson really played a very responsible role. Still, one can understand it.

Earl of Perth The people, on the whole, weren't aware of it; it was kept very quiet in the papers here—they behaved impeccably throughout—whereas on the Continent, things were different.

Philip M. Kaiser (1913–2007), minister, the American Embassy, London, 1964–69 I lived through the abdication.[8] Of course, the most amusing thing was that the British news distributors cut out of our magazines, particularly *Time* magazine, any reference to the affair with Simpson.

Some of us Americans had our subscriptions to *Time* magazine, so we were getting the stories. We were very proud of our college—it was probably the most famous college in Oxford. First of all, we had the best collection of magazines. We had to vote when we proposed a new magazine. When the English boys discovered that this was taking place, the proposal was made to open three subscriptions to *Time* magazine. And it was carried unanimously.

There was among the students a sense of the drama of it. I can't say very honestly that I remember the students taking sides. It turned out to be a real scandal.

* * *

In a radio broadcast a few days following the abdication of Edward VIII, Cosmo Gordon Lang, Archbishop of Canterbury, was thought to have unduly criticized the former king for maintaining a social circle whose "standards and ways of life are alien to all the best instincts of his people."

* * *

Earl of Harewood I was at school. I had no idea of it until I went to get sausages, or something, and I saw a placard: "The King and Mrs.

Simpson." I'd never heard of her until then. We were completely shielded from it.

So was much of the country. There was a press conspiracy, a rather good conspiracy, a very considerable conspiracy, I think—meaning that to let everything hang out, all the time, all over, regardless, is just completely idiotic. And it was blown by a bishop in his sermon. I believe that rationing all that is good for everyone. It means that mistakes sometimes are treated as mistakes and not trumpeted as if disasters.

Lord Armstrong As it happened, my father was a strong supporter at that time of King Edward VIII, whom he thought was being scurvily treated by Mr. Baldwin and Archbishop Lang—the discussion was going on round me, and I was listening to it, even though, of course, I was only ten years old at the time.

In later life, my father would have said that his judgment was mistaken—that like many people, he saw King Edward VIII as a young and forward-looking Monarch who was taking a keen interest in the social conditions of his subjects. That had very much appealed to everybody.

You have to remember that the great British public until December 1936 knew nothing about Mrs. Simpson. And he was seen as a young and attractive figure, committed to new thinking about the role of the monarchy, and with a history of very considerable commitment to relations with the other countries in the British Empire.

When biographies of the King were published much later, in the 1960s, 70s, and 80s—some of it autobiographical—the shallowness of his appeal became very much more evident, not least his apparent preparedness to see some great merit in Fascism—the Nazis in Germany.

Rt. Rev. Hugh Montefiore (1920–2005), vicar, Great St. Mary's, Cambridge, 1963–70; bishop of Kingston upon Thames, 1970–78; bishop of Birmingham, 1978–87; theologian We thought it was rather the right decision to go. On the whole, people felt that he should abdicate. I know there were people who didn't see that. But, by-and-large, the country was behind Baldwin on that; I think that they thought Archbishop Lang was a bit "archbishopy"—he was a bit tough.

Earl of Harewood I don't think a morganatic marriage would probably have been acceptable at all: it was against the feeling of the times. Baldwin, who was prime minister, canvassed all the prime ministers of the Commonwealth [Empire], who all, I suppose, asked their cabinets, and he [Baldwin] was totally against anything of that kind.

THE DUKE OF YORK BECOMES KING GEORGE VI

King Edward formally ceased being the Sovereign when, on December 10, 1936, the day before his emotional radio address to his subjects, he signed a document, the Instrument of Abdication.

The next day, December 11, following a meeting of the Accession Council, Prince Albert, Duke of York, became His Majesty King George VI and ten-year-old Elizabeth became the heiress presumptive.

* * *

Sir Gordon Jewkes She must have been very much aware of the burden on her father of assuming the monarchy when he did, because he was a very sensitive man.

And then she saw her father's sense of duty displaying itself in the early years of the war. And I believe it was communicated to her, and she was marked out in a way that Margaret never was—Margaret could be frivolous; Elizabeth couldn't.

Even that first time I saw her—she was the heir, the Princess Elizabeth—she didn't really smile. It was an athletics contest at a small hall in Shropshire. I'm sure she played a very gracious role *en passant,* but she was always on duty.

* * *

King George, as the Duke of York, had treasured family life—as King, he would attempt to maintain their privacy and identity, referring to himself, the Queen, and the two Princesses as "we four."

But in his mind had been the thought that he might one day become King and that his elder daughter, Elizabeth, would succeed him on the Throne.

* * *

Philip Ziegler They were singularly united; they formed a very strong quartet; the King loved the idea of this family fervor.

And the King actually doted on his elder daughter: he was rather resentful when his daughter wanted to marry out of it. But it was genuinely an extremely close, very affectionate relationship.

When the Princesses Elizabeth and Margaret were children, the Duke of York was neither on the Throne, nor heir to the Throne: it seemed highly unlikely that he'd ever be King.

By the end of 1936, when he actually found himself—to his indignation—popped onto the Throne, Princess Elizabeth was ten years old, and so these enormously important formative years had been spent as a kind of informal family.

Then you had a war, during which the burden on the King and Queen was enormous. But there was far less pomposity, far less formality, far less royal flummery, so the time he did have to spend together with the Queen and Elizabeth [and Margaret] was much easier.

CHARACTER BUILDING: ELIZABETH'S SENSE OF DUTY

Philip Ziegler Both her father and her mother were completely dedicated to the job. In a way, her mother's input was more important for the Queen than her father's.

Sir David Scott I think King George definitely saw her as a future Monarch and intended to make sure her training was right. I believe it was a lot of support and training—a lot of telling her what the duties of a Monarch would be, when it happened.

* * *

It appeared at the time that Princess Elizabeth had made a seamless transition from being the Duke of York's daughter to being the heiress presumptive.

* * *

Earl of Harewood That impression is absolutely accurate. Her father was a shy man, although he did a number of public duties. He brought up his daughters very much in the country—although often in London—but I believe they had very normal, if rather privileged, lives.

When he became King in 1936, when she was ten, I'm sure that, to some degree, life changed, and gradually it became more so: she grew up in the war and joined the ATS [Auxiliary Territorial Service], and fiddled away with motorcars and things of that kind when she was seventeen. But there must have been an element of spotlight on her, to put it mildly.

However, she certainly behaved well. However agreeably, decently, the other people round her were behaving, they must have known that she was the heir to the Throne and that was a noticeable thing, much more than with a boy playing games, which was a different thing when the fun of hurling him to the ground was legitimate, so to speak. But it wasn't with a girl, learning how to strip cars down.

It was absolutely true that her life must have changed. And she must have known, however skillfully her parents treated the situation—and I'm sure they would have, because that was how people did in those days—I'm sure she would have been conscious that life wasn't going to flow as it had, and, indeed, as her parents' lives had until then: it's a big shock to discover that you've got to do far more public engagements, and take a far more prominent public position than you were expecting—and more than your parents had been taking.

WAS QUEEN ELIZABETH RELUCTANT TO HAVE HER HUSBAND BECOME KING?

Lady Longford There was plenty of reluctance, but it was all in the King. If she'd been reluctant too, and had gone about with him saying: "Neither of us is any good for this; we're not trained for this job; it's not our thing," it would have been absolutely fatal.

She understood it wasn't a disaster; it was going to work. And, therefore, she made her daughters in the end accept the change.

It was really largely because she was with him, and boosted him, and helped him in every way, and believed in him, that it worked so well.

There are all sorts of stories. I've quoted one in one of my books: when Princess Elizabeth heard all the noise of the cheering when George became King—the two girls were in the house at Hyde Park Corner—she ran downstairs to see what all the excitement was, and a footman told her that her father was King.

She came back and told her little sister, who was six at the time. And Princess Margaret said: "Does that mean you'll be Queen?" And she said: "Yes, some day." And Princess Margaret said: "Poor you."

VIEWS ABOUT THE NEW KING AND HIS FAMILY

John Eisenhower (1922–2013), personal aide to his father, President Eisenhower Dad, I would say, wasn't a royalist, he was much more of an organization man—he'd been in the structure more than most—and I believe he was quite captivated with them. He had something between respect and awe of the British monarchy, almost more than any other institution.

Archdeacon George Austin I can always remember King George VI and Elizabeth coming on a tour round the country. I was at the high school then, and I can remember coming to school and saying to one of the teachers: "He had makeup on." Both of them looked like wax dummies.

After that, I used to see them every year because my father was involved in football and he used to get tickets for the cup finals at Wembley, and we always used to go, and the King and Queen would always come. And I'd always watch out for the makeup—which, of course, wasn't as sophisticated as it is now; it would be much more subtle now—for the photographers.

We always listened at three o'clock on Christmas Day afternoon. You had to get your lunch over by then because you must listen to the King's broadcast. You knew he was having difficulties. He was regarded as a very courageous man. He hadn't wanted the job—it had been thrust upon him by his brother's activities—and you knew that it was painful to him, and you sort of wanted to help him get it out.

He was held in tremendous affection. And a part of it was his own courage in overcoming, quite considerably, this speech disability.

Sir Kenneth Bloomfield I do remember seeing King George VI. I was quite a young boy, and I'm certain it was before the war, on a visit to Belfast. I remember him driving past the area where I was at school, in a car that was lit from the inside, and, actually, he looked just like an unreal figure. I think he may have been made up, in fact, a bit like a waxworks, sitting in the car. But I do remember that—and great enthusiasm.

Bishop Hugh Montefiore There was great worry about what would come, because this poor fellow couldn't even speak—it was pain and grief to listen to him; he just couldn't get it out—and he smoked, of course. He won enormous respect, however.

THE POST-ABDICATION LIFE OF THE DUKE
AND DUCHESS OF WINDSOR

Following the abdication, Edward left almost immediately for France to wait until Mrs. Simpson obtained a decree nisi, dissolving her marriage to Ernest Simpson.

The former King married Wallis Simpson at a chateau near Tours on June 3, 1937. Now styled the Duke and Duchess of Windsor—Wallis, to her and Edward's outrage, was denied the coveted "Her Royal Highness"—the couple embarked on a thirty-five-year marital odyssey that would take them to Hitler's Germany; to *de facto* exile in the Bahamas, where the Duke became the island chain's wartime governor-general; and to the U.S. on numerous visits, where the Windsors were fêted by cafe society, roaming from watering hole to watering hole in a seemingly aimless existence; and back to France, where they established themselves in an elegant house in Paris.

* * *

Lady Longford [...] One of the things that she [the Queen Mother] was criticized for after the abdication was that it was assumed that she was the powerful voice that kept the Windsors out of the country.

Well, we don't know exactly who was responsible. But if it *was* her, it was to her credit because it could never have worked: it was difficult enough for George VI to forget that the adored brother David, who, he thought, was the most marvelous man that had ever been, had abdicated and he himself had taken his brother's place.

And to have his brother living next door, being boosted by the press—We have lost this wonderful man who would have been such a good King; now we've got this second-rater. Why did we do it?

No abdicated King ever goes back to live in the country from which he's abdicated. How could it work? There would have been no end to backbiting and troubles.

Sir (Arthur) Michael Palliser, GCMG, PC (1922–2012), private secretary to Prime Minister Harold Wilson; permanent under secretary of state, Foreign and Commonwealth Office, head of the Diplomatic Service, 1975–82 I was never particularly impressed with the Duke of Windsor when I did meet him. I don't remember her at all. We saw him mainly at stag affairs of one kind or another. I remember a dinner at the Travellers' Club in Paris, which was all male. There was a dinner at the embassy. But, again, it was just for him.

Larry Adler (1914–2001), American-born harmonica virtuoso blacklisted in the U.S. during the 1940s; resident in the U.K.; a friend of the Duke of Edinburgh He [the Duke of Windsor] was a stuffed shirt. When you tried to talk to him, he answered in clichés. You didn't feel that anything came from his own brain, just things he had been told to say.

I was playing at the Waldorf-Astoria, and Richard Boomer, the owner of the Waldorf, was going to give a private party for the Duke and Duchess of Windsor, and he wanted me to play at it.

My agent called me about it and I said: "Okay, what's my fee?" He said: "What do you mean?" I said: "My fee for this party." And he said: "Larry, it's for the Duke and Duchess of Windsor." I said: "Well, is it for a charity?" He said: "No." And I said: "Then why should I do it for free? My answer is *no!*"

Two days later, the head of MCA[9] said to me: "Larry, if you don't play at this party, we're going to lose the whole Waldorf account." So I was blackmailed into playing for it.

But while I played, I kept looking at the Duchess of Windsor's left ear, because she kept turning around to see what I was looking at, and I wanted to make her feel uncomfortable. She dressed very well. That's all I can say. I didn't have much of a conversation with her.

THE DUKE OF WINDSOR'S SEEMING FLIRTATION
WITH HITLER

On October 22, 1937, two years after the promulgation of the racist Nuremberg Laws, depriving Germany's Jews of their civil rights, and with increasing evidence that Nazi Germany was rearming in violation of the Versailles Agreement, the Duke and Duchess of Windsor met with the Nazi Führer, Adolf Hitler, at his mountaintop villa, the Berghof, above Berchtesgaden.

That meeting was the high point of a visit by the Windsors to Germany, during which they dined with Nazi officials Rudolf Hess and Hermann Goering and their wives, who pleased the Windsors by referring to the Duchess as "Your Royal Highness."

The visit had been arranged by Charles Bedaux, the wealthy business entrepreneur in whose chateau the Windsors had been married earlier that year. Bedaux, who had major business concerns in Germany, was seeking to ingratiate himself with the Nazi regime and believed that the way to the Führer's heart was through the propaganda coup of delivering the former King of England.

The Windsors' visit to Germany was announced to the press in Paris as one of two such trips, the other being to the United States, "for the purpose of studying housing and working conditions."

News of the impending visit infuriated both the British government and the Royal Family, with King George exclaiming to an adviser that it was "a bombshell and a bad one."

* * *

Earl of Harewood Hitler in 1937 was the head of a friendly foreign government. The mere notion that he [the Duke of Windsor] was a dedicated Nazi—he spoke German—or had any Nazi feelings whatsoever, is absolute bunkum—total and absolute nonsense.

I believe the thinking was: they're pretty competent, aren't they? They've turned the country round and the Communists are worse. That was thought in many parts of the world, including the United States, that that was all.

And the enormity of Hitler wasn't really known to the world at that stage. And until Kristallnacht,[10] it was only known because it was in *Mein Kampf*,[11] but it wasn't thought of as being a major issue for the rest of the world.

Larry Adler He accepted a decoration from Goering, and you must know what you're doing when you accept a decoration from one of the highest Nazis. He knew. And England was lucky that he didn't stay as King because he was very pro-Nazi.

Philip Ziegler His attitude towards Germany was not that different to either his brothers', or to two-thirds of the Conservative cabinet. At the time when he went to Germany, probably at least half of the Conservative government would all have agreed with him that the Communist menace was far more serious: that there were some very, very nasty things about Fascism, but it probably wasn't as bad as they make out, and once it [National Socialism] established itself, the nastiness would die down, and we'd got to do what we could to get on with them.

Lord Thurlow It was a notable illustration of his detachment: he was nobbled [won over] by these Nazi intriguers and influenced by that curious figure Mr. Bedaux—I think that Mrs. Simpson knew Mr. Bedaux—who got quite close, with his efficiency thing, to some of the German industrialists.

And one way or another, he allowed himself to be seduced into going to pay what was a completely informal visit—he had no formal position. And, no doubt, when so many efforts were being made by [Prime Minister Neville] Chamberlain, and everybody else, to come to some kind of reasonable arrangement with this impossible brute—people lived in a wishful world, in which they liked to believe some of his assurances—I think that the Duke of Windsor saw himself as hoping to build a social bridge, as it were, and showing that the British from their side had tendencies, or friendly feelings, towards Germans as a whole. After all, he had a lot of German blood.

He was basically taken for a ride. I don't accept at all that there was anything more than poor judgment: he was suckered into this situation, and he had nobody to advise him—he had no official staff at all.

And he enjoyed being made a fuss of: it's very difficult, if you've been made a fuss of all your life and then suddenly find that nobody is interested in you, so it's rather nice to be made a fuss of.

I have no doubt that Hitler had a perfectly clear-cut, ulterior motive: he expected to go to war with us; he expected to win—indeed, many of us at the beginning didn't see how he could help it; and then, he was going to make him [the Duke of Windsor] King of England again.

And whether he would have in his weakness of judgment allowed himself to be manipulated to that extent I doubt: I don't believe he'd have been because he remained, after he abdicated, a loyal subject to the new King, his brother, and so I don't think he would have allowed himself to serve their purpose.

Lady Longford Somebody suggested it—probably one of his German friends said that the Führer would love to meet him and that it would be very interesting and good for the world if these two great characters met and became friends.

I don't think he had very good judgment; he wasn't very clever in those kinds of ways, though he had great charm, and intuitive feelings about people. But he didn't have a great deal up here [in his head].

Sir Michael Palliser It was a complex of motives. I think he wanted to do something; he had a genuine sense of duty to the country. In a way, he abdicated partly out of a sense of duty. But I think he felt he wanted to do something for the country.

If you think back, there had been enormous support for Chamberlain—what is nowadays called, rather pejoratively, appeasement. It was not an unpopular policy at the time and, I think, probably the Duke of Windsor was a bit sort of colored by it, if you like, and also, he was fairly right wing in his political attitudes.

I don't say that he felt sympathy for Hitler and his regime; I don't really think he did. But there was a strong sort of undercurrent of: couldn't we make peace with Germany?

Philip Ziegler He genuinely admired the achievements of National Socialism in Germany, when it came to unemployment, and housing the workers, and things like that—this was a field in which over forty years he had registered some expertise.

And so he genuinely wanted to go there, and to be perceived taking the liberty: he knew the Germans would fawn on him, would address the Duchess of Windsor as "Your Royal Highness," would give him a chance of showing off to her as being somebody who was still a royal. That, I believe, was probably the greatest single factor. He certainly also took some pleasure in annoying his family.

Sir Rex Hunt, CMG (1926–2012), governor and commander-in-chief of the Falkland Islands, 1980–82; high commissioner of the British Antarctic Territory, 1980–85 He always did flirt with the idea of Nazism. He rather admired Hitler for what he had done: he thought that Hitler had the right ideas and was really doing something for his people.

At the same time, he was certainly very, very bitter at his brother, or mainly at his sister-in-law [...] because they wouldn't grant HRH [the title of Her Royal Highness] to Wallis Simpson, and he wanted to get his own back.

I felt very sorry for him. It was very moving, his speech, when he abdicated. But after that, I learned a lot more about him, and I can't have any respect for him now. I believe he was a very little-minded man.

WOULD THE DUKE HAVE ALLOWED HIMSELF TO BE USED BY HITLER?

Lady Longford He never would have done that. And I don't think she would either.

Earl of Perth I was, perhaps, surprised by the visit to Hitler. But, more important, one can't tell, but I believe he would have put his country first, and if there had been an overrunning—if Hitler had won—it's possible to say that he would have done whatever was best for his country.

He was definitely a patriotic man, and although he may have had some sympathy with one or two of the Hitler ideas, I wouldn't put it further than that.

Earl of Harewood I have no idea. He might have. But he might have refused to do it. He might have done it to try and mitigate the damage. All of those things can be true and can be sensible.

I'd be very surprised. I don't know whether King George VI talked German. I know his brother did. Most of them were taught German—my mother[12] was taught German; she had a German governess before the First War and was very unhappy that she had to go back to Germany when the war was declared in 1914. I don't think my mother kept up her German but she certainly understood German. And the King did too.

The Duke of Windsor went from Paris to Brussels. He had an American friend there, and the American friend was supposed to have been pro-German—perhaps was pro-German; you don't get kneecapped for being pro-German at that stage, although it's regrettable.

That was supposed to have been an act of great treachery. I suppose if you're friends with them, you might even try to persuade them they were wrong.

Sir David Scott There does seem to be quite a strong belief that when he went to Portugal that he would, in fact, establish contact with the Germans and he wouldn't have been averse, if things had gone wrong, to being called back to be the King.

I don't know to what extent that's rumor, or not. But certainly, the story of that event convinces me he certainly did maintain contact with Germany before he went to the Bahamas. If he'd been invited to come back as King, I strongly suspect that he would have accepted. I don't believe he did a great deal of lobbying for that; I believe that he kept his options open.

Earl of Harewood There was a big program about him on English television, and it tried to bring out that he was a kind of traitor—I think it called him "the traitor-King," God help us—and one of the things it did, it found a broadcast he'd made to the United States—under what circumstances I don't know—in 1938 or 1939 in which he said, in effect: I'm speaking to you from Europe, and I want to emphasize how crucial it is that the world remains at peace. Any of us who were in the last war will know the horrors of war and will know the crucial advantages of staying at peace. Whatever happens, we must accommodate whatever goes on in the world to preserve peace.

That was never broadcast in England; it was considered to be a terrible piece of appeasement, which was considered a terrible thing when the war began. But, of course, it wasn't a terrible thing: peace is a pretty valuable thing.

WHY WAS THE DUKE SENT TO THE BAHAMAS?

After much discussion in the wartime government of Prime Minister Winston Churchill, on July 9, 1940—barely one month after the end of the "phoney war" with Hitler's invasions of France, Denmark, Norway, and the Low Countries—the Duke of Windsor was appointed governor of the Bahamas.

The Windsors' service in the Bahamas was marked by controversy— and even the Duke's involvement in a reported cover-up in a sensational murder case.

Earl of Perth He wanted to serve. And they wanted him out of this country, to serve abroad. I remember very well when during the phoney war he used to be in Paris and I think it was always a little bit awkward.

But, given also his very real wish to serve in some capacity, to send him out to be a governor in the West Indies was an ingenious solution. I believe he wanted perhaps to get back into things, but it's very difficult if you've got somebody who's the Monarch, and the ex-Monarch: you want to get the Crown unimpeded.

Eric Moonman I believe the fact that he had a very small role during the war—he was governor-general in the Bahamas—was just to get him out of the way.

In fact, my brother-in-law at the time was with the intelligence in the same place, and it was the posting of a lifetime—to go there while the war was on, in this beautiful place, and just to get a dispatch every morning as to what was happening—it must have been pure delight.

I believe it was demeaning and I can only think that it was to get him out of the way. But then why did he take it, unless they offered him nothing else?

Earl of Harewood I don't think he was tremendously effective, because the position was very ill-defined. He had very bad luck in the Bahamas: a prominent citizen[13] was murdered who was quite possibly a villain. But that's not the point. He was well-known in this very small place and they pointed the finger at somebody who was said to have murdered him, his son-in-law.

The Bahamas, I suppose, was not very well provided with sophisticated detective methods, and the Duke of Windsor called for the police in Miami to come and help. And that was thought to have been a mistake. It was a very minor mistake.

And he went occasionally to the United States from the Bahamas. But that was the extent of the "wickedness" in the war. I thought he should have been given a more responsible job. A lot of people thought that, and a lot of people thought not.

Lord Thurlow It was a long time before I was there.[14] Of course, a lot of people remembered them, and used to come to Government House when he was governor, and so we picked up quite a lot of gossip.

Regrettably, I suspect, rather under the influence of Mrs. Simpson, the Duchess, there was a very distinctive color bar in Government House: I don't believe any black Bahamian would have got near any sort of social relationship with the governor and his wife; they were supposed not really to like black people. And their senior servants they brought in from France, and elsewhere.

But the Bahamas, after all, in those days was still run as it had been run for three hundred years by the white Bahamians who ran everything and owned everything: it was very much a Deep South attitude to the races and color.

And so one has to make allowances for that: the Windsors arrived in a social setting which was totally set in, as it had been for three hundred years.

* * *

Following their return to France after the end of World War Two, the Duke and Duchess of Windsor resumed their frantic social pace, traveling from shore to shore, and living together in their Paris house until the Duke's death, from cancer, in 1972.

After the Duke's death, a thaw occurred in the House of Windsor when Wallis Warfield Simpson Windsor returned to Britain to bury the former King Edward VIII and was received by the Royal Family, including Elizabeth the Queen Mother.

On her return to Paris the Duchess resumed her social round for a time, but her health began to decline and she became a recluse. She would remain in the house she had shared with the Duke, frail and living in splendid isolation, until her death in 1986.

CHAPTER 3

The War and the
Royal Family

A T 5:45 ON the morning of Friday, September 1, 1939, a force
of more than one million Wehrmacht soldiers invaded Poland,
unleashing Hitler's almost six-year reign of terror in most of
Europe, as well as a war in the Pacific that would in August 1945 cul-
minate in the use by the United States of two atomic bombs over Japan.

The war clouds had been gathering for some years. As early as November
1934, Winston Churchill stated in a speech in the House of Commons
that Germany's armaments industry was operating "under practically war
conditions." Churchill predicted that by 1937 Germany's Air Force would
be double the strength of Britain's. And by March 1935, the specter of
German rearmament had become so alarming that plans were announced
for the expansion of the British Army, Navy, and Air Force.

Hitler soon began a series of land grabs, marching into the Rhineland
on March 7, 1937. Flying in the face of the Versailles Treaty, he demanded
lebensraum (living space) for Nazi Germany in a massive rally at
Nuremberg on March 5, 1937. He annexed Austria on March 14, 1938,
in what would come to be known as the *Anschluss*.

And on September 30, 1938, in Munich, in an act that would ensure
war with Britain, Hitler concluded an agreement for "peace for our
time"[1]—the dismemberment of Czechoslovakia—with the leaders of
three European nations.

In the early hours of that day, following nearly twelve hours of nego-
tiations punctuated by Hitler's rantings and ravings, Prime Minister
Neville Chamberlain of Britain, Edouard Daladier of France, and Benito
Mussolini, the Fascist premier of Italy, in the absence of a representative

of Czechoslovakia, agreed to Hitler's demand that the Sudetenland, inhabited by a German-speaking minority, be ceded to the Third Reich.

On April 27, 1939, the House of Commons endorsed the government's decision to introduce military conscription for twenty-year-olds. And three days later, on May 1, the Military Training Bill was formally introduced.

On May 17, King George VI and Queen Elizabeth—in the first visit by a reigning British Monarch to the United States—embarked on a more than six-week North American tour, seeking support for the now inevitable conflict with Nazi Germany.

Going first to Canada, they arrived in Quebec on May 17. On June 7, they arrived in the U.S., visiting Washington, where they were guests of President Franklin Delano Roosevelt and his wife, Eleanor, and New York City, where they attended the World's Fair then underway. The King and Queen also spent time with the presidential couple at the Roosevelt family home in Hyde Park, New York.

The King and Queen returned to London on June 22 to face a summer of increasing tension as Europe moved closer to war.

July was marked by the King's approval of the formation of the Women's Auxiliary Air Force and the government's announcement that Britain would borrow £500 million for defense spending.

On August 23 came the stunning news of the signing in the Kremlin of a nonaggression pact between Nazi Germany and the Soviet Union. Four days later, the first flight of a new gas turbine aircraft that would come to be known as the "jet" took place in German skies.

And on August 31 perhaps the most disturbing pre-war event of all for the British public occurred on the homefront: the start of the evacuation of 1.5 million children from cities across Britain to safer areas in the country. As of 5:30 that morning, parents began to say tearful goodbyes to youngsters clutching only a few possessions—and government-issued gas masks.

In another ominous development on August 31, Britain's historic Coronation Chair was removed from its customary place and taken by train to an unannounced hiding place.

September 3, 1939, marked the beginning of what would come to be known as the phoney war. After the Wehrmacht's lightning subjugation of Poland, there were skirmishes, sinkings of Allied shipping, and air attacks. But full-fledged conflict was still months away. That lull would be shattered in the spring of 1940 with the invasion by Nazi forces of France and the Low Countries. But nobody could have known that on September 3.

Sunday, September 3, 1939, was a beautiful, sunny day in London. At noon, following the expiration an hour earlier of Britain's ultimatum to Germany to cease military operations against Poland, Prime Minister Chamberlain declared in the House of Commons: "This country is now at war with Germany. We are ready."

Half an hour after the prime minister's historic declaration, air raid sirens sounded in London. That sounding would prove to be a false alarm. An unidentified aircraft—later found to be "friendly"—had triggered the alarm as it approached Britain's south coast. It was one of the last of such false alarms for the British people.

That evening, in a broadcast to his subjects in the Commonwealth, King George VI declared: "We can only do the right as we see the right, and reverently commit our cause to God."

* * *

Yehuda Avner (1928–2015), formerly of Manchester, immigrant in 1947 to the then-British Mandate Palestine, now Israel; political adviser to Prime Minister Menachem Begin of Israel, 1977–81; Israeli ambassador to the Court of St. James's, 1982–88 Then it was "King and country; King and country." There was a patriotic community. One of the biggest flags I've ever seen in my life was opposite where I was born—we were not living there at the time. My father's small drapery shop was opposite the Strangeways jail; and it was one of the largest flags I've ever seen. It was draping over the front entrance of Strangeways jail.

Adm. Sir Henry Leach It was a *Dad's Army*—the idea that you'd take a kitchen carving knife, or a hay fork, that you're going to beat them. There was great spirit on that. What we thought in the military was another matter.

Baron Merlyn-Rees, PC (1920–2006), life peer, cr. 1992; Labour M.P., 1963–92; secretary of state for Northern Ireland, 1974–76; Home Secretary, 1976–79; member, the Falklands Islands Review Committee, 1982 They must have been mad, but nobody in 1940 thought we were going to lose. If the Germans had crossed the Channel, there was very little we could have done to stop them.

"WINNIE'S BACK"

On September 4, 1939, a signal was flashed to the British Fleet: "Winnie's back." With those two words the nation learned of the return from the political wilderness of Winston Churchill as First Lord of the Admiralty, a post he had held at the outbreak of World War One twenty-five years earlier, but had resigned over the disaster at Gallipoli.[2]

* * *

Philip Ziegler In a way, for a small boy during a war, Churchill was the crucial figure, and he rather overshadowed the Royal Family in the minds of everyone who was in Britain at the time and got this picture of the slim, tired figure of the King, climbing over bombed sites in the East End, and doing all the things Kings are supposed to do. He undoubtedly inspired respect and affection, but he was not the kind of glamorous rallying point, which was Winston Churchill.

Canon Paul Oestreicher Churchill was a unique figure in world history. Churchill would have been respected because he was Winston Churchill, not because he was prime minister of the United Kingdom. Churchill was a figure in his own right, who won a world war, and who was respected for that reason. But he was thrown out of power as soon as the war was over.

The King would have been respected because he was head of state of this country and this country was the motherland. New Zealand was a very patriotic country; New Zealand sent a lot of troops into the war—in fact, the percentage of New Zealanders killed in the war was higher than the percentage of British people—and that patriotism was there to that extent because Churchill represented the war's spirit: he would be respected as a great figure.

Lady Young Under our constitution, of course, Churchill was a very powerful figure. And, of course, Churchill's speeches were of immense encouragement. That isn't in any way to downgrade the role of the monarchy because, of course, the fact that the King and the Queen stayed in London, and the Princesses stayed there, was very important to everybody.

Archdeacon George Austin Winston Churchill was seen as the great war hero, the great war leader, but *they* [the monarchy] were the nation, encapsulated in the person of the Monarch and his wife.

THE ROYAL FAMILY AND THE BLITZ

On September 7, 1940, Luftwaffe bombs began to fall on London's East End, ushering in horrendous physical and psychological suffering that would last for many months, sending Londoners into the Underground train stations to seek nighttime refuge. Many Britons in key ports or industrial centers would be killed, or severely injured. Many homes, blocks of flats, and public buildings would be pulverized. Landmarks, such as Coventry Cathedral, would be left in ruins.

And the Royal Family was not immune: one day in September, as the King and Queen sat in a small upstairs room in Buckingham Palace, six bombs fell on the grounds below, blowing windows in and creating craters in the area known as the quadrangle.

Following the direct hits to the Palace grounds, the Queen stated that she could now look the East End in the face.

* * *

Lord Merlyn-Rees It goes without saying that George VI wasn't as popular as his brother. Then the war came, and they stayed in London; they visited the East End of London, where all the bombing was. And he became, if not a popular King, a respected King. Nobody in the general public realized the nature of his problem—he was a bad stutterer. And he had a turn of temper, and frustration, over the way he couldn't speak.

Lord Healey Water was rationed and you weren't allowed to have more than two inches in the bath. And George VI and his family, they painted the two inches on their bath, and they observed the same restrictions as everybody else.

I would say that that was when the "people's monarchy" really began. It wasn't true of George V, or his predecessors, who were very much above and apart, whereas George VI made the point of getting around a great deal. And, of course, his children and grandchildren have done so as well.

Lord Thurlow The King and Queen were nearer to the people in the Second War than in the First War because at the time of the First War the Monarch in those days didn't bother about public relations, and they did their own thing—Queen Victoria, after all, didn't bother to come to London for years—and they didn't bother what people felt about them.

Claire Rayner, OBE (1931–2010), journalist, advice columnist, author of ninety books, anti-monarchist Propaganda was not just the province of Goebbels. That business about the King and the Queen staying in London during the war is a lot of crap! I was an East Ender and we were not impressed: essentially the royals were very cushioned and protected—they certainly weren't experiencing the privations we were—and we knew this.

Sir Bernard Ingham, chief press secretary to Prime Minister Margaret Thatcher, 1979–90; later *Yorkshire Post* **columnist and television commentator** There was an undertone of resentment of privilege. I have to tell you, that died with the war, because whatever else you may say about the King and Queen, during the war they certainly conducted a magnificent public relations operation of identifying with the people in the bombing, and their problems, and their difficulties.

It is fair to say that the King, who had a problem with stammering—I remember that his Christmas broadcasts, which we always listened to, were felt to be a triumph of courage, in a sense of sheer willpower over a natural disability—was looked up to, and they emerged from the war with much greater respect. There was less, perhaps, an overt concern about privilege, although that has always been there.

Gen. Andrew Goodpaster Eisenhower always had a very high, and personal, regard for the King, who had brought stability to the country when he took over after the abdication of his brother and became head of the Royal Family.

Eisenhower felt that the King had really displayed great leadership in his personal presence during the war, that he was a steadying and inspiring figure to the British people during that time.

He was an inspiration to his people. The Queen had a very steadying effect as well. And she was so greatly admired by the people. And, of course, they stood their ground all through the war, so that there was a personal regard on Eisenhower's part toward all of them in the family.

A WARTIME VIGNETTE

Adm. Sir Henry Leach I met the King in the war years when he came up to Scapa[3] to visit the fleet. He stayed with the commander-in-chief, Admiral Bruce Fraser, in the flagship.

I was then what was called the sub-lieutenant of the gun room in the fleet flagship, the battleship *Duke of York*. It was a big gun room—it had forty-three in it, including sub-lieutenants, but I was the boss of that little community.

King George was up there about two or three days, and one evening, which was a great honor for me, he came and dined in the gun room, which was interesting, an evening in very close quarters, which was never to be repeated. He was charming, and you were not unduly aware of his stammer—it was noticeable.

He smoked quite a lot and I remember upsetting the messman because this was in the middle of winter, December or January, in Scapa Flow in 1942, the middle of the war, and it was difficult to get exotic fruit and stuff like that because it simply wasn't around. And the messman, who, like most messmen, was a bit of a crook—but he was a naval crook—managed to get strawberries and cream. So that was what we had as a dessert.

But the King wanted to have a smoke. And as a result of that, the strawberries and cream were forgotten, and we went straight on to coffee, and port, and all that sort of stuff. Maybe I should have insisted on serving the strawberries and cream. I was, obviously, fairly new at this.

THE YOUNG PRINCESS AND THE WAR

Although many parents who had the means to do so chose to send their children out of the country for the duration of the war, the Princesses Elizabeth and Margaret Rose were not evacuated.

While they did spend much of the war outside London, they were sent only as far as Windsor Castle, within easy striking distance of Hitler's Luftwaffe (Air Force).

Princess Elizabeth became personally involved in the war effort on October 13, 1940, when, at the age of fourteen, she made her first radio address, directed at British child evacuees to North America. Palace advisers hoped the broadcast would influence public opinion in the U.S.

At the end of the broadcast, Princess Elizabeth introduced her younger sister, whom she urged to say goodnight to their listeners. Obliging, Princess Margaret said: "Good night and good luck to you all."

In January 1942, Princess Elizabeth joined the adult war effort, becoming honorary colonel of the Grenadier Guards and carrying out her first inspection of the troops at Windsor Castle on her sixteenth birthday.

On April 21, 1944, Princess Elizabeth celebrated her eighteenth birthday, a milestone made more significant in that she was now entitled to succeed directly to the Throne without being represented by a Regent.

Then, early in 1945, it was decided that Princess Elizabeth would join the Auxiliary Territorial Service (ATS). In late February she was registered as #230872 Second Subaltern Elizabeth Alexandra Mary Windsor and was instructed in driving and vehicle maintenance at a training center in Aldershot.

On the last day of her ATS service the Princess was taken aback when the King chided her for not being able to restart a stalled engine. Only later did the King inform his daughter that he had removed the distributor as a prank.

* * *

John Eisenhower Elizabeth was not the one that impressed me of the whole group She was pretty serious, she took herself pretty seriously, was authoritative. I guess she never had a youth.

I tried to banter a little bit about how, in Germany, they had the relatives running around in kilts. She did not laugh.

Princess Margaret, who was fourteen [in 1944], was a tremendous admirer of Dad. She insisted on going off at Windsor for a walk with him. She was much more interested in Dad than Elizabeth was. But she could be. She didn't have the weight of the world on her.

D-DAY

The long-awaited Allied invasion of the Normandy peninsula began in the early hours of June 6, 1944.

* * *

Gen. Andrew Goodpaster Winston Churchill had wanted to accompany the invasion and Eisenhower thought that was very unwise, very risky, and he was strongly opposed to it. And Churchill pressed on this and Eisenhower said: "Well, I will go to the King, if necessary."

John Eisenhower Churchill demanded to be aboard a ship that watched the D-Day landing and King George objected to that. I believe he felt that *he* was the titular commander of the Army and the Navy, not Churchill.

* * *

King George had also wanted to witness the invasion. After much reflection, however, the King wrote to Churchill: "We should both, I know, love to be there but, in all seriousness, I would ask you to reconsider your plan ... I have very reluctantly come to the conclusion that the right thing to do is what normally falls to those at the top on such occasions, namely to remain at home and wait."

VE DAY, MAY 8, 1945

Stephen Peter Day, CMG, ambassador and consul general, Qatar, 1981–84; ambassador and consul general, Tunisia, 1987–92; senior trade commissioner, Hong Kong, 1992–93 I was a very little boy. It's a very clear "snap-shot" memory of the street party, with the trestle tables all put up in the street. And we each had a little china mug to celebrate.

And also, an extremely vivid memory of my first American soldiers, two of them, I caught going along the road in their big gray coats. The funny papers had a saying: "Any gum, chum?" So I tried it on them and I got some gum!

That gave me an enormous affection for Americans, you see, because to be brought up in the war when we had no sweets, the luxury of having chewing gum—the joy of having that chewing gum—was something I don't think I ever experienced again.

* * *

On the evening of VE Day among the celebrants joining the street parties, linking arms in the streets of London and singing "Roll Out the Barrel" and "Hang Out the Washing on the Siegfried Line," were the Princesses Elizabeth and Margaret.

They were encouraged to do so by the King, who recognized that due to wartime privations the Princesses had "not yet had any fun," as he noted that evening in his diary.

Escorted by Guards officers of the Household, Elizabeth and Margaret slipped out of the Palace, made their way unrecognized as far as the Ritz Hotel on Piccadilly and back to the Palace, where they joined the crowd beneath the balcony where the King and Queen stood acknowledging the cheers of their war-weary subjects.

CHAPTER 4

The Marriage of Princess Elizabeth to Prince Philip

O N AUGUST 14, 1945, the day Japan surrendered to the Allies, Britain had been at war just twenty days short of six years. While there was jubilation throughout the British Isles and the Empire, a somber note was sounded on August 24 when Britain's new Labour Prime Minister, Clement Attlee, who had succeeded Winston Churchill on July 26 in a stunning defeat for the Tory Party,[1] stated in Parliament that due to the abrupt ending by the United States government of its Lend-Lease policy, Britain was facing a dire financial situation, requiring major cuts in imports of such necessities as food, cotton, and gasoline, as well as such non-essential items as tobacco. And those meager amounts of goods produced in Britain would now have to be exported.

Adding misery to austerity, in February 1947, heavy snowstorms and freezing temperatures, combined with a major fuel shortage, caused Britons to shiver in their homes and workplaces—when they could work, as layoffs necessitated by power outages forced the shut-down of much of the nation's industry. Buckingham Palace was not exempt; the vast building was being lit by candlelight.

Then on June 30, the government ordered a further economic cutback. New slogans emerged, such as "Export or Die," and "Work or Want."

On August 27, the government announced the implementation of further cuts, among them a reduction in the already meager meat ration; the need for the use of ration books in hotels for more than a two-night stay; the cessation of all non-essential driving; and a ban on holidays abroad. The government also acknowledged that worse was to come.

* * *

Archdeacon George Austin It got worse after the war, actually. It was very harsh—the butter and sugar rations decreased, as far as I remember, after the war.

I went to university in 1950 and we had to line up every Friday for a butter ration of two ounces—there was a little room, which was called "the buttery," a kind of butler's pantry—and our sugar ration. And sweets were rationed a long time.

I can't remember us going hungry. Everybody knew somebody who could get you something; we used to get duck eggs.

We lived in a seaside resort on the west coast and I can remember going by rail—it was a very tedious journey, because there were delays for troop trains—and we stopped outside the station of a big city en route, and an American G.I. troop train was opposite and they were throwing oranges—I think they were telling them: "Throw them towards the girls, not towards the boys"—I'd seen oranges before the war, but, of course, not since. It was appreciated.

* * *

On February 1, 1947, in the midst of the worst weather Britain had yet endured in the twentieth century, the Royal Family boarded Britain's newest battleship, HMS *Vanguard*, for an almost three-month visit to South Africa—Princess Elizabeth's first trip outside the British Isles.

For the government, as well as for the King and Queen, the visit was necessary for political reasons. For the young Princess, the South African experience was an introduction to what for her would become one of the driving passions of her reign: the Commonwealth of Nations. In an address to the Empire and the Commonwealth broadcast from Cape Town on April 21, her twenty-first birthday, the Princess pledged:

> I declare before you all that my whole life, whether it be long or short, shall be devoted to your service and the service of our great Imperial family to which we all belong, but I shall not have the strength to carry out this resolution alone unless you join in with me, as I now invite you to do. I know that your support will be unfailingly given. God help me to make good my vow and God bless all of you who are willing to share in it.

Princess Elizabeth, however, had another concern during the royal tour: the King and Queen were testing her devotion to her handsome third cousin, Prince Philip, the grandson and nephew of Kings of Greece.[2]

Tim Heald There were a lot of reservations about Prince Philip from people who were senior at court, or senior members of the English aristocracy; senior people at court weren't terribly helpful to Prince Philip.

I don't know that there's any evidence—the Queen Mother's brother was always supposed to have been very hostile to Prince Philip.

When I was researching my book, I had lunch at Clarence House with the Queen Mother, and beyond directly saying: "Did you approve of it?" we talked quite extensively about him. I remember, for instance, saying to her: "What nationality do you think of Prince Philip as being?" and she said: "Oh, he's an English gentleman."

He's intensely patriotic and very *British*, but he's still very aware of the fact that he comes from somewhere else, and he's part of that big, difficult to define, European monarchy, rather than being specifically British—in the way of Queen Mary.

But I thought it was very interesting that as far as the Queen Mother was concerned: he's just like the rest of us; he's thoroughly *English*.

I certainly didn't get the slightest impression—and this is forty years, or more, after the marriage—of any sort of reservation, certainly in the present, nor in the past.

Lady Pamela Hicks They whisked her off to South Africa. It was purely that they felt that he was the first person she had fallen in love with, and she was only twenty-one, and it's a life-long commitment, particularly in *her* position, and that she ought to be very sure, and she ought to look around, and meet other people, and be very sure of herself. It was a very sensible precaution to have taken.

When they came back she still was of one mind. She was dazzled by him when she was a little girl, and she found, when she was older, he was still very good looking; he was still very amusing; he was still very enthusiastic—he had the kind of charisma that dazzled people. Although she liked going dancing with several other people, various quite suitable people, I don't think any of them had the dazzle that Philip had.

I think then the King and my father[3] did talk about it in those days. And I'm sure my father actually proposed it because I think he thought that Prince Philip would be the ideal kind of person. He is a remarkable man and I think my father probably guessed that he was going to become a remarkable man.

Could there have been a more suitable candidate for marriage to the heiress presumptive?

Philip Ziegler I can't think of a good royal, really. There were a fair number of British grandees who would have been perfectly eligible, but, on the whole, everyone slightly preferred the idea of her marrying into the royal circle because it avoided picking one British family over another British family.

So I think that the Establishment, on the whole, rather welcomed the fact that she was marrying into a foreign royal family. It was the best of both worlds, in a way: Philip, who was educated almost entirely in England, was a British naval officer, was a British citizen [subject], and yet was a foreign royal.

Tim Heald The King and Queen thought he was very good news in all sorts of ways, and also, that there wasn't really an alternative: there wasn't anybody in the European monarchy field, basically, who wasn't either patently inadequate, or already married, or who hadn't fought on the wrong side in the war.

And I don't believe—there were various sorts of suitable English dukes walking around—that anybody would seriously have entertained the idea of the future Queen of England being married to anybody other than a member of a royal family.

LORD MOUNTBATTEN

Like Princess Elizabeth, a great-great-grandchild of Queen Victoria and Prince Albert, Prince Philip was the son of Victoria's great-granddaughter, Princess Alice, and her estranged husband, Prince Andrew of Greece, and due to the circumstance of his family's exile from Greece, an impoverished royal.

He had been taken under the protective wing of two uncles—Princess Alice's brothers, George, Second Marquis of Milford Haven, and Louis, Earl Mountbatten of Burma. And following the death of the Marquis of Milford Haven in 1938, Lord Mountbatten became Philip's chief advocate in Britain.

Lord Mountbatten and his brother were the sons of Queen Victoria's granddaughter, Victoria of Hesse, and the German-born Prince Louis of Battenberg, First Marquis of Milford Haven. Despite having distinguished himself in a forty-six-year career, lastly as First Lord of the Admiralty at the outbreak of the Great War in August 1914, Prince Louis was forced to resign three months later, due to public antipathy to all things German.

* * *

Adm. Sir Henry Leach Lord Mountbatten always had a slight chip on his shoulder because his father had had to resign as First Sea Lord in World War One. And Dickie was convinced that he was going to make it, and he was going to be this and he was going to be that, and he was pretty arrogant in his latter days: he could be utterly charming, but he could be very difficult.

Tim Heald He was not an easy person to interview. I only interviewed Mountbatten once, when I was doing some work for Prince Charles, and I found him extraordinarily difficult, because he was one of those people who didn't respond to questions: he told you what *he* wished you to hear, so you would say: "Lord Mountbatten"—we were talking about fishing—and I would start to say: "When did you actually first put a fishing rod into Prince Charles's hands?" And I was halfway through the question when I would be aware that Lord Mountbatten was talking, and he was saying, in the third person: "Lord Mountbatten, on a certain ..." And I would say: "Excuse me. I'm going to ask you a question and then you give me an answer." "Don't be *ridiculous*; you are here to listen to what I have to say!"

Earl of Harewood The charm was *fantastic*. We used to send out a lot of Christmas cards, and we used always to send Dickie a Christmas card, forgetting that he'd given up Christmas cards at the time of his wife's death.[4]

But he always used to write back a postcard—it was much more trouble than sending a Christmas card—saying: "Thank you very much for your Christmas card. I, as you possibly remember, have given up sending Christmas cards, but I enjoyed getting yours ..." More trouble than sending a Christmas card!

Lord Healey He was an exceptional man. He was always rather pro-Labour. There was a famous story about how, during a general election, a Conservative canvasser called at Broadlands, where he lived, in the country. He answered the front door, you see, and the chap said: "I'm a canvasser for the Conservative Party," and Dickie said: "Ah, well, I don't have a vote, of course, because I'm a peer of the realm. But if I had one, I'd vote Labour. But you can talk to my butler; I think he's a Conservative."

Gen. Andrew J. Goodpaster He came and participated in our annual exercise in which the senior commanders of the NATO Command, along with the senior military leaders of each country, came together at SHAPE.

Field Marshal Montgomery, who was Eisenhower's deputy, charged by Eisenhower with the training and the organization of the troops in NATO Command, set up this exercise, called Shape Up. And he had these strict rules for all people who were in attendance. He said: "There will be no smoking." And he said: "Now I do not want coughing. Here is a box of cough drops, and anyone who feels the need can take a cough drop."

Well, he was talking a little later, and in the midst of something, and all of a sudden, Mountbatten got up, strolled over in a very leisurely, easy-going way, reached his hand into the box, took a cough drop, thrust it into his mouth, and took his time walking back. The place, of course, absolutely broke up.

Lady Pamela Hicks It was absolutely fun being around my father! And until he died life was one big excitement.

PHILIP'S RELATIONSHIP WITH LORD MOUNTBATTEN

Tim Heald He gets very, very irritated about being misunderstood. I've seen that often. As he put it: "People think that Lord Mountbatten was my father. Well, they forget that I have parents."

He was deeply devoted to his "Uncle Dickie," and they were very close, and he wouldn't ever deny the fact. Nevertheless, he had a mother and father, of whom he was extremely fond—their portraits are still in his private office.

And yet, if you went out into the street and talked to a cross-section of people, you would probably find a significant number who would think Mountbatten *was* Philip's father.

Philip Ziegler Prince Philip is a man with very much a mind of his own: he tends to get very cross if you suggest that he'd been subject too much to his uncle's influence. And I believe that once he ceased to be a boy, once he'd become a naval officer, he was very much his own man.

He respected his uncle: he would listen quite carefully to anything his uncle said—both Prince Philip and the Queen would always listen with interest to what Lord Mountbatten said.

But he did not have undue influence. In no way was he a master over them, from what I've seen. I don't think it was seen, remotely, that Mountbatten was privately pulling the strings, controlling Prince Philip.

Lady Pamela Hicks My father was the kind of person who was enthusiastic, and genuinely interested in almost everything, and probing, and wanting to know why—of course, Prince Philip is very much the same—and he had the secret of being very interested in young people and they were very much akin to him, and thought him fascinating.

And, of course, the King having died, my father sort of stepped into the grandfather position, really, because Prince Philip's father, Prince Andrew, was also dead, and so there was no grandfather figure. So my father was the grandfather figure. In fact, Charles always referred to him like that.

THE BEGINNING OF ELIZABETH AND
PHILIP'S RELATIONSHIP

Elizabeth and Philip had met before the war, on July 22, 1939, during a visit by the Royal Family to the Royal Naval College, Dartmouth, where the then-eighteen-year-old Philip was a cadet. Princess Elizabeth, then only thirteen, was smitten.

* * *

Michael Parker I wouldn't be surprised if they hadn't met before. To be perfectly honest, I believe they'd met before, at a dinner party, or a lunch, because he was at Gordonstoun [school], in Scotland, and at the end of term he had to go somewhere, so he might have gone to the Palace—he didn't always go to Mountbatten, but it might have been there. And you see how it could have happened before.

* * *

Elizabeth and Philip corresponded during the war, and he spent the Christmas of 1943 with the Royal Family at Windsor Castle. Soon there was talk in royal circles of a possible future marriage of the cousins.

Amid much controversy due to the political situation in Greece, Philip became a naturalized British subject in 1946, hastening speculation that he was being advanced as a possible husband to the heiress presumptive.

The public got its first inkling of the royal romance when, in the autumn of 1946, newsreel footage captured a tender exchange between Elizabeth and Philip as Elizabeth arrived at the wedding of their cousin

Patricia Mountbatten to Lord Brabourne, when Philip, an usher, helped Elizabeth remove her coat.

* * *

Imogen Campbell-Johnson When we went to Patricia Mountbatten's wedding, the Queen was one of the bridesmaids, and this very young Prince, who became the Duke of Edinburgh, was amongst the guests.

WAS LORD MOUNTBATTEN THE
ROYAL MATCHMAKER?

A source privy to a conversation between an American president and Lord Louis Mountbatten recalled Mountbatten's having said: "I hope Philip doesn't marry the Princess; he's too good a boy."

* * *

Philip Ziegler Mountbatten liked to tell it that he had orchestrated the royal match. He was an ardent matchmaker—he devoted a large part of his prodigious energies to arranging marriages, particularly of royalty: he tried terribly hard to marry his granddaughter Amanda [Knatchbull] off to the Prince of Wales.

He had undoubtedly tried to claim the credit for having organized the royal marriage. Certainly, I think, he probably thought of the possibility when no one else did. It was not, I'm quite certain, a contrived thing, but Mountbatten would have done anything he could to help it along. And certainly King George VI thought that the pace with which the affair was developing was partly Mountbatten's fault so he had justifiably claimed some credit for it.

But there was no way at all that Prince Philip would have gone into this relationship simply because his uncle wanted him to.

Lady Longford The Mountbattens were very much in favor of it, for obvious reasons, and helped in any way they could.

But I don't believe they made the initial move; the Princess was too young; nobody thought of her as falling in love, and remaining in love, with that person for the rest of her life when she was only thirteen. I mean she was a child. Therefore, in that sense, it was not arranged. It was a genuine love match.

* * *

A source close to the situation, preferring to speak off the record, told us: "I believe that the late King and the Queen Mother, bless them, were not happy with Mountbatten. He was, perhaps, a bit of a showman, and they were very straight-laced about things like that."

* * *

Tim Heald He was a person who excited very extreme reactions. I think, the family took him with a pinch of salt—all the stuff about medals, and uniforms, and all that—they all thought it was ridiculous.

Baron Powell of Bayswater, Charles David, KCMG, life peer, cr. 2000; special counselor for Rhodesia negotiations, 1979–80; personal private secretary and adviser on foreign relations to Prime Minister Margaret Thatcher, 1983–90, and to Prime Minister John Major, 1990–1991 I am not one of those who regards the late Lord Mountbatten as a great man. He was vain, garrulous, with great ambition, a sense of self-importance. How about that for starters?

He was a glamorous figure, no doubt about that, because he wore his uniform at breakfast, lunch, and dinner—all gold braid for as far away as you could see. He did play a role in the Royal Family.

Adm. Sir Henry Leach He exerted considerable influence when the present Queen married Prince Philip. He was—I was about to say "the wicked uncle"—in the background, but he was the *eminence grise*, and I think he did exert a great influence there.

Lady Pamela Hicks I think they would have married absolutely on their own. In fact, my father happened to be there when the King and Queen took the two girls to Dartmouth when Princess Elizabeth was only about twelve years old and Prince Philip was one of the senior cadets and, of course, this absolute Greek god—he looked stunning—and he was a great show off, of course, as all boys of that age are. And the Princess fell in love with him at that moment. My father was there, certainly, and probably was quite amused to notice.

WAS IT A LOVE MATCH FOR *PHILIP?*

Larry Adler At first I thought he was in love with her. I think then the job got to him. I think it was inevitable that he could not sustain that love. It evolved. I believe he still respects the Queen. And he does everything else correctly, except for these gaffes he makes when he goes overseas.

Lady Pamela Hicks Prince Philip began to take her seriously when she was grown up enough for him to realize that this little girl cousin had blossomed and was now a young woman—an attractive young woman.

Probably also, it's always very nice to feel that somebody adores you. But, of course, because he was in the Navy, and there had been a girl in every port sort of thing—round the Mediterranean, round Australia; he obviously had had a few flings before he married—his was really a much more serious choice.

He really did realize that he did love this girl, because it would be quite an undertaking for a young man in his twenties who is a career naval officer—and a very serious career naval officer with a lot of potential—to realize that eventually she would succeed to the Throne.

But, of course, at the moment when they got engaged to be married, they were thinking that they would be making this commitment when they were of an age you would expect to make it.

Tim Heald There's something in Chips Channon's diaries, and elsewhere, that really it was regarded as being the ideal match, and that they were all being manipulated.

And one of the things that made him *really* cross when we were discussing the book were suggestions that he had, in some way, been manipulated into this dynastic marriage.

It made him so angry that I don't think that it was just an insult to his honor; I think he was actually saying: "I was very much in love with her."

There were people who suggested that he was on the make in the way that Uncle Dickie seemed to be. But I'm not aware of any evidence, at any time, to suggest that it wasn't a genuine love match. And certainly that's the way that he talks about it—not that he talks about it very much— but it's something that makes him very irritated. He gets very, very cross when you suggest anything to the contrary.

Again, it's the *shape* of the evidence: Okay, fine. So he gets to be married to the Queen of England, but he also had to give up a career to which he was temperamentally suited, which he absolutely adored, and which he was very good at, and in which he would have gone right to the top. So he's made many sacrifices, as well; it's not only a gain.

Michael Parker He's a chap who can hold his feelings quite well. I knew him very well and I could say this: that in all our wartime experience— we went all over the world and we wound up in the Pacific, in Japan—in all that time, there was never another girl on the horizon.

There were plenty of girls, showers of them, and I made *the* most unfortunate remark in my lackadaisical way: I said there were "armsful of girls." And of course the press has never let that die. I wish to God I'd never said it, but what I meant was, it was abroad, and there were a lot of them, plenty. For example, he came to Australia and met all my family— my sisters, and their friends, and so on. But there was never anybody—I say this absolutely categorically—over those years.

* * *

Princess Elizabeth remained firm in her devotion to Prince Philip during the royal tour. The Royal Family returned from South Africa on April 27, 1947. On July 9, King George and Queen Elizabeth finally announced the Princess's engagement to Prince Philip, who was in the year of the royal marriage created Duke of Edinburgh, Earl of Merioneth, and Baron Greenwich.

THE ROYAL WEDDING

The royal wedding date was set for November 20, 1947, at Westminster Abbey. And despite harsh post-war austerity in Britain, the royal nuptials were choreographed amid all the splendor and pageantry the British are known for, as an elaborate affirmation of Britain's place in the post-war world.

* * *

Larry Adler I knew Prince Philip very well. I had a very good friend who was a photographer named Baron[5] and through him I met Arthur Christiansen, the editor of the *Daily Express*, and Baron and Chris formed a club called the Thursday Club. One of the first people who joined was Prince Philip, and one of the next people was me, so I got to know him very, very well. He was the only one of the Royal Family that I knew really well.

I was at his bachelor party the night before his wedding to Princess Elizabeth. There were about thirty people there. And they were all making dirty jokes about Philip.

But I couldn't take part in that because I knew that this man was so nervous—he was scared; his face was *white*. This man just began to realize what he was getting into. And now he finds he doesn't like it. He wanted a friend, and at that party, no one was able to give him that.

Michael Parker I arranged that party. He, like the rest of us, was elated. We were all elated that Prince Philip was getting married to Princess Elizabeth because most of us had met her, and most of us had fallen in love with her. I went: Boy!, like that. I thought she was *Christmas*!

What most of us liked, and spotted, was the fact that she was already a complete person in wisdom and judgment. We all respected and understood that she had been brought up in this atmosphere, and she'd got it totally but, at the same time, she was extremely human about it, and she could make jokes, and laugh, and carry on, in the same way as we did: I'd make a crack and she'd roar with laughter, and say something else that would carry it on.

So we were all delighted for him, absolutely delighted. So that party was a really joyful affair. It was arranged so that his uncle was there, and we had all of those captains and first lieutenants of the 27th Destroyer Flotilla present at that party—the 27th Flotilla was the flotilla that wound up in Japan with the British Pacific Fleet at the end of the war. So it was a pretty great party; it was terrific fun.

* * *

The bride's wedding dress, designed by royal couturier Norman Hartnell, was made of ivory silk encrusted with small pearls—reportedly ten thousand—arranged in a pattern of York roses.

* * *

Fourth Viscount Younger of Leckie, George Kenneth Hotson, KT, KCVO, TD, PC, FRSE (1931–2003), life peer, cr. 1992; secretary of state for Scotland, 1979–86; secretary of state for defense, 1986–89; later, chairman, Royal Bank of Scotland Certainly the royal wedding was the first glimmering of a peaceful world, because it was quite soon after the end of the war, and in those days, a thing like having the materials to make a wedding dress was quite an effort. And so it was a great, glamorous occasion.

And I know that all of us hardened schoolboys were avidly watching every move of that wedding. It was definitely a *big* event—even for us.

Lady Pamela Hicks It was peculiar, of course, when you think that in 1947 we still had clothing rationing so somebody would donate their coupons so that a bride could have an even better dress.

They were doing a television thing—my younger daughter had been bridesmaid to the Princess of Wales and so she was talking about how they had done her dress. And I with great pride showed the dress I had worn as bridesmaid to Princess Elizabeth. My daughter was horrified!

She was quite wrong because it was a very, very pretty dress. But it was yards, and yards, and yards of mesh, with little satin stars, and so on, sewn on. But it was also a strange dress because it was ideal for rationing—nobody would ration that kind of material.

Lady Longford I'll always remember their wedding. We were invited to it, which was great fun. But I'd just had a baby, my last, my eighth, a wonderful son called Kevin, and I was nursing him, hoping that I wouldn't get back and find him a testy baby, saying: "You keep me waiting for my dinner. I'm going to be a republican and bring the monarchy down!"

It was the look of happiness on the face of the Princess—by great good luck, Frank was a member of the government of the time,[6] so we had front seats and we could really see what people were looking like as they walked in. A lot of brides look nervous, or have no expression, but she did look wonderfully happy.

* * *

Whatever his misgivings may have been prior to Princess Elizabeth's betrothal to Prince Philip, King George expressed his happiness for the newlyweds, albeit with a longing for the happy family life of the past. In a letter received by Princess Elizabeth during her honeymoon with Prince Philip, the King wrote:

> I was so proud of you & thrilled at having you so close to me on your long walk in Westminster Abbey. But when I handed your hand to the Archbishop I felt I had lost something very precious …
>
> I have watched you grow up all these years with pride under the skillful direction of Mummy, who, as you know, is the most marvelous person in the world in my eyes, & I can, I know, always count on you, & now Philip, to help us in our work. Your leaving has left a great blank in our lives, but do remember that your old home is still yours & do come back to it as much & as often as possible. I can see that you are sublimely happy with Philip which is your right, but don't forget us is the wish of
>
> Your ever loving & devoted
>
> Papa

CHAPTER 5

The Coronation of Queen Elizabeth II

F OLLOWING THE NEW Queen's accession in February 1952, planning for her Coronation began. At that time, post-war austerity continued in Britain.

* * *

Bryan Forbes (1926–2013), author; film director, including *The L-Shaped Room, Only Two Can Play,* **and** *The Stepford Wives;* **friend of Princess Margaret** There was still tremendous austerity—we had even more stringent rationing after the war than during it; bread was rationed after the war—and we had rationing basically until 1955.

And on the day she was crowned Queen, Hillary ascended Everest, so there was a feeling that things were happening. Mostly, I think, it came out of the awfulness of the war, and the Blitz. So people suddenly saw a young Queen, and the name "Elizabeth" obviously struck echoes of the first Elizabeth, which was one of the golden ages of English history. And, therefore, people tended to equate the two.

That, as I say, came purely from a national feeling of relief that the war and everything was behind us, and that there was a future at long last. And the Coronation of a young Queen—a very beautiful young Queen—was a factor.

I don't know whether it had any more significance than that. But I was conscious of it myself: I stood in the street—the corner of Piccadilly and St. James's—to watch the procession.

It's difficult to really recreate the emotions of fifty years ago. Certainly one was very proud of it all, and the fact that we put on a show rather well.

Baron Rees, Peter Wynford Innes, PC, QC (1926–2008), life peer, cr. 1987; Conservative M.P., 1970–74, 1983–87; minister of state at Treasury, 1979–81; minister for trade, 1981–83; chief secretary to Treasury, 1983–85 I'm afraid at the time that George VI died and she came to the Throne, I was very conscious of the first stages of the contraction of our Empire—my father having been a general in the Indian Army, I was very conscious of the passing of power—the handover of power to the Indian and Pakistani governments.

And it was quite a painful process. I don't mean so much for us British in the sense that we were giving up power and all that—although I had been brought up with a sense of Empire.

Sir Rex Hunt I was a colonial officer in Uganda and I hoped there would be a resurgence of dynamism and good leadership from having a new Queen, and I was hoping this would mean that the Empire would go on. I hoped that it would rather than thought that it would because I'd been in India during partition and I could see what was coming in the rest of the Empire.

In fact, when we went to Uganda, I said to my wife: "I think we will be lucky if we have ten years before independence." Well, I wasn't far off: we had eleven years there.

* * *

Planning for the Coronation began almost immediately after the death of King George VI. First though, there were issues to be resolved, such as the new Sovereign's style and the name of her Royal House.

Following an emergency cabinet meeting as soon as the government had learned of the King's death, an Accession Council was convened that afternoon to discuss the wording of the proclamation of the Queen's accession. The Queen would attend her first official public engagement as the Sovereign at a full meeting of the Accession Council held on the afternoon of February 8, 1952, at St. James's Palace.

It was decided at the earlier meeting to amend the Sovereign's titles to reflect politically generated changes: a reference to the "Imperial Crown" was removed and a reference added describing Elizabeth as "Head of the Commonwealth." And the designation "Great Britain and Ireland" was changed to "The United Kingdom of Britain and Northern Ireland."

* * *

Michael Parker We were in Clarence House because that was her home. And we thought: Okay, this is good, because we had our little office at the back—she wanted us to be in that house. We said: "No, that is *your* house." So we found this little office at the back and we built a hole in the wall so that we could go to and fro.

One of the things was that the Queen used to ask us to have lunch with them whenever possible, and we could go on talking business at lunch, and laughing, and having jokes. And I raised the question: "Ma'am, wouldn't it be marvelous if we could stay *here*—the Royal We—and you could go daily to the office in Buckingham Palace?"

"Oh! A wonderful idea!" So we grew on with that idea—we talked about it; we discussed it—and I talked to Martin Charteris, and I talked to Boy Browning—General Browning—who was our Comptroller, and I said: "Boy, we've got to do this for her; she's happy here. And you know the Palace, and it's not so intimate and happy as Clarence House. And the Queen Mum is over there, anyway."

So we started to really think of this, and see how it would work. And then Churchill came on the scene. And he said: "I am sorry. The flagpole [at Buckingham Palace] flies the Queen's Standard and that's where she must be."

Oh, we thought: you old bastard! We loved him dearly, but he did things like this. It wouldn't have mattered a hell of a lot when you think of the context today: they live at Windsor; Buckingham Palace is open to the public—it's an office. We were ahead of our time.

WHAT'S IN A NAME?

Another issue, which generated much controversy at the time, affecting the Sovereign and the Duke of Edinburgh, was the name of the Royal House.

The Duke wished his children to be designated as being of the "House of Edinburgh." Following much debate, it was decided that "Edinburgh," a title given Prince Philip and not the name of any Royal House, was inappropriate.

"Mountbatten" was out too, due to negative sentiment aroused by the mention of the controversial Lord Mountbatten.

* * *

Tim Heald I've always had the sense that that was a subject that mattered enormously to Uncle Dickie. It didn't actually matter very much to Prince Philip. He was very keen to say that getting the job done is what matters.

And whether he's called "Prince Consort," or "Prince Philip," or "Duke of Edinburgh" doesn't mean anything.

I believe he would say: "You can take me, or leave me, and what you call me is *your* business. But as far as I'm concerned, I'm getting on with the job at hand, doing the best I possibly can."

Robert Lacey Prince Philip is not himself a Mountbatten. His mother was a Battenberg, but he has the name of the Danish Royal Family[1] and "Mountbatten" was just a name he took for convenience in 1947. If he wanted the Royal Family called anything, he wanted it called "Edinburgh-Windsor," picking up his title, which he considers personal to *him*. He doesn't actually have any great, special feelings about "Mountbatten" as a surname since he knows it came to him as part of marrying Princess Elizabeth.

Sir Edward Ford I was aware of the fact that Prince Philip, having not really got a name, in a way, was very keen that his name should be taken by his children in some form.

Of course, Dickie, Lord Mountbatten, played a very considerable part in trying to get the Mountbatten name into the family. To be quite honest, I don't know that the Queen, other than wanting to accommodate her husband, had any particular view. I never heard them expressed.

Winston Spencer Churchill (1940–2010), grandson to the late Prime Minister Winston Churchill; journalist and author; Conservative M.P., 1970–97 I can well believe that Dickie Mountbatten was pressing for anything—there was nobody more pushy than Mountbatten—although I hadn't heard of such a conversation.

Incidentally, when after her Coronation she did a world cruise with the Duke of Edinburgh on *Britannia*, the Queen wrote to my grandfather on half a dozen occasions beautiful letters in her own handwriting.

Most of it was telling of the wonderful receptions that they had. But the Queen had one request which, actually, was never fulfilled, either by my grandfather, or by any successor: the Queen wanted Prince Philip to be given the title of "Prince of the Commonwealth."

* * *

The matter was soon partially resolved. On February 20, Prime Minister Churchill informed his cabinet that the Queen had agreed that she and her descendants would continue to bear the Windsor name.

Then some years later, on February 8, 1960, the Queen would decide that those of her descendants not styled "Royal Highness" would bear the name "Mountbatten-Windsor."

THE QUEEN MOTHER LEARNS TO ADJUST

Robert Lacey She went through a very black spell—she retreated up to the Highlands [of Scotland]—understandably unhappy about shifting out of what she'd come to see as her own Buckingham Palace, to Clarence House.

There was about a year, of course, when Queen Mary was still alive and, thus, technically the Queen Mother, although somehow that title never sat very easily on the rather stiff shoulders of Queen Mary.[2]

But once again, here's an example of her [Queen Elizabeth the Queen Mother's] professionalism: she didn't let it show in public; it didn't get in the way of the job; she was willing and happy to subordinate herself to the Royal Family, in which she saw herself at the end of the day as just one serving member.

And this is the difference between her and Diana Princess of Wales several decades later. There was that famous overheard telephone conversation on the so-called Squidgy tape,[3] in which she's talking to a young man who calls her "Squidgy," and she complains at one point about the Royal Family, and says: "When you think of all I've done for this lot!"—or words to that effect—"You'd think they'd show more gratitude." That, by any standard, overstated her importance. But it's certainly something you could never imagine the Queen Mother saying.

The Queen Mother came into the Royal Family in the 1920s, very much a Lady Di figure: she taught the Royal Family how to smile—the family of George V and Queen Mary was very stiff and wooden; she gave it a human face; she was the first non-foreign Princess for generations to come into the Royal Family; and there were all sorts of ways in which she was presented by the press as the savior of the situation.

But never did she ever feel that that made her bigger than the family. And she was always very conscious that, at the end of the day, the magic that surrounds *her* is *borrowed* magic, and no matter what she does to enhance it—which she certainly does—it comes from this family, and this institution which she belongs to, so she's ultimately loyal to it in a way that Diana proved not to be.

Lady Pamela Hicks It really was terrible for her. And, of course, because she had been such a help to the King—they were much closer than most couples are—in a way, very often you find that the person who supports is more bereft than the person who is supported. So if you're no longer needed in that way, you are absolutely adrift as to what to do. It took quite a long time, actually, for Queen Elizabeth [the Queen Mother] to leave Buckingham Palace, to make the changeover.

I was told she did contemplate going into retirement, not being Queen Victoria after the Prince Consort died—of course she wasn't the Queen regnant—but still very much thinking she would withdraw into retirement. And Prime Minister Churchill talked her out of it and said: "Absolutely not! This young Queen is going to need you by her side an awful lot. And this is no time for you to go and sit in Scotland."

Sir Michael Oswald If I say "Monday" and I meant "Sunday," the Queen Mother will correct me. She has lost nothing, has not slowed up mentally, in the last fifty years.

* * *

An interviewee, speaking off the record, recounted a story told to him by Bob Hawke, former prime minister of Australia:

> When he [Hawke] first came over here as prime minister—we were opening a memorial home to [another former Australian prime minister] Menzies—opening it was the Queen Mother, and Bob Hawke told me that he took one look at the Queen Mother and fell in love. He held her hand, and, when he left, he held her hand even longer, and whispered something in her ear.

I happened to see the Queen Mother about three days later, and I said to her: "Tell me, what did Bob Hawke whisper in your ear?" And she said—and I knew what she was going to say because President Carter had said exactly the same thing to me—"Oh, you *do* remind me of my mother." The Queen Mother was very amused.

* * *

Larry Adler She did something that is amazing. I did a concert at Clarence House, and she came over and asked could she see the harmonica?[4] So I handed it to her. And I swear to you, she said: "No one will ever believe me when I tell them that I held Larry Adler's organ!" And she knew what she was saying because she gave me a wink.

Robert Lacey It's no secret now that Queen Elizabeth the Queen Mother has many views that are politically incorrect—nostalgia for the Empire, reactionary, particularly in the New Labour Britain [of the late 1990s].

And again, it's one of the paradoxes which is puzzling but somehow explains something about the Royal Family—that the most popular member of the Royal Family is this elderly lady, whose private opinions would shock most of her subjects. She has much less in common with ordinary people in the street than anybody else in the family.

But she is the member of the family that people revere and love most. They don't want to hear any ill said of her. They tolerate her massive overdraft and tales of drinking because of what she offers, which is a matter of tradition, history, folk memory, escapism, and glamour. She's a great actress; she makes people feel good. And people, therefore, are happy with that warm sensation that she generates, and don't feel the need to probe beyond that—she's an old-fashioned royal.

Rt. Rev. Michael Mann, KCVO (1924–2011), bishop of Dudley, 1974–76; dean of Windsor and domestic chaplain to the Queen, 1976–89 The Queen Mother was going out to Oman to dedicate a new standard for the regiment my son had served in[5] and she asked me and my [late] wife, Jill, to join her on the trip. After the dedication, on the plane returning to London, she sat down opposite me. She turned toward the window and put her hand up to her face. I thought: she is tired. Then, she looked at me and I noticed tears streaming down her face. She said to me: "I'm sitting here, thinking how hard the ceremony must have been for you and Jill."

* * *

The Queen Mother, a most beloved member of the Royal Family, died peacefully in her sleep, the Queen at her side, at the age of one hundred and one, in her residence at Royal Lodge, Windsor, at 3:15 P.M. on March 30, 2002. Her death occured a mere seven weeks following the passing of her daughter, Princess Margaret Rose.

The former Elizabeth Angela Marguerite Bowes-Lyon, who had been married to the future King George VI since 1923, kept an active schedule until days before her passing. Following her funeral service at Westminster Abbey, she was buried at St. George's Chapel, Windsor, alongside her husband and daughter.

HOW MUCH DID THE PAGEANTRY OF THE QUEEN'S CORONATION FOLLOW THAT OF KING GEORGE VI'S?

Earl of Perth I was very much involved really because my cousin the Earl of Norfolk was Earl Marshal. And clearly we—the family—were guided very much by the past, but trying to bring in the reality of the present. And I wouldn't have thought there was a very, very great difference. You've got a protocol.

The Earl of Norfolk was a great showman. I always remember when we were boys Lew Grade[6] saying: "If only you weren't *you*, you would be tops!" I think those things hadn't really changed. They give all sorts of chance for display of tradition, and so forth, and the country liked it. It's a pageant, to a degree, and it's got its sacred side too.

Adm. Sir Henry Leach It followed very closely [the style of King George VI's Coronation], in fact. Comprehensive records had been kept, of course, and they could all be looked up.

I was then, personally, involved in the naval side of the Coronation ceremonies. Indeed, it was one of the hardest jobs I've ever had. The Navy was allocated certain jobs—it had a section of the procession; it was responsible for lining certain streets.

I had just got a half-stripe—I was a very young lieutenant commander, attached to a naval division in the Admiralty and you were attending a high-level conference chaired by a major general and the next minute you were literally out on the streets, having worked out on a large-scale map how many men would go in what space, holding one end of a tape measure, and painting in a mark on the streets.

The decision was taken that the service lords would ride white horses. Now for the Army that, of course, was very easy, they were used to it; for the Air Force it was not, nor was it for the Navy.

All sorts of stories started to be dug up then, how at the Coronation of King George VI, the mounted record was held by a midshipman and it was from Marble Arch to Whitehall.

The Second Sea Lord of the day and the Fourth Sea Lord of the day were both rather plump men, and I can distinctly remember seeing their minute, which said: "This is a ceremonial occasion of international importance, not a circus; we will not ride." And that ended it.

So they had to find another two to make up the team. And, at that point, they started to run out of white horses, and they had to dredge the British Army of the Rhine, over in Germany, to find pom-poms and all-white horses. And they did.

We had a chief-of-staff who was a captain, and we had an admiral appointed but he hadn't taken over the job. I briefed them on who went where—I had maps, and things—what it was all about, and where they would have fallen in, and how they would march to their positions, and then took them out to show them round the course.

I came to the position of the first company, and there were no marks. And I thought: I look rather an idiot. And I went on to the next one, and there were no marks. And I couldn't understand it because I'd checked on the marks, which had been done two or three weeks before.

And so I gamely went round the course with them in a taxi—some of them were quite senior captains, and colonels, and so forth—and you could see them all tittering behind their hands, and saying: "What's that upstart up to? He's talking a load of quack."

And it wasn't till we got halfway back up Whitehall that I realized what the problem was: one of these very high-burning fire furnace things that blister the tarmac when you're resurfacing a road is going along, covering everything up!

The Metropolitan Police had looked up the records of the 1937 Coronation. It had been a blazing hot day. And when the street liners, and particularly the police—hence it was noted in the police records—when the police came to move on at the end, after the procession had finally passed, the bobbies' great big, thick boots had stuck to the tarmac.

TO TELEVISE OR NOT TO TELEVISE

After much debate, among the prime minister and other officials, Queen Elizabeth, on December 8, 1952, granted permission for the Coronation to be televised.

* * *

Archdeacon George Austin They wanted to keep the television out— Churchill and the dean of Westminster didn't want television because they said people might watch the service while drinking beer! But Buckingham Palace insisted.

Earl of Harewood For the Queen, it was probably the first big influence she had. Probably the first big effect she had was in the drama of television.

I'm sure there were voices both ways. But she believed that she was really right, and I believe Churchill believed that she was not. Churchill was by then heftily a traditionalist. He wasn't before—he was an anti-traditionalist, a radical figure, but by then he certainly wasn't. He changed his path.

Sir Edward Ford The original decision was that it could be broadcast, but not televised. But when this was put to the Queen, she said: "Oh, no"—this was something she wished to see the whole nation take part in and, therefore, it should be. And she overruled an original decision—a tentative one, perhaps—that it should not be televised.

I believe that in the taking of communion, which is part of the Coronation service, they did not have the cameras on them when they were doing that. That was the only concession there.

And, of course, she was absolutely right, because it was a stunning performance, which was enormously appreciated in pubs, and churches, and everywhere else.

THE IMPACT OF TELEVISING THE CORONATION

Lord Younger We hired a television set for the day—it was the first time I had ever seen television. It was only black and white, but it was astonishing. I watched the Coronation ceremony avidly, and the crowning moment was very emotional.

Sir Malcolm L. Rifkind, KCMG, PC, QC, Conservative M.P., 1974–97, and 2005–15; secretary of state for Scotland, 1986–90; secretary of state for transport, 1990–92; secretary of state for defense, 1992–95; secretary of state for foreign and Commonwealth affairs, 1995–97 My family first acquired a television set in order to be able to watch the Coronation in 1953. We were the first house in our street to get a television set. It was a relatively rare object in Edinburgh in those days, so a number of our neighbors came to watch it—it was all in black and white.

At the time it seemed very exciting watching what was actually happening. When one sees the old film now, it's so faded and flickering, you wonder why you got so excited over that.

Sir Adam (Nicholas) Ridley, special adviser to the Chancellor of the Exchequer, 1979–84; special adviser to the Duchy of Lancaster, 1985 It was the first time I ever saw a television set. It was in the bank my grandfather was then chairman of, and they had installed a television—they were tiny, inadequate little black-and-white things—so all of us could watch.

Robert Lacey On the day of the Coronation itself, we all went next door to our neighbors, who had actually bought a television—they were considered quite affluent people: they went away every summer on a foreign holiday.

They had their children, but all the children from the neighborhood were invited, and we sat on hard wooden chairs. We started relatively early in the morning and watched this little blue flickering screen in the corner at the table from nine o'clock in the morning until teatime. I can remember coffee in the morning—"elevenses" it's called—and the mothers collaborated on producing sandwiches for lunch for us.

REHEARSING THE GREAT EVENT

Adm. Sir Henry Leach I taught the headquarters staff how to salute, because the admiral hadn't the foggiest idea. And then there was the question of what was the correct uniform for a naval officer mounted. We got the manager of Gieves, the service outfitters, to come along to the Admiralty Quadrangle one day at a quarter past two, and the First Sea Lord, who was a man called [Admiral of the Fleet Sir Rhoderick] McGrigor, at the time, looked up the records, and he [the manager of Gieves] said: "You have to wear, of course, full dress, all that sort of thing. But under your trousers, you'll need to have a piece of elastic, and it goes under the instep of your boot, and that keeps your trousers from riding up."

Then later it was discovered that to be proper, a naval officer should wear box spurs when mounted. And, of course, we had none. So the records were looked up as to what were then the parameters of a box spur, and acceptable spurs for the Admiralty board members were produced.

The members of the board were very diffident about rehearsing, because they were pretty shaky on horses, and didn't want to make asses of themselves in public. They arranged that they would do their rehearsing in Hyde Park at seven o'clock in the morning.

They'd been at this lark for a couple of weeks or so. They regarded it as a piece of cake and used to go twice round the circuit—the First Sea Lord, McGrigor, was absolutely bored rigid—he had other things to do—and he sat like a sack of spuds on his horse, and he rode sort of swinging his feet to and fro, to and fro. But the first day they were wearing their box spurs he inadvertently touched his horse's flank, forgetting that he had his spurs on, whereupon his horse bounded forward, and nearly threw him. And you know what it is if you have a line of steeds: all the others started doing the same, and the horses all flashed past the line, disappearing into the distance—they still hadn't quite completed their first circuit—flashed past the entrance to the camp and went on.

The Controller, the Third Sea Lord, was a great big, heavy man called [Sir] Ralph Edwards. His horse took off—he had no control over it at all—and he decided he would, obviously, follow his senior officer's motions. But his horse decided that he wouldn't half mind his breakfast, so he headed for his stable, and he threw this great, heavy man, who landed on his head and was knocked out.

The first I knew about this was when I was rung up by a dear old colonel of the Blues, who had a flat by Marble Arch. The Controller had been rescued. They took him to the flat, apparently poured out a tumbler full of brandy, started to hold it to the great man's lips, who suddenly remembered [the treatment for] shock: hot, sweet tea. So they put the kettle on and the colonel drank the tumbler himself.

LAST-MINUTE PREPARATIONS

Adm. Sir Henry Leach One of the things I had to go into in some detail was what steps we needed to take to survive this very long day: there we were, lining in the streets, and if you wanted to "spend a penny" [relieve oneself] there was a problem. I went and consulted the medical director general of the Navy, and he said: "You don't drink any liquid for the previous twenty-four hours—not a drop—and then you'll have a chance."

And I said: "Well, supposing it's a blazing hot day and someone gets heatstroke." "You can't have it both ways," he said. The night before, dining in the *President*, they passed the port and I gave the royal toast, so I did have a sip.

CORONATION DAY

Adm. Sir Henry Leach It was blowing, it was raining, and it was bitterly cold. We fell in, and we'd hardly got them all sorted out when along came a senior Army officer, and said: "Wet-weather routine; oilskins."

There would have been a shambles, and we would have looked scruffy. And so I legged it to the head of the naval line just in time—they'd just started to dish out bundles of oilskins—and I got hold of the Army sergeant who was in charge, and said: "Take them all back—the whole lot." "But it's wet-weather need, sir." "Never mind about that: the Navy doesn't wear oilskins; take them all back. And drive off. Drive anywhere. I don't care where you go. But don't come anywhere near here"—I was quite unpleasant about it. I was wearing two-and-a-half stripes, and that was good enough for him.

And shortly afterwards, an adjutant came down and started bellowing why were the Navy not wearing foul-weather dress? And so I told him: "The Navy doesn't." And that was that.

Lord Healey I had just been an M.P. for a few months and I went to the Coronation in the Abbey, and they let you keep the chairs you sat on, so we have got them at home. They're blue velvet, with the royal crest.

Lady Longford Frank's uncle, Lord Dunsany, gave Frank and me a lift. He came round in a car and we set off. And he suddenly said: "I'm just going to stop for a minute; I left my coronet in Ireland by mistake. I'm going to try and borrow one from one of the peers I know is away and won't be using his."

He tried somebody like Lord Astor, and we stopped outside—it was somewhere in Berkeley Square—and he got out, went to the front door and rang the bell. The butler came downstairs. They had a little confabulation. And then Uncle Eddie, as we called him, came back into the car with a large box in his arms containing the Astor coronet—if it was Astor.

That gave me a feeling that this Coronation was a bit off—people forgetting their coronets.

MEMORABLE MOMENTS IN THE
CORONATION PROCESSION

The Queen traveled to Westminster Abbey in a golden state coach pulled by eight gray horses.

* * *

Lord Wright I actually watched the Coronation procession from under the arches of the Ritz [Hotel], in pouring rain, and my main memory—it was quite a moving sight—was not only of the Queen in the golden coach going by, but of seeing Winston Churchill, actually the only time in my life that I ever saw him. And also Queen Salote, of Tonga, with the Emperor of Ethiopia [Haile Selassie, 1892–1975], in the same carriage.

Lord Rees I had quite a good ringside seat in Regent Street. I remember the great figure of the Queen of Tonga—it was a wet day—wiping her face, waving at the crowds, who all loved her. There was a rather small, Malayan, I think, potentate who was with her, and wasn't enjoying the rain so much—he wasn't an extrovert.

Baron McNally, Tom, life peer, cr. 1995; international secretary, Labour Party, 1969–74; political adviser to Foreign Secretary, 1974–76; political adviser to prime minister, 1976–79; M.P., 1979–83; later, minister of state for justice and deputy leader, House of Lords, 2010–13 Most people will tell you where they saw the Coronation. And they'll remember the Queen of Tonga was the star because it rained and she was a big, fat lady, and she drove through the streets in a golden carriage and was clearly enjoying it. So that was really the first awareness of the monarchy.

Sir Michael Oswald I took a leave from [the Army in] Germany and watched the Coronation procession from a window above Park Lane.

People who were too young to have seen, or watched the Coronation ceremony on television, have never really understood the implication of it. In a political job you can give it up. The Queen sees it that it's something she's consecrated to do, and to do for the rest of her life to the best of her ability.

MOST MOVING MOMENTS IN THE
CORONATION CEREMONY

Philip Ziegler Like everybody else I talked to, I found enormously moving the moment when she was stripped of all of the robes of state, this small girl with all the harpics crouched round—the archbishops, the dignitaries, and all the potentates of state clustered round her—this small, shy, exposed girl who was robed again, and came back as the titular Monarch. It was a wonderful spectacle, very moving indeed.

Brigadier Johnny F. Rickett, CBE, leader, Falklands presentation team, 1982; regimental lieutenant colonel, Welsh Guards, 1989–94; ADC to

Queen Elizabeth II, 1993 To have two days off from school to go and watch it was wonderful! My father had friends in St. James's Street, and we watched from the office. And we saw it on television.

The pomp and circumstance was impressive, the way it all came over; the actual crowning ceremony; the pageantry; the anointing—that was wonderful. The anointing, particularly. One didn't really understand what it was about; the same sort of ceremony has gone on since 1066.

Lady Angela Oswald I was very moved by the consecration with the oil. And that very much means something special to Her Majesty. You hear people saying: "Is the Queen likely to abdicate?" And, of course, the Queen will *never* abdicate because she feels she's been consecrated by God with the holy oil and that is her mission, if you like, in life—that it is not for her to just throw in the sponge.

Robert Lacey I remember being very intrigued as a nine-year-old boy by talk of the sacred moment of the anointing, when the Queen would be under a canopy, alone with the archbishop, and this was something that would not be televised; this was very secret and private.

I wondered if she took off the top of her dress to be anointed on her bare breasts, although that is a horrific thought for a respectable young boy to have about the Queen of England—it's like one doesn't think about them going to the lavatory; that's a taboo subject.

Baroness Greenfield, Susan Adele, CBE, FRCP, life peer, cr. 2001; professor of pharmacology, Oxford University, 1996–2013; senior research fellow, Lincoln College, Oxford 1999–2018; founder and CEO, Neuro-Bio Ltd, 2014; interviewed in 2021 The anointing being the most sacred coronation ceremony, the notion is that the Monarch is chosen by God, having a special endowment from God.

People will struggle with that idea, literally, but this said, my own view is that it is a mistake to treat the monarchy as if they are *Hollywood* royalty.

Earl of Harewood The sight of the Queen, who was indeed very young and vulnerable in this ancient ceremony—I had seen her father crowned as well—was very moving.

You could say that all ceremonies are totally unnecessary. But actually they aren't; they do fix things: President Kennedy saying: "Don't ask what your country can do for you; ask what you can do for your country" was wonderful. He may not have made that remark up, but whoever helped him write that speech, it was great. And that was a ceremony.

These things are important: they fix things for people and they give a certain satisfaction to people. I think people like that.

Lady Longford I got a slightly prejudiced view of the Coronation. The service was wonderful, and very enjoyable. Somebody—I think it was Churchill—described "the swan-like arms of the Pharisees, these white arms, like the necks of swans, holding up their coronets at the moment when she's crowned."

When we all called out our own enthusiastic support for the newly crowned Queen, I would like to have really given tongue and bayed like a hound. But we were all a bit timid and didn't quite know how loud you were supposed to shout, so it wasn't quite as loud as I would have liked. But I was very moved, being able to do it at all.

GLORIANA

The Earl of Harewood, with his deep love of music, wished for a musical component to the festivities surrounding his cousin's Coronation, so broached the idea of an opera celebrating the British nation to Benjamin Britten,[7] and the composer complied, writing *Gloriana*.

The opera, vetted in advance by Queen Elizabeth and the Duke of Edinburgh, was performed before them on June 8, at Covent Garden, to rather negative critical response.

* * *

Earl of Harewood I was keen that there should be a musical celebration because I was very keen that the arts should take a more prominent part in this "new Elizabethan age."

And I thought that the celebration of the Coronation, of a high musical event, would be very valuable. It turned out not to be; it turned out not so much to divide people, as alienate an awful lot of people.

Okay, they may have been ignorant and stupid people, but ignorant and stupid people have a voice too—and maybe it was only I who thought that everyone was stupid.

Lady Longford It was slightly ahead of the time. Now everybody would be delighted to think that we had Benjamin Britten because, far from being too modern, he's one of the glories of the state.

Lord Younger I'm afraid I agree with that. I have to be honest. Perhaps I shouldn't say it, but I also felt that about Elton John's contribution to Princess Diana's funeral. That makes me very old-fashioned. My family gave me a hard time for that: they were horrified when I said that. They thought it was wonderful.

WAS THERE A FEELING OF A NEW ELIZABETHAN AGE?

Larry Adler That was hype—all such phrases are hype. Nothing changed—in life around the Palace, nothing changes. They have advisers and they have civil servants who talk to them. But they don't talk to them as people; they talk to them as people from another planet.

Duke of Norfolk There was a great press outpouring, saying: "We've got a new Elizabethan age." She's done jolly well. There may be one or two awkwardnesses, the way the children have got divorced a bit, you know, but she and Prince Philip are very successful.

Lord McNally There was the feeling of a new Elizabethan age. Now that I'm in public relations, I realize that it's not so new a profession, because they announced the ascent of Everest[8] on the eve of the Coronation.

Earl of Harewood In my case, the feeling of the new Elizabethan age, and the prospect that it held out—the prospect of starting again, and the excitement, and all that—was very considerable; it was complete optimism. I believed absolutely in it. Disillusion came later, but I did believe in it, completely.

I believe a great many people in England did. There was a real feeling of excitement—being born again is going too far, but there was something like it.

Philip Ziegler She's presided with considerable dignity over fifty [and now seventy] years of steadily diminishing national status, which is a kind of inverse Elizabethan age, you could call it, I suppose.

Eric Moonman Whether people viewed it as a new Elizabethan age is hard to say. If it was, it didn't last long, because we certainly had gone from one war to the likelihood of a new war, and by the time it got to 1953, you had the Korean War. So there were a lot of very worrying clouds.

Stephen Day It was the excitement of having a new Queen, and a new era—a new Elizabethan era. It was a feeling that maybe we'd turned a corner and now, maybe, things were going to pick up again after a very difficult period.

Lord Healey Bullshit! It was all done up by the press. In a way, the New Britain began in 1945, with the end of the war, with the Attlee government, and a great explosion of creativity in the arts, and poetry, and so on.

I don't believe the succession of Elizabeth made very much impact, in that sense, on what was going on. I was a busy M.P., and it was nice to know that she was taking over, because she was a *very* attractive young woman at that time and he was a very attractive man.

CHAPTER 6

The Consort

S HORTLY AFTER THEIR marriage, the heiress presumptive and the Duke of Edinburgh had moved into Clarence House, a newly refurbished royal residence close to Buckingham Palace.

The Duke of Edinburgh resumed his naval career. Stationed on the Mediterranean island of Malta, he was joined there for a time by Princess Elizabeth for what would turn out to be the only relatively normal period of the young couple's married life.

* * *

Michael Parker Bear in mind that Clarence House was a little piece of heaven, for them a big piece. And she was being the Princess and working very hard; he was still in the Navy, coming and going all the time; and I was whizzing to and fro, keeping the communications.

Now, it's very hard for me to describe what a wonderfully happy, enchanted atmosphere it was then. The war was over; we were building— we were putting the country together if we could, we were doing everything we could to help; you had a sense of achievement coming from that.

And he was going on with the Navy as much as he could, because that was his profession. I was out of the Navy, so to speak—still in uniform but virtually out of the Navy—because I was in waiting on the Princess and Philip.

Now, in our innocence, we thought this was going to go on for a very long time—after all, the King was quite young; there might have been forty more years for her as Princess. And it was a lovely horizon. And there were visits abroad—we went to the United States and to Canada, to Australia, and elsewhere, all over the world.

That was going on until we were on our way to Australia and we stopped off in Africa. And bang! the King died.

* * *

Within less than a year after the royal wedding, Princess Elizabeth gave birth to Prince Charles Philip Arthur George, "the heir," born on November 14, 1948, at Buckingham Palace.

* * *

Sir David Scott I was duty officer in the Commonwealth Relations Office overnight, and about ten o'clock I had a call from the Palace: would I activate what was the already-in-hand telegram to all the Commonwealth countries, saying that an heir to the Throne had been born?

I actually got that off about midnight. I rang my wife. She was one of the first people in the country to know that Prince Charles had been born.

It wouldn't have mattered, but at that time, the fact that it was a *male* heir was regarded as being rather appropriate.

* * *

Two years after the heir's birth, the Princess gave birth again, to Princess Anne Elizabeth Alice Louise, "the spare," born on August 15, 1950.

As Queen, Elizabeth would bear two more sons. On February 19, 1960, she would give birth to Prince Andrew Albert Christian Edward. And four years later, on March 10, 1964, the Queen would give birth to Prince Edward Antony Richard Louis.

* * *

Earl of Harewood So much of the life of a King or Queen is completely circumscribed by the duties, the functions, the rituals, the decisions, the travels, and the people they have to meet, and the official parties that they have to go through. Too little of it is private life. That's just how it is.

Lord Merlyn-Rees Prince Philip had a difficult passage to run when he was first the Queen's husband— "Phil, the Greek," and all that sort of thing. I think he's had a far more difficult time than his wife.

Lady Longford If the King had lived to eighty, say, they would have had a long naval life.

As it was, they just had those few years at Malta. She was a naval wife: she went to the hairdresser's; she went out for coffee, and all the rest of it. It must have been great fun to have that short period.

It's a very interesting question whether Prince Philip, with all his talent, was throwing himself away. I honestly don't think he feels that, and I'm sure he didn't.

The further back you go, the less he would have felt that because when you think of the family he came from and their fate, and all those things that were happening in Europe—the monarchies that were going down like ninepins—to maintain a strong, democratic monarchy was something quite big, and needed character.

Sir Michael Palliser Prince Philip at that time was commanding a little frigate called the *Magpie*—in the Mediterranean Fleet—and the Princess Elizabeth, as she then was, two or three years after their marriage came out to visit him there.

There was a great reception for her at the embassy [in Athens]. She came into my consciousness then, when, as the third secretary, I had to do most of the arranging of the reception and all that.

She was very shy, and rather formal, and sort of withdrawn. In a way, she must have inherited a mix from her parents—and certainly as a young Princess, at that point, you felt she was making an effort to get to meet the British community.

There's an outgoing quality which she developed, and now she has no problems. She is always conscious of being Queen. But, I think, in those days, she was conscious of being the Princess Elizabeth, but not in an aggressive way. There was a substantial degree of shyness and not really being very used to that kind of gathering, and how to do it.

Michael Parker It was a magic period of their early life. We were set up in Villa Guardamangia with a lady-in-waiting, and myself, and she was to be "Mrs. Prince Philip," if you like, and she was really to know what it was like to be a naval officer's wife.

So there we were. And Uncle Dickie was there, and he had to be very much *the Admiral*, and she had to be "Mrs. Philip." And the King made it clearly known to everybody that when she was out there she was still Princess Elizabeth, but she was out there as "Mrs. Philip."

And she had a ball; she had a wonderful time—we went all over the island and visited people. She would like to have shopped, but didn't. It wasn't the practice, and it wasn't done.

And she would be wearing the sorts of clothes the other wives were wearing. There was one particular dress—a black dress—that she wore. She looked *stunning* in it—simple, absolutely perfect in it. They were a stunning couple—separately and together.

Adm. Sir Henry Leach He was a very able naval officer. I never served in a ship with him, but we took the [destroyer command] exam at the same time. He was failed in one subject. I only discovered this [...] because I met his examining officer out shooting. And I asked him deliberately whether he'd done it as a gimmick, so as to be able to go round afterwards saying: "Well I failed the Duke of Edinburgh . . ."

And he said: "No, not at all. He just hadn't done his prep on that particular subject, which was torpedo anti-submarines, and he admitted it to me." So he had a rescrub.

And the local admiral, who was later to be my father-in-law, was consulted about this and stood no nonsense at all. He said: "No, no, of course he's going to do it again." And that was that.

There's no question that he's a highly intelligent person and I would say that, had he been able to follow through a full naval career, he would have stood a very good chance of going right to the top.

Michael Parker And then the King died, and she became Queen. She's well able to cope with it; she's wonderful. But, there it is: she's the Queen. And he, perforce, is the husband. So what does the husband do? Go off to sea and stay out at sea? It just isn't reasonable.

So then he had to work out a new existence, a new series of responsibilities for himself, with nobody there to help him—nobody there to suggest anything.

I do think that the King when he was alive had quite an influence on Prince Philip as to what was expected of him, and the King was a pretty wise man. He was wonderfully easy to get on with, too, an absolutely delightful person. I believe that a sort of osmosis could have taken place. He evolved, and grew, with all of that.

WERE THE COURTIERS UNHAPPY WITH THE DUKE OF EDINBURGH IN THE EARLY DAYS?

Philip Ziegler People like Tommy Lascelles, in particular, would not have been against Prince Philip for being a Greek Prince, or a German Prince, or whatever you like to think of him as, or for being a pauper.

But they distrusted him as a rather brash, arrogant, pushy young man; they did think that he was a rather aggressive young man, with ideas of his own, who would not necessarily follow their wise advice, who would want to do things his own way, who would muck up accepted patterns of life.

Earl of Harewood Look, they were much older. He was a radical and he probably didn't want to conform to all sorts of things which they were used to conforming to: they had old-fashioned ideas. And as he was the boss—or, at least, the assistant boss—he could ride roughshod over them. I don't think he did ride roughshod, but he may often have disagreed. It would only be reasonable if he did.

WAS THE DUKE OF EDINBURGH FRUSTRATED IN HIS NEW ROLE?

Larry Adler You don't know until you're in it. It's wrong that they don't give anybody who's about to come into the Royal Family a tuition course on what their duties are, and what their jobs are, and what they're expected to do. The Duke of Edinburgh certainly was never given any course at all on what to do and how to behave. And he took it very hard.

Before she became the Queen, he could call her by her first name. After they were married, he, so help me God, had to call her "Your Royal Highness." And he didn't like that at all.

Lady Longford I remember reading one of the first really good lives of Prince Philip, by Basil Boothroyd. He gives a picture of him that does really convince me that Prince Philip is, in a way, a dual personality: he's the very active, creative man, with his career, but he also does believe, in his real being, in the monarchy.

And, therefore, as some men would find it irksome to be always walking a step behind the Queen in every way, I don't think he feels that; I think he feels he's carrying out a necessary job, and doing it as well as possible. Personally, I admire him very much.

Peter Jay The rules of that game were perfectly well understood: the consort cannot interfere with the constitutional process, and, of course, the consort has in all ceremonial ways a role to play, which is symbolized in the State Opening of Parliament, when the consort stands to the side of the Sovereign, or a bit behind her, when she reads her speech.

Beyond that, he can play a very active role, as a citizen in society with an exceptional position, encouraging and promoting good causes—not getting involved in controversy, obviously.

I believe that nothing about his life can have surprised him, or would have surprised anybody else at that time; they would have expected him to be the constitutional consort—to be a half step behind her in ceremonial matters, and to play an active part in good causes. And that is exactly what has happened.

Tim Heald I'm sure all the protocols are adhered to; I'm quite sure that Prince Philip has never sat in on the weekly meeting with the prime minister, because that is not allowed. And I'm quite sure that he does not see the boxes.

But, equally, I would be absolutely amazed if after the Queen had seen the prime minister on one of her evenings that, at least some of the time, they'd take tea, and she'd say: "Philip, do you know, the most extraordinary thing . . ."

If you go back to the time of the wedding, I think that Prince Philip would have reckoned on, at most, only another ten years or so, if he had ever put it into a chronological formula, of being able to continue a conventional naval career—he only commanded one ship, and at a very low level. And he would know, intellectually, that that was going to have to come to an end—that he would have been involved, and would have to come home.

But, having said that, there's never been any sense, that I'm aware of, of complaint: he went into the job, if you like, with his eyes wide open. And I know he complains about all sorts of things, but I've never had any sense that he's complaining about the way that life has actually come to pass.

He knew very well what he was in for when he got married; he knew what was involved. He knew what his job was with his wife—what he was supposed to be doing—and he was acting out what he was supposed to be doing: he supported her; he knew what limitations that imposed on their behavior.

Obviously, there must have been times when it was very tough in all sorts of ways, but I certainly don't get the impression that at any point he felt hobbled by her.

Joe (Joseph) Haines, press secretary to Prime Minister Harold Wilson, 1969–70, 1974–76; chief political editor, the *Mirror*; author, *The Politics of Power* (1977) He had nothing to do with the government. Indeed, one evening when Wilson was talking to the Queen, he burst into the room to say something to Wilson. He immediately had to leave; the Queen told him to go because these conversations are totally private between the two people.

Larry Adler I'll tell you one thing, he doesn't like his job. He said as much. We'd give an annual dinner for Philip and gave one once at which Prince Bernhard, of the Netherlands,[1] flew over. And all through dinner, Philip was making cracks, telling Bernhard that he [Prince Bernhard] can go anywhere he likes and nobody recognizes him. And Philip said: "I can't go anywhere without six Secret Service men trailing me."

When Bernhard left—he had to leave early to get back to Holland before the lights were turned out at the airstrip—Philip got up from the table, and said: "Give my regards to Her Royal Highness, the Queen of the Netherlands." And I said: "Oh boy! This guy doesn't like his job at all."

Peter Jay What matters is whether he has conducted himself in a way which is supportive of the institution or damaging to it, and the picture that almost everybody has is of a man of duty, who has meticulously carried out his functions in quite an extraordinarily long career—and with quite extraordinary self-discipline.

Lord Healey It's an awful job to be the spouse of a Monarch!

THE *BRITANNIA* CRUISE

The royal marriage would be severely tested when, in 1956, the Duke and his closest friend, Michael Parker, boarded the royal yacht, *Britannia*, for what was officially characterized as a six-month royal tour but was rumored to be more of a voyage of adventure, taking in the more obscure and unvisited corners of the Commonwealth and scheduled to coincide with the opening of the Olympic Games in Melbourne.

* * *

Larry Adler Mike's a very nice man, and I see him whenever I go to Australia. What made things tough for Mike Parker was that he was a divorced man, and the Royal Family were very, very stuffy.

I didn't hear any gossip about that trip. But I do know—lots of people thought—that he [Prince Philip] had girlfriends all over the place.

He can't be discreet; he's always being followed by Secret Service men. I don't think that there's any conscious effort on the media's part to be good to him, because all his gaffes get very prominently reported.

He was completely at home with Mike Parker. Losing Mike Parker was a blow to him. Mike Parker was the one confidant he could rely on not to gossip to the press. He could behave as he liked with Mike Parker.

If Mike Parker came to England, there would probably be a meeting arranged because they were very close friends. And if the Royal Family goes to Australia, it is somehow arranged that Mike Parker meets Prince Philip.

But there can be no closeness any more. The Queen has absolutely forbade that.

Michael Parker My wife had decided to divorce me. I only mention this because it coincided with the return of *Britannia*, and the British press made much of it—so much of it that I got very introspective about it, I suppose.

I telephoned to the Queen and I said: "Ma'am, I don't like the idea of me sheltering behind you while this is going on. I'd very much like to resign." And she said: "No way! I want you to stay." And I said: "Well, Ma'am, I will be followed by forty or fifty press people every day, right up to the door of Buckingham Palace. And I'm sorry, I frankly can't stand that." So with reluctance we agreed. The Queen was wonderfully kind to me, and sympathetic, and understanding.

However, it didn't stop the press from using me as a bit of a lever as far as Prince Philip and the Queen were concerned. But there was nothing in that whatever, nothing whatever. The rift was cooked up by one or two British press.

You can imagine that after all my years with them, it was a pretty black moment for me. It took me years to get over it, absolute *years*.

Tim Heald There were good reasons for actually showing the flag in that specific way in parts of the Commonwealth that weren't normally visited.

What are we talking about? Nine or ten years of the marriage, and, eventually, four fairly tough years of being married to the Queen. I believe he needed a bit of a break.

Adnan Khashoggi (1935–2017), international financier; uncle to Emad [Dodi] Fayed He knows his place; he behaves very well. He has a lot of charisma with the British, even though his origin was not English. He has managed to comport himself as the Queen's husband in a nice way: he has his funny life, like Clinton and others, but he is discreet.

THE DUKE OF EDINBURGH'S PERSONALITY
AND CHARACTER

Lord Powell He was much more of a professional military man—a German by birth,[2] a martinet, not at all interested in cultural aesthetics, very much into shooting and horses.

John Eisenhower We sat next to each other at lunch. And we had a couple of Scotches, and we kidded about each other's babies. He was, as he has always been, quite approachable and open. I had a feeling that he was fighting a hard battle with his status.

* * *

A high-level source in the Navy described his annual custom of briefing the Prince, which usually took place at Buckingham Palace. At the time of his scheduled third briefing, however, Prince Philip's office said:

"No, no. He doesn't want you to come to the Palace. He will come to the Ministry of Defence." And the Prince would come to the south door, which was the wrong door—it was miles away from the office—and he didn't want to be let in by anyone, which was unhelpful, because it meant that you had to go round everybody and make quite sure that they knew that this was happening. Otherwise they'd blow their top because they hadn't been informed, and they'd think you were doing something undercover.

The naval officer had to go down to the south door and meet him, and they walked—it was about a quarter of a mile back to the officer's room.

Prince Philip was given a cup of coffee, and the naval officer sat him down, and started off very easy. And the officer hadn't been going more than about three minutes when he said: "Well, what you really ought to be doing is … *roar, roar, roar.*"

So you wait for the clock to run down, and then say things more or less like: "Would you like me to continue, Sir?" And so it was difficult.

* * *

Donald Stovel Macdonald, PC, CC (1932–2018), Canadian M.P., 1962–78, posts include president, Privy Council of Canada, Government House leader, minister of national defense, minister of finance; high commissioner of Canada to the U.K., 1988–91 The guy is a bully, and the least I had to do with him the better off I personally would be. I believe the greatest thing he could do for Canada would be to stay home.

He was rude. One of my colleagues hadn't landed on D-Day, but he had been in one of the reenforcement groups that came up afterwards, and he was wounded almost to death. And he was the host for Prince Philip, and Prince Philip made some disparaging comment about the Canadian Armed Forces—and here was a guy who had almost lost his life.

And the following day, one of the officials from Buckingham Palace said: "There may have been some misunderstanding; His Royal Highness said . . ." I think the man is an oaf.

I remember him saying something to me at another function, in London. He said: "None of the British papers think we are fairly treated in Canada." And I was about to come back to him and say something when he turned and walked away.

Of course, he was a bully in the sense that a bully knows that the person that he's injuring can't hit him back. And most of the time, he can be as rude and as uncultured as he likes to everybody, and courtesy requires them to do [nothing]. And I think he turned away because he realized that I just might take him on.

But it's typical of him. He's not a very nice person.

Dr. Ivan Leigh Head, OC, QC (1930–2004), special assistant and counselor on foreign relations to Prime Minister Trudeau of Canada, 1969 through the 1970s; delegate to numerous Commonwealth Heads of Government Meetings (CHOGM) He was viewed [in Canadian government circles] as a smart aleck—of no consequence at all, an embarrassment, really. He was always putting his foot in his mouth when he was present at formal occasions.

He became the butt of jokes. There's one that's told very fondly—and it's not apocryphal, apparently, because the individuals there had passed it on to a number of people:

He was in Yellowknife, up in the Northwest Territories, a number of years ago, when it was still a pretty frontierish place, and there was a dinner given in his honor.

As in any small-town cafe, the cutlery was somewhat limited. And when the time came to change from one course to another and he left his knife and fork on the plate, as one always does, the waitress was said to say: "Save your fork, Duke, there's pie."

This is told with great good humor, but there's a bit of a barb to it, as well.

Sir Donald Charles McKinnon, PC, ONZ, GCVO, deputy prime minister of New Zealand, 1990–96; foreign minister, 1990–99;

secretary-general of the Commonwealth, 2000–08; interviewed in 2021
He did have a reputation for being quite rude. I would see him [...] two or three times a year at conferences or special functions in London, as well as when my wife and I were invited to Balmoral. He was an intellectually curious person who would become bored when things were not moving fast enough and would make shocking comments as his way of drawing people into conversation.

Sir Bernard Ingham; interviewed here in 2021 He lent quiet support, *except* when he occasionally made some curious remark, and was a rock of stability.

Baron Howard, Michael, PC, QC, CH, life peer, cr. 2010; Conservative M.P., 1983–2010, cabinet positions include employment secretary, environment secretary, and Home Secretary; leader of the opposition, 2003–2005; interviewed in 2021 Her Majesty's relationship with Philip is steadfast and remarkable; they are a team.

Baron Steel, David Martin Scott Steel, PC, KBE, KT, life peer, cr. 1987; Liberal Party and then Liberal Democrat M.P., 1965–97; M.S.P. (Member of the Scottish Parliament) and presiding officer, 1999–2003; Lord High Commissioner, General Assembly, Church of Scotland 2003 and 2004; interviewed 2021 I knew Prince Philip very well, he having been chancellor of Edinburgh University at the time I was Rector and we did a lot together during the fortieth anniversary year, and I was with him privately when he was doing his carriage driving [of which Lord Steel is an aficionado].

He was always extremely amusing company but was apt to make remarks that you could take offense at if you wanted to do so.

As he once said to me when I was wearing a gaudy tie: "You have got courage to wear it."

Some people might think he was being rude, making a gaffe, a word used by the press that I don't like.

On another occasion, during a ceremonial event in London regarding plans to open a hotel in Tanzania, my constituency for four years, where I had contacts and was very friendly with that nation's then-president Julius Nyerere,[3] I made a slight boo-boo as I did not realize that the ceremony would be followed by a luncheon.

I was sitting there, dining with Philip, when I realized that I must depart before he would in order reach the airport for my return flight to

Tanzania, so I said: "I am terribly sorry, Sir, but I will have to break with protocol and leave before you do."

Replying, Prince Philip exclaimed: "Oh, that is an original excuse! When you get there, you might remind them that I liberated them! I pulled down the Union Jack on Independence Day!"

Two weeks later, on seeing Prince Philip again, I would report: "Well, I did tell them that and they remembered very well that you liberated them."

Baron Butler of Brockwell, Frederick Edward Robin, KG, GCB, CVO, PC, life peer, cr. 1998; private secretary to five prime ministers, 1961–98; secretary of the cabinet and head of the Home Civil Service, 1998–98; interviewed in 2021 Bear in mind that his gaffes were intended to put those who were nervous about meeting him at ease. Prince Philip was very good at recognizing people and the truth is that although he—as well as the Queen—would do everything according to protocol, he would secretly enjoy it when things would go slightly *wrong*.

As head of the Civil Service, I was fortunate to meet with the Prince from time to time. My wife and I were very fortunate in being friendly with Sir Robin Fellowes, who is married to the sister of the late Princess Diana. Sir Robin and his wife would often have the Queen and Prince Philip to informal suppers, to which they kindly invited us, affording us the opportunity to talk with the royal couple under quite informal circumstances, and we regarded this as a great privilege.

On one occasion, while riding his pony and trap at Windsor, Prince Philip had fallen off and the cart had capsized and he had fallen into the lake, and the Queen was very amused about the incident.

I said to her: "Do you think that Prince Philip should give up driving that trap?"

Replying, she said: "You try to make him!"

That evening, my wife was sitting with Prince Philip on the settee after supper up in Norfolk, where Sandringham is. As it happened, my wife's father had worked on the Sandringham Estate during the war in jute manufacturing, making parachutes. Prince Philip really enjoyed talking about that and so my wife had a very easy conversation with him lasting about half an hour.

Baroness Neuberger, Rabbi Julia Babette Sarah Neuberger, DBE, life peer, cr. 2004; chief executive the King's Fund, 1997–2004; senior rabbi, West London Synagogue, 2011–20; chair, University College

London Hospitals; interviewed in 2021 We had a Jewish, Christian, Muslim meeting which he was part of with the Crown Prince of Jordan. Prince Philip certainly was a brilliant, incredibly supportive Righteous Gentile.

Bishop Michael Mann I have the most enormous respect for Prince Philip; he's a man who would have got to the top of his profession, whatever he was going to do. He has never tried to be a Prince Albert.

Lady Longford I don't believe the Duke of Edinburgh likes being compared too much to Albert because he's got his own ideas.

But there is a very strong parallel in their practical activities: they have both tried to modernize the Palace and the Monarch. And they succeeded. Albert made enormous changes.

On the other hand, I would have to say that any intelligent man would have started making changes. I remember when Frank came back from the first dinner party he chaired—it was about prison reform—Frank said: "This man would rise to the top in whatever career he'd have gone in for. And he certainly would have in the Navy."

John Grigg, formerly Lord Altrincham (1924–2001), having renounced his title due to his objection to hereditary seats in Parliament; journalist affiliated to the *Guardian* and *The Times*; critic of the monarchy He's a very underrated, slightly combative, figure. He's been very important. In the early years he helped her. I was very glad to see that it [the golden wedding] was the occasion for rather more favorable comments.

Baron Archer of Weston-super-Mare, Jeffrey Howard, life peer, cr. 1992; Conservative M.P., 1969–74; bestselling novelist; one-time candidate for the office of mayor of London Charles is much more sensitive; he likes art, the theater, music, and the ballet. Prince Philip wouldn't know where Sadler's Wells[4] is if his life depended on it.

Duke of Norfolk Prince Philip's a very attractive person, you know, and has a very Cartesian mind.

Bishop Michael Mann Prince Philip is like a terrier with a bone; every single thing has to be chewed over and gnawed, torn apart: I want people to know I've got an inquiring mind.

Larry Adler He is a goddamn good joke-teller and he made one crack about me which I think is very funny. He said: "I think, in Larry's honor, 'whitebait'[5] on the menu should be changed to 'redbait.'"

Lady Longford He's quite a tease. Sometimes I've felt he was going beyond the limits. A friend of mine had sent me *part* of a hat from Paris, fixed with some feathers and flowers on it. At one garden party we were talking to him [the Duke of Edinburgh]. He looked at this hat and said: "Where did *that* come from?" I told him and he said: "Oh, I see. It's a do-it-yourself hat."

Hugh D. Segal, OC, OOnt, CD, principal secretary to the premier of Ontario, 1975–77; chief-of-staff, office of Prime Minister Brian Mulroney, 1992–93 There is a story that he flew his own flight on his way to Canada and he stopped at Gander, where we have a Canadian Forces base, for refueling and a cup of tea, so our commanding officer was out there with his wife.

They were standing at the bottom of the stairs, and down he comes— he's not in a very good mood at all—and the commanding officer says: "Hello. How was the flight, Sir?" And the Duke says: "Have you ever flown before?" And the commanding officer says: "Yes." And the Duke says: "Well, it was a lot like that." And he strides off to get a cup of tea.

Lady Greenfield Concerning his comments about Asians,[6] which were not thought through well, he did not intend them to be nasty; they were meant to be funny.

Baron Howe of Aberavon, [Richard Edward] Geoffrey, CH, PC, QC (1926–2015), life peer, cr. 1992; Chancellor of the Exchequer, 1979–83; secretary of state for foreign and Commonwealth affairs, 1983–89; leader, House of Commons, and deputy prime minister, 1989–90 It was a lighthearted remark; it was intended sort of jocularly—the students had been there for five years, or something—which anyone might make *en passant*. It did look very foolish in print, there's no doubt about it.

Michael Parker Dickie was a great P.R. man. Now P.R., in my opinion, was Dickie's great field; he was excellent, a past master at that.

But I believe that Philip is far better—and comparisons are odious— in a broader sense, but he's certainly no P.R. man.

Baroness Featherstone of Highgate, Lynne Choona, PC, life peer, cr. 2015; MD of own design firm, Inhouse Outhouse Design, 1980–87; Liberal Democrat M.P., 2005–15, minister, crime prevention, 2014–15; interviewed in 2021 I know lots of old people—Philip was ninety-nine when he died—who make difficult or racist remarks.

It was a difficult job, however, for a man of his era to take second place to a clever woman all the time.

He was quite a character and he and the Queen were a great team.

* * *

Prince Philip's funeral service, viewed in the United Kingdom by 13.6 million people, as well as by millions more throughout the world, was held at St. George's Chapel, Windsor, eight days following his death on May 9, 2021.

The Queen, who on the occasion of her Diamond Jubilee in 2012 had described her husband as "a constant strength and guide," sat alone during the one-hour ceremony, which included musical selections chosen by the Duke of Edinburgh and buglers sounding "Action Station"—a call summoning sailors to battle readiness.

In his moving eulogy, the Right Reverend David Conner, the dean of Windsor, spoke for multitudes of Her Majesty's subjects saying: "We have been inspired by his unswerving loyalty to our Queen, his service to the nation and Commonwealth, his courage, fortitude and faith. Our lives have been enriched by the challenges that he has set us, the encouragement that he has given us, his kindness, humor and humanity."

PRINCE PHILIP'S LEGACY

Lady Greenfield He was not stuffy although he had every reason to be, and he had the ability to debunk, a marvelous way of bringing people down to earth.

Lady Featherstone He brought people together who would not automatically have come together, enabling discussion. The further we are from his death, the more we will see how extraordinary he was in doing that.

Lord Butler People will know of his encouragement of what I would call his "good activities."

Seventh Marquess of Cholmondeley, David George Philip, KCVO, DL, joint hereditary Lord Great Chamberlain of England, 1990–; film director; this interview 2021 He did an enormous amount in many fields for young people; the public learned quite a lot about these things only following his death.

Rt Honorable Andrew (Andy) Burnham, PC; Labour M.P. 2001–17, chief secretary to the treasury, 2007–08, secretary of state for culture, media and sport, 2008–09, secretary of state for health, 2009–10; mayor of Greater Manchester, 2017–; interviewed 2021 While politicians, prime ministers, and members of the Royal Family have causes they believe in, there is a tendency for these things to come to an end. The Duke of Edinburgh Award is the complete opposite, however—an enduring program that through the decades has touched the lives of so many young people, and still *does*.

PART TWO

The Institution of
the Monarchy

CHAPTER 7

Who Is the Queen?

T HE NEW QUEEN's subjects had been aware of her first as a tow-headed, rather serious, angelic-looking toddler—"Lilibet" as she called herself from the age of two-and-a-half; then as a patriotic teenager in wartime, broadcasting encouraging words to the world and serving her country in the ATS; then as a young woman very much in love; then as a lovely bride; later as a daughter grieving for her father; and more recently as a conscientious Monarch who took her Coronation vows with an air of great dignity and sense of responsibility.

While her family and Palace courtiers, as well as a select group of friends, were aware of the qualities of the young woman who had just come to the Throne as Queen Elizabeth II, the public did not know at all the human being behind the royal façade—and could not, due to the tradition of maintaining the Monarch and the monarchy apart from all others.

THE QUEEN'S PUBLIC PERSONA

Sir Adam Ridley She absolutely naturally took it over. Nobody seemed to be worried lest she should be unable to rise to expectations. It was, right from the start, a flawless performance.

Bishop Michael Mann She has this very sincere belief that she is consecrated to her post, in the same way that I am consecrated. When my late wife was very ill, I went to the Queen and said: "Ma'am, I'm afraid I'm going to have to resign, retire." "Ha!" she said: "That's all right for you. I can't."

Sir (John) Oliver Wright, GCMG, GCVO, DSC (1922–2009), private secretary to Prime Minister Alec Douglas-Home; ambassador to the Federal Republic of Germany, 1975–81; ambassador to the United States, 1982–86 In private, she has the most girlish giggle you can think of, and it is so beautiful when her face lights up in a smile; in private she is a very normal person. But just as soldiers put on uniforms for doing their duties, so she has to be regal when she performs her duties in public.

Bryan Forbes She's rather a beautiful woman. She's got this wonderful skin—both she and Princess Margaret have this Vivien Leigh, translucent sort of, almost porcelain, wonderful skin, and wonderful eyes—and I've always thought she's a very attractive woman. And as a young girl, when she was crowned, she was exceedingly beautiful.

Sir Edward Dillon Lott du Cann, KBE (1924–2017), minister of state, Board of Trade, 1963–64; chairman, Conservative Party, 1965–67, chairman, 1922 Committee, 1972–84 She is a performer who knows her role, has great experience in it, and realizes that she must perform.

I was [...] at Sandringham with a group of thirty for an official function. As we stood in a circle, the Queen and the Duke of Edinburgh greeted each of us, chatting with us for a minute-and-a-half each.

She was warm in her greetings, but it was as if she had assumed the role of a performer, knowing what her role was and understanding the roles of those whom she was greeting. It was a rather awkward moment.

Chief Sir (Eleazar Chukwuemeka) Emeka Anyaoku, GCVO, CFR, CON, Nigerian diplomat; deputy secretary-general [political] of the Commonwealth, 1977–83, 1984–90; secretary-general of the Commonwealth, 1990–2000 It is difficult to draw a clear distinction between the public and private personalities because her whole existence is symbolism: she as the Monarch serves a particular image, a particular role. She *lives* that role.

Michael Deaver (1938–2007), President Reagan's deputy chief-of-staff, the White House, 1981–85 I was introduced [to the Queen during the advance trip for President Reagan's 1982 state visit to Britain] and we talked a little bit about the visit. We then went on a tour of the Castle.

She was in plain attire. Later, I found out, in traveling with her, and being around her, she was pretty much a regular person. There obviously was a difference when she was in public. There were two or three levels of her—levels of relaxation, I would call it. So she was very kind, but very proper, and it was clear that she was going to be given the deference of her position. And, after all, we were at *her* house.

At Windsor Castle, they were very relaxed, at home. On that first night when we got there, we had obviously had a big day, but we all dressed for dinner, and it was just them—Princess Anne was my dinner partner—and the Reagans, and Carolyn,[1] and me. So it was just family, it was just a dinner—the corgis were at everybody's feet, and chasing cats around the dining room table.

Ivan Head We were at Windsor and she and Prime Minister [Pierre Elliott] Trudeau went in and had a little tête-à-tête. We went later to lunch. There were six of us at the table: the Canadian high commissioner to Britain, the British high commissioner to Canada, and someone from the Household who was responsible for these sorts of things.

We went down into a tiny little room to have lunch, and as we went into the room, the Queen said to me: "Mr. Head, you sit there and be Daddy; I'll sit here and be Mummy."

THE QUEEN AS A STICKLER FOR TRADITION
AND FORMALITY

John Eisenhower There was some talk about a ceremony playing only parts of the National Anthems—any time Dad could make a ceremony shorter, he would do it, no matter what. So Philip said: "That sounds good to me. But you know, she [the Queen] said no." So that was that.

Michael Noakes, PPROI, RP (1933–2018), portrait and landscape painter, portraitist of the Royal Family Certainly, in my case, I've been very aware of who she was all the time: I never got casual with her, but we did see occasions where people were being a bit pushy [...]

In the Millennium Dome, for instance [on New Year's Eve, 1999], Tony Blair was there, and he was pressing the flesh. The Queen came in. And at the end, when she was about to go, some working guy wanted to shake her hand—she was up on the platform.

She takes flowers from people, but she doesn't very often shake people's hands if they stick them out from behind a barrier—she will do formal lineups, of course, but not to people just lining the route—and she just gave him sort of a little half-smile and walked past.

I felt sorry for him really. I thought it wouldn't have done any harm had she felt able. But I suppose she feels it diminishes her. And she's not a performer in that sense; she doesn't see why she should perform.

And during this past year [at a visit by the Queen to a hospital] the press were lined up and there was a small child in a hospital bed. The press were willing her to go near the child in the bed, not to clasp him to her bosom, or anything, but just to go *near*, just so they could get a shot where the picture was: there was a great emptiness in the middle; you can't have a child, wall, Queen. It doesn't make a good picture. Why can't she? She must be aware of that need, but she won't do it.

Vivien Noakes It's interesting, because she's very aware of the press; they have press office who set things up for them to get the best pictures. And yet there's this point beyond which she isn't prepared to go.

I imagine she's always been like this: she is the Monarch and has always been in the distance; she was never in on the touchy-feely thing before becoming Queen in the way that the Princess of Wales was before becoming a Princess.

People are looking out for it more now; they expect it more. They want it more. They're very happy for the Queen just to be there. But now they would also like her to move in a bit closer.

The thing that we've noticed—and have tried to convey in our book[2]—is the element of celebration that accompanies her presence—the sheer joy of the event when the Queen arrives; the people's pleasure.

And if it's a walkabout, we've been in one or two walkabouts, and it's been such *fun*. The Queen's enjoyed it; they've enjoyed it; we've enjoyed it. People have been laughing, and it's so easy, and relaxed. And in that way, she's right in with the people.

It's more when she's being taken around formally, from room to room: "Ma'am. this is the surgeon, and here is the child." Then she's sort of [stiff and formal], really.

Michael Noakes It's exaggerated the problem now, in a sense, because she obviously doesn't want to give the impression that she's trying to do a sort of queenly version of the Princess of Wales.

It's electric, actually, when she goes into a room, isn't it?

Lord Archer She's formal: she will say: "Lord Archer," where all the children will say: "Hello, Jeffrey."

Bryan Forbes The first time you go in and greet somebody like the Queen, you would go in and say: "Good evening, Your Majesty." But beyond that you don't have to preface everything by "Your Majesty"; you would call her "Ma'am," or "Sir," if it's Prince Philip.

Lord Healey It's a difficult thing, you know, seeing the Monarch. I always found it a little difficult, and awkward.

It was the formality, really: ridiculous things, like you're never allowed to turn your back on the Queen, so you have to walk backwards out of the room.[3] There are lots of odd little things like that which make it difficult. But, again, a prime minister is in a much better position than a member of the cabinet, because he sees the Queen a great deal—both formally and informally.

The only time I felt quite natural was once when I was meeting with the Queen about the budget and Princess Anne came in—she looked exactly like my daughter at that age—and said she wanted to go up to Sandringham. And the Queen said: "Well, darling, do be careful how you drive," exactly like my wife and my daughter.

Geoffrey Arthur Holland Pearson, OC (1927–2008), son of the late Lester Pearson (prime minister of Canada, 1963–68); director general, Bureau of U.N. Affairs, 1975–78; adviser on arms control and disarmament, 1978–80; ambassador to the USSR, 1980–83 My father was an usher at the Coronation in 1937 of King George, when he had to dress up in a special uniform—he was always talking about that.

But he didn't like that kind of thing—he was always making fun of it. So when he came to know the present Queen, he would talk about it, and she didn't like it either, so they got along famously because of this common dislike of too much official pageantry of one sort or another. She was a down-to-earth person.

Bishop Hugh Montefiore She's not starchy, but she has a public face, and she's very conscientious about it: she reads her speeches passively; you have no idea what's going on inside because you mustn't have any idea of what a Monarch is thinking.

Gen. Andrew Goodpaster One thing really startled the British people. They showed on the T.V. the president arriving at Balmoral[4] and being greeted by the Queen there. Of course, there was the Royal Salute, and then they met with each other, and as they walked away, he [President

Eisenhower] took her elbow—he did it out of personal affection, really. They were astounded. No one ever touches the Queen!

* * *

This caused Michael Noakes a similar problem when planning a composite royal portrait. In order to assemble the separate studies on the final canvas, he would need a scale of everybody's height as an aid to perspective.

* * *

Michael Noakes I therefore explained to Heseltine[5] that I'd got a cardboard screen which was marked off in one-inch things, and I'd like to ask the Queen to stand against it and be measured.

And he said: "Measure *the Queen?*"

And I said: "Well, yes."

And he said: "Well, leave it with me and I'll have a word with her about it. It might be all right."

Well, the next day, I had taken all my gear out and was waiting for her. And he later told me he'd forgotten; he'd looked at his watch and it was a quarter-to-three, and he hurried along to her room. But she, thinking the new painter had better be on time, had gone.

And he also hadn't told her a thing about being measured. So when she came into the room with somebody she'd picked up in the corridor who wore a funny red waistcoat and had never done this sort of thing before, and came in and said [whispering loudly]: "Her Majesty!" and fled, she was a bit thrown, and I was a bit thrown.

Anyway, I said: "Has Mr. Heseltine explained, Ma'am, about the construction of the cardboard?" And I thought she was going to say it was all right.

But she said: "No."

And I said: "What! He hasn't explained about how I need …?"

And she said: "No."

Well she has a curious thing—she's got two expressions: one is dour. And one is ping! And she's got really very little in between. And while she's listening to something, she's always dour. And I didn't know whether this meant she was saying: "Is this man *mad?* Have him *measure* me?"

And there was a slight mini-pause and then she said: "Yes, it's all right." So she went and stood against this thing, and by then I was in such a state, I so nearly got black felt-tip marker all over her blue silk robe. So Bill was not my number one, favorite person, I'm afraid, for quite some time.

Michael Deaver During the Queen's visit to Los Angeles [in 1983], I always sensed that when we were going through the ropes, officially, and when she was in public, officially, she was sort of carrying the purse—the Monarch.

Then, when you got into the limo, there was a little bit more relaxation, perhaps an aside. When the gangplank would come up on *Britannia* in the evening, she was very relaxed and enjoying herself.

Sixth Baron Carrington, Peter Alexander Rupert, KG, GCMG, CH, MC, PC, DL (1919–2018), leader of the opposition, House of Lords, 1964–70, 1974–79; secretary of state, defense, 1970–74; energy, 1974; foreign and Commonwealth affairs, 1979–82; secretary-general, NATO, 1984–88 I don't think the Queen minds not being regarded as a pop star. She's never sought easy popularity and the people who criticize her, in her view, don't understand the monarchy in their country; it's a much more serious affair than being a pop star. That's not the Queen's style—nor should it be.

Stephen Day As the Queen has been shown an extraordinary affection and respect she has never sought to be popular, and one's never had the impression that she is fashioning her image, or anything like that. She gets on; she does her job. And in this day and age, that becomes more and more impressive.

John Grigg She is very easy, and fun. But there's no question that she lacks the ability—a lack she's had throughout her reign—to respond to public enthusiasm in a way that makes it clear that she's enjoying it and that she appreciates the enthusiasm that's being shown.

She's not good at responding to crowds. When she does walkabouts, she's really good. But, compared to the Prince of Wales, and compared with her mother, she's not good at responding, dramatically, to the enthusiasm shown by crowds.

People now accept her rather reticent style; people realize it's how she *chooses* to bear herself in public: she isn't an actress and she can't get into the actress business.

Lord Armstrong She has become much easier over the years she's been doing it: she does it now with much greater self-confidence; she comes out, as it were, to the people more.

But she can never escape the fact that she is there as the *Queen*. That is the fact of her life; that is why she is doing what she is doing. I keep saying it: she's a very professional lady, and she's got a very clear idea of what her profession requires of her. And she is very committed to carrying her duties out with a very high degree of professionalism.

THE QUEEN'S SENSE OF DUTY

Archdeacon George Austin The Queen is someone with a very high sense of duty, instilled in her by her parents and her grandmother, not least because of Edward VIII. So it's very much part of how she grew up—the historical situation of how she grew up. And I would think she would think: If I am Defender of the Faith, I will keep that vow as firmly as I can.

Lady Angela Oswald The abdication obviously would have had a very big effect on her. It was a great shock to the Royal Family, generally, that the Duke of Windsor should have put his own personal feelings ahead of his duty to the nation. The members of the Royal Family felt very strongly that duty was always first.

Sir Michael Oswald If she didn't get that feeling firsthand, because she was a bit young at the time of the abdication, she almost certainly got it from the King and Queen Elizabeth [the Queen Mother]—that it was generally felt that you should put your duty to the nation first, and your own personal happiness second.

Adm. Sir Henry Leach There was a mammoth luncheon at either the Mansion House or Guildhall [...]—it might have been the Falklands ten years on, or something like that—and the Queen was due to speak. And, poor thing, she was very hoarse. Her voice problem was sufficiently acute that she was going to say her few words at the beginning of lunch—it was a bit unusual—and not at the end because it might have faded away altogether by then.

It was an occasion when the chiefs of staff formally gathered. The good and the great were shepherded into a particular anteroom, where they were all going to be presented, and she went through the assembled VIPs like a dose of salts.

She came out into the much bigger anteroom, where us lot were moving around, and, hoarseness, or not, chatted away—absolutely delightful and natural. She wasn't going to not do her stuff just because she was ill and at risk of losing her voice, which I thought was a very brave act. She was a natural. And she's a marvelous person.

Bryan Forbes They are different not because they are not human, but because they have been placed in the position through an accident of birth, and they have to go through with it. There is no alternative. And therefore it's difficult for us to envisage, or imagine, what that does to you.

I get up in the morning and put on a tee-shirt; the Queen has to dress up every day, and not wear the same thing twice in succession. And then she's criticized for what she wears: "Why is she wearing *that*? Why doesn't she go to Armani?"

It must be difficult. You go out to a big dinner—it's a set meal—and something is put in front of you which normally you would throw up, rather than eat it.

Imagine the meals that she has to eat when she goes abroad and somebody brings her boiled rattlesnake, or something. Now you can't insult your host; you've got to at least get through it somehow. It must be a nightmare!

Michael Deaver The Queen was always right there, ready to go—standing there like: "Mr. Deaver, where have you been?" And she would always have a nice comment after every event: "Oh, I *enjoyed* that" or "Wasn't that *interesting*?" It was very impressive to me. And she had a full schedule.

Ivan Head There's an informal photograph of Sonny [Ramphal], and Her Majesty, and me on my wall—it was Commonwealth Day and I just happened to be in London, and Sonny said: "Come on, she's coming over to Marlborough House and you've got to be here."

The three of us were just having a chat. But her attendance on her duties is evident in her face: the Queen is getting to the end of a long, hard day. You just know she's having trouble with her shoes, or something.

Sir Donald McKinnon I would meet with the Queen three or four times a year to discuss what was happening in the Commonwealth, presenting a Commonwealth view of the world, in contrast to that of the Foreign Office.

These were very good meetings in the sense that there were no note-takers, just the Queen and I, these sessions lasting between thirty minutes and an hour on days she would have shorter meetings with ambassadors heading out to their posts, as well as diplomats from abroad paying courtesy calls.

From the Commonwealth's point of view, there was generally a very warm relationship with the Palace.

I believe that Her Majesty handled her relationships with Commonwealth leaders remarkably well, having had seventy years' practice doing so, during which time she had to dine with some of the world's most notorious bandits. Imagine her government insisting that she host a state dinner for President Nicolae Ceausescu, the General Secretary and President of Romania's Communist Party![6]

Sir Peter Kenneth Estlin, Kt, BSc, FCA, Lord Mayor of the City of London, 2018–19; non-executive director of Rothschild & Co and chair of FutureDotNow; interviewed in 2021 While the Monarch's role as the head of state is largely symbolic, hers is a very powerful, influential, and sustainable model amid today's accelerating political swings via the social media.

And although the institution of the monarchy is not perfect—nobody is saying that—I would find it hard to find people not viewing Her Majesty as giving her utmost to duty, at the age of ninety-five taking a leadership role, and fulfilling major speaking engagements. Her constancy is *amazing*.

Lady Featherstone She sets the tone for the country and to my knowledge has never refused to give assent; she is in this sense a figurehead. She does, however, have her weekly meetings with her prime minister and receives red boxes on affairs of state daily.

Her Majesty keeps an eye, if you will, but will not intervene regarding the laws of the land, which is the job of Parliament.

THE QUEEN AND PRINCESS MARGARET

The Queen's sense of duty was severely tested early in her reign, regarding Princess Margaret's ill-fated relationship with an RAF officer, Group Captain Peter Townsend, who had served as an equerry to the late King.

The Princess's feelings for Townsend became public knowledge in 1953, when at the Queen's Coronation she brushed a piece of lint from the tunic of the group captain's uniform.

As the group captain was divorced—although he was the innocent partner, his former wife was still living—Margaret's relationship with him assumed crisis proportions in 1955 when she had to decide whether to marry him and thus forfeit her place in the succession.

Margaret's situation tugged at the hearts of romantics the world over.

Her marriage to a divorced man, albeit the wronged party, was, however, unacceptable to the government and the Church of England.

Privately, the Queen was sympathetic—hadn't *she* married for romantic reasons? But as the Monarch, she had concerns that overrode her feelings for her younger sister.

Had she chosen to do so, Margaret could have married Townsend without the Queen's consent under an option contained in the Royal Marriage Act of 1772, had she been willing to wait one year and to forfeit her place in the succession, as well as her funding from the Civil List.

The drama ended when, in a terse statement to the press on October 30, 1955, the Princess announced: "I would like it to be known that I have decided not to marry Group Captain Townsend."

Group Captain Townsend left Britain immediately for Brussels, to assume duties as air attaché in the British Embassy, and eventually married again.

On May 6, 1960, there was much rejoicing in the realm when Margaret married a commoner, society photographer Antony Armstrong-Jones, later created Earl of Snowdon, in a lavish ceremony in Westminster Abbey.

Despite the romantic promise of this union, and the births of two children, David Albert Charles, created Viscount Linley, and Sarah Frances Elizabeth, the marriage was not happy and was dissolved in 1978.

Increasingly, following the end of her relationship with Townsend, and exacerbated by the failure of her marriage, Margaret's unhappiness found expression in the emergence of a side to her personality: whereas she had been conscious of royal protocol from childhood, she became difficult, even with old friends, if due respect was, even inadvertently, not paid to her.

* * *

John Eisenhower In 1965, Princess Margaret came to Washington and there was a dinner at the White House. When I went through the receiving line Princess Margaret said: "I'll see you later."

Later on, I made my way over to her and we had a very, very friendly conversation. And then I said: "How's your mother?"

She turned into an iceberg, right in front of me, and said: "You mean Her Majesty the Queen Mother."

Bryan Forbes It is difficult for Princess Margaret to have close friends— she doesn't like sycophants. I've never felt uncomfortable with the situation because our friendship goes back almost thirty years,[7] but it must be difficult because people don't behave naturally.

Princess Margaret has proved a very loyal friend through all the vicissitudes of her own life, right up to the present day. Every year she arranges a treat for her friends. One year, she took us to the Tower of London, on a very foggy November night, and we had dinner in the cell where Elizabeth I was incarcerated. The Queen was there as well, and we went out to the battlements to witness the ceremony of the Keys. The Keys are symbolically the Monarch. The Queen had never seen the ceremony because she's never there when it takes place, so it was a revelation to her as well.

THE QUEEN'S ATTENTION TO DETAIL

Lord Wright The headmaster of Wellington College[8] had been killed by a bomb in 1940. Very soon after that King George VI, and Queen Elizabeth, and the two Princesses came down to Wellington, really as a sort of marked condolence. It was a touching gesture: they came down to express sympathy, and there was a service in the chapel.

My father was a housemaster, and his house was chosen as the place for the Royal Family to visit. I was actually away at prep school quite near by, but was allowed to come home for the visit, and was presented to the King, the Queen, the present Queen, and Princess Margaret. That was my first direct awareness of the Royal Family. I was terrified. I'd been briefed about how you bow, and so on, and I'm sure that I got it all wrong.

I was able to remind the Queen of that first meeting [...] when she came down to visit Wellington. She had her private secretary, Robert Fellowes, with her. I said to her: "Your Majesty, if I may remind you, this is actually the second time we've met at Wellington; I met you when you came with His Majesty, King George VI." And she said: "There you are. I told Robert I'd been here as a girl and he wouldn't believe me!"

Stephen Day The old Emir of Qatar realized that the state visit just had to go right because every one of the neighbors would be watching him minutely.

And so he [took] very great care to know *exactly* what was happening, and as he was preparing for the dinner, he said to his right-hand man, his minister: "You just go down and do a final check, and make absolutely sure where we sit, so I know exactly where everything is."

The minister went down. And as he got to the door of the state dining room, one of the flunkies said: "I'm very sorry, Sir, you can't go in." So the minister said: "I'm checking it out for the Emir." And the man said: "We're sorry; it's Her Majesty making her final check."

She *herself* had done the final check to make sure everything was right. That deeply impressed the Emir. That was his instinct, too, about how it should be done.

Bishop Michael Mann One day I received a letter saying just: "Can you and your wife come and spend the weekend with us at Windsor? We'll give you the choice of three dates." Signed Elizabeth R.

Well, in this country, you don't just turn *that* invitation down. And so down we went and arrived in time for tea. There was a dinner party that night. It was quite clear that everyone had been invited to scrutinize us. Then I celebrated communion in the chapel and preached at the morning service.

We were taken in to meet the whole Royal Family, and then the Queen extricated my wife and me—Prince Philip was away—Princess Margaret was with her, and we drove from Royal Lodge, which is in the Great Park, down to the Castle for lunch. I had quite a lively argument with Princess Margaret at lunch—it was over a theological issue—and I could see my wife, who thought I shouldn't argue, getting more and more irritated with me. After lunch, I was taken off in one direction by the Queen and my wife was taken off in another direction by Princess Margaret, and we were grilled for about an hour and then dismissed. And on the way back, my wife said: "Well, you've blown *that* one!"

Then we heard nothing more for about six weeks. I understood, retrospectively, three more people were put through the process—there were four candidates, a weekend for each one. It's typical of the Queen; she does take the greatest of care. And then one morning about six weeks later, the telephone went and a voice said: "This is the Queen. Will you come and be my dean of Windsor?" I said: "I never take a decision without consulting my wife." She said: "How long will that take?" I said: "About five minutes." She said: "Ring me back." So I rang back and that is how I became dean of Windsor.

Andrew Burnham There were other, more formal, occasions. When serving on the Privy Council on Remembrance Day, it would be my duty as a minister to receive the Royal Family at the Foreign and Commonwealth Office, hosting them until it would be time to guide Her Majesty through to Whitehall and the Cenotaph (the war memorial).

I was, as you might imagine, panic stricken that I might lead her to the wrong part of the building, thus making her late.

As Her Majesty had done this countless times previously, however, she required no guidance at all, even knowing the exact moment to arrive at the place.

Rt. Honorable Jean Chrétien, PC, OM, CC, QC, three-term prime minister of Canada 1993–2003; counsel, since 2014, Dentons LLP; interviewed in 2021 In 1978, my wife and I spent time here in Canada with the Royal Family. At that time, the Queen presented me with the Order of Merit and she practiced her excellent French with me.

The Queen Mother's French was better because she had spoken the language with her French governess as a child in the Scottish castle where she grew up.

John Eisenhower She really works at her job and takes her job very seriously—takes herself seriously. I don't think she's having a happy life at all.

THE QUEEN'S SELF-DISCIPLINE

Peter Jay Civil servants, BBC broadcasters, ambassadors, archbishops, whatever, all sorts of people learn that in certain roles they have to button their lips in certain respects, that they have to bear it with dignity, discretion, and prudence, and that they have to abstain from controversy—or at least certain kinds of controversy. That is clearly fundamental to the idea of a constitutional monarchy, as the constitutional Monarch who is visibly taking sides between two political parties would undermine the public confidence in the institution.

Therefore, that must not happen. And if the Sovereign can't do it, then nor can close members of her family, because otherwise it would appear that she really was secretly a Tory, or a socialist. In her refereeing function, she would have a conflict of interest.

Sir Malcolm Rifkind When she is with people she knows very well— her Household who she sees every day—she will, even then, be very careful.

Not all members of the Royal Family are. The Queen Mother I've heard make some very controversial remarks. And the Duke of Edinburgh is well-known as someone who makes controversial remarks.

But I don't think I have ever heard the Queen say something that would have been embarrassing for her to say in public. There's a much greater discipline there.

Sir Michael Palliser It is the difference between being the Queen and being immensely conscious of that all the time—always in her mind is that she's got to behave. It's a sensitivity to what public reactions will be to almost anything she does, that's developed over the years—and particularly with the greater intrusion of television, and cameras, and all that. Television has really transformed all of these sorts of things. The Queen has got to be accessible without being *too* accessible; there's a balance there which has to be very carefully struck.

I think she simply says to herself: I must show no emotion; I must walk straight on and not look right or left. He [the Duke of Edinburgh] isn't inhibited in the same way; there's no doubt about that. I think he rather enjoys being different; I've often spotted it. It no longer surprises me. It is part of the way they are when they're together, particularly on a big public occasion.

Lady Longford She thinks, *all the time*; she never sort of throws herself into the situation and just bubbles away and enjoys it. She has always got a reserved part of her that's thinking.

Bishop Michael Mann I remember her once saying to me: "My father told me that I must always remember that whatever I said, or did, to anyone, they would remember it."

THE QUEEN'S RELIGIOUS FAITH

Bishop Michael Mann The Queen has a deep faith, very sincere faith.

Canon Paul Oestreicher I don't think the Queen is particularly religious. It is one of the hallmarks of Anglicanism—as it is of Roman Catholicism—that if you're receiving of communion, you're entitled to salvation of the Eucharist, which is at the heart of Anglican worship.

At least in public, the Queen is never seen in Eucharistic worship. She comes to the more formalized morning and evening prayer, which is non-sacramental. When she's in Scotland, she goes to the local Presbyterian church and listens to long sermons.

She doesn't behave like a devout Anglican. She behaves constitutionally like a Monarch who goes on Sundays to one of her royal chapels. But being religious in the sense of having a particular pleasure in church-going, and the warp and woof of the life of the Church of which she's head, no. I think it bores her.

Now as to what her interior life is—what her spirituality is—that's a different question again: whether she has a personal relationship to God; whether she prays; whether she has a religious adviser to whom she even might confess her sins, for all I know, [she may].

Father Michael Seed, Franciscan friar; ecumenical officer, archdiocese of Westminster; author The Queen has been here [Westminster Cathedral]. She was the first Monarch ever to come to our Catholic service here, in 1995, which had never happened since the Reformation.

Privately, the Monarch in the past has been to Mass: when the King and Queen of Spain at the turn of the century would visit Edward VII, Edward VII would go with them to Mass, and he'd be in the congregation, but the King was there in a private capacity.

But it wasn't until 1995 that the Queen attended a Catholic service in state, officially, publicly, which was quite incredible. It was the centennial of Westminster Cathedral and she was invited, and she came. All the Church leaders of the country were here. Cardinal Hume presided at it, and it was very spectacular, a tremendous success.

I believe that people live in their mythology of this Catholic-Protestant thing, and of connecting the Monarch purely with Anglicanism. It just isn't so. There is a technical link with the Anglican Church. I think for her personally, she is an Anglican.

But then, I understand, when she goes to Scotland, she is Presbyterian. And this is very unusual because she's not the head of the Church of Scotland but she's the kind of protector of it—she's got a special title in Scotland.

Michael Deaver My wife and I were married in a church on the floor of Yosemite which was built in 1848. I knew that the Queen would like to go to church on Sunday [during her visit to California], so I said to her: "There is this wonderful Episcopal church on the floor of the valley; it was built during the Gold Rush and I think you would enjoy it."

I was kind of horrified because I didn't know anything about [its level of churchmanship], nor did I know anything about who was going to preach. He was a kind of a fundamentalist, fire and brimstone guy from one of the neighboring valley towns, a very nice guy. And so when we were driving back, I said to her: "I'm very sorry. I didn't realize." And she said: "No, actually, I liked it better than the big, pomp service. I really enjoyed it. It's nice to be in a little church and hear the preacher."

THE QUEEN'S HUMAN SIDE

Michael Deaver The Queen had a wonderful time [in California, in 1983]. When those torrential rains came, they decided they weren't going to "steam" [travel in *Britannia*] because she doesn't like rough weather.

But that caused me a terrible problem because it gave us a whole night that I hadn't planned. And so, after whatever festivity it was in Los Angeles, and we Beat Retreat, and the gangplanks were up, and the tiaras were off, and the bar was open, I went up to the Queen and said: "We have a free evening tomorrow in San Francisco, and I have called Trader Vic's and they're going to give us a special room and I just thought it would be fun."

And she said: "Oh, a restaurant! That's wonderful!" And the Queen turns to the Duke of Edinburgh—he's standing over here—and says to him: "Philip, Mr. Deaver has this wonderful idea about going to a restaurant!"

And he turned around and said: "A restaurant? Surely you are kidding? A restaurant?" And she turned to me and said: "We'll talk about it tonight and I'll tell you." And she came down later and said: "We'd be delighted to go to a restaurant."

We did have a wonderful time at Trader Vic's. And to see Susan Hussey, and the Duchess of Grafton, the lady of the robes, with these drinks—they hit you like *that*; they're powerful things! And so we had a wonderful time. And, of course, Vic sold that dinner for years: you could go in and get the royal dinner.

That evening, when I took them back up to their suite at the St. Francis,[9] when we got to the door, the Queen said to me: "Thank you, Mr. Deaver. That was a wonderful evening. It was the first time we have been in a restaurant in seventeen years!"

Adm. Sir Henry Leach I had to take the Queen round the assembled flag officers,[10] and present them. And the further up the line you went, the longer their names, or their ranks, or their positions became, but the more did she know them. Therefore, knowing them, the quicker she went through.

We then went down to the cabin, where there was a selected, smart young steward. I had been at great pains to find out from Peter Ashmore, who had been the Master of the Household, what the Queen would drink before going into dinner. And I was told that she would have a dry martini.

But to be quite sure, I said: "Now what do you mean?"—thinking that the Queen, having to have so many nips, on so many occasions, would probably go for something barely alcoholic—that there might be something out of a bottle marked "Martini."

So I pointedly asked him this. And he said: "Oh no! Gin and French vermouth, shaken up properly in a shaker, with crushed ice. And no ice in the glass. And the Duke will have a gin and tonic."

Now I have to admit that I haven't actually tasted either. When the Queen went into the cabin, I turned to her and said: "Would you care for a drink, Ma'am?" And she took one look and said: "What on earth is *that*?"

I said: "It's a dry martini, Ma'am, which I understood to be your preference." "Oh," she said, "it doesn't look like it to me." I was getting a bit appalled, and so I said: "Well, Ma'am, would you care to try it? And if it's not to your taste, we'll try and do another."

And with the utmost reluctance, she reached out her hand as if she was about to fondle a snake, and she picked this up, and wrinkled her nose, and she took a tiny sip. And then a look of immense delight came over her face.

Baron Blunkett of Brightside and Hillsborough, David, PC, life peer, cr. 2015; Labour M.P., 1987–2015; education and employment secretary, 1997–2001; Home Secretary, 2001–04; work and pensions secretary, 2005; interviewed in 2021 Both of us having dogs, mine being my seeing eye dog, Her Majesty and I had something in common and we always used to talk about ours.

During Vladimir Putin's state visit to the United Kingdom [in 2003], my dog barked at the Russian visitor and Her Majesty patted him, as if to say: "Good dog! *Good* dog!"

Sir Peter Estlin I fortunately met the Queen on several occasions, both before my appointment as Lord Mayor of London and during the year of my service, the most spectacular time being at Buckingham Palace for the

State dinner for Donald Trump, where I had the honor of sitting on High Table with Her Majesty and President Trump.

While one does not normally reveal conversations with the Monarch, I can say this: I am a six foot, five inches tall individual, Her Majesty is considerably smaller, (former) President Trump is a rather large gentleman, and on introducing me to him, she first commented on the diamonds I wear on the brooch of office around my neck.

Well, my eyeline was very much with Her Majesty's tiara and its large number of rubies. As she commented on the quality of my diamonds, I noted the quality of her rubies, at which point Trump, having neither diamonds nor rubies, might have felt a bit naked!

THE QUEEN'S PERSONAL INTEREST IN PEOPLE

Bishop Michael Mann She is immensely interested in all those people who serve her. I was expected to keep her informed of whether the cowman's wife had had her baby, or whether the man who ran the dairy had come out of hospital. She really wanted to know and be informed of everyone around her.

Yehuda Avner My wife and I were speaking with the Queen about youth—their education—and she knew a lot: she knew about the fact that our eighteen-year-old was going to the Army. She asked us about what percentage of girls go into the Army. And then we discussed the benefits of national service, in respect to education, generally, and the fact that her kids went into the forces—though not all of them did—and she saw the benefits of it.

I have to say that literally all our conversations with the Queen—a half-dozen over the almost six years that we were there—in general were very domestic and family conversations.

Anson Chan GBM, GCMG, CBE, JP, chief secretary of Hong Kong, 1993–1997, 1997–2001 I recall the Queen's visit [to Hong Kong] in 1986 very well because I was actually involved in organizing one of the functions which she attended. I also took part in introducing the Queen to a group of guests at Government House.

I remember being very impressed with the Queen's genuine interest in people. For example, she clearly had read up on the background of the various people that she was meeting, and I was quite impressed with the fact that she asked the individuals that she met relevant questions, clearly having some idea about their background, and their area of work, and their interests. It was really very, very impressive. I had the sense that she really *cared* about people.

Third Baron Glentoran, (Thomas) Robin (Valerian) Dixon, CBE, DL, front bench opposition spokesman House of Lords on Northern Ireland, 1999–2010 You can talk to them about almost anything—it doesn't matter whether you talk about the Duke of Edinburgh's Awards Scheme, or whether you talk about wildlife, or whether you talk about politics, in the general sense, or almost anything you like. Her main love is horses.

Michael Noakes The Queen talks non-stop during sittings. There are not long periods of silence at all. And she's also very interested in what's going on outside because she doesn't see that side of the Palace very often; she doesn't work in rooms which overlook the Mall and Birdcage Walk.

So if you get her settled and you say: "Ma'am, would you mind turning your head a little bit?" then she does what you ask, then she says: "Oh, what's that down there?"

And then she gets off the platform and goes and looks out the window: "I told him not ... I told Mummy: 'You mustn't do that!'" And she comes back and you start all over again.

In the mid-1970s, I painted the Queen once wearing robes for the Order of the Bath, which are a bright, pinky red, in satin. They're very striking.

We had an afternoon session once where the light was awful, so I put lights on. It was a big picture I was painting—eight feet tall—for the City of Manchester, and to get to her head, which was six feet up on the canvas, I had to stand on a trolley. And to get her in the right height relationship, she stood [on] a trolley, as well. But meant that raised up, near what natural light there was, and artificial light as well, she could be seen from outside, which can't normally happen.

She kept up a running commentary, either on the scene, or on people's comments [about glimpsing the Queen]: "Oh! They think it is. No, he's grabbed her. No, they've gone away now." And that, I thought, was a comment about her standing as Queen, which was quite interesting: she was amused at people saying: "Wow!"

And then there was a taxi that got hit by a car and she carried on a running commentary about that. Again, I thought it was quite fun because they didn't know that the Queen was saying: "Oh! He's got out now; there's going to be a fight, think."

And, of course, because of who she is, her comments on yesterday's investiture or last night's royal film performance are doubly interesting. I don't mean that they are deeply intellectual, but she brings with her that particular view.

THE QUEEN'S CARING SIDE

Nelson Rolihlahla Mandela (1918–2013), leader, African National Congress (ANC); prisoner of the former government of South Africa; president of South Africa, 1994–99 If I can be a little bit long-winded, [my first meeting with the Queen] was at the CHOGM[11] in Harare. Somebody asked me: "Have you received an invitation from the Queen to the banquet?" I said: "No." He said: "No, no, no. You have been invited. You must come." And I said: "I am not happy with going there—an affair of this nature—without me receiving the invitation in hand." He said: "No, no. You are invited."

So in the evening I went. And when I walked into the building, there were the British officials in the foyer, and a lady says: "Ah, there's President Moi.[12] Let's give him his ticket." She was so certain. And, of course, she was tall, and regal, and very certain. And I didn't want to disappoint her, so I took the card, and I went to a gentleman who was standing there, some distance away, and I said: "Look, I've got an embarrassment here: they think I'm Arap Moi, but they were so certain that I did not want to disturb them"—because the British, they've got the British grace—and he said: "Don't worry. You are welcome. Go in."

So I went in. We had dinner. And after dinner I was standing with Brian Mulroney[13] and Bob Hawke[14] and I was facing—I was against the wall—and I saw Her Majesty come up, and so I said to my friends: "There is Her Majesty." And they turned round, and then Her Majesty came forward.

That was the first time I met her. And we had a very pleasant conversation. And the fact that she walked from the other side of the room to join us flattered me a bit. I did not know whether she was coming because I was there, or because she wanted to speak to the prime ministers. But she made a statement to one of the presidents, [Sir Ketumile] Masire, of Botswana. She said: "You know, I didn't invite Mr. Mandela, but I like the fact that he's here." That strengthened my attachment to her.

Larry Adler I played for her in Edinburgh. We did a party called "The Great Events," about the fortieth anniversary of her accession to the

Throne. She came back to meet us and I said: "I played for you when you were twelve." She said: "Oh, when was that?" And I described it.

And for a moment I thought something regal was about to come out, and she said: "How kind of you to remember so far back."

Bishop Hugh Montefiore People always notice her side of humanity: when she addressed her father, or she addresses the Queen Mother [it is]: "Mummy, are you all right?" People are awfully cheered by that because it shows she's a human being; she doesn't give that impression in public.

Lord Howard A remarkable listener, she is brilliant about establishing relaxed settings, a case in point being on an occasion when Her Majesty invited a British doctor to lunch who had been doing fantastic work with people suffering in Syria while witnessing the most terrible things.

When asked by the Queen to describe these episodes, the clearly traumatized physician could not go on.

Responding to her guest's distress, this royal hostess asked that her corgis be brought into the room, an example of the Queen's grace and sympathy.

The corgis' calming effect allowed the doctor to go on with her report.

* * *

Following Prince Philip's funeral, the Queen was glimpsed at the wheel of her car, driving through Windsor Castle's grounds. With her were her beloved corgis.

One might conclude that having just buried the love of her life, his grieving widow was seeking, and drawing, comfort from the closeness and calming effect of her treasured canines.

* * *

Andrew Burnham Her driving that day was a moving and powerful picture of who the Queen really *is*; she has a resilience that most of us can only dream of possessing.

This drive illustrates her independence as a very capable person who knows her own mind.

Baron Desai of St. Clement Danes, Meghnad Jagdishchandra, Ph.D., life peer, cr. 1991; economist; Honorary Fellow 2005 London School of Economics and Political Science; interviewed in 2021 Her Majesty knows how to deal with people's nervousness; she is amazingly good at this, and it is very impressive how she does that.

I met her at garden parties and receptions, for example, one when the Queen had a function at Buckingham Palace with Tony Blair involving India, which I attended with my [now former] wife [Gail Graham Wilson], who was much better than I in talking with Her Majesty. We also met the Queen at Windsor Castle at a dinner for the President of India during Gordon Brown's term as prime minister.

While I did not actually have much time with her as others were awaiting their turns, one had the impression that she had noticed you and that is an *art*.

In fact, the next time I saw the royal couple, Prince Philip, astonishingly, would not only remember me, but recall what we had said. He had obviously read my profile.

As for the Queen, what is amazing, really, is her absolute consistency and her trying not to disappoint or upset anybody. And even if somebody says something that is very gauche, Her Majesty just passes on.

Andrew Burnham I am fortunate to have spent time with the Queen on numerous occasions. I vividly recall at the time of my appointment as secretary of state for Culture, Media and Sport taking a long train journey to Sandringham to receive my seal of office from Her Majesty.

I recall the simple lifestyle maintained in that royal residence; there was a half-completed jigsaw puzzle on a table and her corgis were running about the room—a moment I remember fondly.

On another occasion, when Her Majesty came to my former constituency to open a sports complex when I was a Member of Parliament, she didn't just depart afterwards but stayed on for two hours, having a meal, and a glass of Dubonnet, and chatting with the attendees.

A HUMOROUS INCIDENT WITH HER MAJESTY
AT THE WHEEL

Lord Steel When the Queen was driving out from Windsor to London, with a detective beside her, of course, they were held up by a procession: the Princess Michael of Kent—known as "Princess Pushy"—was passing by. It was a very amusing episode for Her Majesty to be held up by a minor royal!

On another occasion, Her Majesty and I were having coffee following the Thistle lunch at Holyrood Palace and she remarked very critically about somebody we both knew—a public person she had appointed, and I said: "I am so glad *you* said that Ma'am, because I thoroughly agree with you."

Sir Kenneth Bloomfield In 1991, I was about to retire from my job as head of the Civil Service here [in Belfast, Northern Ireland], and I was invited to have a farewell audience with the Queen at Buckingham Palace, which is an interesting experience.

I dressed myself up in morning coat and off I went. I had twenty minutes or so alone with Her Majesty, and, of course, she was then revealed to me as an entirely different person from anything I'd met before, because this was a proper conversation.

One of the things we talked a bit about was my own experience, because I was nearly assassinated in 1988 [by the IRA] and any briefing the Queen would get about me would surely mention that, so there was a mention of that.

And one was able to see her warmth, her humor—she has a considerable sense of humor—and tremendous knowledge of what's going on in the world, because this is someone who's met absolutely *everybody*, and is regularly briefed by the prime minister about what's going on on the political stage, and all that. That was very impressive.

And it just struck me as sad, in a way, that so seldom can the Queen be detached from this rather formal position, so that people have a chance to judge her as she really is.

Lady Angela Oswald If the Queen or the Queen Mother had a really bad disaster [at a horse racing meet], they would worry first, obviously, about the horse, secondly about the jockey, thirdly the trainer, and for the boy or girl who looks after the horse, before they would think about their own disappointment.

Michael Deaver One of the things that struck me about the Queen's trip to California was that she called Princess Margaret every day, and excitedly told her what was happening, and what they had done that day—it was one of the Queen's first trips to California—and how interesting *this* was, and how much fun they had doing *that*. It was sister stuff.

IS THE QUEEN A GOOD LISTENER?

Sir Shridath Ramphal Is she a good listener? Yes, very much a good listener, and very involved, but someone with views, which she wouldn't hesitate to put, even if they weren't in total harmony with what you were saying.

In my terms, I found her—and looked to her as—a great support because the things I would be talking to her about were things that, in my judgment, were designed to further the interests of the Commonwealth. So we started off on the same premise and, invariably, we were of the same view. I benefited from the discussions; I'm sure she saw some value in them.

The Queen has a great capacity which, I think, is part of her overall success in whatever she does, in the Commonwealth, or in Britain. And for the moment of any encounter with you—for example, when I am having discussions with her—she is totally focused on that. I don't have the impression that she's squeezed me in between a lot of other things.

She may be at a Commonwealth Day reception, a big occasion when the secretary-general receives her at Marlborough House and takes her round to some five hundred people, all of whom are dying to shake her hand; she would be shaking hands with nearly two hundred of them. It would be maybe under half a minute, maybe a minute, that she'd stop in her progression along the way, and for that moment in time, she is totally focused on *you*.

And you are aware that she is: she isn't carrying the images of the one before you, and looking ahead from where you are. She is for that brief moment all yours—and that's a tremendous asset; it makes all the difference to people.

Bishop Michael Mann She is a very good listener and she always picks up any mistakes; she's very quick. She'll say: "I thought you told me ..." She never forgot—or missed—a thing. She'd come back and say: "You never told me ..." and I might say: "Well, I didn't actually know that," and she'd be delighted.

THE QUEEN'S SELF-ASSERTIVENESS

Michael Noakes It is said that when the German president arrived [for a state visit] and she was being driven down that hill by Windsor, and an over-zealous young trooper, or policeman, on horseback came alongside, in a protective sense; the Queen leaned out and said: "I think they've come to see me, not you!"

It implies an understanding of the significance of her office, and what it means to people, rather than vanity. Anybody else saying: "They've come to see me, not you," would seem arrogant. But not in the Queen's case, I think.

Joe Haines There was one occasion when Wilson made his secretary, Marcia Williams,[15] a peeress, and the Queen said to the private secretary from Number 10 [Downing Street] on the day that I was due to announce this appointment—with the greatest reluctance on my part— "Mr. Wilson does know, doesn't he, that if he wants to change anything, he can do so right up until the last minute?"

Now that conveys a keen political sense. She also, I am told, raised an eyebrow when the list was first put in front of her; that's the same as Muhammad Ali hitting somebody.

Adm. Sir Henry Leach The Queen was utterly charming—very relaxed and very easy to talk to—and I had Jim Callaghan, the prime minister of the day, on my other hand.[16] Somehow, he got into a discussion with the Queen on the relative merits of *Ark Royal*, where we were, and *Eagle*. I knew that the Queen Mother had launched the *Ark Royal*, but I couldn't remember who had launched the *Eagle*. And the two ships were really rather different: *Eagle* was equipped with more up-to-date things, sophisticated radar and that sort of thing, for most of the latter part of her life, and was a very smart ship, but didn't have such an operational record, had had more flying accidents, and, arguably, was not such an efficient fighting unit.

Ark Royal was always pretty crummy from the outside. Inside she was immaculate. But her flying record was super, and she had much more spirit, and a much more vivacious ship's company, top to bottom.

I was expounding on all of this, really as a conversational piece, until the Queen said, with a bit of a smile: "Steady on, Admiral. You'll remember who launched the *Eagle*!"

And, of course, it was her. And I had forgotten. So that set me back a bit. Recovering, so to speak, I said: "Well, Ma'am, I've only been speaking my personal impressions, but I believe them to be true."

"Yes," she said. "You see, Mummy has green fingers, and everything she touches grows."

Michael Deaver I remember going out to Windsor on that first advance trip[17] and landing in helicopters out on the lawn, and walking up with somebody from Windsor, and somebody from the Queen's protocol office at Buckingham Palace who had flown out with us.

We were with our backs to the Castle and I was saying: "Now the president will arrive here, to this assemblage of about forty people, and he will walk up here, and the Queen will be standing over here."

And I heard this voice behind me saying: "No, I don't think so." And I turned around. And it was Queen Elizabeth. And she said: "I think I'll be standing *here*."

And I said: "Yes, Ma'am, I didn't realize you were going to be here today." It was a very surprising way to meet the Queen.

* * *

Prince Charles and Princess Diana's wish to visit Gibraltar during their honeymoon cruise on *Britannia* in the summer of 1981 generated controversy due to Britain's dispute with Spain over the territory, which had been ceded to Britain in 1713 under the Treaty of Utrecht.

According to an official close to the Queen, she insisted that the visit take place, exclaiming: "He's *my* son; it's my yacht; and it's *my* colony!"

* * *

Lord Carrington She can be quite formidable. There has been over the years a great discussion about the royal yacht, *Britannia*. When I was First Lord of the Admiralty, in about 1961, the *Britannia* was going to be refitted, and it was going to cost a lot of money. There was a journalist who used to run the *Sunday Express*, called John Gordon, who was always very critical of the expenditures of the Royal Family, and particularly critical about the yacht. And the yacht was going to be refitted for £2 million, which was in those days a lot of money.

There was an outcry in the *Sunday Express*. I was sitting in my office in the Admiralty when the telephone rang and it was the Queen's private secretary. And he said: "The Queen would like to see you at 6:30." Well, I knew, by the tone of his voice, that I wasn't going to get a medal.

So, I went to Buckingham Palace. The Queen said to me: "I see that the yacht is being refitted." I said: "Yes, Your Majesty." "Why?" she said. And I said: "Well, you know, she wasn't really all that well built just in the aftermath of the war, and we can't have the yacht breaking down in the middle of the Atlantic with the Queen on board." And she said, rather icily: "I see." There was a pause, and then she said: "Who's paying?" I said: "Well, it's all on the Admiralty." And she said, rather icily: "I see. You pay and I get the blame."

I thought that was splendid! I was given a rebuke, but, I thought: that's not outside the bounds of her constitutional duties.

Lord Heseltine, Michael Ray Dibdin Heseltine, CH, PC, life peer cr. 2001; Conservative M.P. 1966–2001; secretary of state for defence,

1983–86, for the environment, 1990–92, for trade and industry, 1992–95; first secretary of state and deputy prime minister, 1995–97 I hope that *I* have never been in a position where I needed deflating!

* * *

IS THE QUEEN FRUSTRATED AT TIMES BY NOT BEING ABLE TO VOICE OPINIONS PUBLICLY?

Lord Desai I do not think that is the case as when she was growing up, being the child of the second son, she had no expectation that she would be queen.

She obviously learned very quickly; her father taught her to restrain herself. But, of course, she keeps tabs on what is happening.

Lord Steel One of the glories of our constitution is that Her Majesty is above politics.

Lord Blunkett I have met Her Majesty on several occasions, both before and during the time I was a cabinet member, and for that matter, since then. She is almost inscrutable and that is part of how she has managed to survive as a respected Monarch for so long. But it is quite difficult to get inside the shell which she has constructed to avoid people's accusing her of getting involved in the political arena.

Sir Peter Estlin While the role of the monarchy in British society, where the Monarch is the head of state, is largely symbolic, but in quite an influential way, it is very powerful.

Lord Butler While the Monarch's role is now mainly formal, the government remains *her* government and while she appoints its ministers, she does so on her prime minister's recommendation. As for other appointments of state, such as judicial, military, and academic ones, Her Majesty makes all of these on the advice of the elected government, which is mainly the prime minister.

It would be very exceptional that the Queen would have to exercise any discretion. Indeed, great efforts are made to avoid putting her in that position, thus always protecting her from appearing to take a controversial political role.

Rt Reverend Nicholas Baines, Bishop of Leeds We are not supposed to reveal what we talk about with Her Majesty, and I stick to that. But what I can say is that she is very reasonable, very funny, and asks very good questions, handling everything with great grace and generosity.

Lord Steel Her Majesty does not pontificate and is quite capable of taking her prime ministers' advice and not going off the rails. That is very important because, quite unlike being the head of any other state, the monarchy is a unique institution; it is very valuable that the head of state is not controversial.

Sir Donald McKinnon I believe that if the Queen, who was very interested in the issue of land distribution in Zimbabwe—many of our conversations involved land, farming, and farm animals—could be somewhat divorced from the monarchy, she would be living in a rural area as she is very much a countrywoman.

Patrick Jephson, equerry, private secretary, chief of staff to Princess Diana, 1988–96 It is said—it may well be true—that she has more time for animals than for people.

But bear in mind the fact that she has experienced the deaths of a great many people, including family, prime ministers, even most of her ladies-in-waiting.

I am sure that her grief is very personal and very private, and that her instinct is to get on with *life*. I find this to be very commendable.

Sir David Antony Haslam, CBE, FRCP, FRCGP, chair, 2001–04, president, 2006–09, Royal College of General Practitioners; president, British Medical Association, 2011–12; chair, National Institute for Health and Care Excellence, 2013–19 As Her Majesty must remain buttoned up in public—the British tradition is to keep a stiff upper lip—you would think: This is not good for her mental health.

DOES THE QUEEN BECOME ANNOYED EASILY?

Lord Glentoran She can be quite fearsome if she senses that people are seriously being offensive, or wanting to be crude or offensive, or anti things she believes in.

Sir David Scott In New Zealand after the Commonwealth Games [in 1976]—I don't know who took the initiative—there was a photograph taken of the Queen with her high commissioners. There were about six of us—from Australia, New Zealand, India.

It all went wrong because the photographer's flash didn't work, and after about four attempts, the Queen got a little bit irritated, and we were having hysterics in the background because the poor man was actually going out of his mind with anxiety. Eventually he got a very good photograph, which I've still got hanging on my wall.

Adm. Sir Henry Leach We moved in to dinner[18] and there was trouble about sitting down. Everybody was standing up [because the Queen was]. It's a naval practice—which I thought the Queen would have known, actually—that you have grace by the parson at a formal dinner *seated*, and you just got on with it.

The Queen stood behind her chair and turned to me and said, rather coldly: "Well, do we have grace, or something, now?" I didn't think it was the right thing for me to say: "We prefer to be seated because that's the naval drill" and so I banged with my gavel and hoped that the chaplain would pick up the tone. And he did.

Bishop Michael Mann When I went to Windsor, her private secretary said to me: "I'll give you three bits of advice: never let anybody come between you and your right of access; never let the Queen hear of something that you ought to have told her, which you haven't done, always make sure she knows; and, thirdly, never believe that the Queen has said anything unless *you* have heard her say it."

THE QUEEN'S SERIOUS SIDE

Lady Longford The Queen's smiles are there, and they're gone, and they come back, and they're gone. When she's facing you, she smiles and she looks very young—she has wonderful teeth and a lovely expression. But if you see her in profile, in between, when she's just thinking, she looks very serious, and she looks her age.

And she's got all those Hanoverian traits in her features. In other words, when you see her, she's much younger and more beautiful in front-face than in side-face. But you see the two aspects of her very clearly, which is very interesting.

Adm. Sir Henry Leach She can look quite sulky and probably doesn't know when she is looking it. And if she's photographed then, it's rather unfortunate because she isn't sulky, really. If anything, with what she's got on her plate, she's got enough to be sulky about.

Sir Michael Oswald Somebody once asked me—somebody I thought might have known better actually—why the Queen always looks so serious at something like the Birthday Parade, and why didn't she smile and wave? And I said: "Well, she's not a politician, for a start, she is an officer on parade. And if you're on military parade, you don't wave and grin."

And another thing, when the Queen is thinking, and concentrating on something, she does look serious—it's just a way that she has. People say that she looks "poker-faced." Well, I know that look, but when you *see* the Queen looking very grave, it's because somebody is telling her something, and she's thinking about it, and concentrating on it.

HER LESS SERIOUS SIDE

Bishop Michael Mann One weekend, we were driving from Buckingham Palace to Windsor and stopped at some traffic lights, and a man walking past the car suddenly stopped dead, turned around, looked into the car and made a thumbs-up gesture. And the Queen was delighted.

Nelson Mandela I was very impressed by her sense of humor; she was very humorous. She immediately put us at rest, and I said to her: "Look, you have got a very powerful competitor, a person of whom you must be careful, Your Majesty, and that is Princess Anne." And she said: "As a matter of fact, she might eventually win."

Lord Healey Jim Callaghan[19] was very good at joking with her, even making, sometimes, slightly naughty jokes, and she didn't mind that at all—up to a point, obviously.

Vivien Noakes David Attenborough is a friend of ours and he was telling us one evening about the time when he used to critique or correct the Christmas broadcasts. And they thought it might be rather fun, because of Christmas, if they had it in the Royal Mews. So they asked the Queen if she would stand in front of a horse, with the horse over her shoulder, or just behind her. And she thought about it, and she decided yes, that would be fine; she would be quite happy to do this.

So they went down to the Mews and they set up the cameras and they ran through, before she came, what they were going to do. And the Queen arrived, and the cameras rolled, and she said what she was going to say.

And David, who's not obsequious at all, said: "That was wonderful, Ma'am. That was marvelous. Thank you very much."

And the cameraman said: "David, it's no good. David, she's got to do it again."

The horse, behind her while she was talking, had actually bared its teeth and over her shoulder was looking at the camera with bared teeth! It was explained to her. She thought it was very funny and did it all again. She loves silly things. At the stables, if a horse is brought out and misbehaves, she just thinks it's very funny because she knows it's what horses do.

Rev. Ian Richard Paisley, PC (1926–2014), leader, Ulster Democratic Unionist Party, 1971–2008; M.P., 1970–2010; first minister of Northern Ireland, 2007–08; member of the European Parliament, 1971–2004
The Queen is a great mimicker of me when she has her friends around, so I suppose that is a form of flattery, isn't it?

Bishop Michael Mann She has a great sense of mimicry; the Queen imitating the Concorde landing is one of the funniest things you could see. It's a great pity she gives the impression very often that she's a bit sort of stuffy and dowdy.

Michael Parker She always had a lighthearted, wonderful way of doing things. She is very serious when seriousness is required, but oils the wheels with a lot of humor.

She's super at doing imitations of people. She can imitate brilliantly. There's a funny book written about the Australian accent. I got hold of that and we were all reading it before one of the visits. She adored all that.

I remember once when I was introducing her to a chap in Gibraltar, a major who had done something extremely brave and was coming to be decorated, and I told him to wait just outside the door, I'd just be a minute.

I went in to her and said: "Ma'am, the major is there. Should I bring him in now?" And she said: "How is he?" And I said: "Well, he's a bit taut and twangy"—"taut and twangy" is Australian for throwing up—"at the moment, but I think he'll be all right when he sees you." And she thought that was heaven.

Canon Paul Oestreicher It's fun to talk to her. She's easy and relaxed as soon as she gets out of her representative role and can sit around the table and chat. She's a very, very nice person. And she has a lovely sense of humor; she can laugh.

She never smiles in public. I've never known her to make a joke that isn't formally written into a speech—to sort of go off the cuff and make a joke, *in public*. It's not dignified, and dignity goes before all else.

But behind that dignity is a real person, which most people don't know about, which is a pity, I think. I was present at a gathering, a dinner party, with about twenty tables, given by the Lord Mayor for the Queen.

I wasn't at the Queen's table; I was at the next table. But her sheer laughter throughout that meal was very natural. She was obviously quite different in that small circle of people sitting round a table, having a meal. She no longer felt herself to be the representative, and she was just "me."

* * *

A military official, who preferred to speak off the record, recounts a social occasion with the Queen:

We wanted to give her a present because she had presented the colors. And her private secretary had let it be known that she would be very grateful to have usable wooden candlesticks, because they spent quite a bit of time in Balmoral out in the lodges, where there's no electricity, they are lit by candlelight—they do their own cooking, and she has a really marvelous time.

What about buying her half a dozen wooden candlesticks? We did more than that. We got the best craftsman from York Minster, and we said: "Can you make six, with the Air Force crest and the Queen's crest?" And he said yes.

But he was a typical artist—very unreliable—and instead of having six candlesticks to present to her at this dinner, they had only one, because the artist had the habit of disappearing, and hitting the bottle for a week, or two.

The honorary commandant got extremely worried. He said: "What am I going to say to her about this?" He came up with the magic solution: he turned round to her and said: "Ma'am, you may have plenty of butchers and bakers in your realm, but you are damned short of candlestick makers." And she hooted with laughter—she really has got a lovely, musical laugh, quite uninhibited—and she really thought that was marvelous.

I said to her: "Rest assured that we shall get the others." We did manage to get the craftsman to finish them and we heard that she was very grateful, and that they had been put to good use in Balmoral—and, as far as I know, they still are in use.

Joe Haines It was great fun.[20] The Queen was very funny—very offhand. I did not realize it, but she was not speaking from one of those formal scripts, written by people who have never made a speech—and probably would never.

She said that one of the things she and the prime minister had in common was that they both lived in "tied cottages"—in this country it related particularly to farm workers, whose housing was tied to their job. They would live in a "tied cottage": as soon as they lost their job, they lost their house—and she was describing Buckingham Palace and Number 10 Downing Street as "tied cottages"!

It was very good, very informal, and very relaxed. And she spent a lot of time talking to Michael Foot,[21] who in those days was one of our great left-wingers, who was there in evening dress and wearing a Miners' Union lapel badge.

Lord Glentoran I was invited to a lunch at Buckingham Palace six years ago. We were only twelve for lunch, including the royals, and I sat next to the Duke of Edinburgh. And that was a very memorable occasion: we arrived and went into the White Drawing Room and had a gin and tonic, and talked.

Then we went into lunch, and conversation flowed—the Queen or the Duke would tend to drive the conversation, but it's less formal than it used to be now; you get one or two extra words out when you have a gin and tonic—and then we went out and had coffee, like a normal lunch party. But the humor, and the sense of humor, was lovely. They both have a marvelous sense of humor, rather dry.

One of the guests was a well-known international sculptor, a funny young man, and he said: "Ma'am, do you ever watch television now?" And she didn't really answer him. He said: "I just wondered if you watch *Spitting Image*?"[22] And she said: "What did you say?" And he said: "I wondered if you ever watch *Spitting Image*, and you saw the occasion where you said: 'Now, Mr. Major, what do *you* do?'"

He was very brave. I thought she was going to fall down. She said: "I thought it was the funniest thing!"

* * *

In 2012, displaying her warm sense of humor, the Queen would appear in a video with James Bond—aka Daniel Craig—that played at the opening ceremony of the London Olympic Games. In this sequence, Bond arrives at Buckingham Palace and is greeted by two of Her Majesty's beloved corgis as he is ushered into the Queen's presence. Upon realizing that a visitor is in her study, the Queen rises from her desk, saying: "Good evening, Mr. Bond." He then escorts her to a helicopter, from which it appears the Queen is to abseil to her box in the Olympic stadium.

CAN THE QUEEN EVER ESCAPE FROM HER PUBLIC ROLE?

Sir Michael Oswald One great thing about racing, or indeed dogs, is that because the Queen's work always follows her around—it's always there; there's never any real escape—racing and breeding race horses is a marvelous therapy for her.

Two different private secretaries have told me they thought it was very important because it is something that is totally divorced from her everyday work of being Queen and head of state, and it is something she can get very deeply immersed in, not just the horses, but the people looking after them—a retired stud hand has got arthritis; how can we help?

The Queen can get really deeply involved in it and, if only for two or three hours, switch right out of her everyday work. And that's very, very important indeed.

Bishop Michael Mann When Field Marshal Montgomery was being buried she decided to just put on a headscarf, because she wasn't involved in the ceremony, and watch the procession through the streets of Windsor. Of course, she was on her own, without the courtiers—nobody noticed her. That's why Windsor is so precious to her.

Sir Michael Oswald The Queen uses Wood Farm when she or the Duke of Edinburgh want to come up to Sandringham without having to open up Sandringham House, which involves an awful lot of people, when they want to come up on their own, or, indeed, when other members of the Royal Family want to come up for a few days.

They would bring a very, very small staff and it doesn't involve a tremendous upheaval, or a lot of expense. It's a very sensible thing to do.

The Queen might come up here at any time—spring, or autumn. Sometimes when she's been on a foreign tour she might come here afterwards just to unwind and relax a bit. It's very small—just one room thick. It can actually house quite a few people, although the bedrooms are very small.

And there's a barn attached to the main house with a solar heating panel at the top—that's the Duke of Edinburgh's idea, I'm sure. You go in the front door and there's a little sitting room on the side, and a little dining room on the other side. It's all very small, very simple, but very, very useful.

This is by far the best place for the Queen to relax and unwind. And the Duke can do some of his carriage driving staying here. And the Queen can look at the farms, and the gardens, and the stud, and the dogs—everything she wants to do up here.

ARE THERE TIMES WHEN THE QUEEN HAS TO PSYCH HERSELF UP TO GET THROUGH THE DAY?

Sir Shridath Ramphal She's disciplined, and she's got a lot of stamina. I can tell you that for all of those fifteen years that I had to be with her, everything was consistent: it didn't go up or down.

I've always thought that it was a good thing that she graduated from being ordinary in those early days, and did not carry the burden of "Oh, my God! I've got to watch out what I'm doing," as Prince Charles has.

Lord Healey It's basically her private secretary who's responsible for seeing that she's fully briefed—and that's a very responsible job, a difficult job. Of course it's difficult [for the Queen]; it's very exhausting.

I remember when Charles was invited to attend a meeting with cabinet, which, of course, was a phoney meeting, really—we wouldn't discuss things in the way we would if he wasn't there—but he said what a terribly tiring job it was. And it is.

CAN THE QUEEN HAVE FRIENDS IN THE NORMAL SENSE OF THE WORD?

Michael Noakes My own feeling is that she picks her friends from too select a group—the Duke of Westminster, and people like that. I think it would help if she didn't always have immensely rich people for her friends.

I do think that when she is with people that she trusts, she does become quite unbound. She does, occasionally, during sittings say things which are quite startling, perhaps, about people.

Lord Younger That is certainly a problem in the sort of position that she's in. She does have a wide circle of her own friends, which come not all from the top echelons of society. Through racing, for instance, she's got some very close friends who are probably jockeys, and trainers, and all that.

Earl of Harewood I used to see her as a child: I'm three-and-a-half years older; I was in the war and she was only a young person in the war.

I suppose it's perfectly normal to see some cousins more often than other cousins. You're expected to have a complete rapport with them, and you may, or may not. I've always got on very easily with her, but I've not seen her very often: if I've seen her a hundred times since she was Queen, I have no idea.

The interesting thing, of course, is the perspective that it gives you: it's very, very, very different from what you know as a child, where you go riding, and to dancing classes, or whatever nonsense you do as a child.

That's a very different relationship from the one you have with somebody who is, so to speak, your contemporary. And, of course, you become more and more somebody's contemporary as the years go by. The little gap disappears: I think of people as my contemporaries who are twenty years younger.

Lady Pamela Hicks The Queen is quite a private person. But this is, of course, where Prince Philip is such an essential part of the whole thing, in that he has remained her stalwart support and adviser, whom she can confide in, whom she can talk to, she can be advised by.

She's very close to her mother and her sister, both of whom, I think, cause her great problems. But she's got a family bond like that.

She has a few very close friends, but very few. But I believe she's the kind of person who because inevitably she's such a public person because that's her job, most of her time it's such a relief to her to be private, and to be quiet, that I don't think she has any desire for a large circle of friends.

And her family—her mother and her sister, but particularly her husband—are what she needs and what she has. And it's probably quite lucky that she hasn't a more extensive circle of great friends, because she's not running the risk of their being indiscreet—she knows that the ones she's going to be speaking to are like sponges and they're not going to leak in any way.

This is why it's much more difficult for people like prime ministers when they suddenly come to the pinnacle of power, because they're unused to being self-contained; it's quite new. But she's been brought up all her life to be self-contained, and is by nature self-contained.

Sir Michael Oswald She and the Duke have plenty of friends who are a good deal younger than they are, which is good. They have a pretty wide age range of friends, more than most people. There are people from quite different backgrounds and interests.

Of course, you must remember even the slightest relationship is used by the press: if they want to make a point, they can make it seem much closer. Take the Prince of Wales: if he meets somebody, or he's seen to speak with somebody, that person is labeled as his "close friend." That may not be the case at all.

Robert Lacey It is very difficult, but she does have a small group of friends that most of us would characterize as aristocratic. Obviously they are pretty elderly, conservative with a small "c," and, above all, absolutely discreet—she has this great sense of privacy, and a condition of friendship with the Queen is that if she says something personal, then you do not repeat it. And on the whole, that's worked very well.

In a way, you can compare the importance of her friends and the seriousness with which they do not pass on what she says to the function she offers the prime minister of the day—he can come and speak to her and know that it won't go any further.

In contrast, Prince Charles has a group of friends who are much more leaky, and much more chatty. Of course, this is related to the public relations problem he's had [...] to do with his failed marriage, and his relationship with Camilla, and the need that his friends have felt always to justify him and present his side of the picture.

John Eisenhower You don't have a rapport with the Royal Family. Prince Philip and I very temporarily came close to it. But you don't.

· There was no personal relationship [between the Queen and President Eisenhower], at least so far as I can determine. There would undoubtedly be protocol, or other things, announcing the assumption of office, or something like that, by her government. But there would be nothing like the Roosevelt–Churchill correspondence.

Lady Longford I knew that James Callaghan got on very well with the Queen and often spent much longer than usual in their weekly interview, and I asked him: "Would you regard yourself as being a friend of the Queen?"

He thought for a minute and said: "No, we're not friends of the Queen, but we get real friendliness, even friendship." But he would not call himself a friend. And he said none of them [the prime ministers who have served during the Queen's reign] did—that's not what they are. But that doesn't mean that she isn't friendly; that's a different thing.

Of course, she can talk to her inner circle of staff, her private secretary. They're a great help; she had some wonderful ones in the past—Martin Charteris was a man in a million, and she was very lucky to be helped and trained by him.

I just think if she didn't have that, she couldn't cope. No human being could. That's what she depends on. And people may criticize the Palace— it's become rather a dirty word—but without the Palace, we would have no Queen. No human being could endure.

Ivan Head Callaghan—"Sunny Jim," just a wonderful guy—described it [his relationship with the Queen] very accurately. Nor would the Queen want it to be otherwise: she is the *Queen*. And the Queen is different: one of the people but apart from the people. And it is sad. I can't imagine that the Queen has any friends at all—of her choice. And it may well be a factor contributing to the present difficulties in which the monarchy finds itself—absolutely unprecedented attacks in Britain.

CHAPTER 8

What Does the Monarchy Mean to British Subjects and Others?

Lord Glentoran The Monarch and I share the same birthday and when she was sixteen [in 1942] and I seven, my birthday treat was to go to Windsor Castle to watch the Princess Elizabeth, as she was then, taking her first major parade, in which my father was participating, as she inspected one of the battalions of the Grenadier Guards.

I can remember it—I have a photographic memory—it was in the big quadrangle at the top of the long walk. It was wartime and she was colonel of the regiment.

Other than that, the monarchy has always been a part of my life, really, from school, learning the National Anthem and history lessons—I still get the Kings and Queens mixed up.

Robert Lacey Every Monday we would buy national savings stamps—we were encouraged to bring two-and-six-pence into school, as a sort of hangover from the war days, and we'd buy national savings stamps, which had the faces of the young Prince Charles and the young Princess Anne on them—I think Prince Charles was the more valuable one than Princess Anne.

In some way, this family was deliberately associated with our actual welfare in a way that I didn't understand at the time. But the reverence that this whole group of people was treated with showed that they were totems of some sort, although at that stage of my life I didn't think about the paradox of them exercising such power over the national imagination but, actually, exercising no *real* power, in any political sense.

Lady Pamela Hicks As very small children we'd go and play with the Princesses at Buckingham Palace. I suppose from the time one was about five one was being taught to curtsy.

But then, on the other hand, I had a grandmother who was Queen Victoria's granddaughter—my father's mother[1]—and so, as she had been born Princess Victoria, we always curtsied to her and kissed her hand. That was how we were brought up. When you brought your friends home and you had to explain to them about curtsying to your grandmother, they were very startled.

Michael Richard Whitlam, director general, British Red Cross Society, 1991–99, who traveled with Diana Princess of Wales on humanitarian missions; chief executive of the Mentor Foundation, 1991–2001 One of the things I've found fascinating over the years I've worked with various members of the Royal Family is that time, and time, and time again, you come across people who are anti-monarchists even to claiming that the monarchy is a waste of time, a waste of money, a drain on the United Kingdom's resources—the usual arguments—yet those very same people, if presented with a chance to meet a member of the Royal Family, forget all that and are desperately keen to meet them.

We used to have incredible problems in all the charities I've ever worked in trying to organize who should be the people to meet members of the Royal Family when they arrive at a project, or at a headquarters, because everybody wants to meet them, royalists, or not.

Joe Haines I grew up in a rather militantly socialist area, on the Thames, where most of the men were employed on the docks, as my father was, and my grandfathers, and my cousins.

I was the first to break away, so my first impression [of monarchy] wasn't one of respect—one was against authority and all symbols of authority; that's really how I grew up.

Indeed, I think I was a passive republican until I met Richard Nixon, which turned me into a monarchist; it just seemed to me that the presidential system doesn't work if it produces Nixons—and Clintons.

Margaret A. Ewing (1945–2006), Scottish National Party M.P., 1974–79, 1987–2001; M.S.P., 1999–2006 Like most young people growing up in basically a working-class background in the country, it was something you were expected to revere—there was the monarchy, there was the Church, there was the schoolteacher, the village policeman—and it was just something that was *there*; it was an institution to whom you gave respect, and you weren't really expected to question it at all.

So my early memories of the monarchy certainly were of Mum and Dad standing up for "God Save the Queen"—when I was a wee toddler, two or three years old, it was "God Save the King"—and we were just expected to stand up for that.

And for school groups like the Brownies, and the Cubs, and the Scouts, and the Girl Guides it was: "I promise to do my duty to God and the Queen" and all that kind of thing. And that was just the way you would grow up. It was just *there* and nobody really questioned it at that stage.

I suppose a few rebels did, but it wasn't something that made headlines, or appeared in radio programs, or television—working-class people didn't have television until the 1960s.

Sir Michael Oswald My first memory was as a small child being told about the Silver Jubilee of King George V. I could only have been a year and a bit, but I can still remember the word "jubilee."

The next thing I can remember was the Coronation of 1937. As a very small child I didn't understand much of anything, obviously, but I was interested in the golden coach and gray horses. And the great excitement, and flags, I can remember all that.

And I can remember I'd been taken to a railway bridge to watch the royal train on the way from Waterloo to Southampton when the King and Queen went on a tour of the United States and Canada [in the spring of 1939].

And then the war started in 1939, which I remember very well indeed. I first saw the King and Queen at the victory parade, which I was taken to watch.

Winston Churchill The eighth of May, 1945, was VE Day. I was four-and-a-half years old and I was part of the throng—probably half a million strong—outside Buckingham Palace, clutching with one hand my Union Jack, which I was waving furiously, and with the other, the hand of my Scottish nanny, Mrs. Martin.

And suddenly on the balcony on the front of Buckingham Palace, there appeared the King and Queen, and my *grandfather*. But that was no surprise at all because every little boy is convinced that his granddaddy is the most important granddaddy in the whole world. So what could be more natural?

Michael Noakes I remember on what we call "VJ Night," which was when Japan surrendered [ending World War Two], my parents took us up to outside Buckingham Palace, where the King and Queen, and the Royal Family, and Winston Churchill appeared on the balcony.

I remember how we had to climb up a lamp post; there was only one other guy up there and we shared a little tiny ridge. Every time I go past the lamp post—it's just by that big monument outside the Palace gates—I think of that still. And it was very exciting.

But it was very exciting partly because they—the Royal Family and the dogged Churchill—epitomized having come through the war. I can't see myself doing something like that just for a politician. There was something beyond it.

Lady Young I don't remember a time as a child when I *wasn't* conscious of the monarchy. When I was a child, a long time ago now, I just remember seeing Queen Mary coming to open part of a new hospital.

I can remember hearing one of King George V's very early broadcasts to the nation. It had a tremendous impact on everybody because, of course, most people had never heard him speak. I can even remember when the National Anthem was played, we stood up at home—certainly when there was any question of the King speaking, we wouldn't lounge about.

And, of course, I grew up in the time when I was told the sun never set on the British Empire—and all the stamps and everything I used to collect—you were very conscious of all the symbols of the monarchy, all the time.

Baron Weatherill, (Bruce) Bernard, KStJ, PC, DL (1920–2007), life peer, cr. 1992; Comptroller of Her Majesty's Household, 1972–73; treasurer, Her Majesty's Household and deputy Conservative chief whip, 1973–74; Speaker, House of Commons, 1983–92 The standards were quite different in those days; we were brought up with great respect for the monarchy.

Even as children, if "God Save the King" was played on the radio, my parents would have stood up, and so would all of us as children, from quite an early age. So we were brought up with it. And my father had the Royal Warrant of Appointment because he had founded the family business.[2] So we were imbued with it.

And then, of course, came the war, and I had the King's commission, as it was in those days. There was the King-Emperor, and I served in the old Imperial Indian Army, the Bengal Lancers—and I never met Errol Flynn either. I was in the 19th, King George V's Own Bengal Lancers—the King was Colonel-in-Chief of the regiment. This was a sense of pride for me; it had been for generations.

Seventh Earl of Longford, Francis Aungier Pakenham, KG, PC (1905–2001), life peer, cr. 1999; lord-in-waiting to King George VI, 1945–46; First Lord of the Admiralty, 1951; Lord Privy Seal, 1964–65, 1966–68; Labour leader, House of Lords, 1964–68; secretary of state for the colonies, 1965–66 You don't think of anything else. There's nothing to compare it [the monarchy] with; it's just part of life. I'm Irish—my family home is in Ireland; my brother died forty years ago. My son succeeded him, so the family home has kept alive in Ireland. But, nevertheless, I had an English education—Eton, Oxford, and I became an Oxford don.

Michael Parker I'm an Australian who joined the Royal Navy in 1937 because it was a bigger Navy, it had aircraft carriers, and I then thought I would like to fly.

That Navy was very conscious of the Crown, and the position of the Crown, so I grew up in the Navy very, very much imbued with the King as being the leader, and so on.

And I also realized the further dimension, when I got to England, of the Royal Family, because I began to take an interest in exactly what did the King do. What was he?

And then I discovered, to my absolute delight and joy, that he was not in any way a politician—which happens all round the world—but that he was above all that, and he was there to advise the politicians and to steer them away from the rocks, or to help them, and suggest things—to advise and suggest was the thing I thought was brilliant.

Then, to hark back to Australia, I used to drive cattle up in the mountains when I was much younger, with a lot of the drovers, and it was up in the mountains when I heard on a little crystal set of the abdication of King Edward VIII. And there were these tough mountain chaps who live out in the open, and I explained to them the news that was coming through. And all around the campfire—a most dramatic sight this was—all I could hear them say was: "He shouldn't have done that; that's an abuse of privilege"—and this is coming from tough mountain chaps.

Later on, when working with the Royal Family, I was able to tell the King that story. He was quite intrigued that it would penetrate to that degree.

Baron Ouseley, Herman George, life peer, cr. 2001; chair, Commission for Racial Equality, 1993–99; member, advisory council, Prince's Youth Business Trust; chairman, Uniting Britain Charitable Trust I was born in Guyana—British Guiana at the time—so for me it was part of being a colony. The Queen was the head of the Empire. We were British in an overseas place, compared to here; you didn't know the difference until you came here.

Growing up in British Guiana in the 1950s, before I came here in 1957, we were very mixed in terms of all our racial groups, and as a youngster, being more naive about those things, I didn't realize differences were so important until I came to Britain.

In Guyana there was a feeling of being part of something. The Union Jack was always out; there was a sort of reverence and respect without knowing totally what it meant at the time.

When I came to this country as a boy, there was more of a feeling of detachment. The Queen was the head of state but she seemed so distant. So although the monarchy here was physically closer than in Guyana, it seemed much further away because of the class system.

From my point of view, the situation was one of realizing there was the Queen and a Royal Family but they were much further away from me than they had been when I was in Guyana. The Queen was the head of state but very untouchable, almost unreachable. That was a strange feeling for me.

Lord Cholmondeley; interviewed 2000 We were brought up with the idea of the monarchy; everyone in England was. And standing up for "God Save the Queen," as all children were.

We knew my father officiated at the Opening of Parliament, and we'd seen him on television, and I was taken to watch the Opening of Parliament as a child. So in that sense, yes, we were aware, probably more than other children.

And I was made a page, as well, to the Queen when I was thirteen, for two years. It's usually children of those who are involved with the Queen in some way who are chosen to be pages—either an equerry or, in my father's case, Lord Great Chamberlain, or sons of friends. It's a gift of the Monarch. And there are usually four at a time. And when you get too old, or too tall, you give it up.

There are just two functions as a page: the Opening of Parliament and the Garter ceremony at Windsor, and at each one you wear the same tunic. And you have one rehearsal the day before with everyone in civilian dress. And then when it's over, it's over and you go home. It's purely just taking part in those ceremonies.

Lady Angela Oswald The monarchy to us was just something that was *there*, like the sun coming out, and you admired it because it was just *there*.

Stephen Day I was brought up in the outer suburbs of east London—my father's family were Cockneys—and my earliest memories were of the war and the enormous importance of the Royal Family to Londoners during that period. The fact that the King and Queen stayed in London—that their family stayed in London—created a very, very special bond with Londoners that I recall from my earliest years.

And there was the excitement when the young Princess Elizabeth came to Brixton, where I was a young boy. The school was let out and we went down to the end of the road, and she swept by in a big car, and we all waved our flags. It is a very vivid memory, and one of my first memories.

Professor Stuart Macintyre, AO, FAHA, FASSA; historian and author; dean of the Faculty of Arts, University of Melbourne; Ernest Scott professor of history, University of Melbourne On my first day of school—I attended my primary school with a cousin of mine who was living next door—I came back and I remarked that all the famous people had their birthday on the twenty-first of April.

I said: "There's the Queen; there's Miss Friday, who was our new infant teacher; and there's me!" And my cousin John immediately took the wind from my sails and said: "But *you're* not famous yet."

So clearly I knew when I was a five-year-old that the Queen's birthday was the twenty-first of April, although how I got to know it I don't know. But monarchy, and particularly the Queen, were an element of the public culture—certainly at school. That was in 1952.

Neville Wren The British monarchy was the idol of Australians when I was a child. At school, for instance, each Monday morning we would sing "There'll Always Be an England" and "Rule Britannia." And then we would sing one verse of "Advance Australia Fair." Then we would sing everything of "God Save the Queen."

And the Australian flag went up one flag pole, but the flag we saluted was the Union Jack. That was the *important* flag.

England was the dominant country. We felt ourselves almost as an extension of England, and we referred to England as "home." We would say: "I'm going home." And it wasn't around the corner; that meant that we were going back to some miserable village in England somewhere.

And there was a thing called Empire Day. The Empire was very important. We all cherished our map of the world with all the red—it was actually in salmon pink—indicating the British Empire. And we knew we were part of something that was very strong, and very tough, within the pink, and it was very reassuring.

And you would buy books, like *Chums* [the annual of the boys' newspaper]. And one of the notations in the foreword of *Chums* was: "To the children of the Empire, upon whom the sun never sets."

And when I was a child in the 1930s—it seems a hundred years ago the way it is now—there was not very much mix of the races here; it was almost an exclusively British-based, or English-based conclave—you'd get some Scots, and lots of Irish—but by-and-large we were *English*.

Professor Sir Zelman Cowen, AK, GCMG, GCVO, PC, QC (1919– 2011); governor-general of Australia, 1977–82; provost, Oriel College, University of Oxford, 1982–90; pro-vice-chancellor, University of Oxford, 1988–90 Did the monarchy have an impact? The answer is: "Not really at all." You knew something about the King—when I was born George V was King—but you knew him from photographs, and motion pictures, but really nothing more.

So far as the governor-general, or the governor, of the state is concerned, we're very, very different from Canada in the sense that we don't have the lieutenant governor. We have a governor system and the governor is appointed by a process which is preferable to the process by which the governor-general is appointed.

But for the greater part of my life—certainly as a child, as a boy, and as a young man—there was a great remoteness, not only in relation to the Monarch, but remoteness in relation to the governor-general and the governor.

So I wouldn't have questioned that there was a King; I wouldn't have questioned that there was a governor-general, or a governor, but it was something quite remote from my life.

Thomas Keneally, AO, novelist (*Schindler's Ark*, 1982); a leader of the Australian Republican Movement I can't remember a time when I was *not* aware of the institution of the monarchy because in those days—the 1930s and the 1940s—all the civil pieties attached to honoring were in place in a way that they're not now, even in Britain.

I didn't celebrate Empire Day because I went to an Irish Catholic school and the Irish Catholics in those days, when I was a kid, tended to soft-pedal the connection with the monarchy—it didn't worry them, and they didn't want to worry about it.

[My father] said that on Empire Day, in the small country town he lived in during the 1910s and during World War Two, the state schools would march to the show ground with Union Jacks, which were considered virtually the flag of Australia, and the nuns would have the convent school kids march to the show ground with the Australian flag, which at least had the Southern Cross on it.

So although I belong to that slightly excluded, then somewhat excluded, minority, whose loyalty was suspect, despite service in two world wars, despite that I was always conscious of the presence of the monarchy.

George VI was much respected. As soon as I started going to the movies, round about the age of five, there he was. And he was our *King*; I just stood up for him at the start of the "pictures," as we called them. Only my grandfather didn't stand up in the pictures. But that was considered an acute embarrassment to the entire family.

The monarchy was omnipresent; I was aware that all letters from the government, or even letters from my father when he was in the Middle East, were stamped "OHMS," On His Majesty's Service. So I found that the observances, and the liturgy associated with the Crown, were universal.

All our governors general in those days were British noblemen, or soldiers, and they were the viceroy of the Queen. It's since become an entirely Australian institution—the first time an Australian held it was 1931, and he was Jewish by some wonderful miracle, Sir Isaac Isaacs.

Anson Chan To be quite frank, the monarchy wasn't anything that I was specifically very conscious of. Of course we realized that Hong Kong was a colony, and that Britain was the sovereign power, and that the Monarch was the Queen. Specifically how it related to Hong Kong was that the governor was not elected by the people of Hong Kong, but actually appointed by the Queen herself, on the advice of her government, her prime minister.

Because the Queen is so far away, and the monarchy is so far away, it isn't anything most people would think about every day of their lives because it doesn't have a direct impact.

Hugh Segal I grew up in the immigrant community of Montreal—my father was a cab driver and an immigrant from post-Tsarist, Communist

Russia; my grandparents on the other side came from Austria, and so on.

I went to a [Jewish] parochial school. We had in the front of the school pictures of Moses, the various prophets, and a huge picture of Her Majesty the Queen and Prince Philip. And we would sing "God Save the Queen" in the morning, if we were starting with our English course—our non-religious activity. If we started with our religious activity, we would pray, and when we began the English course, we would sing "God Save the Queen."

I didn't get it as a kid, obviously. But what I began to get, never having asked why that picture was there—the same picture we had on our money—was an answer from Mrs. Handelman, she was my grade four teacher: "In this country, because of the structure of our system, because of the Crown, because of that lady, the Queen, we are all equal under the law—Protestant, Catholic, Jew, the new immigrant, whatever."

And there was the notion of the Crown representing the public interest: we don't have "The people vs Mrs. Smith," we have "The Crown vs Mrs. Smith." And that was the first notion for me.

But the actual event that just crystalized it for me was 1956—I was six. Her Majesty had come to Canada, as had President Dwight D. Eisenhower, to open the St. Lawrence Seaway.

That produced a tour through Montreal, and she was going to visit our City Hall. So I'm there on my father's shoulders with the rest of the public, watching the arrival of Her Majesty in the big car. Standing on the stage were all the local politicians—the Pooh-bahs—and all the Catholic priests from the local church, and Protestant ministers, plus the rabbi from our synagogue, a small synagogue. When you grow up in an immigrant community, knowing that you're different, you're not quite sure how you connect, particularly if you're going to a minority school.

So out of the car gets Her Majesty to crowds, and the Royal Salute, and all that. And then she goes to the stands and she shakes everybody's hand—she shook the rabbi's hand. Now, this would all strike us today, in 2000, as a pretty normative thing for the head of state to do.

When you were a kid and you were taught that you were different—perhaps not as good, perhaps somewhat outside the mainstream—to see Her Majesty the Queen, whose face is on the money, and whose picture is in the front of the room, shake everybody's hand struck me as one of the most inclusive things that any head of state could do—And she isn't running for office! This was because, under the Queen—under the monarchy—everybody is equal. And that became a very huge emotional touchstone.

Canon Paul Oestreicher I remember the Queen's visit to New Zealand when she was very young—she was of my generation; when I was twenty, she was twenty-five. The whole country was excited.

There was a great flash flood when she was there and a train was thrown off a bridge by the river, and a couple of generations later, everybody remembers the flash flood when the Queen came.

That was a very, psychologically, good thing for the people: she would represent home; she would be the personification of what people regarded as their roots. And it would feel absolutely natural that the head of state of the United Kingdom should also be the head of state of New Zealand: although New Zealand was proud of being an independent state politically, yet, psychologically New Zealand was a chip off that old block.

Those days are long gone. If the Royal Family, including the Queen, came today, they would be received politely, with a little bit of cynicism and with, at the least, a section of the population saying: "Can't we get rid of this?"

Donald Macdonald I was born in 1932, and King George VI and Queen Elizabeth came to Ottawa, my hometown, in May 1939, the first-ever visit by a sitting Monarch to Canada. This was a big event for a seven-year-old. The monarchy was very important.

At that time—but especially during the war—on Christmas Day there would always be a pause in whatever the family was doing when the King would broadcast to the Commonwealth, to the world.

It was a very important institution in my youth. But since 1945, as Canada has acquired its own political record, Britain generally has had very much less influence in the last forty-five years.

To the extent that people have known and have dealt with the Queen, their judgment would be the same as my own: people may not know her, but she has respect.

And I believe that if it came down to a decision having been taken to disestablish the monarchy, an awful lot of people, at least in my own generation, would say: "Well, yes, but let's not be rude to the Queen." There's that personal element there. So the change that's going to occur will occur when she is no longer there.

Ivan Head I was born and raised in Calgary. I was a youngster during the Depression, just before the war, and what I remember, in the negative sense, was the fact that in those days, there were still persons with British titles—the Crown was able to give titles to Canadians. No longer.

These weren't so much titles as decorations—MBE, Member of the British Empire, and OBE, Order of the British Empire—and I had a mother who was a bit of a schizophrenic in these respects: she was born in the United States and her claim to American citizenship was, I suppose, as a result of the fact that there was no border back at the turn of the century—none at all. Her father was a Canadian who just happened to be on that side of the border for a short period of time. She nevertheless felt that there was something innately wrong about things of this kind.

On the negative side, there was also the fact that during the war some of these people put on immense social airs—it was just astonishing, I thought, that in a tiny little cowboy town like Calgary, we had all this stuff.

On the positive side, just south of Calgary, the Duke of Windsor, Edward VIII, had his famous ranch. He visited very infrequently, but the aura that surrounded his presence was absolutely extraordinary.

And then, in a formal sense, studying history, as we all had to do in those days in public schools, the whole narrative of the British Crown became very firmly embedded in all of us.

Earl of Harewood My mother was the King's daughter and we—my brother and I; he was eighteen months younger than me—saw the King and Queen regularly, as grandparents, in of course very grand surroundings: Windsor is fairly grand; it was very grand then.

We often went on ceremonial occasions, like the King's birthday, the Trooping the Colour—a lot of fun. So we saw a lot of these things in these rather grand trappings, and we were aware of it.

But my parents were very skilled about this: they treated it as perfectly normal, which indeed it was—it was my mother's parents we were going to see—and we never thought of it as peculiar, or abnormal.

We used to go and stay at Windsor for Easter, which was fun because the food was very good—not that we noticed that as little boys. But the more particular thing, there was a French chef who caused wonderful Easter eggs to be made at Windsor. Of course, it was rather less grand than parties at Buckingham Palace.

It was, let us use the words "borne in on us"—my brother and me—that my grandfather was the King and my grandmother was the Queen, and that that was that. We were *not* treated oddly. Nor, of course, at school were we treated oddly. The danger would be the opposite, but the danger wasn't realized—we weren't given a horrible time because we were the King's grandsons.

But it was such a mild awareness, and such a normal awareness, that it didn't really fill, or even blight, our lives at all. And that was the skill of my parents.

Cardinal Cahal Brendan Daly (1917–2009), Roman Catholic Archbishop of Armagh and primate of All Ireland, 1990–96 That question raises the whole issue of the nature and composition of the Northern Ireland population. There are, as the world now knows, two communities, with two distinct identities and two distinct senses of national allegiance.

And the majority population—it's not a huge majority; it's about sixty percent—will see themselves as British and would have a strong identification with the monarchy, and *this* Monarch, and their sense of Britishness.

But the other community, the *nationalist* community, would see themselves as *Irish*, not in any aggressive way, but they are Irish: they belong to Ireland; they don't see themselves as British; they don't see the Queen as *their* Queen; they would aspire peacefully—and in the longer term and with consent—to reunification with the rest of Ireland under a president in Dublin, at least psychologically, belonging to the Republic of Ireland already. Quite frankly, I would fairly agree with them, as a member of that broad community. And I'm not talking politics so much as just a sense of who I am, and who we are, as the nationalist community in Northern Ireland—forty percent plus of the population of Northern Ireland. So that while having no kind of animosity towards the Queen, I would not have seen myself as identifying with the monarchy.

Now that doesn't mean that I don't respect the Queen, nor that the community that I come from doesn't respect the Queen. But she wouldn't be *our* Queen in the sense in which she'd be regarded by the Unionist community as our Queen.

And in the Northern Ireland context, there is another factor: for historical reasons the Protestant community in Ireland, particularly in Northern Ireland, values and honors the Queen in part because she is Protestant, because she is seen as representing the Protestant tradition and the Protestant succession.

Rev. Ian Paisley We were introduced to the monarchy with our mothers' milk. This province [Ulster, Northern Ireland] was Unionist in politics, and brought up its children with fierce and intense loyalty.

I have always had great respect for the monarchy, and great respect for the Williamite Revolution Settlement[3] and all that that entailed.

Also, of course, there were the great sacrifices made in 1917 at the Battle of the Somme. That really tied us by experience, because there was hardly a home, or a family, in the whole of Northern Ireland that hadn't some relatives, some family member, or some distant cousin, who had either been butchered, or had been seriously wounded in the massacre. And that tied us in. That's like the old blood relationship between the dead who were tied in by blood into the system.

That has come down very much so through the generations. And it would still be very staunchly held by a vast majority of people who wouldn't even admit to it. But there's a gut reaction here to the whole conception of trying to do away with the monarchy.

Conor Cruise O'Brien, Ph.D. (1917–2008), minister, government of the Republic of Ireland, 1973–77; senator, University of Dublin, 1977–79; author and editor Well, rather early in my life, in 1936, there was a kind of impact. This was after the abdication of the King and there was the question of his successor. There was a controversy in Ireland. Up to this point, and indeed, for some time after, under the settlement of 1919, the Monarch of Great Britain was Monarch of Great Britain and Ireland— that was part of the settlement.

All along, Irish Nationalists had been trying to detach themselves from this. So it looked to some people in Ireland at the time—which happened to include me at that moment—that this was the moment that the break with the Crown could be made.

De Valera, who was the taoiseach—prime minister—of Ireland at the time, didn't at that time want to make the break. He had the idea that the link with the Crown was something around which Ireland could be reunited—that to break with the Crown would be making the break with Northern Ireland more decisive.

But I was young, and rather foolish, and didn't think that way. So I joined in a street demonstration in O'Connell Street, Dublin, for the break with the Crown. And in the course of this carry-on, a big man, whom I realized to be a detective, offered me a gun with the idea that I would shoot somebody and then they could proceed from there. But though foolish at the time, I wasn't *that* foolish, and I didn't take up his offer. But that was my first memory of a serious involvement with the Crown.

After that, of course, after the First World War, Ireland remained nominally under the Crown, while remaining neutral during the war [World War Two]; we were the only part of the dominions which remained neutral during the war.

And after the war, the then-coalition government declared Ireland a republic, which was basically a nominal thing, a formality—there had been no real link with the Crown for a long time. So from that time on, basically, the institution of the Crown hasn't meant much to us, formally, here in the Republic, although I do note that events in the Royal Family, like Diana's marriage, for example, everything closed down here while that was being broadcast: there was an absolute fascination with the thing, which is rather similar to America, because they, of course, were the first to make the break, but many of them still do take a lively interest in the Royal Family. So there is, apparently, an abiding charm to the institution. *I* don't feel it very strongly.

Garret Fitzgerald There isn't a typical Irish person. There are, and always have been, although in diminishing number, people who are very hostile to Britain, and who see the monarchy very negatively, as a symbol of the Crown that we have tried to free ourselves from.

I never had that feeling at all. But, at the same time, even amongst people who would express no interest in the Coronation, and the wedding, and all that, I can tell you that there is a great interest—and all those people watching the television. So there's a certain inner contradiction amongst many Irish people on the subject.

Thinking back on the role of the monarchy in regard to Ireland, one actual negative factor, in a particular way, was that Queen Victoria never came to live here, and never showed an interest in Ireland. It would have made a difference, I thought, if she had.

Lord Merlyn-Rees I come from Wales and in the mining valleys of South Wales, the monarchy is a very curious dichotomy; on the one hand, nobody stood for the National Anthem. For the immigrant population that had come in, the monarchy didn't loom large. And yet, on the other hand, there was a sense in which the monarchy—the Prince of Wales and all that sort of thing—meant something.

But, in general, to ask somebody from Wales from my background, the monarchy didn't loom very large. The name of the prime minister meant more, in one sense, than the monarchy.

But certainly, until I became an RAF officer during the war, and an Army minister after the war, I don't know that I'd ever realized the full import of the monarchy. In the services, you have allegiance to the Throne.

* * *

During our discussion with Lord Merlyn-Rees, which took place in the large, ornate Queen's Waiting Room in the House of Lords, a fellow Welsh peer passing by greeted Lord Merlyn-Rees. Upon being introduced to us, the peer offered the following view:

> We are staunch royalists and yet the monarchy didn't mean very much. That's the best way to sum it up. We don't talk much about it, but we are staunch royalists. And yet, when we were going to the pictures on a Saturday night and they always played "God Save the King," nobody stood up; everyone walked out. But if the Prince had come to Wales today, or the Queen, the people would jam the streets.

* * *

Gordon Robertson, PC, CC, FRSC (1917–2013), clerk of the Privy Council and secretary to the Canadian cabinet, 1963–75 In public school we opened every day with "God Save the King," as it was at that time. And so we were aware of the monarchy, and it was part of what was taught to us in school. So the consciousness came quite early, and we simply learned about it as a fundamental part of what the country was.

And from that early awareness, it simply became one of those accepted facts—that Canada was part of the British Empire, as it then was.

I remember when I was quite young my father giving me his collection of stamps he had made when he was a boy. On one of his Canadian stamps— it was 1887, for Queen Victoria's Jubilee—was the British Empire, all the countries in red, and all the rest of the world in a sort of gray-green. And across the top was: "We Hold A Vaster Empire Than Has Been"—"We." So "we" in Canada didn't think of ourselves as being a colony, or anything; we were part-proprietors of this great Empire—and there was the Monarch.

I suppose there is a mingling of feelings. There was never a great enthusiasm about the English—the English were different. And, in fact, there used to be in the West a story that various employers had signs when employees were wanted: "No Englishman need apply."

The Scots were looked upon very favorably; the Irish a bit less favorably. But the English were thought to be snooty, thought themselves superior, and, in fact, were rather incompetent. So there was a mixture of feelings about it: the Empire, yes. The monarchy, yes. The English? We're not so sure. In another part of our rather split personality, there was no great enthusiasm for the English.

Nor was there in public service—the part I went into, the Department of External Affairs—any great enthusiasm for English institutions.

Indeed, there was a growing feeling that Canada should have more of its own institutions and be more identifiable as *Canada* than as part of the Empire.

Now this didn't mean any antagonism toward the monarchy; the Monarch was something different: exalted, special. But the governor-general didn't have that kind of mystique, or respect, attached to him. And governors-general could be quite a nuisance at times if they acted too *English*.

London seemed vastly remote in the geographical sense, in actual sense, but not remote in an emotional sense, as far as the Monarch was concerned. But the vastness of this enormous Empire was part of its great mystery. And there was a kind of pride in the whole thing—a kind of civic pride, in a way: we were proprietors. We had nothing to do with it, except to be part of it.

We didn't have honors. In 1921, there was a resolution passed in the House of Commons, and this, too, indicates the split personality, a motion to the effect that British subjects resident in Canada—I say British subjects resident in Canada because at that time there was no such thing as a Canadian citizen; it didn't exist; we were British subjects—should no longer receive honors and awards, because the honors and awards were *British* honors and awards; we had none of our own.

That motion carried by the House of Commons, and fully supported by Mackenzie King,[4] who was prime minister at the time, reflected the feeling, not of animosity, but that we didn't want to have titles here; we didn't want to have these British honors and awards. We wanted to be distant from that.

Again, that didn't reflect on the monarchy: the Monarch was something different. These institutions that were British, and English, were quite another thing.

Archdeacon George Austin I was a very small child—we lived in Lancashire[5]—and my grandmother took me to see King George V and Queen Mary traveling round on their Silver Jubilee, which was in 1935; I was four years old.

Then, of course, Edward came to the Throne and we had new postage stamps, and I collected postage stamps, so I was aware of that. I was aware that something was happening with Wallis Simpson, but I was too young, really—I was about six or seven then—to take it in.

And then King George VI came to the Throne and we had a day off school, and we were given a mug with his portrait on it.

Eric Moonman Often the working classes have been extremely supportive of having a royal family as a concept, and periodically I think, they react. But in the 1930s—when I was just a little child—and the 1940s, it wasn't the case. For the large part of that period there was no question about it: the Royal Family was held in awe—there was none of the cynicism.

S. A. (Saved Aziz) Pasha, OBE (1930–2012), general secretary, Union of Muslim Organizations of the United Kingdom and Eire When I was born, Britain was ruling India so I was born as a British subject—not a citizen, but a subject. India was a colony of Britain, and when it became independent, India became part of the British Commonwealth, so they have got historical links.

By birth I am a British subject and by affiliation I am a Commonwealth citizen. When I went to America, it was a foreign country. When I came to Britain, it was nothing new for me; I thought I was coming to my homeland.

It was my homeland because in my history books I used to study English history—the English Parliament, monarchy, how the constitution functions—everything was in my mind. When I first came to Britain, I wanted to see Buckingham Palace; I wanted to see the British Museum—things we had known already in history.

Nelson Mandela The British Empire extended to almost every part of the world and King George V was a highly respected Monarch. And also, the British heir to the Throne at that time, the Prince of Wales, became very popular because he was an unorthodox figure. And the involvement with the American lady made him well-known to us.

And then, of course, King George VI visited our country in 1947. And he had become prominent because of the war. And also Queen Victoria was a well-known Monarch in South Africa and we grew up then, as youngsters, before we had developed any political approaches, we regarded the British Monarch as *our* Monarch, and really admired them. And so my first impression was one of great respect: this was our Monarch.

And at school, of course, we used textbooks where on the very first inside page there was always the British Monarch, King George V.

Adnan Khashoggi Definitely we are aware [of the monarchy] because the British people are very loyal to tradition. You see in their faces, in their reactions: "To the Queen!" You see the reaction is there. Even we don't go that far for our royalty in the Kingdom of Saudi Arabia.

There's a lot of respect for the Queen. I've dealt with a lot of generals and foreigners in the Army, and they are obsessed by what they call the traditional. I don't see any resentment except when I see it on T.V. that people are against her.

Canon Paul Oestreicher I was very conscious of living in the context of British culture and I loved it: I chose to live here [in Britain].

I could have gone back to Germany—I'm bilingual; I handle German with equal ease to English; I feel in one sense at home in Germany, although I've had to overcome a lot of bitterness because the Nazis killed my father's family, but I got through that; I could have gone back to New Zealand; I could have gone to the States, where we had a lot of friends. But I chose to live in England and the institution of the monarchy is, therefore, part of what I chose.

You can't choose a bit of a country; you've got to take it as it is. And how did it impact on me? No more than any other single aspect of society, but it's part of the backdrop—it's almost like the scene on a stage: it's the play that matters, but if the play has the wrong set, you feel the set and the story don't coincide.

Royalty is not part of the play. That's not the English tradition: the Queen has no power—the Royal Family have absolutely no power. And yet they're part of the scenery; they're painted into the scene.

Ian Adams I'm a George V child and my earliest association with the monarchy is of King George and Queen Mary—and clearly a very old-fashioned idea of royalty, in a way, particularly as far as Queen Mary was concerned.

What used to have its effect on one as a child was the King's Christmas broadcast, which, of course, started then. I can remember the broadcast very well, at the time of the [King George V's Silver] Jubilee, in 1935, and being rather impressed when the King did an address to the "children of the Empire." I can still hear that rather whiskery voice saying: "Remember! The King is speaking to *you!*" And I thought: *Me!*

In a way, my family were natural monarchists; we never really doubted it. And I don't think I have ever doubted it since. There was the disaster with Edward VIII, of course, when I don't think we had any doubt that wanting to go was clearly the right thing. And we made a very good exchange, of course, by the process, because we got an admirable King and an admirable Queen in those two; we couldn't have done better.

And with the war coming ahead of us, they were an absolutely indomi-
table and inspiring pair, which, I'm quite sure, Edward VIII would never
have been. So I don't think we ever had any doubt about the institution.

Bishop Hugh Montefiore I was brought up with an awareness of royalty:
my father made us always stand for the Christmas speech—we had to
stand, literally, when the anthem, "God Save the King," was sung, and
then listen in silence to the old man, George V, speaking.

The Christmas speech was the moment when you really heard him in
a more personal way. It was the most important thing that he did, really,
for ordinary people; he was a symbol of the country. But so far as getting
across to the people, it was about the only time he spoke to them.

Sir Michael Palliser My first awareness was during the war, when my
father was in the Navy. At the outbreak of the war he was captain of the
Naval Gunnery School at Whale Island, near Portsmouth, and we lived
in a house just across the bay from Portsmouth.

King George VI came and visited Whale Island. I was at school then—
but I remembered my father talking about it, being conscious of the King
as Admiral of the Fleet, as a senior naval person visiting the Navy.

During the war, you had the King's commission when you became
an officer. And, actually, somewhere upstairs there must be a rather
tattered document appointing me as a second lieutenant in His Majesty's
Coldstream Guards. You're conscious of the importance of the Royal
Family if you have that kind of career, from quite an early stage.

Lady Longford When I was a small child, my parents were Liberals—
Lloyd George Liberals—that kind of ordinary Liberal. But they weren't
enthusiastic about the monarchy.

My mother was descended from the Chamberlains, Joseph
Chamberlains[6] of Birmingham, and they were all Unitarians, which was
very republican. And Joe once invited a member of the Royal Family
to a meeting and they didn't come, and he announced on the platform:
"Nobody missed them." That was the kind of attitude.

But then as I grew up, I realized there had been a great change—they
began taking different newspapers—and when my father was invited
to go to the Coronation of George V, to represent the non-conformist
Churches of England, he was absolutely thrilled to bits: he even put in
to be allowed to buy the blue velvet stool that he had sat on during the
service, which came home and we all gaped at.

But I myself, after being at the University of Oxford and being introduced to politics by the man I later married, Frank Pakenham, as he then was, I became a parliamentary candidate for the Labour Party. And though we weren't actually outright republican, we weren't enthusiastic about the monarchy, and we were certainly determined to get rid of the House of Lords.

* * *

Lady Longford's view of the monarchy changed when she was given access to the Windsor archives to write her biography of Queen Victoria.

* * *

Lady Longford And I got so interested in the family because it's so wonderfully well documented—I should think better than any other family in this country, probably in any country, going back so far—that you couldn't help being interested in it as a family, with its ups and downs.

And then, of course, I began to study the monarchy. Well, the upshot was that I became a very keen monarchist, and very interested in all the present descendants.

Claire Rayner I have no personal animosity towards the royals, although they bore me out of my socks. I was twelve when it first hit me that an hereditary Monarch was rubbish. I had read Walt Whitman, where he said that animals do not worship one of their own kind. I thought: that is very powerful. After all, rabbits don't have rabbit gods; rabbits don't have rabbit Kings.

* * *

In a recent observation on Her Majesty's enduring impact in America, in an article entitled "Life Lessons from Queen Elizabeth" which is excerpted from Bryan Kozlowski's new book *Long Live the Queen*, and published in the October–November issue of the magazine of the American Association of Retired Persons, AARP, the Queen is described as espousing such time-honored principles as: Recharge your willpower; stick to a schedule; develop your sense of purpose; serve others; brush aside vanity; keep the faith; be open to change; and cherish your crowning years.

* * *

Lady Featherstone When an American president gets an invite to a state visit to Buckingham Palace, we are very good at all that pomp and circumstance and the Americans *love* that.

Lord Heseltine There is *no way* that one would expect Americans, or the French or the Germans, to feel about the British Royal Family the way *we* do.

What people like me know is that in their way, the royals have devoted their lives to their onerous responsibility of uniting our country in a way that no politician can. People will on occasion ask me: "Do you think we should have a republic? Should we have a president?" "No!" I say: "For God's sake! Then you would have people like *me* in charge!"

That is something I would not advocate. There is such a difference between the American head of state, who can be deeply controversial, and ours, and we have managed through our darkest days in ways that inspire people in their loyalty to the British interest.

Having lived through the Second World War, I remember King George VI and the Queen standing among the common Brits in London's bombed-out East End, creating an image of stellar quality.

Their daughter Queen Elizabeth II has herself lived such a life, her overarching preoccupation being, quite obviously, the preservation of everything she believes to be good about the British monarchy.

Lady Greenfield Her Majesty is *tough*. That generation, my mother's, were bombed every night during the war. They slept in the Underground and did not know whether their houses would be standing the next day. And the Royal Family stayed in London, the Queen Mother saying at the time: "Now I can look East Enders in the face."

CHAPTER 9

The Queen and the Institution
of the Monarchy

Q
UEEN ELIZABETH II's title to the Crown derives from statute as well as from common law rules of descent. In addition to reigning in the United Kingdom, the Monarch is also Queen of Antigua and Barbuda, Australia, the Bahamas, Belize, Canada, Grenada, Jamaica, New Zealand, Papua New Guinea, St. Christopher and Nevis, St. Lucia, St. Vincent and the Grenadines, the Solomon Islands, and Tuvalu.

The Crown represents both the Sovereign and the government and is the symbol of supreme executive power. And as the Sovereign, the Queen is the person on whom the Crown is constitutionally conferred. Thus, while the Crown is vested in the Queen, its functions are carried out by ministers who are responsible to the Parliament and, in effect, the nation is governed by Her Majesty's government in the name of the Queen.

While the Queen is quite limited in the way in which she may exercise power, she is constitutionally crucial to the workings of her government. Although, constitutionally, the Queen exercises her power on the advice of her ministers, she is responsible for summoning Parliament, suspending it, or, when indicated, dissolving it; she opens Parliament annually by delivering the Queen's Speech, in which she enunciates her government's agenda for the coming session; she gives assent to bills passed by the Parliament; appoints the prime minister, who is almost always the leader of the majority party in Parliament; is empowered to declare war, to make peace, to recognize foreign governments, to conclude treaties, and to annex—or cede—territories.

In addition, the Queen must be informed by her ministers on every aspect of the United Kingdom's national life.

* * *

Sir Oliver Wright The hereditary principle is in life; we are all children of parents, and most of us hope to be parents of children. The continuity of the nation, as represented by the continuity of families, is a very important, cohesive thing for a nation. The monarchy symbolizes, at top level, the continuity of the nation's life, which doesn't prevent change but means that there is a continual adaptation to modern circumstances.

So the constitutional monarchy is the most sophisticated form of government. And it gives the added advantage that you have a symbol of the nation's life who is not a political figure. That is an enormous advantage.

Mind you, I'm not suggesting that the United States should call back George IV. But we have managed to achieve through constitutional monarchy what Winston Churchill once described as the broadening down of liberty from precedent to precedent. This suits our temperament very well.

Sir Bernard Ingham She's the head of state. But she doesn't have any political role at all. She's not supposed to have a view—and this is one of the arguments for the republicans here: it is all a matter of form; it is totally unnecessary.

But, in a curious way, it is *not* unnecessary because if a prime minister has to go through this hoop—and the prime minister has to think very seriously about the hoop he's having to go through—it's most unlikely to happen. Technically, under the constitution, the Queen can ask questions. If the Queen never does anything else but advise—if you're being advised—you at least have the right to ask questions; it's one of these checks and balances that exists in our society. Now, you may say that it's more chimera than real. But it's there.

Lord Healey It always struck me as an irony of European history that almost all the European countries which have had social democratic governments have constitutional monarchies—the three Scandinavian countries, Holland, Belgium, and Britain.

Joe Haines The constitutional monarchy is a perfectly good system for us because we have a symbol which has no power but which has respect—or did until Charles started mucking about. I gradually moved. I don't think it was a question of age: it was more of experience: I don't believe in taking a great deal of time to change things that don't matter, and the monarchy—in any sense of life in this country—doesn't matter. But it does have some respect.

Earl of Harewood There's no doubt a Monarch, even only a constitutional Monarch, can influence many things in a country, and really can influence them quite a lot. That is actually the strong part of the republican case, let's face it, that an elected person is more likely to use the best influence on the country, and the most up-to-date influence, than the person born to it. That's not necessarily true, but it's logical.

We sometimes speculate about who our various presidents would have been if we didn't have a monarchy: one isn't always happy at the results. Therefore, her personality in the job is absolutely vital.

Ben Pimlott, FBA (1945–2004), historian and biographer, *The Queen* (1996), *Harold Wilson* (1992) There is a legacy of the British Royal Family being the world's *premier* royal family, which goes back to Empire. But even post-Empire, there is no rival. And it does touch some ancient myth.

In the British political system, there is a role: if we didn't have a Monarch, there would be a gap in the constitution. It would be a gap that could be filled, but it's not quite easy to see how it could be filled very easily just by a president, because you'd have to change the constitution in more ways than just remaking that slot.

We have, probably, the most powerful executive in the world, in the parliamentary system: it's very, very large. There is a way, ultimately, for the monarchy does provide a sort of strange historical traditional legitimacy, which is separate from the prime minister and can, under some circumstances, very intangibly offer a kind of counterweight.

Rev. Ian Paisley The monarchy is a great constitutional institution, and it has a valuable contribution to make to the evolution of an Empire into a Commonwealth. I don't think the Commonwealth would have come about without the monarchy, as it was. Because if you hadn't had a monarchy that wasn't a presidency, you could never have had the evolution of the Commonwealth.

The monarchy is a great institution, as developed, and as a *constitutional* monarchy, it should be defended. I fear to think what would happen if every second year we went for a retired political figure.

Lady Longford I absolutely accept that the basic business of the Monarch now is that they reign, but they do not rule. Well, somebody rules; Parliament rules; and within Parliament, the cabinet.

The gray area has been quite important in the past, but I just don't think that in the end there'll be a gray area: it will all be the constitutional—playing the executive on the side of the politicians and the moral and patriotic influences, and the head of state and all that that stands for, and does, for the Monarch.

I'm not in favor of their being left to choose. It wouldn't be strengthening to the monarchy to have this indeterminate moment, when they might suddenly find that the whole future, or fate of the country, was in their hands again.

Earl of Harewood I think that the old definition of a constitutional sovereign in the British constitution was always a very good one: the right to be informed; and to advise. One of those pundits said that in the past, and I think it's very good to be informed about everything, and to advise about everything—to be allowed to say: "I think you're making a mistake."

It's always said—I believe it to be true; I hope it's true: in 1931 Ramsey MacDonald[1] came to see King George V and said: "I place my resignation in Your Majesty's hands because of the difficult financial position." And the King said: "You've got us into this bloody position; get us bloody well out of it." And he did.

Winston Churchill The thing that's really amazing is the survivability of the British monarchy when you see the revolutions that took place in France, and in a large number of European countries.

The continuity of the British Crown in its ability to adapt has been quite remarkable, and moving from being absolute sovereigns to constitutional monarchs with only token political power, but nonetheless, enormous prestige.

And what I believe is terribly important to appreciate is the significance of divorcing the glory, on the one hand, from the political power. Having the power and the glory united together can lead to problems and there is huge merit in having the power divorced from the glory: the prime minister has the power; the Queen has the glory.

And by my book, that is as it should be. And we're blessed to have such a system.

Lord Weatherill We're a country of tradition, and there's something very mystical about the monarchy—the Crown itself, and the Scepter, which is almost a fairy's wand. It goes right back with the mythology; it's a symbol. It's almost divine.

And, bear in mind, the Coronation is an exact replica of the consecration of a bishop—it's actually the same service; she is a consecrated Monarch. And she takes that very seriously.

There's a very interesting chapter in *Enigmas of History* on the death of Charles I.[2] They could not find anybody to cut his head off—he was a consecrated Monarch, and the official executioner[3] refused to do it, and Cromwell put out an order that any of his troopers who was prepared to do this would be made into an officer.

One man stepped forward and did this. And the assistant executioner was alleged to have been Cromwell's own chaplain, who instead of giving aid and comfort to the Monarch, read the riot act to him.

And the chap who actually cut off the King's head confessed on his deathbed that he'd done it—the thought of killing a consecrated Monarch in those days was too much.

Winston Churchill The Queen is more than symbolic. She is a unifying force. And though it may not be fashionable [...] nonetheless, deep down, there is enormous love and respect for the Royal Family, centered on the Queen and her mother, above all. And there is no question that there are millions of people in the country who would lay down their lives for Queen and country. There are very few Frenchmen, or Belgians, or Dutch, who would have such a concept.

There's an emotional attachment, deep down, less so in the younger generation, but above all that generation that went through the war, that felt that the Royal Family, though at the pinnacle, were nonetheless sharing the dangers. And there was the young Princess Elizabeth in uniform doing her bit in the armed forces. And people have a lot of admiration.

THE QUEEN'S SO-CALLED RESERVE POWER

Lady Young The Monarch, of course, enjoys very considerable residual powers, which she has never used. It would be possible for her to use them, but under our constitution, she doesn't. They haven't been repealed, or anything, so it would be untrue to say her powers have eroded.

CAN THE QUEEN EXERT INFLUENCE BY THE WAY
SHE PHRASES A QUESTION?

Baron King of Bridgewater, Tom (Thomas) Jeremy, CH, PC, life peer, cr. 2001; Conservative M.P., 1970–2001; cabinet posts include secretary of state for employment, 1983–85; secretary of state for Northern Ireland, 1985–89; secretary of state for defense, 1989–92; interviewed here 1999 Absolutely. She might well say: "Really?" Or: "Why are you doing that?" She would ask intelligent questions. Very much so.

And she's very wise to listen to, very experienced—particularly on the foreign affairs side because there's nobody in this country who has had more connection and recollection of the leaders of every country in the world.

And she's got this over this amazing period—it's sixty-nine years that she has been meeting all the leaders of almost every country in the world. And so if you're a new prime minister, if you're a new foreign minister, or defense minister, she can say some very interesting things.

Lord Cholmondeley The Monarch is not supposed to take political sides; the Monarch shouldn't do it on any issue, and that's the difficult thing, isn't it? But even with the Queen in her speeches, there's often a veiled reference to her feelings, or what her constitutional role is, the importance of her role as Monarch—how she was crowned Queen of Great Britain and of Northern Ireland and so she's always upheld the importance of that, which is a very strong political point of view, if you like. But it's upholding what she was crowned to be.

[I]t's quite a controversial, strong point of view.

Lord Weatherill Don't underestimate the big influence of the Queen. She gives the prime minister an audience every week and none of us ever know what is said. But it would be very true to say that any prime minister who in these private conversations sought her advice and didn't take note of it would be very foolish.

CAN THE QUEEN VOICE HER OBJECTION TO A
GOVERNMENT POLICY?

Raymond G. H. Seitz, ambassador of the United States to the Court of St. James's, 1991–94 It would all depend on *how* she objected: if she objected in a public sense, she would violate one of the fundamental understandings. A lot of this works on understandings; one of the fundamental understandings about the conduct of the Royal Family is that you don't pick a political fight. And when they get close to it—Charles, or whoever, gets a little close to it—you will hear about it: people will write editorials, or [there will be] big headlines in *The Sun*, that sort of thing.

It would have to be almost national life-and-death before the Queen would ever say something publicly about her discomfort on a particular issue.

Lord Howe I've never been conscious of it, oddly enough. There is a tremendous body of experience and wisdom there, but I've never myself consciously, as I've said, actually said: "What do you think?" But I think she'd be very hesitant to offer an opinion.

Peter Jay I don't imagine she has ever said—or could have said: "I will not appoint this man." The role of the [U.S.] Senate and the role of the Queen are sometimes described in rather similar words: to advise and consent in the case of the Senate; to advise and warn in the case of the Crown.

I suppose there could be a case where the Queen would say to the Foreign Secretary, or the prime minister: "Have you considered the fact that this man, or this woman …?" But to my knowledge, no such thing has ever occurred. No, she would not be in the position of saying: "Mr. Prime Minister, why don't you appoint Mr. Jay?"

IS THE QUEEN EVER FRUSTRATED AT THE CONSTITUTIONAL LIMITATIONS ON HER POWER?

Winston Churchill I suppose it must be a little frustrating at times. But what is important—and what I imagine Her Majesty feels is important—is that someone with her experience likes to be able to impart her views, and give her advice, and hope that it will be given fair consideration and, as appropriate, acted on.

Now I'm not a fly on the wall, so I've got no idea what passes between the Queen and Mr. Blair. But if he treats her with the same contempt with which he treats the House of Commons, I can imagine that it must be quite a frustrating ordeal for her.

On the other hand, there were prime ministers—such as Harold Wilson, possibly even Jim Callaghan, and unquestionably Harold Macmillan—who would give very serious consideration to points that she would make of a political nature, or foreign policy nature, on the basis that she is such an experienced player in the game, and she has a lot to contribute.

And maybe I'm maligning Mr. Blair; maybe Mr. Blair does in fact have the good sense to give full consideration to her points of view. I would certainly hope so. But I'm not convinced.

Lord Weatherill Bear this in mind of the Monarch: we have in this country an elective dictatorship; the prime minister is all powerful—he appoints absolutely everybody, including the bishops—it's all done through Number 10.

So it's nominally in the name of the Monarch, whose main responsibility is to choose the prime minister. She would normally choose the prime minister from the majority party. But there have been times when it looked as if in the general election, particularly in 1992, that there would be a hung Parliament. And it was up to the Queen to decide who she wanted to be her prime minister.

Furthermore, of course, she is not only Queen of the United Kingdom, but Queen of [several] other countries. When I was Speaker, I went to the opening of the new parliamentary building in Canberra, Australia. And one thing that struck me most on the building was that it was [the Parliament of] "Her Majesty, Queen of Australia."

And it's not just the old dominions, but also, of course, Fiji, and other, smaller territories. And she receives red boxes from all these countries, and she's very well-informed.

Peter Jay She reads all the dispatches and as many of the telegrams as she can, but she doesn't write back and say: "Why did you take this action?", so you don't know what she thinks about it, but she reads them; she's very dutiful, so it is very constitutional.

Robert Lacey The question of how much power the Queen has, in my view of the monarchy, takes for granted that she has no power. And if I have to justify the monarchy to somebody, her powerlessness—and the powerlessness of any modern Monarch—is the essence of what it stands for.

[...] Prince Charles canceled a trip to Austria [in 2000] to reflect the British government's unhappiness with the allegedly Nazi-inclined Mr. [Jörg] Haider and there was a very good article in *The Times* by Kenneth Rose pointing out how important it was to realize that this was not his personal decision, that he was absolutely the tool of the government in this, and that it's the job of the constitutional Monarch—and to some extent, the heir, therefore—to subordinate their own decisions.

And when people say how disgusting it is that the Queen has to shake hands with a dictator like the president of China, they're misunderstanding the situation if they think about the Queen's personal feelings. She knows that her job involves rubbing shoulders with tyrants if that is what she's required to do by the British government because that's her value—that she is absolutely a cipher.

And the question of her personal knowledge, and wisdom, and stability of judgment, which successive prime ministers have paid tribute to, is a bonus to that, but shouldn't be mistaken in any way as a reason for her existence.

Philip Ziegler I don't believe *she* feels it. She takes her role for granted: she accepts it; she thinks that she can be useful, despite her limitations. And that's what she wants to be.

I believe that possibly Prince Philip would like to be playing a less circumscribed, more active role.

PRINCE PHILIP'S ROLE

Sir Michael Palliser He's been an extraordinarily successful consort, and an extraordinarily supportive one. He really has, right from the beginning, mastered the ability of being half a step behind her when she was Princess, and more when she became the Queen, but, at the same time, always being there.

He's not always a very easy man—sometimes puts his foot in his mouth. But in terms of the role of a Prince Consort—it's a very difficult role, particularly for a man who probably could have had a career in his own right, whether in the Navy, or whatever—I just think he made a determined effort to support the Queen in every way.

[...] He's been a very remarkable figure. Now he's no longer a young man and the question of advancing years has become emphasized.

I find it impossible to believe—they've been genuinely happily married for however many years it is—that in those circumstances they don't exchange confidences.

On the other hand, one's seen this in the past, it's less now, but there was a reluctance to have Prince Charles be involved in affairs of state.

I think she's felt that that was the Queen's prerogative. It's not quite so noticeable, as with past Monarchs and Princes of Wales, but it's always been a little bit her position: she reads her boxes with the state papers; I don't think she passes them on to anyone else. But I find it impossible to believe that she never *discusses* anything in private with Prince Philip. I think she must.

Sir Shridath Ramphal In all my life I have placed great store by pillow talk, so I think it would be very unrealistic to believe that a husband, or a wife, does not exercise some influence.

But he [Prince Philip] has always come across to me as being scrupulous in leaving her to follow her instincts, and to listen to her advisers, not intruding, as it were, his opinion. I believe he has disciplined himself to letting her be.

Peter Jay I assume that they, like many non-royal husbands and wives, discuss the office at some times. I assume they do so on the basis that she knows that he will never betray her confidences—and if she didn't know that, she wouldn't let herself discuss such matters. And I suspect that as she takes the constitution very seriously, that there are probably some things she doesn't discuss.

You can guess that the kind of things that they *might* have opinions about are likely to be things that affect the integrity of the United Kingdom; things that affect the health and success of the Commonwealth; things that affect the morale and integrity of the armed forces and the other public services which are wearing the Queen's uniform, metaphorically; and, I think, the whole area, broadly, of social equity, for which the Monarch, not just this one, tended to be caring about social issues, and has been less happy when government policies seemed to be very harsh.

THE QUEEN'S GRASP OF ISSUES

Sir Oliver Wright Walter Bagehot[4] has said that the functions of the monarchy were to encourage, guide, and warn. In order to fulfill those functions, the Queen has to probably be the best-informed person in the realm.

Lord Healey That's a great exaggeration. The most important person at the Palace is the private secretary. I've known many of them, and still do—Martin Charteris, Philip Moore, Robert Fellowes—and their job is to see that the Queen knows all about the issues which she has to discuss with people—not necessarily about other ones.

So, for example, when I was Chancellor, she was always very well briefed about the state of the economy, and we could have a useful discussion. But she would never try to influence my decisions, and I suspect, really, the only area where she had much influence was on the Civil List—how much money the family got, and who got the money, and on what conditions, and so on—which was, obviously, in the end, the thing she had to agree. Those responsible had to persuade her to agree, and so she discussed that in detail.

She has to know not only about politics, she has to know about all the problems of any city she happens to visit; of any institution of which she is a patron; or anything like that.

I wouldn't say she knew more about the things that mattered than anybody else, but she had to be well briefed, and she's been a hard-working Monarch, there's no question.

Joe Haines "Well-informed"? What does it mean? The phrase "advise and consent" comes into my mind. Harold Wilson told me once that unless he had read his papers, there was a real danger that she would catch him out—she does read all the papers. It's not *that* time consuming. It was part of my daily job; I used to read all the same papers, and there was time for other things.

But he would consult her—she has an incredible knowledge of the Commonwealth, probably more than any prime minister. She also has—because she's been there since 1952 and because she's an intelligent woman—this knowledge of foreign affairs over the period, which is probably unequaled [...]

If you have seen it all before, if you've been there, done that, and got the tee-shirt—she must have a whole wardrobe of them by now—then there is a value, although not a value to someone who thought that he knew it all.

Lord Weatherill As Vice-Chamberlain of the Royal Household, I used to take the messages from the Commons to Buckingham Palace. We carried what were called the "white staves"—you see those ancient pictures of courtiers with white staves. When she dies, you're supposed to break them and chuck them in the grave. And when you retire, she unscrews them and gives them back to you. I think I'm the only person known to have three of them, for those three offices which I held.

But I had to go in with messages. And one of my early messages, there was a double taxation order for the territories. I didn't know anything about this, and she said to me: "How many people does this involve?" So I said: "I'm terribly sorry, Ma'am, I don't really know. Nor do I really know whoever we're supposed to ask." And she said: "In that case, I'd better tell you!" I never made *that* mistake again.

Bear in mind, it's a very long time that she's been on the Throne. And she takes it very seriously. So she sees red boxes not just from the United Kingdom, but from her far realms and territories.

I went to a dinner when I was the Speaker, in Number 10 Downing Street, where the Queen said that Queen Victoria was able to boast that during the course of her sixty years' reign, she had been served by twenty-eight prime ministers.

And the Queen said *she'd* had a hundred and twenty-eight, because of some of these smaller countries. Bear in mind that she's not only just Queen of *them* but head of the Commonwealth.

Peter Jay We had about forty-five minutes of what I thought on her part was remarkably intelligent and interesting conversation.[5] I felt rather inadequate because she was actually talking rather knowledgeably about the unemployment problem in Wales, and various issues of the paradox of unfilled vacancies and permanent unemployment, and having people with the right skills, and so on—Americans have analogies for all this. And I was very awed; that was supposedly *my* subject, and I couldn't get two words out together.

She thought this would be interesting, which indeed it was. On all three occasions I've seen her, I've always been extremely impressed by how sharp and knowledgeable she was. Now that doesn't mean that she was saying: "Now you tell that Jimmy Carter this or that message from me." That's not what was going on. But in fulfilling her constitutional role, she sees you, she discusses with you.

Donald Macdonald She was, from a Canadian standpoint, very interested in Canada. On a public occasion—it was at a garden party—we had a chat. There was a standoff between an Indian reservation and the Quebec community just at that time. She said: "What's the aftermath of that situation?"

I said: "There is a certain sense that it has been overtaken by the government. What do you call them [the Indian tribe] now?" And she said: "Oh, you mean the Mohawks."

It was current, and she was totally up on her brief; she knew all about it. And that really impressed me because she wouldn't have known that she would talk to me about it.

Lord Carrington People don't realize how well-informed she is. You would be very ill-advised to suppose when you're talking to her that she doesn't know quite a lot about the subject you're talking to her about. That's what people don't really quite understand. Why should they? The ordinary man-in-the-street thinks: there's the Queen in Buckingham Palace. But underneath she sees people the whole time, and not just her ministers; she sees all of the foreign ambassadors and foreign ministers who come here and really is extremely well-informed—a very, very well-informed person. But she would never try to overstep the bounds of what she should do as a constitutional Monarch.

Lord King She does have a tremendous knowledge of Commonwealth and of other countries. [...] A prime minister may be deeply involved in certain issues, with certain countries; a new prime minister may find them on the map, but he may not know much more about them than that.

The Queen may have some interesting reflections, or comments because she's gone round the country. I'm sure that in the private audiences she does that. But that falls far short of seeking to interfere and say: "Now I want us to establish a special trading relationship," or "establish a new treaty," or "I want us to join the European Union," or whatever it is. She wouldn't interfere in that sort of way.

But in terms of being fairly well-traveled, and extraordinarily experienced in terms of people she's met, and countries she's been to, because she's been unchanged in that position for all the years she has, it's a terrific archive of experience.

Sir Oliver Wright I have been astonished in my own experience in how well-informed she is. She has become the sort of "tribal memory," because she can remember things which happened during her lifetime, when a young man like Tony Blair was not born.

Sir Edward Ford Her knowledge certainly is there. When high commissioners are appointed, they come to "kiss hands," as it's called, and I think very often they think: this is just a formal ceremony.

I can remember very well when a high commissioner was appointed in Ghana. He came—he'd just been an M.P. and so he'd never met the

Queen before—and he was wondering: "What do I do?" And I explained: "The Queen merely wants to be able to meet you and talk to you." "And how long would that take?" he said. And I said: "Oh, she'll probably talk to you for about ten minutes, and she'll make it quite clear when she wants you to go."

And he went in, and about forty minutes later, he emerged, and said: "Well, I'd been going round the Colonial Office, and the Foreign Office in the last three weeks to find out all about my post, but I've learned more in the last forty minutes than in all that time."

Lord Howe As I arrived at Buckingham Palace for my first one-to-one meeting with her, I was immensely struck by the fact that here was I, full of authority, going to present my budget to the Queen, and I had forgotten that it was only one of forty-five budgets she has to know something about—I must have been the eleventh Chancellor of the Exchequer she's dealt with.

And I thought to myself: it's this extraordinary record of continuity, which is a distinctive feature of it, and it's quite impossible that any Johnny-come-lately prime minister could match her depth and breadth of experience that the Monarch has accumulated.

One is always conscious of this great body of experience. And, in a sense, it's rather sad, although it's perhaps entirely right that it isn't ever deployed to shift people's opinion. I mean, she certainly wouldn't have dreamed of saying to me: "Well, do you think it's wise to raise VAT?"[6] I suspect that to the prime minister she's said more.

Peter Jay The Queen can "remind" prime ministers of things which many of them never knew. I had an example of how this can be true: I fell into an argument about one aspect of our constitution. The issue we were inquiring about was: when the Monarch dies, does the incumbent prime minister resign because the prime minister has the commission from the Monarch?

The person I was arguing with said no, he thought that the administration continues: Winston Churchill between 1951 and 1955 had only one administration, and so he was continually prime minister during that period.

Anyway, we had a great argument and we planned to have a bet on it: whoever lost would buy a good dinner for the winner. And then I asked a good friend of mine—an old tutor and friend, Geoffrey Blake, the greatest authority on Britain's constitution—and he thought not; he said he wasn't sure.

I then consulted the person who would normally get consulted, namely the recently retired secretary of the cabinet, who was the holder of these matters, and he said he was sure that the prime minister would *not* resign. But he couldn't quite put his finger on *why*. So I asked the private secretary to the cabinet, who was a personal friend of mine. *He* got the papers out of his cabinet and looked it up, and said: "Definitely, he *doesn't* resign, but it doesn't say here *why*."

So I then rang up Buckingham Palace's information site and said: "This dispute has developed between myself and my friend, and we want to resolve it." And the voice asked whether my inquiry related to the present reign or previous reigns, because in previous reigns, the wisdom is all concentrated in the library at Windsor, whereas in the present reign, it is concentrated at Buckingham Palace.

And I said: "By about one day, the present reign," and I asked: "When Sir Winston met the Queen on the tarmac at Heathrow, did he resign, or did she ask him to form a government?"

The question was duly noted and after about three weeks, they came back and said: "Mr. Churchill did not resign; he did not receive the commission; and the reason he didn't was Section Thirteen of the 1901 Demise of the Crown Act, passed just after Queen Victoria died."

Well, the point of this story is that the only institution—from all the high authorities, both academic and Whitehall—I'd been to which knew the answer was Buckingham Palace. And I suspect that the actual answer came from the Queen herself, and that nobody else in Buckingham Palace knew. And she knew because she'd been there—and because it was her job to know such things. I like the idea of a head of state who is the final authority on constitutional issues.

CHAPTER 10

The Queen and her Prime Ministers

T HE FIRST PRIMARY governmental adviser to the Sovereign to be officially designated as the prime minister was Sir Robert Walpole, a Whig statesman who assumed office in 1721, during the reign of King George I. In the ensuing years, there have been additional Whig prime ministers, as well as Tories, Peelites, Liberals, Conservatives, and Labour.

The present Monarch has been served by fourteen prime ministers to date—from Winston Churchill to Boris Johnson—reflecting the profound changes that have taken place in the United Kingdom in the last sixty-nine years.

The prime minister and staff work from Number 10 Downing Street, a rather modest town house—according to both European and American standards—in central London, and the Chancellor of the Exchequer resides next door, at Number 11.

* * *

Joe Haines The Downing Street staff, including the messengers, the drivers—we didn't have any luxuries—was about one hundred. It's two old houses. The U.S. White House had the advantage of being burned down.[1] Downing Street was built on very unsound land—they designed well, but they built badly—and has been a constant drain of money ever since.

THE QUEEN'S ROLE WITH HER PRIME MINISTERS

Sir Malcolm Rifkind The proper role of a constitutional Monarch, certainly in Britain, is to advise, to encourage, and to warn. And in the way in which that opportunity is exercised more than anything is that the weekly meeting would take place in private between the Queen and the prime minister. And ever since Winston Churchill, every week, almost without fail, unless she is abroad, or ill, she is having about an hour-and-a-half.

Lord McNally There are people who have looked at her role, and I've never heard any of them suggest that she was anything other than diligent, meticulous, well-informed, professional—all the right descriptions of somebody who took the job very seriously indeed.

In all her reign—and with occasional points when the Palace could have got it wrong—there has been hardly any criticism that they've used their constitutional position improperly.

The only criticism was probably at the time of Harold Macmillan's resignation, when there was some doubt whether Lord Home, Sir Alec Douglas-Home, had the backing [of the Conservative Party].

But the fault was not so much the Monarch's as the Conservative Party's rather opaque way of choosing the leader—this magic circle of senior figures who took soundings and then came to a conclusion. But that is the only time, I believe, that anybody has even suggested that the Palace might have done something different.

And now, of course, the Conservatives—as do all the parties—have a transparently democratic way of electing their leaders, so the Monarch doesn't have to take advice from magic circles who may, or may not, have got it right when they came to the conclusion.

So the general impression of constitutional scholars, politicians, and media commentators is that the Queen and her advisers have played their role properly. And when you consider the opportunity in a modern democracy to get it *wrong*, that's a pretty well-kept record over such a long period.

THE PRIME MINISTER'S WEEKLY AUDIENCE
WITH THE QUEEN

Lady Longford Part of her duty was to see her prime minister, whoever he [or she] was, once a week. I think she saw it as her duty to get on with him as well as possible. If her prime minister was an outgoing kind of person, all the better, because she's not outgoing in the sense that her mother is.

Lord Wright I got the clear impression that Wilson[2] and Callaghan[3] enormously valued their Tuesday evening audiences, both because they genuinely found the Queen, as she is, a very charming and easy person to discuss problems with, and also respected her enormous, now unequaled, knowledge of world events, in which she played a part.

Lord McNally The two prime ministers of which I am aware, Harold Wilson and James Callaghan, took very seriously the weekly audience with the Queen, and found it useful and daunting—in that, of course, by the time they arrived on the scene you had somebody who had considerable experience of both domestic government and world government and, therefore, who could bring that experience to bear, and who was a good listener on issues and comments on them.

Joe Haines There is always something happening if you're running a country like this—foreign affairs, Commonwealth affairs, and domestic affairs. The Queen usually has some questions she wants to ask; the prime minister may go along [to the meeting] with something particular in mind, but she may wish to raise something else. And she has the right to do it; she has the right to advise, in a symbolic, theoretic, sense—and to consent.

Sir Oliver Wright I know from my firsthand experience that all prime ministers value, more than they can say, the weekly audience with the Queen, because being prime minister is a very lonely job; you have no one to talk to because anyone around you with a chance for leadership wants your job. The one person who *doesn't* want the prime minister's job is the Queen.

In my day, the private secretary at the Palace would make a checklist of the subjects which "the prime minister may wish to discuss with the Queen." But, of course, there was no compulsion for the prime minister to discuss those subjects, or not to add to the list those areas he wanted to discuss.

Sir Malcolm Rifkind I would be astonished if these were not occasions in which the Queen expresses opinions and views. And because she is Queen, but also because she has such experience, background knowledge, and awareness—she is a very bright woman; she's not an intellectual, but she's a very intelligent woman; she's very shrewd, and she's got very good judgment—I would be very surprised if Mr. Blair, or Margaret Thatcher, or any of the prime ministers, have not been often influenced on some issues.

It depends on the kind of issue—issues which are not party-political, but have a national significance: on constitutional change; on some aspect of foreign policy; on judgment of people, for example, her views on an American president, or a French president, or a German chancellor.

When Churchill was prime minister and she had just become Queen, I'm sure it was the other way round: she looked to the prime minister for guidance. But increasingly, when she became Queen—Mr. Blair was born almost exactly the year she became Queen—you can see what the respective experiences are in that situation.

Lord McNally I suppose for prime ministers under the pressure of their office—probably a psychiatrist would explain it to you—it's almost like a visit to the confessional, when they must feel shriven and refreshed, so it's probably quite a clever way of just giving them a different, and very special, focus that takes them away from the pressures of the day.

HOW IS THE PRIVACY OF THE AUDIENCE ACHIEVED?

Sir Oliver Wright Those weekly meetings are the best-kept secrets of the realm because no one has an interest in leaking.

Joe Haines There are two secretaries there, for a start—the principal private secretary will accompany Wilson to the Palace; then he will go and talk to the Queen's private secretary. The only two people in the room [during the prime minister's audience with the Queen] are the Monarch and the prime minister, and, therefore, it's very difficult to leak—and nobody did.

Wilson was quite good: he wouldn't come back and say: "The Queen told me … and I told her …" He would occasionally let little things out, and occasionally, the private secretary would say something. But you won't find any prime minister who's gone on record to any extent about his relationship with the Queen.

Lord Heseltine The idea that gossip will flow from Her Majesty's conversations with her prime ministers is extremely unattractive.

Sir Bernard Ingham, interviewed 2021 Mrs. Thatcher *never* discussed her audiences with the Queen, regarding them as being entirely confidential, according to the constitution, and it is one of the great things about good government that things can be done confidentially.

THE QUEEN'S EVOLUTION FROM LISTENER TO SPEAKER

Sir Malcolm Rifkind I would say 1964, when Harold Wilson became prime minister. Before then, she had Churchill, she had Anthony Eden, she had Harold Macmillan, Alec Douglas-Home—they were all much older than her, and they had all been statesmen when she was a child. And that inevitably affects the relationship of two people.

When Harold Wilson won in 1964, she was dealing with someone who was older than her, but more of her generation, and who was a post-war politician—he was the first post-war politician to become prime minister. All the previous ones really went back to the 1930s or the 1940s.

Eric Moonman John Major would be the turning point. When Elizabeth came to the Throne as a young girl, she couldn't have contributed very much to issues, dealing with older men.

She had to stand up for herself when Margaret Thatcher was there; they didn't get on. The Thatcher thing started to show her the whole area of argument and debate.

But, on the other hand, if you're in a situation with a colleague in business and you've got two directors, if there's a creative tension you actually learn from that, as well, and so the next time round, you're in a better condition to deal with the next person in.

THE QUEEN'S RELATIONSHIPS WITH SOME OF
HER PRIME MINISTERS

Philip Ziegler It is more a question of personalities than of parties: she got on very well with Harold Macmillan; she found Eden difficult—who didn't? She found Ted Heath difficult.

She never really had a very happy working relationship with Mrs. Thatcher. But I believe that was probably as much a kind of sex problem as anything else; I don't believe it was because she led the Conservatives at all.

It is a curious case, but, in fact, the two prime ministers she probably was closest to have been Wilson and Callaghan, both socialists. But I don't think it was because they were socialists. It was their personalities.

Lady Longford She's said to have got on particularly well with Harold Wilson, which rather shows their kind of relations, because they never could have been friends. But he amused her. I knew him quite well and he never stopped talking, and would tell little stories, and she liked that.

WINSTON CHURCHILL

Winston Churchill was seventy-eight years old and serving his third term as prime minister in 1952 when the young daughter of his close friend King George VI came to the Throne as Queen Elizabeth II.

Lord McNally In those relationships, it must be, in part, the chemistry: Churchill had an almost Victorian kind of approach to this—he obviously saw himself as Melbourne to the Queen's Victoria—and, being an emotional old fogey, an emotional fogey with a sense of history, he was particularly enchanted, I believe, with the idea of this young Queen.

Winston Churchill My grandfather was a great monarchist. He had it in his genes going back to the father of John, the First Duke of Marlborough: the first Sir Winston Churchill had been a Cavalier soldier at the time of our Civil War, in 1642, and had fought for Charles I.

And then came the Restoration of the monarchy in 1660. He and many other royalists looked forward to the Restoration as being the moment that they would be restored to their estates and properties which had been sequestrated under Cromwell.

But he and many other royalists didn't get their sequestrated lands back. Hence the Churchill family motto: "Faithful but Unfortunate." It was a reproach to Charles II: I was faithful to you, but it did me no good. And to this day it is the Churchill family motto.

For her part, the Queen revered my grandfather as her first-ever prime minister. And I have no doubt whatever in my mind that he was also her favorite prime minister. He treated her with great courtesy and respect. And she embodied for him everything—his concept of monarchy.

He was very much a father figure to her, and of course, there was the huge span of age: in 1952, my grandfather was seventy-eight years old and she was twenty-five.

Sir Edward Ford He came out once after a meeting with her, he was grumbling, saying: "The Queen told me she had an awful time last night" because she'd been to a film, *Beau Brummell*, which was about George

IV, one of her ancestors. Churchill took this very seriously. He came out saying: "We mustn't have this!"

And within twenty-four hours, the Home Secretary had been told by the prime minister that he must arrange for the films that were going to be presented to the Queen on the occasion of a gala to be censored by, or to be changed, by a committee. And the committee was appointed under Lord Radcliffe, who had chaired the commission about the partition of India. He was appointed as the chairman of this committee to choose the Queen's films!

I don't think the Queen had the slightest knowledge that he was going to do that! It was very like Churchill, in the way in which he would take up, in that sort of romantic way he had, almost anything that she said—and, also, his determination that if a thing was to be done, then it had to be done within twenty-four hours.

Jeremy Thorpe Churchill used to look at her and the tears would pour down rather like Lord Melbourne with Queen Victoria.

Churchill had been very careful not to involve the Queen in [Conservative] Party politics. It was her government but *their* speeches; they wrote her speeches.

But Winston did ask whether she'd come to dinner at Downing Street the night before he retired from office forever, and she accepted. And he said to her: "Would you mind, Ma'am, if I toast your health?"—this was unheard of as she was the Queen—and she said: "Yes, go ahead." And so he said: "Ma'am, when I consider my life, I was First Lord of the Treasury; I have served in office under Your Majesty; and I served in office under Your Majesty's father, King George VI; and Your Majesty's great-grand-father, King Edward VII; and I had a commission in the Army under Your Majesty's great-great-grandmother, Queen Victoria, and I am proud to put on my gravestone that I am a loyal subject of the Crown. To the Queen!"

The Queen got up and she said: "It is my pleasure to drink to your health. To our host and my prime minister!" And Churchill was in tears.

Winston Churchill At Chartwell there is a wonderful photograph of my grandfather in his britches, and silk stockings, and his Garter, beaming with affection and love at the Queen on the doorstep of Number 10, bidding her farewell.

I believe I'm right in saying it was the first time that a Sovereign dined at Number 10, and it's happened a few times since.

ANTHONY EDEN

Anthony Eden, who was married to Prime Minister Churchill's niece Clarissa, the daughter of his younger brother, Jack Churchill, succeeded Churchill as prime minister in 1955, when the elder statesman, dogged by ill health, resigned.

In 1957, following the debacle over the Suez affair, which will be discussed in chapter twenty-one, Prime Minister Eden became ill, left Britain for medical treatment in the United States, and on his return resigned.

* * *

Sir Michael Palliser Eden was an elder statesman with a great reputation, and extremely popular.

I never thought much of Eden, but that's a personal thing. But in British political terms, Eden was one of the leading political figures, and I think the Queen, only very recently on the Throne, whatever her feelings—perhaps she didn't have many, you know, she hadn't got at that stage her knowledge of state affairs and knowledge of the Commonwealth, and all the rest of it—I wouldn't be surprised if she hadn't done more than register what the prime minister was intending to do.

Winston Churchill Anthony Eden was an enormously attractive, good-looking, charismatic figure, and he was Foreign Secretary during the war years, and he had long been the unspoken successor-in-waiting to my grandfather.

I have a cartoon, which I've given to my son Randolph, which is a montage of about six different cartoons forming all part of the whole: one is of my grandfather's getting sick and Eden's looking very perky and eager to take over; then my grandfather through stages of dramatic recovery and, meanwhile, Eden gets sicker and sicker; and my grandfather decides that he has to hang on for a few more years.

I think the problem with Eden, which my father, Randolph, identified, was that he was a very good number two, but was not up to the number one job, and certainly was not the person to fill my grandfather's boots. And, of course, by the time that he became prime minister he was already a sick man.

HAROLD MACMILLAN

Harold Macmillan, another father figure to the still very young Queen, succeeded Prime Minister Eden and held his post until 1963 when, following prostate surgery, he resigned. An unprecedented action by the Queen was taken at that time.

On October 10, 1963, Macmillan announced his resignation due to illness, setting off a furious battle for leadership of the Conservative Party.

On October 18, the Queen—invoking the Royal Prerogative—appointed the Earl of Home[4] prime minister, having decided to do so on Macmillan's advice and in consultation with Sir Winston Churchill, as well as other political figures.

The Queen's action enraged the supporters of R. A. ("Rab") Butler, the deputy prime minister in the Macmillan government, who claimed that a "magic circle" had conspired to keep Butler from succeeding Macmillan.

There is little doubt that the Queen was influenced in her action by Macmillan's desire to be succeeded by Home, a personal friend of hers with strong aristocratic credentials, rather than by Butler.

In time, the power engendered by the Royal Prerogative would fade when the major political parties opted to elect their leader on the understanding that that individual would become prime minister.

* * *

Sir Oliver Wright Macmillan, from his sickbed, conducted a poll of all strands of his party, for two reasons: one, to discover for himself what the opinion of his party was, and secondly, to relieve the Queen of any controversy surrounding whatever choice she made, so that he, the outgoing prime minister, would be able to give advice to the Queen which the Queen was constitutionally required to accept. So his desire was to remove any possibility of controversy.

I was Lord Home's private secretary at the time, and I remember the incident rather vividly. Alec was the preferred choice of the Conservative Party, so this did not reduce the power of the monarchy.

What would have reduced the power—but in reality the *influence* of the monarchy—was if the Queen had made a controversial choice. If she had taken R. A. Butler, who was a marvelous man but had one defect—he could see every side of a problem and could never make up his mind—that would have been far more damaging.

Sir Edward Ford I don't think that an outgoing prime minister like that has a right to advise the Queen about his successor. And, particularly, if, in fact, he has already resigned.

Certainly, the Queen is not bound to accept that advice. I don't think, as long as he is prime minister, he can say who his successor should be. She can ask him: "Now who do you think I ought to appoint?"

Harold Macmillan, I believe, was determined, for one reason or another, that it should not be Rab Butler and so he had to find out from the party as a whole who they would like because there had been, of course, an unseemly sort of rush to be prime minister: he had put forward the announcement of his resignation by a day so that it came well within while the Conservative Conference at Blackpool was on.

Well, I don't think she asked him; he volunteered that. And it was thought to be what a retiring prime minister shouldn't do unless he was personally asked by the Queen. The Conservative Party needed to ask the Queen to choose who should be their leader because they hadn't got a designated leader once Harold Macmillan was out: they couldn't decide among several candidates. They said that in the end Home, who was in no way a compromise candidate, was wanted by all.

But it wasn't very satisfactory because after that the arrangements of the Conservative Party were changed so that they would immediately have to decide who was the leader of the party.

And then the Queen would obviously send for the leader to form the next government. So now it would be difficult for her to exercise her personal choice if the person had not got the previous recommendation of the majority party.

Earl of Perth Macmillan paid great attention to monarchy; he was a traditionalist and I believe he would really prepare his ground very, very carefully for his interviews.

I believe the others hadn't got quite the same—I don't want to use the word "reverence"—that Macmillan had. Mind you, Macmillan was a most attractive man, in every sense of the word. And when he wanted to put himself out, he could win anybody. And he had a very good historical knowledge relating to the past.

HAROLD WILSON

When Sir Alec Douglas-Home lost the 1964 election, Harold Wilson became prime minister for the first time, serving until 1970, when the Conservatives, led by Edward Heath, came to power.

Prime Minister Wilson would become prime minister again in 1974, succeeding Prime Minister Heath. He would serve for two years until, beset by diminishing mental prowess, he decided to resign.

* * *

Lord Healey Harold, in a sense, was very opportunistic: he was very good at getting on with people he *had* to get on with.

Larry Adler He took me aside and he said: "Larry, I know about you, and I know about your politics. You won't like what I'm about to say. The greatest president you have ever had is Richard Nixon. I know what you think. But remember what I said." He mentioned the fact that Nixon opened up China.

Margaret, Countess of Mar, thirty-first in line of premier earldom of Scotland; later deputy Speaker, the House of Lords As prime minister, his government was liberal—flower power, and love, and all the rest of it—so we were beginning to lose self-discipline.

Lord Armstrong Nobody's had a greater respect for her, and he valued the connection with the Queen very highly. He used to enjoy going to his regular audiences, and would come out saying how interesting it was to talk to the only person he could really talk to who'd been around in that business, at that stage, for years.

Philip Ziegler Initially, his audiences would last the regulation hour. But as the years had gone on, they'd got longer, and longer, and longer. He became more excited by them, and he'd come back with a kind of glow of satisfaction.

He undoubtedly attached very great importance to his relationship with the Queen, and valued very much the chance of talking to her. He said, several times: "She's the only person in this country who I can talk to about anything, because she's not after my job."

Joe Haines Harold didn't talk a lot about his relationship with the Queen—it's a convention that they [prime ministers] don't, not even to their closest assistant. But they got on very well; there were one or two occasions when Harold got back from the Palace on a Tuesday night that I thought he had had a whiskey or two too many with her—she liked to drink, and she liked to gossip; they were both gossips, you know.

I remember Harold telling me one day when we had been to the Palace and come back [to Number 10 Downing Street]—I forget now what the issue was, but it was a big issue at the time—that she was far more interested in discovering whether rumors about a prominent French politician were true—that he would ride back home in the early hours on a milk cart, having been womanizing somewhere—[her interest] was foreign affairs in the widest sense!

Sir Michael Palliser I worked for Harold Wilson for three years. I know that he immensely looked forward to his Tuesday evening meetings with her. He came away from them, always, in very good form.

Harold was a paradox in many ways: he had a real devotion to the Queen and to the concept of the Royal Family—even though he'd been ostensibly on the left of the Labour Party. I say "ostensibly" deliberately, because he was a mix of very Conservative attitudes and rather radical Labour attitudes. I've no doubt that he respected the power—and had real affection for the Queen. Whether that was reciprocated, I don't know, but it may well have been.

He's had so much written about him that, understandably, the majority thought he was a difficult person. He was a very kind person to work for; if for whatever reason you wanted to get away for the weekend, or whatever, he would always say: "Go." It was that sort of reaction always, which is nice when you're working for someone—it makes you work harder. In fact, I'd be more reluctant to ask, so from his point of view, it had its advantages. It was a genuine thing. At the same time, there were always "conspirators" under every hedge; he had a kind of fixation with conspiracy and plots.

And there was no doubt he had a degree of vulnerability as well. He was an extraordinary character. All of that doesn't overlay that he was a very brilliant man.

PRIME MINISTER WILSON'S RESIGNATION IN 1976

Joe Haines The Queen knew before most of them. He told her in the first part of December, he announced it on March 16, and he told her, finally, in December—this was after I'd worked out the timetable for his going.

But he didn't tell his colleagues—the last thing you should do is tell your colleagues if you're about to resign; if you're going to do that—apart from a horrid farewell—they're going to spend all their time squabbling to try and succeed you.

He'd had enough; it was as simple as that. He felt that his powers were failing, and I felt they were too—he was only fifty-nine.

He and I had an enormous argument one day, over his industrial policy and his wish to bring in a compulsory wages limit policy. We argued for a long time, and at the end of the argument, he said: "The trouble is, Joe, when old problems recur, I reach for the old solutions; I've got nothing [new] to offer."

That was the crucial thing; he felt that his mind wasn't as good as it had been—I certainly felt that, and so did one or two others who were close to him, like Bernard Donahue.[5] We felt that it was noble of him to recognize that and not cling to power.

Sir Michael Palliser Sadly, he had Alzheimer's disease in the end; he had a very sad end. But I remember at that time someone with whom I was working said: "It's extraordinary, really, when you think of all the brilliant people who were in the cabinet when Harold Wilson was prime minister." I said: "All I can tell you is that if you were able, as I am, to be a fly on the wall in a cabinet meeting, you wouldn't think it's extraordinary at all; he's got not just as powerful an intellect as any of them, but he's got a sense of how to manage them, and how to manage the cabinet, which I believe is better than any of the others would have. It's absolutely natural that he's there."

Anybody working for him was bound to have some reservations. But in terms of his intellect—his ability to grasp a problem with tremendous speed, what an extraordinary memory he had. He'd say: "I can't remember the page, but it's about three-quarters of the way down the right-hand column of a right-hand page; you'll find it in the speech I made on such and such a date." He had an incredible memory, which, again, made the Alzheimer's even sadder.

Michael Noakes Ben Pimlott [the biographer] came to see me—he wanted to talk to somebody who had painted the Queen. He'd also written about Harold Wilson, and I just happened to mention to him that when Wilson resigned, I was having a sitting with the Queen when it was announced, and I said: "That was a surprise, Ma'am."

And she said: "Well, it didn't actually surprise me because he'd told me eighteen months ago that he was going to come out at about this point," which I thought was interesting, because everybody thought he'd been caught with his hand in the till, or he was being blackmailed, or had got Alzheimer's and he'd seen the first mark of it.

Ben Pimlott said: "I would like to mention that in the book." And I said: "Well, we'll have to get permission because it was a conversation." We applied for permission and it went from Sandringham to the Palace, and then they came back and said that the Queen would have no objection to the conversation being mentioned.

But some fool in the publishing house—the presses were trembling, ready to go—took a blue pencil to it and said: "What's this painter person carrying on about?"

So they got it as me saying: "Gosh, Ma'am, that was a surprise!," and her saying: "Well, it didn't surprise me." Full stop.[6] And of course that, apart from being a pointless conversation, could be interpreted, really, as her saying: "Well, that old crook, I'm not surprised."

EDWARD HEATH

In 1970, following Prime Minister Wilson's first six years in office, the Conservatives were returned to power with Edward Heath as prime minister. An aloof, remote personality, Prime Minister Heath would serve until 1974.

A major political crisis erupted on the evening of February 28, 1974, when in a general election the Labour Party won the largest number of seats but failed to achieve a parliamentary majority.

For the next few days, the Queen, who had interrupted a visit to the Pacific, returning to London to await the election returns, and her advisers looked on as Prime Minister Edward Heath attempted to remain in office by striking a coalition deal with the Liberals, the small party led by Jeremy Thorpe, which held the balance of power.

The Queen's position, as spelled out by a key aide, was that the prime minister holds that office until he resigns.

Finally, on March 4, following the failure of intensive and exhaustive negotiations between Heath and Thorpe, the prime minister tendered his resignation, leaving the Queen with the option of inviting someone other than Heath or Labour Party leader Harold Wilson to form a government.

The Queen decided, however, to pursue constitutional safety, calling on Wilson to do so, resulting in some risk to Labour: while that party held the largest number of seats, its lack of a majority could result in defeat on a specific item of legislation, returning the Party to the situation extant on February 28.

The threat to Labour did not materialize as the Wilson government endured, winning a narrow majority the following October, in the second general election to take place in 1974.

Lord Armstrong Her role doesn't come into play unless and until the prime minister resigns. I lived through these days, so I remember them very well. On 1 March, there was the result of the election: no conclusive result, with the largest number of seats to the Labour Party; a large number of votes in the country to the Conservative Party—discussions with the Liberal Party.

She had no role during those days because the prime minister had not resigned; he was still the prime minister. I was keeping in very close touch with her private secretary about what was going on—I'm sure he was briefing her. There was no formal duty for her to perform.

Then Mr. Heath did resign. He advised her to send for Mr. Wilson. That was obviously the right thing to do: he [Wilson] was the largest party in the House, although he was a minority. The Conservatives, as it were, the official opposition. It was Heath's duty to advise. Even if he had not done so, I'm sure she would have sent for Mr. Wilson.

There is a more interesting issue really: the system is that after any general election, proceedings in the House of Commons start with the Queen's Speech, prepared by the new government, and that is debated in the House of Commons over a period of six working days. And at the end of that, there is a vote.

If that vote is a vote, technically speaking, on the address, in reply to the Queen's Speech, that vote is by custom a vote of confidence, so if the government loses it, then that raises serious issues. The government can't continue as it is; the prime minister has to be prepared to offer his resignation.

At that point, in my own view, and in those circumstances, if Mr. Wilson had brought forth his Queen's Speech and had lost the vote, he might have thought that he should advise the Queen to dissolve Parliament and have new elections.

There were those of us who thought that before the Queen accepted that advice, she would have been entitled to satisfy herself that the government couldn't be carried on by somebody else, at least for a time, in order not to have another set of elections three or four weeks after the one that had just happened, and in order not to put the country, and everybody else, to the expense of a second election.

The question never arose because Mr. Wilson won the debate, so his position as prime minister was confirmed, and the elections were put off until October of that year.

It was an issue I certainly discussed with Mr. Wilson, and with others, at the time. The view was taken that it was actually rather unlikely that Parliament would cause a loss of the vote because it was in the interest of nobody to have another election so soon, so the expectation was that what did happen would happen.

But if it had gone the other way—there was a debatable point; the Queen couldn't have very well sent for Mr. Heath because he would have tried to form a government and failed.

Joe Haines Ted Heath decided to try to bring down the government on the Queen's Speech—at least that was our understanding, that he was going to vote against it. And so Wilson, by a circuitous route—which was the use of the Lord Chancellor—found out from the Queen's private secretary, and asked: "What would the Queen's attitude be if the government were defeated and Mr. Wilson were to ask for a dissolution?"

If they hadn't only been in office for a month, the Queen would have turned to another political leader. The Queen said that if Mr. Wilson asked for a dissolution, she would grant it, which would mean another general election.

And so the message was then conveyed to the Conservatives that in the event of a defeat there would be another general election. And so the vote wasn't pressed, because they did not want another general election.

Jeremy Thorpe What was quite interesting about the 1974 election was that Heath made it sound like I was involved in a cold canvass of Downing Street. In fact, I received a telephone call on the night before [Friday, March 1]. Number 10 rang me at my home. I was out and it was suggested to Number 10 that I would be back by 10:30 P.M., and they indicated they would call back. No call came through, so I decided to ring Number 10.

I went up to London the next morning. One point I made was the mathematics of the situation. I said: "As we sit here, I have half as many votes behind me as you have. But you've got 296 M.P.s and I've got fourteen." Heath turned to me and said: "Do you want a course in representation?" and then mentioned the existing formula. He's a strange man. Wilson was much warmer; Wilson was fun, too.

WAS THERE A MOMENT WHEN THE QUEEN
COULD HAVE INTERVENED?

Joe Haines No possibility. No question of it. That would be outrageously unconventional; she would have followed convention. Mr. Heath could not form a government. If Mr. Heath had told her that he could form a government with Jeremy Thorpe, then he would have carried on, because he doesn't resign—the problem of a new prime minister doesn't arise until the present one resigns—and he would not have needed to resign if he had been able to cobble together a coalition with the Liberals.

Had he done so, we would have exposed the story of his [Thorpe's] relationship with Norman Scott, and that would have made Thorpe's position in the government impossible, and would have made a deal with the Liberals impossible, and Heath would have gone a few days later, rather than the day he did.

Jeremy Thorpe It was a tricky situation. First of all, when it was dead-locked, she would have been bound to have allowed Heath the chance to form a coalition. And he would have been right to ask her. And if he had done his best to try, the Queen would have allowed him the power to do it.

But who knows? Was she entitled to impose the solution? In theory, yes, she could have done. Ultimately, she would have had the power.

It was a very fascinating time for one or two days.

Sir Adam Ridley [What happened in 1974 is] an illustration of something that may return to us, because—let's just cast our minds forward a bit—if it's the case that we have a major voting reform in this country and we have some kind of qualified proportional representation, what you then get is a situation which is much closer to, at the very least, Germany's, and, possibly, to some of the other countries, where you would have a polychrome House of Commons.

Under those circumstances, the role of the person who summons people suddenly becomes very, very important.

WHY WOULDN'T THE QUEEN GO ELSEWHERE?

Joe Haines Any Sovereign would act as the Queen did in 1974. There are academics who toy with theories, but the reality of politics is that she will always send for the leader of the largest party. And that's what she did in 1974, and there's no possibility of her going somewhere else; she's not like that—nor is any Monarch. The Monarch doesn't have power, in that sense; she has a formality of power, but it's not *real* power.

Lord Healey Her responsibility is clearly and strictly defined: she's got to choose the person who she's assured will get a majority in the House of Commons—it's as simple as that.

And this is where her private secretary and his contacts with Parliament and with the government played the key role, inevitably, in Wilson's coming to power: Heath didn't have a majority and Wilson did. And, of course, he increased it substantially as soon as he had the chance to hold another election.

Lord Rees As it did work out, it wasn't at all difficult for the Monarch to determine whom she should ask to attempt to form a government.

There could be, though, rare cases, situations where at the end of the day the Monarch may have some quite important constitutional role to play. The republicans, and the more left-wing members of the political spectrum, say this would be an outrage and that the monarchy should not have any power of choice in this—that it gives them too much political power.

In Britain, we're pragmatic people. So far, the system has worked.

Lord Armstrong She had a good relationship with Heath, an absolutely correct relationship.

Lord Healey I don't think Ted got on terribly well with the Palace: he's a very buttoned-up chap himself, whereas Wilson was very hale-fellow-well-met with everybody, including the monarchy.

JAMES CALLAGHAN

James Callaghan succeeded Prime Minister Wilson in 1976 and served until 1979 when the Labour Party was defeated following a very difficult time in Britain, which came to be known as "the Winter of Discontent."

Lord Healey Jim is much less opportunistic, but he actually had a very good, human relationship with the Queen; they quite liked one another.

WAS THE QUEEN'S GOOD RELATIONSHIP
WITH CALLAGHAN DUE IN PART TO HIS HAVING
BEEN A NAVY MAN?

Philip Ziegler I don't believe so. I believe it was much more personalities: Wilson and Callaghan made it clear that they were not merely [showing] the prime minister's respect for the Queen, but genuinely liked her—and it's very nice to be liked, and I think she felt a genuine warmth about it.

Lord McNally Jim Callaghan, if anything, the formative thing from him was that he came from a naval background, a service background, and had that sense of duty that made him feel [he was] "the Queen's first minister."

It's funny that it hit two Labour prime ministers. But that's partly also the fact that they also would be representing very much the views of their voters, as well, and there's certainly no republicanism, or hostility, to the Queen among the rank-and-file Labour voters, working-class voters, in this country. They no more than represented the kind of small "c" conservatism and the small "m" monarchism of the working class of the British people.

But Jim enjoyed his visits, and he would be highly protective of what went on, but still would coyly give you the impression that it was a very pleasant occasion—a very warm occasion.

MARGARET THATCHER

The succession in 1979 of Margaret Thatcher, a grocer's daughter who rose to become the Conservative Party leader in Parliament, was newsworthy in that she was the first-ever woman to serve as Britain's prime minister; that she was the longest-serving prime minister of the twentieth century; and that, during her tenure as prime minister, Mrs. Thatcher dealt with a series of crises in domestic and foreign affairs.

Among the domestic concerns Mrs. Thatcher dealt with were racial tensions; changes in Britain's economic structure; and the very complex issue of Northern Ireland, including IRA terrorism, which hit home for the Royal Family with the assassination in 1979 of Lord Louis Mountbatten, as well as for Mrs. Thatcher, who narrowly escaped death in an IRA bombing in Brighton in 1984, during a Conservative Party conference.

As for major foreign affairs concerns, Mrs. Thatcher played a leading role in the evolution of Zimbabwe-Rhodesia; the controversial issue of sanctions against South Africa; the Falklands War; and her period of office saw the U.S. invasion of Grenada and the beginning of the demise of the Soviet Union.

MRS. THATCHER'S RISE TO POWER

Joe Haines Gradually, she built up her reputation. Somebody sneered at her and called her the "iron lady," and the people liked it, the same as there was a famous hostile cartoon of Harold Macmillan, which described him as "Super Mac"; it went down a bomb; it was wonderful. So the myth of Thatcher was greater than the fact, but politics is all about myth.

Bishop Hugh Montefiore She struck a chord. She was a conviction politician—it's quite rare—and made no bones about it. She was a powerful woman, with a strong persona, and policies, which people felt when she came and the country was going to the dogs. And she said: this has got to stop! I'm going to take on the unions, and I'm not going to throttle industry anymore. And people respected her for that.

The trouble was that, in the end, the power went to her head and they got rid of her. But she re-asserted the individual—she over-asserted it—but still the reassertion struck a chord.

* * *

Mrs. Thatcher, as she was styled—reflecting her long, reputedly harmonious marriage to business executive Denis Thatcher—soon generated much controversy due to her rumored personality clash with the Queen: many of the prime minister's colleagues regarded the prime minister's manner to be abrasive and opinionated.

And despite the fact that implicit in the Queen's role as a constitutional Monarch there is the understanding that she may not comment publicly on any issue, there has been speculation that there existed major political differences between the Queen and Mrs. Thatcher.

THE QUEEN'S POLITICAL VIEWS

Sir Michael Palliser To the extent that she has a political concept, it's a Conservative one. I don't think that has affected in any way, or has colored, her relationships with prime ministers of whatever political complexion, or ideals, or personality.

I suspect that her relationship with them is affected more by how she feels personally about them—what the personal chemistry is like—than the political chemistry.

Joe Haines I doubt if she was in any ideological conflict really with Mrs. Thatcher, except that Thatcher—and Heath—didn't really think much of the Commonwealth, particularly, and would want to get rid of it, whereas Wilson was very much a Commonwealth man.

Thatcher was more of a revolutionary than many of the other prime ministers. I think that the Queen would have worried about the attitude when Thatcher said—she claimed that she had been misrepresented— "There's no such thing as society." That would have disturbed the Queen.

I think that there was not a happy relationship between them, not so much that it was ideological, because the Royal Family are, by nature, Conservative, but in her manner of doing things.

You could argue that Mrs. Thatcher wasn't a Conservative at all, in U.S. terms, "radical"—although in this country, "radical" is a *good* word, as is "liberal," which in the United States isn't either.

IS THE QUEEN "WET" POLITICALLY?

Lord Healey That was a phrase Maggie Thatcher used. The Queen had strong social feelings because, as a matter of fact, she's one of the few people from her class who, because of the nature of her job, actually sees poverty, and visits people who are suffering—who are out of work, or suffering some illness or other. I believe, inevitably, that has made her more sensitive than many dukes and duchesses would be.

Joe Haines "Wets" and homosexuals—Mrs. Thatcher didn't like either, but I don't think there was any rivalry woman-to-woman, because the Queen wouldn't accept any suggestion of rivalry; you cannot rival the Queen—any more than the Speaker of the House of Commons could.

Bishop Hugh Montefiore Mrs. Thatcher didn't *have* any social conscience—at least that was the impression she gave, whereas the Queen did, even though she lived in the lap of luxury. There are certain things she does—like the Maundy money[7]—a symbolic showing that shows that she cares for the poor.

Lady Longford I would think that there was quite a lot in that. I know that years and years ago, at the beginning of her career, I had a short chat with Thatcher at a garden party, and mentioned the word "compassion"—we were discussing something—and she immediately said: "I'm against compassion! It's so patronizing."

Sir Michael Palliser The Queen has a greater degree of what you might call "social conscience" than Margaret Thatcher has. Margaret Thatcher's social conscience is very tough: if you can't stand on your own two feet, you'll probably fall down, and that's just too bad.

I don't think that would be the Queen's view. She's probably seen much more of Britain than any of her ministers have—and not just the Commonwealth; she's traveled all over the country. And although her journeys to different parts of the country tend to be within a rather formal framework, she nonetheless is really quite perceptive enough to read between the lines of what's being said, and to see how things are.

Although she's a tough person—obviously she wouldn't have done all the things she's done if she weren't tough—I think she's also probably more compassionate than someone like Margaret Thatcher.

That would color the relationship—not beyond a certain point, because she inevitably has respect, if not liking, for her prime minister, who wouldn't be prime minister if he, or she, wasn't a pretty formidable personality.

Of course, there are exceptions always, but a prime minister is a significant person in the way that the Queen is a significant person. It's more: do you like that man, or that woman, or not? That she would never say, except, possibly, to Prince Philip. That, rather than her political attitude, may well have been why, in talking to Margaret Thatcher, at times she seemed to have rather "wet" reactions to what was being said.

Sir Adam Ridley Was she really, as it were, not sufficiently supportive of Mrs. T's policies? I've no evidence of it. I suspect that, in reality, like very many people at the time, there were moments when she felt that the government was driving too hard, too fast, and too toughly.

I suspect that, in retrospect, she would say: "I think that they were probably right on a lot of things, and in some cases not."

Jeremy Thorpe I strongly disapprove of Mrs. Thatcher's views on the community at large, and on the social responsibility of the state.

I think she's a bad woman. And I think she's also slightly unhinged. I think she has really gone a bit over the top—some of the things she said and did were simply awful—and I think the Queen certainly would not be going along with the "dry" policies of Mrs. Thatcher.

They were two ladies who did have respect for each other. But I feel that the Queen was more *au courant*.

WHAT WAS THE QUEEN'S RELATIONSHIP WITH
MRS. THATCHER REALLY LIKE?

Jeremy Thorpe I can tell you they had a very healthy respect for each other. But you know there was the time when they arrived [at a Commonwealth Heads of State Meeting in Lusaka, Zambia] in the same dress—someone had packed the same dress.

Mrs. Thatcher's secretary had said to the Queen's secretary, actually: "Let us know what she is going to wear so they don't clash."

Nelson Mandela We were aware of stories which showed that relations between the two were not so good. There is a story that at one function, they had similar dresses, and so Margaret Thatcher then said to Her Majesty: "I'm sorry about this. Next time we attend a function together, we must speak to each other to see what we are going to wear, instead of us wearing similar dresses." And Her Majesty says: "Her Majesty never notices what another person is wearing!" I thought that was beautiful.

Sir Michael Palliser [regarding the story that the Queen once kept Prime Minister Thatcher standing during one of their Tuesday evening audiences] It could be. I mean, you don't sit down with the Queen until *she* sits down. If she chose *not* to sit down, the prime minister wouldn't sit down.

Joe Haines The truth is that at one time, she was *not* on good relations with Mrs. Thatcher. Indeed, she told Harold Wilson that Thatcher had fainted at a Downing Street reception, which was indiscreet if she *had* really admired Thatcher.

Lord Healey Thatcher was a difficult person for anyone to have a normal relationship with because she was the boss, and she saw herself as such, and behaved as such; it had nothing to do with party politics.

Lord Wright I suspect that the Queen might have been as surprised as all of us were when Mrs. Thatcher stood on the steps of Downing Street and said: "*We* have become a grandmother!"

Nelson Mandela She really amazed me because I regarded her as a lady with no blood in her veins, just water. When she picked up the phone, she said: "Mr. Mandela, I don't know what you are going to talk to me about, but I must warn you; your program is too heavy for a man half your age! Cut it down! You are going to the United States. If you carry on the way you do, you won't come out alive!"

You know, I was so shocked because I did not expect her to have any sympathy with anybody. But when I came to the real topic of why I phoned her, she was totally different person. I said: "Mrs. Thatcher, it is now the beginning of June. I believe on the 26th of June you are going to move a resolution in Dublin, calling for the lifting of sanctions against South Africa. I will be seeing you on the Fourth of July. I would like you to postpone it until I brief you on sanctions."

"Mr. Mandela! I am totally against sanctions!"

I said: "No, Mrs. Thatcher, I don't want us to discuss their merits. We will discuss them when I see you on the Fourth of July."

"Sanctions are very disastrous to the economy of a country. You see, you and I know nothing about sanctions. You should talk to my husband, Denis, who knows more than you and I put together."

Sir Edward du Cann While the relationship was positive at the beginning, the Queen grew to like Mrs. Thatcher less and less as Mrs. Thatcher's role as prime minister continued. Margaret became more arrogant as the years went on, and that was troublesome to the Queen.

Sir Bernard Ingham We at the Downing Street press office did not have a regular relationship with the Palace; we didn't need to. The Palace had to handle its own press relations and did so entirely separate from us.

The only time that we came together was in 1986, when the *Sunday Times* did this article [claiming there were major differences in point of view between the Queen and Prime Minister Thatcher][8] and I was telephoned on the Saturday afternoon by a friend at the *Sunday Times* who was working on the story, to say: "What do you say to this?"

And I said: "Very simple. Since I don't discuss any relationship, I'm not doing anything; you won't get another word out of her. We are not going to say anything."

Now, it is fair to say that there was enormous speculation inside Number 10 as to how this story had arisen. But we did not say anything to the public. It is very true that I got onto the Palace and said: "Look, this is a story that's appearing. I don't know what *you're* saying, but I can tell you what we aren't saying." And that was it.

We did, after that—it may have been before—but during half my time at Number 10, every six months or so, the Number 10 press office and the Palace press office met for drinks in the early evening, just to say hello. That was all. But there was no formal working relationship at all, other than when there was a crisis on of the kind I've explained. But there were no proposals.

Peter Jay In some of her policies and attitudes, I think the Queen probably found her fairly unsympathetic. On the other hand, whatever she may have thought about Mrs. Thatcher's way of doing it, the Queen would have regarded Mrs. Thatcher as a pretty loyal upholder of the kingdom: she certainly was not anxious to devolve Britain to a United States of Europe.

Her style was to lecture people. It's possible she even lectured the Queen; she really hasn't any other way of communicating. It might not have been entirely congenial.

Claire Rayner That dreadful, dreadful Thatcher woman! We met Thatcher. Good heavens!

She didn't get on with the Queen. I recall one of my newspaper colleagues who covered the Royal Family saying that the Queen had come back from the country and was in a foul temper; they all knew this would happen when Thatcher had been there.

Frankly, it was one of the few times I found the concept of Queen quite endearing. I thought anyone who could dislike Thatcher can't be all bad.

Lord Archer There is in Margaret Thatcher's bedroom a picture of the Queen Mother, the Queen, and herself, together. The picture in her home would suggest to you her great admiration.

Winston Churchill I have no doubt that Mrs. Thatcher has the greatest respect for the Queen, as she does for the institution of the monarchy. It's easy for scribblers to write scenarios that there was inherent conflict between them. But I've got no reason to believe that that is true.

Sir Bernard Ingham A lot of people say that two women could never get on—two *powerful* women could never get on. That's just stupid, because Mrs. Thatcher would be absolutely determined to get on with the Queen; she'd be horrified at the thought that she couldn't.

Probably Mrs. Thatcher suffered in the eyes of the hangers-on at the Palace because she probably tried too hard and, because she was a woman, she was always a target for some kind of criticism. But mainly because she would be too serious, too businesslike, too uptight, too formal, too correct. And they would laugh at her.

There is some evidence from my time at Number 10 that some of the people around Mrs. Thatcher felt that the Queen's hangers-on—as distinct from the Queen—were disparaging. But not the Queen, I don't think.

You have to examine two events after Mrs. Thatcher had left. Mrs. Thatcher did not set out to demonstrate that she had a good relationship with the Queen. I did not cultivate that idea; I did not cultivate *any* idea about their relationship other than one of being businesslike—and constitutional.

It may be that previous prime ministers have set out to cultivate the impression that they got on brilliantly with the Queen—and, of course, there was tremendous temptation to do that in Labour times, because it was always felt that Labour prime ministers might find it more difficult to get on with the Queen than the Tories. I don't know why it should, but nonetheless you can see in the sort of class structure of Britain a reason for that argument.

Coming back to the time when Mrs. Thatcher left, the Queen very quickly bestowed upon her the honor of Companion of Honour. That is the clearest possible message to people to say: "You've got it all wrong. I have great personal respect for her. As my personal gift, I'm conferring this upon her." And indeed it did come very quickly. There has to be a vacancy before you can confer it. But nonetheless it had gone through.

The Queen didn't have to do it. And, second, she waited less than her predecessors for the honor of Lady of the Garter, which is another form of honoring our leading people. And she said to me that she got that rather quickly.

Sir Rex Hunt There's a lot of criticism that Margaret Thatcher was acting as if she were the Queen. I never got that impression: she was always extremely polite to the Queen. And, contrary to what a lot of people have said, I felt they got on well together, and I never heard the prime minister say a bad thing about the Queen.

Lady Mar I'm very biased: I don't see how *anyone* could love Margaret Thatcher.

She's a typical, small-town Baptist shopkeeper's daughter—narrow-minded. Her foreign policy was fine, but her domestic policy was absolutely appalling.

I'll give you an example of what she was like: there was a chap, a minister in her cabinet, who had a beard. Margaret said she didn't like beards, so the man shaved his beard off at her behest.

Yehuda Avner At the end of the meal [during a state visit to Britain by the then-German president Richard von Weizsäcker], the Queen made a toast to the president of Germany, and the German Anthem was sounded by the musicians in the gallery. The words were different, but the tune ["Deutschland Über Alles," the Nazi Anthem] was the same.

I could not stand up. That was one of the most extraordinary experiences of my life: the body wanted to rise and the spirit did not let it. Everybody was standing to the German National Anthem; I felt an extraordinary sense of Jewish history on my shoulders: this was not Yehuda Avner; this was an ambassador of *Israel* who could not rise to those musical notes.

After the dinner was over, in the chamber where we were having coffee, cigars, and brandy, I went up to von Weizsäcker and introduced myself, and told him what had happened, and he nodded, and he said: "I understand, I understand."

I did not realize that Margaret Thatcher was two steps behind me. Then—by this time she was calling me Yehuda; I always called her prime minister—she said: "Yehuda, you did well to apologize to the president"—these were her words—"Think of it like this: here you are in the Queen's home, who is hosting the president of Germany."

John Grigg They were very different characters and until Margaret Thatcher became prime minister, the Queen had always been dealing with men—and all considerably older than herself. They tended to eat out of her hand, and were rather dazzled by it. They didn't exercise their right to make suggestions to her, which would have been helpful. They were just pleased to be there, and they passed the time of day in a rather lackadaisical way.

When Margaret Thatcher came along, it was very different. She was the same age and the same gender. And although certainly a strong monarchist—there's no question about that—Margaret Thatcher was a strong woman. Her values and the Queen's values in many other respects were different.

Philip Ziegler The Queen is quintessentially a consensus animal: her ideal prime minister is one who avoids head-on confrontations with anyone; who avoids extremes; who conducts the affairs of the nation in a quiet and decorous way—which is not at all Mrs. Thatcher.

And I believe it caused severe disquiet to the Queen that she was adopting social policies which the Queen held to be divisive and were likely to be damaging to the framework of the nation.

The Queen also took immensely seriously her role as head of the Commonwealth and believed that the Commonwealth was an important and potentially far more important unit, and that Mrs. Thatcher was totally indifferent to it.

Lord Younger Mrs. Thatcher never said to me: "Oh God! I'm having a hell of a lot of trouble with the Queen." And as I was the defense secretary, she would have done. She would have said to me: "Can you explain this better so as I can explain it to the Queen." But she never did.

Lady Longford It's always said she didn't get on with Thatcher. I believe that. They just didn't click; it was a personality difference; it wasn't what Mrs. Thatcher said, or believed, because, in fact, I think the Queen would have agreed with most of the things she did.

She may have thought she overdid it and set up differences in the country: after all, the Queen's job as head of state is to unite the country, so she wouldn't be pleased if her task was made more difficult. And I believe she felt Thatcher made her task more difficult. So that was a rational reason for not getting on so well with her.

Sir Rex Hunt I feel very sorry for our monarchy; our press are the first to go at them. Our media are far worse than the American media: if they can stir anything up, they will. They sell papers by having *bad* news, not good news. They have a headline: "Who Is Our Queen: Margaret, Baroness Thatcher, or Elizabeth II?" They love that sort of thing. That's why you hear such a lot of bad reporting about the monarchy.

Sir Malcolm Rifkind She's a very sensitive woman, Margaret Thatcher, and people might not realize this sometimes—when it comes to protocol.

I'll give you a small, indicative example: when I was minister of defense—she was no longer prime minister—we were at some grand reception. I was chatting with her, and then the announcement came that they wanted us to go in to dinner. Quite properly, I said to her to go in front of me. And she stopped me and said: "No, no, no. You are a minister of the Crown; I am no longer. You must go first." I was a young whipper-snapper as far as she was concerned, but because I was a minister and she was not, she insisted on me going first.

Now multiply that dozens of times for her relationship with the Queen.

TONY BLAIR

Mrs. Thatcher's successor, John Major, was no more born to wealth and privilege than she had been. There the similarity ended, as he was considered to be mild-mannered. As prime minister he would serve two terms until the Conservatives were defeated in 1997. During the second campaign, Mrs. Thatcher declined to endorse him.

Tony Blair had brought the Labour Party to a more centrist position. He also brought public relations savvy and an air of youth to his office—the latter image enhanced no doubt when, in May 2000, Mrs. Blair, a barrister, gave birth to the Blairs' fourth child, Leo. Tony Blair was still prime minister when the first edition of this book was published.

* * *

Jeremy Thorpe Blair has modernized the monarchy extensively; he's done a good job. I would think their relations were very good.

Winston Churchill "Cool Britannia"—excuse my language—is crap! The people don't go for it and even Mr. Blair seems to have let it pass.

On the other hand, they're not doing what they ought to do in terms, for instance, of making sure there's a proper celebration of the Queen Mother's Centenary. Not a penny of public money is being provided for that. Of course, if we had a presidential system, the sky would be the limit!

One of the arguments trotted out by the republicans is that the Royal Family costs a lot of money. A wonderful case in point was that the Queen had traveled to Australia as a first-class passenger on a British Airways scheduled flight.

The prime minister took one jet to Portugal, the Foreign Secretary took another, and the Chancellor of the Exchequer took a third, all private aircraft, at the taxpayers' expense! And they don't seem to think this is strange.

But if the Queen had gone in a plane of the Royal Flight, questions would have been asked in Parliament about the extravagance. Who do these people think they're fooling?

Eric Moonman Tony Blair has made a real effort to try and understand, and interpret and, I think, they get on quite well.

He's an attractive personality. I don't say she feels the same way about him as Queen Victoria did about Disraeli—she's probably saying that he talks too much.

But the age range has something to do with it; it's the power of the personality rather than the power of authority, I think.

Lady Mar One of the problems in our government at the moment—and it's been said in the House of Commons, and the subject we're [the House of Lords is] debating today—is that we've got a "presidential" government at the moment, without the controls that the U.S. president has.

Lord McNally There have been stories of him giving advice to the Palace on areas of communications and public relations. And, certainly, he was decisive in getting them down from Balmoral, which was important, because in the week after Diana's death they so badly misjudged the national mood. That was the only time, in my knowledge, that you actually felt a national displeasure aimed at the Queen herself—a national displeasure in a way which really put the monarchy on the line.

I suspect that his relationship will be in the Wilson-Callaghan mold—rather sympathetic, rather close.

Philip Ziegler The idea that Blair is a kind of manipulator, using the tragedy [of Princess Diana's death in 1997] with the Queen, would be fairly nonsensical: the Queen is perfectly capable of looking after herself and is not easily used.

I would doubt whether Blair particularly wanted to. I think he had appalling problems after the death of the Princess of Wales: Tony Blair felt that things had gone badly wrong and that they ought to come in and take advice.

And on the whole, so far as I know, which is very limited indeed, the Palace appreciated Blair's advice, and thought it was good advice, and appreciated his motives and the fact that he wanted to take an interest and help.

Larry Adler He is the easiest person to talk to of any of the prime ministers. I've met several. I first met Tony Blair on the night that John Smith, who was then the head of the Labour Party, made what we did not know was his last speech: the next morning he was dead. But I shared a table with Tony Blair and we got on very well indeed.

When he became prime minister, I sent him three little mouth organs for his children. And he wrote me back a handwritten letter and said: "P.S. Could you send me a fourth for my wife?"

Lady Mar You have to remember that the British people never vote *for* something; they only vote *against* it. And they'd had enough of the Tories.

CHAPTER 11

The Monarch as Defender of the Faith

THE ACT OF settlement of 1701 states that only Protestant descendants of Princess Sophia, a granddaughter of King James I,[1] are eligible to succeed to the Throne.

The Act of Settlement was confirmed in 1707 by the Act of Union, which brought Scotland into the London Parliament. And in 1931, the Statute of Westminster was enacted, stipulating, among other things, that the succession may only be amended by common consent of all of the member-nations of the Commonwealth over which the British Sovereign actually reigns.

* * *

Canon Paul Oestreicher "Defender of the Faith," which is what is written on the coins, is not a bad term. It is actually what the Pope gave a King[2]— who mightily abused it.

I don't object to that title very much; I would just like to broaden it to all faiths. "Defender of the Faith" simply means you're not ruling over the Church; you're safeguarding its right to be the Church. In that sense, "Defender of the Faith" is a good title.

It's the *other* title—"Head of the Church of England"—that I object to. It's not the one we've defined on the coins, "Supreme Governor," because she's not, in practice, the "Supreme Governor," so she shouldn't be called the "Supreme Governor." It is a fiction.

I think she would be quite glad to be rid of that title because she knows she makes no attempt to be the Supreme Governor of the Church of England.

In fact, not even constitutionally does she do any supreme governing. It is pure fiction, whereas King Henry VIII really was: he—and the Kings that succeeded him—ruled the Church. Without any question.

And it's a damaging fiction, because it gives the general public—and people from other nations—the idea that the Queen of England runs the Church of England.

Frankly, the non-Anglican Christians in this country, be they Roman Catholic, or Protestant—Presbyterian, or Methodist, or Baptist, you name it—used to be most irritated by this; they used to be angry with the Church of England for having this prerogative of influence and status.

Those days are gone. Most Free Church leaders nowadays say: "It's an amusing fiction; we know the Church of England doesn't abuse this power." They'd like to see it go, but they're not going to make a fuss about it.

Duke of Norfolk She's Supreme Governor of the Church of England; she takes that very seriously.

At the Reformation, when the Elizabethan Settlement was—Elizabeth was 1558 to 1603—there were some very definite laws passed after Mary, "Bloody Mary," who was a Catholic, and they established the Church of England as it is now. And it was treason to say Mass, or to go to Mass, or to believe in the Pope.

And the Queen was made "Supreme Governor." The Archbishop of Canterbury was the senior spiritual man, but the Queen was the senior lay person. And, of course, if the Church got disestablished, the Queen would cease being the Supreme Governor, I suppose.

Bishop Hugh Montefiore The actual symbol of royalty is profoundly religious—a firmly religious concept: she is given authority from God, symbolized by the Archbishop of Canterbury at the Coronation, and she hands that authority to those elected by the people to govern on her behalf, which she exercises herself—the higher authority is a human being, which is very difficult for the family as a whole.

People get this wrong about the Queen being "Defender of the Faith." Yes, she has the title, but as a constitutional title. I don't think most people realize where it came from: it was given by the Pope to Henry VIII. It was removed, naturally, and then the government reinstituted it, but the Queen discharges her function for the Church of England through her first minister and, therefore, the title "Defender of the Faith" really means that she is head of the country—defends the faith through the Establishment; she is not defending the faith.

She is a bit troubled by the secularism, but that's not her role. The role of the "Defender of the Faith" is really an act of the Supreme Governor of the Church of England. She doesn't govern the Church of England; insofar as it's governed, it's governed by the appointment of bishops from the first minister.

Fr. Michael Seed There are tremendous advantages for keeping things as they are—that the Queen is Governor of the Church of England, and that the Church of England stays as the state Church.

I'm on the side of that; I would rather keep that as it is because if you remove that, then there will be a void where religion in terms of the nation would be just thrown out the window. So I'm quite happy to leave the Monarch as the Governor of the Church of England, and to leave the Church of England where it is in its place in society. So I don't see much point in changing things.

I'm very happy with it because it means that we gain benefits from it. For example, some Catholic schools will receive funding from the government, as Church of England schools do. We receive the same funding, so we can have religious schools—you could have Jewish schools, you could have Muslim schools, Catholic schools, and so on, mainly because the nation has got a Christian Church actually within the structure of society.

So there are tremendous advantages in keeping the *status quo* of the presence of the Christian group in the Parliament—we have Anglican bishops in the House of Lords. It's very helpful for others, and we benefit, so I'm certainly not for changing things at all. And I would rather keep the Church of England as it is, and the Queen's role in that.

Sadly, I think, it is inevitable that it's going to change, the way the House of Lords is being reformed—it's radically been reformed. It's gone; what we've had for eight or nine hundred years is gone forever, so it's quite possible that in the signing of the bill anything could happen and the Anglican bishops could be thrown out tomorrow; the Church of England could be disestablished tomorrow, easily, by decree.

Archdeacon George Austin The Church of England is the established Church: everybody has the right to be married in a parish church, and buried, so you actually have a relationship.

When I was a vicar of a large parish, I met all sorts of people through burials and marriages whom I wouldn't have met otherwise.

Fr. Michael Seed The Cardinal [the late Cardinal Basil Hume], I think, had a tremendous effect on the Royal Family because number one, he epitomized to the country—not just to the Royal Family—the kind, perfect gentleman. And he was impeccable in his behavior and his language. And he was immensely charming.

And yet he wasn't even English! It was funny: his mother was French and his father was a Scottish Anglican. But he had this charm and I think the members of the Royal Family looked at him as, in a sense, the spiritual leader of the country—as everybody did.

It was never, ever, his intention to undermine the Archbishop of Canterbury—there were three archbishops of Canterbury during his tenure. But if you were to ask ordinary people who was the practical spiritual leader of the country, you would find it would be the Cardinal.

And that became very obvious to the Royal Family. The Queen used to call him "my Cardinal," and it was a term of great affection—there was tremendous affection between them, and mutual respect. He just drew affection from anyone, whether you were the Queen or a homeless person.

And in a very funny way, even though he didn't mean it, even he, probably, in a negative sense contributed to: Well, why do we need a Church of England? What can they do?

No Catholic bishop has a voice in the nation—he can't go to the House of Lords. But twenty-five Anglican bishops can go in there every day if they want, but they haven't really created very much; nobody remembers what was said.

And yet, Cardinal Hume was invited to go to Parliament to speak at *their* invitation. And it was incredible! They all came out of the woodwork to hear him, hundreds of them.

Lord Steel Her Majesty is not dogmatic in her faith, nor does she put up with some of the wilder fantasies of Christian denominations. A regular church-goer who never misses a Sunday service, in her role as Defender of the Faith, she stood by her principles when dealing with the issue of her sister Margaret's love affair with the divorced Group Captain Peter Townsend, but it was very tricky for her.

Lady Greenfield Her Majesty is a Monarch of deep faith. Her relationship with the United Kingdom's Jewish community, contrary to that totally misleading idea that the British monarchy is racist, is very warm. That notion of royal racism has not been my experience, nor that of my colleagues.

As for Prince Philip, he was interested in inter-faith dialogue and established a program in Windsor Great Park for precisely that purpose. While Philip had a great interest in technology, at the same time he possessed a deep religious faith; one does not exclude the other and he held both, side by side.

Bishop Nicholas Baines Her Majesty's faith, which was instilled in childhood, is clearly personal.

THE MECHANISM FOR APPOINTING BISHOPS

Duke of Norfolk In things like the appointment of bishops, where the prime minister recommends to the Queen, she could easily say: "No. I want somebody else"—and probably does.

The Church of England is all so muddled up with the Elizabethan Settlement, and that's got amended. And now the Church of England itself—the bishops of the Church of England—meet, recommend two or three bishops to the prime minister, who decides which will become the next Archbishop of Canterbury, or Archbishop of York, or something, and the Queen implements it.

Bishop Hugh Montefiore What happens is that the patronage secretary and the archbishop's secretary visit the diocese—visit all the chief people in the diocese, the mayor, and lots of other people, and get their views. There is then a commission of the Church of England, which, after consultation, decides upon two names, and these names are sent to the prime minister.

If they wish, they can put a priority; they don't have to. The prime minister chooses a man and the Queen rubber-stamps it, although she could really have the power, if she didn't like him, if she had strong views against a person, properly, she could inform the prime minister.

And if the prime minister didn't like either of the men—as happened for the first time [in 1997], with the See of Liverpool, after the retirement of the bishop of Liverpool—he asked for two more. The Church has the choice; the prime minister has the selection.

Canon Paul Oestreicher The fact that she does that constitutionally is a scandal of a different kind because the prime minister reserves the right to veto who should be the bishops of the Church. That's a political decision, of course, because prime ministers now have power. That is scandalous. And wrong.

Now prime ministers very seldom abuse their power, and sometimes because they've got it, might even do something that does the Church some good. The Church chooses two candidates for every bishopric that becomes vacant—it's entirely a Church choice; the state is not involved.

But in order to maintain the fiction that the state can make a choice, two names are sent to the prime minister, and the prime minister has the right to choose the second person, as well as the first. And sometimes the prime minister—in fact he did it twice—chooses the second name rather than the first, whereas it is known that the first name is the one which the Church would prefer—that the second name is another name that the Church has also put forward, therefore it is acceptable to the Church.

Now it was thought until now that the prime minister didn't have the obligation to choose either of them—he could send both names back and say: "Send me two more names; I don't like either of these." But it was always thought this would never happen.

But Tony Blair has proved us wrong on the [...] Liverpool story. Tony Blair sent back both names and said: "I'm not happy with either of these names. Start again. Send me two more." Now that proves in a way that the state has power it should not have.

In fact, I don't think Tony Blair's actually abusing his power, but using it quite intelligently because the Church sent two names which were really inadequate to the job and Tony Blair's advisers said to him: "Look, these names are just not good enough. We need somebody better for Liverpool. The last bishop of Liverpool was a great man; we want somebody like that."

Paradoxically, he shouldn't have had that power—and I still maintain that he shouldn't have had it—but he used it well. That's one of the ironies of history.

Now the Queen wasn't involved *at all*. The Queen has to sign all legislation in Britain, but she has no choice—she has no say in what's in the government law. And so in the way in which she signs legislation, she also puts her signature on for the appointment of bishops. But she doesn't *choose* bishops—she has no voice in it—and, as far as I'm aware, she doesn't even try to influence it. She could get on the telephone and say to the prime minister: "I don't like that name. What do you think?" But it is not something she has ever done.

She will certainly be consulted on the staff of Westminster Abbey, and Windsor, and the Chapel Royal—those are royal chapels. It's okay, if you have a court, that there should be a few churches that are, basically, court churches. I have no objection to that at all.

I would expect the Queen to take an interest in the most important of those positions, the dean of Westminster; he is the direct servant of the Queen, not subject to the bishop of London, although the church is in the diocese of London.

That's okay with me. I don't like the Queen of England with political influence, but she doesn't try to abuse it—there is no criticism of the Queen involved there.

Archdeacon George Austin I once asked—in fact on the first occasion I was very rude—we had a briefing meeting for new members and I said: "One thing I'm not clear on. What happens after the two names leave the commission and go to the prime minister and the Queen?" The prime minister decides which of the names he will take to the Queen, and I was told very firmly: "That is none of your business."

That's the problem area—the Church then loses control of who they want. And, of course, if a secretary has his own strong feelings then he's going to favor the one over the other. And if the one identified as the favorite candidate got through to the last two, you could be sure that he would get it. It's not the people who are corrupt; it's the system that's corrupt.

When the system was first introduced in 1978, we tried to get it so that just one name went forward. And we were told from the prime minister's office: "No, the Queen must always have a choice; you can't just present her with one name."

The prime minister says: "This is the one we want," and her choice is that, because that's what happens under constitutional monarchy.

ARE OTHER DENOMINATIONS THREATENED BY THE EXISTENCE OF THE ESTABLISHED CHURCH?

Canon Paul Oestreicher I'm sometimes a little surprised that they're not more irritated by it than they are, but they don't seem to be.

I believe they've recognized it to be like the Beefeaters at the Tower of London in their funny uniforms marching up and down carrying ancient weapons. It's part of a tradition that's doing nobody any harm.

But one would also say that it's not doing anybody any good and, therefore, on balance it would be a good thing if it was removed. But again, no Free Church leader is going to campaign for it to be removed because that would look like anti-Anglicanism. And the churches at the leadership level work so well together: the Church of England doesn't pull influence and power.

I often say that the illustration is that Church of England is only established in *England*; it is not the established Church in any other part of the United Kingdom. It used to be the established Church in Wales. The Welsh decided to disestablish it in the 1920s.

Now, what has changed in Wales? Almost nothing. The Church in Wales lives, though fundamentally differently to the Church of England: it doesn't have an established Monarch at its head; a Welsh bishop is appointed by a Welsh synod—the government has no voice in it, whatever.

Is it a better church? No. In other words, this ceremonial stuff makes very little difference. So that while the Welsh Church did the right thing in disestablishing, I'm not naive enough to think by doing it, it made a better nation. It didn't. It is a side issue.

Bishop Hugh Montefiore First of all, you really must dispossess yourself of the fact that this is a very multi-faith country. There are minority religions. If you actually look at the statistics, there are one million Muslims out of 53 million people; if you look at the Jews, sadly, it's a small number; the Hindus aren't that large, about one percent.[3] So when we talk about a multi-faith society, we must take care what we are talking about.

Now, admittedly, there aren't a large number of deeply practicing Christians; there are a very large number of people who are attached to Christianity without being practicing Christians.

It's getting clear what we mean about being a multi-faith society: certainly there are these minorities, and by-and-large they are in favor—the Chief Rabbi has said he is in favor—of the establishment of the Church of England, for its religious values are at the heart of the nation.

THE ROMAN CATHOLIC COMMUNITY

Lady Longford Actually, I was a member of the Church of England[4] for a very short time, but it didn't make me feel any closer to the monarchy.

Fr. Michael Seed I didn't really become Catholic until I was eighteen. Prior to that, my family were Salvation Army and Independent Baptists, so I came from a very reformed evangelical tradition—the opposite of Catholicism.

I went to an Anglican church for a few months when I was seventeen. But I wasn't conscious that the Queen was the Governor of the Church of England; it didn't have a great impact whether the Queen was involved in the Church, or not. Even now, it's more of a courtesy; it isn't practical.

Cardinal Cahal Daly A lot of weight should be attached to the fact that the Queen, constitutionally, has to be a Protestant. Naturally, that presents difficulties for Catholics. And it so happens, for historical reasons, that [Ulster] Catholics are, in the great majority, nationalists—they see themselves as *Irish*.

And for the same historical reasons, the Unionist community is almost entirely Protestant—at least sociologically Protestant, politically Protestant—and they would identify with the Queen, not only as the Queen of England, but as the symbol of Protestantism—of the Protestant faith—and the head of the main Protestant Church in Britain, the Anglican Church, because the Unionist population would be in considerable part composed of people who four hundred years ago came in as part of the plantation policy of the British governments at the time, the British Monarchs of the time, to Anglicize and Protestantize the population here in Northern Ireland at a time before any white person existed in the United States of America. So their descendants are Irish now, but they don't see themselves as Irish; they see themselves as British—and they see the Queen as the Defender of their Faith.

Duke of Norfolk I happen to be a Roman Catholic, and I'm a senior Duke. And when the Queen came to Vespers—Evensong—at Westminster Cathedral, that was something we were all very pleased about because after the 1688 revolution, when James II was so narrow-minded that William III kicked him out,[5] the Catholics were really in a very awkward position; you couldn't be an Army officer, or a Navy officer; you couldn't be an M.P., or take part in the House of Lords—you just couldn't go; you couldn't be Earl Marshal, until the Catholic emancipation in 1829.

And now we have Catholic emancipation. But we were not fully recognized, even though we were fighting everywhere, as being totally part of England till really in this present reign.

Fr. Michael Seed Westminster Cathedral was opened in 1903. Before that time we had little churches. There were no Catholic bishops until 1850. In fact, on May 4 of [2000], we're celebrating 150 years of the restoration of the Catholic hierarchy.

But Catholic emancipation was in 1829—a very important historical date. It was in 1829 that Catholics could become normal: they were
allowed to vote; they could go to university, they could join the Army and
become officers; they could become M.P.s.

But Catholic churches—not just Catholic churches, but all non-conformist churches—were not allowed to be built in public; they had to be built
behind roads, in little streets—they couldn't be seen. Westminster Cathedral,
of course, wasn't built as it is today. The piazza is only twenty-five years old.
Victoria Street connected, so Westminster Cathedral was hidden behind—
you couldn't see it. Anything that wasn't Anglican couldn't be prominent.

We weren't allowed to have church bells either. Some of our Catholic
M.P.s are very funny. They keep saying that we want to repeal—bell-ring-
ers peal bells—the act and allow Catholics to ring their bells. It's a joke;
we ring our bells every Sunday, but it's a silly law, because the Catholic
Church is not there to ring bells. But to this day, officially, the police could
come and arrest us.

The Catholic clergy are not allowed to even dress as clergy on the
street, according to the law. We have silly little laws. There are probably
hundreds of eccentric little laws which are in need of repealing. Many of
them are never used; this country is full of eccentric little things.

I believe all of these things, inevitably, are going to change. And the
Royal Family, I think, would be the first to want to change them. The
reason they don't is that they're worried about the Northern Ireland situation—that it would cause problems.

It could happen that it could be removed any day. It will be ultimately.
And the Anglicans themselves want it removed, so we don't have much to
do about that. The Catholic Church doesn't actually need to do anything
about any of this; it's inevitably going to change.

The main person who is actually requesting that at the moment is the
Archbishop of York, David Hope, and he has publicly demanded the Act
[of Settlement] be removed. And he's also started to ask questions about
the disestablishment of the Church of England.

THE MUSLIM COMMUNITY

S. A. Pasha I came from India, which is predominantly Hindu; there
the Muslims are a minority. Here, in this country, Christians are the
majority and we are a minority, so I found no particular problem to
accommodate myself.

On the contrary, I thought—as a Muslim, as a religious person—we are much closer to Christians than to Hindus, because in our book, the Holy Koran, there is mention of Jesus and Moses. This is a predominantly Christian community; there is a Jewish community. These are very close to the Islamic religion; we have common tradition coming from the prophet Abraham.

Robert Lacey The Muslim faith is the one faith in the world which in its own view incorporates Christianity, and acknowledges Christianity, and treats Christians as People of the Book. And the Muslim community that's entered Britain [...] is, on the whole, the most respected of all the immigrant communities by the white Establishment as being hard-working and its members are very influential in the media.

Bishop Hugh Montefiore I was very touched when I was in Birmingham and they [leaders of the Muslim community] used to come to me and say: "Look, will you see that our nurses can wear pajamas [referring to the style of the Muslim dress for women]?"

They look to me, as an Establishment religious person, to help them—and by-and-large that's true. Of course, there are some fanatics—there are always people who wish to do away with the Establishment.

THE JEWISH COMMUNITY

Rabbi Dr. Sidney Brichto (1936–2009), executive vice-president and director, the Union of Liberal and Progressive Synagogues (Reform movement), 1964–89; served as director, Joseph Levy Charitable Foundation As a group in this country the Jews are more integrated into the community than they are in the United States of America. In the United States of America, the Jews, as a group, felt very secure in the country. While a very small minority—2.9 percent—they have lobbies and power, and so forth; as *individuals* in America, there was a lot of discrimination—golf clubs, and this and that—ghettoization; Jews sticking together.

In this country, as a group, while they had their recognized institutions—the Board of Deputies, the Chief Rabbinate, and the like—they felt very shy of using their muscular power in terms of the influence they had.

But as *individuals*, they were totally acceptable; Jews, as individuals, I found, were much more secure—to the extent that any minority has been accepted. Britain is a very eccentric country and encourages eccentricities; it enjoys its individuality as a country of individuals and, therefore, Jews are able to take advantage of that appreciation of individuals. The anti-Semitism is *there*, but it's based on: what do they really believe? What are they really thinking? Fears of difference—and of jealousy. [...]

Eric Moonman Historically, there are two organizations that have earned the right to be identified, or recognized, by the monarchy: one is the Anglo-Jewish Association, and the other is the Board of Deputies.

The Anglo-Jewish Association 150 years ago got some letters—a formal warrant—which meant that they could be consulted. But, more importantly, the Board of Deputies, which began 240 years ago, is the central body of the Jewish community with constituents—the people come together once a month; it's unique; it's around the world—they come together representing either a Jewish organization or their synagogue.

Now there isn't anything like this in the United States; American Jews have come over and said: "Gosh, we ought to do something like that."

We meet with the prime minister on a regular basis, and with the foreign minister on a regular basis. And on any legislation the Home Secretary might wish to put forward, he would consult us.

Sometimes it's more than consultation: we might be pre-emptive in handling arrangements. We're a secular body, we're not a religious body—that's the Chief Rabbi's business. But we're also, I suppose you could say, a political body, so we're more likely to get involved with the politics of legislation than we would with the Royal Family.

DOES THE QUEEN REALLY HAVE A SENSE OF THE PRESENCE OF THE JEWISH COMMUNITY?

Eric Moonman A lot of people would say she does. She does things, and so on. And somebody might say: "Wasn't she good? She wrote something or other."

I don't think so. And I think that's something that reflects on two levels: one is the advisers that she deals with are people who themselves don't know what the sense of the Jewish community is.

And us—that we didn't really go beyond perhaps the protocols, or the formal relationships. Maybe we've been too shy.

We can do the right things: we can meet with her at remembrance parades; we can send her congratulations when there's been some [royal] function. And when there was Charles's fiftieth birthday, the Chief Rabbi was invited [...]

But I believe it's a challenge for the minority people with the monarchy, because part of the dealing with the image of the monarchy in the last five years is that it's still changing—it's trying its best to change.

The public perception is also changing—at a faster rate. The public expectation is also changing at a faster rate, so the monarchy is not the most desirable product, if you're going to use marketing terms.

In a way, this is also why, perhaps, people haven't tried to get close to them; they will get close if they can get them to the function, because it's still a very important thing, if you're putting on a function. But I don't believe that she [the Queen] has got that close—and I believe the fault's on both sides.

Larry Adler I never heard anything even remotely anti-Jewish from any member of the Royal Family. But there is still very much of an anti-Jewish feeling—there are still golf clubs a Jew can't get into.

THE HINDU COMMUNITY

Professor S. N. (Surender Nath) Bharadwaj (1918–2009), president of Arya Phatinidhi Sabha, U.K., and Arya Samaj, London I came here thirty-eight years ago [in 1962]—as in everybody's case—for economic reasons because my family was growing; everything was costly; the salaries we got in India did not give us financial security. So in search of a better financial position, we came here.

When I came here, you would not find Indian priests to perform these ceremonies, and there were many Hindu marriages which used to be performed in churches.

Because I knew the rituals, I started doing them. And so I became popular; they had a priest in me—an honorary priest. And they just pushed me and I became their president.

They call us on UNESCO Day for International Peace and I go to Westminster Abbey and participate in the prayers. All of the different societies go there.

The Royal Family come to our community. The Queen has been here many times, and her husband, and other members of the Royal Family if she cannot come. But in the most important functions she has been here.

There is no direct dialogue with the Queen. There are some societies who are financially more secure than our society, like the Swami Narayan Society. They are big people, very rich people, so many times they call in the members of the Royal Family—Prince Charles has been there, and he makes a statement there, appreciating all that.

CHAPTER 12

The Queen's Travels Abroad

T HE QUEEN HAS traveled extensively throughout her reign, both to fulfill her constitutional duties by undertaking state visits, and privately, often making the latter trips in pursuit of her interest in thoroughbred horse racing.

While the Queen has traveled widely in the Commonwealth of Nations, these trips will be discussed in the context of her role as head of the Commonwealth in Part Three. Beginning with the Commonwealth tour of 1953–54—undertaken as Princess Elizabeth, on behalf of the ailing King George VI, but interrupted by his death—she has, to date, traveled to many non-Commonwealth nations as well.

They include the United States, Mexico, Chile, and Brazil in the Americas; Austria, Belgium, Denmark, France, the then-Federal Republic of Germany, and then Germany, Hungary, Italy (including a visit to the Vatican), Luxembourg, the Netherlands, Norway, Portugal, Spain, Sweden, Switzerland, Turkey, and the then-Yugoslavia, in Europe; Hong Kong, Indonesia, Japan, the People's Republic of China, South Korea, and Thailand, in Southeast Asia; Iran, and Nepal, in Asia; Algeria, Ethiopia, Liberia, Morocco, Senegal, Sudan, and Tunisia, in Africa; and Bahrain, Jordan, Kuwait, Oman, Qatar, Saudi Arabia, and the United Arab Emirates, in the Middle East.

THE PLANNING OF THE QUEEN'S STATE VISITS

Sir Michael Palliser The Queen makes two state visits outwards in any given year. Each country has a different system and, basically, she does what the country she's visiting would like her to do—subject to her being

happy with what's been [planned]. Of course, there's a good deal of negotiation about that.

Stephen Day There is a planning machinery which brings together the
Palace and the Foreign Office, a Royal Visits Committee, which looks ahead,
first of all, obviously, at the Queen's priority of visits, the balance between
Commonwealth and non-Commonwealth—which country should be in
which priority—and then, once the Queen's visits are established, [visits of]
the Prince of Wales and other members of the Royal Family.

Clearly there are bids coming in from all over the world—ambassadors
who need a royal visit; or that the British need; or something is happening; or because a head of state is aggrieved that they haven't been visited.

All of these things are juggled, every so often, by a very senior committee, bringing together the Foreign Office and the Palace, where they make
recommendations to the Queen—clearly, the Queen's own staff advising
her, giving her views, and discussing it with her, and her courtiers. There
is a balance between all the considerations.

I had been involved in planning the Queen's launch [in the Arab
world]. I had seen all the things that had gone right; seen all the things
that had gone wrong. I did a planning paper about a year before the
event, and I said: "Above all, on this tour, we need a 'scapegoat'"—that
was the word I used—"things will go wrong; taking the brunt of the
inter-reaction, particularly with the protocols of the different countries,
smoothing things over, keeping calm, requires the presence of a minister."

Sir Michael Palliser In good Whitehall tradition, there was a committee.
If you were thinking of a visit say in 1990, the Royal Visits Committee
would be planning it in 1988, possibly even at the end of 1987, and there
would be discussion of which countries the Queen had been to; which
she hadn't been to; which were the most suitable politically, commercially,
whatever, for her to go to; and which *she* would like to go to. The Palace
would have a view: which did the Palace think would be useful for her
to go to?

You'd have that sort of discussion and a program would then be
mapped out, for first the Foreign Secretary and prime minister to mull
over, and then for it to be put to the Queen. And if she didn't like it, or
whatever, well, she would say.

Lord Howe The occasions would arise when I accompanied the Queen on
her state visits. As the Foreign Secretary I was with her on all state visits to

countries other than Commonwealth countries; in the Commonwealth countries, she was advised by the secretary of state in that country. For example, I went with her on her state visit to China. I went to Nepal but when she went on to Australia and New Zealand, she left us behind in Nepal. We went back to the United Kingdom; she went on with her trip.

She would be accompanied by the Australian and New Zealand Foreign Secretaries. There was always a minister with her to deal with issues that might arise during the course of the visit.

It is quite a difficult operation because you're not meant to use a state visit as an occasion for promoting ordinary business with the country you are visiting. She has courtesy calls on the president, or the Monarch, of that country, and I would sit in with her on these.

But it would be improper for me, for example, visiting China, to use that as an opportunity to advance the Hong Kong negotiations, which we had substantially completed two years before in that case. And the discussions she would have with the other head of state would normally be a matter of courtesies.

On the way out, when I traveled with her on the royal plane and talked through some of these things, she would express her interest and offer her knowledge. She might, for example, express a personal opinion to me.

It sounds rather blasé but, I think, as one of her Foreign Secretaries said: "It's the Foreign Secretary who gets really tired."

The wear and tear is reduced to the minimum because conditions are extremely good: the timetable for the Monarch's tours is always relatively relaxed, and, obviously, there are interesting aspects of almost every visit. So I never got the impression that she was ever bored there. Like any job, however, there are peaks and troughs.

THE QUEEN'S STATE VISIT TO CHINA, 1986

Lord Howe The state visit to China was the first visit by a British head of state ever—and it was sensitive due to the Hong Kong affair.

By September 1984, we had completed negotiating the Declaration of Hong Kong, so that a major stumbling block had been cleared out of the way. And at the end of these discussions Deng Xiaoping[1] said to me: "We have decided that we can trust the British government and the British people. We would like to extend an invitation to Her Majesty to visit this country on a state visit as a mark of achievement, and talk to your prime minister, Mrs. Thatcher, if she would also sign the Hong Kong Declaration."

The prime minister went to sign it in December 1984, and that was a full, working heads of government meeting—a full, working political meeting—in which Margaret Thatcher met all the senior people in the Chinese government, and talked through all the things working prime ministers would talk through with each other.

When the Queen went two years later, again, I was at the meetings she held with the different Chinese leaders, particularly one with the president. You see, in mainland China he is a relatively nominal figure—he is the head of state rather than the head of government.

And that was the discussion which was broadly concerned with generalities, so it was quite different from the Margaret Thatcher meeting. There was concern with: How is the Hong Kong legislature going? And are we keeping on track on the Joint Declaration? And are we going to do all that trade with each other?—all the usual agenda things.

So the one visit had content of a working, day-to-day kind; the other visit had content of a much more symbolic value. The Queen went to Peking [Beijing], Xi'an, Kunming, Canton [Guangzhou], Shanghai, and Hong Kong—a very extensive visit.

On the Shanghai leg of it, for example, we drove through the city, back to the royal yacht, *Britannia*. One had literally millions of Chinese dying to see the Queen. It was a strong manifestation of a new bridging relationship between the countries; it was very important.

And then Deng Xiaoping, representing the Chinese government, came to dinner on the royal yacht. So it was a very moving occasion as well.

THE DUKE OF EDINBURGH'S COMMENT IN CHINA

Lord Howe That [the worldwide uproar over the "slitty eyes" comment] was due very much to the pursuit of the whole of the British press corps, who were yearning for that kind of thing to happen. And as soon as it had happened, it was immediately released around the world the following morning; it was all over the press.

We had a great discussion between myself and the Palace private secretary, Bill Heseltine, as to what we should do about it. And there were really two things: one, we had to discover how far the Chinese government were offended; and then two, to talk to the Duke of Edinburgh and see how far he realized that he had committed a minor gaffe. And we decided, frankly, that Heseltine should speak to the Duke, and I should speak to the Chinese foreign minister.

As soon as I spoke to the chairman, he responded entirely to our advantage. We all knew he's a very sincere man—there's no doubt about that—and it never got in the Chinese press. So it was an event of no international significance.

Anson Chan The Duke has been known from time to time to make headline remarks. It is not anything most people pay a great deal of attention to. He's probably not viewed much at all here [in Hong Kong], to be quite frank. As he's viewed, he's viewed as the husband of the Queen.

Michael Parker My God! Amongst his own people like us, or people who worked for him, he was a delight to work for: he was funny, direct—it's marvelous to work for somebody who's direct, absolutely fantastic.

If at any time he got steamed up about something, he would apologize like anything. He would say: "Well I'm sorry about that. I was wrong; you were right." He was marvelous at that. We all loved him dearly. And we still do.

THE QUEEN'S STATE VISIT TO THE GULF REGION, 1979

Stephen Day I was involved in the whole question of planning a royal visit to the Gulf in the 1970s. There are a lot of rulers in that part of the world, and they all wanted to be the first, and there was the particular problem of the Shah [Mohamed Reza Pahlevi]. And on top of that, there was the tradition, naturally, that if she was to go there, she would invite him to come back, and there are only two or three state visits a year, and the problem of how to slot in the Arab rulers.

In the mid-1970s, we in the Middle East Department bit on the bullet and we set out the parameters for the Queen's first visit to the Gulf: we decided to which countries she would go; how she would balance it against the Shah of Iran, and how it would be done on board *Britannia*.

And never, in our worst nightmare, did we imagine that on the eve of her departure, the Shah would be deposed. But he was. But she went ahead with the visit, regardless, obviously omitting Iran, and it was a very great success, that she began by visiting Kuwait.

She had been concerned about this issue. She had met various Arab rulers back in the United Kingdom—but she had not gone there [the Gulf] herself. She had been, I believe unfortunately, ill-advised by certain people about the complexities of the Arab world, the difficulty for a woman, a female

Sovereign, to go to that part of the world. All the questions of etiquette that the so-called experts on the Arab world had a graveness about are actually far less important and I believe she had been over-advised on the complexities.

When she went there, she discovered, as it worked out, that actually it was an extremely hospitable part of the world, and it went swimmingly.

The brief [for Kuwait], which was based on a reconnaissance that had been carried out before, was that she would enter a Rolls-Royce belonging to the Emir with the Emir *and* an interpreter, because somebody had reported that the Emir spoke no English.

In practice, the Emir jumped into a Cadillac with the Queen. The door was slammed on the interpreter, who was scratching at the window, trying to get in. The Emir raced off, leaving behind the rest of the cortege. And the Queen was startled that the Emir spoke excellent English. That's a perfect example of the planning issue in parts of the world where traditions are very different.

THE QUEEN'S STATE VISIT TO SPAIN, 1988

Lord Howe When we went to Seville, we went to the Library of the Americas. It's a marvelous library and topography place, and the Spaniards had laid on a very interesting exhibition of books and maps there.

And the feeling that was unexpected was a sense of humor: all the maps of the Falklands and of the West Indies, some had the British [names] on them, some had the Spanish on them, so you had one of the "Falklands," and the next of the "Malvinas."

It was a slightly humorous insight into the problem. I think it also showed the Queen had been offered "Hispaniola" as a sop to Gibraltar—that sort of thing—and the Queen was obviously very interested to see all this. So there was a lot of real enjoyment in the visit.

THE QUEEN'S STATE VISITS TO THE U.S.,
1957, 1959, AND 1983

The Queen has a special feeling for the United States, which she has visited many times, both on state occasions and privately.

* * *

Lady Angela Oswald That is very true. And she gets that from the Queen Mother—I believe the Queen Mother felt this very strongly from the visit she made just before the war—and the Queen Mother always feels it. And there always has been that special relationship between Britain and the United States.

John Eisenhower They call that room [in the White House, used by the Queen in 1957] the "Queen's Room." My wife and I stayed in there when Dad was first inaugurated. But then Mother decided it was too dignified for us, so we were banished after that first time.

The Queen was very uptight. She was pretty frank, you know, in conversations with her. There was no kicking off of shoes. It was not a "down home" thing at all. The second floor of the White House is an elongated thing, and so when the two families were at the two ends of the hall, they were not exactly on top of each other. I don't mean to say it was an unfriendly atmosphere at all.

Now, in December 1957, Dad had a minor stroke. He went to Paris by way of the United Kingdom. We were going down the street in London— it was after Suez—and Dad expected a cool reception, and the streets were so full of people that Macmillan said: "If you ever had a state visit now, this would upstage it."

The British are terrible—my God, they were so concerned about the status of their Royal Family. They wanted to avoid having a state visit being an anti-climax after this [President Eisenhower's reception in London].

* * *

A source informed us that during the Queen's visit to Canada in 1959 with President Eisenhower to inaugurate the St. Lawrence Seaway: "The Queen was upset about what they had done to her up in Canada: they had worked her to death. And she was complaining about it. She was exhausted."

* * *

Michael Deaver The president asked me to take charge, and to be with the Queen when she was in California [during the Queen's state visit in 1983].

Prince Philip was very irritated, *constantly*, about the security—how unnecessary all the security was. For the president, you had to have control of all the vehicles and, of course, every time they moved, we treated it as if it were a presidential motorcade. And it drove him crazy. I don't know what it was about the American security that was so overdone. He made his comments in no uncertain terms on what he thought about it.

And then we had a terrible tragedy: three people were killed protecting him. That was the result of some deputy sheriff in Merced County getting all excited, and racing to meet the motorcade.

Sir Gordon Jewkes The Queen likes the United States. She had a very warm welcome during her visit to California. When three of her Secret Service escort got killed—it had happened on my territory—she took it very personally: she sent a very warm tribute to the families on that occasion.

FORMALITY ON A STATE VISIT

Raymond G. H. Seitz When the Queen went to visit a housing project,[2] there was a big black woman there. The Queen walked through the door and she just walked up and hugged the Queen. In the U.S. this was great; it was warm, it was nice, there was nothing phoney about it at all. In Britain one just does not *do* that!

Michael Deaver The first night on *Britannia*, I had come in from Washington, so I was on Eastern time. They had "steamed" [traveled], as they put it—they had been on a leisurely cruise to Mexico—and they were in the same time zone and had been for some time.

So when the first night was over with—they had dinner onboard the *Britannia* for guests of the City of San Diego, and they had other guests who had come on for Beating Retreat—it was 11:30 and they'd pulled up the gangplank, and everybody relaxed and had a drink, so I got a drink.

And then I realized how tired I was, and I just slipped off, down to my little room. I had a valet assigned to me who had laid everything out, and I had just gotten into bed and turned the lights off when there was a knock on the door. It was the Queen's private secretary. And he said: "Michael, are you in there?" And I said: "Yes." And he said: "Are you in *bed*?" And I said: "Yes." And he said: "Well, one shouldn't retire before the Queen." And I said: "I'm terribly sorry"—it was midnight—"It's three A.M. my time, and I know we have a full day tomorrow, and I didn't think I would be missed." And he said: "Well, you ought to remember that." And I said: "I certainly will."

And the next morning, getting up, when the valet came in and asked did I want a shower, or a bath, he said: "I've laid your clothes out." He had laid out a pair of slacks, and a sweater, and a sports shirt, and loafers. I said: "I don't think this will do. We have to go someplace on some official function." And he said: "No. This is only for *breakfast*."

I wasn't used to all this. I went to the salon, where the men were all eating, and in their casual clothes, and then they all came back down and got dressed for whatever the function was. I thought it was a terrible waste of time.

THE REAGANS' WEDDING ANNIVERSARY
ON BOARD *BRITANNIA*

Michael Deaver It was just wonderful. We'd had a beautiful state dinner at the Legion of Honor in San Francisco, which was much more elegant, of course, than the dinner in Los Angeles that we had on the 20th Century Fox lot, which was kind of a "Night in Hollywood," with Sinatra, and George Burns, and all of that crowd. And the Queen loved that.

But the dinner in San Francisco was where she made her official state dinner remarks, and she was in her tiara, and beaded dress, and there were limousines, and all that, and it was very glitzy.

I think she was very excited about that trip. We tried to put together an interesting, representative schedule so that she could see various parts of California, and various kinds of people in California. She obviously got to meet a lot of public officials, but she also got to meet the "royalty" of Hollywood at that dinner we gave there.

But the drive from San Francisco to Yosemite was very interesting because we went into rural communities and there would be pockets of farmers and their kids standing out there with flowers, and signs which said: "Hello, Elizabeth." It was very, very wonderful.

They [the Queen's staff] were really superb, maybe a little insular. It was always the Crown moving around. You never got the sense that they had a feel for California as someplace different. I mean, none of them "went" to California in the ten days, whereas another visitor might want to go and get a Planet Hollywood tee-shirt, or something like that.

We had *Air Force One* for traveling until the Queen left the United States and I remember the Duchess of Grafton getting on the phone and calling home—she thought that was wonderful. And the Queen called Princess Margaret from the airplane.

* * *

In May 1991, during the administration of President George Bush, the Queen became the first British head of state to address a joint session of the United States Congress.

The day before the Queen's milestone address, however, she was inadvertently hidden from public view during the first public ceremony of her state visit.

* * *

Raymond G. H. Seitz This was the arrival ceremony at the White House. The president is a very tall man. [He] stood there at the podium. And then the president stepped back, and the Queen went to the podium. Of course, somebody should have been there to adjust it.

But the photograph the next day on the front page of the *Washington Post* showed the podium, the Queen's eyes, and her hat! And that was *all* you saw. From where I was standing, I didn't quite see it, but anybody who had been at the front—where all the photographers were—could see it. It was a great picture, very funny—one of the protocol-area things that go wrong.

But the best part of it was the next day. The Queen was to address the joint session of Congress, and she showed up and she began with something like the line: "I hope you can all see me." It just brought the house down, for three reasons: it was funny; it was from the Queen; and the audience were all politicians—they'd been there before.

It was a wonderful connecting first line. But saying that first line was the subject of discussion between the Queen, [her] private secretary Robert Fellowes, and David Airlee for at least three hours—the whole morning: "Should I do it? Shouldn't I do it?"

The last thing she wanted was to say something that would be a lead balloon, not a joke. She risked it. I don't know who suggested the line. In fact, Robert Fellowes probably suggested the line. While *she* was amused, she wondered whether it was funny. It wasn't a debate; it was a discussion among them. She did it and it was such a great hit. That tells you something about her; it showed her good instincts.

In virtually any Commonwealth country it would not have gone down well; the joke wouldn't have been gotten.

I just keep coming back to the Queen's professionalism: her job is to go on a state visit. When she gets into her hotel suite and kicks off her shoes, I doubt whether she says: "Jesus Christ, did you get a load of that guy?"

THE QUEEN'S OVERSEAS VISITS TO HORSE RACES
AND STABLES

Lady Angela Oswald If you go back a bit, Monarchs always have had an interest in racing. In the case of Queen Victoria, she was a very successful breeder of race horses. But most people if you asked them would be absolutely amazed, whereas everyone knows that Queen Elizabeth is passionately interested in both horses and dogs.

When you have races—and in the case of the dogs, the Queen goes herself to the field trials—it's something where she can compete on level terms with anybody else, and nobody can turn around and say: "She only won that because she's the Queen." If her horse wins, it wins on its merits, and she bred it and it won.

Sir Michael Oswald The Queen goes to races, and sometimes to a stud farm, in places like Australia, New Zealand, Hong Kong—all over the world. The more that racing becomes internationalized, the more the Queen takes an interest in it all. But she has always known what's going on on race tracks all over the world.

The Queen has won races in the United States. She started in one, and she was third in another big race just the other day. She's won one race at Arlington Park; she's been in races at Saratoga. She's won races in France, Germany, Italy, Spain.

Now, as for scale—and this is quite an important point—for 150 to 200 years, racing in Western Europe was dominated at any one time by about twenty major owner-breeders, the principal racing countries being England, Ireland, France, Germany, and Italy.

Then things became much more internationalized with the advent of the wide-bodied, pressurized jet, and you had all the American-bred horses coming to race over here, starting in the late 1960s and early 1970s, when the competition hotted up.

And then, when the price of oil went rocketing up in the mid-1970s, the Arabs came in—in a very big way indeed.

Most of the old families had more or less either gone out of it altogether, or were reduced to an almost token involvement, with half a dozen brood mares and fewer than ten horses in training. The very few kept going—there have been one or two newcomers, but not too many—so the Queen is completely eclipsed in size: from being a big fish in the pond she is now a minnow compared to these people.

However, somebody produced some statistics [...] on the 1999 racing season, and it turned out that the Queen had the highest percentage of winners, including the Arabs.

But the Queen is, invariably, very much smaller. And she cannot inject huge sums of money into it because there is a certain sort of public relations issue here.

So there are many advantages in being Queen, but there's a big downside and that is that you've got to keep one eye on what people say and think. Even if they've got the wrong end of the stick altogether.

And because of her work, she is unable to race or, indeed, visit stud farms anything like as often as she would want to do. Her diary program is worked out roughly about a year in advance in some cases, and in some detail about six months in advance.

You can't tell when a horse is going to run. So there are certain major race meetings which are kept clear in her diary, for instance, the [Epsom] Derby and Royal Ascot. And probably we'd get one or two where she can go and race which are very easy for her to get to, and where an attempt will be made, if possible, to have some runners for her.

Otherwise, it's a matter of luck whether the Queen can go to see a horse. Nowadays, of course, it's made easier with the Racing Channel and Sky, so the Queen can watch it. And every race is now taped, so she can actually see later what every single horse does.

But it's not quite the same thing as being there. So you have to act as eyes and ears and try and tell the Queen what people are up to, and what they're saying, or thinking.

Lady Angela Oswald When the Queen paid her first visit to Kentucky, she took me as a lady-in-waiting—I was actually lady-in-waiting to the Queen Mother but the Queen borrowed me on that occasion—while she was in Kentucky because we knew our way around—we'd been out quite a lot, visiting the mares every year and so that was very nice for me.

Sir Michael Oswald The Queen was staying with Will [William F.] Farish— Will Farish's grandfather started Humble Oil—[at his farm in Kentucky, Lane's End] so that she could have a look for the first time at the stallions at one of the big stud farms out there, and she very kindly took us along.

We flew in an Air Force plane and when we got to Lane's End, a beautiful place, it started to rain—the sky got dark—and the Queen said she wanted to go for a walk outside. And there was absolute horror. In her party were Secret Service agents and they said: "Do you really want to go for a walk in *this*!"

And the Queen put on a head scarf and wrapped it around her head, and had on a raincoat, and these chaps were in some shock. But being good boys, there were a few volunteers to go on this trek, and they were absolutely horrified that anybody would go for a walk in the long grass in the rain!

But the Queen did. And she had a marvelous time, an absolutely wonderful, fabulous time. It was a private, informal visit—she's done it four times now—and she was able to meet all the people that mattered. Some came to lunch, some came to tea, and they talked about horses, and had a really, really good time.

But with her private secretary there all the time, there really wasn't any work that came up that wouldn't follow her, even on a trip like that. But most of it was fun and relaxation.

CHAPTER 13

Life at Court

FINANCING THE MONARCHY

COURTS, AND COURTIERS, have been mainstays of monarchies throughout history. And court life, with varying degrees of pomp and circumstance—among the most splendid being the British court, with its impressive castles and palaces—has been chronicled as far back as the reign of King Bridei of the Picts,[1] who maintained a court replete with a council, treasury, priests, slaves and messengers.

The monarchy is funded through three sources:

Firstly, the Sovereign Grant, which comes from a percentage of the profits of the Crown Estate revenue. Prior to April 2012 the Queen had received the Civil List for her expenses as head of state and head of the Commonwealth, which was again granted in exchange for the revenues of the Crown Estate, in addition to grants-in-aid from Parliament for upkeep of the royal palaces, and royal travel. Prince Philip and the Queen Mother had also received lesser amounts from the Civil List.

Secondly, the monarchy is funded by the Privy Purse, which provides income from the Duchy of Lancaster—a landed estate held in trust for the Sovereign since 1399—for both the Queen's public and private use.

And finally the Queen has her personal income, for her own expenses.

The Queen covers the expenses of the other royals, with the exception of Prince Charles, who derives his income from the annual net revenue of the Duchy of Cornwall.

While the Queen's income was for many years tax-free, in the wake of the fire that heavily damaged Windsor Castle in 1992, she has since 1993 paid personal and capital gains taxes, as well as on that portion of her Privy Purse allotment for personal expenses.

Prince Charles, who on the Queen's accession became the twenty-fourth Duke of Cornwall and is obligated to pass on the estate intact, pays a tax on his income from the Duchy.

While the Queen is extremely wealthy—estimates of her personal fortune range from £50 million to more than £400 million—it should be noted that the royal palaces, most of the art treasures in the Royal Collection, and the Crown Jewels are held by the Queen as Sovereign, and may not be disposed of, as they must be passed on to her successor.

* * *

Sir Oliver Wright The Monarch costs the taxpayer nothing. The reason is a deal struck in the nineteenth century, whereby the Queen, who is a very considerable property owner, gave these properties to the Treasury in return for what is known as the Civil List [which was replaced in 2012 with the Sovereign Grant]. They get enough to run the monarchy, but just because it comes out of the Treasury doesn't mean to say it is the taxpayers' money.

It is past generations of the Monarch's money that is now being used to finance the cost of the monarchy, so it is quite wrong to say that the upkeep of Buckingham Palace, the upkeep of Windsor Castle, costs the taxpayer money.

Lord Rees Obviously, she's got her private fortune—I don't think it's as big as the Getty fortune, or the Rockefeller fortune, but it's quite big. She has to maintain these palaces; she has to maintain a civil service of a kind—her private secretary and all that. They are not part of the Civil Service as properly defined; they are servants in the highest sense of the Crown. That costs a lot of money.

Sir Adam Ridley Basically people haven't the *faintest* idea what the Civil List is, and some newspaper picks out one item, and says: "300,000 to the Queen's Corgis," which probably turns out to be a load of rubbish. But it makes a good headline and sells the paper.

As to the operation of what one might call the various bits of property and sources of income and authority owned by the monarchy, you've got the Duchy of Cornwall; you've got the Crown Estate; you've got the Queen's own personal property; you have the Duchy of Lancaster; and so on, and probably things I haven't even thought of. They tend not to get written about, or understood, very much.

[...] I've never seen a serious campaign, let alone a sustained campaign, saying: "This is outrageous!" You get specific things occasionally: "Isn't

it a shame that it isn't possible to walk through some of the great parks?"
Or: "Is the Monarch going to permit the right to roam across her estates
at Balmoral?"

Joe Haines The Civil List was dealt with [by 10 Downing Street during
Prime Minister Harold Wilson's tenure] without great difficulty. There
were always a few Labour M.P.s who objected to it. The revenue that the
government got from the Queen's estates was greater than the amount
given back in the Civil List.

Some people would sooner turn her into a bag lady in Piccadilly Circus.
But the Queen is a wealthy woman in her own right: the Civil List was
never really excessive, and the income that the government got—particularly from the estates and the Duke of Cornwall, the Duchy of Lancaster
and all that—was quite substantial.

Lord Healey The argument will always be: which things should be put on
the Civil List? How much money should she have to do the things which
are her responsibility, rather than those of the taxpayer? But there's never
been a very big argument about that, even when there have been changes
in the Civil List. I believe it works very well.

Sir Michael Oswald There is a very, very clear, and carefully observed,
dividing line between what is public, or state, money and what is private.
And in racing, and indeed in any other equestrian sport, it has strictly
come out of an absolutely, totally private pocket—even down to the last
postage stamp and telephone call.

We have to be whiter than white. If some Member of Parliament got
on his hind legs and tried to say that public money was being spent on the
Queen's racing, we'd have to be able to shoot that one down. And it's no
good cutting one corner, you've got to be absolutely whiter than white in
this thing.

Although every penny involved in the Queen's racing is strictly
private—not a penny of public money involved—nonetheless, because
perhaps people don't want to understand that, it would look wrong, or
they think it would look wrong, if the Queen bought something very
expensive. It would raise a lot of questions and it would attract attention
from outside the racing world. And, generally speaking, you don't do that.

If on rare occasions the Queen is going to spend a significant
amount of money, we will sell something which would more or less
balance that, so if they say: "Where does she get the money to do that?"

We can say: "We sold …" Otherwise, somebody will find something to complain about.

THE QUEEN'S HOUSEHOLD

Robert Lacey The old-fashioned word for them is "courtiers." In fact, they are a highly skilled professional cadre of largely men, but now a few women, who have sprung up and developed in the course of the twentieth century to mediate and work the levers of operational, constitutional monarchy.

Many of them hold ancient titles but their jobs have been modified in various ways. But the private secretaries themselves only date back to the last years of Queen Victoria.

Of course, the private secretaries are dealing with the government of the day, but also keeping very close contact with the leaders of the other political parties.

And then you have the most recent group of officials of all, the press secretaries, and the press officers, mimicking the world as a whole, where public relations media specialists have become a semi-professional group prepared to deal with communications problems, as lawyers deal with legal problems, and as accountants deal with money problems.

So the press secretaries play that sort of role in the Palace, as the people who make the Royal Family's image.

And also, it's about charity work and philanthropy, and it's based on the idea that all these limousines and helicopters that go out from Buckingham Palace every day, ferrying all sorts of senior and junior members of the Royal Family—like Princess Alexandra, and the Duchess of Kent—to hospitals, work that is conventionally thought of as a chore, is actually more and more the very heart of what the Royal Family is about, and that these semi-holy figures, to use religious metaphor, are going out to meet ordinary people in the community and bless their activities and say: "You are observed, and you are good, and you are praised." This is really what the function of the Royal Family is.

Every healthy society has a very important element of self-help and philanthropy, and that is what the British Royal Family nourish, and maintain, in a very healthy way. And, of course, they are besieged every day with requests to come and open this, attend that.

These requests are filtered by the courtiers, who are specialists in it, until it is decided what, not just the Queen and Prince Philip, but every junior member of the Royal Family should attend, and bless, and treat as important.

Sir David Iser Smith, KCVO, AO, official secretary to the governor-general of Australia, 1973–90; attached to the Royal Household, Buckingham Palace, 1975; secretary, Order of Australia, 1975–90 I've always wondered and marveled at the way they sift through all the information, whichever of the three private secretaries was available. I knew roughly that there was a division of responsibility to try and spread the load, and one knew who to talk to on a particular issue.

But there would be an occasion when you were in and the one was out on duty with the Queen on an engagement and one of the others was in the office at the Palace, and you needed to talk to somebody.

I could talk to whichever of the three of them was currently available, even if I had been dealing with one of his colleagues, because they obviously have some miraculous system of keeping each other informed on all sorts of things.

Certainly Bill Heseltine was the Australian expert.

Lord Weatherill The Vice-Chamberlain writes a daily message to the Queen, even today, of up to five hundred words. You can say anything you like, and it is not seen by anyone. It goes down to Windsor Castle and is put into the archives.

I gave her what I would call a "private eye" message, which was purely personal—I was able to give her the gossip—and I've preserved [copies] amongst my papers.

Then, after some eighteen months, I was promoted to Comptroller of the Royal Household and, in parliamentary terms, if you've got a new job and are rather overwhelmed, they don't say: "Poor chap, it's a big responsibility, really, and the fellow wasn't up to it."

So I wrote to the Queen's private secretary of the day, Martin Charteris, and said I knew the Queen had a great deal to read and I'd got this newer, and onerous, responsibility; would it be a good idea if I did it [wrote to her] once a week?

I preserved his reply:

Dear Jack,

I've been told by the Queen to reply to your letter and say that this is one of the parliamentary papers Her Majesty enjoys reading *daily*.

Sincerely yours,
Martin

Lord Younger One of the keys, of course, to the British monarchy is the system of the Monarch's Household. When you go to see the Queen, whether it's official, or whether it's social, the first people you meet are the Household—the Queen's private secretary, and the Comptroller of the Household, and those sort of people.

There are quite a few of them, and they have medieval sort of titles, but they are an extremely important and effective "front of shop" for the monarchy.

They are extremely professional: every time you go there, it always appears that you're the *one* person the Household has been longing to see; they're so good at making you feel that you are really welcome. And they do it to absolutely everybody: I've seen them do it to people of all sorts—a trade unionist, coal miners, shopkeepers, everyone. They will come into the room and the Household will absolutely make them feel at ease. That's a very important part of the Queen's presentation of herself to the world.

Lady Angela Oswald With the Queen Mother you are in residence—you do it in two-week increments. The Queen Mother is the only one who still has her lady-in-waiting living in.

At my level, I'm called a "woman of the bedchamber," and we live in with the Queen Mother wherever she might be—either in Scotland or at Clarence House. But the Queen's ladies-in-waiting don't, on the whole, live in any more; they go in each day and do engagements. Obviously they would stay when the Queen was in Sandringham, but not when she was in London.

You could say it's a position of a mixture of a personal assistant and a companion. The role is slightly different with the Queen Mother in some senses, because she's on her own, so one's companionship is, perhaps, needed rather more. Whereas the Queen, of course, has the Duke of Edinburgh, and she moves around rather more.

You do the letters. The Queen, of course, has such an enormous post bag that all her letters are divided up: some go to her private secretary's office, and some go here, and some go there, and the ladies-in-waiting get various ones.

Whereas the Queen Mother's post bag is so much smaller—not the volume of the Queen's—anything that is addressed to the Queen Mother gets opened either by the Queen Mother herself, or by whichever one of us is doing our two-week increment.

There are a lot of different things—a lot of "fan mail," and there are a lot of people writing for help, because the Queen and the Queen Mother are great patrons of many organizations. And when people are desperate, they very often write here to see if help can be given.

And because the Royal Family has got so many interests in the different organizations, you can usually find one of them that they might be able to help in whatever the situation is.

Buckingham Palace and Clarence House are pretty separate. There are certain occasions when something is quite close to home, like the WI, the Women's Institute [countrywomen's clubs], and then the Sandringham WI, which was started by Queen Mary, which is very important in the Queen and the Queen Mother's lives. The Queen Mother is president of the Sandringham WI; she presides over the January meeting each year, and the Queen always goes too, and if Princess Margaret is there she would go too.

Every year the Sandringham WI would have a raffle. The Chairman of the Sandringham WI would write to the Queen Mother and the Queen, separately, to ask whether they would give a raffle prize. And they basically do. And the Prince of Wales has given one too. So with three raffles you can raise a lot of money.

You might have a glass decanter, or a clock, or a barometer, or sets of silver teaspoons, or something like the Prince of Wales's [place] mats for which he did paintings, and he, perhaps, would give a set of those.

They're not going to be things that would cost you hundreds of pounds if you bought them in a shop, but they would be something nice, of good quality. And they would have a little card saying that they are given by the Queen, or the Queen Mother. So people are very, very thrilled.

And you find that a raffle, a royal prize like that, would pre-sell the tickets far, far beyond what it would fetch if they just had an ordinary raffle.

Funnily enough, when we went to live at Sandringham, I carefully didn't join because I thought: well, it's for people who don't have quite enough to do with their time and I always had much too much to do with my time, and never enough time to do it in.

We lived at Sandringham for some years before I was made lady-in-waiting to the Queen Mother. And then one day, the Queen Mother said to me that I should join the WI. So I said: "No, Ma'am, I really don't have time."

And then a few weeks later, the Queen Mother said: "You know, Angie, you really *ought* to join the WI." So Michael said to me: "Well, you know where your duty lies."

So I then joined the WI. And, in fact, the Queen Mother was quite right because it meant that I met an awful lot of the older widows of the estate workers—the average age of a member of the [Sandringham] WI is about eighty, and there are younger ones too.

It meant that I was a great liaison to keep the Queen Mother informed as to who was ill, and who had fallen and broken their hip, and who was having their Diamond Wedding, people who I would not otherwise have met.

Vivien Noakes One thing I observed during the year is how much the Queen seems to enjoy the company of her ladies-in-waiting.

They're very important to her on her away days. When she's in her car, she arrives with her driver and her protection officer, and generally, the Duke of Edinburgh. If he's going on to another event, the lady-in-waiting will go in so that she will have some companionship for the next part of the journey.

And they do seem to be people she is very much at ease with—she's known all of them for years and they, I would say, would be her real friends, somebody like Lady Susan Hussey, who would be somebody that she considers a real friend. But there would be very few of them.

Michael Noakes Some of them are very nice; some of them are very remote. The Duchess of Grafton is very grand, very jolly and lovely, but she doesn't talk to us.

The senior protection officer is very chatty to us always, and he would sit in the front of that big Rolls-Royce, and when they would arrive somewhere, he would slip out, and stand; he'd open the door for the Queen, and he'd stand there on duty, and he'd turn his head, and he'd go— [gesturing in greeting]—which I thought was charming.

Sir David Smith The purpose of my stay in London [for six weeks in June and July of 1975] was the administration of the honors system and also in relation to the opening up of royal residences.

Sir John Kerr [the then-governor-general of Australia] suggested to me one day that instead of being constantly on the phone to talk to them about these things, that it would make a lot more sense to spend a few weeks on the spot. Well, I wasn't going to object to that.

When I reported to the Palace, they gave me, very apologetically, as my office, because office space was at a premium, the center room, the room that has the balcony that the Royal Family come out on and wave from [on ceremonial occasions]. That room behind the balcony was my office for six weeks. Bill Heseltine had told the Queen I was coming, and he said that she had thought it was "interesting."

As well as doing the meetings and appointments that had been set up for me, the Queen wanted me to be regarded as an extra member of the Household, and to accompany her, as a supernumerary private secretary, if you like, on all her public engagements. That was an additional, and unexpected honor, and gave me another insight into the operation of the public presentation of the monarchy.

I alternated between going with the Queen and her duty private secretary of the day, and the lady-in-waiting, and the equerry—I was the funny mug from Australia who wasn't wearing a bowler hat and wasn't carrying a furled umbrella—and I accompanied the Queen on some very wonderful occasions, including a magnificent night at Stratford for an anniversary performance of *Falstaff*.

The Queen's private secretary saw her daily—and sometimes more than once a day—because they would have to go and see her with the "boxes," and the paperwork, just as I would be in and out of the governor-general's study at Government House several times a day, and he'd be on the phone to me several times a day.

But the lady-in-waiting, and the equerry, and the supernumerary's duty, in the time I was there, was simply to be down at the side door when it was time to go, and wait for the Queen to come down and get into her car, and away we'd go.

And when we'd come back, she had a habit of always stopping in the hallway and reminiscing for a few minutes about where we'd just been, and what we had done, and whom she'd talked to—just to unwind. And then she'd pop on the lift and go up to the private apartments, and we'd go back to our office.

The Queen is a great observer of human character. It seemed to me that, first of all, it was just an opportunity to relax and unwind. But it's also part of her very special skill of treating the immediate Household as people with whom she wants to enjoy a very happy and relaxed relationship.

The alternative to what she does would be to come down, nod, and just get in the car, and when you come back, get out of the car, give you a nod, and disappear. That's not her style.

It's developing a rapport, and a relaxed relationship with the people who are physically the closest to you in your public duties, and on whom you rely for your public presentation, and that makes them feel that they are more than just employees, public servants. That they are, in fact, part of the team.

So it is very important that the people whose home life you are disrupting, and whose time on the job imposes great demands on them, should feel that it is appreciated.

LIFE IN A ROYAL RESIDENCE

The Court of Queen Elizabeth II is conducted in three official residences in the United Kingdom: the six-hundred-room Buckingham Palace, the London residence of British Monarchs since Queen Victoria's accession in 1837; Windsor Castle, approximately thirty miles west of London, built by William the Conqueror in the eleventh century and the world's largest inhabited castle, where the Queen often spends the weekend, as well as conducting certain official functions; and the Palace of Holyroodhouse, in Edinburgh, the Queen's official residence in Scotland, the present building dating from the seventeenth-century reign of Charles II.

In addition, the Queen owns two private residences: Sandringham House, in Norfolk, where since childhood she has spent many holidays, and where her father, King George, died in 1952; and Balmoral Castle, in the Scottish Highlands, Queen Victoria's retreat, where the Royal Family customarily vacations in the late summer.

* * *

John Eisenhower It was incredibly informal [at Balmoral Castle in 1946]. That was not expected. I was really taken aback by their procedures when you get there.

And the equerries had duty hours. The [then] Princess [Elizabeth] called out to one of them: "Peter! Peter!" and she gave some instruction to him. And he said: "I'm off duty, Ma'am."

Sir Michael Oswald The Queen by nature is essentially a countrywoman. I believe that if she wasn't Queen her choice would be that she would live in the country, if she could afford it, surrounded by horses and dogs. That's where she's happiest. She has a natural empathy with the countryside; I don't believe she's a town person at all.

A lot of ladies, for example, love big cities because of the bright lights and, above all, the shops. Now I can't imagine the Queen liking shopping; I can't imagine the Queen enjoying spending money in shops, or in restaurants. That's just not *her*.

Michael Noakes [At Buckingham Palace] the Queen started looking round. She said: "I must do something about these curtains." It's a Chinese drawing room—from the Pavilion at Brighton which I believe Queen Victoria brought back—so you can't get any old stuff stuck up.

[During a sitting for one of the Queen's official portraits] the Deputy Marshal of the Household arrived with a little swatch of material while I was laying out all my gear, and said: "The Queen said she wants to get the curtains reorganized in here," and laid it out. And then he said: "Do you think you could ask her to go through it?"

Well, I wasn't very keen, frankly, about losing sitting time for her choosing curtains. But I did say: "The Deputy Marshal of the Household came in, Ma'am, and he asked if you could have a look at the curtains."

And she obviously didn't do it because the next picture I went back for, which was four years later, the swatch was still lying on the sofa!

Anyway, the time came when the Queen did move herself to make the choice. And I found myself on my knees while she was holding these things up and saying: "Do you think that goes well? Does that go against the paper all right?"

At Sandringham, we had arranged that we would meet her at the kennels at ten o'clock in the morning. And at ten o'clock, we were there, on duty. And one of the equerry fellows came along and said: "There's been a change of plan, I'm afraid. Would it be all right if we do it at four o'clock this afternoon?"

The delay was a bit of a nuisance—this was in winter and the light was not very good. But you don't argue, of course, so we said: "Fine."

And again, we were on duty well before four o'clock, and a Land Rover came along, and we said: "God! It's *her*!" She was driving the thing, and she was wearing specs [eye glasses], and a head scarf, and an old waterproof coat, and waterproof leggings, and clogs. The difference between her when she was done up in her tiara and after a day's shooting was terrific.

Vivien Noakes It was very much unstuffy [at Sandringham]. It was helped in its unstuffiness by the presence of the dogs: the Queen has the most extraordinary rapport with dogs.

At Fotheringhay Castle[2] last summer—she does these garden parties— she was walking down in a space between two rows of people, and one of the people she stopped to talk to was blind and had a guide dog with him.

She was talking to him, and not talking to the dog. But as she talked to him, the dog came up and went right against her, and she was just stroking the top of its head and it was gazing up at her. It was the same thing we had seen in the kennels, where these dogs, who were working dogs, not lap dogs, were jumping up into her arms. They were thrilled to be with her.

It is said that when her car approaches, the dogs start barking before the cars arrive; they know she's coming.

Sir Malcolm Rifkind I've had two jobs in government which enabled me to see the Queen at firsthand; first of all when I was secretary of state in Scotland, and then when I became Foreign Secretary—whenever the Queen goes on a visit overseas, she is accompanied by the Foreign Secretary.

It's not true now because of the changes that have taken place, but until [2000] the Queen spent a whole week in Edinburgh, at Holyrood Palace, every year, quite apart from any incidental visits. And during that week, the secretary of state for Scotland became a temporary member of the Royal Household and had to be with the Queen throughout all her engagements. And I did that for three or four years.

It was extraordinary—like being a fly on the wall. It was quite a difficult experience because there are no written rules but there are hundreds of *unwritten* ones, which you absorb—a very curious mixture of formality and informality; obviously, during public engagements it's very formal.

But what I was most interested to find out was what happens when you get back to the Palace, or when you get back to wherever the Queen happens to be staying. How informal does it then become?

And the answer is: quite informal. She chats very informally with the Household about what has happened, about people she has met—she's got a marvelous sense of humor; she does very funny imitations.

But there is always a requirement to remember that she is the Queen and the rest of us aren't. For example, there is this story about Princess Anne—and she is very unstuffy; she's the most informal person you can think of—and somebody in her presence referred to "your mother," and the Princess Royal said: "I think you mean *the Queen*."

Even in the Palace in the morning, for example, when the Queen would come for the first time into a room where the private secretary, the equerry, and the lady-in-waiting were, the lady-in-waiting would curtsy and the men would be expected to bow—just a small bow, not a deep bow—as a mark of respect. So these protocol requirements are maintained even privately, even though the conversation might be much more informal.

What you don't have nowadays, you sometimes hear that if you're sitting next to the Queen, you're expected to wait until she opens the conversation. In practice, with the Household, that would not happen. I've sat next to her probably a dozen times and, during lunch, I might very well start the subject with her rather than wait for her to start it with me.

But she would always decide when she wanted to speak to the person on her left: I would keep speaking to her until *she* decided she wanted to speak to somebody else.

Michael Deaver They [the staff of the Queen's Household] were very deferential. They were relaxed, but you could see clearly that she was the Queen and they were her staff, although they were all titled people. If there was going to be a joke, it would be her joke, not their joke.

Michael Noakes I believe that even inside the family, they've preserved the formality of her being Queen; I think that even the family are expected to pause when they go into the room.

And they might do it, of course, when strangers are there; that I could understand more, certainly inside the Palace.

When we were buttoning up a few things which were in our original agreement,[3] but which we hadn't accomplished, having to do with the greeting of ambassadors, we took up our positions when we realized that—I don't think the Queen noticed—from the private secretary's point of view, we should have paused at the door and gone [indicating a slight bow], and we didn't.

We had a session of the Queen at her desk because we wanted to start [the book] with her with her boxes, and her with her private secretary, and dealing with correspondence.

Janvrin, the private secretary, for some reason had gathered a big bundle of unpaid bills, or something, and he'd plopped them down in front of her, you see, to "dress the set," so to speak.

And the Queen said: "Have you got a pen?" And he said: "Oh, for God's sake, Ma'am, don't sign those. Any recipient getting those back with your name on the bottom would be extremely surprised!"

Michael Parker People when they go to meet the Queen are inclined to be somewhat introspective, or scared, only because they don't know how to behave and they want to do the right thing.

You've got to get over that little barrier. So to help them, you give them some advice on what to do. And you say: "It might be a help to you to listen to what the Queen is saying, and then answer that. Or, if you know of something that would interest her, say it." Then things would start to roll. She's very good at getting people to relax, and talk. And she loves a joke in amongst it all.

We heard just during this visit [to Australia in the spring of 2000] that the Australian high commissioner in London—he's the ambassador, if you like—and his wife suddenly rang up the Queen and said: "You're just off to Australia. Would you like to come and have dinner with us, an informal dinner? And we'll tell you anything you want to know about Australia."

"Delighted! What time?" And so they went. And they had a few martinis, and a lovely dinner. And apparently, it was a very hilarious evening, and went on till quite late. And then off they went home. And then they were off to Australia. It can be as spontaneous as that.

Sir David Smith There's a friendship that develops—and I don't use that in any presumptuous way—there's just a great warmth between members of the team and "the boss."

And that's why, whenever the Queen comes out [to Australia], she sets aside one occasion to meet those people—the retired has-beens like me— who did work with her, and for her, and did render service, and who were part of the system. It was just her way of keeping up, and continuing to say "thank you."

[...] As one of the private functions the Queen had during her [2000] visit, on her second Sunday here after she returned from church to Government House, there were just six of us and our spouses, and another who wasn't married—two former official secretaries, two former directors of royal visits from the prime minister's department, and two now-retired service officers who had been attached to the Queen as equerries for recent visits, and all in one way or another were members of the Royal Victorian Order—and we were invited back just for a private get-together and chat.

The Queen had just expressed the wish to meet some of those, I won't say old friends, but old retainers on the Australian scene, and we were invited by telephone to come and have drinks and a chat with the Queen and Prince Philip.

It was just a very informal occasion and we were having a conversation and you gave as good as you got—perfectly frank, and perfectly relaxed.

Sir Michael Oswald I'm just the luckiest man I've ever met! I owe my position to being at the right place at the right time. I was a young stock manager at a very well-known stud farm in Newmarket and I just happened to be the right age.

The job of manager of the Royal Stud really meant being responsible for the whole race horse breeding operation. Before I started the job, which was on January 1, 1970, the stud farm manager had been also the racing manager and, quite likely, it was decided to split these two jobs because it was too big a job for one person to handle—maybe something important was happening on the stud farm and the stud farm manager needed to be there, or there was some emergency, or he could have been watching an important horse running at York. So they—I think quite rightly—split the two jobs and I became the stud manager.

My responsibility was really only for the breeding stock. There were then four stud farms, small ones compared to the big spreads you see at Lexington [Kentucky], or somewhere like that. And I reported to the Queen.

And in all of these things, quite honestly, the Queen was really the manager, but because, for obvious reasons, she hadn't the time and couldn't be there, you had to act for her.

For instance, at the bloodstock sales, you had to be the eyes and ears, and talk about the catalogue—what was coming up—the day before, and then tell the Queen what the various horses looked like.

The Queen has an encyclopedic knowledge of pedigree and blood-stock and you had to be very careful when you were looking through the big catalogue that you didn't miss anything that she'd already noticed—that if she asked you what lot 1,064 looked like and you had slipped past it, not realizing that its great-grandmother was someone the Queen had bred, you hadn't done too well.

And also, in running the stud, the Queen called all the shots—all the major decisions. You'd always discuss anything really, really important with her—checked it out with her first.

I suppose one rang up on the average of two or three times a week. We had a hot line, far more, in fact, than some much more important members of the Queen's Household ever did.

You tried to brief the Queen on everything you thought she ought to know about, and on everything you thought she ought to hear, not just about the horses, but about the people involved, and the whole business of race horse breeding and owning race horses as well.

The racing manager would discuss all of the forthcoming races with the Queen. And after a race, he would ring up the Queen and tell her what happened. And, indeed, in many cases the trainer of the horse will ring up—some far more important people are often very surprised that the Queen can pick up the telephone, without going through anybody else. Most of us involved in this sort of business just ask the Buckingham Palace operator to put us through. And they are very helpful: if the Queen is out, they will tell you when the Queen is due back.

The racing manager is the link between the Queen as owner and the race horse trainer. They would talk to her directly after a race, particularly if it's an important one, so that we could try to keep the Queen in the picture as much as possible.

The Queen is extremely economical—very, very economical—and likes plain, simple food, for example. And the Queen is a great person for turning off electric lights, that sort of thing.

A lot of people working, say, in Buckingham Palace—certainly from the Queen's early days in the job—tended to write to each other on rather smart writing paper, embossed writing paper with the coat-of-arms and "Buckingham Palace" written underneath, or "Sandringham," or "Holyrood House," and I had some printed paper made up especially for writing to the Queen.

I got answers to my letters, memos, and notes back on some very, very inexpensive paper torn off a pad—about the cheapest sort of paper you could get anywhere—and then I very soon got the message.

I believe it's that there's a certain amount of Scots blood in the Queen. She deplores any form of extravagance and left to her own devices would live a far simpler life, eating fairly plain, simple food, and wondering about horses and dogs in the countryside, which she understands and loves.

CHAPTER 14

Visiting a Royal Residence at the Queen's Invitation

THE QUEEN ENTERTAINS approximately thirty thousand individuals annually at royal garden parties, three of which are held at Buckingham Palace, and one at Holyroodhouse; hosts weekend house parties at her various official and private residences; presides over special functions on occasion to mark milestone events; invites noted musicians and others to perform; grants audiences to diplomats and others in service to the Crown; presides over a diplomatic ball held in November for ambassadors to the Court of St. James's; holds investitures at which she presents orders, decorations, and medals to individuals who have distinguished themselves in public life; and holds luncheons and dinners—including gala affairs for visiting heads of state.

THE GARDEN PARTY

S. A. Pasha Only last July [1999] they asked us as a representative body to send a few Muslims to their annual garden party. So we went and I saw the Queen.

It was a very useful gathering, with people from different walks of life, and the Queen, the Prince of Wales, the Duke of Edinburgh, the Queen Mother, cabinet ministers.

This was the first time they had invited us. They wanted to reach out. And they wanted to show that she is the Queen of all the communities, not just the Christians: she is the head of our Muslims, the Jews, Hindus, Sikhs. There was a simple greeting because there are so many people. But she comes round and shakes hands with people and talks to them.

That was very important because now we are feeling as part of the country; we are not something separate; we are not different. We are part of the society, although we have a different religion, we have got a different way of life. But still we are part of British society. That gives recognition to this fact—that this is a multiracial, multireligious society.

Sir Gordon Jewkes I have met her at garden parties. But even there, she's on duty—and nobody's been on duty quite as much as she has been—and it's *work*: if you've done it a hundred times before, it's a job.

And she's not a normal human being. And that's what I like about her—her sheer constancy. But she does have a warmth about her, which may be a little difficult to break until a personal note is struck. It may have something to do with the family—something about their health. But she does share with them, regardless of the circumstances.

THE WEEKEND HOUSE PARTY

Hugh Segal There is a long tradition of inviting high commissioners to Windsor for a weekend. That usually involves a reception and dinner on the Friday night; a luncheon and some activity on Saturday afternoon; and a Saturday dinner. And you'll be with other elements of British society, so the new young conductor of the London Philharmonic may be there; and a well-known athlete who has just come back from the Olympic Games may be there; and an outstanding business person; and there might be one other foreigner.

But, normally, *you'd* be the foreigner of record. And that would achieve a level of intimacy and open up some relationships, because what the Palace knows is that that person is probably talking to the prime minister, or the prime minister's staff, once or twice a week.

So that's a linkage which goes beyond the traditional Privy Council—High Commission, High Commission—Palace. And that allows Her Majesty to set up her own back channels, which she has every right to do, if she chooses to.

Lord Howard I met the Queen several times, including when I became leader of the opposition and then when I took leave.

On one occasion, a Tuesday, when my wife and I were invited to dinner and to stay overnight, at Windsor Castle, my wife was very cross with me because I insisted that we must leave before breakfast the following morning so that I would reach Parliament in time for Prime Minister's Question Time, beginning at noon. I am not sure that my wife has ever forgiven me!

Lord Heseltine I stayed the night and had lunch there the next day. There is, obviously, an atmosphere of regal splendor about the Castle and one is very conscious of being in the home of the Constitutional Monarch.

Windsor is, of course, a great piece of British history, filled as it is with the most extraordinary treasures, including many works of art. On one occasion, the Queen herself took several of us on a tour of the pictures.

A MOST MOVING INVITATION TO BUCKINGHAM PALACE

Sir David Haslam Prince Charles would preside in 2018 over my knighting, an extraordinary experience. The ceremony had, in fact, been scheduled to take place a year earlier, but would be postponed upon my diagnosis of throat cancer.

On the newly appointed day, the Palace staff could not have been more helpful. Due to the effects of the malignancy on my throat, I would always be very thirsty and so I requested that I be provided with a bottle of water to sip from and the staff arranged that I could drink from it almost to the last minute before Prince Charles would knight me. As I was standing at the side of the hall, I passed the bottle to one of the staff, went over to Prince Charles, was knighted, and proceeded to the other side of the room. There, the bottle was immediately handed back to me. What a thoughtful thing to organize!

In 2004, on the awarding of my CBE, another amazingly choreographed event, my wife, Barbara, and my son and daughter would join me, as they had for my knighting.

THE ROYAL RECEPTION

Lord Younger The Queen and the Duke of Edinburgh are not austere, or distant, or posh. They're very friendly.

For example, I'm chairman of the Royal Anniversaries Trust, which was set up to celebrate the Queen's fortieth anniversary. We had a great big pageant to do that. And the money we raised from that was devoted to giving every second year a series of Queen's Awards for Higher

Education—we conduct a competition every second year where all the universities make submissions and we choose about twenty or so of them to win the Queen's Award for Higher Education, a very coveted award.

When we give the awards, the Queen and Prince Philip invite them into Buckingham Palace, and they invite not just the head of the university, but some students—about ten people from each of twenty universities— and they spend the whole morning in the Royal Gallery.

The Queen and Prince Philip come round and take time to talk with all these people. And the comment these people always make, some of whom have never met the Queen before and never will again, is: "It's so easy to talk to her; I talked about my daughter's A Level results …"

And it is the Household that lubricates that because they make everybody feel at ease first, and they all chat them up before the Queen and Prince Philip come anywhere near them. And they [the guests] suddenly realize that these grand surroundings don't mean that they're to be petrified all morning: a few minutes' chat with the Queen's private secretary, or one of these posh-sounding people, and they're chatting away as if they were in the local shop. And that is very important.

Now it's pretty natural to me because I know so many of the Household personally as well. I have to cast my mind back to when I first was involved in meeting the Queen, which is more comparable to where these people are now.

It was a very mystical moment to feel you were in the same room as the Queen. When I was twenty-five, or thirty, I felt very awestruck, wondering if I was going to do the right thing. And that is what people initially feel.

It wears off. I'm now able to know the Queen so much better that my respect for her is even ten times greater than it was then.

STRICT FORMALITY AND GATE-CRASHERS

Jeremy Thorpe I gate-crashed once with the Queen. On April 1, 1968, I announced my engagement to my first wife[1] and we had a photograph taken at Marlborough House.

That night there was a dinner at Lancaster House to mark the fiftieth anniversary of the RAF. I had a picture in my mind of me photographed in white tie and tails, while Caroline, I knew, would be at home, in the kitchen, standing over the sink, poor, wretched girl.

A recent innovation at these dinners was that after the dinner, there would be a reception for spouses, and I was pretty certain that this would

apply on this occasion, and so I said: "Look here, there's a new development: if they have the Queen at dinner, then the wives are invited into
the reception afterwards, so come to the reception afterwards and ask for
me." And she said: "I hope it's all right."

I sought out [Minister of Defense] Denis Healey to clear the arrangement with him, and Denis told me that no wives had been invited—that
the only ladies present would be the Queen, the Queen Mother, the
Princess Margaret, the Duchess of Gloucester, Princess Marina of Kent,
their ladies-in-waiting, and a few WAF officers. But, he told me: "She has
probably got out her frock, so she'd better come."

When Caroline arrived at the reception, the Queen Mother came over
and said: "We needn't ask who *this* is." Then the Queen said: "Is this …?"
I said: "Yes, it is, Ma'am."

Since we were only engaged that afternoon, gate-crashing the royal
dinner that evening and a royal presentation was pretty good going! We
were photographed, and we got in the newspapers.

PERFORMING AT THE PALACE

In addition to attending Command Performances at public theaters, the
Queen invites noted actors, musicians, and performance artists to entertain at royal palaces.

Larry Adler To me it's another show. You see, rank means nothing to me at
all. There's a lot of pomp around it. There is a certain protocol to it. But not
to me. I don't bow to anybody; nobody makes me bow. People kiss their ass
like crazy. It's rather embarrassing to watch. But when I give a show, I give
the same show I always give—I'm not encumbered by whom I'm playing to.

THE ROYAL AUDIENCE

Sir Gordon Jewkes You arrive at the Palace. The doorman will open
the doors. You step out and a lady-in-waiting greets you. She takes you
through the labyrinth of the Palace, to an anteroom, the robing room of
the guards, where you will meet an equerry first—there was a famous
equerry by the name of Johnny Johnson; in the 1950s he was still alive.
He, for example, would meet you, and he would say: "Now we want this
to be a very, very happy event for you. I know there is a certain formality,

but don't worry if you put your foot wrong. Now I will take you to the door and announce you, and Her Majesty will be in the drawing room, and as you go through the door, just bow, and walk towards Her Majesty, and she will offer her hand and invite you to sit down."

The Queen is in the room when you come in, seated. It was a little unnatural because if three people[2] are cast into a room, it's up to the main person, the hostess, to break the ice. The Queen is astonishingly good at that. You still feel a bit stilted—it is not from *her* side, but from our side that the conversation was a bit stilted.

But because I was going to the Falklands, and because Prince Andrew had been there, there was, obviously, some common ground toward a start.

But it was not in any way comparable to the previous, private discussion that I had with Mrs. Thatcher some months earlier, who truly did discuss the issue—although "discussion" is not the right word for Mrs. Thatcher; she "addressed" me on the issues. The Queen did not go into that depth.

Then, as you have been warned, you know when the conversation is finished. She says: "I wish you well." You stand up as though you're a puppet on a string. At that time, we were enjoined to walk backwards.

Peter Jay It is not formal like the Queen's Speech[3]—you're not got up in medieval clothes; you're wearing a morning coat. She's not wearing her Crown, she's wearing a modern suit, and [carrying] her handbag.

There's no messing about: you bow, you go straight into the conversation—she starts the conversation, you have the conversation, and back out. It's serious, dignified, and businesslike.

Gen. Andrew Goodpaster The Queen put us completely at ease. She had obviously talked to her counselors about NATO, about the things we were doing. Interestingly, all of the royalty on whom I have made calls followed very closely the work of NATO, and the importance of NATO to the future security, safety, and wellbeing of the country. That's characteristic of the royalty.

The nature of the meeting was very, very positive, and really quite warming. To me, and to all of my colleagues, it built and solidified the sense of responsible level that each of us has had, not just to our own country, but to each of the [NATO] countries.

The Queen was completely at ease, just completely confident in the position she was exercising. And you had the feeling that you were a moment in a long history, meeting with a really very beautiful young woman—a youngish woman, I would have to say.

For my wife and myself, it was really a thrilling moment to be able to actually see her, and converse with her. She spoke with knowledge and assurance of how my duties pertained to the interests of her country.

One of her assistants, who had escorted us in, kept a close eye on the proceedings, and then, when the time came for us to say goodbye, she completed the discussion, and it was done with complete grace and cordiality.

Lord Wright Actually, as I got to know the Queen better, and because of the presentation of credentials, which when I was in the country I always attended, I had pretty frequent meetings with the Queen, alone, before and after those occasions.

I really began to feel that one was making a sort of personal friendship. And I think it was, in a way. But on the other hand, I had to keep putting myself back, and remembering that, traditionally, you treat the Sovereign with a degree of awe and respect, and ceremony.

That has gradually diminished over the years. But there still is ceremony, and you bow when you come into the room and bow when you leave the room. And much of the Queen's life is taken up with ceremony and, therefore, quite understandably, she likely attaches quite a lot of importance to it.

THE ANNUAL DIPLOMATIC BALL

Lord Wright There is an annual diplomatic reception for the entire Diplomatic Corps—every head of mission—and they're allowed to bring a certain number of their staff with them, held in Buckingham Palace every November.

One new high commissioner was rather nervously asking the Lord Chamberlain what he had to do: Did he present the Queen? What did he call her? And how did he do it?

And the Lord Chamberlain said: "Look, don't worry. It's very simple. Do this, that, and the other. But if you're in any doubt, just watch the head of mission next to you."

Fijians when they meet the Queen bend down on one knee and clap three times, which is the mark of respect for their paramount chief [Queen Elizabeth]. Well, it is alleged that the man next to him was the Fijian, who got down on one knee and clapped three times. Thereupon whoever the high commissioner was did the same!

Yehuda Avner At the annual diplomatic ball, you are lined up according to seniority—I found myself between Iraq and Lebanon. Seniority is a matter of who presented credentials ten minutes before you and who presented credentials ten minutes after you. The more junior you are, the further you are down the line; the more senior you are, the closer you are to what's called the Music Room.

So you're somewhere in the line and, eventually, the Queen comes, attended by her ladies-in-waiting and by an equerry, and she chats. This is an enormous skill—to go over to each one, and their wife, and the minister—the number two, and two or three other ministers of the embassy with their wives, all in full regalia. She was able to totally compartmentalize: "Aren't we having miraculous weather today?" Or "How is Mr. Peres doing?"—that kind of thing.

Coming along after her was the Prince [Philip], always with a sniping look. He would always have something to say about Iran and Iraq—and you knew it was going to happen. My impression is that the man is utterly *bored*; highly competent and intelligent.

Then would come the Prince of Wales—I'm talking about a two-minute chat, which is quite a lot. Then would come Princess Diana, always with a self-deprecation; always with a chuckle about the kids—"little monsters."

Ivan Head At Buckingham Palace, at big receptions, Her Majesty would receive her guests, and the Duke would be elsewhere, circulating in the room, which is quite all right.

He seemed always to be vitriolic; he always had some garbage to say about things. On one occasion, I'd been racing around, right up to the last minute, and I hadn't had an opportunity to change from a green suit and brown shoes, and so he made a point of letting me know that he hadn't seen brown shoes in his presence for some time.

The Queen is certainly not going to say anything, or make a face, in his presence.

Hugh Segal I suspect HRH [His Royal Highness] is an equal opportunity, small "b" bigot—probably not actually a bigot, but just condescending towards most people.

When I worked for Premier Davis,[4] who was the premier of Ontario for fourteen years, the Queen and Prince Philip were over, and there was a dinner on the royal yacht *Britannia*, at the base of Toronto Harbor.

Apparently folks were quite embarrassed because His Royal Highness was into a series of Irish jokes: we have Irish jokes here in Canada, called

"Newfie Jokes," about New Foundlanders, and they are quite inappropriate, and quite unacceptable. They generally imply a level of intellectual capacity somewhat beneath a normative human standard.

KISSING HANDS

Newly appointed Privy Counselors and government ministers[5] have an audience with the Queen at Buckingham Palace in a ceremony known as kissing hands. In the brief ceremony, the appointee kneels on a footstool before the Queen, who offers her right hand, palm downward, fingers closed. The appointee will in turn extend the right hand, palm upward, take the Queen's hand, and kiss it with a mere touch of the lips.

Ambassadors of the Court of St. James's, governors general, and Church officials, however, will not literally kiss the Queen's hand during the Palace ceremony. The term "kissing hands" is used in that instance rather to denote a certain kind of audience.

While the ceremony must have at one time involved an actual act of osculation performed on the Monarch's hand, that is no longer the case—most likely to the Monarch's relief.

* * *

Archdeacon George Austin When bishops are appointed, they have to kiss hands. If I were the Queen, I wouldn't want to be kissed by certain of the bishops, with their greasy beards. And when they do it they make an oath, handing to the Queen not only the temporalities[6] of the diocese, but also its spiritualities.

Bishop Hugh Montefiore The Home Secretary is there, in top hat and morning coat. I put my hands together and she puts her hands over my hands—and you swear an enormous litany of oaths: that no foreign pope, or prelate, or potentate will have any jurisdiction in the Realm of England.

And then you have a talk with her. She gets an agenda, so she talks very intelligently. And they ask you, before you go, what you want to talk about—just to show how conscientious she is, she wants to know what *you'd* like to talk about and clues herself up. I talked about the inner cities [of which] she is very knowledgeable.

One of the things that strikes you when you talk to her is that she's very *small*—she never appears small in photographs—when you actually see her, she's not very tall.

Lord Wright My wife was invited to accompany me, and we were invited to sit down, and there was a very informal conversation. It was formal in the sense that I bowed and my wife curtseyed on arrival, and then on leaving. But otherwise, we sat down and then talked, just the three of us. It was very pleasant, I must say.

The Queen was rather surprised to discover that I was being transferred from Luxembourg, where, of course, the Grand Duke is a close personal friend of hers, to Syria. I've often wanted to ask her, but I think the Queen must have thought that I was found with my hand in the till: nobody could *conceivably* regard a move from Luxembourg to Syria as anything other than punishment.

But if she did have suspicions, she concealed them. And it was very informal, and very easy. And there was absolutely no nervousness about not knowing when to leave because one of the gifts that the Queen acquires—that you have to acquire in that position—is making absolutely clear when the time has come for you to go.

When I attended presentations of credentials, what happened was that I'd be announced by an ADC, I'd go in, bow, and then stand, talking to the Queen—there was no question of sitting down—sometimes for ten minutes, or twenty minutes.

And often [the conversation was] not actually about the country, or the individual who was about to present credentials. She sometimes had things that she wanted to ask me about that were quite unrelated to the presentation of credentials.

And then, when the ambassador, or high commissioner, had presented his wife, and then members of his staff, they would leave and I would stay. And then we'd have, depending on her program, five, ten, fifteen minutes' further conversation, sometimes about the person who'd just been, but more often about something entirely different.

The Queen attaches a lot of importance to dress: in attending presentations of credentials, I had to get into diplomatic uniform, wearing gloves. And on one occasion I was unable to do it, and a colleague of mine who had a uniform—it tended to be rather restricted to those who actually got uniforms—went to the presentation but forgot to put on gloves.

Consequently, there was a note from the Lord Chamberlain, I believe, to an official in the Foreign Office, asking whether the rules had been changed without the Lord Chamberlain's knowledge.

It was pretty clear that he was writing on the Queen's instructions. She does notice things; she's a master of detail, absolutely.

I suppose if you're giving medals and decorations, you're likely to take an interest in it. She notices things like decorations and war medals. I don't have any war medals at all, but she would quite often say to people: "Now let me see, what's that medal for?"

Stephen Day It's a private interview with the Queen—with one's wife—and that happened to me when I was appointed ambassador to Qatar in 1981, and again when I was appointed in Tunis.

She's been extremely well briefed—and on one's wife—but very businesslike. It's not small talk; it's a very clear background briefing on how she sees that part of the world, the country you're going to, the particular points she would like to discuss, or advise on.

It is a very important, substantive interview; it's not simply symbolic—there is a symbolism about it—but that consciousness that you do represent the Queen and, therefore, something more enduring, and permanent than the government alone, is a very real element of the job.

It was the best possible briefing I had on the nature of these regimes and, particularly, the nature of the rulers themselves. I found that very, very helpful. It's a wealth of experience: following the telegrams over the years; meeting the individuals, and the visits she has herself made—in my case, to Qatar.

Sir Michael Palliser One of the nice things about the presentation by ambassadors of their Letters of Credence to the Queen for me always was that after the ambassador and his wife had bowed and gone out, the Queen and I had about five—maybe ten—minutes, depending on what she wanted, of conversation. And that was always extremely easy, pleasant, usually, and a good deal of fun. At the same time, she was never anything but *the Queen*.

Periodically she would grumble about something we'd been getting up to that she didn't like, that for me was the sort of [bonus] in what was otherwise a fairly tedious interruption in the official process: I'd get into uniform—it takes a while—and be there before the ambassador arrived, wait around with him, and then go in—I went in first—and the Queen would usually say: "Do you know this man?" And I would say yes or no. And then: "What sort of person is he?" And we'd have half a minute or so of conversation about the incoming ambassador.

And then *he* would come in, and she'd talk to him. And then his wife would come in and there'd be conversation with the two of them. But then, when they'd gone and we were on our own, it was the sort of [bonus] that made the whole morning worthwhile. It was interesting to see what she was interested in at that point.

She would sometimes comment on the person, or the country, or on what was going on in the country. If there was a new ambassador representing a country with whom we had a problem, she might well ask about that, or comment on it. Sometimes she'd say: "I've seen in the [Foreign Office] telegrams . . ." It was virtually always related to foreign policy when I was with her.

She had read her papers; she usually had her view; and she's got a certain, rather wicked sense of humor—there's sort of a rather sharp quality often to comments that she makes. There is a sort of slightly puncturing sense of humor there. It's not incompatible with her sense of dignity of the status of the monarchy and all that. She's an interesting woman.

Yehuda Avner I'm the youngest of seven—I've got four older sisters and two older brothers, in that order. *All* of them lived in Manchester; I was the only one who came on Aliyah [the Hebrew word for the coming of Jews to Israel as immigrants—a major ideal of Zionism].

An eighteenth-century coach drawn by white horses comes to your embassy and a representative of the Crown escorts you to the Palace in this magnificent coach, drawn by these horses through Hyde Park.

And then, at the same time that you enter the gates of the Palace is the moment of the Changing of the Guard, so that that ceremonial is a salute to *you* as you trot by.

Now, because it's the Changing of the Guard, you've got thousands of people outside there. And outside the gates were all my brothers and sisters. The police were holding them back, and one of my sisters, as the carriage was going through the gates, said to the policeman—with her Lancashire accent—"Here, that's my brother!"

How did I feel at that moment, as I was trotting through the gates of the Palace? I was thinking: Mom and Dad, I wish you could see me *now*!

In a part of the inner courtyard, there was a sentry, and there were the various equerries, and we were taken to a room, called the Bell Room, because it is shaped like a bell, where you have an actual rehearsal beforehand, and you are told to take two steps forward and bow.

And then you are standing at the door—you are carrying your credential—and then you take two steps forward and you bow; you take another two steps forward and you bow again; and then you are within handshaking distance of the Queen.

Now I had a sad task to perform at that moment: my predecessor, Shlomo Argov, was shot.[7] The Queen asked me how he was. When one leaves a position of ambassadorship, one deposits at the Palace what is called the Letter of Recall, and, of course, Shlomo could not do that, so before presenting my Letter of Credence, I gave her [the Queen] Shlomo's Letter of Recall.

It is at that moment [after the presentation of the ambassador's Letter of Credence] that you present your wife, and a set number of members of the embassy staff are also presented at that time.

It was an extraordinary rendezvous with my childhood, and with my sense of pride in representing Israel—coming back after more than thirty years.

When I presented my credentials to the Queen, she said to me: "I do believe this is the first time that I've ever received credentials from a foreign ambassador who was born in this country."

I remembered that [Shmuel Yosef] Agnon, on receiving the Nobel Prize [for literature, in 1966], said to the King of Sweden when the King asked Agnon: "Where were you born?"—and I'm paraphrasing; this is the answer I gave to the Queen: "Your Majesty, though I was born in this country, I was given birth in Jerusalem." She looked at me and said: "Oh?" And then we went on to talk of other things.

Michael Noakes It was quite fun, actually, the ambassador with his Letters of Credence.

They stand, curiously, far apart—uncomfortably far apart for people who are talking. When one is sitting down, that is fine. But when you're in a room, just the two of you, a bit apart from a little army of retainers, and so on, it's sort of distant.

But then the time came for him to pass his Letters of Credence across and they dropped, and the Queen said: "Oh, nice and crinkly."

INVESTITURES

The major orders of chivalry are: the Garter, instituted by Edward III in 1348 and limited to the Sovereign and twenty-four Knights Companion; the Thistle, revived in the seventeenth century and restricted to the Sovereign and sixteen Scottish knights; the Bath, established in 1725 by George I, with both civilian and military categories; the Order of Merit, of which Sir Edward Ford serves as registrar, established by

Edward VII in 1902 and limited to twenty-four recipients, especially in the areas of art, literature and music; The Order of St. Michael and St. George, founded in 1818 and reserved primarily for diplomats; the Royal Victorian Order, founded by Queen Victoria in 1896 for members of the Royal Household; and the Order of the British Empire, created in 1917, following the change of the royal name to Windsor, and comprised of five divisions: Knight (or Dame) Grand Cross, Knight Commander, Commander, Officer, and Member.

Those so honored are invested in formal and splendid ceremonies held usually at Buckingham Palace, although the Queen does confer titles while on visits to Commonwealth countries.

* * *

Sir Edward Ford It's entirely the Queen; she selects them. And she can select them on her own, and her principal private secretary will always keep in a book any record of people who might be considered by her for vacancies in the three orders which she disposes of herself—namely the Garter, the Thistle, and the Order of Merit.

And when there are vacancies, she will no doubt ask him to come and discuss them. Some she chooses on his advice alone; others she asks him to find out more about. I believe he would have taken some trouble to get the opinion, perhaps, from an existing member of the order.

At the end, the only thing that she doesn't do is to consult the prime minister on those considered.

He's got all other honors: peerages, and the honors of the Order of the British Empire, and the Companion of Honor, and knighthoods are in the hands of the prime minister, in which she very rarely interferes at all.

Lord Younger The Knight of the Thistle in Scotland—and the Knight of the Garter in England—is a very enormously high honor in the sense that there are such a tiny number of people involved: in Scotland, there are fourteen Knights of the Thistle, plus the four royals—the Queen, Prince Charles, Prince Philip, and the Queen Mother. That's all there is: out of any generation there only are fourteen, so that's a great honor.

What happens is very little, very formal. Nothing more than that. It's symbolism: we have two big events a year where we put on our robes. We process into the big church in Edinburgh, St. Giles Cathedral, we have a church service, and then we come out again and have lunch with the Queen. That's all that's involved, except that Knights of the Thistle stand very high in the sort of protocol world: one tends to find oneself on the top table when you don't think you would be otherwise. It's just a great honor to someone who has done a great deal of public work.

Geoffrey Pearson Some years before my father died, the Queen gave him the Order of Merit. There are only twenty-four such awards, and she decides, not the prime minister. That was very unusual; there are only two other Canadians, I think, who have ever received it: our long-term prime minister for twenty-five years or so in the 1930s and 1940s, Mackenzie King; and Dr. Robert Penfield, who was a famous surgeon in Montreal—it must have been the Queen's grandfather who gave him the award.

So it was unusual—and not many politicians would get it. It's like the Order of Canada, which we give to people for community work. My father prized his Order of Merit more than almost anything else,[8] although it's not well-known in Canada—there are so few and Canadians aren't aware of it. And the monarchy doesn't advertise it.

Sir David Scott Actually, the Queen gave me my K [knighthood] in New Zealand,[9] so I was in her New Zealand investiture, which actually was rather interesting and impressive because it showed the sort of unity—the fact that there were a lot of New Zealanders being given knighthoods and other decorations—and when the Queen came to me, she said: "Well, it's rather nice to see a familiar face here."

Claire Rayner [Upon being awarded an OBE] I got a letter saying: "You are to go to the Palace on ... and the Queen will give you this honor." My children insisted I should take it in recognition of what I had done for the country in health services. And I said: "There is no power on *earth* that will get me to the Palace; I will not do it." Some friends said: "Of course you should go; it's a giggle, a hoot."

I rang up the Palace—I got through to this frightfully pompous person, who said: "Can I help you?"—and I said: "I've got this invitation. I really don't want to come for this presentation. Can't you just pop it in the post?" She said: "Well, we can arrange for someone else to give it to you." I said: "I don't want this flummery. Just pop it in the post if you want me to have it."

It arrived by recorded mail two days later and Des [Ms. Rayner's husband] opened it and presented it to me on a silver tray. It's a piece of cheap flummery that is now in my top drawer—a piece of rubbish.

Ivan Head This class thing—MBEs and OBEs—Canadians just don't bother. That's the influence, without any question, of the United

States—the republican attitude in Canada—which makes us a much better country, and we have a much better society as a result.

Sir Harold Smedley, KCMG, MBE (1920–2004), British high commissioner in Ghana, 1964–67; ambassador to Laos, 1967–70; high commissioner in Sri Lanka, 1972–75; high commissioner in New Zealand and governor of Pitcairn Island, 1976–80 The staff do their best [to put people at their ease] but it's not an occasion you *can* relax.

You're allowed to invite two people, or something of that sort, and they all wait for you to trip down: we were all lined up in our order of seniority—morning dress, uniforms—and we marched forward at the appropriate moment.

It's not a conversational occasion—she's got two hundred people to get through. It's extended perhaps to the major sportsmen and such types, who get more than the customary few seconds.

It remains, obviously, a major occasion, of which one was always conscious. But, having said that, you know the drill—you know how to bow—and that in itself is an enormous help. The whole thing goes much more straightforwardly than on the first occasion, when you don't really know quite what's happening.

Sir Kenneth Bloomfield In terms of our honors system, which many people regard as Gilbertian,[10] what the ordinary citizen gets is something called the Order of the British Empire, which is quite amusing, because the British Empire doesn't actually exist anymore.

I had a role in that, in my old job [in Belfast, Northern Ireland], of "sieving out" [prospective honorees]. And in the nature of things, quite often members of the Catholic community would come up for their excellent work. And one had to ask oneself: would you actually embarrass somebody by making them an offer, because in terms of their principles, they might say no?

We always concluded that we should look at that absolutely on merit: if we thought somebody deserved it, he should at any rate know that the state thought well of him by getting a letter saying: "I have it in mind to recommend you for this award," because he could then write back in total confidence—this is never disclosed—and say: "Thank you very much, but I'd rather not." And that's the end of the matter. But it was much better that they should know that the state was aware.

The interesting thing is that quite a lot of people who, I'm certain, would vote at an election for a non-Unionist—for a Nationalist party—do accept these awards, so they become members of the Order of the British Empire.

One of the members of the BBC board of governors is a very, very charming man from an Indian background. His father was something like commissioner of the Punjab, a very senior official in India.

In the New Year honors the son was awarded the CBE, which is quite a high honor—it stands for Commander of the British Empire. The chairman of the board said: "I want to congratulate our colleague on the award." And my colleague, very disarmingly, said: "If my dear father were alive, I think he would be quite surprised to find me commanding the British Empire."

Robert Lacey One of the benefits in recent years has been the opening up of the investitures in Buckingham Palace. These used to be secret sorts of affairs. So far as the public were concerned, there was nothing mysterious about them, but you'd see the celebrities turning up at the Palace, and you'd see them come out, and there might be a photograph in the papers of a well-known footballer, or a particularly brave fireman, holding up their award.

Then, for several years, these events were videoed, using the latest technology—small cams—and it became possible for you, if you'd been given an award, to buy the video of the ceremony, which was a mixture of the behind the scenes, and what had happened, and the whole thing, and then it concentrated on your particular thing.

And now all this material is actually put out to the television companies, and so now it's a regular item on the television news every month or so—Sean Connery gets this; this comedian gets that.

This again relates to the royal bounty idea of the Royal Family existing to—if you want to be cynical—just bestow brownie points on people. But that's a very valuable function, and the new P.R. advisers in the Palace have pushed that as a new aspect of the Queen's life.

Month after month, the flow of celebrities, ironically generated by the Labour government, who are suspected in some ways of being anti-royal, creates news stories which reflect the Queen in a good, popular light, and show people some of the work the Queen does.

VISITS BY FOREIGN DIGNITARIES

Sir Michael Palliser The Queen has two state visits inwards per year. We also devised—it's now much more in use—what's called an "official visit" by a head of state, or a prime minister, which, as far as the Queen is concerned, *isn't* a state visit.

And the visitor—the president, or the prime minister, or whatever—does not stay in Buckingham Palace, but is received by the Queen at lunch, or a reception, and then has talks with the prime minister, and does whatever he, or she, wants to do.

The state visit is set to an absolutely rigid formula, and that's one of the reasons why we devised the "official visit," because the state visit formula was too set in concrete. And while the Queen might have accepted to a degree the change, her courtiers didn't like the change—and still don't.

On the state visit, you have to be received at Victoria Station, then drive in the state coach to Buckingham Palace, where there's a banquet that evening in the Palace. The visiting leader would host a banquet at his embassy the following evening. And at a special reception you receive the leader of the opposition.

Broadly speaking, the state visitors were more important than the official visitors. But there was a kind of queue for state visits, and the official visit enabled one to jump the queue for a head of state who wasn't going to grumble too much at not being given a state visit. It required a degree of judgment on the part of our ambassador [to the other country] and their ambassador here.

It was a way of inserting candidates who—either because of time, or whatever—didn't qualify for a state visit, or who weren't important enough to qualify for a state visit. It's a strange, rather typically British, way of doing things because of the sort of set-in-concrete nature of the state visit.

The most difficult negotiation, I may tell you, is the one about the exchange of decorations—who should get what. There's a lot of fuss about the Emperor of Japan being given the Garter—just the tip of the iceberg, I can tell you. There is always a lot of interesting discussion: how many grand crosses, knighthoods, whatever, honorary, and who gets what the other way around.

Adm. Sir Henry Leach When you are in your final year as a captain—I'm talking in terms of the Navy now, or the equivalent in the other services—if you have not been seen picking your nose in public, then you've got a good chance of being made an ADC, just for that final year.

They're strictly honorary accreditation: you are not really called upon to do anything, to wait on Her Majesty, or to participate at all, except when you get a visiting head of state, you are expected to be present, either supporting the guard of honor at Victoria Station, or if they come up the river by barge, and that sort of thing, or even going down to Heathrow—the Queen never goes to Heathrow to meet visiting heads of state.

And then you would go on to the official banquet in Windsor, or Buckingham Palace, afterwards. But you're not actually doing anything; you're just being there. You don't act in any way as an ADC *per se*—as a flag lieutenant, if I use a naval term; you don't do that. I suppose you could be called upon, but you never are.

* * *

During the state visit of a foreign leader to the United Kingdom, the Queen hosts a banquet at Buckingham Palace, to which members of the Royal Family, government leaders, opposition leaders, diplomats, and British subjects distinguished in many walks of life are invited.

* * *

Jeremy Thorpe State banquets are *amazing*! There's a big mahogany extension under the table, with great gold ice buckets, champagne—a marvelous sight. She's very formal. She's very discreet in what she says. She doesn't crack too many jokes.

Michael Deaver The dining room was incredible. I snuck into the dining room that afternoon, and there were these men walking up and down the table, doing whatever they do, wearing their special socks. I was probably one of the few untitled people in the room that night. One of the things that I will never forget was that people would have to walk backwards into the room. No Americans would do that.

U.S. PRESIDENT DWIGHT DAVID EISENHOWER'S
STATE VISIT, 1957

Gen. Andrew Goodpaster That there would be a visit would be worked out with our embassy in Britain, and direct communication, in the case of our visit to Britain, with the prime minister. And, of course, the personal relationship of Eisenhower with [the then-prime minister] Macmillan laid the base for that.

Then, once the decision was made and there was agreement on the timing, the ideas would begin to generate on both sides, particularly on the host side—the British side—as to what the events would be. And our embassy in Britain would have a major hand in putting together kind of a straw map to be looked at.

And they would come up with this quite elaborate schedule that included everything from the initial greeting and inspection of the troops and the Royal Salute.

I had never seen the Royal Salute before President Eisenhower's visit. We got off the plane and the Royal Standard was brought forward. And I thought that the man was becoming ill because the Standard was approaching the ground—they lay the Royal Standard on the ground. That's like laying our national flag on the ground!

Fortunately, my British escort was alongside me and he saw that I was disturbed and he said: "You've never seen that before?" I said: "No. I haven't." And he said: "That's the Royal Salute that is being rendered to the president of the United States." That was quite a moment.

But when it's all put together, there are surprises on both sides. I was in with Captain Timothy Bligh, who was a senior staff assistant to Prime Minister Macmillan,[11] and he said to me: "Now, you shouldn't be taken aback if you don't see many people lining the road. It's not a British characteristic to line the road to greet a visitor."

And as we started out from Heathrow, there were a lot of people along the side of the road, and he said: "Well, that's quite unusual, but I guess that's because we're close to the airport." And as we went along, there were people along the side of the road every step of the way. He said: "I've never seen this before."

The visit was well thought out on both sides. And it did serve, certainly from the American side, to highlight the long-term and very, very deep and warm relationship that we had with the British. And, of course, Eisenhower was anxious that everything be done to show respect for the Queen, and for Britain.

He thought that they had made a terrible mistake in the Suez affair, but that needed to be rectified and the relationship reestablished.

PRESIDENT NELSON MANDELA'S STATE VISIT, 1996

Nelson Mandela I went for a state visit to London. I went with the Queen to a concert at the Royal Albert Hall. There was a South African choir singing. I always liked to join them. But on this occasion, I couldn't leave my seat because I was sitting with Her Majesty and Prince Charles.

But I got up and danced, and Her Majesty got up and danced too! One British paper said I should be charged with treason for making Her Majesty dance, because it was a light one. But I really enjoyed that.

During the state visit, I stayed in Buckingham Palace, and now I saw another side of Her Majesty, as the hostess: she would serve tea herself.

And then I went to Britain on a private visit. And again, she invited me. I enjoyed that very much. She's a wonderful lady, very, very wonderful. I value my association with her.

THE EMIR OF QATAR'S STATE VISIT, 1985

Stephen Day I was involved in that visit—I was then head of the Middle East Department—and clearly for the Emir of Qatar, that state visit to the United Kingdom, without question, was the high point of his life— the acknowledgment that Qatar was fully accepted as a fully sovereign state, bearing in mind that it was a small country that had been under British tutelage for many years. The corollary was that it was not only an enormous event, but that it, in itself, was a great trial for him, person- ally, to measure up, and it was a formidable ordeal for somebody whose background and culture was so thoroughly different, with the heavy cer- emonial of a British state occasion.

But it was great. I saw him [the Emir] at the end of the state visit—he asked me in for a private chat—and he was obviously unwinding; he was on a high. He thought it was quite fantastic.

There was one thoroughly amusing thing about the Qatar state visit: it is traditional that on the second day of the visit the guest goes out for the day, for lunch. And on that occasion, British Aerospace had invited the Emir out to Hackney, north of London, for lunch.

It was a *dreadful* day, pouring down with rain, the car got stuck in a traffic jam, and the Emir looked out and said: "What on earth are we doing here?" So all the protocol people swanned around, saying: "You must, you know; Her Majesty insists." And he said: "I'm sure she *doesn't* insist. I'm not going to sit here and do this; I'm going to go back and I'm going to have lunch in the Palace."

So he turned around and got back into the Palace, at which moment there was growing panic everywhere. And the Palace came up trumps and served a stupendous lunch: his [the Emir's] right-hand man, who realized something was happening, had telephoned a Lebanese restau- rant, which brought in a gargantuan lunch; and his ambassador had telephoned another Lebanese restaurant, and they brought in *another* gargantuan lunch.

PRESIDENT RONALD REAGAN'S STATE VISIT, 1982

Ronald Reagan was the first-ever U.S. president to be invited to stay at Windsor Castle during a state visit.

* * *

Michael Deaver It was because he was Ronald Reagan. President Reagan was a great admirer of the Queen. Ronald Reagan came from pretty humble roots, and so this was a very special visit.

He knew that they would be riding together after the Parliament speech the next morning. He liked to talk to her about horses: they were both familiar with thoroughbreds, and he was somebody who could handle and enjoy big horses.

I believe she admired him—she admired what he'd been able to do in bringing dignity back to the White House. He was a charming person, and did everything right, and I believe she enjoyed very much being around him, and talking to him. And he enjoyed being around the Queen very much.

When we arrived at Windsor, all of our bags that had been on *Air Force One* were taken care of—they were taken to our room. But of course at Windsor you are assigned a valet, for me, and a maid for my wife. They had taken out all of her cosmetics and lined them all up, precisely. And she had a pair of old sheepskin slippers that were dearly loved, but horrible to look at, and they were neatly in front of the bed. And I remember her saying: "Oh, my God! They've gotten into our suitcases!"

We had been on the road for five or six days, so our suitcases were filled with dirty clothes. The problem with me was that they had taken *everything* out [to launder], and I had no pajamas—I had one pair and they had taken them.

So the next morning I came out of the bath with nothing on—just as the maid came in with our breakfast tray. I could have been a grandfather clock as far as she was concerned. She said: "Good morning, sir," and I stood there like I was a piece of stone as long as I could and they discussed what my wife was going to wear that morning. I was so furious with my wife for not dismissing her and getting her out of the room!

The other thing that morning was the Queen's "alarm clock"—pipers at Windsor at seven o'clock in the morning outside her window. I remember hearing the pipers and opening the window and looking at them. And in addition to the pipers, there was a footman, *in tails*, walking the corgis!

PART THREE

The Queen and the Commonwealth

CHAPTER 15

The Commonwealth

Q UEEN ELIZABETH II is the head of the Commonwealth. Comprised of fifty-four independent states—thirty-four are republics and three, Brunei, Lesotho, and Eswatini (formerly Swaziland), are monarchies in their own right—and with a population of 2.4 billion, the Commonwealth is second only in size to the United Nations as an international body.

In fifteen of the sixteen Commonwealth nations in which the Queen is the head of state, she is represented by a governor-general, whom she appoints on the advice of the head of government, and who serves as the *de facto* head of state—a role distinct from that of head of government of an individual nation. The sixteenth country is the United Kingdom, where the Queen is head of state in practice.

In those Commonwealth nations which do not recognize the Queen as the head of state, she is represented by a high commissioner.

All member-states, with the exception of Mozambique, have in the past had a constitutional or administrative link with the United Kingdom or one of the other Commonwealth countries.

The Commonwealth does not have a written constitution, functioning rather through a series of agreements setting out its tenets and objectives. They include the political values of democracy and good governance, as well as respect for human rights, gender equality, the rule of law, and sustainable economic and social development.

These agreements were codified in a Declaration of Commonwealth Principles adopted in 1971 at a Commonwealth Heads of Government Meeting (CHOGM) held in Singapore and reaffirmed in 1991 at a CHOGM held in Harare, Zimbabwe.

Subsequently, at a CHOGM held in 1997 in Edinburgh, Scotland, it was agreed that all future applicants for Commonwealth membership should, in most circumstances, have had a constitutional association with an existing Commonwealth member-state; comply with Commonwealth values and principles as set out in the Harare Declaration; and accept Commonwealth norms and conventions, such as the use of the English language.

The Queen attends all CHOGM meetings. In addition, she visits Commonwealth nations. As of July 2021, she has visited fifty-two of the fifty-four member-states.

The Queen also reaches out to the Commonwealth via the airwaves, in a radio address broadcast annually on Commonwealth Day, which occurs in March, and in her annual radio and television address on Christmas Day—the sole occasion on which she speaks personally to the Commonwealth rather than reflecting the views of her government, which she does on all other public occasions.

The Queen's chief liaison with the Commonwealth is its secretary-general, who is chosen by the nations of the Commonwealth following initial input from those nations' high commissioners in London.

THE COMMONWEALTH TODAY

Sir Bernard Ingham [...] The Commonwealth encircles the world, and there is a very considerable advantage in having that organization because there is always somebody there who could exercise a moderating influence in a part of the world.

It's ex-British Empire; it represents continuity. What it does uniquely in this world is bring together the English-speaking peoples—the ex-colonial territories and the colonial powers—in discussion.

Secondly, it brings together the largest democracy in the world, India, and the smallest which is Tuvalu, which is about twenty-three square kilometers [nine square miles]. It's quite remarkable: India, getting on to a billion people now, and Tuvalu, with a few seagulls.[1]

Sir Rex Hunt It's really a tribute to the way we administered our overseas possessions that so many of them have wished to stay in an organization that may be pretty loose.

I've served in Indonesia and in Vietnam, as well as in the Commonwealth countries, and certainly the Indonesians have said: "Why did you let the Dutch back after the [Second World] war? We didn't want them." And the Vietnamese said: "Oh, why didn't you stay? You look after your colonies far better than the French looked after us." So if you're going to be a colony, then we were better administrators than most of the others.

Bishop Hugh Montefiore If it hadn't been for Queen Elizabeth II, the Commonwealth well might not exist, because for some reason, her first ministers were not interested.

It was a time of reconstruction after the war, a time when they were beginning to be interested in Europe and the United States of America, and they were not interested in the Commonwealth.

But the Queen was. And, what's more, her relationship as head of the Commonwealth—the famous dance that she gave, when she danced with the black ruler of Tanzania at a Commonwealth meeting—was a symbol, really, of the Queen doing something for the Commonwealth.

Nelson Mandela The Commonwealth is very important. In the first place, it has representatives of all continents; it is really a rainbow organization. They took resolutions at [the 1999] summit centering on poverty, which is the greatest single challenge to society.

Queen Elizabeth is heading this organization. And as she is a popular person, not controversial. Very-difficult-to-please heads of state really appreciate her as the head of the Commonwealth. She has kept the Commonwealth together.

THE TRANSITION FROM EMPIRE TO COMMONWEALTH

The modern Commonwealth evolved from the British Empire and came into being on April 27, 1949, when the leaders of its member-nations issued a document, the London Declaration, in which the phrase "common allegiance to the Crown" was dropped as the basis for Commonwealth membership.

* * *

S. N. Bharadwaj That was a correct decision because India could only have dialogued with the outside world if it was in the Commonwealth. Otherwise, it would have remained isolated.

And, moreover, in spite of all the things there, the link with the British rulers was important: we could still learn so many things from them because we were new as administrators—in India the art of administration is a great problem, even nowadays.

By having the link with them, we could learn about commerce, technology, administration, and, moreover, the self-confidence that should always be there.

I remember in India when we were young people, if we saw any white person—British, or whatever—we would say: "Oh, he's great, wonderful." It was a feeling of reverence. But when we went into the Commonwealth, that feeling vanished and confidence was gained.

INDIA'S SIGNIFICANCE TO THE EMPIRE AS "THE JEWEL IN THE CROWN"

Civilization in the Indian subcontinent can be traced back to circa 2500 B.C. in the Indus Valley, in present-day Pakistan. But British involvement in the subcontinent would begin in the early seventeenth century with the founding of the first settlements of the East India Company, which had been established by a charter from Queen Elizabeth I in 1599.

In the reign of Queen Victoria, following the savage Indian Mutiny against the British, the East India Company was abolished and control of the subcontinent was transferred directly to the British Crown, where it remained until its partition in 1947 into two independent states, the Hindu nation of India and the Muslim nation of Pakistan.

Agitation for independence from Britain had intensified in the early years of the twentieth century when the Indian National Congress, led by Mohandas Gandhi[2] and Jawaharlal Nehru,[3] began its struggle.

While the British established a program of gradual power-sharing, the Congress leaders wanted things to go at a faster pace and so during World War II organized the Quit India movement.

Meanwhile, the Muslim League had its own demands: the partition of India into separate Muslim and Hindu states.

Their goal was achieved on August 14, 1947, with the partition of the subcontinent into the sovereign democratic republic of India, with Nehru as prime minister, and Pakistan, with another major player in the struggle, Muhammad Ali Jinnah,[4] as its leader. Independence of both nations would be proclaimed the following day, August 15, 1947.

But that partition, overseen by Lord Mountbatten of Burma, India's last viceroy, and later its first governor-general, came at a terribly high price: more than one million people would die in the bloody battles that followed partition. The effects of partition continue to divide the subcontinent's Muslim and Hindu nations into the twenty-first century.

THE ATMOSPHERE AT THE TIME OF INDIA'S PARTITION

S. N. Bharadwaj There were two types who were there: those Indians who were in government service were pro-British because they wanted to win the favor of their masters; they wanted to be in government service.

The other people were poor, so leaders like Gandhi would say: "It is all due to the British Throne that you are poor." But in the schools, because they were controlled by the educated people, there was no teaching going on against the British.

Then there were the demonstrations in favor of India. There were the processions: "Death to British Imperialism!" That was influence outside the school; within the school, there was all loyalty.

They were the most terrible days, and one shudders to think of what happened there. I saw dead bodies, slain in the trains, with my own eyes. When the trains used to go from Pakistan to the Indian border, they were murdered there. Later on, there was retaliation, and when the trains moved from India to Pakistan, there were murders there.

Amritsar used to be the border between Pakistan and India—from Amritsar, where I lived, the distance to the border with Pakistan was about ten miles. There is no natural boundary between Pakistan and India; at that time, there were farms and fields there. Half of a tree, and the branches of the tree, were in Pakistan, and the other branches were in India.

At that time, those people in the city thought to be good people, when they got the opportunity of looting, and robbing, did not hesitate, because there was no punishment, and a very strange kind of very horrible atmosphere started there.

I saw women and children murdered. I saw many hundreds of dead bodies. Unfortunately, we had to witness all these ghastly scenes there.

Imogen Campbell-Johnson We had [living] alongside us a maharaja, a great, handsome man, a Sikh, and his men were just running about the countryside chopping people's arms and legs off.

I was up there with my nurse and children and we had Gurkhas[5] to protect us. And they rang every day from Delhi to make certain we were alright. The local people's Muslim servants all came up and lived in our attic for a bit. That's how it was. So you needed one soldier, really, per person to deal with it.

LORD AND LADY MOUNTBATTEN'S ROLE

Elizabeth Ward Collins, secretary to Lady Mountbatten at Southeast Asia Command, Ceylon (Sri Lanka), 1943–46; secretary/assistant in India, 1947–48 He [Mountbatten] was so devoted to the Navy that it was a great wrench, in a way, for him to leave it to go and do it [the partition of India], but he did. Mr. Attlee, who was prime minister, thought he was the only person who could do it so successfully.

It took at least thirty hours to fly to India then. It was a little exhausting. But they made the job so full with all of their own terrific inspiration: if you picked up a pin from the floor, you would feel as though it was a terribly important thing you were doing.

The Mountbattens really did so much for the people of India and I'm sure they felt that they were appreciated. And I don't believe the Mountbattens were ever taken for granted; the Indian people became genuinely fond of them.

And they asked Indian people to the viceroy's house. That hadn't been done before; they didn't get so close. The Mountbattens were really crucial to the process. As I say, they had got real affection from the people.

She [Lady Mountbatten] was absolutely marvelous in what she did. She worked hours and hours a day. And she was the most wonderful person—she had the greatest compassion and sympathy I've ever known, and loyalty. They really were wonderful people.

Lady Mountbatten would sometimes leave the house at five o'clock in the morning—I would accompany her—to visit refugee camps—she really did see for herself; it could be a rotten job. Lady Mountbatten did what she could to help them all. And the numbers were so vast in the camps.

Lord Thurlow She [Lady Mountbatten] was very widely respected, and she played quite a significant part during the post-independence period.

She had a very close relationship with Nehru. She was a very intelligent woman indeed, and Nehru liked and respected her. There is absolutely no foundation, I believe, for the suggestion that it had a physical side to it, but they were very close friends.

Nehru, as a Kashmiri, had this very strong feeling—a sentimental feeling—for Kashmir. And Edwina Mountbatten was very pro-India on Kashmir—too much so—and so we working in the High Commission in Delhi regarded her as being a damned nuisance, because there were times when it would have been possible for India and Pakistan to have got together.

They had many Pakistani friends, of course. It was inevitable that there would be a Pakistan because they [Jinnah and other Muslim leaders] wanted it so much. Jinnah wasn't an easy man, by any means, in any sense. He was very difficult to negotiate with. Of course he was a very sick man. It was a tremendous challenge to Lord Mountbatten and I think it was wonderful the way he did it.

DID LORD MOUNTBATTEN ACT TOO QUICKLY IN BRINGING ABOUT PARTITION?

S. N. Bharadwaj He should have waited. When there was a mixed military, then things were under control. But then the time came when he said that they would fix the date of independence, and that was sudden, and very quick.

In that situation, they had to train their military, and Hindu military men from Pakistan were taken to India and the Muslim military people in India were taken to Pakistan, because they asked them: "Where would you like to opt to be?" And, naturally, the Muslim military said: "We want to move to Pakistan." And the Hindu military said: "We would like to go to India."

And with the change of military, feelings were very high. The military at that time also, on both sides, had people who wanted to wait longer. So he should have waited. There is blame there: an uprising could have been much averted had he foreseen the situation.

Elizabeth Ward Collins Things moved at such a rate, and so quickly, that one hardly had time to really think about it.

It had to happen, you see, because it was the Indian people themselves who wanted the transfer of power and independence—and Pakistan too. And the level of violence could have been ever so much worse, in the sense of the number of people who lost their lives.

It was inevitable. To my mind, it just had to be. And all these people who do criticize it just don't know.

S. N. Bharadwaj And one thing more: the majority in the military at that time were the Muslims. The Hindus were influenced by Mahatma Gandhi and his movement of nonviolence, and a person who believes in nonviolence does not like to join that profession.

Even apart from Mahatma Gandhi, Hindus have always been believers in nonviolence: they have never believed in killing.

I remember a very significant remark by one of the military leaders. He said: "If you have a Hindu military, you will not be able to create Pakistan. But if you have a Muslim majority in the military, then you will definitely have Pakistan there."

I'm speaking from the point of view of a student of history, not from the nationalist point of view: because they [the Muslim military] helped the British in the war, they [the British] had to give consideration to this fact.

Sir David Scott There wasn't enough preparation, and it did go too quickly. I believe that Mountbatten was right in the sense that it had to go quickly, but the homework hadn't been done properly: the boundaries had not been properly worked out in quite a number of areas.

I simply don't know if it had taken longer whether the Kashmiri problem, which is the one really difficult problem outstanding now, could have been solved. Perhaps if somebody else had been the viceroy it wouldn't have been rushed as much as it was.

We certainly left behind a lot of very unhappy people who may have been Muslims but who would have been better, perhaps, if there hadn't been a move to Pakistan, who would have much preferred to have stayed in India.

In my time it was still the Army, particularly, that had an extraordinary attachment to the British Army, and, indeed to the Crown: if you were invited to a regimental dinner, there was an enormous amount of beautiful silver, most of which had the Crown, or the royal coat-of-arms, on it, and they were terribly proud of this.

There was a great feeling that Britain was something more than a foreign country. That sometimes worked to our disadvantage: when it was a question of going to take sides between India and Pakistan, it was almost impossible to do the right thing.

Sir Rex Hunt I believe the criticisms are absolutely justified. Mountbatten was the cause of an awful lot of unnecessary deaths in India by rushing the independence through: I believe he was ultimately responsible for the loss of thousands of lives in India because he hadn't got the boundary lines even drawn by the time of the partition of India.

I saw the most terrible atrocities in the Punjab: we were flying over them and told simply to report on mosques burning, or if we saw Hindu temples burning, or Sikh temples burning. We weren't allowed to go armed. If we'd had our rockets and our guns, and our bombs, we could have saved lives, because we could see crowds gathering to ambush a train and kill everybody on it. A few rockets, even over their heads, would have dispersed them before the train came through.

But Mountbatten wouldn't allow us to have arms; when he had some fire power at his disposal, he wouldn't allow it to be used. And it was downright deceit, because he was telling Attlee and the government back here that he would stamp on any rebellions or civil uprisings—and do it with all the power at his disposal.

Philip Ziegler I don't agree. I believe that Mountbatten was given an impossible task—that, somehow, we've got to get independence through. But the idea that he rushed it just to get back to his naval career is just so silly as to be laughable. He concluded—and in this all the old India hands agreed with him totally—that the one thing we could not afford was delay.

There is a theory that if you had had the time, you could have moved in troops and secured out safe areas, and secured safe points on the frontier. It didn't work because there weren't any troops who could be relied upon, who would have been really prepared to behave with impartiality.

The government were never going to allow Mountbatten to commit them in what could be the midst of a war: his instructions were to get out, not to take on India, Pakistan, or both, in a war. And so I believe that the price of further delay would have been critical—and infinitely more dangerous—than the course he did take.

Imogen Campbell-Johnson Lord Ismay,[6] who had been chief of Winston Churchill's cabinet, had been a cavalry officer in India and knew India very well. Ismay accepted the job with Mountbatten because he said he liked working for lucky men. Mountbatten induced luck; Mountbatten wouldn't face defeat. Mountbatten wouldn't face not getting things right.

But the fact remains that Ismay said: "We're on board ship with ammunition in the hold and fire on the deck." And that's what we were. We were very, very lucky.

Winston Churchill My grandfather once famously said: "I haven't become His Majesty's first minister to preside over the dismantling of the British Empire." But, effectively, that was what had happened.

Of course, if we had been prepared to be ruthless in the way that we had been one hundred, or two hundred, years before and put down insurrections with a considerable amount of bloodshed, we could have sustained an Empire to this day. But it's something that very few people in this country would have wished.

But certainly, in regard to India, my grandfather felt that we were moving much too fast, and that Indian independence was premature and would lead to massive bloodshed.

And he was right. There was a bloodbath: a million and a half deaths resulted immediately from that cut-and-run decision of the post-war Labour government.

Sir Harold Smedley India was the Jewel in the Crown. But looking at the Commonwealth development and the ending of Empire, we *gave* it up: a lot is made of fighting for freedom in these countries, but in a lot of them the fighting wasn't very much more than a slight argument, and it was the lack of will on the British side to maintain an Empire as much as the giving way to new circumstances.

We were in no position to maintain large forces overseas, and our economy was weak, on the one side. And the number of people who were really interested was relatively small, and that was the reason.

There certainly was never a will to try and hang on to the Empire. If the will had been there, we could have gone a lot further down that path than we chose to.

COULD PARTITION HAVE BEEN HANDLED DIFFERENTLY?

S. N. Bharadwaj Definitely. I have thought about this question many times. I believe that there was a proposal from Mr. Jinnah at that time that the exchange of population could be done in a proper way: the Muslims in India should be shifted to Pakistan because the country was divided on the basis of religion there—they should go there, into the new homeland; and those Hindus who are in Pakistan should be brought back to India.

If they had taken consideration of our leaders, this kind of arrangement, there would have been much less murder, and things like that.

But our Indian leaders blundered in this way because they thought: No. We don't believe in the two nation theory; there is only *one* nation.

But that was wrong because they contributed largely on the basis of individual nations. They just ignored it: from our point of view, there is no difference between a Hindu and a Muslim. They overlooked the fact that the bases were different.

So things happened there that shouldn't have, which could have been controlled, had they listened to that view.

VESTIGES OF THE EMPIRE IN INDIA AND PAKISTAN

John Eisenhower We went to New Delhi in 1959. At that time—that was eleven years after independence—Nehru still had a statue of George V in his office. I understand it's gone now.

The Indians and Pakistanis used to man a military unit, the Lancers, who, except for the color of their faces, were British. And when the split up came in 1948, half this unit went to Pakistan and half went to India. But they still kept the same uniforms, and they still did the same demonstrations. The Pakistanis, more than the Indians, kept their Britishness: the Pakistani president, Ayub Khan,[7] looked and acted like a British officer.

Sir Harold Smedley It had changed, but there were echoes, undoubtedly. One of my jobs in India—I was a counselor there—was the responsibility for keeping in touch with citizens of the United Kingdom in India.

There were quite a lot of them who had settled in retirement in India because they were happy there. And there were others who couldn't understand the complications of immigration and nationality—you could only be a U.K. citizen in certain, fairly circumscribed, circumstances.

And these people, who never thought of themselves as being anything but British, were, perhaps, disgusted and horrified to find that they couldn't get a British passport—it's a bit like the feeling about Hong Kong was a few years ago.

And there was, certainly, the Indian Civil Service: you couldn't mistake its background when you saw them in action. But they were, of course, a fiercely independent nation, and they could make life difficult for a British diplomat at time, because there are obvious sensitivities – one saw that when the Queen was there recently [in 1997].

Philip Ziegler We all realized from the moment at which India became independent that, in a way, it was just a question of timing as to how rapidly the rest of the British Empire would also become independent. The only thing that surprised us was the speed with which it actually got going, because there was a rush to independence.

Imogen Campbell-Johnson It was a great, great triumph, that transfer of power. We kept their friendship. And it was quite amazing: all the big embassies came, as soon as independence came, and settled in.

S. N. Bharadwaj If Mountbatten had not been there, things would definitely have been different because he had such a dominating position that whatever came to his mind, it was in his power to get the rulers here to agree to whatever he wanted to do in India.

And there was no check on him. And he got agreement from the rulers there. If there had been a nonmilitary man—some political guy—it would have been better.

Elizabeth Ward Collins It wouldn't happen again, but I would do it again, certainly. I think it is very bad, very unfair, when people talk about it as if it was all a mistake, because they don't know. They weren't there at the time and they don't understand what happened.

Lord Thurlow Mountbatten and India played a key part in determining the constitutional shape of the Commonwealth; this was the single most important factor in determining the constitutional relationship between the new Commonwealth and the old structure of the dominions and the Empire.

Because India decided to become a free and independent member of the Commonwealth, and Pakistan took the same decision, under the influence of India, that determined the decision of every successive colony that came up.

Sir Emeka Anyaoku There was originally some inconsistency between the British Monarch and the Commonwealth countries that chose to become republics. Before India and Pakistan joined the Commonwealth, the Commonwealth was one of dominions; the original five members were all dominions. They had the King—the British Monarch—as head of their state.

But when India and Pakistan joined the Commonwealth upon obtaining independence in 1947, a formula had to be found, and the essence of that formula is that irrespective of what your constitutional arrangement is—whether you are a republic, or a monarchy, or whatever—you accept the Queen as head of the Commonwealth.

So she has been, and still is, the head of the Commonwealth, and she takes that responsibility very seriously and in that capacity takes continuing interest in the wellbeing of the Commonwealth.

Sir Shridath Ramphal Literally a month or two before April 1949, Ireland had left the Commonwealth on the basis that Commonwealth membership involved allegiance to the Queen. And fresh out of the revolutionary period, which had all to do with allegiance to the British Sovereign, they just found it unthinkable that they should be a member of a Commonwealth, which, they assumed, must imply allegiance to the British Sovereign—and in constitutional theory at that time it did.

But that was also the time that India had become independent. And Nehru, who was very farsighted, had taken the decision that, yes, India had become a republic—it would not have the King as the head of state in India—but it wished to be a member of the Commonwealth.

So it had to be revamped, if you like: the constitutional theory of it had to be adjusted to accommodate India's wish—and the wish of any future country emerging in independence that opted to be a republic.

The King of England would be head of the Commonwealth, but not necessarily head of every state—so that was a very fundamental change in constitutional doctrine affecting the Crown.

THE MEANING OF THE OLD EMPIRE

Eric Moonman Empire Day, which later became Commonwealth Day, was a chance to look at the enormous red patches on the map, and you were very proud to see that we owned the world—this was before the United States came on the scene.

Imogene Campbell-Johnson It was the Empire on which the sun never set. But I don't think there was any glorification over it; I don't think people went round pompously patting themselves on the back. It was just something that had happened. And I think, in a way, that's how the British Empire *did* happen; it *happened*, you know.

Joe Haines The nature of the British people has changed enormously in my lifetime: the old "Queen and Empire"—or "King and Empire"—was actually a rallying cry. If you read any of the books from the First World War, where we were the only European nation to have a volunteer army, so many of those men were moved by the thought of King and Empire; you see it in the poetry—whether it's Housman's *Shropshire Lad*, or some of the war poetry.

The Empire was something that was greatly admired, loved, and cherished. People were loyal to the concept of Empire because it gave the British—and particularly the English—a kind of ineffable superiority that the rest of the world hates so much. I don't think that exists today.

Donald Macdonald I can remember one of my first readers in primary school in Ontario. On the inside cover, it wasn't the old Canadian flag; it was the Union Jack. I can't remember whether it said: "One Fleet, one Flag, one Empire." But if it didn't say that, the whole context was that.

That was what I was brought up in. And, I think, an important disestablishment between that contact and the Second World War is an important difference. It became perfectly evident that Britain was no longer in the age of power—that it could barely manage.

Lord Howe It's an extraordinary story. I had served in East Africa in the Army of the late 1940s with Swahili-speaking troops, and one of my jobs there was to conduct a weekly current affairs course with them, and to explain why Bwana King George was a better guy than Bwana Joe Stalin.

They had all fought for Bwana King George in the Burma campaign—they had received letters from the King; they had come to the victory parade in London, walking past dignitaries and so on, so they were subjects of the Monarch. And the message at that time was that we were all fellow-citizens of the British Empire, because for the first time since the Boer War it was about colored people—the very phrase "colored people" dates it—in Britain, of which there were then thirty-five thousand, in total, in this country, half of them sweepers and half of them seamen, located in Stepney, and in east London, and in Liverpool, and so on.

And ten years later, there were a million, because they had begun exercising their freedom of movement within the Commonwealth, because it had become just cheap enough that they could afford to get on a liner from the Caribbean, or somehow get to England.

They were untrained, and all of them were in tatters and shambles. So we had to take this agonizing decision, really rupturing the concept of *Civis Britannicus sum*, and saying they couldn't come at all.

But you can see that we all had an emotional desire to maintain the *Civis Britannicus sum* for the whole lot, and the Commonwealth, in a sense, represents that for them as well as for us. And the Queen was very, very important in ensuring the continuity of that relationship.

THE QUEEN'S SPECIAL FEELING FOR THE COMMONWEALTH

Lord Wright You have to remember that there's a particular section of the Commonwealth of which she is actually the Sovereign. In the presentation of credentials, heads of the monarchical missions in London—like the Australian high commissioner, the Canadian high commissioner, the New Zealand high commissioner, and Grenada and a few others—don't present credentials; they present letters to the prime minister. And they call on the Queen.

But they are not accompanied by the permanent under secretary; they call on their own Sovereign, alone, which is entirely right and proper. These are the sorts of distinctions that probably mean a lot to the Queen.

Sir Malcolm Rifkind She's not just Queen of Britain. She's Queen of Australia; she's Queen of Canada; [...] she's Queen of Jamaica. She's Queen of about a quarter of the Commonwealth, so that's one very important factor—she is the constitutional Monarch of twelve [now fifteen] countries in the United Nations.

Secondly, the Commonwealth is the consequence of the Empire: her father was Emperor of India. If she'd become Queen five years earlier, she'd have been Empress of India. So the Crown was the symbol of what the old Empire was all about.

Also, the Queen has perhaps found it easier, and at a much earlier date, to contemplate the fact that Britain is a multiracial society because her family ruled a multiracial Empire and she is head of the Commonwealth.

Perhaps the most important point, by the wishes of all members of the Commonwealth, she as Queen of Great Britain is officially head of the Commonwealth, even for those countries that are republics. So because that is part of her job, she will, obviously, see a special interest.

Sir Emeka Anyaoku It would be right to go back to her first commitment to the wellbeing of the Commonwealth, which was a commitment she made as a young Princess during a visit to South Africa, when she actually pledged to devote her life and work for the Commonwealth. She has kept true to that commitment.

Nelson Mandela That was the moment when we had developed some political attitudes. His Majesty, King George VI, was invited to South Africa by General Smuts,[8] who, though he was famous in the British world, was our enemy because he belonged to a ruling group that had denied us all opportunities for self-expression, and embarked on a very brutal method of racial discrimination ever seen in the world.

So at that time we developed a negative attitude towards the British Crown, because of the link with the South African government. And especially since 1948, when the National Party, under Dr. Malan,[9] came into power.

We saw pictures of the visit by Malan to London; he was warmly welcomed by Sir Winston Churchill. And that, of course, prejudiced us because Dr. Malan was our mortal enemy.

So the British visit in 1947 was tainted by that. We did not even want—we as politicians—to come near the Royal Family and that visit did not exercise much impact on us at the time.

Sir Michael Palliser She genuinely, and strongly, feels that the Commonwealth is a continuing, postcolonial, if you like, link between a large number of English-speaking peoples.

She genuinely feels that her role as head of the Commonwealth is helping to hold together a group of countries who, anybody recognizes, have different systems; they have different degrees of democracy, or none at all; they're different in so many ways—but they have a common factor, which is, or has been defined in the past by economic assistance, but a common experience. There is a legacy there, which is up to her to sustain, and support, and nourish. And she does it remarkably well.

Sir Edward Ford Of course, the first thing she decided to do after being crowned was to do a Commonwealth tour, which she did. So it's always been very much in her mind.

It must have impinged on her a great deal—masses of people of different nationalities, races, and colors, and so on. And, of course, she has had extraordinary experiences since she was very young […] in every corner of the Commonwealth she, or possibly Prince Philip, has been to.

Lord Armstrong The fact that she's been anointed Queen gives her a duty to carry out the functions of the Sovereign to the best of her ability for the rest of her life—not only in relation to England, or the United Kingdom, but also in relation to other parts of the Commonwealth.

With the Empire breaking up, and India becoming independent—Canada and Australia, obviously, were virtually independent before the war—and other parts of the Commonwealth becoming independent in the succeeding years, she felt that the role of head of the Commonwealth, which had been devised at the time of the Indian independence, largely, I believe, thanks to Pandit Nehru, gave her a unique ability to focus the Commonwealth and keep some measure of unity in it.

Sir Shridath Ramphal Another part of it is that the Queen came to the Throne as a young person, and what were to become the new and substantial members of the Commonwealth, which were the old countries of Empire, were being led by young men who were almost contemporaries [of the Queen] in terms of age—people like Julius Nyerere, in Tanzania;[10] Kenneth Kaunda,[11] in Zambia; Lee Kuan Yew,[12] in Singapore. The ones that were coming to the fore increasingly were going to be of *her* time, and she related to them in terms of their aspirations.

I don't believe she saw the Commonwealth as a dimension of her role as Queen of England and as bringing something additional to just the old-fashioned monarchy. This was the newness, this was the value added, this was something that meant that the Queen of England, that the British monarchy that had survived the war, when monarchies all over Europe were coming down, had about it something that went beyond country, that had a character that was partly international and, therefore, set it apart and gave it a justification, which the others didn't have; that would work to its being sustainable. And in that, she was absolutely right.

THE QUEEN'S GRASP OF COMMONWEALTH ISSUES

Sir Emeka Anyaoku When she meets with the heads of the individual countries, they are quite amazed as to how well she is briefed on the affairs of their nations. Long before I assumed my present post in 1990, years before that, I was the head of our political affairs division. We had a meeting of the cabinet secretaries of all the Commonwealth countries and the Queen held a reception for this group at Buckingham Palace.

It was my task to escort her around, to meet all the senior officials and to identify what countries they came from. She chose which direction she went, and I was quite amazed at how she had something relevant to say to each one about his or her own country.

Sir Adam Ridley I sense from when I was working with her that she did not want to be lectured. And there was a period when one or two of the Commonwealth leaders would read her a short homily on racism; it was basically because it was thought that she was too pro the Rhodesian whites in South Africa. But she was certainly not uninterested in the wider Commonwealth conflict.

Sir Shridath Ramphal I believe few people are quite aware of how much she is in touch with Commonwealth affairs, through Palace arrangements—her prime ministers of the Commonwealth don't come to London without calling on the Queen—which keep her in touch with Commonwealth leaders. And the prime ministers would feel free to convey to her matters they think she should be aware of, through their channels of communication.

In the countries in which the head of state is a representative of the Crown—like Australia, or Canada—the governor-general would call on her, and communicate with her pretty regularly.

Duke of Norfolk She's a person of great sagacity. She knows how to play the card of humility very well—she can be very humble—but very *determined*. She loves the Commonwealth, and she doesn't lord it over [leaders of the Commonwealth countries]. She's very much Queen. Of course, she does dominate quite a bit, but always through her prime ministers.

Sir Michael Palliser When with her, when talking about a Commonwealth country, the Queen would nearly always say: "I remember when I was there ..." She related the current question to her own experience, and I remember thinking, on a number of occasions: this woman knows far more about the Commonwealth than any of her ministers, because the ministers, and the government, the Commonwealth secretary will be Commonwealth secretary for a year, or for two years; he may have had prior experience in Commonwealth affairs, but it's very unlikely that any Commonwealth minister—and any Commonwealth officers—have the range of experience and knowledge of the Commonwealth and the countries, and the prime ministers, and so on, that she has acquired over fifty [now seventy] years. It's a very remarkable personal corpus of experience that she's had.

Philip Ziegler There is no doubt at all that [in the late 1970s] she was much closer to the various Commonwealth leaders than any British politician was likely to be. And if the prime minister of the day wanted to know what Kenneth Kaunda, or Hastings Banda[13] was going to do, or what [Australian Prime Minister] Robert Menzies, or the Canadian prime minister Lester Pearson was going to do, the Queen would probably give a far better judgment than the secretary of state for Commonwealth relations.

This is not so true now, in part because the Commonwealth has very largely grown much looser. And, also, another generation has come on the scene, and she is an elderly lady who very well may not keep as closely in touch as she used to with their predecessors.

Nelson Mandela When she came here for the Commonwealth, I spent about forty-five minutes with her. And again, we recalled fond memories, and she's a lady I really respect and love—very graceful.

The real contact that I had with her was when I invited her to pay a state visit. It was necessary for us now to change that relationship which was disturbed by the association of the British prime ministers with South Africa, so I invited her, to remind her that we were part of the British Empire. And though we have now ended that association, historically we are closer to Britain than any other Western country. Her Majesty behaved very, very well, and because she turned up, showed the impact of the British Monarch on South Africa.

In fact, the late Canon [John] Collins, who was canon of St. Paul's, the Anglican Cathedral, came here in 1952 and the South African government wanted to impress him. And they had an African, who was employed by them, to take him to certain places which were selected by the South African government to impress Canon Collins, because he was already developing as an important critic of the South African government.

So they went to hospitals, to schools, and so on. And this African chap was praising this government, saying: "We are free here; it's only agitators who are creating trouble." In the room now, there were present some members of the government. But during the course of the talk, Canon Collins saw that he sat alone, and he said: "I'm very happy to hear that you are free. When I go back home, I will tell Her Majesty that she does not have to help to free your people because you are free."

And this fellow says: "Please, no, no, don't do that. Tell Her Majesty that we are oppressed, that she must come as quickly as possible to liberate us." Now what had a real impact, I felt, was when Her Majesty came for a state visit.

Sir Shridath Ramphal The prime minister of England is not her adviser on the Commonwealth—on her role as head of the Commonwealth— any more than any other single one of the heads of government of the Commonwealth. Collectively, if you like, they are *all* her advisers.

The Commonwealth secretary-general comes closest, I suspect, to being the channel of communication to the Queen on Commonwealth affairs, and the exerciser of influence on her in these matters: if the

Queen were to want specific information, or advice, on a Commonwealth dimension of something, it would be to the secretary-general that she would turn. Whereas in domestic affairs, of course, the Queen does not act solely on advice from her prime minister.

The trick, of course, is to have this freedom and use it with such seamlessness that she does not appear to be using it—does not appear to be exercising a direct influence—and what appeared to be, particularly in the apartheid situation, fighting with her prime minister at home.

The Queen over the years has developed a tremendous skill in deploying these freedoms and acting on them.

THE BIENNIAL CHOGM

Ivan Head We went from being around a single table in Marlborough House to Singapore, where it was in a huge, air-conditioned convention center with massive space—a great big, hollow, circular table with floral bouquets in the middle. And the individual prime ministers were at a distance from one another; you almost had to yell across at the other guy. It was just too much.

The pressure was on the Brits to allow the Commonwealth Conference for the first time ever to go elsewhere than London—in a massive departure from convention. And, of course, it would go to Canada. So the P.M. said to me: "What about this?" And I said: "Not on your life!" And he said: "Why not?" And I said: "Of course we should have it. But you see what they're doing—this is the British view: Canada is the senior Commonwealth member, then Australia, of course, and then New Zealand. And we'll go way down. This is idiotic. Either we're all equals, or we're not. Talk to a couple of the others and see if one of the developing countries—one of the newly independent members—will have it. And then we'll take it the next time round, and get it done that way."

And Singapore wanted it—they were ready—so in 1971, we went to Singapore. In some respects, it was even more formal than in London.

We went back to London in 1975 for a variety of reasons: it was a Jubilee year, so the Brits wanted the Commonwealth to be there—everybody wanted to be there for the same reason that Julius Nyerere liked to go back; it was a special treat.

On that occasion at Buckingham Palace, we were being presented, and just as at Government House in Ottawa, they would check you out first, so that they were able to introduce you. And on that occasion, the Queen said: "How nice it is to see you again."

And right behind me, there was a guy from either Australia or New Zealand, and she said: "How do you do?" And he said: "Your Majesty, don't you remember me? We've met." When you think of the millions of people who go through that line!

Sir Shridath Ramphal [Of the Queen's private meetings with the heads of government] They attach immense importance, great value, to that fifteen or twenty minutes, or whatever it is, when she talks with them. It used to be quite often on *Britannia*, or in the presidential palaces in a country like Zambia.

And out of all that comes a relationship that is quite personal, not just based on ambassadors' reports. And they are all quite amazed: many have said it to me directly after those meetings how impressed they were by how well the Queen was briefed on their national affairs, and how much their country's welfare meant to her.

When the Queen travels in the Commonwealth you see with what enthusiasm she is received by the people of those countries, some of whom have struggled for freedom from British colonialism—and here is the very symbol of old Empire—and yet the Queen relates to them, and they to her, in a marvelously wonderful way.

Sir Bernard Ingham Quite frankly, I didn't like going to Commonwealth Conferences because I knew that there would be an unpleasant atmosphere, and I knew very well that we would be in a minority of one, and that they quite deliberately sought to put us in a minority of one, and that created considerable problems for the Queen.

And there is at least reported evidence that the Queen began to show concern about the effect upon the Commonwealth, which she led, and that was part of the 1986 criticism [of Prime Minister Thatcher] that came out of the Palace.

The evidence since is that it didn't do the Commonwealth much harm, because now people are wanting to join it: they've admitted Mozambique, which is Portuguese-speaking [...]

Now, to the extent that Mrs. Thatcher helped to get rid of apartheid strengthened the Commonwealth. We can't deny it made for difficulties for the prime minister, and it made Commonwealth summits very unpleasant places.

HOW IS THE QUEEN REGARDED IN THE COMMONWEALTH?

John Eisenhower Nehru came to Washington in 1961. He met with Dad and he talked about how they had refused to recognize the Queen. And he said people were wondering, and were tearing their hair out: How can you be in the British Commonwealth and not recognize the Queen? And he said: "Well, we're just in it. That's all."

Raymond G. H. Seitz The white members of the Commonwealth have a feeling for the monarchy that is not wholly shared with the non-white members.

In Kenya when I was there, there was always a lot of respect for the British. The British were very, very good colonial administrators—certainly better than the Belgians, who weren't very good. What they left behind was, on the whole, very creditable.

Because of a lot of disorder in a lot of the countries that were once British colonies, there was a kind of nostalgia for the stability, if nothing else, of British administration. The Queen benefits from the view. While I abhor colonialism, if I had to be colonized, I'd rather be colonized by the British than by anybody else.

THE QUEEN'S VISITS TO COMMONWEALTH COUNTRIES

The British Sovereign's responsibilities as Queen and as head of the Commonwealth require her to visit Commonwealth member-countries, especially the fifteen—in addition to the United Kingdom—where she reigns."[14]

The Sovereign has traveled to all those member-nations in which she reigns, with particular emphasis on Canada, Australia, and New Zealand.

* * *

Sir Emeka Anyaoku It is difficult to know if the Queen has favorites among the Commonwealth countries because she treats each one of them with the same degree of concern, which is very much appreciated. For example, on the eve of the celebration of the Queen and Prince Philip's fiftieth wedding anniversary [in November 1997], I had suggested to the heads of all of the Commonwealth nations that it might be appropriate for the Commonwealth to give the two of them a present in appreciation of her long and committed service to the Commonwealth.

I received such an enthusiastic response that the two levels of contributions I had recommended were oversubscribed, the only Commonwealth venture for which I have had oversubscription.

Sir Shridath Ramphal It would be wrong for me even to say that she had a closer feeling—a more intimate feeling—for the old Commonwealth: I believe the Queen is just as happy in India as she is in Australia, or in Kenya.

I've seen her nearly every year in the Commonwealth. She doesn't have any favorites, if you like. She is a person; she's entitled to her own special kind of likes and dislikes, and she would have views of some of the characters she's encountered.

But in terms of her being a Queen who is happy in the white Commonwealth but takes the rest of the Commonwealth—Africa and Asia—on sufferance, absolutely not!

IS THE QUEEN MORE RELAXED IN THE COMMONWEALTH THAN IN LONDON?

Sir Shridath Ramphal The whole aura of majesty does not accompany the Queen to the Commonwealth—it's part of the ambiance of the Commonwealth. It's much more relaxed, much more friendly.

How happy the Queen always seems to be—because she is—in a Commonwealth setting. You can take the Queen in Zambia, or in Samoa, or in the Caribbean; she is jolly, and smiling, and involved, very happy.

When you see the Queen going round Britain, I don't think you will see the smiles, and the brilliance, and the general involvement that you see in any Commonwealth photograph. She's just very happy in the Commonwealth—this Commonwealth that she relates to so well, and that gives her so much affection.

PERCEPTIONS OF THE COMMONWEALTH IN POLITICAL/GOVERNMENT CIRCLES

Stephen Day It's a symbol of stability—the continuity of certain institutions in any real sense is the continuing relationships, which are largely unaffected by the change of government: educational exchanges; technical cooperation; discussion of parliamentary and legal issues—they're very important; certain traditions of military training; the whole, tremendous network of these that go on, regardless of government.

And that's why, if you talk to the average diplomat, and he's asked about the priorities of British foreign policy, he clearly wouldn't think of the Commonwealth until fairly late on. That's not because it's unimportant. It's just that he doesn't need it; it just works terribly well.

I've always found one of the fascinations about representing Britain is that one does have to have a certain humility as a diplomat, because those aspects of Britain which are most successful are, by-and-large, outside the control of government.

Sir Shridath Ramphal All of the British prime ministers had different attitudes to the Commonwealth. Ted Heath had a fearful row at a Commonwealth meeting in Singapore, but it didn't derive from his general attitude about the Commonwealth; it arose out of a specific issue.

Attlee was very much a Commonwealth man, a deep believer in the Commonwealth.

Wilson was supportive of the Commonwealth without being visionary about it: he saw the Commonwealth as an economist, in terms of its economic potential of cooperation, and so on, and he made an effort in relation to the issue of UDI,[15] which was the issue in his time.

I believe that Callaghan was very genuinely fond of the Commonwealth —a strong Commonwealth man. He had come out of the Labour Party's stable, which had over the years very close contact with Commonwealth countries in Asia and Africa. Callaghan would have been of that generation who would have known Nehru; who would have known Nkruma; who would have known the next generation of Nyerere, and Kaunda, and so on.

Mrs. Thatcher knew nothing about the Commonwealth. Her husband had done business in Africa, but clearly not with African governments, at the corporate level. She had never been to Africa—it was all very new to her. She was very much a domestic politician. In international terms, she was of suburbia.

Bob Hawke (1929–2019), prime minister of Australia, 1983–91 The Commonwealth has been a very useful institution. What you've got to remember though, when you're talking about the monarchy and our view about it, and the Commonwealth, is that the majority of the members of the Commonwealth are republics, so there's no question of the Queen remaining Queen of our country being in any sense as an essential part of membership in the Commonwealth.

The Commonwealth played a very useful role in a number of areas—and in two, in particular, in which the Australian prime minister has been very much involved. The first was in 1979, during the Commonwealth Conference, when Malcolm Fraser was very much involved in the discussions then which led to the emergence of Zimbabwe—you have to wonder at the moment how propitious that was.

And of course I was the leader of the group in the Commonwealth in the fight against apartheid in South Africa, and the Commonwealth did play the leading role in mobilizing world opinion against apartheid.

GENERAL PERCEPTIONS OF THE COMMONWEALTH

Anthony Eggleton, AO, CVO, press secretary to Australian Prime Ministers Robert Menzies, Harold Holt, John Gorton, 1965–71; Commonwealth director of information, 1971–74; federal director, Liberal Party of Australia, 1975–90 I don't believe that the average Australian walks around thinking daily about the Commonwealth. But even Australians today who are not of British heritage see the virtue of this particular international grouping and, while a lot of those kinds of people would like to see the change to the republic, they certainly wouldn't have the same feeling about wanting to break from the Commonwealth.

Generally, most people are positive about their Commonwealth relationship only because it reminds them that there is a link through the Queen as head of the Commonwealth.

But also they are conscious that lots of things seem to happen at a Commonwealth level which work very effectively—that every now and again, all these prime ministers get together and this seems to be a useful thing to do, that it's quite a lot smaller than the United Nations, and because of it's being somewhat smaller, sometimes more useful things can be achieved.

And it's one of the few organizations where the actual leaders themselves sit down around the table and talk to each other and not just make set-piece speeches, but actually say what they think, sitting around the table together—that there's an exchange of a kind which doesn't happen in many other organizations.

And so while they wouldn't necessarily spell all that out, there is the feeling that the Commonwealth is harmless, in the sense that there's nothing for us to be worried about it, and yet it does, rather, good.

And they're aware that it provides links between a whole range of people, whether it's exchanges between schoolchildren, common interests in education, common interests in law, common interests in architecture. There is a multitude of nongovernmental organizations that form the basis of this relationship with the Commonwealth.

So I believe that the Commonwealth enjoys good support. And you'd find that support equally among republicans and monarchists.

Thomas Keneally The man-in-the-street likes the Commonwealth, feels that it's a useful set of connections, and feels the fraternity with other Commonwealth countries.

We have this four-yearly event called the Commonwealth Games, and that's very important to Australia because not only do all our Olympic-level athletes win gold medals, but most people who wouldn't otherwise get in win gold medals. For this reason, there's a warm, fuzzy feeling about the Commonwealth— [...]

If you went beyond the warm, fuzzy feeling and asked people what they remember about the Commonwealth, those who were a bit more informed would say: "Well, it slapped some very important sanctions on South Africa, against the wishes of Maggie Thatcher, so, look, we can even make the British do what we want them to do."

Bob Hawke How far does the man or woman in the street identify with the United Nations? How much do they identify with their membership of APEC [Australia Pacific Economic Community]?

The answer is that in a day-to-day sense, it's not the normal topic of conversation around the dinner table in the normal Australian home. It's just like so many things that are in our lives, in our political life: they're accepted, but they're not talked about a great deal.

But it's something that's there and I think that the overwhelming portion of the Australian people would regard membership in the Commonwealth as a good thing, and would recognize the good things that have been done through it.

Ivan Head It's largely a mystery to the average Canadian. Anybody who's fifty or sixty years old would have warm recollections. But even those recent arrivals in Canada from India, Punjabi communities in Canada, wouldn't have any particular affection for it.

In the Caribbean it's a little bit different—the Eastern Caribbean more than the Western Caribbean, Barbados much more than Jamaica.

Geoffrey Pearson The Commonwealth is difficult to imagine. Where *is* it? If you ask the average person, they don't have the faintest idea, except that they know it has something to do with the British.

It used to be called the *British* Commonwealth until fairly recently [1949], when we dropped the "British," partly at my father's insistence. But it's not well-known.

There is a Commonwealth Association here—it has a few members. But partly because we're a country of immigrants—the Chinese [population] is the third-largest, after the English and the French, and then you go down further a bit and you find Ukrainians—these people don't think about it; it's not a big deal.

S. A. Pasha Generally, Muslims are in favor of the Commonwealth because that shows us our link, particularly the first generation, who has immigrated from their home countries. They feel more at home if Britain has a Commonwealth.

But the new generation who is coming up here may not be so much attached. I'm not saying now what is going to happen, but they might not be so attached to the whole idea of the Commonwealth.

But for Britain to occupy an important position in the world as the head of the Commonwealth is something any British citizen will be proud of—regardless of whether they're a Muslim or a Christian, because Britain has an important role.

If Britain is head of the Commonwealth, that is much more favorable to us because a lot of Muslim countries are part of the Commonwealth.

Raymond G. H. Seitz Certainly, as an operating organization, if you say "Commonwealth"—the sort of footprint of Empire—then yes, it does excite a lot of things: they watch movies about the colonial wars; books, biographies, are out all over the place about Britain's imperial era. So the Commonwealth as a continuing life—or a kind of outline of what used to be—is of some interest to the public.

But the Commonwealth as an organization that *does* things and meets the heads of government and heads of state level, that tries to decide things and passes general resolutions on one thing or another—sometimes people will leave the Commonwealth, and sometimes they will come into the Commonwealth—I don't think that matters a whit.

Sir Donald McKinnon British high commissioners in Commonwealth nations saw themselves as primary sources of information concerning the countries in which they served, so I would insist that they be part of the information flow to Buckingham Palace.

This was not a question of *primus inter pares* as they were all equals. The British have a remarkable way of handling foreign policy, which means that what they were doing in bilateral terms on the left hand has nothing to do in Commonwealth terms on their right hand.

Lord Steel The Commonwealth is a very remarkable institution.

I was heavily involved at the time when the Queen was extremely influential regarding the South African issue during the August 1979 Commonwealth Heads of Government Meeting in Lusaka, Zambia.

My friend Sonny [Sir Shridath] Ramphal always says how important Her Majesty's role was in keeping the Commonwealth together at that point following her slight argument with the then-Prime Minister Margaret Thatcher over the latter's attitude toward South Africa.

* * *

During the 1999 Durban CHOGM, which the authors attended in preparation for the first edition of this book, the Queen would demonstrate her skill in dealing with disparate delegates, such as the late, controversial Robert Mugabe.

* * *

Sir Bernard Ingham, interviewed 2021 While the Queen is seen to be a good figurehead who takes the institution seriously, it is fair to say that quite a few Commonwealth member-nations and their people are republicans.

Lord Heseltine Creation of the Commonwealth from the British Empire is a remarkable, historic achievement.

Everybody knows that the practices of imperialism had unattractive aspects, that our country would morph into the Commonwealth, whereby people would voluntarily want to be associated with it—there is no doubt that this is a tribute to the imperial achievement, and the Royal Family has the responsibility of heading the Commonwealth. In doing so, they have spent a good deal of time traveling, encouraging the Commonwealth's unity and, indeed, have achieved remarkable popularity across an incredible diversity of nations and peoples.

CHAPTER 16

Canada

B RITAIN'S INTEREST IN Canada can be traced to John Cabot's claim over that territory in 1497 in the name of King Henry VII.

France acquired an interest when in 1534 explorer Jacques Cartier discovered what is now the Gaspé Peninsula, and rivalry soon developed between the two nations, mirroring their tensions in Europe, notably in conflicts known as the French and Indian Wars.

Modern Canada would evolve through a combination of British settlement, conquest, and cession of territory by France. French Canada, encompassing New Brunswick and Prince Edward Island, was ceded in 1763.

Later, Vancouver Island was recognized as being British through the Oregon Boundary Treaty of 1846; and British Columbia was established in 1858.

Then, with the British North America Act, the shape of Canada as it is known today evolved, beginning in 1869 with the purchase of the Northwest Territories from the Hudson Bay Company and culminating with Newfoundland's joining to Canada in 1949.

Through the British North America Act of 1867, Canada became the first dominion within the British Empire.

THE QUEEN'S ROLE IN CANADA

Ivan Head When I was in the Foreign Service the Queen actually signed the appointments of Canadian ambassadors and high commissioners within the Commonwealth—it was *her* signature on these things. She appointed them.

Other appointments within Canada—and there are still many made in the name of Her Majesty Queen Elizabeth II of Canada, Defender of the Faith, and all of that—are no longer signed by the Queen herself; they'd be signed by the governor-general, acting as the deputy, the representative, of the Queen.

Gordon Robertson It's very, very rare for anything to come up that really requires the attention of the Sovereign herself; almost everything is part of the system and the governor-general is the representative for those parts where it happens.

And there's no need for the Queen to meet with the Canadian prime minister. She, in a sense, is part of the system because she has a representative doing this.

Hugh Segal There was very little the government of Canada asked of Buckingham Palace that Buckingham Palace didn't respond to positively—they were always going out of their way to be accommodating. And that's important.

And it would be an issue we would think about: Is there a role for Her Majesty that would be constructive, where Canada gains? And oftentime the answer was yes, and they were always very, very responsive.

Ivan Head We decided at a certain point that the signing of the appointments of ambassadors and high commissioners was a vestige of the past and that it should be given up because we were gradually pulling away from those kinds of things.

The Queen was quite reluctant to do that. The Queen and prime minister had a conversation about it at Windsor. That was not a difficult conversation, but one in which she wasn't just going to give in: she felt that this was a personal link—her interest as the Monarch in her subjects—that this was a severance of an element of her awareness of who was doing what, and when, and she felt that this was one of the few remaining personal functions that she had with the functioning of the government of Canada; this allowed her the occasion to read the C.V.s of the individuals that were being appointed.

Never would she say: "I don't think this is an appropriate person for this appointment." But it kept her informed. I think that was much closer to her than the formality of it—the fact that her signature appeared on these documents.

There was never any doubt that a) Pierre Trudeau was going to carry it through, or b) that she would agree to it; she would never have held it up. But her reluctance was a bit stronger than had been anticipated.

She purposely wanted to do this in the old-fashioned way—of the Monarch with her prime minister; there was nobody else there.

Donald Macdonald The monarchy is not important in this country. It's just part of the structure of the domestic questions that are driven on their own merits. If you thought about the monarchy at all, it was on a purely formal basis. It was quite clear that the serious roles you had with the English were within Parliament. There was no local political dialogue.

Geoffrey Pearson Canadians are natural democrats, in the small "d" sense—we don't believe in lords and ladies. We're not allowed to accept foreign decorations—we stopped accepting British orders in the 1930s. We cut our ties to England, in that sense, except for the Queen.

We created our own order—in fact, in my father's time—called the Order of Canada, which was the first time we had ever done this. It's given to people who have made some mark on our society. There are only about twenty or thirty every year.

The military [in Canada] identifies with the monarchy more than anybody else does because of the sense of [British] tradition—these things remain important for historic and symbolic reasons. But otherwise, they're anachronistic.

Hugh Segal We're a conservative society. The guiding principle of our constitution is "Peace, order, and good government." And when you get to "Peace, order and good government," you get to a constitutional monarchy, and a parliamentary system, and a slightly greater role for the state.

The monarchy has become one of the few distinguishing differences between the Americans and us. There aren't many left, and the homogenizing force of technology is probably going to reduce some others.

Interestingly, the Indo-Canadian population, people of Sikh and Hindu background which we have in some cities in very large numbers—in some parts of Canada, in Vancouver, and Toronto, there are parts of the city where twenty-five to thirty percent of the population are Indo-Canadian in one form or another—tend to be strong monarchists, in the long tradition of service: they served, or their parents served, with, for example, the imperial forces up against Japan. So that's quite a positive force.

THE QUEEN'S RELATIONSHIPS WITH SOME OF THE CANADIAN PRIME MINISTERS

There have been twelve Canadian prime ministers, to date, in the reign of Queen Elizabeth II.

LOUIS STEPHEN ST. LAURENT (1948–57)

Gordon Robertson St. Laurent was a French Canadian. While he was a very strong Canadian—you couldn't expect a French Canadian to have a vast enthusiasm for things British—there was never the slightest thought of any disrespect, but he would never have thought of himself as partly a proprietor of the Empire. He would have seen the Sovereign as the legal head of state, to be regarded with respect. Period.

LESTER BOWLES PEARSON (1963–68)

Gordon Robertson Mr. Pearson would have taken a rather lighthearted view of things formal. When there was a proclamation to be signed for the new [Canadian] flag, in 1965, we were going over to London for the funeral of Mr. Churchill, and the prime minister decided this would be a good time to take the proclamation with him for signature by the Queen, which had to be done.

He didn't get around to signing it until we were on the aircraft going over. He decided to sign it on the aircraft and there was no desk there, and so I got out my briefcase and put it on the end of a trunk, and took out the proclamation, and he started to sign it.

He got to the "L" of "L.B. Pearson" and the plane gave a lurch, and his pen slipped. And the proclamation ever since, to this day, has an "L" that goes like that— [gesturing to indicate a broad stroke downward.] This was a reflection of a less-than-serious view of even things like a royal proclamation.

Donald Macdonald I would think that the relationship would have been very good, because it was very difficult not to like him. Everybody thought he was just a soft guy, that you could push him around. But inside he was very tough. He accomplished a lot as prime minister, but he had a very good personal manner, and I'm sure that she would have found him delightful in her relations with him.

I'm not sure what the Queen thought when Mr. Pearson said in a formal interview that we should move away from the British tradition and establish some of the Canadian symbols.

Hugh Segal Mike Pearson, who had an extensive background in foreign policy, would have been someone she would enjoy to spend time with—and vice versa—because she would learn things. One of the first criteria for a Queen is: are you learning something from the prime minister about the country over which you have some responsibility?

Geoffrey Pearson We knew Queen Elizabeth as a family; my father knew her when she was a Princess. And because he went to conferences in England once he became the minister of foreign affairs, he met her when he went over to pay his respects to the King, at that time.

Part of the Queen's liking for my father was that she had known him as a girl. When you know somebody when you're young, you don't usually forget.

They would come here. We have pictures in our home with the Queen, and Prince Philip, and our children. When they came in 1967, our centennial year, they came to the house where we lived—prime ministers of Canada live at 24 Sussex Drive [Ottawa].

The Queen was interested in our foreign policy, and, especially, the Commonwealth, which was her major interest. So as my father became even more active later on in African questions, especially in Commonwealth Africa—Rhodesia had been a colony and he helped to create the country that became Zimbabwe—obviously, there were a lot of common interests in questions about the future of the Commonwealth; could it act as a bridge between East and West? Could the Commonwealth be a force for good?

So she regarded him, and Canada, as a useful sounding board for her. The British might tell her what she wanted to hear and she felt that here people would speak to her more frankly about Commonwealth issues.

PIERRE ELLIOTT TRUDEAU (1968–79; 1980–84)

Donald Macdonald When I was there, he had only become a member of the Privy Council for Canada and there were occasions when he would meet the Queen in that capacity. He would not be an unfailing admirer of the institution.

Princess Elizabeth, the future Queen Elizabeth II, greets the officer of the guard at the Aldershot tattoo, 1935

At Sandringham, Norfolk, April, 1944

Waving to the crowds on Victory in Europe Day, May 8, 1945.
Left to right: Princess Elizabeth in her ATS uniform, Queen Elizabeth, Winston Churchill, King George VI, and Princess Margaret

King George VI and
Princess Elizabeth, *c.* 1946

With her fiancé,
Lieutenant Philip
Mountbatten,
Buckingham Palace,
July 10, 1947

Princess Elizabeth and
the Duke of Edinburgh
on their wedding day,
Westminster Abbey,
November 20, 1947

Princess Elizabeth accepts a present for Prince Charles from Lieutenant Michael Parker, *left*, and the Hon. Piers St. Aubyn at the Flower Ball in aid of St. Loyes College, Savoy Hotel, London, May 23, 1951

The Royal Box at Ascot, May 13, 1951. *Left to right*: Princess Margaret, Princess Elizabeth, Group Captain Peter Townsend, and Queen Elizabeth

The Duke of Edinburgh and Princess Elizabeth with their children Charles and Anne, September 8, 1951

Princess Elizabeth walks ahead of Governor of Kenya Sir Philip Mitchell at a garden party at Government House, Nairobi, Kenya, February, 1952

Leaving Clarence House for Windsor after George VI's death, February 7, 1952

Queen Elizabeth II, Queen Mary, and the Queen Mother at King George VI's funeral, February 15, 1952

Presidents and leaders follow George VI's coffin from Windsor Castle on the way to the funeral service at Westminster Abbey, February 15, 1952

With Princess Anne
and pony at
Balmoral Castle, 1955

Captain A.W.R. McNicoll,
commander of the HMAS
Australia, conducts Queen
Elizabeth II on a tour of
inspection of the ship, off
Townsville, Queensland,
March 20, 1954

Greeted by Winston and
Clementine Churchill
when arriving for a
dinner at 10 Downing
Street, April 4, 1955

With Frank Sinatra at
the royal film premiere
of *Me and the Colonel*,
July 10, 1955

Meeting Queen Salote of Tonga,
Tongatapu, December, 1953

A wet day at Oban, on the Royal
Tour of the Isles, August 14, 1956

Greeting US President Dwight
Eisenhower at the British
Embassy, Washington, D.C.,
October 19, 1957

With the Ghanian President
Kwame Nkrumah, during a visit
to Kumasi University, 1961

Inspecting cadets in New Delhi with
Prime Minister Nehru, January, 1961

The Queen Elizabeth II and the Duke of Edinburgh watching stockmen round up cattle near Alice Springs, on the Royal Tour of Australia, March 18, 1963

Prince Edward, Prince Andrew, Earl Mountbatten of Burma, and the Queen on the Royal Yacht *Britannia*, Southampton, August 7, 1974

Greeting Prime Minister Harold Wilson at 10 Downing Street, London, March 24, 1976

In Brisbane, during the Silver Jubilee Tour of Australia, accompanied by the Lord Mayor of Brisbane, Alderman Frank Sleeman, March 9, 1977

With Premier Pierre Trudeau in Toronto, on the Silver Jubilee Tour of Canada, October 1, 1977

With the corgis at Balmoral. *Left to right*: Prince Edward, the Duke of Edinburgh, Queen Elizabeth II, Prince Charles, Prince Andrew, and Princess Anne with her son Peter, January 11, 1979

The Queen approves the marriage of Prince Charles and Lady Diana Spencer through the Privy Council, at Buckingham Palace, March 27, 1981

Visiting wounded soldiers from the Falklands conflict at a military hospital in Aldershot, June 29, 1982

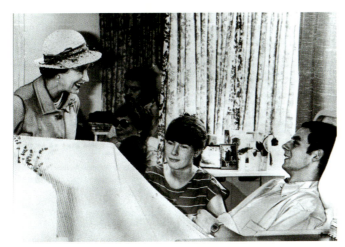

Horseback riding at Windsor Castle with President Reagan, June 8, 1982

A welcome fit for a queen on Tuvalu, during the Tour of Australia and South Pacific, October 28, 1982

Queen Elizabeth II, with Princess Diana and Prince Charles in the Chamber of the House of Lords for the State Opening of Parliament, November 3, 1982

Walking the dogs on a beach near Sandringham, Norfolk, July 27, 1984

Prime Minister Margaret Thatcher addresses the 32nd Commonwealth Parliamentary Conference in the Westminster Hall, September 25, 1986

Meeting the Anglican Archbishop of Cape Town Desmond Tutu with Sir Shridath Ramphal, secretary-general of the Commonwealth, at a Commonwealth Day Reception at Marlborough House, March 9, 1987

Derby Day, Epsom Downs Racecourse, with Princess Anne and the Queen Mother, June 1, 1988

Escorted by the chief fire officer around the grounds of Windsor Castle, November 20, 1992

Standing with South African president Nelson Mandela before a banquet given by Mandela at the Dorchester Hotel, July 11, 1996

In Portsmouth, for the last annual trip to Balmoral via the Western Isles aboard the Royal Yacht *Briannia*, August 7, 1997. *Left to right:* the Prince of Wales, Prince Edward, Prince Harry, the Queen, Peter Phillips, Zara Phillips, Princess Royal, Prince William, and Captain Tim Laurence.

After attending a private service at Crathie church, the Royal Family stop to look at floral tributes left for Diana, the Princess of Wales, at the gates of Balmoral Castle, following her death on August 31, 1997

Prince William, Earl Spencer, Prince Harry, and Prince Charles follow behind the cortege that carried the Princess of Wales's body to Westminster Abbey, September 6, 1997

Queen Elizabeth II and the Queen Mother at Westminster Abbey for the Princess of Wales's funeral, September 6, 1997

Queen Elizabeth II, accompanied by Prince Philip, attends the State Opening of Parliament, November 24, 1998

The Royal procession in the Royal Mile, Edinburgh, for the first State Opening of the Scottish Parliament in 292 years, July 1, 1999

The Prince of Wales, Prince William, and Prince Harry outside Clarence House, London, on the day of Queen Elizabeth the Queen Mother's 101st birthday, August 4, 2001

Queen Elizabeth II arrives in Iqaluit, Nunavut, Canada, October 4, 2002

Camilla, Duchess of Cornwall, Queen Elizabeth II, Prince Charles, Meghan, Duchess of Sussex, Prince Harry, Catherine, Duchess of Cambridge, Prince William, Princess Charlotte (*front left*), and Prince George (*front right*) on the balcony at Buckingham Palace, for Trooping the Colour, June 9, 2018

The Duke and Duchess of Sussex with their baby son, Archie, St. George's Hall, Windsor Castle, May 8, 2019

Queen Elizabeth II during the funeral of the Duke of Edinburgh in St. George's Chapel, Windsor Castle, April 17, 2021

Queen Elizabeth II and the Duke of Edinburgh, Windsor Castle, June 1, 2020

Hugh Segal Pierre Trudeau saw the whole thing as quite an anachronism. And the relationships would have been correct, but you're probably overstating it when you get to "cordial." But in terms of any kind of warmth, or back-and-forth, I'd be stunned if there were any.

Gordon Robertson Trudeau—a French Canadian—didn't have very much respect at all for these institutions. None of this Empire nonsense. Of course, the Empire was long a thing of the past.

His attitude was reflected in a famous photograph of him doing a pirouette in Buckingham Palace when he was at a Commonwealth meeting [in 1969]. The Queen always gave a state dinner for the heads of state who were there and before he went in—I believe the press had been warned that he was going to do it—he did a pirouette, and a photograph was taken, and that photograph received a great deal of circulation.

I suppose the photograph shocked a lot of people. But a lot of others would have just laughed at it. Or a lot of others would have discussed it and have said: "Well, what else would you expect from that fellow?"

[MARTIN] BRIAN MULRONEY (1984–93)

Hugh Segal Mulroney had a good relationship with Her Majesty. He understood the importance of the monarchy to the structure of the political party he was the leader of, the Conservative Party, which always had a strong bias in favor.

He also understood that the network that Her Majesty represented across Europe and the world was an important network for him to be part of as prime minister. There are not many people in the world outside Canada who say: "I wonder what Canada's up to?"

JEAN JOSEPH JACQUES CHRÉTIEN (1993–2003)

Hugh Segal The Chrétien relationship would be in the category of correct to cordial. One of the Federal Liberal ministers, Mr. Manley, the minister of industry, actually floated the idea quite formally [...] that perhaps we should begin a debate as to whether or not we should be having the Queen as our head of state and be heading towards a republic.

It died pretty quickly because under our constitution, Her Majesty could stop being the head of state in a whole bunch of countries before she could ever be banished from Canada because our constitution requires that on any matter as fundamental as the monarchy, or parliamentary democracy, you must have unanimity, which means that the Parliament of Canada has to vote for it; the Senate of Canada has to vote for it; every province—not nine out of ten, not four out of ten, not seven out of ten—every province.

And the minute brother Manley made this reference about perhaps changing the system, the premier of Prince Edward Island, population 110,000—there are more people in apartment buildings within vision of this window [in downtown Montreal]—said: "We'll never approve it; matter *closed*." And it is. Because we don't have the constitutional capacity to change that part of our constitution without unanimity.

THE QUEEN'S KNOWLEDGE OF CANADIAN ISSUES

Ivan Head The Queen had a good knowledge of what was happening in Canada. She was kept well-informed. But again, that was partly because of the close relations that Gordon Robertson had with his counterparts in Britain. And [in] those earlier days, the Commonwealth was handled in a fashion other than as a foreign country, as it was supposed to be; it was a Commonwealth country. So those channels of information—those informal, back-channel conversations that happened by telephone, were taking place all the time. So she had a great interest.

And I don't recall a single instance when Pierre Trudeau was in Britain on an official visit that he did not call on the Queen to keep her informed. They had a very close personal relationship. I was involved in some of those: I would sit in. They were kind of fun.

Geoffrey Pearson I don't know that she had expertise. She was always well briefed and knew what she was talking about, but I don't think she was a scholar—she didn't read very much, herself, about politics in Canada.

She was aware of the issues and was prepared to talk about them. But I'm not sure that she took a deep interest in our political culture.

She spoke good French, which was important, compared to American presidents who try out their French when they come up here. So that was useful for her, because she would always speak in both languages when she came, and nobody ever said that she didn't know how to speak French.

THE ROYAL FAMILY'S VISITS TO CANADA

Gordon Robertson King George V was a very remote figure as a person: there was no television and not much radio. And so I don't think there was an awful lot of a sense of George V as an individual.

Now George VI was totally different because he was King during the war, and he, plus the now-Queen Mother, earned tremendous respect by their courage and the way they handled things, partly in contrast with his brother [Edward VIII].

But I believe that the present Queen—partly because she is a woman—has earned a greater personal enthusiasm than any of the others. And, also, because she has visited here several times; she has been seen. And there is a greater sense of her personal presence, through television, when she is here.

She's not coming in a substantive way; she's coming partly to give Canadians a closer sense—a more intimate sense if you can call it that—of the fact that she *is* the Sovereign.

For older Canadians, there is a great deal of affection, and for younger Canadians, when she comes there is a good deal of excitement—she stirs up great, great interest.

I was commissioner of the Northwest Territories for a number of years, and the Queen was to visit there. We got representative people from all the tiny communities across the north and brought them into Yellowknife, which was the capital, for her visit.

Well, the Queen had previously toured in the Yukon—she was pregnant at the time but we didn't know it. And when she was there, there was something that disturbed the doctors and she was advised not to go to Yellowknife.

We knew nothing about the fact that she was not coming because communications up there were very bad. Well, all these kids and all the others from across the Territories were in Yellowknife, and the excitement was intense.

When the plane landed on the field, there was tremendous excitement. And when the door opened, everybody was thrilled: they practically thought she'd be wearing the Crown. And out stepped this man, in a very unexciting gray suit—it was the Duke of Edinburgh, taking her place—and you could just hear the wind going out of the whole crowd—whoosh. It was nothing compared to the Queen. She was the Queen, and that was it.

The Inuit, or Eskimos as they used to be called, had been found quite early on to have a real talent for stone-carving, and we were encouraged as a source of income, apart from everything else.

One of the Eskimos in one of the settlements where they do the carving had decided he'd carve a little statue of the Queen. He had a picture of the Queen in her Coronation robes to go by. I was the one who, as commissioner, presented this to the Duke of Edinburgh for the Queen.

It really was beautifully done. We took it out of the box to take a look at it and admired it enormously. But the only thing the sculptor had not been able to see was what the Queen had on her feet because the robes went right down to the floor. And when we turned it over, she was barefoot! Every toe was beautifully carved.

The Duke of Edinburgh has a very good sense of humor. He enjoyed this just enormously: he laughed. But his wit *can* be cutting. To be fair to him, he picked up the ball just as well as he could; he did very well.

Donald Macdonald I've never known—or heard anyone ever say—that when she came here she was carrying any brief for the British government, or British interests. I know they're very sensitive to that. She would recognize that this was a political issue wherein trade policy was a matter to be conducted between governments—that she should not get into that.

A couple of times there was a question as to whether the Queen should come. There was going to be an election, and they had already booked a royal visit, and the question was: "Can you tell Her Majesty to stay home?"

Ivan Head In 1973, Ottawa was the site of the Commonwealth Heads of Government Meeting. And Gordon Robertson and I had heavy responsibilities in the organization of it. As a result of that, at the conclusion of the Queen's participation, before she left, she gave personal audiences to three or four of us.

These things are kind of old-fashioned: she's standing, of course, and you're brought into the room, and she doesn't say: "Nice to see you. Sit down." She then handed me an autographed photograph, a beautifully framed thing, of herself and Prince Philip.

She was aware of the fact that for the first time ever, Pierre Trudeau, as host, had taken consultations with every other single prime minister to find out what was on their minds: he wanted to make sure this was a substantive meeting that reflected the desires, the interests, of the other prime ministers—not just a pro forma thing. So that was what we talked about. It was not lighthearted, but not heavy.

Hugh Segal I was involved in the planning of the 1992 visit when the Queen came over for the celebration of Canada's one hundred and twenty-fifth anniversary. And that's essentially a process in which the federal government says: "Here's the agenda we would like Her Majesty to have." That is submitted to the Palace; the Palace responds.

The Palace never responds negatively—they never say: "We can't have seven events that day." I've never seen them respond in any way to suggest that Her Majesty wouldn't take on whatever work they would deem her business.

Often they will respond in a very thoughtful way; they will say: "Reception Parliament Buildings, with Parliamentarians." And she'll notice that she actually doesn't get to see any ordinary Canadians that day—except through a walkabout—so often the Palace will write back and say: "Could young achievers, or young scholars, or bright people involved in the arts, be invited to that reception?"

And there are some security issues, which I always left to security—like food, and facilities, and where she is staying. There are certain things. For instance, you never serve her fish—whatever the menu is, if it's fish, she isn't eating it.

Of course, no one ever sees Her Majesty eat: at our state events, there's always a card in front of her—you can see her tiara, but you don't actually see the food entering her mouth at the event.

The monarchy has a very special relationship with our Aboriginal people. If you talk to our Aboriginal leaders, elected and otherwise, they would say: "We signed all our treaties with Queen Victoria. That's who we signed our treaties with. This lady here [Queen Elizabeth II] is the one we trust."

So there's always a huge Aboriginal presence when she comes. And she always insists on spending time, sometimes in the poorest parts—the way we've handled our Aboriginal circumstance is a matter of no great national honor: we have mortality and morbidity rates amongst our Aboriginal population which are amongst the worst in the world, Third World level—and she engages fully. And it makes a big difference.

And one of the things which drives public policy, where there's a great desire to improve the circumstances, is the knowledge that the Royal Family has a proprietary interest.

And if Canada ever disengaged from trying to keep on moving things ahead, and forward, for Aboriginals, I'm not quite sure what would happen in terms of the Royal Family engaging on the issue. But the notion that they would be utterly silent, and totally disengaged, is probably optimistic.

For our own Aboriginal tradition, it's much more akin to a monarchy, or a matriarchy, than a democracy. And the Royal Family, and the monarchy, are at the present time a matriarchy. So there's a natural affinity there.

Our Aboriginals will have a much higher regard for the elders than for the elected council. Her Majesty is on that side. She's all for democracy, et cetera, but it must be clear, she didn't get elected; she's there because of her inherited presence and responsibility. So that's where part of that affinity comes from.

Ivan Head She has always taken a great interest—like the Pope – in traveling. These are great tourists!

What takes place, well in advance of any Queen's visit, is really a wish list. There will be invitations: "It's been six months since the Queen was last in Victoria [British Columbia], so she must come again."

It just couldn't happen at all that changes could take place in the Queen's schedule. It's sort of sad that that can't happen. But the protocol is just such, and all the ladies of the place would be in such a tizzy—that they've planned their church social and she's going to drop by.

Her visits here are very people-oriented, but they're not heavy on substance at all. Generally speaking, she will deliver one speech of substance and the text will be shared in advance with us.

She's not speaking in a political fashion, but she's nevertheless here, speaking as Queen of Canada. And, therefore, the procedure is that she consults with her prime minister. There's never the need, nor a suggestion, that a word, or a comma, could change. But it's just the way it's done.

No formal arrangements will be put in place until the prime minister has agreed that this is the proper time. There is some tension on occasion in that respect. The Queen says: "I want to come!" The prime minister says: "That's all very well, and we'd love to have you, but this isn't the time. We've got other things; we've got an election coming."

And the Queen would never come during an election, because she just could not be seen to be independent of the prime minister of the day, and it would convey such a sense of partisanship. So she stays out of it on those occasions.[1]

CHANGES IN ATTITUDE TOWARD THE CROWN

Hugh Segal The polling numbers indicate that young people don't have any greater disaffection for that institution than they do for any other. But they're disconnected from it.

Remember that none of the kids who are arriving as freshmen at college would even remember *Jaws*. And so all of the historical relationships that would have built my sense of Her Majesty the Queen just don't exist for that generation.

The real challenge for the monarchy, I believe, is to identify itself as a force for good in a way that people begin to see it as a constructive part of the new galaxy.

I believe she's actually quite modern. If you look just at her own inter-action with the public, if you look at just how the change has taken place in the Queen's Message, over which she has tremendous control—the focus on children and young people, and different sorts of values.

Whether the institution can follow along, with all its trappings, suffi-ciently to move public opinion so that her position is stronger all the time, or whether the institution can survive her ultimate demise—hopefully, not for many years to come—I don't know the answer to that.

Ivan Head "God Save the Queen" is no longer sung in Canada. It stopped in about the early 1970s. It was rather an unusual thing when you think back about it now, but nobody thought twice about it as the first movie of the performance started, whatever time of day it was. If it was a matinee, or if it was in the evening, the first film—it wasn't done between films—we stood up and sang "Oh, Canada," and then at the conclusion of the performance—around 11 or 11:15—we sang "God Save the Queen." This just petered away after a time.

Hugh Segal The federal government, which used to be an exponent, is now quite ambivalent. So, for example, the crown has been removed from lots of stuff: the crown used to be on every postal box—it used to be the crown and "ER"—it's now "Canada Post"; the coat-of-arms of Canada with the crown on top has now been replaced with the ubiqui-tous maple leaf. You still see it on police officers' badges. And, of course, the military still has it in a heavy dose. But the linkages and the presence aren't as much.

And the only places where there are toasts to the Queen now are all our luncheon clubs where Canadian speakers come—usually Rotary, Kiwanis, and all those folks. And you can't go to a B'nai B'rith[2] event where there isn't a toast to the Queen—and, often, to the president of the United States if there's an American speaker. That's still part of the formal structure. Whether it will penetrate to the next generation is unclear.

Donald Macdonald I don't know of any organized antipathy to the Queen, or to the monarchy, such as apparently exists in Australia.

There is a very broad area of indifference: there is a tiny group, the Monarchist League of Canada, and there are some scattered, not very influential, abolitionists.

But basically, I believe, the view is denying that they're interested. We've got a lot of other difficult things to argue about in terms of national unity.

Geoffrey Pearson We have had something called the Monarchist League—it's not very big, but it does exist. And English Canada, for obvious reasons, has always been pro-monarchy. My father and mother and their generation were brought up to believe in the British Empire. And this was partly because of the dual nature of our country: the French part of our country did not feel that way, while the British part of it became even closer to the monarchy—or the *idea* of the monarchy, because these other Canadians wouldn't fight in the [Second World] War; there was conscription and they objected. So the English Commonwealth became even closer in the war to the monarchy, by showing that they were loyal.

Not the French, although our French-speaking prime minister Sir Wilfrid Laurier[3] was a great friend of the Monarch. But that was in the early part of the century. As the years went by, nationalist sentiment rose in Quebec, especially because of the last war.

Yes, the monarchy is not a big issue here, partly because it doesn't matter in the end whether we have a Queen, or a governor-general, or somebody else. Who cares? There's nobody saying we've got to change the system. You may find the odd person, but there's no *movement*—no political movement—because it's just not of interest to people.

I believe that if Prince Charles became the King, people would then begin to raise the issue. But this Queen is very popular.

The Australians may feel they're further away, since they are. But we live beside our Great Neighbor, and we've got to, in every way we can, demonstrate that we're not American. And this is one way of doing it.

Jean Chrétien Her Majesty is very aware of these problems. She is well briefed, follows the political situation very closely, knows quite well what she is about, and asks pertinent questions.

WHEN CHARLES BECOMES KING, WILL THERE
BE A FURTHER CHANGE?

Hugh Segal The issue will be reborn. At the time of transition, there will be some who will say this is a chance to ask the question: "Do we even want to be subjects of this King?"

And the relevance of that question will be determined by the circumstances at the time: if the country is in economically good straits, or not facing any national unity crises, or is getting on with getting on, then there might be people saying: "Why don't we do this?"

But if we're involved in any kind of major debate, or difficulty, people may say: "We don't have any room for this; this would just add to the burden, add to the divisiveness."

So the government has to say to itself: Why aren't we doing this? Because we're going to get some trendies in Toronto, and maybe a few Quebecois, on our side?

It's important to know this: [Jacques] Parizeau, who was the premier at the time of the last referendum, when we came so close, and was quite a nationalist, and wanted Quebec out of the Confederation, wants Quebec to stay in the Commonwealth.

He's Oxford-educated, and his mannerism is very much Oxbridge High Table.'[4] And he would want to be part of the Commonwealth. He'd be delighted to have Her Majesty the Queen not as head of state, but in a titular sort of role: she speaks impeccable French; she's never said, or done, anything that's been the slightest bit insensitive to Quebecois national interests, in terms of language and culture; if anything, she's been supportive.

So it doesn't really solve that problem in a sense; becoming a republic is not really going to make them happy. And you'd be stirring up more of a hornet's nest than it's worth.

Gordon Robertson Charles certainly hasn't established any great accumulation of respect. I suspect that the Canadian public—to the extent that they think of him at all—think of him as a rather fumbling person who hasn't done very well.

But I don't think that it will amount to anything significant if in ten years, or fifteen years, or twenty years, it becomes a question of his succeeding to the Throne. I don't believe Canadians would want to wrestle with something else.

THE QUEEN AND QUEBEC

Gordon Robertson The 1960s were really quite a bad period in Quebec: there were bombings, and explosions, and manifestations by quasi-terrorists, not extreme terrorists, who put bombs in mailboxes to attract attention. It was really at the early stage of the separatist movement. But because it was the early stage, it was rather more extreme than it became later.

Jean Lesage[5] was premier of Quebec; he was the Queen's host at the time. And there was concern: there were large numbers of troops on the streets for riot protection because they wanted to be sure that no incident would hurt her.

That was one of the touchiest periods as far as the monarchy was concerned. I believe that now even the separatists in Quebec don't have any great animus about the Monarch and the monarchy. If they were to separate, of course they wouldn't have the Monarch. But as long as they're part of Canada, I don't believe there would be much support in Quebec for any manifestations against the Monarch, or any indication of disapproval, or opposition. Certainly since 1964 there has never been any serious concern, or attention, about royal visits.

Donald Macdonald The domestic political debate was already going on, and the Queen was always very gracious to take advice as to how to avoid that.

Around that period of time, my colleagues and I, as ministers, would host the Queen, with Prince Philip, in various parts of the country. I was the minister having to do with Western Ontario and traveled with them there.

The principal impression made was by the accompanying staff, who were voracious to know the public reaction in the press, in places where the Queen visited. They were very concerned.

The demonstrations were in Quebec. And that would be really a manifestation of the separatist movement. I don't believe that would be regarded as general. A demonstration against the Queen in Quebec goes back to the time and an age when the majority of English-speaking Canadians—even now—would say: "Don't be rude about it; she's not just an important constitutional figure, but she's a great lady. Don't be rude."

Ivan Head Even among the wildest of the separatists in Quebec, there's no animosity towards her; it's the institution—what it represents—that would bring out some of the young bloods into the streets to do silly things. She has acquired, through her own personality and through her own commitment, an aura of great love and respect on the part of persons who know her, and persons who only know of her. And as time has gone on, and she has become more familiar with what's happening, and, perhaps, in particular, more knowledgeable about the individuals, they regard her really very warmly as a human being.

Geoffrey Pearson Nineteen sixty-seven was the more important occasion, the Centennial—General de Gaulle and all of that. De Gaulle arrived on a warship. And the way he talked! He talked from a balcony in Montreal: *"Vive le Quebec libre!"*

He had stopped at Quebec City, and there was a procession from Quebec City to Montreal, in which he waved to the crowds for most of the procession as though he had liberated it; he really did pretend to be the liberator of Quebec!

The Queen certainly heard about it, and everybody else was unhappy. And then my father said [to de Gaulle] in response: "We don't think you liberated Quebec, although you think you do."

CHAPTER 17

Australia

B RITAIN'S INTEREST IN the huge continent "down under" dates to the reign of George III, when in 1770 Captain James Cook sailed into Botany Bay, claiming the eastern coast of Australia for Britain.

Australia's first penal colony was established in 1788 when the first shipload of convicts, both criminals and political prisoners, many of the latter Irish dissidents, arrived on the site of present-day Sydney.

Free colonization replaced the penal institutions by the middle of the nineteenth century. By that time, new settlements had been established in Tasmania, Western Australia, South Australia, Victoria, and Queensland.

The settlements soon flourished due to wool and wheat exports, as well as gold rushes in 1851 and 1892, which attracted additional settlers.

In 1901, the colonies were federated as states of the Commonwealth of Australia and in 1927 the seat of government was transferred from Melbourne to Canberra, the capital of Australia today.

The present Queen and other members of the Royal Family have had over the years a deep involvement in Australia. The Queen's uncle Prince Henry, Duke of Gloucester, was Australia's first royal governor-general, serving from 1947 to 1949.

Later, the possibility of Prince Charles becoming governor-general was discussed, but shot down in several quarters. But Prince Charles in 1966 spent a semester at the Geelong Church of England Grammar School in Melbourne, the first-ever member of the Royal Family to attend an overseas Commonwealth school.

The Queen visited Australia for the first time in 1954 with the Duke of Edinburgh during their post-Coronation Commonwealth tour, the first there by a reigning Monarch.

THE AUSTRALIAN MENTALITY

Neville Wran We are inclined to be a difficult, truculent people underneath this nice exterior for several reasons: one is that we started as convicts; and two, we have a disproportionate number of people of Irish descent, compared to the other migrant groups here. And the Irish are a fascinating people, and quite difficult, in their own charming way.

To the extent that they thought about it at all, in the earlier days people didn't talk about their antecedents because to have come as a convict and to be a descendent of a convict was not regarded as the sort of thing to push you up the social tree.

But as time has progressed, people are more honest about why people were sent here, and now people would be proud to say: "My great-great-uncle arrived in 1832 on a fleet where thirty-seven people died of scabies."

Thomas Keneally Transportation has become more a matter for celebration than shame. You can play the card both ways, even to the extent that on the popular level, you will meet people in pubs who say: "All the Irish were political prisoners," which, of course, is not true.

In an index of how people think about transportation, there is huge interest in ancestry. And generally if you can find a convict, you've really hit it big. It's like finding that you're of noble blood.

ATTITUDES TOWARD BRITAIN AND THE QUEEN

Thomas Keneally There's an incredible ambiguity towards Britain: if you hear my father's war stories—he was in the Middle East with the British Forces—they're all about humiliating officers, borrowing Australian officers' uniforms and going into Shepheard's Hotel in Cairo, and picking a fight with British Guards officers, and that was far more important than the Afrika Corps.

The Australians had a way of making British officers snap a salute. They would walk along the streets of Cairo, or Alexandria, and as a British officer approached them, they would raise their hand, the British officer would snap a salute, and they [the Australians] would wipe their nose.

There was ambiguity towards the British, but not towards the Monarch. George VI was much respected because we used to see him on the newsreels reviewing troops and walking round bombed-out sites.

In every public school there was a picture of the Monarch on the wall. I went to a school run by the Christian Brothers of Ireland. There was no picture of the Monarch when I was there. In the seven years between my going there and my little brother going there, there was a picture of that young Queen on the wall.

She got a spin from the fact that suddenly we Catholics became very anti-Communist—we had versions of McCarthyism in Australia—and the Queen, with this young, fresh face, virginal figure, looked a much better bet than Joe Stalin. And so the Cold War helped cement the monarchy to us.

Neville Wran It's very difficult to say, or to define when the attitude towards the Queen changed. But the period was Sir Robert Menzies.'[1]

Now he was a monarchist to his bootstraps. He was a very clever politician, but he is famous for [saying of the] the Queen at Parliament House, in Canberra, in a speech: "I only saw her walking by, but I shall remember her until I die."

Now that was the high point. She made him the Warden of the Cinque Ports, and he loved getting into his garters and buckled shoes, his fat belly hanging out of his pants. The relationship with the monarchy was fostered strongly under him.

Whitlam won in 1972. Whitlam wasn't anti-monarchist, but he was pro-Australian. And we as a nation started turning away from Europe, and turning to Asia.

Bob Hawke While it hasn't got the wilder degree of enthusiasm it had in the earlier years, there's still a genuine affection for her here.

That affection is not across the board; it's obviously rooted in those of British origin. Those of Irish origin are not madly enthusiastic about the Queen, or anything to do with the British Monarch. And in a sense, those of our citizens who've come from non-British stock don't have the same degree of affection, but there's an acceptance of her.

Neville Wran She was a chilly sort of person. That might have been because of my inadequacies, not hers; I wasn't used to greeting Kings and Queens and maybe I didn't generate any warmth.

Everything was very, very correct; no warmth anywhere. There was enormous protocol. As time went on, it has got less—there's much less protocol now—but everything was protocol.

On the first visit here, I remember, she brought the *Britannia* out. I just thought it all starchy—very stiff and slightly uncomfortable. The Royal Family are all starchy.

There were lunches and dinners where there'd be twelve people around the table. The first time I met the Queen when devolution was on the agenda, I was trying to think of something to say, and show what a good chap I was, and I said: "Ma'am, what is your view about Scottish devolution?"

Well, a block of ice descended from the ceiling. If she doesn't like the question, she's got a terrific technique of just not answering.

Thomas Keneally In her demeanor on visits to Australia, especially [since 2000], she's perceived to have behaved properly. Her sense of duty was seen as generally her valiant attempts, rather than her mean-spirited attempts, to keep the family together. So it's based purely on her demeanor as a fairly good stick, even though some republicans point to her huge wealth, and her ultimate indifference to our destiny.

In 1977, when the Queen came to Australia, a weekly newspaper called the *National Times*, which is now defunct, asked me to go and cover it, as a republican, so I was introduced to the Queen at Government House at the press reception.

It's the only time I've actually met the Queen because I don't go to monarchical things. I've been invited many times to monarchical levees, on the yacht *Britannia*, and elsewhere, and always refused, out of primitive Australian republicanism, but always politely; I've never said: "To hell with her!"

I was already a republican and I had knocked back a CBE, so I was not as interested. I was still young, so I was almost egregiously disinterested. But I was polite.

The Queen was very cordial and probably I was a bit internally snotty at that stage in a way that I would not be now. I must say I've never felt a warmth for her. But I don't feel a rancor.

Prince Philip asked me what the *National Times* was—the circulation, and so on. And he was quite nice. But it was not the fulfillment of a life's dream. But still in 1977, for many Australians it *was* the fulfillment of a life's dream.

FEELINGS ABOUT THE DUKE OF EDINBURGH

Sir Zelman Cowen There is an institution called the Duke of Edinburgh's Commonwealth Conference—the Duke of Edinburgh is president of the conference. A number of people who are already showing promise in business, in administration, in unions, are brought together from a number of Commonwealth countries for a Duke of Edinburgh's Commonwealth Conference.

It happened in 1986—this was after I had ceased to be governor-general—that I was asked to be chairman. As chairman I would rub shoulders with the Duke on something virtually every day of the conference.

He is a dogmatic man and I found that the only way in which I could respond was to say, if I believed in a thing: "Well, I think you're wrong. And I'll tell you why I think you're wrong." And it worked.

But I was startled when I received a letter from him saying that I had done the job beyond the call of duty. I didn't think that he did that sort of thing.

Stuart Macintyre He's regarded as cranky, conservative, and difficult. Mind you, he's got an impossible role. Looking on from the outside, he does not appear to be the world's most caring father.

But if you think of what his life consists of! The extraordinary thing is that he hasn't had more outbursts. Especially this idea towards the end of your life, when you think: Why am I doing this? Where am I going? When is it all going to end? And you find yourself attending ceremonies, having to make small conversation to people with whom you have nothing in common, or will never see again, and you're only there because it's your wife and so you have to be invited.

* * *

A leading Australian politician from the Labor Party, who wished not to be identified, said that Prince Philip was "a monumental pain in the ass."

On one visit to Britain, our source had an important matter to discuss with the Queen, regarding a constitutional issue of how advice or information should go to the Palace—whether it should go through the governor-general, as the Queen preferred, without direct access.

We were having tea at Buckingham Palace, and we were talking about this—the Queen was sitting across from me and Philip was talking to somebody else. And then Philip butted in and said something which was absolutely bloody stupid.

The Queen was marvelous the way she handled him: she said in so many words: "You don't know what you're talking about. Let us get on with it." She did it very politely.

* * *

Neville Wran I don't believe most people here would regard him at all. He's acerbic. I can understand it—if I had to walk behind my wife, I think I might be a bit sour too; he's not altogether the fun of the party, you know.

I believe he's quite cynical about a lot of what he does—the formalities he has to comply with, and very short—indeed, some people might say he's an ill-tempered individual.

Anthony Eggleton [In 1970] I watched the Duke in action every day, and he would look for ways of sort of provoking the press a bit. If we were somewhere where there were some hoses, he would say: "Why don't we turn on the damn hoses and get the press wet? That'll keep them away!"

He does have a good sense of humor and sometimes he says things which I'm sure he thinks are funny, and often are, but which can then be misinterpreted and get him some flack from the press.

I'd quite like to sometimes have been sitting at the breakfast table with the Queen and the Duke when some of these stories were hitting the front page, and the Queen having to say to the Duke: "Why did you need to say *that*?"

FEELINGS ABOUT PRINCE CHARLES

Anthony Eggleton I believe you'd find very mixed feelings about Charles in the Australian community. He was very popular of course when he went to school here at Timbertops, down in Victoria. He got quite a lot of coverage out of that. And he was then—and I think he is still, to this day—very fond of Australia.

And there was a period when thought was given seriously to him becoming governor-general of Australia. Malcolm Fraser was prime minister at that time, and the thought from the Palace was: the Queen is carrying on as Queen, so what about a role for the Prince? Wouldn't it be quite nice for him perhaps to be governor-general of Australia, a country that he's very fond of?

But that didn't work out for a range of reasons. And then, I suppose in more recent years the unfortunate publicity which the Royal Family, apart from the Queen, had been subject to has certainly affected Prince Charles.

Indeed, the republicans as part of their campaign were raising the issue: Do you really want to wake up tomorrow morning and find that Charles is the King of England?—and that's the King of Australia. Do you really want Charles to be your King?

In Australia, if he did become King tomorrow, it wouldn't cause great shock waves and people wouldn't worry too much. But he certainly wouldn't enjoy the popularity that the Queen does today.

Neville Wran He had a good standing in Australia until Diana took over. And rightly or wrongly, I think most Australians really liked Diana.

I can remember her coming out here when they were first married, and she was a shy, retiring flower. And then we had her out here just a year or so before she got killed and she was a very different woman—very much in charge of herself and calling the shots. But very attractive; I liked her very much.

And I think most Australians liked her. And her problems with Charles didn't help Charles's standing with the public out here. She was the winner there, I thought.

Stuart Macintyre I believe that because he was sent here for part of his secondary education, there was the conceit on the part of certain Australians that he had a particular affinity for Australia and would be an appropriate governor-general.

But the difficulties of reverting from an Australian governor-general to a British one were insuperable. You would need to be a very rash politician to think that we would go back to having a non-Australian as governor-general.

Australians like to think that all sorts of people have an affinity with them. But the affinity might not be returned with quite the ardor that they think. I believe that Prince Charles as an adolescent enjoyed himself *to a degree* in Australia, but never really thought of himself as having much in common with Australians at all.

Bob Hawke There was indeed talk of his becoming governor-general. When I was prime minister, suggestions were around, so I instructed the governor-general to make it quite clear that he would not be appointed as far as I was concerned.

I get on well with him by the way. But there was certainly no way I could have changed the way from what had become a reasonably well-established schedule to appoint Australians. There was *no way* we would have had a non-Australian as the governor-general!

And interestingly, this was the intrinsic paradox of the Monarch's position here: I was saying: "The Queen is not really the head of state; it's the governor-general of Australia."

And the governor-general of Australia said: "What you're saying is that it's improper to have the head of state as a non-Australian. But constitutionally, the Queen is the head of state."

So I said to him: "You're contradicting yourselves, by the way."

Sir Zelman Cowen One thing was sure: Prince Charles would never be a governor-general of Australia. It's anomalous.

In the case of Prince Charles, the fact is that the Australian government is wholly Australian-grown; the governor-general is the nominee of the Australian prime minister; and the powers the governor-general exercises, he exercises to the exclusion of the Monarch.

But to take Charles was, as it were, to turn the clock back. And after all, why take Charles? Well, because here he was approaching middle life without a real job.

But when you come to reflect on it, if he'd been appointed as governor-general, you couldn't have expected the price to be paid. There would still be significant jobs for the person who was to be successor in the United Kingdom. And whatever he said about attending exclusively to Australian affairs, for one reason and another, he'd have been called to assist his mother at home.

* * *

The Queen's role as Sovereign of Australia would be tested when in November 1975 opposition leader Malcolm Fraser, using his party's majority in the Australian Senate, blocked enactment of Labor government budget legislation.

In order to break the ensuing deadlock the then-governor-general, Sir John Kerr, on November 11, acting "in the Queen's name," and exercising the reserve powers of his office, broke the deadlock by sacking the prime minister, Gough Whitlam,[2] and appointing Fraser acting prime minister.[3]

Kerr's action raised the issue of the Crown's sovereignty in Australia, fueling calls by republicans for the removal of the British Monarch as head of state in Australia.

Questions were asked at the time: Did the Queen know in advance of the governor-general's intentions? How should she have acted throughout? Was the governor-general's sacking of an elected prime minister a constitutional crisis?

* * *

Sir David Smith It was not a constitutional crisis. The constitution worked perfectly, as it was intended to work. It was a parliamentary crisis.

In 1974, when Whitlam was prime minister, when the then-opposition threatened to block supply, he called on the governor-general. He said: "The Senate is blocking my appropriation; the proper thing to do is to advise a double dissolution and an election." And it was held in 1974, and he won.

Confronted with the same situation in 1975, but a political situation in which he wasn't going to win the ensuing election, suddenly twenty-five years of constitutional and parliamentary history are ignored, thrown out the window. He defies our constitutional conventions; he refuses to call on the governor-general and recommend an election; he can't govern because he has no supply—no money from Parliament; he proposes to coerce the banks, illegally and unconstitutionally, to, in effect, lend him money—underwrite his government—until the Parliament can fix the situation; and stubbornly says: "The governor-general can't do a thing."

Well, the governor-general said: "I'm sorry. The constitution gives the governor-general the reserve powers." He exercised his reserve powers and that was to dismiss a prime minister who was seeking to govern without parliamentary authority, and unconstitutionally.

He dismissed the prime minister and commissioned a new prime minister as a caretaker on the sole condition that he would immediately recommend the dissolution of Parliament and the holding of an election, and the parliamentary controversy—the parliamentary deadlock—was to be remitted to the people to resolve. All the odium attaches to Sir John Kerr because he simply applied the constitution.

Bob Hawke Of course it was a crisis. It was the biggest constitutional crisis this country has had. There could have been a solution. But of course I'm not surprised by the way Kerr acted.

Anthony Eggleton It was pretty traumatic in the sense that no one expects the prime minister of the day to get sacked by the governor-general.

It wasn't a crisis in the sense that as a consequence of it the country faced a crisis: democracy took over the necessary processes and so you suddenly had someone being appointed as a temporary, caretaker prime minister. And the governor-general immediately called an election so the people could make their own judgments.

But it was certainly an unexpected, an unprecedented, act that the governor-general should sack his prime minister. And the drama—I still remember the scenes outside this building [the Old Parliament Building, in Canberra]; it was on those steps outside Parliament House where the sacked prime minister, Gough Whitlam, made some very dramatic statements. He said something like: "God save the Queen because nothing will save the governor-general!"

And indeed there was great fury in the streets at that moment: people felt that the wrong thing had been done. But the fact was that the country was really wanting a change in government, that the incumbent government was running out of money because it couldn't get its bills through the Senate and was even talking about issuing IOUs in order to run its business. So it was quite clear that something had to happen.

And so the governor-general did give the prime minister the opportunity to call a general election, as opposed to just an election for the Senate. And when he sat in his office and said: "Sir, I will *not* call an election," the governor-general handed him an envelope and it was the notice of dismissal.

Sir Zelman Cowen By-and-large throughout the country after the shock there was a good deal of strong disapproval of what was done.

But on the other hand, there was strong approval. For example, Menzies said in his last years, in retirement, that he supported Kerr's exercise of power as legally what he was entitled to do. And having come down on one side, he said he would have approved what Kerr did in the circumstances.

There were others who conceded that Kerr had the power to do what he did, but that he should not have exercised the power in that way.

What should he have done? What could he have done, other than what he did? Most of us who conceded the power would have said that this is not the sort of power that ought to exist—that there is something fundamentally troublesome about the dismissal of a duly elected prime minister by a non-elected person.

But, having said that, there's still the question: If you have this crisis and if your money is running out, there has got to be some means of dealing with this. What is it? Well, you got few good, convincing answers to that.

Stuart Macintyre It's odd how afterwards not only historical reputations, but also historical significance stuck to us. The tide's still going out on

Gough Whitlam's reputation: he's probably thought of less favorably than he was fifteen years ago. There's great affection towards him, but he's no longer seen as the towering figure of politics cut down in his prime.

Sir John Kerr remained governor-general for several years. Malcolm Fraser eventually got sick of him, shortly after Kerr had been down in Melbourne, presenting the Melbourne Cup, which is the major race meeting in this country.

He had overindulged at lunch. There was a crowd of about a hundred thousand there. He got a fairly hostile response and he started giving them two-fingered salutes, and began trading insults with them. And this was regarded by Conservatives as distinctly disturbing. They had been supporters of the governor-general, and he had turned out to be sort of a drunken buffoon.

Shortly afterwards, Zelman Cowen succeeded him and Kerr became UNESCO ambassador, based in France.

WHY WASN'T THE QUEEN TOLD BEFOREHAND?

Sir Zelman Cowen Kerr published an autobiography not long after he left Australia and he was very positive about not advising the Queen in advance. He said:

> I never told the Queen beforehand, though once I had exercised the power, I talked to her straightaway. And I didn't inform her first because the power was mine and not hers.
>
> It is my power, not hers. So, therefore, I didn't want to get her involved in some way so it could be said that if I told her before, she knew about what I was going to do and stood by. It was particularly undesirable to tell her what I was going to do when it was in respect to a matter in which she had no constitutional power.

Sir David Smith The Queen was immediately informed by me. Whitlam was sacked. Fraser was brought in and sworn in as prime minister. And I immediately went to the phone and called the Palace.

I was ringing a very sleepy private secretary at three o'clock in the morning, their time. They could see it coming, just as everybody else would. That was the first advice they had of its intention. It had only come to the governor-general's attention over the weekend.

Thomas Keneally The Monarch was in no way responsible. Whitlam asked Kerr: Had he consulted the Palace? And he said: "I don't need to because I have such powers under the constitution as the Queen's viceroy; I can operate independently of her under the Australian constitution."

The Queen herself, of course, was well aware after it happened in 1975 that this was a dangerous thing to do. It wasn't like a Pakistani dismissal of a prime minister or a military coup. The governor-general did call an immediate election; he put the prime ministership in the hands of a caretaker prime minister, who happened to be the leader of the opposition, who then won the election. But he didn't let the government run its natural course, and he shouldn't have been able to do it.

The ignominy attached chiefly to Sir John Kerr's governor-generalship was not directed at the Monarch. Australia is a country of working-class refugees who have a kind of lower-middle-class sense of politeness, which wouldn't allow them generally to be too obstreperous towards a Monarch.

The anger was directed at the idea that the institution should be rubbed out of the constitution. But it wasn't any personal enmity at the Queen because she had not been asked.

Sir John Kerr used imperial honors—like knighthoods, Commander of the British Empire, and Member of the British Empire—to garner support in the wake of his political assassination of Whitlam.

He wrote to me and offered me a Commander of the British Empire, not a knighthood, but the next one down—the one above what the Beatles got, actually—and I wrote a polite letter back saying: "Not only is there no British Empire left, but I would not have much trust in one of which I was a Commander."

THE QUEEN IN AUSTRALIA

Thomas Keneally On a morning in 1788, two million square miles of Australia were claimed—later more would be claimed—in the name of the monarchy. From 1788 to 1954, the Monarch is totally absentee, and then in 1954[5] she turns up and there is universal enthusiasm, except by a few grouchers like me.

I was an adolescent grouch then, but I was also locked away in a Catholic yeshiva,[6] studying for the priesthood, so I didn't have to participate. But my little brother's school went and queued up for hours and were very excited to see this young woman come along, and her young, gallant-looking husband in his uniform, and there was huge enthusiasm.

It makes an interesting contrast to the most recent royal tour [in the latter part of March and into early April 2000], which was extremely low-key; news of the Queen's progress was not front-page news and yet she is our head of state.

In 1954, you wouldn't have believed that the monarchy would ever fade. The streets were full by then of immigrants. It seemed that Australia would never *not* be a constitutional monarchy. And under that constitutional monarchy, you could do whatever you liked, anyhow—you could sit in a corner, if you liked, and have a beer, and have a chat about the Irish Famine.

But you always knew that if you were going to enter the society, you would have to take to the monarchy, which after all, you interpreted in a way as an oath to Australia.

In 1954 there was no question of taking the Queen out of the oaths and affirmations. Last Australia Day, I attended a citizenship ceremony, and the oath and affirmation are now entirely an oath to Australia—the Monarch is not mentioned.

So you can see that psychologically, by comparison with 1954, the monarchy is dying. And the affection is, definitely. In 1954, the affection was for the institution and the person; in the present, the affection is purely for the person—for Elizabeth II.

Neville Wran By that time, I was a young attorney, and one of my clients was the state-owned power company here. And I remember I was given a window in the building to look down at the procession when the Queen arrived.

Well that was a euphoric occasion—the biggest occasion that Australia had ever experienced, to see this peaches-and-cream lady dressed as you would expect a Queen of England to be dressed—very graciously, and beautifully—and with a young husband, and driven in a Rolls-Royce. We thought that was *great*! Now when she drives down the street, no one looks.

The Queen would be less than human if she didn't sense those changes because in 1954 the whole city was abuzz for a week; you had to push your way through crowds everywhere, and if the Queen was coming down the main street, they would rush from one side of the city to the other, just to get one glimpse of this almost God-like personage.

Whereas, she came out three times when I was the premier and we had to rent a crowd. I would always get packs of schoolchildren, with their little flags. In a way, it was good for them—it was good politics; I didn't mind them at all.

Each visit she made was of decreasing significance and impact—people just couldn't be bothered. And the visit she's just made here the itinerary was even more tailor-made than I used to do because they took her to places like Burke, which is a very famous little town in western New South Wales—if you sent Jack the Ripper up there, he'd get a big crowd because nothing ever happens in Burke. So she was taken to these sorts of places. It was really a bit tough on her, I thought.

Anthony Eggleton I was in charge of the press side of the royal visit in 1970. At the time they did extensive tours so I spent about a month traveling with the Royal Family in Australia.

There was a nice thing I remember from that tour. It was the Queen's actual birthday and we—the Queen and her party—were up in Queensland, on the coral reef, and we went in a little launch out to this reef. The press had gone out ahead because there were too many of them.

And as we came alongside the wharf, all the press were lined up to start doing the story of the Royal Family's arrival, and they all broke into singing "Happy Birthday to You!"

And these were Australian and international press. Here they were—they quite deliberately got together, singing "Happy Birthday" to the Queen as the Queen came alongside. It was a very moving moment. The Queen was very moved.

Now that wouldn't happen today. But in 1970, even the toughest of those Australian press people felt quite happy to stand there with the British press, and other press, and welcome the Queen by singing "Happy Birthday."

Bob Hawke In 1977, the twenty-fifth anniversary of her Coronation, I was up in Canberra and a political leader and I were talking, and then he said: "We've got the twenty-fifth anniversary of coming to the Throne. We should think about what we're going to give her."

And I said: "Well, don't give her a dinner set; the vaults of Windsor Castle are full of dinner sets and all that sort of thing. Why don't we give her a horse?"

And he said: "That's a great idea!" So he got on the phone and rang up the prime minister and said: "Malcolm [Fraser], I've got Bob Hawke here. Are you free? Can you come round?"

So he came round. The prime minister was told my idea about the horse. Malcolm thought it was a great idea and asked me whether I could organize it.

So I said: "Well, one of my friends is one of Australia's leading trainers and breeders." So I got on to him, and he said: "Yes, we could breed one in the northern hemisphere in time." So that was organized. And the horse went over there and it was absolutely no bloody use; it couldn't get out of its own wagon!

And so we had a bit of a giggle about that one. And the Queen thought it was the best, most imaginative gift she'd ever had.

Thomas Keneally Sadly, the gift that they gave the Queen was appropriate, but kind of surreal: the foal from the next standing of a champion Australian stallion with a champion Australian mare.

The conjunction had not occurred yet; it was the next standing they were giving the Queen. And, therefore, not only had the foal not been born, it had not been *conceived* and yet it had to be praised to the Monarch.

To the average person, the encomiums offered this as yet unconceived horse in King's Hall, on a very hot night in 1977, to flatter the Queen were extraordinary. And Gough Whitlam, the supplanted prime minister, later said: "I've never heard a horse so fulsomely praised since Caligula made one a consul."

But there was a fundamental Australianness about the thing because then the Queen departed and all her colonial children, including myself, went to the Rose Garden and listened to military bands and drank too much.

And indeed I saw a future prime minister, Bob Hawke, whom I admired and wanted to flourish, get inebriated—this was the same night that Big Ma'am was there, but this was the naughty children misbehaving in an Australian manner after Ma'am has departed. That's the way the Australians are when the Queen's not there, as opposed to the way when the Queen is there.

Even though you were at an institutional level capable of excessively praising an unborn horse for the sake of the Monarch, at the level of the street, the monarchy had lost its punch from that point on.

Raymond G. H. Seitz When the Queen got off the plane and was on the tarmac [during a visit in the 1980s], some little girl—she was just five or six years old—came up to present a bouquet of flowers. She curtseyed and asked the Queen: "May I kiss you, Ma'am?" And the Queen said: "Oh no, dear." There was an ocean of difference on those kinds of things [between Australia and the United Kingdom].

Sir Zelman Cowen I saw quite a bit of her a few weeks ago [during the 2000 visit]. Knowing that her visit was announced—I'm not sure whether before the referendum was itself called—there was a good deal of discussion: what form will it take? She'll have a program made for her in various parts of Australia. And it will be opening this sort of building, or going on one of these hand-waving tours.

In fact, it was a visit that really didn't have much point. Assuming she was interested, it was a success: she was nicely received; she went on walkabouts in various places; and everywhere there was courtesy.

Stuart Macintyre I actually went to one event because I'm on the board of a museum down in the city. And when the invitation reached my home and I said I wasn't going, one of my daughters—she's a republican—said: "Oh, yes you are. You're taking *me*!" She wanted to be able to tell her children she'd seen the Queen—it's just the idea of the Queen being a celebrity.

And it was just bizarre. There is a real problem with royal protocol; we had to be there an hour in advance. It was the only day in that month that it hadn't been hot weather and it was actually quite cold, and we had to assemble outside the museum at a particular point and wait for an hour.

There were about a hundred pro-monarchists in the crowd and about sixty republicans round the side, and the Queen—the Duke of Edinburgh was there—came bustling through and moved around, then asked everybody: "Hello, how are you?"

They finished that in about a quarter of an hour and then they went up the hill and at the entrance, as they reached the top of the steps—there were about a hundred of us standing there—she gave one of those royal waves and every single person—with the exception of my daughter and I—imitated the wave.

REPUBLICANISM AND THE MONARCH'S FUTURE
AS QUEEN OF AUSTRALIA

Since the mid-twentieth century, public support has grown for a process in which Australia would move from its current constitutional status to that of a republic.

* * *

Thomas Keneally The truth is, there's always been republicanism in Australia. But the reason it never succeeded was the fact that the Crown never stood in the way of institutional development in Australia, and never, of course, did the fatal thing of imposing taxes, as it did in the American colonies.

And on top of that, most of the people were from the British Isles—even Ireland was then under the Crown—and so the Crown was an institution they looked to. And they depended upon Britain too for capital for developing Australian resources, and they were certainly not about to let some nascent colonial radicalism stand in the way of the capital they needed.

And there was perhaps the dominant influence upon the survival of the monarchy: the sense of being Britons far away. Australians no longer describe themselves as "Britons," and if anyone tried to describe them in those terms, they'd be pilloried and laughed at.

But as late as the end of World War II, politicians like Evatt[7] and Curtin[8]— Curtin was a child of the Irish—spoke of "We Britons." Evatt used the phrase in a speech out here.

And there was a sense of being psychologically connected to Britain but enormously distanced from it by the strangeness of various Asian nations, and the Turks, and the Egyptians, and all sorts of strange Europeans. All this, twelve thousand miles of this, lay between us and them.

And so in the 1980s and 1990s, when republicanism emerged again, it was on a popular level, but it never could stand up against those realities of that dependence, which was psychological.

Neville Wran And with that shift to Asia, the value system changed a lot here and older people were still attached to the Queen, but younger people could see no relevance in the Queen. They didn't turn against the Queen, but she just didn't count. She was a nice lady in London, with a lot of pomp and ceremony. But what was her importance to us?

And I think there was no anti-monarchist movement, no relevant movement, against the Queen, or against the British monarchy. But it was just a very gradual, very incremental move towards being in control over their own destiny.

We founded the Australian Republican Movement somewhere about 1989. I had been about three or four years out of politics then and I felt that we had a ten-year period to get this thing up and running and use it as an educational tool—and I don't use the word "education" in any pejorative sense of ignoramuses out there; the truth is that we haven't got [public] indoctrination to our history and our constitution.

Thomas Keneally In modern times my republicanism is based on the different diplomatic and trade orientation of Australia—the fact that Australia is multicultural but the monarchy is a monolithically British institution and, therefore, we hide the truth of our multiculturalism under the bushel of the monarchy.

When I joined the Australian Militia, the Citizen's Military Forces, I asked the sergeant major if I could take an oath to Australia and not to the Queen. And he told me not to be a silly bugger—which is a common phrase in Australia—and just *do* it.

And so my republicanism is based partly on a sense of being marginalized from that institution in childhood. I suppose psychologically it's based on that.

Rationally, it's not based on that: it's based on really important Australian issues, and our standing in Asia, which is our market, and our community, and living down the reputation for racism and the White Australia policy in the past, which is one to which the present government is returning.

THE 1999 REFERENDUM

On November 6, 1999, a referendum was held in which fifty-five percent of the voters turned down a proposition which would have resulted in the establishment of a republic.

* * *

Sir David Smith The Labor Party at its 1991 conference in Hobart suddenly resolved to turn Australia into a republic before the centenary in January 2001, and resolved to embark on a ten-year education campaign to help the Australian people make the right decision. And Keating[9] set up a Republic Advisory Committee, headed by Malcolm Turnbull, an Australian republican.

And they produced an advisory report, bearing in mind that their terms of reference were to advise on *how* Australia might become a republic, not *whether*. The prime minister had said: "We're going to become a republic. That's that." The only advice he wanted was how to do it.

The Republic Advisory Committee traveled the length and width of the country. Most of these meetings could have taken place in telephone booths; the biggest crowd they got in one country town was fifty and one of the members of the Republic Advisory Committee waxed lyrical about this huge audience—most of them were between half a dozen and twenty people, so that's the level of interest. And they stumped the countryside and produced a report on how it could be done.

Keating went out of office before he could do anything about it. And Malcolm Turnbull and the republicans kept beating the ground for what they wanted—a republic.

But, of course, everybody had a different version of the republic they wanted; they wanted to make this change, or that change. The republicans wanted to get rid of the Queen, but each had a different gloss on how it might be done, and what would be put in her place.

And so because they didn't understand how to cope with the reserve powers of the Crown, which would only reside in the republican president anyway—if the republic gets in a mess, it will turn to the monarchy to find out how to deal with the problem.

So you see the importance of the principles of constitutional monarchy in our constitution. They thought they could simply replace the Crown. And to make sure that the president could never act like a governor-general, turned him into the prime minister's puppet. And there's no other democracy in the world where the head of state is instantly removable without reason by the head of government, at the stroke of a pen.

Neville Wran We should have won, but everybody who was likely to go against you went against us. But the major thing that went against us was that it was a change of government, and the new prime minister, Howard,[10] is a frenetic monarchist—he's probably got a large Union Jack over his bed, and a picture of the Queen.

He determined to put every obstacle in the way. But he did it very cleverly because he pretended that he was being even-handed. And there's never been a referendum succeed in Australia that didn't have the support of the ruling government.

But what the referendum *did* do was that it made more people think about the constitution; it made them think about why is the Queen the head of state? Why haven't we got an Ozzie[11] as the head of state?

And finally, the reason we lost the referendum was that there was a schism in the Republican Movement, and the schism was not on the issue of whether Australia should be a republic; but it was on the issue of how the president should be elected, or appointed.

Thomas Keneally A number of older Australians, men and women who survived World War II, are extremely devout monarchists. They would see their efforts in World War II as negated by a move to a republic.

It's a psychological thing. We're not talking about a cultural revolution—a scrubbing out of the Victoria Reginas, the "VRs" on the country courthouses, or the taking down of pictures of the Queen in the bowling clubs of Australia. We're not talking about a discontinuity with the past, but they see it as a cultural revolution, which would negate their childhoods.

Neville Wran I believe that British royalty would breathe a sigh of relief because what does this really mean to them now? And it would have been a neat way to cut the tie.

Except for a minority, there is no anti-monarchist feeling in Australia, and we have been very careful not to promote, or engender, anything that could be construed as a hatred of the monarchy: we say that the Queen is a fine woman, she's done a great job, her country is England, and it is as appropriate for her to be the Queen of Australia as it would be for the president of France to be the King of Australia—that they are independent, sovereign countries and have nothing to do with us.

Anthony Eggleton You wouldn't find many republicans who would be critical of the Queen. In fact, even during the campaign, they went out of their way to say: "This has nothing to do with the Queen; she'll always be welcome in this country." And she would have been very welcomed just a few weeks ago when she was here, whether or not the decision had been made to become a republic.

She is highly regarded. So it would certainly have nothing to do with the personality of the Queen, *per se*. If and when the change takes place, it will be evolutionary; it will be the fact that one day, inevitably, Australia will become a republic.

It will more likely do that in a natural, evolving way than trying to make a political issue of it. So one of these days it will happen. One of the brakes on it a bit is the Queen, in that there would certainly be some people who would vote no, who would have done so because of their fondness for the Queen.

And when you have a different personality—a different person—on the Throne, some of those links will be lost. But whenever it happens, the members of the Royal Family will continue to be very welcome in this country—whoever is King or Queen would be always most welcome here.

And that will always be the case, I believe, because of the great sentiment of the link of history, which will always be there. And if they're performing their tasks well, there will be admiration for the fact that they're doing that.

Thomas Keneally When I was chairman of the Republican Movement, Bob Hawke said to me—he later changed his mind on this, but only a long way down the track—"If you guys want to win, you should campaign that we become a republic upon the death, or abdication, of Elizabeth II. You'll win then."

I said to him: "We cannot do that because then we're in the demeaning position of waiting upon the convenience of another nation, and we've been doing that too bloody long. Even if it takes longer, we can't do it."

But, nonetheless, his suggestion, which had a lot of political savvy to it, is based on the reality that the affection for the monarchy is now an affection for Queen Elizabeth II.

Stuart Macintyre The Queen was at pains to emphasize [in a speech she made in Sydney on March 20, 2000] that she thinks this is something that Australians should decide and she won't be offended. And, indeed, she was more or less distancing herself from John Howard in that respect. She was more or less saying: "There's going to come a time soon when you won't want us, and that's only natural."

It was her first chance to say anything about all that had transpired, and it was quite carefully thought out. It was really saying: "In the end it's up to you, and I'm not going to be here."

That's not to say that she won't be back again, but that she realizes that major changes are possible, and she was wanting to indicate that this is an Australian decision, and one in which she's not taking sides.

She could have said: "I hope you'll preserve the link. Please don't let me down." But that would have been counterproductive, in a sense. Her speech was generous in a realistic way.

Michael Parker Since their visit, and since the Queen's speech in Sydney shortly after their arrival, one of the greatest speeches that's been made in Australia in my time—it was not a prime minister's speech; it was not a politician's speech; it was not a corporate leader's speech; it was not a speech of a social leader of any kind; it was a *Queen's* speech—a lot of Australians who have never heard a Queen's speech before suddenly sat up and took note.

Since that visit, things have got very quiet, and very cool. It's almost as though she's steadied the ship with what she said. It's been a remarkable result.

Bob Hawke She made a magnificent speech, which disconcerted the republicans no end. And she addressed head-on the question of the republican vote in this country, and she said in her speech that she wanted to say here, in front of this audience, what she'd said on the night of the result, that what happened in terms of Australia's constitutional arrangements was entirely a matter for the people of Australia, and she would happily accept whatever that was.

And then the real stinger was when she beautifully said though: "But whatever you may do in the future in regard to your constitutional arrangements, I will always maintain a deep and abiding affection for Australia—and Australians."

Which is really saying to people there: "What in the bloody hell are you doing? Why don't you get on with it?" So yes, she can subtly make points. But she can't make decisions.

Thomas Keneally Maybe in five years optimistically, ten pessimistically, there'll be a republican Australia.

The Republican Movement opted for a model which made the least intrusion into the present constitution. They did that for fear of conservatism; they ran into a public backlash against the idea that ultimately there wouldn't be a popular, direct election for the president. And thus it will take some constitutional rearrangement.

I always thought that that problem was superable; I always said that if you put a modern Jefferson for a weekend in a Travel Lodge motel with a pack of Heineken's, he'd have it done by Monday morning if you just trusted it.

Constitutionally I don't think it's as big a problem as it is psychologically. But we'll have to gear up the entire proposition again because the prime minister helped defeat the first one very cleverly by taking the monarchy out of the debate over yes or no. On the day of the referendum, the question didn't say: "Vote no for the sake of the Queen; she's been a good old stick—as she has—she likes us; what harm has she done? At least she's above politics." That wasn't the rhetoric; the slogan was: "Vote no for the politicians' republic."

Bob Hawke If we had a referendum which said: "Are you in favor of Australia becoming a republic and it coming into effect when the Queen ceases to be Queen of England?" I think you would probably have about seventy-five or eighty percent, because I think there are a lot of people who, in principle, go with the concept of a republic, but have a real affection for the Queen and thought it would be seen as a rebuff, or a rejection of *her*.

Harry Robinson, Australian journalist and commentator We are not unmannerly. I see the occasion as calling for a final royal visit marked by a garden party at Yarralumla,[12] a command performance at the [Sydney] Opera House, and an open air mingling in one of the Olympic stadia, we [Australians] to be the hosts all through, she [the Queen] to be the honored guest.

The Queen could then depart, flags flying, bands playing.

Lord Heseltine I cannot in any way foresee what will occur on Her Majesty's death, but it seems to me that Prince Charles and Prince William are building a reputation across the Commonwealth that which will stand the Monarchy in good stead.

Lady Greenfield Australians are very fond of Her Majesty, and so the people there will not want to break with something that is doing them no harm.

Lord Steel I do not think it matters very much if the Australians decide to become a republic as there are plenty of them in the Commonwealth.

It would be rather sad, however, as Australia has got such strong ties with Britain; like Canada, it is part of the *old* Commonwealth, and I think Australian public opinion has moved quite a bit *against* going the republican path.

But if it *does*, so what? That nation is entitled to do as it chooses.

Sir Bernard Ingham, interviewed 2021 While this [leaving the Commonwealth] is clearly a matter for *the Australians* to decide, I find it difficult to believe that it will be popular among all Commonwealth member-nations.

One of the problems of modern communications is that those with a mission try to color everybody else's views. They don't have such problems in Communist states, *do they?*

CHAPTER 18

Africa

A T PRESENT, NINETEEN African countries are members of the Commonwealth. The Queen has strong emotional ties to Africa. They stem from her visit there as a Princess in 1947 and her address to the Commonwealth and the British Isles from Cape Town, and more personally, from her accession as Queen in 1952, while visiting Kenya with Prince Philip.

And the Queen as head of the Commonwealth has played an important role in African affairs, particularly on the issues of Rhodesia, now Zimbabwe, and on sanctions against the apartheid governments of South Africa.

* * *

Nelson Mandela At the CHOGM in Harare, Dr. [Datuk Seri] Mahathir [bin Mohamad], the prime minister of Malaysia, proposed a toast. He said something which was remarkable. He made a very good speech, and he then said: "I ask you to rise to drink a toast to Her Majesty, Queen Elizabeth I."

Chief Emeka Anyaoku thought Mahathir was making a mistake, and he said, quite loudly: "No. Elizabeth II." And Mahathir just continued, and repeated: "Queen Elizabeth I."

What he was saying was that this is the *real* Queen Elizabeth. It would not be diplomatic to say this. Perhaps. I don't think that there is any head of state more popular than Queen Elizabeth.

Sir David Scott Until the independence of India, Pakistan, and Ceylon in 1947, nobody had looked ahead to the independence of the African countries. I don't think it was in anybody's mind at all in 1947 or 1948.

I believe it then became very quickly inevitable. And the various Empire statesmen began to see that there were top jobs available, and that they were coming up to the moment when independence would be appropriate.

When I went to South Africa the first time, in 1953, when independence for African colonies was coming up, I drew the parallel with what had happened when the Roman Legions left the British Isles in the beginning of the fourth century A. D. It took something like five hundred years for tribalism in this country to get sorted out, and [for the country] to get unified.

I said that tribalism was bound to reassert itself in independent African countries, of which I had no experience at the time. But obviously the world now, with communications being what they are, wouldn't be able to deter this for all that long. They would help; they were building up their own countries.

And this has happened—and is happening. The central government maintained communications and general oversight of what was going on. And when that was withdrawn, the locals all decided they wanted to be Kings themselves. And I'm sure that process is not, by any means, being treated in Africa at all.

Ghana was the first. I believe that there was still quite a lot of surprise among quite well-informed people in the United Kingdom about Ghana getting its independence quite as it did.

I knew the last governor-general, who then became governor-general, with Nkrumah[1] as his prime minister. He makes much of the story that when he had his first cabinet meeting as governor-general—it must have been roughly just before independence—he said: "Well, gentlemen, I've been doing my homework and I discovered that I'm the only one in this room who hasn't got a degree." He was a nice man, and I believe that went down very well as far as the transition was concerned in Ghana.

Subsequently, of course, independence has gone to [more] smaller countries than anybody reckoned would be practical, or possible. In the end, there were some very small countries, indeed, particularly in the Pacific.

It's been an evolving thing, and I think at each stage there's been a certain inevitability about it. But the inevitability wasn't foreseen back in 1947, which was the key date.

Lord Thurlow I was in Ghana just before, and after, the transfer of power. I knew Nkrumah very well—I did things for him: I created his foreign service—and Nkrumah was a firebrand, a nationalist firebrand;

for his own reasons, he was a Marxist—a half-baked Marxist at heart. He attached quite considerable weight to maintaining an appearance of a strong connection with the Queen. He went and stayed at Balmoral.

RHODESIA

Sir Harold Smedley After UDI,[2] various attempts were made to get our relationship with Rhodesia back on a reasonable footing, and Sir Alec Douglas-Home, whose private secretary I had been, incidentally, made a major attempt.

He had reached an agreement, subject to the approval of the people of Rhodesia as a whole—a fine statement—but then you've got somehow to implement it. And the way they chose to implement it was to form a commission and go out there to assess opinion, and I was appointed secretary-general.

We devised a scheme to take the opinion of people in the African population of Southern Rhodesia, and we decided that the only way to set about it was still to do it informally, through groups. And so we appointed commissioners who were people with previous African experience.

Our commissioners went round talking to people, and they interviewed people in Salisbury [now Harare], they made assessments, and we distributed copies of the proposals.

We all started with a feeling that it would be very difficult to get the African population to express its views; it would be frightened of doing so. But then, on the contrary, in fact, we formed the virtually unanimous conclusion that these proposals were not acceptable to the people of Rhodesia as a whole.

We tried to be scientific: we tried to have a public opinion poll. But the more we went into it, the more difficult it seemed to launch it, for political reasons. And so they didn't have the vote of most of the Africans to do it. I don't think anyone will ever appoint a commission like that again.

Raymond G. H. Seitz I can at the moment think of only one issue that distressed the Queen a lot, and that happened in 1979, right after Margaret Thatcher became prime minister.

Thatcher in her campaign—and in all the period before that, when she was the opposition leader—seemed bent on recognizing what was called the "internal settlement" of the, at the time, Rhodesian issue. And the person who was head of what most people believed was a skewed election was Bishop Muzorewa.[3]

There was a sense that when Margaret Thatcher became prime minister she was going to recognize—the British equivalent of recognizing—this government. And many people felt that that would be a serious error.

But she was stuck with it. It's one of those things where there's a lot of history; it seems so simple but turns out not to be so simple.

But the Queen was displeased at the prospect of the [British] government moving in too hasty a fashion on Rhodesia and recognizing a government whose legitimacy was questionable, and if it were recognized then it would almost surely split the Commonwealth—that was her particular interest—and probably split it on the race issue. This was something the Queen thought would really be a serious mistake.

There were also many other people advising Mrs. Thatcher not to do something too quickly here which she would regret later. In the event, she did not. The Queen had a major opinion that helped relations.

Sir Emeka Anyaoku In 1979, when the Commonwealth was at the risk of breakdown in cohesion over the crisis in Rhodesia, as it was then called, there was going to be a meeting of the Commonwealth heads of government, in Lusaka, Zambia. The security agents that had gone on an advance visit to Lusaka had returned to London and said that the security situation in the Zambian capital was mixed.

That was in the first few months of Margaret Thatcher's term as prime minister. The then-prime minister of New Zealand, Robert Muldoon, who was visiting Mrs. Thatcher, gave a press conference in which he said that he did not think Lusaka would be safe for the Queen of New Zealand to travel to. His comments were regarded as views he had formed after meeting with Margaret Thatcher.

Sir Shridath Ramphal There were right-wing elements in Britain, and in some Commonwealth countries, like New Zealand—I shouldn't say New Zealand; it was very much the prime minister of New Zealand, Robert Muldoon—who knew where the Queen stood on apartheid and these issues, UDI, because it was Rhodesia that was the [major] issue at the Lusaka CHOGM, and they would rather she had not been around.

I had been in communication to a degree that I knew how strongly she felt—that she would be there. I wanted her there because we were dealing with a brand new prime minister of Britain, who would turn out to play an enormous role in the Commonwealth, Margaret Thatcher, whom I, and the Commonwealth as a whole, hadn't known in advance.

So the Queen's presence, as the continuing link out of Britain, was very important, not just [the presence of] Mrs. Thatcher, who was coming to Zambia against a record of having taken a very bad stand against the Freedom Movement—who would call them "terrorists"; whose manifesto was for recognizing Muzorewa, and all of that. So it could have been a very difficult meeting.

The South Africans had bombed Zambia, and Muldoon used that as the pretext for saying that he did not approve of his Queen—the Queen of New Zealand—being exposed to danger by coming to the Commonwealth Conference.

Well, it was nonsense! The Queen would never have been deterred by that danger—there wasn't really a danger. I don't believe that her going was really ever much in doubt.

The Queen in these situations had a healing touch, and her presence would be an opportunity for the Commonwealth to benefit from that. I knew this; she knew this. I don't believe she had given a moment's doubting to her going there. But voices would have been reaching her—perhaps even voices from here—that perhaps she shouldn't be in Zambia.

It didn't take her long to scotch those ideas, and she announced: "I will be going to Zambia." And she went. It turned out to be as important as we all thought it would be.

Sir Michael Palliser The Queen said: "To hell with that; of course I'm going to go. You can see that I don't get shot."

Sir Emeka Anyaoku The Queen came to Lusaka and held a function for the heads of government and their ministers—Mrs. Thatcher was there, of course. This type of event would normally end about ten-thirty in the evening. It did not end until a quarter to midnight because she was keen to talk to everyone. And that was what saved the Commonwealth at that time of crisis. The heads of government were encouraged to find a solution.

So the Queen's headship has had the beneficial effect of encouraging the continued cohesion of the Commonwealth. And the Commonwealth in the intervening years has become sufficiently strong so that threats, like the one over Rhodesia in 1979, are unlikely to reoccur.

Sir Michael Palliser The Lusaka Commonwealth meeting in a way put the seal of approval on what the government was trying to do over Rhodesia.

And, of course, the Queen's presence there made a big difference. I have to admit also that, in all fairness, the combination of her presence and the influence she exerted, plus Margaret Thatcher dancing with Kenneth

Kaunda, and all that, plus Peter Carrington managing the politics, was a very formidable combination.

If the Queen had not gone, I don't believe that conference would have succeeded. I think she feels that, and that is why she is so attached to it, and why she gets her children to go off to visit Commonwealth countries: she sees her Commonwealth experience as having been tremendously valuable to her in terms of being Queen.

Jeremy Thorpe Buckingham Palace had that suite in the [Lusaka] Intercontinental Hotel, on the fifteenth floor, and Prime Minister Thatcher was there, on the tenth floor.

The Queen sent for her and said: "I've just had a state visit to two countries in the African part of the Commonwealth, and I'm not going to preside over the break-up the Commonwealth. We can negotiate with Zambia and Uganda, and we have to settle the thing."

And she really did pull her weight on this occasion, so much so that the prime minister expressed an enormous amount of gratitude to her for what she'd done.

SOUTH AFRICA

In 1961, during the regime of H. F. Verwoerd,[4] South Africa had resigned from membership in the Commonwealth in order to forestall expulsion due to its policy of apartheid.

Throughout the following years, other Nationalist Party regimes continued their harsh policies, igniting passionate debate in Western nations, including whether the imposition of sanctions could undermine these racist regimes.

Sir Bernard Ingham Of course, the Commonwealth was very keen to get rid of apartheid; so was the prime minister, Mrs. Thatcher. The argument was not over whether you want to get rid of apartheid; the question was how best to do it. They all felt that sanctions were the only way; they had no other idea in their brains but sanctions.

Mrs. Thatcher argued that sanctions are always *ineffective*. Look at Saddam Hussein.

Sir Emeka Anyaoku The question over sanctions was a rather tricky situation. The Queen could not take any view on the political issue of sanctions.

The Queen was on the side of the Commonwealth in terms of caring for the Commonwealth and its wellbeing and cohesion, but I would hesitate to say that that meant that she was for sanctions.

The cleverness of her position was that she made her caring for the Commonwealth evident without taking sides on the basic issue of the controversy.

Nelson Mandela It was, of course, difficult to verify it, but we got information that Her Majesty was not in favor of the attitude of the British government.

According to our information, the Queen understood the sanctions issue. But she is a constitutional Monarch; she would be careful not to give any trace of a difference between herself, and her prime minister, and her government.

And, quite apart from the fact that she is a Monarch and will be trained how to handle problems, she as a person is really a very, very gracious lady. I have the highest respect for her.

Sir Emeka Anyaoku You could say that at one point, Prime Minister Margaret Thatcher was prepared to damn the rest of the Commonwealth. In 1987, at a press conference following the meeting of the Commonwealth heads of state at Vancouver, a journalist asked her if she was worried that the rest of the Commonwealth took a view different from hers, and she answered that she was sorry for the rest of the Commonwealth.

So it was possible to interpret her position as not being too concerned with the wellbeing of the Commonwealth. I am not sure that this interpretation is correct, because I knew of her concern for the Commonwealth.

Lord Wright It was a view which applied towards Callaghan, as well. It is an important point in terms of the Queen's view of the Commonwealth. And I believe she was as distressed as many of us were by the fact that successive Heads of Government Meetings were actually sort of Britain against the other forty-nine [Commonwealth nations], or however many we were then—a situation which, I believe, Margaret Thatcher rather enjoyed: she was quite happy to be one against forty-nine because she was convinced that the forty-nine were wrong.

But it did mean that some of the Heads of Government Meetings— at least the ones I attended—were really quite bad-tempered. Not, of course, bad-tempered against the Queen, who was there as head of the Commonwealth, and not as the Sovereign of Britain.

It must have saddened her that there was this row. It did, undoubtedly, sour the Heads of Government Meetings. But that, happily, is a thing of the past.

Lord Howe I believe that the Monarch certainly would have been more concerned to hold the Commonwealth together and to avoid issues which divided it.

But Margaret Thatcher, particularly at the time of the Commonwealth Heads of Government Meeting when we took the vote to call on sanctions, was very impatient of that decision, of course, and tried to avoid the next step in the whole thing, in London, at the end of July.

Nelson Mandela I just couldn't make a dent [in a telephone conversation with Prime Minister Thatcher]. After about fifteen minutes, I hung up.

I returned on the Fourth of July and saw her. She was most surprised, and she was so generous—she had investigated my habits in regard to diet, and so on, and she knew everything that I liked.

We were supposed to meet for an hour. We met for *three* hours, and I had to ask for an excuse; I had to see Neil Kinnock.[5] I went to see Neil Kinnock and the first question was: "How is the Iron Lady?" I said: "She was warm and motherly." He said: "Warm and motherly? You must have met *another* lady!"

Lord Howe The Monarch would not have been involved in discussing the specific issues, although she would have discussed it with, probably, every head of government.

I think that Margaret probably never attached as much value to—tended not to attach as much value to—these kinds of debates that took place at Commonwealth meetings with the Commonwealth heads of governments and as I, for example, did.

It's a subject of speculation. I don't believe Margaret Thatcher did feel as positively about the Commonwealth as the Queen because, after all, the Queen has been associated with it directly, in one form or another, since her childhood. And Margaret Thatcher has been more of a U.K. nationalist. The Queen found that sometimes Margaret Thatcher took up positions which she didn't entirely wish to accommodate.

Sir David Scott The problem with sanctions, I believe, was that the example of Rhodesia obviated and demonstrated that sanctions were extremely difficult to operate in there, and tended to be highly ineffective.

And it was only in the question of arms collaboration where we had any sanctions as far as South Africa was concerned.

There was a general disapproval of the South African regime, and particularly in the light of what was happening elsewhere in the Commonwealth. Certainly, that was pretty universally held, with only a few exceptions, in high places in this country.

I remember, when I sailed out of South Africa—I came back on a little ship—we sailed past Robbin Island, where Nelson Mandela still was, and I commented that there was the big unknown, still languishing in this island prison, which was just off the coast of Africa.

What I didn't know was that, in fact, the South African government, by the time I left, was already in touch with the African National Congress. And so things were, under the surface, beginning to shift slightly.

SOUTH AFRICA'S RETURN TO THE COMMONWEALTH

F. W. De Klerk, who had become president in 1989, yielding to international condemnation of the National Party's racist policies, removed the ban on the ANC and other anti-apartheid parties.

And in a most momentous act, De Klerk ordered Nelson Mandela released from his twenty-six-year imprisonment.

All remaining apartheid laws were repealed in 1991 and an interim constitution ending white rule was implemented in 1993, giving way to the formation of a multiparty transitional government council.

Then in April 1994, elections were held in which the ANC won more than 60 percent of the vote and Nelson Mandela was elected president. Shortly thereafter, on June 1, 1994, the newly democratic South Africa returned to the Commonwealth.

* * *

Sir David Scott The Queen said to me [in 1976]: "Do you think there is going to be any chance of my visiting South Africa while you're ambassador?" And I said: "Well, Ma'am, I don't think it's very likely. But I hope the day will come when South Africa will be back in the Commonwealth." And I believe she felt very happy about that.

Sir Emeka Anyaoku The Queen was absolutely delighted that South Africa came back to the Commonwealth. On June 1, 1994, the day of South Africa's return to the Commonwealth, we had a special service at

Westminster Abbey. After the service, I hosted a reception at Marlborough House [Commonwealth headquarters] which was attended by the largest number of royals to go to one function.

Nelson Mandela There is no doubt that it is a very significant development because it is evidence that now we are no longer the pole cat of the world, because South Africa was expelled from the Commonwealth. And the fact that we're now a member of the Commonwealth means that we are fully accepted by the international community. And there are advantages, for example, in regard to visas and passports, trade preferences. We enjoy those advantages.

* * *

The Queen's most recent experience in South Africa, the CHOGM held in Durban on November 12–14, 1999—the last CHOGM of the twentieth century—was both an occasion for deep satisfaction over the return of South Africa to the Commonwealth, and a milestone in that Mozambique had joined the Commonwealth, the only non–former colonial territory in Africa to do so, after having survived years of Portuguese domination to attain independence in 1975.

In recognition of Mozambique's entry into the Commonwealth, following the CHOGM, the Queen paid a twelve-hour visit there on November 15. Flying in a chartered British Airways aircraft, and accompanied by Prince Philip, she landed in the capital, Maputo, at exactly noon, in sweltering heat.

As she descended the steps of the aircraft, the Queen observed not only the nation's president, His Excellency Joaquim A. Chissano, and the usual, requisite number of local officials and members of the British High Commission standing at attention on the tarmac to greet her, but also a crowd of banner-waving members of FRELIMO,[6] of which President Chissano was a founder-member in 1962.

No representatives of the opposition party were anywhere to be seen, a significant factor as Mozambique was only weeks away from holding a presidential election, in which President Chissano would be re-elected.[7]

The Queen, who is constitutionally protected from becoming involved in local political issues must have been surprised. She did not, however, betray the slightest reaction, walking briskly down the red carpet laid out before her, reviewing the troops with the president, and then walking to a covered platform to deliver her greetings.

Later that afternoon, still in sweltering heat, but having changed from her arrival attire, a blue ensemble, to a brighter, red-white-and-blue dress, the Queen greeted Mozambiquans as well as British subjects resident in the country at a colonial-era hotel overlooking the ocean before opening a trade show there.

The Queen was lighthearted throughout as she paused to greet youngsters holding Union Jacks and teenaged girls arrayed in colorful garb who danced for her.

That evening, the Queen, accompanied by the Duke of Edinburgh, arrived at the presidential palace for the culminating event of her brief visit, a dinner held in a wing of the palace overlooking a wide expanse of lawn, amid the sounds of noisy peacocks who strolled there oblivious to the fact that the Queen was dining within.

And despite the heat and growing humidity, the Queen was attired as she might be in London, in an elegant, floor-length gown with a gold lace bodice and gold chiffon skirt, and bejeweled with a pearl necklace and diamond tiara.

Shortly before the pre-dinner speeches were to begin, three of the Queen's highest aides, their expressions grim, were seen racing from the dining wing toward the main house where only moments earlier the Queen had presented gifts to the Chissanos.[8]

Being present on the lawn with the official press corps covering the event, we raced after the aides, only to see them emerge from the residence moments later, all smiles.

What crisis could have precipitated their concern and mad dash, we wondered. Then, looking closely, we noticed that one of the aides was carrying a pair of eyeglasses, the Queen's, as it turned out.

The aides then returned to the dining room and within a matter of seconds the British and Mozambique National Anthems were played, and then the Queen began her address.

Given the timing of the aforementioned activities, it is obvious that the Queen was clearly unable to begin her address until the eyeglasses were retrieved, as she was required to read it rather than speak extemporaneously, due to the constitutional requirement that she reflect the government's message, not her own.

Official message or not, the evening was clearly a triumph for the Queen and her entourage. But at eleven o'clock, the royal party left the gathering, entered their cars, and proceeded to the airport.

It was wheels up at precisely midnight. The Queen had been on the ground in the Commonwealth's newest member-nation for precisely twelve function-packed hours.

CHAPTER 19

The Future of the Commonwealth

As of 2021, the Commonwealth, international in scope and spanning the globe, consists of fifty-four countries. Since 2002, Zimbabwe withdrew its membership, in 2003, and Rwanda joined, in 2009. Will other countries opt to join?

* * *

Yehuda Avner There were in the 1950s initial feelers put out for Israel to become a member of the Commonwealth, but it didn't happen. Among other reasons, not only political, it was made clear [in the 1980s] that while Mr. Shamir was still prime minister, these things couldn't happen.[1]

Stephen Day Arafat asked to join the Commonwealth. Would he be welcomed? Not at the moment [as of 1998]; he'd have to improve his human rights record quite powerfully. That is a very important part of it.

Sir David Scott Actually, one of the very extraordinary things is the fact that the Commonwealth is extending outside the Empire now: Mozambique has come in [in 1995], and there is an application on hand [as of 1999] from Yemen.

Of course Yemen did have a connection through Aden, but at the moment, Yemen is not going to be a very likely member of the Commonwealth. [...]

As far as success, or otherwise, with the Commonwealth, I think it's very important not to believe that because a country is in the Commonwealth it will automatically behave as we—or any other Commonwealth member—thinks it ought to behave.

Lady Young There's a lot of debate going on about whether or not we ought to really make more of the Commonwealth than we do, where we have a certain influence in these countries.

And, of course, in today's world it crosses all nationalities [...] all peoples of every continent are members of the British Commonwealth. And there are a huge group of them in the United Nations, for instance.

Anson Chan In legal terms, since Hong Kong is no longer a member of the Commonwealth, it's not possible for us to have legal constitutional links. But we will always have a link with the Commonwealth countries by virtue of the fact that the common law system will continue to be practiced in Hong Kong. [...]

Sir Emeka Anyaoku Australia seems decidedly moving towards becoming a republic. At the same time, they have continued to make it clear that this will not affect their allegiance to the Commonwealth, of which the Queen will remain the head. Even the diehard republicans in Australia have said so [...]

Bob Hawke I don't believe there'd be any significant move—certainly none coming from Australia, and I doubt from any other country—to replace the British Crown as head of it.

There's a neutrality about her: she's not the executive head of Britain; she's titular. If you're looking at other members of the Commonwealth, most of them are much more than titular heads, and I can't see any argument that I find convincing for changing that.

Stuart Macintyre The Commonwealth has already embraced republics so it's not necessary to have a monarchy to have a Commonwealth of Nations.

There is a problem if Britain finds its way toward some republican status: then what do you do with your Royal Family? Traditionally, you used to have royal families going into exile after some revolution overthrows them. But if there's a general agreement that the British monarchy doesn't work anymore, where do they go? And what do they do? What is the post-monarchical role for the Windsors?

Neville Wran It's never been an issue. And we [Australia] don't even envisage, or talk about, any change to our position in the Commonwealth—that's part of our history and our heritage and unless there are good reasons for us *not* to be part of the Commonwealth, we will remain part of the Commonwealth.

Sir David Smith Under the rules of the Commonwealth, a country that changes from a monarchy to a republic, in effect, must reapply for read-mission under its new status.

A single Commonwealth prime minister can veto the admission of this so-called "new member." [There was a] bitter personal relationship between Prime Minister [Dr. Datuk Seri] Mahathir [Mohamad], of Malaysia, and [prime minister of Australia] Keating. Keating once called him "recalcitrant" and Mahathir was very insulted and since then, both during the Keating government and during the Howard government, has consequently stopped any attempts by Australia to get closer to our Asian neighbors. He's gone on [record], saying: "Australia is not Asian; Australia is not part of Asia." Keating, of course, used to say we *are* part of Asia, and we've got to have a republic to get closer to them.

While a republican Australia would be eligible to remain in the Commonwealth, with the Queen as head, and participate in the Commonwealth Games—everything in this country revolves around sport—it was not clearly cut. And we sought to say: "Yes, that will happen, *provided* ..."

I used to say to audiences when I addressed them: "Is there anyone here who is prepared to bet their home on Dr. Mahathir allowing a republican Australia back in the Commonwealth?"

And of course we were accused of scare-mongering, but we had to bring home the reality that our continued membership was *not* automatic under the rules of the Commonwealth. We got a letter from the secretary-general confirming that for us, and we publicized it.

Sir Rex Hunt I believe that the fact the Commonwealth has carried on for so long since our colonies have gained independence shows that it's of some benefit to them.

And as long as Charles, or William, carries on in the same way as the Queen, and doesn't try to rule the Commonwealth, then I believe it will [continue].

Sir Shridath Ramphal There's almost bound to be a generational aspect to it. There will come a new leadership that hasn't known those years, or known the Queen in those years. How will the Queen relate to them? That is probably going to be the role of her successor.

But I am sure that so long as she is around as Queen, she's going to work very hard at relating to them—whether they're young prime ministers arising in Barbados; a new school of prime ministers arising in Asia, not the Congress Party types that she has known; the new African leadership emerging in this second phase.

Donald Macdonald It's entirely conceivable that Charles might continue as the head of the Commonwealth. My generation is not going to have to make the decision on this question—I'm just three years younger than the Queen: due to her Bowes-Lyon genes, she's going to long outlive me. My children's generation will have to decide the question.

Joe Haines It won't carry on from her. Charles *couldn't* have the same personal experience of Empire and Commonwealth; by the time he began to grow up, it was fading fast—people were getting their freedom.

Lord Howe He certainly has enormous interest in it. There are so many bonds with the Commonwealth, through the division of funds, and secretariats, and scholarships, and organizations, and the Prince is very, very interested.

Tim Heald The Commonwealth is something that England is going away from. I have cousins who emigrated just after the war, so it was a very immediate thing for my generation; much less so for my children's generation.

Charles is very good about the Commonwealth and has spent some time in Australia. But I don't feel it means quite as much to him in that gut way: Philip fought a war alongside them; he was on one of those ships in the Australian Navy. It's a different, sort of gut feeling in his case than you could possibly have if you're thirty years younger.

Ivan Head One of the concerns that I would have with the succession of Charles is that he's such a formal dolt—to have a discussion with this guy: "I feel very strongly about the Commonwealth's business. We must, must, must ..." and all this. You want to kick him in the kneecap, at least.

On one occasion in the 1970s, he was interviewed at some length by CBC [Canadian Broadcasting Company] while in Ottawa, at Government House. And if there was a reason to get out of the Commonwealth, there it was. He was so pompous and pretentious. It was just awful. And I don't think he's changed.

Jeremy Thorpe He has got great interest and is thoroughly informed on the Commonwealth. A friend of mine from Scotland went to [a function] in the Commonwealth with Prince Charles, and everyone went straight to the high commissioner's afterwards and they were all excited by his enthusiasm for the Commonwealth. Obviously he won't have the experience. But he'll have the enthusiasm.

Sir Shridath Ramphal He has grown up with these events in the Commonwealth development unfolding. But it was the next King of England side of things that concerned him, and preoccupied him, not the next head of Commonwealth.

And he did not trample on the Queen's Commonwealth turf, so he never became a royal insider in Commonwealth affairs. He has not been an intimate part of it because he has felt very consciously that the Queen regarded the Commonwealth as *her* thing.

Now, when he accedes to the Throne, the Commonwealth will have been full-grown, and he will come to the position of head of the Commonwealth in a way that almost doesn't require of him the nurturing that it required of the Queen.

The Commonwealth has grown up, and as King of England, he is going to relate well to the new Commonwealth. It's going to be a very different kind of role, but I believe he will rise to the challenge.

Lord Wright I believe he would hope to continue as head of the Commonwealth. That is not automatically the case. And it may well be that they will find that others want to take over the leadership of the Commonwealth.

His interests outside the Commonwealth are probably stronger than the Queen's, his interest in the Middle East, for instance, to which he really attaches a lot of importance. I've served in the Middle East, and I've very often talked about the Middle East with him.

Part of the respect that the Commonwealth has for the Queen is the fact that she has been there for so long. All the heads of government know of her enormous experience and knowledge. And not only are they flattered by the Queen's interest in the Commonwealth, but they genuinely value the expertise that they can draw on in talking to the Queen.

That does not apply in the same way to Prince Charles. And so he will have to make up for it in some way.

Lord Desai The real Commonwealth started after Indian independence and the condition was that the Queen would be its head and India would no longer be obedient to her but would *respect* her.

It is not obvious, nor has it been decided, that the Monarch will be the head of the Commonwealth, either *de facto* or *jure*.

The Queen has fulfilled her role with dignity, without ruffling feathers in the day-to-day running of the Commonwealth, but I do not know whether it can make the transition to the next Monarch, who will be head of the Commonwealth *by definition*, and the Queen knows that if she were not present, the discussion about succession would be contentious. As she is a very clever woman, that is why she designated Charles as her successor as head of the Commonwealth.

In my view, the Commonwealth will not stay the same after Her Majesty is gone.

Lord Steel Prince Charles is very Commonwealth-minded thus I believe that as King he will be a very good Head of this institution.

Sir Donald McKinnon The question of whether he would succeed the Queen as head of the Commonwealth was an issue very much under discussion during my tenure as secretary-general and I got into trouble with British press when I said that his succession in that role would not be automatic on the Queen's death, as this position is given to the British Monarch by the leaders of the Commonwealth's nations. The media and the Foreign Office would ultimately agree with me.

During the London CHOGM [of 2018], however, the Commonwealth leaders would recognize that Charles would succeed to that position upon Her Majesty's death. In practical terms, it is very important that the British Monarch be its head.

PART FOUR

Major Issues of
the Reign

CHAPTER 20

Northern Ireland

THE ORIGIN OF THE SECTARIAN CONFLICT

B ARON FITT, GERARD (1926–2005), life peer, cr. 1983; co-founder of the SDLP (Socialist Democratic and Labour Party of Northern Ireland) The beginning of the present political turmoil in Northern Ireland began in the first Queen Elizabeth's reign, when in 1588 she decided to send over mostly Scottish people—there were some English—in what was known in Ireland as the "plantation."

It is from that generation of settlers that you now have the Northern Ireland Troubles: the Orangemen are their descendants.

They brought with them not only their physical presence but their religious beliefs—they were nearly all Calvinists and Presbyterians, whereas the majority of the Irish were Catholics. And that's where you have the big debate that exists now, because some people regard them as imports who have no right to be there: "Why are they here? They are not Irish; they are imports."

Other people say: "They are here, so there's not much you can do about it. We can't go out of our way to annihilate them all; they are here, and they are a fact of life."

So the Unionists had a majority in Northern Ireland, and that's where our troubles come from today.

* * *

By an act of Parliament in 1920, Ireland was divided and Northern Ireland was constituted from six of the nine counties of Ulster.

Southern Ireland, whose population is now mainly Roman Catholic, became a dominion in 1921, was declared the sovereign democratic state of Eire [Gaelic for Ireland] in 1937, and by Irish legislation passed on December 21, 1948, was created a republic, withdrawing from the Commonwealth.

Northern Ireland's population is approximately two-thirds Protestant and one-third Catholic, resulting in the latter community's serious grievances over discrimination in employment, housing, and social programs, and leading to continuing agitation for separate political status or for union with the Irish Republic.

These grievances, coupled with strong opposition to British rule, led to a new, prolonged period of sectarian violence known, like the earlier one, as the Troubles, during which more than three thousand people were killed, beginning in 1969 and lasting into the 1990s.

During this time, many bombings, shootings, and torture were carried out against civilians, mainly in Northern Ireland, but also in the Irish Republic, and in mainland Britain itself. The violence caused death and injury to politicians in Northern Ireland, the Republic of Ireland, and Britain, and in the British military.

Several of these acts of violence stand out. They include "Bloody Sunday," January 30, 1972, when thirteen people were killed by British paratroopers in the Bogside area of Londonderry after a civil rights protest had turned unruly; car bombings in Dublin on May 17, 1974—likely planted by Protestant militants—killing twenty-three people; the bombing deaths of eighteen British soldiers on August 27, 1979, the very day of Lord Mountbatten's assassination as he sailed his boat, *Shadow V,* in the harbor of Mullaghmore in the Irish Republic; the bombing on October 2, 1984, of Brighton's Grand Hotel during the annual Conservative Party conference, in which five people were killed and Prime Minister Thatcher escaped death only because she had left the room for a moment; and the bombing deaths on November 8, 1987, of eleven people, including three couples, as they gathered in Inniskillen, Northern Ireland, for the town's annual Remembrance Day observance.

While acts of violence against Catholics and Protestants received widespread media attention, perhaps nothing in the history of the Troubles captured the public's attention and galvanized support for the republican cause more than hunger strikes, particularly the one conducted in 1981 by nationalist prisoners at the Maze Prison. Joint efforts by the governments of Britain and Ireland to end the mayhem resulted, in the latter part of August 1994, in the IRA announcing a ceasefire, which it broke in February 1996 and reinstated in July 1997.

A major breakthrough occurred with the signing on April 10, 1998, of the Good Friday Agreement, an accord approved by referendum in May and followed by elections for a 108-member constituent assembly to govern Northern Ireland.

The fragile peace achieved in April 1998 was sorely tested on August 15 of that year when twenty-nine people were killed in Armagh by a bomb detonated by a group calling itself the Real IRA.

Then in 1999, protracted discussion between the parties, brokered by former U.S. Senator George Mitchell, resulted in a reaffirmation of the Good Friday Agreement and the establishment of a cabinet which included two Sinn Fein seats.

While home rule was suspended for a time over the issue of weapons decommissioning, by 2002, when the first edition of this book was published, the new government was again functioning at Stormont and was now grappling with the complex issues before it. The key issue was whether the IRA and the Protestant militia groups would cooperate in the process.

BRITISH ROYALTY'S ROLE IN IRELAND, NORTH AND SOUTH

Garret Fitzgerald Thinking back, one negative factor was that Queen Victoria never came to live here [in the Republic], and never showed an interest in Ireland. It would have made a difference, I thought, if she had.

Cardinal Cahal Daly Our interest in the Queen, or in Prince Charles as a possible future Monarch, is that she's the Queen of another country. As the nationalists would think: she's not the Queen of *our* country.

But we respect her. And we know that our fellow-countrymen have a perfect right to do so. And that's what the nationalists are being asked to accept: that the Unionists have a perfect right to remain, to be British, and to have their identity and their culture fully protected, and are guaranteed full equality. And that the mindset that they shouldn't be here at all, that they were brought here as foreign implants in this country of ours, has to change.

Lord Fitt The Palace has identified with the Unionist majority, and every now and again they would send a member of the Royal Family to pay a visit to some Unionist establishment, or some Army or police establishment. But they never really identified with the Catholics.

But the Catholics actually didn't want to identify with them, either; the Catholics didn't want to know them. They called the Queen "Mrs. Windsor."

When I was the leader of the SDLP, I could detect no antagonism against the Royal Family, but no particular liking for them either. But if I had gone out of my way to meet any member of the Royal Family, I would have lost the next election. It's only lately that you would have members of the minority meeting with any member of the Royal Family.

Rev. Ian Paisley I've met the Queen on many occasions and have had conversations. She's very well-informed on the issue of Northern Ireland. I don't know where she gets the right information from, but it's a lot more accurate than the government's sources. And I always say when I come away from speaking to her that she's not briefed by Whitehall people—that she must have her own briefing people: they seem to tell her more of the truth than you would get from Whitehall.

* * *

In 1994, Queen's University, Belfast, in response to students' views, voted to replace the British National Anthem with the European Union's anthem, "Ode to Joy."

* * *

Sir Kenneth Bloomfield There was a very passionate issue here at the Queen's University of Belfast. The graduation ceremonies always used to be concluded by the singing of the National Anthem, "God Save the Queen." But increasingly in recent years, under all the stresses of the situation here, some not inconsiderable part of the audience would remain firmly glued to their seats.

Finally, the government of the university decided it would be better if it was not played at all. Now there was an initial, frightful, row about that. You might imagine, people were saying: "The university hasn't been true to its heritage; it's swinging irreversibly in a particular direction."

I can understand why that was done, although it was bound to outrage some people—almost anything you do here is going to outrage somebody.

Conor Cruise O'Brien The monarchy now concerns us in Ireland mainly through Northern Ireland. As long as a majority in Northern Ireland wish to remain subjects of the Crown, we ought to leave them alone and let them get on with it. I feel very strongly about that particular matter, and have been very vocal regarding it. The link with the Crown is there.

THE ROYAL FAMILY'S VISITS

The Queen first visited Northern Ireland in 1977. Other members of the immediate Royal Family have gone there since, and Prince Charles has expressed interest in the victims of violence, visiting families in Ulster and inviting groups of individuals from the province to his Highgrove estate.

Lord King The Royal Family were regular visitors. I used to encourage them to come when I was secretary for Northern Ireland. I used to give an annual garden party. There was always a member of the Royal Family there: Princess Diana came—she was an extremely popular visitor; and in the early days, the Duke and Duchess of York; Prince Charles came. That was actually appreciated right across the community.

And they also came when we had a very bad bombing—Inniskillen was one, and Remembrance Day. And then there was a very bad attack on a bus carrying soldiers—a number were killed and a lot were badly wounded—and they came; they came to the hospital. And they used to come and see the Royal Ulster Constabulary widows.

And they were quite involved in different elements in which their presence and their involvement was felt, of course, particularly, to the Unionists, who were worried about the linkages of the United Kingdom. There was an intensity of enthusiasm for royalty in their loyalty to the Crown and the Monarch is the symbol of that unity.

The warmth was enhanced by this living symbol of that unity and that they weren't being sold out—as they saw a united Ireland—to a country which they were, in a way, divided from, and hostile to.

Lord Glentoran Demonstratively, the monarchy can help, just by being there. And we have had over the thirty years a tremendous support from the Royal Family: every single one of them has been over, and they're all wonderful.

[...] Princess Anne goes over on a variety of her Save the Children things; the Queen has been over irregularly, not all that often; but the Queen Mother's been; and Prince Charles was there almost right after the Armagh bombing.

And just by being there, demonstrating care and concern, and fostering that sort of relationship with the population has done a great deal of good. They are in the hospitals, they are in the police stations, they're at the Army bases—they're everywhere.

Garret Fitzgerald There were no visits of the Royal Family here [the Republic of Ireland] until the 1960s when Princess Margaret came and stayed.

I am not sure she was that sympathetic to us. It was said that she was not. They chopped down trees in the area, but basically people were very happy with her. The government didn't have any problems with her.

Prince Charles came here on an official visit [in 1995]. There was a dinner in Parliament given by the then head of the government, John Bruton.

I had met him a few times before that. He has always been very interested in Ireland, and very positive about Ireland, since I first met him in 1977. And on that occasion he went from dinner to the galleries to watch the Jubilee bands of the Guards playing on the lawn. And he joined in asking questions about Ireland. He obviously had done his homework: he knew what questions to ask.

The next time he came, in 1981, with the royal party, there was a tour of the ministers of the European Union—the heads of government and foreign ministers. He was sitting straight across the circle from me and he spent half an hour talking about us. His interest was very genuine and positive.

The 1995 visit, obviously, was seen as a prelude to the Queen's visiting here. There was a man in the government who said: "The only way to have the Queen come here would be to tell nobody—not even the police—and have her arrive by helicopter at the racecourse. If nobody knows she's coming, nobody will try to shoot her. Telling it to the police, there'll be trouble."

Cardinal Cahal Daly Visits of the Queen, or members of the Royal Family, to Northern Ireland in the past were really visits to the Unionist community: they would have been confined to areas of Unionist majority, and they would have been celebrated as sort of national holidays by the Unionist community. And in that sense, our community was unaffected by the movement through the streets to welcome Her Majesty.

During what the republicans call the "war years" of armed conflict before the ceasefires, there would always have been visits to the British Army bases, and the Royal Ulster Constabulary bases, and to places where security was guaranteed, and therefore, on security reasons, as well as political reasons, they would have avoided nationalist areas.

The Queen visited Armagh [in 1995] in order to confer the honor of the title of city on Armagh as the ecclesiastic hub of Ireland. It was a different kind of visit from the ones that had historically been.

I was there; I was archbishop at the time. There was a very different atmosphere—it was harmonious and positive. It was, I think, probably the first time in which Elizabeth the Queen was recognized and welcomed by representatives of the nationalist community.

Whereas in the past she would have been greeted by the Union flag, by children waving the Union flag, and by the rendition of the British National Anthem, when she came to Armagh, a very conscious effort was made to turn the visit into a cross-community event: there were no flags; there was no anthem; people from the nationalist community were invited and accepted the invitation—they'd been invited formally in the past but didn't come.

Prince Charles has visited Northern Ireland. He has visited Armagh. And on that occasion I was impressed by his sincere interest in the problems of Northern Ireland. I certainly had the impression that he was very well-informed, thoughtful, and intelligent.

Sir Kenneth Bloomfield I was asked by the government [in November 1997], as the Northern Ireland Victims Commissioner, to consider how the sufferings of victims of violence here over thirty years could best be recognized, and I produced a report, *We Will Remember Them*, which was published [in May 1998].

By chance, in the more or less immediate aftermath of its publication, the Prince of Wales was visiting in Northern Ireland and, somehow or other, this had been brought to his attention.

He then said: "I'd like to meet a number of the victims if I could." So a gathering of people from both sides of the community was brought together at Hillsborough Castle.

I was present because I had to introduce these people, acting as a master of ceremonies. And he was absolutely wonderful—so nice, and so sympathetic and caring—and when the thing was over, he actually said: "I know what I'd like to do next summer; I'd like to have some of these people to Highgrove."

It was followed up, and [in June 1999] I went with a party of the victims to Highgrove, where they were entertained by the Prince of Wales as if they were heads of state—and these were very ordinary people; some of them had never been outside Northern Ireland before. They were absolutely staggered by the whole thing.

Again, he was wonderful. And I'm sure there were in that party people who wouldn't *dream* of voting for the Union, but one could not fail to be impressed by his concern, or by his own personal involvement in the thing, through the death of Mountbatten, because he, in particular, was very close to Mountbatten.

And I told him: "As it happens, I've recently been in Mullaghmore"—where this bombing took place, where Mountbatten was killed—"My wife and I were on holiday nearby, and I said: 'Let's go and have a look at Mullaghmore.'"

And he said: "You know, I would love to go there myself but, so far, security advises it's a difficult thing to do."

John Dixon, an Ulsterman severely injured at Inniskillen I haven't had any contact with the Royal Family. Tom King, the Northern Ireland representative, came to visit me. I highly respect the Royal Family and believe our country would lose a lot. One of the greatest things this country has is the Royal Family.

I think the Royal Family have been isolated from the situation, and I don't think that they can do much about it. We are being led by a pro-terrorist group. Our British government is pro-terrorist.

ACTS OF TERRORISM

Lord Fitt When I was the leader of the SDLP, the IRA were doing quite a lot of murdering, blowing up people, and killing people, and I was going to different funerals.

Naturally, I would go into some television studio and they would ask me [about the killings], and I would condemn it without qualifications: I said that the people who were responsible for this were murderers; that they were dragging the name of Irish nationalism in the gutter; that they weren't representative of the Irish people; that they were murdering psychopaths.

There was no way that anybody could have misunderstood what I was saying. And Sinn Fein could have looked at me through the television screen and said: "He's our enemy; he's against us."

So they began to attack my house; they began at nighttime to throw stones, and bottles at the windows. And then I had to get protective devices to make sure that petrol bombs didn't come in the windows. And then they put bombs at the doors. It was a hell of a time.

They started to do that in 1972, and they continued to do that almost nightly. They were around the house with petrol bombs, and stones, and cans of paint. And then in 1983, I came over here [to England]—one of my daughters was over here—and when I was away, they got into the house and burned it.

John Dixon These men are guilty of heinous murders. I was sitting beside a lady the other day, and she said: "We had twelve people put out of their homes. There was five men held my husband and a red-hot iron poker was pushed down his throat."

I could tell you stories after stories where men's insides have been gouged out and bombs put in them.

Sir Kenneth Bloomfield I used to live on the County Down coast, and about ten past six one morning in September 1988, we were blown out of bed by a bomb going off. And then another bomb went. And then there was a loud crack, which, in fact, was the detonator of the third bomb going off, which didn't detonate the bomb.

My wife and I, and our son, then eighteen, were in bed. My daughter, thank God, was in law college back in England, because her room was cut to ribbons; she would certainly have been killed.

We had a fortuitous escape because if all four bombs set around the house had gone off, as intended, we would certainly have been buried under the house.

And why didn't they? Almost certainly because my wife, who's a very healthy person, unusually, was a bit queasy in the night, and she got up to go to the loo at six o'clock in the morning. She put the light on in the bathroom, and, almost certainly, seeing the light come on, they thought they were observed and just didn't complete their preparations, so the last two devices were not properly primed. It's as simple as that, really.

A large part of the house was destroyed, and both our cars were blown to pieces, and we emerged from the house, as you might imagine, in some disarray.

We were very lucky; there were those who were much less lucky: about three thousand six hundred dead and as many as forty thousand injured, in a tiny place.

I believe that as long as you're not killed or injured it's possibly quite a good thing to happen to you, although it doesn't seem so at the time, in that it does inculcate a proper sense of proportion: you're not so inclined to take seriously things which may be unimportant.

Cardinal Cahal Daly My reaction to all violence is one of horror. And, of course, I condemned it. But then, because I accompanied my condemnation with calling for equality of rights—civil, human, justice, opportunity, housing, equality in access to education—I was thought on the Unionist side to be partly condoning violence, to talk about justice and equal rights, because it seemed to be supporting the republicans. Whereas, when I condemned the militants, and condemned the murder of Lord Mountbatten, I was seen by some of the nationalist community as being pro-British, anti-Irish.

Nationalists, too, were victims of IRA violence, as we now know from the stories of the disappeared. And all of these people who disappeared, whose bodies are being searched for now, were Catholics, murdered mainly because they were accused of being informers.

I have officiated at the funerals of scores of innocent murdered Catholics. I would have sympathized with the families of members of this group, particularly those murdered by the IRA.

In all of these cases, I would have found that there were no words that were going to help in the situation, but that my presence could be of some help, and some support—that I wanted to be with people in their grief, and to listen to them express their grief, and show that I wanted to be with them in their sorrow.

So whoever the perpetrator in the attack, whoever the victim, whatever the allegiance, I felt the presence with them in their sorrow was the only thing that I could offer, and yet the thing which they seemed to value.

THE ASSASSINATION OF LORD MOUNTBATTEN

The 1979 killing of Lord Mountbatten, second cousin to the Queen, uncle to Prince Philip, and great-uncle and mentor to Prince Charles, was reported to have "deeply shocked" the Monarch.

Lord Mountbatten's teenaged grandson, one of the twin sons of Mountbatten's elder daughter, Lady Patricia Brabourne, and a teenaged crew member were also killed in the explosion, and Lady Brabourne's mother-in-law, the Dowager Lady Brabourne, died hours later of her severe injuries, adding to the deep sense of horror felt by the Royal Family.

* * *

Lord King Obviously, it didn't enhance the IRA; it didn't increase any sympathy in this country for them, or for any causes they might be seeking to espouse. I believe it was damaging to the IRA.

And then, of course, it happened in the Republic, which was also, therefore, very offensive to a tremendous lot of Irish people whose sense of hospitality and generosity of spirit were grossly frayed: he'd lived there for a long time; he had a holiday home there and was very popular. So that was very damaging.

And it was upsetting for the Royal Family as he was, obviously, very popular and very close to Prince Philip and to Prince Charles.

Lord Fitt I was at home with my wife in Belfast the day it happened. And when I heard on the radio that he had been killed, I thought to myself it was a very cowardly way to kill him: he was nearly eighty years of age, and he loved Ireland—he used to go to Ireland all the time—and the people round there all loved him; he was an easy target. And they killed an old woman and a young boy from County Fermanagh. And I thought that was a very, very nasty thing.

I have made lots of statements condemning the murder of Mountbatten because not only was *he* killed, but on the very same day, eighteen paratroopers were killed [at Warrenpoint, County Down].

As a Catholic, I was on television condemning both crimes. There were some of our Christian brothers who indicated I wasn't supposed to go on television and condemn the murder of a member of British royalty, or members of the British Army. But I did, because I didn't agree with murder.

The English papers had gone mad when Mountbatten was killed and they had big headlines: "Assassins! Bastards!" We had a meeting of the SDLP about a fortnight after. I had condemned Jack Lynch for not coming back[1] because he was the taoiseach of the country in which it had happened, and my own party executive said: "You shouldn't have attacked our taoiseach." I said: "He's not *my* taoiseach. I don't live in the Republic; here is where I live."

And then you could see the difference emerging between me and the rest of the SDLP. One of them said: "It's up to you to defend the national interest." And I said: "What do you mean, 'national interest'?" And they said: "Well, we mean you're Irish and you're not supposed to condemn the people who murdered Mountbatten."

And I said: "Hold on a minute. That's IRA murder talk. And I'm not happy with that." So within a few weeks after that I left.

THE GOOD FRIDAY AGREEMENT

One of the prices of the Good Friday Agreement and peace has been the release of known terrorists, including the murderer of Lord Mountbatten, Thomas McMahon.

* * *

Lord Fitt The man who set the bomb at Brighton is free, too. I feel badly about some of those people who have been released because they murdered—and some of their victims were Catholics.

Sinn Fein said: "We will have nothing to do with this agreement unless you agree to release all our prisoners." And the Unionists said: "That's very hard to accept because a lot of those prisoners are in there for shooting our brothers and fathers," and the Unionists find that very, very difficult to accept.

But Blair said: "There's no way that they will agree unless you agree to release their prisoners." So Trimble, the leader of the Unionist Party, agreed, and he said: "I agree. But could we not relate the decommissioning to the prisoner release?" In other words: if they give up some of their arms, we will then release some of their prisoners.

And Blair again said: "No, no, no. Sinn Fein will not come on board if decommissioning is written into this agreement." In fact, he was fighting for Sinn Fein to get the agreement without decommissioning being written into it. Now that spells itself out; the actuality is that he wanted to keep Sinn Fein on board at all costs to stop them from bombing London.

Sir Kenneth Bloomfield The prisoner release thing is extremely difficult, not least for the kind of client body I was dealing with when I did this work, because the way to do this work—and the way I did it—was to actually meet face-to-face with hundreds of these people who had been through these horrible experiences—widows, amputees, blinded people.

All of us could see that even if a prisoner had served his full term, the moment when he comes out and, perhaps, returns to the very town you all lived in, and you, the widow of the victim, meet him in the supermarket, that's not going to be easy anyway. And when the person is, as it were, prematurely released—released before anybody would have expected—it's all the more difficult.

Now, I think the community—and that includes the victims—are divided on this issue. There are people whose views I understand, and even respect, who say: "I can't tolerate this; I can't deal with it."

And to be honest, if—as was entirely possible—my wife had been blinded by that bomb, I don't know, I might have been in that camp. I have the luxury of only having lost material things; you get over that. So I'm with the not insubstantial number of people, including some of the victims themselves, who would say: "Well, of course I don't like it;

in principle, it's a very unfortunate thing to have to do. But if it means that other people are not going to be exposed to these experiences in the future, well, we'd better swallow it."

Garret Fitzgerald It's possibly a necessary development: you weren't going to get a solution until this is resolved. We've always known that that would come in time. However distasteful, however much we dislike them to do it, it's just a precondition of peace.

Lady Pamela Hicks My sister and her family—and I say my sister with feeling because, of course, her son and my brother-in-law's mother were killed—don't have the same feeling, but this man who was convicted had spent something like twenty years in jail. You can't leave a human being to rot after that. You *can't*.

It was quite right that he had a heavy sentence. But he's paid the price. And there's no room in life for bitterness. Bitterness is counterproductive: bitterness destroys the person; it doesn't destroy the person you're bitter against.

THE STORMONT DELIBERATIONS OF JUNE–JULY 1999

During a visit to Belfast, Northern Ireland, in the summer of 1999, at the time of deliberations at Stormont, we observed both tensions and signs of hope in a people with yearning and aspirations for future peace.

Heading from the airport to the city by taxi, we came upon the Belfast Channel, which leads to the Irish Sea. At that point, our driver pointed out the Harland & Woolf Shipyard and, with great pride, informed us that it was "where the *Titanic* was built."

In response to our observation that the great liner had indeed come to a bad end, he shot back without missing a beat: "Well, she had a British captain!"

We got into a political discussion with the driver—June 30 being the day of the deadline imposed by Prime Minister Tony Blair for the Unionists and the Sinn Fein–IRA, as well as their satellite groups, to come to terms and to set up a power-sharing government at Stormont.

This conversation was the first of many we had over the next few days with taxi drivers, a most readily available segment of the vox populi. We did not ask them about their religious or political affiliations. Where we make such references, the driver has volunteered that information.

Our driver coming in from the airport on June 30 expressed his aspirations for peace, saying:

I was born and raised in the Shankhill district. They [the IRA] will have to accept the terms offered. Most people want to pursue normal lives: the boys are chasing the girls; the girls are chasing the boys, And that's the way it should be.

We arrived in short order at our hotel. Settling into our room, we switched on a television news channel to learn whether there were any developments at Stormont. The legend "Breaking News" appeared on the screen. We rushed forward only to learn something about Manchester United, the latest on a sporting event.

A Catholic driver, a woman who appeared to be in her mid-thirties, picking us up in front of our hotel later that afternoon for the short ride to our first appointment, greeted us cheerily, and then inquired: "You're staying *here*? It is the most bombed hotel in Belfast. It has been hit twenty-seven times!"

We were later told that the hotel, the Europa, had been heavily bombed in the 1970s, having been the hotel of choice for many foreign businesspeople, as the IRA sought to disrupt the economy of Northern Ireland.

After lunch, the next day, July 1, we went up to Stormont to mingle with the media and observe the "spinners" of the disparate positions of the Unionists and the Sinn Fein–IRA.

As we arrived there, in the distance, set in a magnificent park, lay Stormont Castle, the stately seat of the former government of Northern Ireland, which has become the seat of the new coalition government.

Some distance away from the Castle, in one of the buildings in a cluster of low-slung, unprepossessing structures known as the "Castle Buildings," Prime Ministers Tony Blair and Bertie Aherne of Ireland; Ulster Unionist leader David Trimble, and Ulster Democratic Unionist activist Ian Paisley; Sinn Fein leader Gerry Adams, and his chief nego-tiator Martin McGuinness and others were going at it, hot and heavy.

Outside, a media tent, media trucks, media towers, and porta johns littered the landscape. Print and broadcast journalists, as well as photog-raphers, stood about, talking, smoking, interviewing each other, their activities suspended every time a "spinner" emerged from the Castle Buildings and strolled over to articulate his group's latest position.

While spinners from both the nationalist and Unionist sides appeared regularly, the Sinn Fein people struck one as being the more experienced in dealing with the media.

From time to time the negotiators themselves came out to speak with journalists, among them the Reverend Ian Paisley.

* * *

Rev. Ian Paisley I say to you today: terrorists have no place in any government of Northern Ireland. Those that have guns must have the guns taken off of them. They must restrict their power to sow mayhem, and murder, and anarchy, among the people of this province.

If you had listened to the two prime ministers here today, and hadn't heard, or seen them, and you asked what came after them, you would have thought that they were all on their way to heaven.

* * *

On the afternoon of Friday, July 2, we went by taxi on a tour of the Catholic area of Belfast—the Falls Road, and Ballymurphy Road, among others, and of the Protestant Shankhill Road, viewing some of the many politically inspired murals that adorn the sides of local buildings.

Our driver told us on that occasion: "My mother was a Protestant. Her sister was killed by an IRA bomb. They all killed innocent people. I have no time for them."

Then, speaking of the British monarchy, he said:

I wouldn't like to see the end of the monarchy, to be honest. It's a British tradition and it would be sad to see it go. It's only the Unionists who would go to see her; she'd have more warmth than in the home country.

On the afternoon of Saturday, July 3, we engaged a driver to take us to the Milltown Cemetery, established in 1869 and located at 546 Falls Road, having only just glimpsed the Catholic cemetery the previous day as we toured the neighborhoods, but wanting to see the IRA's burial plots.

The driver met us in the lobby. As we strolled out to his car, he asked: "Where is it you want to go?" When we said: "Milltown Cemetery," he handed us the keys to his cab and said: "One of you drive!"

Of course he was joking. But his little jest said volumes about lingering tensions and fears between Catholic and Protestant, between nationalist and Unionist.

Milltown Cemetery is located across the road from a fortified police post. In a large section are the tombstones and monuments to fallen IRA fighters, including people killed in the first quarter of the century, the 1981 hunger strikers, and the three IRA soldiers "murdered" by British SAS forces on a Gibraltar street.

While there is no comparable graveyard in the Protestant part of the city, the memories of fallen Unionists are no less vivid.

As we walked among the many IRA burial plots and monuments, we noticed fresh flowers placed on many of the graves. There were inscriptions, heartrending ones: "Killed at the age of nineteen. ..."; martial-seeming ones: "Killed in action. ..."; and incriminating ones: "Killed on the way to an action. ..."

At the conclusion of our visit to the cemetery, our driver told us that only a few years ago, he would not have ventured into the Milltown Cemetery.

WHAT THE VOICES OF 2002 THOUGHT THE FUTURE HELD

Cardinal Cahal Daly There are extremists on both sides who are being intransigent and desperate. But they are sufficiently voicing the traditions, and the convictions, and the fears of their respective communities as not to be totally alien to the community.

The violent republicans are using methods which the vast majority of the current community abjure and detest. But the violence is claimed to be used on behalf of the principles and convictions which are broadly shared by the nationalist community. They condemn their methods, but not their convictions.

And equally, on the Unionist side, there are loyalist extremists who have carried on a counter-republican campaign with equal violence, with equal ruthlessness, and who still carry lists, and who are still a law into their own hands in their military "campaign" against Irish nationalists.

But what unites the great majority in both communities is a weariness with violence, a disgust with violence, a longing for peace, and, broadly speaking, a sense, and an agreement, on the need for change if there is going to be peace.

John Dixon I'm very opposed to terrorists taking a seat in government because you can't have peace made from terrorism; peace only comes from law and order. And we have been cajoled, and bribed, and demonized in every direction by the government; we are the decent people, and I represent the victims—there are thousands in Northern Ireland—we've been the forgotten people in all of this. We're bottom of the line on everything. Terrorists coming out get money, get set up in jobs. The victims haven't got anything. We haven't got one good representative in the entire North of Ireland.

Sir Kenneth Bloomfield The prevailing British view about Northern Ireland is one of pervasive boredom and fed-upness: if you asked the average English voters what are their principal concerns, Ireland would come pretty low down.

To Tony Blair's great credit, he's put it much higher up. That's where it belongs: if one part of your own country that you govern has been wracked by violence for years, it needs to be very high up on the agenda.

If you profoundly believe in the republican goals—which I don't happen to do, but clearly, they do—people like Adams need to be able to say: "Well, look lads, let me tell you, we're going to gain more movement through the political process than ever we did by the gun, and if we go back to the gun, we will do worse, rather than better."

If he could say: "We have a potential to play a much bigger part in the political stage, and you throw all that out of the window"—a lot of the kind of thing they quite enjoy in America, going to the White House and all that stuff—I hope they'd pause.

Lord Longford Personally, I'm hopeful. For the first time, the Protestants and the Catholics are really talking.

I asked Gerry Fitt the other day what he thought, and he said: "They hadn't had strong support in the British government, but this time, the British government are very keen on it."

Ideally, they'll have a power-sharing for some years, and then it will become a united country. In Northern Ireland, you don't have a satisfactory union; you've got no reality at all on either side: if you're British, the Irish don't want you.

I think the only remedy in the future lies in a united Ireland. And Ireland has been very successful economically. When we went to school, the Protestants were mostly well-dressed, but the Catholics were wearing rags, literally; they were barefoot. And now, they're up to the English level. Now that's a tremendous change.

It won't happen in a hurry, but there's movement. This government are keen on it. And that is something.

Sir Kenneth Bloomfield I don't believe there's such a thing [as reconciliation in this generation]; I believe there's movement in the right direction, and one shouldn't be overambitious.

I remember using a phrase some years ago, to which I'll adhere, to the effect that: "as far ahead as I can see, the task of government in Northern Ireland will be the civilized management of diversity—if you can achieve *that*."

It's one thing bouncing the rhetoric around; it's another thing bouncing bombs around—there's really a difference in kind between those things. So I don't think you're going to create at a very early date a society where people are going to run out into the street and embrace each other.

Lord Glentoran Perhaps the most encouraging thing that has happened is the statement from the IRA saying that they've put their arms out of use, signed by "P. O'Neill." Sinn Fein–IRA have told so many lies over the years. But nearly always it has been the case that when they have issued a statement under the name of "P. O'Neill": "We're going to kill Glentoran next week," or "We're going to blow up Stormont," they've always done it; they've always kept to it.

So it does encourage one to believe that they have crossed the Rubicon and really decided that the guns have got to be taken out of politics.

Cardinal Cahal Daly How can we trust the IRA not to begin their war again? Are people really committed to democratic methods if they still feel that they need weapons, that if their politics fails, they can start their weapon-getting again?

You can understand that point of view; it's a very reasonable point of view. Many, many, whatever their politics, would agree that even if the IRA were to destroy all its weapons tomorrow, they can buy it all again.

Rev. Ian Paisley The truth here in Northern Ireland will prevail. And I believe that we have people, both Protestant and Roman Catholic, who are decent and likeable. And I believe that that tough, centered mark of wisdom of Ulster will come through at the end. It is tough, certainly. But I believe it will come through at the end.

I am not a lover of the dogmas of Roman Catholicism. Everybody knows that. But I have every respect for a Roman Catholic who strongly believes in the religion of his own Scripture. I don't care for what it says, but I admire him, and I will fight for him. All I want for myself is what everybody else has.

* * *

Tension between Catholics and Protestants has lessened considerably in the years following the inception, in 1998, of the Good Friday Agreement. The onset of Brexit, however, has created issues involving trade with European Union nations as well as with England, Scotland, and Wales.

CHAPTER 21

Suez and Hong Kong

I N ADDITION TO the Queen's deep interest and involvement in the Commonwealth, she has a keen awareness of Britain's past role in both the Middle East, where Britain ruled the then-Palestine by a mandate following Turkey's defeat in the First World War, and in the former Crown Colony of Hong Kong.

THE SUEZ CRISIS

The first major Middle Eastern issue of the Queen's reign was the Suez crisis, which occurred in the fall of 1956 when Britain became involved, along with Israel and France, in a military action to protect Western interests in the region.

The crisis had its roots in the action taken by Egypt's president, Colonel Abdel Gamal Nasser, on July 26, 1956, when Nasser announced that he had nationalized the Anglo-French Suez Canal Company.

Nasser's action—the result of the failure of the United States and Britain to fund Egypt's Aswan High Dam project—was viewed at the time as having the potential to jeopardize the flow of oil to the West through the 103-mile waterway running from Port Said to Suez.

The Egyptian leader's bold move prompted Britain's prime minister at the time, Anthony Eden, to observe that Nasser had placed "his thumb on our windpipe."

Three months later, on October 29, 1956, Israeli forces—with the likely assent of the British and French governments—swept through the Sinai peninsula, moving to a position just twenty miles east of the Canal.

Two days later, following Egypt's rejection of repeated Anglo-French requests to pull its forces back from the Canal, British warplanes bombed military targets both near the Canal and in the outskirts of Cairo.

The Queen, being both head of state and Britain's military leader, was fully briefed on these events. The Duke of Edinburgh was at that time several weeks into his six-month cruise in *Britannia*, leading one to conclude that the events of July had not been thought serious enough by the government to question the timing of his trip. Nor, following the Allies' military action, had the government viewed it as being of such consequence that the Duke should be recalled.

Whether or not the Queen was influential in ending the crisis, it is known that several of her key advisers had been against the military adventure, whose progress they observed within the context of two major international events: the Hungarian Revolution with the brutal repression by Soviet forces of the freedom fighters; and the huge re-election victory in November 1956 of President Eisenhower, who strongly opposed the Suez intervention.

* * *

Philip Kaiser The British Ambassador [in Washington] told London that if they moved into Suez there would be a strong reaction on the part of Eisenhower.

Eden didn't want to accept that so he sent Eisenhower's buddy Macmillan, who had been liaison, to talk to Eisenhower. He spent forty-five minutes with him and reported back: "Don't worry about Eisenhower; it will be all right."

Sir Michael Palliser While Eden did not have to tell his cabinet until the last minute, I can't believe that he wouldn't have told the Queen what was going on.

You've always got to put yourself in the position of the people on the spot at the time. In the Queen's case, she was a very young woman. At that stage, she had only been on the Throne for four years.

The military action continued and on November 6, British and French forces captured the Canal Zone, while Israel established firm control over the Sinai and Gaza.

* * *

Adm. Sir Henry Leach I had nothing to do with it at all, for which I am deeply grateful because I believe it was one of the more major historical out-and-out mistakes from the word "go." There isn't a good word to be said about it. It was ineptly handled, but it involved quite a lot of loss of life. It was an appalling thing.

John Eisenhower They sent out a boy to do a man's job in that operation. You bombed so that the pictures of dead children come out in the press five days before you invade by land! It was stupid! That was not their finest hour. I believe there was some resentment against our action.

* * *

Three days later, bowing to immense pressure from the United States, as well as other nations, the British and French forces accepted a U.N.-brokered ceasefire.

Less than three weeks later, in the wake of a warning by the United States that it would not assist in averting the collapse of the sterling monetary unit unless the British backed down, the British withdrew from Egypt.

* * *

Gen. Andrew Goodpaster The British were faced with a severe financial problem, and with the severe problem of access to oil, on which their industry was dependent.

Those were President Eisenhower's overriding concerns—that the British financial system would be destroyed, which it could have been.

The president talked on the telephone with Prime Minister Eden—he got him off the floor of the Parliament, which was almost unheard of.

It was said that he had used barrack-room language to the prime minister. Not at all. He said: "I think you've made a terrible mistake. The problem now is: how do we get beyond it?"

He felt that on this matter, there was such a level of importance, and urgency, and immediacy, that he simply had to have communication and understand the views of Eden.

Over the spring and summer of 1956, they had had numerous exchanges. And in those exchanges, it was quite apparent that the two men were missing each other.

I recall Eisenhower saying, on occasion, that Eden would not respond to the question he had raised: "To what end do you aim to bring this?"

Eden's response was always that Britain would not go down without a fight. That was the essence of it. But despite the exchanges, nothing was reconciled.

* * *

The political consequence of Britain's involvement in the Suez affair was the resignation of Prime Minister Eden, ostensibly due to illness, and the coming to power of Harold Macmillan, who took office on January 10, 1957.

* * *

Winston Churchill Within eighteen hours of total victory, Anthony Eden had chucked it in under massive pressure from the United States. He had had major surgery and was going to have further major surgery. And as a result, he ended up totally bungling the Suez affair.

That was the [subject of the] first political conversation that I can recall with my grandfather. I was a boy of fifteen-and-a-half at the time—this was in 1956, just in the wake of the Suez disaster—and I was lunching with my grandfather alone at 28 Hyde Park Gate, my grandparents' London home once he ceased to be prime minister. I said: "Grandpa, what do you make of all this Suez business?"

[Mimicking Prime Minister Churchill's distinctive, sibilant pronunciation, the younger Churchill recounts his grandfather's response]: "Hm, I don't know that I should have had the courage to start it all in the first place. I certainly wouldn't have dared stop halfway."

Geoffrey Pearson My father was instrumental in helping to get the British and French out of there in favor of a U.N. force. The Canadians offered to become part of the force, and our national defense people sent the Queen's Own Rifles.

Well, Nasser said: "Who are *they*? We just got rid of the British!" He didn't want to bring them back.

Hugh Segal We moved all our troops for that U.N. peacekeeping operation on our own hook, in a period of two weeks. And there was a fascinating situation for the Royal Family in that context because the Head Office, if you wish, was heading in one direction and the Dominion was heading in another direction.

Historically, that had never been the case. Historically, the dominions were the first to stand with the Head Office, so that would have been a real departure for us, in terms of breaking that traditional U.K.-Dominion.

THE QUEEN'S UNDERSTANDING OF
MIDDLE EAST ISSUES

Lord Wright She doesn't know the Middle East terribly well. She's been to Saudi Arabia; she's been to Jordan; she's probably been to Tunisia—Charles has been to Tunisia quite extensively—and, of course, down the [Persian] Gulf: she's visited Kuwait and Bahrain.

I believe she regards the Middle East as slightly mysterious, and she's rather uncertain about her contacts in the Middle East. And, of course, there is no Middle East country in the Commonwealth, and the Commonwealth actually ranks very high in her vision of the world. This does not say that she doesn't take an intelligent and close interest [in the Middle East].

Stephen Day The Queen was concerned about the Middle East. She had met various Arab rulers in the United Kingdom. But she had been, unfortunately, ill-advised by certain people about the complexities of the Arab world, the difficulty for a woman, a female sovereign, to go to that part of the world—all the questions of etiquette that the so-called experts on the Arab world had a graveness about, but actually are far less important.

When she went there, she discovered that actually it was an extremely hospitable part of the world, and it went swimmingly.

I went later with the Prince and Princess of Wales and, of course, the journalists there stirred it up to an absolutely outrageous degree, inventing stories of shock, horror, and, of course [the headline]: "The hem was five inches above the floor"—as if any of the Arabs had noticed that. They were largely fictitious stories; they were invented to inject a bit of drama into the whole exercise.

In practice, the tour was a great success. And then that enabled the machine to grind into action to arrange return visits for the Gulf rulers, the first one being a Saudi Arabian emir. All those rulers have now had their state visits.

THE RETURN OF HONG KONG TO CHINA

The Queen's interest in Hong Kong is, no doubt, informed by Britain's long occupation of the colony, which began during the Opium War of 1839–42, and was consolidated in 1898 by a ninety-nine-year lease of the New Territories from China.

A sparsely populated area in the nineteenth century, Hong Kong as a British colony grew to be a major East-West trading center, as well as the commercial gateway to, and distribution center for, South China. Hong Kong was conquered in 1941 by the Japanese during World War II and reoccupied by the British in 1945.

Following the Communist revolution in China and the establishment in 1949 of the People's Republic of China, Hong Kong absorbed hundreds of thousands of refugees from the mainland.

Hong Kong's population swelled further in the late 1970s with an influx of additional mainland Chinese, as well as Vietnamese following South Vietnam's fall in 1975, prompting stringent controls in 1980 on the Chinese border.

In 1991, six years before the scheduled return of Hong Kong to China, in Hong Kong's first direct election for thirty percent of its legislative seats, most of those positions were won by liberal, pro-democracy candidates.

Britain's further efforts to introduce democratic reforms in the run-up to the return of Hong Kong to Chinese sovereignty, advocated by Christopher Patten, the colony's last governor-general, prompted a strong negative response by China. The reforms, however, were passed in 1994.

On July 1, 1997, Hong Kong was returned to China in elaborate ceremonies presided over by the Prince of Wales, who arrived in *Britannia* in the royal yacht's final voyage before its decommissioning.

The former colony is now known as the Hong Kong Special Administrative Region.

* * *

Anson Chan I joined the Hong Kong Civil Service in 1962. The governors associated with the earlier history of Hong Kong were more distant and removed from the mass of the Hong Kong people. They did not speak the language and an overwhelming proportion of the local community are Chinese-speaking.

But certainly governors like Lord MacLehose, David Wilson, and particularly Chris Patten were moving with the times, were seen to be much more involved with the local population, and much more in tune with what the community wanted in terms of things like priorities of provision of services, of participation in government.

WAS THE RETURN OF HONG KONG REGRETTED BY THE QUEEN?

Anson Chan I didn't have any sense that the Queen found it a matter of regret. Particularly following the signing and the ratification of the Joint Declaration [in 1984], people just accepted it as a reality, as something that both sides wanted to make sure that they were as well-prepared for the handover as could be possible.

Hence they set up the Land Commission, they set up the Joint Liaison Group to flesh out the details of the important principles that are laid out in the Joint Declaration.

Lord Howe There's no way in which anyone could feel a sense of loss because we were there on a lease which was term-fixed.

This is the great misunderstanding. I always feel irritated when I hear people talking about the "handover" of Hong Kong; it was the "hand-back" of Hong Kong.

But even if you respect our right to carve out the lease in somewhat unequal circumstances in the nineteenth century, at least the Chinese respected that, and we therefore had to say: "Well, our root of title, which we claim legitimacy for, is a lease which runs out in 1997."

So nobody who takes the right seriously could imagine that we were giving away a birthright. We were complying with a contract which was, probably, from the Chinese's eyes, an unfair one anyway.

Stephen Day When I was appointed to the Colonial Office in 1961, I was told by a very senior official—he was very upset—that it was inconceivable that we would ever give independence to Singapore, or to Aden, or to Hong Kong.

They were the outposts of the Empire at that time. Aden, at that time, was far more important than Hong Kong, strategically. And the Hong Kong deal was brilliant in terms of history—to launch Hong Kong without being swallowed up by China, giving it a chance to retain its very special characteristics.

And Patten always made that point in the foundation of what is rule of law: democracy is irrelevant if you don't have rule of law. It was a fact that this was the solid underpinning of Hong Kong's prosperity; I thought it was a great achievement to see that through.

And, of course, that's what the Queen has lived through: that whole transition from Empire to Commonwealth—the capacity to change, and to see that evolving works.

Sir David Scott It was always a very important feature of the Commonwealth because it was so rich, and a gateway to China—a source of investment into China.

But the Queen would have recognized right from the moment she took over that the days of Hong Kong were numbered. It was all in the treaty; it was inevitable.

It would have been quite inconceivable for us to have resisted that with China because they would have cut off the water supply. And it would have been too easy for them to have blockaded Hong Kong: it would have fallen in a matter of weeks.

As it was, I think it's been a remarkable demonstration of the sort of flexibility, if you like, of the approach to the Commonwealth, which is prepared to take in foreigners, if you like, as well as accepting treaty obligations to cede Hong Kong.

Lord Howe She was very interested in it. I'm sure I talked to her a great deal about it in those days. It's the kind of issue that raised agonies of impossible crisis, because wouldn't it have been nice to people to have given British citizenship to six-and-a-half million Hong Kong people, making it a rather serious bet that they'd never claim the right to exercise it?

If one had conferred that citizenship and China really *did* push the applecart over—to have six-and-a-half million Chinese just turning up here would make five thousand Bosnians look like …

PATTEN'S BEHAVIOR PRIOR TO THE HANDBACK
OF HONG KONG

A high official in Hong Kong, speaking of the role of Chris Patten in his last days as governor of Hong Kong prior to its return to China, said:

The June 4, 1989, incident[1] for many people was a very traumatic experience. And for Hong Kong people, it heightened their sense of nervousness and apprehension because they saw what happened at Tiananmen, and they were very afraid, given particularly their suspicion and their concern that Beijing may well not honor their promises about leaving Hong Kong alone.

The people of Hong Kong were concerned and wanted to hasten the pace of democratization because a lot of people in Hong Kong saw that as a hedge against undue interference from Beijing. So when Christopher

Patten came in 1992, he clearly thought—and I think the British government also have thought—that they needed to do more to shore up the
process of democratization in Hong Kong.

And so Chris felt that it was the people's wish, and that it was the
least that Britain could do to hasten this whole pace of democratization.
But unfortunately, the leadership in Beijing regarded what Chris Patten
wanted to do as being in breach of the previous understanding that had
been reached between the British negotiators and the team here in Hong
Kong and the leadership in Beijing.

Hence, it led to a very unsettled, and in a sense, very controversial
relationship between the governor here and the leadership in Beijing.
So it was not an easy time for Chris. But Chris felt he had to do what
he had to do in order to provide sufficient reassurance for Hong Kong's
people, and to meet what he perceived to be the Hong Kong people's
wishes.

* * *

Lord Howe It was fine as an objective. But not fine when it was done in
the fashion that provoked huge Chinese uproar. So the sadness is that
Chris, during the last four years of his tenure, and the Chinese were at
loggerheads the whole time, shouting at each other. And he went ahead
and legislated for the larger [legislative council], which they said they
would repeal, which they did.

My vision was that Chris would have been very like De Klerk and
Nelson Mandela—along with their handover there, their hands clasped
together so that all could see the taking over—and that the Prince of
Wales would entertain the president of China on the royal yacht. And we
should have had a less turbulent transition.

Sir David Scott A lot of people thought he was going too far, and bending
over backwards to accommodate the Chinese. But I believe it was very
constructive. I'm absolutely certain that he was right, and I'm a strong
supporter of Chris Patten's.

Some of the former governors who knew it was inevitable hadn't done
anything to ease the way through to independence, and I believe he
[Chris Patten] saw it as his job to make sure that, even if he didn't become
personally popular in the process, that he should facilitate this.

THE CEREMONY OF RETURN

Was there a message in the Queen's sending Prince Charles and not going herself?

* * *

Stephen Day It was obviously a very tricky political event. It was more appropriate that he go; it was right and proper that he should have done it.

I don't recall it ever being other than the Prince of Wales [being under consideration as the United Kingdom's official representative]: he had visited it regularly; he knew it well. It was not India; it was a different order of things. I wouldn't read anything more into it than that.

Sir David Scott The Queen has virtually never been to independence ceremonies—it's always been Prince Charles, or another member of the Royal Family; I don't think she even went to Kenya, when she had links to Kenya, to attend the independence ceremonies—in the way that she doesn't attend funerals.

She delegates her representation, usually to the Prince of Wales, although it's been going sometimes to other members of the Royal Family as well. That doesn't in any way diminish her interest.

I just don't think it would have been expected that she'd have gone, and, perhaps, it goes back to this thing that [one of the Queen's private secretaries, Martin] Charteris was talking about—that the magic has to involve a certain remoteness from things.

She might still do a tour which took in Hong Kong, by agreement with the Chinese, if they were happy to do that.

Lord Howe By that time, there had been a rift in the [Sino-British] relationship because of the way Patten had done things. And so the handover was, in some ways, actually a very cool one. And although the royal yacht was there, there was no entertainment of the Chinese on the royal yacht. I was sad about that because I thought that the closing status could have been handled differently.

THE AFTERMATH

Anson Chan Most people acknowledge that the political transition of Hong Kong, as distinct from the economic transition, particularly what happened in light of the Asian financial turmoil, has gone much better than anybody ever anticipated. So from that point of view, we have proved all the doomsayers wrong who had said: "Hong Kong as we know it will come to an end after the handover."

The good thing about what happened after the handover is that you haven't had the anticolonial feelings that you may have had elsewhere.

By-and-large, the British are seen to have done well by Hong Kong. Britain has given Hong Kong two of its best legacies: the rule of law in the way that the judiciary is structured; and the whole structure of the Civil Service, because the Civil Service here is one of the few meritocracies left in the world. And the people of Hong Kong take great comfort in the fact that the Civil Service is apolitical, and based on merit and not on political pressure.

The average, reasonable man-in-the-street who doesn't have any colonial baggage will look at Britain's contribution to Hong Kong in a very positive light because it is the earlier history of Hong Kong and the 135 years of British rule that has made Hong Kong what it is today.

CHAPTER 22

The Falkland Islands War

BRITAIN'S CLAIM TO the Falkland Islands—Las Malvinas to the Argentinians—can be traced to their probable discovery in 1592 by a navigator named John Davis. The Falklands, which lie off the southernmost coast of Argentina, eight thousand miles from the British Isles, were later claimed and occupied by Spain, France, and Argentina.

In 1832, the seizure of an American ship in the region resulted in a punitive military expedition by the United States. The British, claiming sovereignty, occupied the Falklands, which they proceeded to administer as a Crown Colony, beginning a long-simmering dispute with Argentina over the colony's control.

On April 2, 1982, that dispute erupted into military action when Argentinian forces captured the Falklands. Three days later, following heated debate at the highest level of the British government, a task force led by the carriers *Hermes* and *Invincible* sailed from Portsmouth Harbour to liberate the Falklands.

The operation ignited a political crisis in London, resulting in the resignation of the Foreign Secretary, Lord Carrington. At the same time, Prime Minister Margaret Thatcher fended off demands for her resignation by taking a militant stance: responding to a question concerning the chances for the task force's success, the prime minister repeated the words of Queen Victoria: "Failure? The possibility does not exist."

The Falklands War presented a unique problem for the Queen. She was, of course, constitutionally involved in her government's decision to oppose the Argentinian aggression, and as head of the Commonwealth she was concerned over the possibility of losing territory in the South Atlantic.

The Queen's overriding interest in the conflict, however, involved her second son, Prince Andrew, who as a serving Royal Navy helicopter pilot had joined the task force.

As the war progressed, it became apparent that Prince Andrew and his fellow pilots were at risk, in part because the Argentinian military was equipped with modern weaponry, including the devastatingly effective Exocet missile.

In early May, both the British and the Argentinians suffered major losses. The British sank the Argentinian cruiser *General Belgrano* with the loss of more than three hundred lives, giving rise to negative international reaction as the ship had been attacked while outside the British-declared exclusion zone.

In response to the sinking of the *General Belgrano*, the Argentinians fired an Exocet, destroying HMS *Sheffield* with the loss of twenty-one lives.

Later that month, other British ships were sunk in fighting near San Carlos Bay, while on May 25 the container ship *Atlantic Conqueror* went to the bottom. On May 29, seventeen British paratroopers were killed at Goose Green.

Soon after these losses, task force troops moved on Stanley, the capital of the Falklands, which was captured on June 14. A ceasefire ensued.

Britain's victory in the Falklands boosted Mrs. Thatcher's popularity. She was not only cheered at Number 10 Downing Street but upstaged the Queen by taking the salute at the Falklands victory parade.

The Queen, however, had played a major role in the war effort, both supporting Prince Andrew's involvement in the fighting and being a steadfast symbol to the troops, visiting some of the injured among their ranks.

The Queen had also contributed to Britain's wellbeing—even within the constraints of her constitutional role—when she played host to the then-U.S. president, Ronald Reagan, at Windsor Castle, re-enforcing the president's determination to support Britain.

THE ARGENTINIAN INVASION

Sir Rex Hunt The first intimation I had of a pending Argentine invasion came with this telegram at 3:30 P.M., local Stanley time, on Thursday, the first of April. It was marked "Top Secret," and it said we had "apparently" believable evidence—you see how they covered themselves at

Whitehall—they had "apparently" reliable evidence that "an Argentine task force could be assembling off Stanley. Stop. You will wish to make your dispositions accordingly. Stop." That's all they ever said.

I decided that Government House would have to be our operational headquarters. Some of the Marines, obviously, wanted me to up sticks and hide in the hills. I said: "No, this is the seat of government, and I have to stay *here*, and they'll have to unseat me."

I didn't see the point of that [upping sticks]: I thought we were going to be caught sometime, anyway, and what's the point? We might unnecessarily lose lives. Once they got Government House, they were in control and it didn't matter where I was; they were in control.

So we had the Army set up their staff and headquarters in my office. We got the radio in there, and I got a link with the local radio so that I could explain to people what was happening overnight. That took us until about midnight. And then we were waiting.

I wasn't allowed to declare a state of emergency—I wanted to—until there had been a last-minute attempt by President Reagan—at about 4:15 in the morning—to persuade Galtieri[1] not to go ahead with it. But Galtieri rebuffed President Reagan's last plea.

Once I heard that that had been rebuffed, then I could declare a state of emergency, and I went on the radio and did.

Brig. Johnny Rickett I was in the staff car with my regimental sergeant major, on the way to Swansea, South Wales, to attend a regimental association dinner, and we suddenly heard the news that the Argentines had landed. And I remember saying to him: "Well, at some stage, some troops will have to be sent there."

Sir Gordon Jewkes It really was very difficult: you were operating eight thousand miles from the homeland with, at the time, very uncertain transportation; in 1982 the fax was scarcely in use; satellite telephone communications were in their infancy.

A fateful meeting was called on Wednesday, March 31, in the prime minister's office.

Sir Rex Hunt Mrs. Thatcher called a meeting of the war cabinet in her office in the Houses of Parliament. She went round all of them there, including John Nott, who was the secretary of state for defense then, and they all said: "You can't do anything about it; you'd better try and come to terms, because we can't take the military option."

And in came Henry Leach, the First Sea Lord, who had heard this was going on, and the prime minister turned to him and said: "What do you think?"

Adm. Sir Henry Leach Wednesday was traditionally a day that normally you thought you could escape from Whitehall. I had been down to Portsmouth, visiting what was then called the Admiralty Signal and Radar Establishment, where I'd done my first job as a commander in the middle 1950s.

When I got back it was about six o'clock in the evening. I went to my office in the Ministry of Defense and there were two piles of briefs on my desk. One was from the local staff, talking about the Falklands situation, and advising me not to get too agitated about it because it had, after all, occurred annually for the past, certainly, sixteen years, and it was going to be very difficult to find any force of consequence to go down there. And for what purpose? And all that sort of thing—don't touch it. And the other one was from the interpretive people who, in the poorest sense, after long years of little experience, tend to cover their backs and not commit themselves to black and white—yes and no—stuff and they're so absolutely certain, because they've been caught out so often, and one didn't hear from them.

This time they placed their bets, to my surprise, and they said: "We think that on this occasion the Argentinians really do mean business, and we think that they will probably invade one of the lesser islands during the first week in April."

My immediate reaction was: What the hell was the purpose in having a Navy if you're not going to do something about that?

I went storming along to John Nott's office in the knowledge that even then he was being briefed. He wasn't there, and his private secretary, a nice man, a good friend, told me that he was being briefed in his room in the House of Commons. So I grabbed a House of Commons pass off him and hopped into my car and went down to the House.

The only way in I really knew was the public entrance. The rule is that you go up to that well-known burly policeman in the central lobby and say who it is you've come to see, and they locate that person, and then that person comes and collects you.

I said I'd come to see John Nott and could I please be shown to his room? No, no. Nothing would get past him: he would go through the system, and would I please take a seat.

As I sat down, a number of M.P.s passed whom I knew, and they stopped and had a chat. And then, one of the whips, who I didn't know, and whose office was literally just round the corner, said: "Won't you come round and have a glass with us while we're locating John Nott?" And so I did.

They were all ex-soldiers, a very nice lot, and they thrust a glass of whisky into my hand, and we chatted for, I suppose, ten or fifteen minutes. And then they located John Nott; he was with the prime minister, and word was passed down that I should step in.

There were not very many people in the prime minister's room: Peter Carrington, the Foreign Secretary, was away in the Middle East, but his number two was there; John Nott was there; the permanent secretary of the Ministry of Defense, Admiralty ADCA; a couple of legal experts; and the cabinet secretary.

I said: "Good evening, prime minister—it was about a quarter past seven—is there anything I can do to help?" And she sat me down, and off we went.

We were at it hammer and tongs. And although there were a number of interruptions—of course other things went on too—she ordered sandwiches and that sort of thing and that session finished at a bit after midnight.

She was very sharp. She started off by quizzing me on all sorts of things, and when you gave an answer, she'd pick you up on it. The others said nothing at all—John Nott never uttered a word.

She was asking me what sort of force would be required. I was totally unbriefed on this so it was really off the top of my head. I said: "We'd need the whole of the Commando brigade and one or two other brigades."

And then we got to the ships. Now the ships are crucial in terms of air cover. And the only operational ships were *Invincible* and *Hermes*. *Intrepid* was going into a refit—and I simply didn't know whether there was any chance at all of retrieving the same ship's company before they got too dispersed. In fact, there was, and they got something like three-quarters of them back, and associated escorts, of course. And then the submarines came up. And so it went on.

After a number of interruptions, sitting there with a rather penetrating gaze, she said: "Can we do it?" And I said: "Yes, if we contain the risk." And that was as far as I should have gone. In fact, I went further, which was not my job, not my business, and I said: "And we must."

And she leapt forward and said: "Why do you say that?" I said: "Well, because if we don't do this, if we are not entirely successful, if we pussy-foot and delay, if we don't make a complete success of it, despite the odds, then in another couple of months we shall be living in a different country, where our word counts for nothing. Already we are long on advice and short on action to back it."

She took it. Then she started ringing people up. And finally she turned to me and said: "What is it you want from me?" And I said: "I want authority to assemble, not sail, a task force."

"Couldn't that be done clandestinely?"

I said: "No, it couldn't. I think it would be bound to leak if it's too big." I said: "Give me forty-eight hours to assemble it." And we in due course packed up and that was that. It was a risk, but a good risk, a responsible risk.

Adm. Sir Sandy Woodward The military in this country, who are essentially apolitical, when their government says: "Go and do something," say: "Okay. We'll do what we can." You give advice—as was given by the Ministry of Defense to the cabinet—on the feasibility of it.

This was then rephrased by Henry Leach, so that instead of saying: "The official advice is that we in the Ministry of Defense do not think you can win this war because you will not get air parity, or air superiority, for a sufficiently advantageous air situation," Henry said: "We *can* do it, *if* we can get the air situation under control."

I don't know that Henry, even to this day, realizes whether it was simply by presenting the same statement, put the other way round, that he allowed Mrs. Thatcher to do what she had her mind to do anyway.

Winston Churchill There was a whole group of young Turks, as it were—I was among them—who were very anxious lest she be pushed backwards from her determination to go ahead.

She may not have had a great knowledge or understanding of military matters, but she had a very keen sense of self-preservation and realized that having lost the Falklands, she could not hope to survive the next election unless she got them back, and that either she or Galtieri would have had to bite the dust. And she was absolutely determined that it wasn't about to be *her*!

But that said, it took a lot of courage to take those decisions. We're talking of the opposite side of the globe—thousands of miles away from home base. And we didn't have proper flat-top carriers that could carry supersonic aircraft—the Argentines *had* supersonic aircraft—and we were at a very great disadvantage. And it would just have taken a couple more of the larger ships to be lost.

It would have been quite difficult, not necessarily from a public opinion point of view, but from an actual military point of view, to have gone forward with the campaign.

Brig. Johnny Rickett If it hadn't been logistically possible, we couldn't have done it. And it was only just touch-and-go. It was a near-run thing—if one more ship had been sunk, if public reaction would have gone against the government—we were never quite sure, frankly, in our minds whether, in fact, the government had the guts to go through with all of it. But Mrs. Thatcher did.

It all happened so quickly: within one day, Margaret Thatcher decided to dispatch a task force, and within four days, the task force was on its way. It was quite amazing how it could have been done so quickly.

We were told that we'd be going. So we only had three days to pack up our kit, and two days R. and R., and we were off—on the *Queen Elizabeth* [the *QE II*], all the wine, and everything else on board; it was very pleasant, actually.

What was so amusing was that everybody—be he lowly guardsman, or be he the highest-ranking officer—had the same standard of food throughout and it was wonderful!

And when we got to South Georgia, our standards slightly dropped: we had to transfer from the *Queen Elizabeth* to the *Canberra*, who had already been in and out, and their crew's discipline—it was a civilian crew—was pretty poor; it was a different ball game, totally, to the high standards we'd been used to on the *Queen Elizabeth*.

THE COMMANDER-IN-CHIEF

Sir Rex Hunt [Before leaving for his post in the Falklands] I had an audience with the Queen, with my wife. It was very pleasant. And she'd obviously done her homework, and she knew a lot more than I did about the Falkland Islands. But she'd never been there, and she said she was very sorry that she hadn't. She said: "It's the only territory of mine that I haven't visited."

That was because the Foreign Office wouldn't let her. The attitude from the Foreign Office was that it was far too provocative to send the Queen down to the Falkland Islands. I'd like to see her go now; I did say that when I came back.

The Queen was one hundred percent behind the decision to send the task force: she was absolutely, thoroughly indignant at the blatant military invasion—it was the first black-and-white military invasion we'd had since Germany invaded Poland in 1939—that Galtieri should *dare* to invade British territory, and again to occupy the land of peace-loving people who couldn't lift their hands to help themselves.

I'm sure Prince Philip reassured her on the naval side. The worry always—and the Queen is intelligent; she knew—was the lack of air support. Nowadays, you have to have air superiority if you're going to do anything, and we only had these two aircraft carriers. So the big anxiety was that we couldn't have done it if we had lost one of them; they had to be kept safe.

Adm. Sir Henry Leach The prime minister of the day normally held a routine session with the Monarch on a Tuesday evening. This was Wednesday, so we were past a Tuesday evening. I doubt that the Queen would have been informed, although she might have heard something, but I doubt that she would have been formally informed until the decision was taken, probably on the Saturday night, to sail the force on the Monday.

Adm. Sir Sandy Woodward She's not in the executive chamber at all, except to the extent that she can whisper in the prime minister's ear: "I've been here rather longer than you, and you wouldn't be too well advised to do that."

But on this occasion, I very much doubt it. I've not heard of any contacts on that between the Queen and Prime Minister Thatcher. And the Queen would have nothing to say to us, directly, nor I to her.

It's the Royal Navy, but it's the *Navy*. And you're driven by other motivations than the thought: there is the Queen, watching over your shoulder. In the Navy, it's a far more general thing: we know we're the Royal Navy and the Army is called the British Army.

But, actually, perhaps for that reason, there are some regiments in the Army which are far more conscious of the Sovereign than is the Navy; they're almost family-conscious, particularly the more obvious regiments which work directly for the Royal Family, from time to time. It's a far more personal thing for those regiments.

In the Navy it's generic; it's a part of the fabric. And it's completely taken for granted, really. It's not something you have to think about.

THE MOTHER

Adm. Sir Henry Leach [Prince Andrew's being a serving officer in the conflict] really had to be sorted out before the ships sailed. He could have been off-loaded at Ascension, but they didn't think to do so. And anyway, there were rather more important things to think about there and then.

Sir Rex Hunt We had a very nice audience with the Queen when I was thrown out of the Falklands in 1982. My wife and I were invited to go down and see her at Windsor Castle. She had us in to her private room—just herself; there were no courtiers, or secretary, or anything like that—and we had a full forty-five minutes with her.

She was just like any other mother: worried about the role that her son was going to play—this was on the Wednesday; the task force had sailed on the Monday, and Andrew was on the way. Her questions to me were: "Do you think he'll be warm enough?"—with the clothes that were issued by the Army; "Do you think we should send him some extra clothing?"

I spoke to her just as I would to any other anxious mother whose son was going off to war; it was perfectly natural, normal talk. I forgot, entirely, that she was my Queen, and I found myself reassuring her as much as I could that there was going to be rough weather, but nothing like as bad as the journalists had made out. I said to her: "It's nothing like as perilous as you've been led to believe. There's nothing special you have to wear; the weather is nothing like as bad as you've been led to believe down there." She was very relieved.

WAS PRINCE ANDREW SHIELDED FROM THE WORST OF THE ACTION?

Adm. Sir Sandy Woodward Captain Black, the captain of *Invincible*, may, or may not, have been told by the senior management of the Navy to be extra-careful; I expect he was, but I don't know that. But I assume he was. And I expect his aircraft got rather extra care. But why *not*?

He flew a lot of missions as a pilot of the antisubmarine screen for the battle group where I was. But there were no special conditions; it didn't affect how I wanted to use *Invincible*, in terms of risk, or anything like that. We couldn't allow that to happen at all.

Brig. Johnny Rickett I don't believe that's true. You couldn't have done in those conditions: he's a pilot; he has to get on with it. The Queen is a mother as well.

THE TASK FORCE SAILS

Adm. Sir Sandy Woodward When we started out, we didn't have any special charts; we had charts that were publicly available. We didn't have the charts on board when we set off from Gibraltar. They were flown out to Gibraltar and we sent a frigate back to collect them and bring them on to us.

The main planning for it was quite difficult because we didn't actually have a clear political directive until May 12, nearly six weeks after we'd sailed. Up until then, we'd been sent with a directive which said: "Prepare to land with a view to repossessing the Falkland Islands."

Now, if you think about that as an instruction, it is something less than positive, or definite. Indeed, it is about as vague as you can possibly get, pointing people in the right direction in the South Atlantic—maybe the Falklands, too. They'd only got to change to "Repossess the Falkland Islands" on May 12.

Adm. Sir Henry Leach Maggie went to Harold Macmillan at an early stage and said: "How do you run a war?" And Harold Macmillan told her: "You form a war cabinet and you put in it those people that you really have to have. And you confine it to the minimum, otherwise you prolong decision-taking, or even negate it." And this she did.

THE SINKING OF THE *BELGRANO*

Adm. Sir Henry Leach It was absolutely straightforward. The plain facts were that they had two forces, of which the *Belgrano* formed one. And each was of a size, and a strength, so that we would have been not impossibly, but poorly placed, to split our force to compete with assurance with both. So you had to eliminate what you could. And it constituted a threat.

The most convincing statement, I believe, came from the captain of the *Belgrano* himself[2] who said: "If I'd been in the British shoes at the time, I would have done the same." And, of course, her escort disappeared in a cloud of dust; that's why there were so many casualties, because nobody stood there to pick them up—a submarine couldn't.

But it created a great, typical furor by people who didn't know what the hell they were talking about, which is usually the case. All that poppycock you hear is clear, unprofessional—ignorant, if you like—claptrap.

THE LOSS OF MEMBERS OF THE WELSH GUARDS

Brig. Johnny Rickett As I was visiting the forward positions [after the landing of the troops at San Carlos], there was a message on the platoon radio: "To the commanding officer: Would he please make his way down to Fitzroy as soon as possible, as a ship has been hit and there have been severe Welsh Guards casualties."

As I said at the time: "It's funny, only bad news seems to travel." I remember being in a highly emotional state, with tears streaming down my face. I got on the motorbike and back down to Fitzroy we went. And a helicopter came, and the padre, myself, and someone went down to see it. It was a pathetic sight, really.

THE FINAL ASSAULT

Brig. Johnny Rickett We had the task of the final assault on Sapper Hill, which was the hill nearest Stanley—again, the radios weren't working and I didn't hear it on the direct commander's; I heard on the gunners'; the gunners could always get through—the ceasefire had been declared: "On no account are you to shoot unless shot at first …"

By that time, my full platoon was already in contact with the Argentines, and we'd had casualties there. So it was a question of linking up with them, occupying Sapper Hill without making war, if you possibly could; it was quite difficult. And then we occupied Sapper Hill. And that was the end of hostilities.

And then we did the job, of course, afterwards, of policing Stanley—I was the *gauleiter* of Stanley—and to try to instill some sort of discipline into a war zone where troops were relaxing quite hard. And they needed a Guards' battalion there to sort things out.

THE CEASEFIRE

Brig. Johnny Rickett There was enormous relief, quite frankly. When we actually occupied Sapper Hill, I had three reporters who were with me—they farmed out several reporters; I felt very sorry for them; we looked after our people and gave them a shovel, and a poncho, and a blanket, and all that sort of thing—and when we got to the objective, I said, looking at Stanley: "For God's sake! Is that all we've come for? It's a pathetic little place."

THE FALKLAND ISLANDERS

Sir Rex Hunt You couldn't have more loyal British subjects than the Falkland Islanders: they have a picture of the Queen in a window of every private house, and in shop windows, and the Union Jack. You don't see that in any village, or town, in England.

I can understand that they had "Big Brother" in Argentina breathing down their necks for so long, for so many years, that they would be much more showing outwardly their loyalty to the Queen because they were in such an unstable position—a volatile situation.

Brig. Johnny Rickett They were pathetic people. There was some farm which was in my area of operations at the end of the hostilities, and there was a chap there who even had trenches in his front garden—this was about ten days after the fighting had stopped and he hadn't even filled the damn things in; his sheep were all over the mountains.

And he expected compensation because he was born there. And that really sums up my view of the Falkland Islanders.

Sir Sandy Woodward They're often likened to the Outer Hebrideans[3] by their way of speaking—they're quite soft-spoken. The only thing I know about them is that they're unlike anybody I've ever met before. I don't want to be rude about them.

I went down there in 1985 to have a look at the way things were going in the islands' defenses. One lovely morning, as we were flying over Bleaker Island, I noticed some smoke coming out of a chimney, so I said: "We'll land here and I'll have a look."

The owner, the bloke, came out—he was the same color as the ground and we didn't actually see him until he moved. We started talking—at least we did; he didn't say much—and he eventually took us inside the house and gave us a cup of tea. His wife was upstairs and she never came down—I suspect she was in bed with a gin bottle, or something—but that was what was there: him, his wife, who didn't do anything, and 2,300 sheep.

We said, amongst other things: "Do you not miss people?" And he said: "Not a bit. Indeed the supply boat comes round every six weeks. As often I tell it not to bother because I'm all right. And I have a radio which enables me to talk two-way with Port Stanley, but I don't use it."

Eventually I asked him the question which was quite popular at the time: "Supposing the British government were to offer you a place which was twice as large, in South Island, New Zealand, and a million pounds, on top of that to leave this place and go and settle there? What would you do about that?"

"Absolutely not!" he said. "I live here, don't I?" And that was it. "I live here!" and he didn't want anybody else; I don't think he much wanted his wife upstairs, either, for that matter. He wanted to be exactly where he was.

THE PRIME MINISTER TAKES THE SALUTE

Brig. Johnny Rickett There was that feeling that the press built up about the two top ladies—"Maggie's outdone the Queen." The press made that up.

But Maggie's a very strong-minded woman. I have the greatest admiration for her; I think she's a wonderful person.

Sir Rex Hunt I don't believe there was any attempt by Margaret Thatcher to usurp the Queen's position at all. The Mansion House was giving a meal to all the people who'd come back, and to people who had taken part. If it had been arranged by them, and if Margaret Thatcher was the guest of honor, there'd be the Lord Mayor of London, and Margaret Thatcher next to him.

The Queen wouldn't automatically be there unless it was a royal occasion. But if it was—as I believe it was—the Lord Mayor of London inviting the task force to parade in the City, and he had Margaret Thatcher as his guest of honor, then they would be on the balcony of Mansion House, and taking the salute as they [the task force] rode by.

But I don't think she was pretending to be Queen. If it had been a royal occasion, then, certainly, they would have had the entire march-past, and she would have been on the balcony of Buckingham Palace.

Adm. Sir Sandy Woodward Anything that goes on in this country there are some people saying: "This is a disgrace!" and there are some people who are saying: "Isn't it wonderful?" And the press tend to back the "disgrace" because that's more newsworthy—that's the press for you. We all live with that and so you learn to take little notice of it.

I was quite aware that a variety of people felt Mrs. Thatcher was taking rather more credit for it than she might have. But she had been very tough-minded, and she had listened to her military's advice. And when they said: "You have got to have made your mind up by May 1, otherwise you're going to lose it anyway," she proceeded to do so.

And all my experience of her later on, in the mid-1980s, when she was still prime minister and I was working as head of Defence Operations, Tri-Services Ministry, was that if you presented her with facts, although she had made up her mind, she was quite prepared to change it.

If you presented her with a political opinion, she'd bounce you on your head and chuck you out! Quite rightly. I'm not a politician; I'm a military professional.

Sir Gordon Jewkes To be fair to her, I do not think anyone who knows Margaret Thatcher had any sense of [her] setting out to displace the Queen. She saw herself as the victorious Winston Churchill, asking: What would Winston have done in these circumstances?

THE QUEEN VISITS THE WOUNDED

Adm. Sir Henry Leach I helicoptered out to *Invincible* when she was off the coast of Cornwall and they set up a nice little dinner for me. The next morning, we arrived at Spithead in thick, thick fog. The Queen and Prince Philip—and rather at the last minute, Princess Anne—were due to come up by barge.

The Queen was looked after by the captain of the ship, quite rightly; Prince Philip was looked after by Prince Andrew; and it befell to me to look after Princess Anne, with whom I hadn't had many dealings by then.

She was absolutely first class. Coming up harbor initially, we went round various parts of the ship, including the hangar where a cross-section of all departments had been assembled, and the Queen and Prince Philip went up one side, and Princess Anne went up another.

Princess Anne was not prepared to just say: "Good morning. Are you glad to be home? Have you read any good books lately?" She actually got into a conversation, and she lagged further and further behind. And so when we were only about halfway up the hangar, though the Queen and Prince Philip were waiting on the lift, there was Princess Anne.

And then when we went alongside there wasn't a dry eye in the ship, from top to bottom. It was a very, very moving experience.

PART FIVE

The Evolution of
the Monarchy

CHAPTER 23

Pandora's Box

F ROM, THE LATE 1950s ONWARD, changing attitudes toward the
monarchy emerged, with the first-ever public criticism directed
against the Queen herself. In August 1957, journalist John Grigg,
then Lord Altrincham, wrote an article entitled "The Monarchy Today,"
which was widely perceived to be critical of the Monarch and of the institution of the British monarchy.

In the past, such articles had been largely dismissed as being the work
of eccentrics—notably one by Malcolm Muggeridge in the September
1955 issue of *New Statesman*.[1] Grigg's article, however, published in *The
National and English Review,* a political monthly whose contributors were
largely Conservatives and which Grigg then edited and controlled, caused
a sensation in Britain.

Unlike many previous articles critical of the monarchy, "The Monarchy
Today" took the young Queen herself to task, going so far as to criticize
her speeches as "a pain in the neck" due to the primness of their scripted
content—a criticism widely misunderstood, Grigg has said, as having
been a "criticism of the Queen's *voice*."

Grigg, while making it quite clear that he did not wish the British monarchy to become a "bicycle monarchy,"[2] called upon the Queen to, among
other things, "give her children an education very different from her own";
allow Prince Charles, as heir to the Throne, to "mix during his formative
years not merely with future landowners or stockbrokers"; broaden the base
of the Royal Household to include others besides the "tight little enclave of
British ladies and gentlemen" who served as courtiers; and to abolish the
"utterly absurd" custom of presentation parties at court for debutantes.

Grigg's criticisms would hardly be sensational today. But in 1957, he
was denounced by public officials, widely rebuked by British editors,
criticized in letters from the public, and challenged to a duel.

* * *

John Grigg The reason that the monarchy has stayed in business over such a very long time—and, I think, will remain for the indefinite future—is that it's an exceptionally strong institution. The reason for that is that historically it has been subject to criticism.

Even absolute monarchs were not immune from criticism. And since our constitution has evolved—since our monarchy has become a constitutional monarchy—our royal personages have been subjected to considerable criticism. Queen Victoria had a great deal of criticism during her reign, and her son, when he was Prince of Wales, much of it justified. And it is because of that the monarchy has remained so strong.

I've never been remotely republican; I've always been a very strong monarchist. I think that the constitutional monarchy is a particularly good form of the constitution—and particularly for us. And the criticisms I've made of the performance of particular members of the Royal Family at certain times have always been from the standpoint of a very strong monarchist, trying to make the monarchy even more valuable and effective than it already is—or was.

The idea that in criticizing particular aspects of the performance of members of the Royal Family while praising others that that is any way anti-monarchist, or an attack on the monarchy, seems to me utterly absurd because nobody would suggest that somebody who engages in literary criticism is against books. Literary critics are, by definition, in favor of books. And that is true of anybody who criticizes royal personages in the way that I have sometimes done. It's from the standpoint of a very strong belief in the institution.

Lord McNally John Grigg and Malcolm Muggeridge were seminal in that they were the first public figures to actually criticize the monarchy in any serious way. And in some ways, that broke the spell, and the press and television began to question who advised the Queen, and who surrounded the Royal Family, and what they did. And in response, they began to try and handle the media.

Now, whether they've done that successfully is a matter of judgment. My own view is that whatever they'd have done, if they'd have tried to stay aloof, they would have been in trouble. And by trying to open it up, that produced a different kind of trouble. But initially, Muggeridge and Grigg broke the spell.

THE COURTIERS' REACTION TO GRIGG'S CRITICISM

John Grigg Within forty-eight hours after the row starting, I met, in the house of a mutual friend, a very senior member of the Royal Household, whose first words to me when we met were: "This is the best thing that's happened to Buckingham Palace in my time," which shows that opinion in the Royal Household was not monolithic; there were those who obviously felt that changes had to be made, whether or not they agreed with everything that I proposed.

One of the people who attacked me—who wrote me a very rude letter, a vicious letter—at the time of the initial row was a Russian emigre, Baron Stackelberg. He said it was a very inflammatory thing, terrible treason, and all that.

I couldn't resist reminding him that if the Romanovs had been subject to the same free comment and criticism that the House of Windsor was subject to, the Romanovs might still be on the Throne of Russia, and that he might not be in exile!

Sir Edward Ford It was an adoring period, when everybody thought of an Elizabethan age. So when you suddenly got criticism, even as mild as that was, really, it was a great shock.

He [Grigg] had a slight bee in his bonnet and he was perfectly right too. And a little bit unmannerly to criticize the Queen's voice. It wasn't a good voice—the top of it was too high. But I think he might have put it in different terms.

And then he criticized the people around her—me and my colleagues— as being more or less out of the same drawer, old Etonian guardsmen, and that sort of thing. Well, the fact was that he was perfectly right on the facts.

[I]n the court it is a family, the people that she employs; you don't need tremendous qualifications for employment there—you need to be an honest man, and have a certain amount of common sense, and so on—but you've got to be very acceptable as members of her Household; she has always got to have people who are not related to her there. And if it's in the country, they're often sharing in the sporting, or the picnicking.

He did not say—or even think—that we were not competent enough. After all, Michael Adeane had got an extremely good first at Cambridge, and I'd had two degrees at Oxford—we were not academic hoodlums! We were people with a certain standard of knowledge and education—and perfectly adequate from the point of view of capacity for the job. [...]

AN ATTEMPT TO CREATE A NEW IMAGE

In 1968, Lord Brabourne, Lord Mountbatten's son-in-law and a film director, saw the need to project the Royal Family as being more modern and informal, a view shared at the Palace by William Heseltine.[3]

Lord Brabourne suggested to Prince Philip the production of a documentary about the Royal Family's private life, recommending that Richard Cawston, then head of the BBC's documentary department, direct the film.

The Queen was reluctant at first, but at the urging of Prince Philip she agreed to go ahead with filming, which took place over one year, resulting in forty-three hours of raw footage. The Queen gave Cawston free access to both her private and official life, but reserved the right to veto the finished product.

The Queen did consent to the film's airing and *Royal Family*, cut down to ninety minutes' worth of footage, was broadcast by the BBC on June 21, 1969, and by ITV eight days later.

* * *

Lord McNally They responded by trying to explain more, be more accessible. The documentary at least put them in the context because, of course, the next social revolution in Britain was in the 1960s, and that produced a different kind of social revolution, a youth-driven culture, one more disrespectful of authority.

David Frost and the satire boom on television—*That Was the Week That Was* and *Private Eye*—loosened the cement, as it were, and meant that the Palace was more open to criticism and, obviously, trying to respond to those criticisms.

Bryan Forbes It was a watershed—the first time we had seen Prince Philip barbecuing. It was an effort on the part of the Royal Family, or the royal advisers, to bring them into the current mood, as it were, and to get rid of some of the mystique.

But, of course, if you let the genie out of the bottle, you can never put the cork back again. And a lot of people think, with hindsight, that it was a mistake.

When I saw it at the time, I didn't necessarily think it was a mistake. I accepted it for what it was, and I think the majority of people accepted it for what it was.

But then we have a section of our media, especially the tabloid press, which really feast like vultures, and now, nothing is sacred. The only person, really, who has kept aloof is the Queen herself.

Robert Lacey Going way back into the 1920s—and you can go right back to this sort of stuff coming from Queen Victoria—the Queen Mother, soon after she became Duchess of York, allowed trusted writers into the house at [145] Piccadilly, where they [the Yorks] lived.

These writers described the inside of the house, the rocking horses, and the way in which through the bathroom door you could hear the screams and giggles of the little girls as they were having their bath, [in the presence of] their father, because it was quite a shocking thing in the 1920s and 1930s. So these intimate details were getting fed out to the general public.

Bishop Hugh Montefiore It's a very difficult balancing act, isn't it, to be human and then to retain the humanist quality as royalty? The function of the Monarch is really as a constitutional symbol—it's the concept of the Crown coming from God and being handed to them—not as a personality.

In the old days, that's how it was so regarded. That's being substituted by this personalized thinking: we must admire them as people if we're going to keep them. It started at Buckingham Palace with the film of Elizabeth.

Lady Pamela Hicks This is the insoluble problem. They were criticized for being stuffy, and not letting anybody know what they were doing, and my brother-in-law helped do up a film, and now people say: "Ah, of course, the rot set in when that film was made." You can't do right; it's Catch-22.

Imogen Campbell-Johnson When we first came back from India and Alan heard that the Queen and the Duke of Edinburgh were going to open themselves up to publicity, my husband advised against it to everybody he spoke to. He said: "You know, you're opening a sort of Pandora's box."

* * *

That Pandora's Box was soon opened: the Queen and the Duke of Edinburgh began to face scrutiny and criticism as parents. The Queen was said to be too preoccupied with her public duties to be a good mother, as well as being stiff and formal with her children.

And the Duke came to be looked upon as a tyrannical father, thought to be responsible to a great degree for the future misfortune of the royal children, whose every misstep as adults would be eagerly followed by the tabloid press.

Ivan Head There was a coldness there. When you see films now of the Queen returning from a visit, even when the children were small, a nanny would bring little Prince Charles up and she'd shake hands, or maybe, kiss him on the forehead, and then put him aside.

Michael Noakes It struck me in my contact with Prince Charles when he was very young that he was immensely fond of the Queen, and he would call her "Mummy," and things like that, when he was talking about her.

Tim Heald I don't believe that Prince Philip and, indeed, the Queen were significantly different from an awful lot of middle-class, or upper-middle-class British parents in that respect: that was the way you behaved. And you didn't cry in public; you didn't cuddle in public.

Life may be a lot more civilized now, but it wasn't something peculiar to Prince Charles's relationship with his parents. And it wasn't that anybody was being deliberately unkind, or cold. It was just that that was the way you *did* things.

Bishop Hugh Montefiore Her role as Sovereign took precedence over the mothering process. The Queen looks after affairs of state and the Duke looks after affairs of the family. One gets the impression that he's a rather strict father; Charles has given that impression himself.

Tim Heald Anne had the closest relationship with Prince Philip; they were quite alike. When I saw Anne, she talked about Prince Philip exactly the way any father would want his daughter to talk. It was with a mixture of adoration and exasperation: "Oh God! Dad's so embarrassing"—and all that sort of thing. They obviously had a cracking relationship.

His relationship with Edward seems to be pretty good. They do a lot of things together—the Awards Scheme being one of these. And his relationship with Prince Andrew is pretty good.

Philip Ziegler The Queen—whether it's stressful, I don't know—has this crippling sense of duty. But I think she would genuinely have loved to have had the chance for spending very much more time with her children. But always, being Queen comes first.

Once they were off the stage, once the camera wasn't on them, they behaved with total informality, as a normal family. But the opportunity for doing so, once she became Queen, was so small. So, inevitably, there was isolation.

I suspect that one tends to overdramatize this slightly. But it is jolly difficult to be a Queen and bring up small children.

Tim Heald When I was doing my book, Prince Charles actually specifically refused to talk to me about Prince Philip. His words were: "unless specifically ordered to do so," by his father, which is suggestive that their relations were not great.

You've got to remember, of course, that [with] the two younger sons there's a significant age difference, and times have changed. I would guess that it was always going to be different—and more difficult—for Prince Charles, as the heir.

Again, what were the models? For Prince Philip, it was his own father, and he was not entirely satisfactory. And Mountbatten himself was much the same. And then you go back to the Duke of Windsor. It's very difficult to see whom, actually, he's able to model his behavior on—and the whole situation of the Prince of Wales and the King and Queen is a very peculiar one, a very difficult one.

PRINCE CHARLES'S RELATIONSHIP WITH
LORD MOUNTBATTEN

Prince Charles lost his main confidant with Lord Mountbatten's assassination in August 1979. Nearly twenty-one years later, on June 26, 2000, when unveiling a plaque in London's Wilton Crescent, at the site of his late great-uncle's home, marking what would have been Mountbatten's hundredth birthday, the Prince said: "We all know what a wonderfully special person he was. We who knew him miss him continually."

* * *

Lord Powell He was a dominant figure within the Royal Family, particularly with Prince Charles—sort of his grandfather. His grandfather, George VI, was dead and gone; in the Royal Family of that generation there was no other male figure.

John Grigg He [Lord Mountbatten] really did feel that he was an enormous influence on the Prince of Wales. There was considerable influence.

Imogen Campbell-Johnson We'd spend weekends at Broadlands. Prince Charles as a small boy used to be there a great deal and would be looking over the banister.

There did come a point, long before Prince Charles's marriage, that Mountbatten was concerned by Prince Charles's general attitude—what you could do, and what you couldn't do—as far as women were concerned. But it would be quite wrong to think that Mountbatten was any agent, as it were, in influencing Prince Charles to be at all promiscuous.

DECISIONS ABOUT PRINCE CHARLES'S SCHOOLING

Lord McNally It may be unfair, but what is now coming across is a rather old-fashioned kind of parenting, which is now seen as a rather cruel kind of parenting, and I'm afraid that the finger is more regularly pointed at the Duke than at anybody else. Sending Charles to Gordonstoun, even more bizarrely, sending Edward into the Royal Marines, are parental decisions that probably reflect more their own upbringing.

In some respects, what the Queen and the Duke did with their children is no different to what the majority of their generation of parents did: to send them to boarding school. The boarding school would often have strict discipline and the rest, and didn't always produce rounded human beings, emotionally, at the end of the process.

But, in fairness, they were the first generation that had to deal with a media for whom the old restraints, and their own self-disciplines in covering royalty broke down—the intrusiveness, the intensity of coverage, the paparazzi, and the constant and real money to be made out of royals.

Tim Heald I interviewed Prince Charles in the 1970s and saw quite a lot of him at the time when he was being invested as Prince of Wales.

There was an hour-long documentary, pretty good, I thought. The basis of that was carrying on from what Prince Charles says in the Dimbleby book,[4] which was, I thought, actually over the top in what he said about his father—and being sent to all those schools.

He wasn't saying this to me [in the 1970s], or even giving any indication of *thinking* it, when he was in his early twenties.

I believe that there is an element in Prince Charles of being wise after the event, or rationalizing things. I'm not saying that he didn't have a proper childhood, but I believe it wouldn't have mattered what his parents did, or where he'd been to school. Given the fact that he was Prince of Wales at that particular moment in British history meant that he was always going to have a very difficult time.

And the fact that he was, on the whole, a rather sensitive boy, not particularly good at the rough-and-tumble games, as his father had been, meant that there were all sorts of dice stacked up against him.

I don't believe that Prince Philip deliberately tried to give him an unpleasant time. I remember interviewing Prince Philip, years ago, for the *Express*, and asking about Charles's education, and his answer then was: "Well, there was a good British tradition of fathers sending their children to the same school that they went to."

I believe it was more complicated than that. And I believe also that perhaps Prince Philip himself hadn't realized how much Gordonstoun, in particular, had changed: when he went to Gordonstoun it was a tiny, tiny experimental school, only about thirty boys, with this extraordinary, charismatic headmaster. By the time Charles went there, it had grown into an established place, with several hundred pupils, with a fairly ordinary headmaster, and it was very much like any other school, except that it was a long way from home. So it had changed character—perhaps more than he had realized.

They were left with all sorts of talk of consultation, but at the end of the day, I think the schooling was very much Prince Philip's decision. And I'm certainly not aware—again, it's very easy to be wise after the fact—that there was a body of people at the Palace saying: "Don't send him to Gordonstoun; it's too tough; it's going to be hard on the boy. Let him stay at home." I don't believe that was being said seriously; I believe Philip said: "Let's send him to Gordonstoun," and everybody said: "All right."

Bishop Hugh Montefiore I knew him when he was at Cambridge. He seemed a religious person at the time—they were very genuine feelings. I don't know [about] now, but he was a very religious boy. And he used to be interested in the paranormal.

I thought he was happy for the first time. I remember him in the *Trinity College Review* having a whale of a time, as any decent undergraduate would have had. He had to fly off to the other side of the world and all of that kind of thing, but by-and-large he enjoyed himself greatly, and, probably, for the first time. Certainly he didn't when he was at school in Scotland; I don't know what Geelong [in Australia] was like.

A ROLE FOR PRINCE CHARLES

Robert Davies (1951–2007), deputy chief executive, Business in the Community (1986–90); chief executive, the Prince of Wales International Business Leaders Forum, 1990–2007 If you are brought up knowing that you are a steward of resources—that you are going to be there, and your influence is going to be around for a long while—you tend to take a much more long-term view. The Royal Family are brought up with a longer-term view, so the concept of stewardship, handing things on through the generations, is very, very compelling.

Tim Heald When he was born, and certainly at the time when important decisions were being made about his education, and all the rest of it, it was not unreasonable to suppose that the Queen wouldn't live as long as she has, in fact, and that that way, Prince Charles would have thirty-four years, or how many years, of being the heir.

The perception is that Prince Charles's entire life has been an education for the monarchy. But looking at it realistically, the Queen may have wondered about the probability that she is going to go on for a very long time: you've got thirty or forty years of Prince Charles as Prince of Wales. What is the correct role?

I don't have any evidence that the question was ever seriously asked. I'm not even sure it's being asked in a serious way now. He's sort of had to fit it all together as best he can.

Lord McNally [Prime Minister] Jim Callaghan did see the problems that might come from Charles's having decades of waiting, and he did make a number of attempts to get him involved—getting briefed in Whitchall; a day at Number 10—and there was a general sweep around to see if there was something suitable for Charles to do.

I got the impression that Jim asked Ken [later Sir Kenneth] Stowe to look at this very seriously and to see if there was a slot in Whitehall, or elsewhere, which would give Charles a proper job.

Now, I might be being totally unfair to Prince Charles, but my impression was that beyond a kind of general look around, there wasn't very much enthusiasm [on his part] for doing a specific job. Whether it faltered because no such proper job could be found, or whether there was a lack of enthusiasm from the Prince, I'm not absolutely sure, although I did get the impression that part of the problem was a lack of enthusiasm from the Prince. It takes two to tango.

* * *

Princess Anne, Prince Andrew, and Prince Edward, while not having grown up with the pressures experienced by Prince Charles as the heir apparent, were, nevertheless, held up to scrutiny and ridicule, especially by the tabloid press looking for chinks in the royal armor.

Two of Charles's siblings would come in for some bad press, particularly regarding sensational extramarital affairs, failed marriages, and divorces.

PRINCESS ANNE

Anne had been the first of the royal children to marry when on November 14, 1973, she and Captain Mark Anthony Peter Phillips exchanged vows in a glittering ceremony at Westminster Abbey. Although their relationship had flowered due to their mutual equestrian interests and activities, the marriage foundered and the pair were divorced in 1992, amid rumors of Captain Phillips's infidelity.

Anne soon developed a tart tongue, which did not endear her to the media, nor to the public. She did, however, embark on a series of good works, notably with Save the Children, on whose behalf she has worked tirelessly, traveling to remote regions of the world under hardship conditions.

In recognition of her unstinting devotion to duty, she was in 1987 declared Princess Royal, an honorary lifetime title held previously by only six other Princesses throughout the British monarchy's long history.

* * *

Sir Oliver Wright She has now, through sheer hard work, worked her way back into public respect, not, I think, public affection. She works like mad for good causes, like the International Save the Children Fund. She has children of her own but she makes no bones that she is not particularly interested in children. But she is interested in *saving* them. She doesn't see why you have to slobber over a baby in order to be an effective patron.

Michael Whitlam I remember with Princess Anne and Save the Children, she used to come in regularly for briefings about the work in the United Kingdom, to the point where she was very knowledgeable and spoke on the radio and on television.

Her value to Save the Children changed around 1974. There was a time when she was getting quite a bad press. There was a particular moment on a royal visit she made to Norway, where she was wearing beautifully immaculate white clothes and a child with chocolatey fingers went running up to her, wanting to touch her, and the press caught her looking at this child as though daggers would kill. It was not a particularly pleasant photograph.

It was around that point that her advisers decided that that was unfair and that she had a lot more to offer. And there was a very famous trip she took to Africa with a whole planeload of journalists, and that trip completely changed people's image of her, and the press image of her.

She worked tirelessly for charities. And certainly at Save the Children, the work she did was brilliant, and very helpful.

Lord Ouseley I worked with Princess Anne, and I began to understand how members of the Royal Family had a better appreciation of the new, emerging role they were playing—that it was a very vital and helpful one to communities, particularly deprived communities, even if it was done in the context of media coverage that depicted the members of the Royal Family as beneficiaries of public finance, not making a contribution to society as a whole.

Claire Rayner I have always said that if there were an election tomorrow and Anne ran for president, she might well get it. If there were an election tomorrow for president, and the Queen ran for it, she might well get it, but Anne would run a close second. I would have no objection to one of the Windsors running for the presidency.

Lord Archer Anne is the toughest of the three [younger members of the family]. She works the most because she likes work; that's why she does so much, not because she's a good, decent person, which, I'm sure, she is.

Michael Deaver I liked her very much. She was very frank. She said: "You know, I don't like a lot of this, what I have to do. But it's my responsibility, and I try to do it well. I work very hard."

I thought it was a very nice way to look at it. And, of course, I had heard about her as being this kind of sourpuss, and I didn't find her that way at all. I found her charming, and very straightforward, with very little pretentiousness at all.

* * *

In Father Michael Seed's book *Will I See You in Heaven?*,[5] a collection of letters from "the rich, the famous, the poor, the needy, and the notorious," Princess Anne contributed a very revealing letter:

Dear Father Seed,

A sense of wellbeing, of peace with the world and humanity steals over you the minute you set foot in your boat. You are the master and can forget your work and the troubles of the world. You become a part of your ship, graceful as a bird, skimming effortlessly over the waves, testing your skill, not against anyone else's but against nature, your ideals and the person you would like to be.

Sailing on a sunny day, with a fresh breeze blowing, with maybe somebody you really care for, is the nearest thing to heaven I will ever get on this earth.

* * *

Fr. Michael Seed I did write to other members of the Royal Family. I did the first "Heaven" book in 1990. The second edition came out in April 1999. The second one is more controlled. I was asked by the publisher to write to those people.

Princess Anne was in the first one, so she's actually been reproduced in the second one, and the Duchess of Kent.

I didn't write to the Queen; there's no point in writing to the Queen because she doesn't write to anybody.

I wrote to Prince Charles and Princess Diana. Prince Charles didn't send words, but he sent a donation of £500, which I thought was very gracious because he didn't have to.

PRINCE ANDREW

The Duke of York is referred to in some circles as the Queen and the Duke of Edinburgh's "reconciliation child" following the Duke's six-month absence for the *Britannia* cruise—which would have made it one of the longest reconciliations in the making, given that the Duke had returned home in 1957, nearly three years before Andrew's birth in 1960.

Prince Andrew, gregarious in nature, engaged as a bachelor in romantic liaisons with a series of high-profile actresses, earning him the nickname "Randy Andy."

He did, however, pursue a naval career, a factor that would be cited in the break-up of his marriage to Sarah Margaret Ferguson, "Fergie."

The couple, wed on July 23, 1986, at Westminster Abbey, were divorced six years later, following the still-married Fergie's publicized romantic romps, including one where she engaged in semi-nude sunbathing in front of her children, with her American-born "financial adviser" John Bryan kissing her toes.

Although the Yorks divorced in 1992, they remained friendly, even living under the same roof.

* * *

Lord Archer He's warm and friendly, jovial, a nice chap. Nothing more than that.

Claire Rayner By the time it came to Fergie, Andrew—he was called "Randy Andy"—the idea that he was marrying at all cheered the family up. It was general knowledge that she had had a relationship with [race car driver] Paddy McNally, but they didn't worry too much. By that time, the line was set with Diana's son.

* * *

In August 2021, Virginia Roberts Giuffre filed a civil action against Prince Andrew in New York under that state's Child Victim's Act. Ms. Giuffre claims that Andrew engaged in sexual relations with her when she was seventeen years old. As a result of the lawsuit and the Prince's apparent friendship with the late, disgraced financier Jeffrey Epstein, Andrew would largely withdraw from public duties, although the Queen would not ask him to relinquish his office as Colonel-in-Chief of the Grenadier Guards.

PRINCE EDWARD

Prince Edward, the youngest, would be ridiculed for his seeming wimpishness after he resigned from the Marines and pursued a career in the performing arts and as a documentary filmmaker.

Edward's sexual orientation also became a matter for speculation, despite his marriage on June 19, 1999, to public relations executive Sophie Rhys-Jones, his long-time live-in companion.

* * *

Lord Archer Edward's the most sensitive of the three; he really cares about the arts. I find them all easy to talk to—well, *Anne's* not easy to talk to.

Claire Rayner He is interested in the theater; there is a long tradition of that in his family. There were rumors about Edward—that he was a wimp. He has a lot of gay friends. He is so down the line of succession that he has made a conscious decision to keep a low profile. He is a pleasant little lad.

Donald Macdonald We met them all. The one I liked best—and the one I saw most of—was Prince Edward.

My wife and I were rather impressed with him, for the reason for which he had been most criticized in the United Kingdom—that very unfair and foolish decision that had been made that he should become a member of the Royal Marines.

There are a lot of very good people who are never going to make it in the Royal Marines, and this was an ordinary kid, in terms of physical ability, and it took a lot of courage for the Prince to say: "This is not for me; I don't belong here, and I'm going to resign." We all greatly respected him for that.

I've seen him in those television series, where he has talked about royal institutions. For an ex-high commissioner they are revealing because he talks about places, and people, and things, and you didn't always know what was happening, and he may say some things, like putting pieces of a jigsaw together, and he does that very well.

THE YOUNGER ROYALS' BAD BEHAVIOR

A notable example of the erosion of the dignity of the Royal Family occurred in 1987 when Prince Edward, motivated by the noble intention of raising money for charity, conceived and produced a royal version of a popular television program, *It's a Knockout*, in which competing teams take part in silly games.

Edward's idea was brought to John Broome, the owner of Alton Towers, an amusement park near Birmingham, who was enthusiastic, as was the BBC.

First, however, the Queen had to give her consent to the venture. Although her courtiers advised against it, the Queen, possibly motivated by a desire to support her son, gave that consent.

The program, reworked as *It's a Royal Knockout*, featuring the Duchess of York, Prince Andrew, and even Princess Anne engaging in send-ups of royal ceremony, was televised by the BBC on June 19, 1987, to almost universal condemnation as a silly and undignified spectacle, although it did raise one million pounds for charitable causes.

To make matters worse, Prince Edward, annoyed at the negative media reaction, became petulant at a post-program briefing and stormed out of the media tent, prompting the next day's tabloid headline: "It's a Walkout."

* * *

Lord Weatherill I believe the side has been let down by certain members of the Royal Family. The rot started when they went on a television program called *It's a Knockout*.

For the first time, they were knocked off their pedestal, and they behaved as some older people hoped their grandchildren wouldn't behave. And they were human. That actually destroyed the mystique, really. And then there were the divorces.

Joe Haines If you see Prince Edward involved in *It's a Knockout*, and Andrew marrying Sarah Ferguson—it was my newspaper that had the pictures of her having her toes sucked by Johnny Bryan, this tall and balding "financial adviser"—that brings disrespect.

They're basically not very bright. But if you don't like the train, get off. It's a luxury train—there's nothing else quite like it. You get *enormous* privileges—people defer to you—and it gives you a life such as no one else in this country can lead.

So, if you're rebelling, don't just rebel against the part which you find stuffy—give me chastity and give me splendor, but not yet—rebel against the lot.

Claire Rayner The royals have always been an odd lot. Any inbred, upper-class family is pretty much ramshackle. They [the royals] are like any inbred family, anywhere; they are not much different from "trailer park trash."

If you are looking at the monarchy, then you are looking at a host of political ideas; if you are looking at the *Windsors*, then you are looking at just another bunch of soap [opera] stars.

Ivan Head Those idiotic children of hers. Not one person in Canada would attribute this to failings on the part of the mother. It's the father. We all understand that.

Rev. Ian Paisley That's not her fault. You can't blame a parent for the woeful acts of her family. That's unfair, on the grounds of unfounded prejudice against the Queen. And that has come, of course, from people with an axe to grind, who want a republic.

Michael Noakes I believe that what has happened with the younger members of the Royal Family has done an immense amount of damage to the monarchy.

Vivien and I feel rather differently about this—Vivien is more inclined to say: "Why should we set them standards which general life doesn't?"

But I do actually feel that special demands are made on them because of the rewards that are given to them, and they haven't really fulfilled those. And I do think that it has been extremely damaging. It would have been better if it had not happened.

Vivien Noakes I feel quite strongly that we expect too much. They, in a sense, set themselves up as a model family in Victoria's reign: she and Albert, as well, wanted to be seen as examples of probity.

And I believe that we've continued to expect that they should be. I don't really think that you can expect it. It would be very nice if they were like that. And certainly it's been very shabby, all that's happened in [the last fifteen] years.

It *is* damaging. But one has to separate the monarchy from the personalities around it. The monarchy itself is something which matters immensely and, in an ideal world, people like Prince Charles should behave wonderfully well. But I don't see why we should necessarily expect it.

Fr. Michael Seed What family, immediate or extended, doesn't have divorces, and remarriages, and separations, and the lot?

The problem is that the British Royal Family have been protected from this inquisitiveness—the Queen Mother and King George VI never had anything like that, other than Edward marrying Mrs. Simpson. Maybe it all stems back to the period in the late 1930s with the abdication. Until then, everything was innocent.

And then they fought the war; and then in the 1950s the beginnings of change—in the 1950s people were hidden and secretive.

The 1960s not so, and, therefore, even more so with the royals, because everybody's eyes were on them—they had become media stars, so it's not surprising in the slightest that three of the Queen's children have ended up in divorces. Had one had a crystal ball thirty years ago, if someone had predicted that three of the Queen's children would divorce, I wouldn't have believed it—but I'm not shocked because of the pressures they're under.

But on the other hand, we still live in a kind of puritanical society where the Royal Family are meant to be perfect, and we have to have someone to criticize as well. And if they're not perfect, we criticize them.

Stuart Macintyre I certainly have sympathy for the Queen in her difficulties with her children. I think most Australians of middle age can put themselves in the footsteps of someone who sees her children, one by one, breaking up their marriages and mucking up their lives.

* * *

None of the foibles of the younger siblings, however, captured the attention of the media, and of the British nation, as would the drama that began when in 1981 the engagement of Prince Charles to Lady Diana Spencer was announced by Buckingham Palace.

CHAPTER 24

Prince Charles and
Princess Diana

O N FEBRUARY 24, 1981, Buckingham Palace announced the engagement of the thirty-two-year-old Prince Charles to Lady Diana Frances Spencer, nineteen, the youngest daughter of the Eighth Earl Spencer, sister-in-law of the Queen's assistant private secretary, Robert Fellowes,[1] and the sister of one of Charles's former love interests, Sarah Lavinia Spencer, now McCorquodale.

Dubbed "more English than the Royal Family," by virtue of the Spencers' relation to the Marlboroughs, Diana Spencer was at that time a rather statuesque, attractive, but not beautiful, and seemingly unsophisticated girl—the epitome of the perfect "virgin" bride.

In truth, Diana was very conscious of the value of her royal connection, and despite a few early, unhappy encounters with the media, learned quickly to cultivate them, in the process creating the persona of "shy Di."

The courtship had begun in the fall of 1980 when the Queen, who knew of, and was upset by, Prince Charles's liaison with the very married Camilla Parker Bowles, purposely invited Diana to a houseparty at Balmoral.

Aware of the pressure on him to marry—and to marry a virginal Protestant—Prince Charles proposed to Diana Spencer at Windsor Castle on February 6, 1981, and she accepted immediately, setting off more than sixteen years of controversy in which the very future of the British monarchy would be called into question by some of its severest critics.

Patrick Jephson Princess Diana was *every inch* a regal figure.

While people's instinct in the presence of royalty is to freeze, Diana was approachable, tactile, demonstrative, and emotionally articulate.

Although the term "People's Princess" would be used following her death, she fulfilled her royal duties in spades, which some people tend to forget.

Yes, she was young, but not naive and there was no way, given her aristocratic background, that British royalty over-awed her. All the more reason to regret the fact that the monarchy did not recognize what they had in her—the potential she had for *them*.

Lady Angela Oswald When Charles was in his twenties he said he felt he ought to get married round about the age of thirty. So everyone was waiting and waiting. And obviously there were an awful lot of people who were thoroughly unsuitable.

Imogen Campbell-Johnson It's general knowledge that Mountbatten would have been quite happy for one of his granddaughters, Amanda, to have married Charles, but she married someone else. She said publicly […] that there was no question, ever, of marrying him.

Adm. Sir Henry Leach There was probably considerable pressure brought by Dickie Mountbatten to make sure that he did get married. But that said, the Prince of Wales was more than old enough to be his own man.

Ian Adams It's been said that one of the strongest influences [on the Charles–Diana match] was the Queen Mother.

There were undoubtedly pressures because, obviously, one doesn't want to have a very aging Prince taking someone for a wife in order to guarantee the succession.

I often say, rather wickedly, that the trouble is that the Royal Family in the last few decades has tended to marry horses, and anybody who is not a horse is not going to have a very strong chance of succeeding. And even when they are horses, they don't always work, either.

Robert Lacey In that brief interview involving Prince Charles and Lady Diana Spencer on the day their engagement was announced, they were asked if they were in love. And, famously, the future Princess had no doubt, and Prince Charles made this comment that has been much criticized.[2]

That was unfair. What he said absolutely reflected his own rather maturer understanding of how affection grows. But for this future King and Queen, as they then were, to discuss their personal feelings—whether or not they were in love was something, it's easy to say, in retrospect, which should not have been allowed to be asked. Or if it had been asked, they should have given answers by which they retained their privacy.

Mohamed Al Fayed, father to the late Emad "Dodi" Fayed, who was killed with Diana Princess of Wales in an automobile crash in Paris on August 31, 1997; chairman and owner of the Ritz Hotel, Paris, since 1979; former chairman and owner of Harrod's Ltd and Harrod's Holdings, PLC Why do you marry such an angel? In order to use her as an incubator to give you kids, and you don't give a shit about her. Her suffering was horrendous. And she grew up normal; her father didn't spoil her. She was working as a nanny. And she learned life not in the easy way.

And when she got married, she had to follow protocol and it was difficult for her. And she had a husband who didn't give her love, didn't give her care—he's just using her. And she was under this pressure from when she was nineteen.

They didn't want her to be a normal human being. They didn't want her to enjoy life. She had had a terrible twenty years: Charles was involved with Camilla when he got married.

Adnan Khashoggi The strangest thing happened. When Diana married Charles, my nephew, Dodi, was on the boat with us and he took a room in the Hotel de Paris, in Monte Carlo, to watch the wedding [on television]. He was the only one of the boys who did that to watch the wedding.

It was just highly coincident that this happened. Later on he got involved in this [Princess Diana's] ambiance. After he died, we remembered that he had done so: it had no relationship until something drastic happened.

* * *

Only days before the wedding, Diana had been shaken on discovering that Prince Charles was planning to present Camilla Parker Bowles with a piece of jewelry as a token of his enduring love.

* * *

Archdeacon George Austin That was an awful burden to her. Now, what disturbs me considerably is that Robert Runcie, the Archbishop of Canterbury, didn't think she was doing the right thing, that she was taking on something she wouldn't be able to cope with, but he didn't say so [at the time].

I believe that was a gross dereliction of duty. It's part of the deference, of course: he wouldn't have wanted to get on the wrong side of the Prince. It wouldn't have been taken very well.

But he could surely have said to Diana: "I want to see you," and to have said: "Look, you don't need to marry this man. If you are having any doubts about this, please tell me. Are you quite sure you're doing the right thing? It isn't too late to withdraw." As any of us would do if we had a couple coming to us for marriage preparation and we thought one of them really didn't want to do this.

* * *

While Diana is reported to have had second thoughts about going through with the union, she dutifully went ahead when urged to do so by her sisters, revealing none of her indecision to the adoring public.

In fact, those viewing the ceremony, either in St. Paul's Cathedral or on television, or observing the royal couple's postnuptial kiss on the balcony of Buckingham Palace, would not likely have dreamed that tension already existed between the two.

* * *

Winston Churchill Within a month of their wedding, I happened to be taking two busloads of my constituents from Manchester to Althorp, her childhood home, and her father, Johnny Spencer, said: "Why don't you come before your constituents and have lunch with us? I'd love to show you the private apartments."

So we had lunch. And then, before the arrival of my constituency, he said, proud as a little turkey cock: "I must show you the guest room that I had completely redone for the return from honeymoon of Charles and Diana."

He'd had new green silk wallpaper, and the four-poster bed had been completely redone. And he opened the door and he said: "I'm afraid it's a bit of a shambles now." And clearly there had been a battle royal: there were water stains on the green silk wallpaper; there was a Chippendale chair that was broken; there was a mirror cracked.

At the time, my then-wife and I put it down to a sort of lovers' tiff. But now, with the benefit of hindsight, one can see that it [the marital discord] started right at the beginning. And I suspect it was when he told her of his affair with Camilla before they were married.

This seemed to drive her ballistic, and from that moment everything went downhill very rapidly. She became very sick, mentally, in terms of the bulimia, and all the rest of it.

Lady Young He too has suffered. He's a very sensitive man. He's done some remarkable things: he's set up the Prince's Trust—he's done a lot to do with the unemployed and almost unemployable people; he's worked very hard to get them into jobs. He's taken a great interest in architecture, in education, and in farming, and he has made a very real contribution to our national life.

Robert Davies I've worked with him since about 1984. The Prince has a side which anyone who knows him is always surprised by—and people don't completely understand: he has a very deep emotional side, a very deep spiritual side.

He's not self-assured. And, therefore, he's been trying very hard to demonstrate—he feels a compulsion; this may also be a part of his upbringing—the validity of [his many activities and positions on issues].

I had immense admiration for the Prince of Wales and his courage [in the 1980s] when he made a very critical speech in Islington, during a meeting on town development, about President [Nicolae] Ceaucescu of Romania.[3]

Suddenly, in the middle of his speech, out came this outburst about Ceausescu, and how he was erasing the signs of village life, and how this was absolutely monstrous.

Even I gasped. I thought: Goodness gracious me. Who is Ceausescu?, forgetting that not so many years previously, he had been lauded by Britain and driven down the Mall in a carriage, and given an honorary knighthood by the British government.

When Ceausescu and his wife were shot at Christmastime, they were considered monsters, but no one really knew them outside of Romania. And people in Britain thought: Oh my, goodness me, those are those terrible despots who the Prince of Wales was talking about!

Bryan Forbes She had a much greater public persona than Charles did because he's not as much of an extrovert as she was; he's a much more introverted person, a thoughtful person, who feels and thinks deeply about a number of subjects.

Lady Angela Oswald They were so wrong for each other! They each ought to have married somebody like the Queen Mother—they each needed someone warm, who would have really looked after them. They each needed it and neither of them was capable of giving it to the other.

Larry Adler Prince Charles is a very stuffy man. I played at Buckingham Palace once. Prince Charles was sitting about twenty feet away from me, and while I was playing, he began to talk to the lady on his right. I thought: What the hell do I do? I don't like this. I have to go through with it. But when I was finished, I walked offstage.

About a year later, I met him with Dickie Attenborough, and Attenborough said: "Larry, have you met Prince Charles?" And I said: "Yes. And he talked all the way through my performance!" And Prince Charles said: "Where was *that*?" And I said: "In *your* house!"

Then Dickie said: "Larry, get the hell out of here!" Which I did.

Imogen Campbell-Johnson With marriage you need to enjoy doing the same things. I'm not blaming her for this. But if you play tennis and your husband doesn't like tennis, or your husband likes to go off fishing for weeks at a time and you don't like it, it takes up a lot of his free time away from you, doesn't it?

It's very important that royals marry people with whom they enjoy doing the same things, because they have so much duty to do that when they have any time off, don't you think they should be able to spend it together? That was an altogether very injudicious match, just on those grounds alone.

And Diana hadn't had her fun; she was much younger than he was. She wanted to go to pop concerts, and all these kinds of things, which didn't fit in with his kind of life at all.

I say this excluding Camilla Parker Bowles, or anything like that. Looking at it, if it were my daughter marrying, I would think it wasn't right for her.

Winston Churchill In the spring of 1992, Charles was deputed as the royal to be in charge of the forthcoming visit of the president of Portugal to the United Kingdom.

Diana was privy to his diary—he was not privy to her diary—and knowing that he'd be tied up with this state visit, she chose that moment to take herself and the boys on a skiing holiday to Lech, in the Austrian Tyrol.

At the last minute, a general election was called here so the state visit was canceled, and Charles calls up his wife and says: "Darling, I know you'll be thrilled. I'm able to join you and the boys at Lech." "You can't come!" she says. "Why on earth *not*?" "You can't. There's no room."

He was two steps ahead of her. There was a very small hotel and he said: "If you check into room twelve, you'll find that's a Scotland Yard protection officer by the name of Smith. That is your husband." He had to go to those lengths to go on holiday with his wife and children.

And while they were there, her father, Earl Spencer, died and he said: "We've got the Royal Flight sitting at Innsbruck. We'll leave immediately." "No, no. I'll make my own way."

Well she discovered that that wasn't very easy, and so in the end she had to back down and say: "Okay, I'll come with you." But she said—and to me, this speaks volumes of her and the problem of her marriage: "When we get home, I do not wish you to travel in the same car as me to my father's funeral. I wish the British public to see me grieving alone."

And so his private office had to arrange, at very short notice, something that hadn't been planned before, the opening of a primary school in North Wales, to give him the excuse of arriving by helicopter at Earl Spencer's funeral, and then departing the same way.

But what an incredible state of mind to say to your husband—and they weren't separated at that time— "I want the British public to see me grieving alone."

COULDN'T THE PRINCESS'S UNHAPPINESS HAVE BEEN HANDLED BETTER?

Philip Ziegler There was a weekend at Balmoral when they were trying to do that very thing: they had set aside that weekend beforehand for talking over all the problems.

She never came down for lunch—she never came to any meals. And when she did appear, she would run around wearing her wretched booby-bag, with her earphones on, and nobody had a word with her for the entire weekend.

Yes, obviously, it could have been handled better if they had realized really early enough what they had got on their hands—that there was great potential for danger. But it would have been jolly difficult: she was not an easy girl to be married to, and to get on with.

The Queen is alleged to have said on one occasion: "My mother's a star; my daughter-in-law's a star. Where does that leave *me*?"

I don't believe it was a major factor in her behavior, but she would have been superhuman if she did not have a certain amount of irritation—especially if she really thought of her son as being miserably unhappy.

Tim Heald Their attitude would have been: "Sort it out. It's *your* business, but don't let down the Family Firm; don't upset the rest of us with all this that's happening to you. Sort it out."

I know officials at Buckingham Palace who were sworn enemies of the Princess, but who were terribly fond of her as a *person*. They would say: "She's doing something …! Oh what's she doing *now*?" As she passed down the corridor [at the Palace], she'd come in and say hello. And [they'd say] what fun she was, and how she was charming, and lovable.

I believe that the Queen and Prince Philip were clearly upset and exasperated by the situation. But I don't have any sense that they ever disliked her. I don't think they were hostile to her; they wanted it to work.

I believe that they were sad that it didn't work out, and exasperated when it seemed to be turning against them. But all the way through, I don't think they were enemies in that sort of way.

I believe that they thought that she was badly advised, and that she was not doing the things that they wished her to do. But I really don't think that there was ever any sense of personal animosity.

There was one occasion when a story got into the papers that Prince Philip had written her a horrible letter. She was, apparently, terribly upset and said that "Prince Philip has never been horrible to me, and I would like him to know …"

The fact that she, Diana, was unpredictable further complicated the whole question. Let us not forget that, for a long period, at least between her and Charles, developments were extremely hostile, so it was very difficult to get anyone to sit down and say: "Now look, we need to sort this out, and what exactly are you going to do?" They weren't, for a long period, capable of talking to each other about anything at all.

Winston Churchill You have situations which arise where, frankly, the Royal Family find themselves out of their depth, like how to cope with a total maverick like Diana, who was going off the rails, who was a very unstable personality—whatever you think of her, she was very unstable.

And what was a totally new experience for the Royal Family was that she was in day-to-day, indeed hour-by-hour, contact with tabloid journalists, leaking her side of the story to the discredit of her husband, to the discredit, very often, of the Royal Family.

This was something that they'd never experienced before. How do you cope with it? Particularly when she was so glamorous and had such a high profile, and was being touted around in the tabloid press as being second only to Mother Teresa in sainthood, while at the same time never running less than two lovers concurrently.

She had, amazingly, been able to put herself over as "one of us" in terms of ordinary people—"one of us" going every day to the hairdresser, every other day for massage, every other day for this or that kind of therapy.

She couldn't have been more different from "one of us," but she managed to put this over, aided by her incredible beauty and also by her very keen sense of self-promotion.

There were endless stories, like: "Diana was driving alone and saw a vagabond drowning in a pond and there was no one around and she saved his life." Well, if there was no one around, then how do we know about this story? Because she picked up the phone and called a reporter with whom she was at least in daily contact, and so there was the story.

She was playing to the galleries, and in a masterly way! She said: "I'm as thick as two planks." Actually, she was an absolute mistress of the art of manipulating the media.

There was an evolution [from the "shy Di" of the betrothal period], but it happened very, very early. And there was a relentless flow of anti-Charles stories, to which he, without going down into the gutter and returning mud with mud—which would be seen as unchivalrous, would have got him nowhere—had no response.

Lady Angela Oswald And the worst thing is that nobody will come out and say it. In that book that Diana wrote with Andrew Morton it said that the Prince of Wales had had a mistress from the moment he was married.

Well that was just not true. He gave up not only Mrs. Parker Bowles, but he gave up his friends, and he gave up shooting for between four-and-a-half and five years. And so it was a wicked thing that was said.

I've always thought that it was very, very sad that when that book came out, the press office didn't in some way throw doubt on the book. There were things in the book that were true. But there were plenty of things in there that weren't true and that was the most damaging of all, and it was so unfair.

Michael Whitlam When the new Andrew Morton book came out [*Diana: Her True Story in Her Own Words*, 1997], we [the British Red Cross] were to receive a sizeable donation from the royalties because we were told at the time that there would be a reprint with a new foreword.

It turns out that behind all of this were other things that Andrew Morton wanted to say from tapes that he apparently had that he shouldn't have had. And it didn't take me too long, having talked to Diana's sister, Sarah, and one or two others, to say: "Actually, we don't want that money based on the kind of book you're about to write."

And even though he sent the check to us, we didn't bank it, and we sent it back because I didn't want to be part of something where she could be criticized for being human.

Stephen Day I've always had respect for the Prince of Wales; he's a very serious guy who does his job—a very difficult job—to the very best of his ability. He had a marital problem. Well, who *doesn't* in Britain these days?

I find deep skepticism about all these revelations, but I'm probably highly untypical, because I've never read one of those books about him and her. Who reads them? I'm amazed at this appetite for trivial information about them and their marriage.

Larry Adler I found her very bubbly, vivacious, and, God knows, a beautiful lady. I was at an art exhibition at the Festival Hall and suddenly I heard a male voice in my ear: "Would you mind making way for Her Royal Highness the Princess of Wales." And I looked around. And there was Diana. And I said to her: "Did you hear what he said?" And she giggled and said: "Yes." And I said: "Do you really want me to make way for you?"

Sir Bernard Ingham I am not an admirer of Princess Diana. I've never been an admirer of her. I think she was a menace, frankly. She was a complex, self-indulgent madwoman frequently, and I never got any thanks for saying so.

It was only based on glamour. I've always asked the question: what would have been the public's attitude if she'd looked like the back of a bus?

Lord McNally I must say that I am in the pro-Diana camp, and always have been, as a phenomenon. As somebody interested in public relations, you can't write down what she had in a manual: some people have that empathy with mass audiences which others do not—and *she* had it in spades.

It was a pity that the Royal Family could not have harnessed that, and that Charles himself couldn't have harnessed it, because she would have been an enormous asset, properly harnessed. As it was, she was an unhappy and disturbed loose cannon, who they couldn't handle.

As a public relations man, I've got great affection for her. The night that Charles did his Dimbleby interview,[4] how do you top that? You go to

a premiere in the "little black number" to end all little black numbers—
and wipe Charles off the front page!

Robert Lacey It's no secret that the Queen and her husband were horrified
by the fact that Prince Charles discussed his relationship with Camilla
Parker Bowles on television in a documentary about his life.

It is, perhaps, interesting to speculate about what would have happened
if a documentary had been made about Prince Philip, or the Queen, in
which similarly intimate matters were broached—say the frequent rumors
that Prince Philip was in earlier years unfaithful to his wife.

Well, firstly, I can't imagine myself, or any television interviewer, feeling
that they can even broach that question with Prince Philip. It's something
to do with the aura that he, personally, has created around himself, which
is a defensive aura. Even if the question *were* asked, one can see Prince
Philip saying in a salty fashion: "That is no business of yours!"

Sir Michael Oswald She was a brilliant actress. She was the first-ever of
the Royal Family to court the media—the first one ever to ring up the
press to tell them at once where she was going. She was the first one to
use the media and to exploit the media, and she was extremely clever and
manipulative in doing that.

Nothing is black or white in any failed marriage, and certainly not
in this case. But I must say, I had never known the truth turned on its
head quite so comprehensively as was done by most of the media in this
country: things that I absolutely knew to be totally untrue have gone
down as gospel truth and history.

Bishop Hugh Montefiore It's a different generation—a different way of
looking at it. She was a phenomenon; she was the most famous woman in
the world and therefore must be dealt with specially.

And she could be very endearing. I have to tell you, I was always skeptical till I saw her; she absolutely won me over. At the same time, she was
exceedingly manipulative.

Adm. Sir Henry Leach She was immensely attractive. She only had to
give one of those sideways looks and you would fall flat on your face and
grovel. How much was in there, I don't know.

Lord Healey She was quite extraordinary, really. I can't think of anyone
other than Marilyn Monroe who was quite so attractive, and Marilyn

Monroe was just sexy and that's all. There wasn't much else to her, whereas Diana had quite a lot to her, really.

Michael Whitlam She was a highly intelligent young woman, and was competent and able to understand issues that interested her. For those issues that she cared about, Diana read about them; she understood them; she discussed them with people; and wanted to have information.

Diana also needed to understand what was behind things, and read briefs, and watched the videos we sent her. In one of the two documentary programs that the BBC made on Diana in Angola [in 1997, during her campaign against land mines], she corrects me: we were talking about the number of land mines that were in a particular country, and I said: "Well, as you know, we've got ten million land mines here ..." And she said: "Actually, Mike, it's twenty-three million ..."

She'd read her brief; she knew it. She would go through her speeches. Even at the last minute, flying into Angola, we were still rewriting most of it so that it was absolutely up-to-date.

She wasn't a confident speaker—I don't think she really enjoyed it— and she got quite nervous beforehand. So if I prepared a speech for her, it would go to her office, and she would personalize it, and change it, and do all the things she felt comfortable with. So it often came back changed, or requiring more information.

Very often, she would just go to the event and deliver the speech. But there were one or two occasions when she was obviously in a playful mood. There was a fund-raising event for our business supporters. She was speaking at the reception and didn't stick to her script then, so I didn't either and I gave her a video—a fairly controversial video we had made about AIDS for seafarers who sail all over the world, to encourage them to use condoms—and I presented it to her and explained that she could only watch it in the secrecy and quiet of her own home afterwards.

And she said: "Tell me all about it"—this is in front of two hundred businessmen; the microphone is switched on. You could have that kind of banter with her.

Adnan Khashoggi It was the conflict between conservatism and liberalism: these people are conservative, and trained to be conservative. This woman was more liberal and she stole the show from her own family. And once she got divorced it was worse because then she was a loose cannon. So they didn't know how to handle her.

In reality, it was not because they didn't love her—it's like when you have a child who likes to go dancing until four o'clock in the morning, and you say: "We are sleeping then"; you can't tell them more than that.

She was not controllable. And to prove that she was not controllable, she went with Dodi. That was a silly act on her side, being the mother of the future King of England, and getting married to one not of her faith. This was a bit more than being liberal. This was a scandal in the family. So, in reality, as much as they loved her, I think they feared her—that she could be the downfall of William.

Michael Whitlam Diana was a very emotional woman. Certainly in the last years, her emotions swung up and down quite a lot. I'd get a telephone call to go and have tea with her in Kensington Palace and not know why I was invited. Was it in order just to chat? You wouldn't know whether it was because she was down or up. She was demonstrative and shared her emotions.

Bishop Hugh Montefiore She talked to people. People looked at her with respect; people looked at her with *love*.

She was going to visit hospitals, cradling the sick. I am a patron of the London Lighthouse for AIDS. She came to give a speech there. She was absolutely splendid, and then she insisted on going round and talking to us individuals who were there—that's the kind of thing that endeared. And then, of course, she was a ravishing-looking woman.

You have a different kind of attitude to her than to the Queen: the Queen is a symbol of respect; here is a lovely, loving person—the most famous woman in the world. She was stealing the show, but in a different role.

Nelson Mandela She came to South Africa. I received her and I asked her to return to help me launch a campaign against AIDS because of what I saw when I was in jail. In a certain country in Europe, which I will not mention, there was a trial. There was the judge, the accused, the prosecutor, the clerk of the court, and the audience. In the course of the trial, the accused said to the judge: "I have got AIDS." And the judge, and the prosecutor, and the clerk of the court, and the audience went out of the courtroom because the belief at that time was that if somebody has got AIDS and you are in the same room, you are infected.

Diana was one of the principal figures to smash that because she went to a hospital in London where there were AIDS sufferers, shook hands with them, and sat on their beds. And then people said: "A British

Princess has gone to shake hands with people suffering from AIDS, and sat on their beds!"

Incidentally, at the press conference, one of the photographers said: "Would you please kiss?" So I said: "To kiss a British Princess, I would need the written permission of the prime minister; the leader of the opposition; and Her Majesty."

Michael Whitlam I was responsible for the walk that she made through the mined area [of Angola, shortly before her death]. It was a cleared area, but there are one or two people around who walked on cleared areas and lost arms or legs even so. I wouldn't have put her life at risk for one moment, but there was always the outside chance; these were real land mines she had to see.

She knew what she was doing. The real point of her wanting to go there—we discussed it—the reason why she agreed to do it was because she was going to speak at the premiere of *In Love and War*. It was Richard Attenborough's show and, in fact, he'd given it to us in aid of the land mines campaign, and she'd wanted not to just go and be there and generate income; she wanted to say a few words.

And I said: "Well, the only way you are going to be able to do this is to speak from the *heart*. And you need to go and just see it." And that's what spurred her to go. So she saw it and used what she saw.

At that time, with the divorce and all that had been going on, I think there had been a lot of discussions—to which I was not privy—about what her role would be. But she was a fairly strong-willed woman and knew what she wanted to do.

I had suggested she go to Cambodia, not to Angola, and it was actually the Foreign Office that said she shouldn't go because there had been a couple of high-profile hostages taken and a high-profile visit wouldn't have helped that. So I agreed that Cambodia was not the right place to go.

I then suggested Angola and the Foreign Office turned up—they were always advising the Palace, and the Palace took advice from the Foreign Office—and they would have preferred if it had been Mozambique.

And I said: "Well, actually, Mozambique has two million land mines; Angola has fifteen million. It's going to be Angola or nothing." And they agreed. And Diana made it very clear that she preferred to go to Angola.

Canon Paul Oestreicher People liked her for different reasons, some just because she was like a film star; some because she was honest and went on television and said: "I've mucked up my marriage and I had a bastard of a husband who happens to be a Prince." People whose marriages had gone wrong would be unlikely to say that in public about their former spouses. She just managed to be everybody's Princess.

THE PRELUDE TO DIVORCE

On December 9, 1992, Prime Minister John Major addressing the Parliament, stated: "It is announced from Buckingham Palace, with regret, the Prince and Princess of Wales have decided to separate."

The prime minister went on to say that the Waleses had no plans to divorce, that there were no constitutional implications, and that there was "no reason why the Princess of Wales should not be crowned Queen in due course."

That would change on November 20, 1995. That evening, twenty-three million people watching *Panorama*, a prestigious BBC television interview program, were stunned to see before them a somber Princess Diana, clad in black.

The Princess stated that Prince Charles's relationship with Camilla Parker Bowles made her own marriage "a bit crowded," and further stunned viewers by confessing that she, too, had committed adultery.

And then Diana dropped another bombshell: she did not believe that Charles would ever become King, but that William would.

* * *

Lord Archer *Panorama* was the height of her anger. She never said she was going to do it, either before or after. There was a group of us she just cut out; she didn't tell us she was doing it. I think she knew we would have told her *not* to do it. Therefore, she didn't ask us. She would not have listened to us.

* * *

The Queen reacted by writing to both Princess Diana and Prince Charles, stating that she and the Duke of Edinburgh believed that divorce—and as soon as possible—was indicated.

The marriage of Diana Spencer to the Prince of Wales that had begun on a beautiful day in July 1981 would end officially little more than fifteen years later, in August 1996.

* * *

Imogen Campbell-Johnson You had the problem that if she was a very beautiful young woman, was she not to have lovers? The Palace can very silently cut off the lovers. They can't kill them with poison, like the Borgias. But they seal the lovers off from things. I don't think it would have worked in Diana's case.

But it would have if he had married, for instance, a young royal from Europe. But he wouldn't have the young royals from Europe, or they wouldn't have him.

Sir Oliver Wright They were just incompatible characters. We paid for turning the wedding into a fairy tale: the images of Princess Diana marching up the aisle on the arm of her father in St. Paul's Cathedral stick in everyone's brain.

It promised so much but didn't work. And like so many things that have promised so much but don't work, people are very unforgiving. This is because it reflects as much on their own judgment of the people and events concerned as it does on the people concerned.

DID DIANA HARM THE MONARCHY?

Rabbi Sidney Brichto Nobody could have done more to undermine the monarchy than she did. Her boyfriend was the son of Al Fayed; it was an embarrassment for them. It wasn't just that he was a Muslim; he was a Muslim connected to a family who had been a thorn in the side of the British Royal Family.

Michael Whitlam Obviously, since her death I've had to look back many, many times, on the ten years or so that I knew Diana, and think: What kind of person was she? Was she a helpful, positive person? And she gets nine out of ten most times.

Yes, there were occasions when she wasn't feeling particularly happy, and where she and I might have had a difference of view—let's put it that way. But across the time, she—as all the Royal Family who get involved in charitable work do—added greatly to the charity's ability to do its job better.

And from that point of view, those who criticize are probably criticizing for reasons best known to themselves—something to do with their own agenda.

Alfonso, a limousine driver When she was around, she tried to help the monarchy; she tried to put the monarchy in touch with ordinary people—something the monarchy did not know how to do. [In 1998], Charles met in a park with AIDS victims. He tried to be a carbon copy of Diana, but he didn't succeed; people saw that he was going through the motions.

Philip Ziegler Tragically, she could have been such an asset: she was from the word "go" a consummate pro at public relations. She could have been a terrific asset, internationally and nationally, which is why it was such an awful human waste.

DIANA'S POST-DIVORCE LIFE: EMERGING
FROM HER PROBLEMS

Lord Archer Unquestionably, she was in love with him to begin with. She had no interest in her place in history. She will have her place in history through her son William.

Diana had respect for Charles. I remember her saying to me six months before she died, pointedly, what a good father he was, and how much she admired him. And she said it purposely, for a reason. She said it so there wasn't any doubt in my mind; we were on our own, when there was no one else in the room, when we were dining alone.

I saw her three weeks before she died. She was viewing Charles in a different way by then. She was feeling more relaxed about it.

Michael Whitlam That was her sons' idea. I remember her telling—we were sitting on a plane—that she was going to have this auction of all her dresses.

I don't know that there was anything psychologically significant about her casting out the past. I believe she saw a way of using these gowns from different designers to raise money for causes that you find it difficult to raise money for, certainly, in relation to that auction.

She got through the difficult times and she cast off a lot of the charities she was involved with. She was much freer to make the decisions herself about what she would do, and where she would go, and the so-called late night visits to hospitals, and night shelters, and things were all part of her wanting to do her job well and get to know the issues better in a way that she probably couldn't have done if she'd been right in the heart of the Royal Family.

Angola was, of course, for her a very different way of working. I've got a lot of footage that was not shown on the BBC. All the stuff they used shows her chatting away, sitting in there. You could sometimes see the pain on her face as she's looking at the mess, and dirt, and poverty around her.

That moved her in the same way that AIDS victims did, or people suffering from leprosy, or drug addiction, or homelessness. These are the unpopular causes. She wanted to be in there, using not just her skills and her knowledge, but her ability to attract the media, and to use her charisma.

It's a gift that not many people have. But she had this gift, which made people feel better. And people get better not just because of drugs, but because of the care and attention that they get from some people. And she had those feelings.

Angola was a watershed for her. It was very much a point where she had decided on the issues that she wished to support, and she knew the kind of role she could play.

I believe the Angola trip was the first time she had a major overseas trip like that as a *working* visit, and that was stressed time and time again: it was a working visit; she was there, traveling in Red Cross vehicles—she didn't travel in an ambassador's car; she wore the same kind of clothes that we did; there was no fund-raising event—no gala dinner.

And she loved it. And she was very good at it. She had incredible charisma and was able immediately to put people at their ease. On the visit we did to Zimbabwe, she walked into a room with two AIDS patients, away from the press—this was a private house—and she sat for an hour, just she and I, and one of the government ministers, and we just sat and chatted to these two patients who had about three months left to live, and she left them smiling, and with hope.

And that's what she did: she would walk into a room and she would leave people who were quite seriously ill with some hope. That was just her natural charisma and she used it to the full.

The last trip I took with her was about six weeks before she died, which was actually to America, to Washington, to launch the American Red Cross Anti-Personnel Land Mines Campaign. And on that occasion Diana was actually much more relaxed, and jokey, and happy than I'd seen her for a long time.

Diana had to work quite hard there: she had to make three speeches in a day: we had a lunchtime event; there was an afternoon press briefing; and she spoke at the dinner. And she did them all extremely well; the media were very interested in what she was doing, and Washington was full of people who wanted to meet her. And Diana was in a comfortable environment there—she was with friends, perfectly relaxed—and she played jokes on me for the three days.

She invited me on one occasion to have tea with her. I'd been out at meetings all day. She had the room below mine and one of the staff came and said: "Diana would like you to join her and the ambassador's wife for tea." And so I went downstairs to where her living room was.

And she was sitting in there with the ambassador's wife, in her dressing gown and with white stuff all over her face. I, of course, blushed and looked incredibly embarrassed, and they thought this was highly amusing and spent the next two hours ribbing me about it: "Come join the girls," she said. "Come join the girls for some girly chat."

CHAPTER 25

The Death of Princess Diana

A T FOUR O'CLOCK in the morning on Sunday, August 31, 1997, Princess Diana was pronounced dead in a basement operating room of the Pitié Salpêtriére Hospital in Paris by Dr. Bruno Riou, head of the emergency team that had fought for nearly two hours to save her life.

The Princess had succumbed from massive injuries suffered only hours earlier in a car crash as Henri Paul, deputy security manager at the Ritz Hotel, owned by Mohamed Al Fayed, the father of the Princess's companion, Emad "Dodi" Fayed, was driving the couple in a leased Mercedes from the hotel to Dodi's flat. Paul had been speeding through the Pont d'Alma Tunnel in the Eighth Arrondissement when he swerved and careened into a pillar.

According to the official French report on the accident, released on September 3, 1999, following an eighteen-month investigation, at the time of Paul's death his blood contained a much-higher-than-legal level of alcohol—between 1.73 and 1.75 gm per liter—as well as traces of Prozac and Tiapridal, which inhibit sensory function and should not be used in combination with alcohol.

The Princess, Dodi, Paul, and Trevor Rees-Jones, a bodyguard employed by Mohamed Al Fayed, had left the Ritz at 12:20 A.M. The crash occurred only three minutes later. Dodi and Paul died instantly, while the Princess and Rees-Jones were pulled from the wreckage alive—but just.

The switchboard at the headquarters of the Paris Fire Brigade had at 12:26 A.M. received a Code 18 emergency call about a serious accident in the tunnel and arrived on the scene six minutes later.

Meanwhile, a nearby police patrol had been informed of the crash by passersby and entered the tunnel, where they discovered the badly damaged Mercedes S280, registration number 680LTV75, which had come to rest facing in the opposite direction to the flow of traffic.

After being treated for forty minutes at the scene of the accident, the Princess, who had been conscious on the arrival of the emergency services, was taken to the hospital, less than four miles away. The trip normally took only a few minutes, but as the emergency crew feared further injuring the Princess, who was now sinking rapidly, they drove slowly and she was brought into the hospital at 2:06 A.M.

For nearly two hours, the emergency team fought in vain to save the Princess. It was too late, however. Unbeknown to the ambulance crew, the Princess was bleeding internally due to a tear in her left pulmonary vein, and by the time the tear was detected by the emergency room crew, nothing more could be done.

Earlier, having been notified of the accident, Britain's ambassador to France, Sir Michael Jay, had put in a call to Balmoral, where the Royal Family were vacationing. The ambassador was connected with Robin Janvrin, at the time the Queen's deputy private secretary, who in turn woke Prince Charles and informed him of the accident.

The Prince had been in a deep sleep, but once roused, he telephoned Camilla Parker Bowles, and then spoke with the Queen.

The Queen and Prince Charles agreed that the young Princes William and Harry should be allowed to sleep until morning, when there would be an update on Princess Diana's condition.

In the next few hours, news of the accident reached other members of the Royal Family, as well as Prime Minister Blair, and the Queen's private secretary, Sir Robert Fellowes, who called the hospital for further information on his sister-in-law, the Princess, only to be told that she was dead.

Sir Robert turned immediately to Prince Charles and broke the news, to which the Prince reacted by crying out in anguish.

Prince Charles later in the day flew with the Princess's sisters, Sarah and Jane, to Paris to bring Diana home.

Meanwhile, at Balmoral, the Queen, who had been informed of Princess Diana's death by Sir Robert Fellowes, did not return immediately to London, nor did she issue a statement of grief at the Princess's death.

Instead, joined by Prince Philip, Prince Charles, and Princes William and Harry, as well, as other members of the Royal Family, the Queen attended services at the nearby Crathie church, unleashing a torrent of criticism from the public and media alike. Some critics of the monarchy were even to call into question for a time the institution's future.

* * *

Lady Angela Oswald One particularly nasty side of the outpouring of emotion for Diana is that when people feel grieved, they have to blame someone—that's been shown throughout history.

And there were so many really wicked things laid at the Queen's door at the time of the Princess of Wales's death. There were people who for years had been criticizing the Queen for putting duty before family. When the Princess of Wales died, the Queen was up at Balmoral with the two little Princes, whose mother had been killed, and yet she was castigated for not leaving them, and coming to London to mourn in the streets with people who had never even met the Princess. And that was wickedly cruel.

And the other extraordinary thing was that, on the day of their mother's death, the two little Princes decided they would like to go to church as usual—if you're a Christian, you find a comfort in going to church. But the Queen was accused of making the Princes go to church on that day, and she was vilified for it in certain sections of the press, which was so terribly unfair.

Tim Heald The popular press were complaining that the Royal Family had gone to church. Well, I still don't understand what it was that was so unhuman; surely that was the most appropriate thing for them to do—to take the boys off to church and have some quiet moments on their own.

My father was killed in a car crash when he was fifty-eight and I would have very much resented anybody telling me how I was supposed to express my grief, and how I was supposed to behave. We wanted more than anything else to be left alone, to deal with it in our own way, behind closed doors.

For them to be told how to behave by the British tabloid press still seems to me to be completely grotesque, and if I'd been any member of the Royal Family, I'd have been jolly cross.

Which isn't to say that they handled the whole thing incredibly well—things like the flying of the flag at half-mast. There were perfectly good reasons for never doing it, but I can understand that they weren't readily understood by anybody except a few people among the heralds and the generals. And it would have been sensible to have done that sort of thing.

But broadly speaking, I don't have any idea what they were supposed to do—go on television and shed some tears?

And then there was Blair's speech[1] outside the church that morning. I can remember saying afterwards: "I wonder if, when he gets into church, will he actually give Cherie a nudge and say: 'Did I do all right?'"

Lord Archer They were stuck in Scotland and physically didn't see what was happening, and probably would have even missed it if they were in London, because they were enclosed within a house.

They would only have had to walk the streets to know what was happening; *they* don't walk the streets. The moment they *did* walk the streets the first time in their lives—from St. James's Palace through to Buckingham Palace—they just couldn't believe it.

Joe Haines It's not uncommon, is it, that if you're prejudiced against someone, everybody shares your prejudice? A beautiful young woman wasn't necessarily congenial to some of the senior aides at the Palace. They didn't like her; she was becoming a loose cannon; and I bet that somebody, somewhere in the Palace, said: "Thank God!" when they heard she was dead.

They never understood. The British are said to "love a lord." Well, they "love a lady" more. They never anticipated it [the public outpouring]. Remember, they were at war: they didn't like her. As long as she was there, there was always the threat that she would do something that would upstage the Royal Family. In fact, she did, all the time: if Charles was doing something big in the country, she only had to put her head out the window to upstage him.

And she was a different sort—she was going to gyms; she could be seen occasionally in restaurants, and all the rest; she went to hospitals; she got on with the people—and they [the Royal Family] didn't like it; she was the competition.

Well, they didn't realize they were a small-minded—as well as being small in numbers—coterie, and that the British people had a totally different view of her—that they sympathized with *her*, and not with him.

And they don't like Camilla; they can't understand how somebody could not prefer a beautiful young woman to a woman who is not beautiful—she's almost equine, isn't she? So they got it all wrong. From Crathie church the first morning—the vicar didn't even mention the Princess's death; they went through: Well, we can't lower the flag to half-mast because we don't *do* that; the Royal Standard is *never* flown at half-mast. That was their mistake.

Earl of Harewood It aroused a lot of feeling, the way the media played it, mostly in asking questions: Should the Queen be in London? Should she have come back to London? Should she do this? Should she have taken Princess Diana's children to church?

She had two grandchildren, who must have been fairly cut up at their mother's rather sudden death, to look after. Because they were all in relative seclusion in Scotland, to rush them down to London for the hype of publicity seemed to me unnecessary. Why you could be less feeling at Balmoral than at Buckingham Palace, I just don't know. But the press certainly worked it up enough.

Alfonso The Queen reacted very slowly to Diana's death. She was surprised at the interest. She just didn't understand because she is not in touch with the people.

The outpouring for Diana scared her. She was thinking: If that is how much they love Diana, I wonder how much they are going to love *me*? Imagine, people stood for ten or fifteen hours just to be able to write a short message [about Diana]. I don't think they will do that for the Queen.

Adnan Khashoggi This is not part of their [the Royal Family's] tradition. First there was the shock of this thing happening, and before it the shock of the possibility of her marrying a Muslim and changing the history of the structure. So they went through before- and aftershocks.

At the same time, they saw the impact of the pain that the people had for Diana when she died: they realized that their grief had to be more open than just behind closed doors. So they reacted to the people's feelings. They are part of the show: their ruling power is a show power. So, okay, if that's what the people want, let's go.

Now you even see Charles, and the boys, appearing more in *Hello!* magazine, and smiling. Now this is all *after* Diana, not before. So it seems that they woke up to the reality that this is a new generation that doesn't want to see the stiffness of previous generations.

Sir Shridath Ramphal It's much too contemporary to make judgments. It was a horrible time, a time of stress for everyone—nor did we know everything. I would always tend in those situations to give the benefit of any doubts I have to the Queen.

Lord Younger For a short period the public were in shock. They felt that somebody must be to blame: Let's find somebody to blame. And the only person you can blame is the nearest person you see, and they tended to blame the monarchy, the government, the Queen, the Prince of Wales— the whole lot.

Canon Paul Oestreicher People were horrified when the Queen was away from her Palace that the grief of the nation was not expressed by flying a flag of some kind from Buckingham Palace half-mast; there was no flag half-mast at all, because the Queen wasn't there.

Now that bit of protocol was recognized to be stupid, so now when the Queen is not there, they fly the national flag. And when she is there, they fly her personal flag. These are not very important things, obviously, but they are changes. And the Queen agrees to them because their time has come.

Bishop Hugh Montefiore They were very foolish about that. What they did was *correct*: the flag only flies when the Queen is in residence, so no one's at fault. It's a lack of imagination, really—a lack of understanding of the feelings of the people.

They put it right very quickly, with the help of the prime minister. But there was deep feeling against the Queen—at that time public opinion could have turned right against the Queen because there was a surge of anger, and because there was the nation's loss, with their idol gone, and there was the Queen, apparently remote, in Balmoral.

The Queen must have received very bad advice. But, I have to say, they did act quickly to turn things right: there was Charles, coming and talking to the people in the queues; there was the flag flying, and so on.

But they made an initial error—and it was only an error—because if you are full of grief, you don't want to appear in public; you hide yourself away. Look at the way Victoria hid herself away—for years.

WAS IT A CONSPIRACY?

Mohamed Al Fayed They killed Dodi and the driver with laser guns straightaway—they dismantled the whole balance of the guy with the floodlights, which can blind a person straightaway and they shot the two immediately. The laser guns were shot from motorcycles. It was paparazzi camouflaged.

My bodyguard, Trevor Rees-Jones, survived. And it was possible that Diana could have survived. But when she did not die, I think the French police broke the car not to go to the hospital. The hospital was ten minutes from the accident; it took forty minutes to get there.

The Queen and Prince Andrew sent me [a condolence message], but not Charles, and not Philip. They want to shut me up.

But I believe in God. And I am sure God will help me to get the bastards. I can't give up. How can I? I know definitely they killed him. I can't accept that for someone who gave his life to the country. How can they do that? It's just unbelievable. You can't just accept that.

It's a challenge. But God gave me the power, and the means, and the ways. And people are coming out of the woodwork, telling me things, which helps. I have a fantastic team of lawyers working everywhere—in France, here, and in Washington. In Washington now there is a big investigation of the CIA, with all the evidence I have, especially the interference not to investigate these documents.

It's unbelievable that you see how these intelligence services manipulate. It's a democracy: how can they be so powerful and unaccountable?

I am going to continue until all this comes out because somebody killed my child; I'm not going to let them get away with it. No way.

Alfonso I don't believe that Diana died as the result of an accident. Something happened. She had a lot of powerful friends, but she also had a lot of enemies—a *lot* of enemies. Those are the people, I reckon, who killed her.

At the end of the day, there was no way that the British monarchy, that has existed for centuries, would let a Muslim be part of the Royal Family, so a lot of people have it in the backs of their minds that something *did* happen.

Look, someone was able to break into her private telephone conversations; only the Secret Service could do that. And, whatever they do, they cannot be held accountable, never be prosecuted. MI5 and MI6 have the highest technology in the world.

And the only person wearing a seat belt was the security guard, and he survived. But if you look at earlier videos of Diana, most of the time, she wore a seat belt.

Robert Lacey I don't believe that people share the dark theories of Mohamed Al Fayed. But actually I'm astonished by the number of quite ordinary people who say there was something fishy about it—the flash in the tunnel, and all that sort of thing.

Like all conspiracy theories, it speaks to a widely held feeling. It's difficult to say, but there is no doubt at all—objectively, one has to say—that the Royal Family is better off now without Diana.

Conspiracy theories are an irrational way of linking cause and effect. So if the outcome has been beneficial to the Royal Family—and one has to say that it has—the concept of Diana still being alive, having love affairs, creating scandals, giving interviews, represents absolute chaos so far as the Royal Family is concerned.

Therefore, one has to say—linking all the correct reservations about this—that the situation of the Royal Family is better with her dead. Then, inevitably, there's the link that happens in the mind and conspiracy theories leap like electricity to make everything neat and full of explanations.

I happened to have studied, because I wrote a book about her, the death of Princess Grace.[2] The same thing happened there—the idea that a beautiful, beloved, fabled woman should just die in a car crash and might have been saved if she had been wearing a seat belt is not a reality that people want to come to terms with: princesses do not exist to remind us of the dangers of life and how the same thing could happen to us. And so the conspiracy theory is escapism.

Adnan Khashoggi I don't believe it was a conspiracy. I believe it was an option: if I was head of intelligence in Great Britain, I would say: "Maybe we should kill her." That's one option. And they make a scenario. Probably this was one of the options that was there to save the Crown. To save the Crown, millions of people were killed over the centuries, so I would not say it's not possible.

But they cannot implement this option that easily. How would they do it? It just doesn't add up. Now, if I were a fiction writer, I would say they came out. The boy was sitting in the car. They were going through this tunnel. They were chased and they were going very fast. And somebody said: "That's our chance! Send another car to the end of the tunnel and put the lights in the face of the driver, and this will blind him …"

But what guarantee is there that she would be killed? So it doesn't make sense. And it's not a clever way.

DIANA AND DODI: LOVE MATCH OR RELATIONSHIP OF CONVENIENCE?

Princess Diana's romance with Dodi Fayed had begun in the early summer of 1997. Initially Prince Charles had given the affair his blessing.

Shortly, though, the Prince would become alarmed over disclosures about Dodi's private life, including the news that he had been engaged to American model Kelly Fisher, who announced plans to sue Dodi for allegedly breaking off their relationship to pursue the Princess.

The Prince was said to be especially concerned about the affair's possible impact on Prince William and Prince Harry, who had spent time with their mother and Dodi on vacation in France.

* * *

Robert Lacey I don't believe that it was a love match in the deeper, long-term sense. The few comments she made about it before her death to her girlfriends suggest that it was a summer fling that she greatly enjoyed.

And, perhaps, the idea of sticking it to the Royal Family appealed to her—it may have appealed to her sense of the mischievous.

I don't believe anybody who knows anything about Dodi can believe that the relationship would have lasted. But one can see how [it appealed], as a summer fling: it was a rare family who got all these facilities and comforts that mimic the Royal Family's own, although, as it was sadly and tragically proved, those security services and transport services, flash though they were, in no way measured up to those of the family she'd forsaken.

If they had decided to marry, for whatever reason, I do not believe that the fact that Dodi is Muslim would have been in any way an obstacle. And given the racial, ethnic, religious mix of Britain, you can see royal spin doctors turning that to very good effect.

Mohamed Al Fayed Diana was very close; she used to come here. Her father was a close friend of mine. His wish was that if they [the Spencer offspring] needed anything, I was like a father.

And if Diana wanted to come on a holiday with my kids, they came and spent a couple of weeks. She was the happiest in her life to come and see my family with William and Harry.

And it happened that she met my son. He was breaking up with his girlfriend and things just clicked. It was natural, absolutely a love match. There was no "arrangement."

Adnan Khashoggi Dodi was a quiet boy. It was more of the father than it was of the son. And just as the father was manipulative, she was manipulative. And they played the game together. Already the cast has been put on the "romantic" story. But the truth is different: the boy was innocent. He was manipulated. I don't think there was a love story.

What proved to me that it was not a true love story was that he had another girlfriend, in another boat, sitting there. If you are *in love* with such a Princess, you don't have another girl sitting there. He was taken out of his world, pushed into his father's world, and that's what happened.

Lady Longford She'd had a terrible childhood: she was always being deserted by people. And it was terrible for her that she found Charles didn't love her and she wanted to find in Dodi somebody really who loved her, and whom she loved.

But it had to be somebody with plenty of dough, because, after all, her only amusement was shopping. They say the Queen Mother is extravagant, but the word has a different meaning when it's tied to Diana.

Mohamed Al Fayed They would have prevented it by murdering them with the help of the French intelligence and the CIA because they would not accept *me*.

I grew up with different cultures and different religions in Egypt: we had Jews and all types of religions. I'm born a Muslim but it doesn't make me fanatic against any other religion. But they would never accept that my son, coming from Egypt, could be the stepfather of William and Harry, no way.

Lord Healey If she hadn't died, she'd almost certainly have married Fayed, and they'd have lived in the Prince of Wales's [the Duke of Windsor's] old house in Paris.[3]

Adrian Khashoggi I don't believe that she would have gone through with it. She was more clever than people think. She would have related this relationship to achieving some ground within their [the Royal Family's] house.

Dodi was my nephew. If he had asked me, I would have said: "Get out of here!" Forget about feeling, and all this rubbish. How much pressure could he take to live in this ambiance? It's like the Windsors: the press were after them forever. So it would have been better for him to have walked away.

A GRIEF-STRICKEN PUBLIC'S UNPRECEDENTED OUTPOURING

Peter Jay I was surprised. Not least was I surprised to find myself part of it, and my overwhelming impression was that the public was surprised in exactly the same sense.

Obviously, it was an immensely tragic event—a beautiful young person in the prime of life, with children, gone, shockingly killed in this way. So in one sense, it's not surprising that people should be shocked by such an event.

But I believe that people were, very widely, quite amazed by the strength of their own reactions, not the others' reactions, but their own: they crept up on them; they were really moved.

Other things happened later, in which the media played a thoroughly distorted role. But the initial reaction to the accident—to the death—was immense, spontaneous, and genuine.

Stephen Day I was absolutely amazed; I've never come across anything like it. It was unreal—an extraordinary shock; everybody felt that. But I never anticipated the magnitude of the public reaction.

I couldn't understand it, given the criticism that had been made of her beforehand: these same newspapers turned 180 degrees, which they're very good at doing, and turned her into a martyr.

I thought the whole thing was very sad. However, from an historical context, it is far from unique; it happened in earlier times in our history when certain members of the Royal Family turned into martyrs.

Joe Haines I was talking to a government minister the other day, an old friend of mine, and she told me she sat in front of the television and cried all day. This is a *Labour* minister! That's really amazing.

Those people who misunderstood it, who failed to realize just how strongly, or failed to understand these people who reacted so strongly, tend to dismiss the reaction as mass hysteria, which I don't believe it was.

Stuart Macintyre I was surprised by the reaction in Britain. I saw some of the footage. There was that sort of contrast between the English, who like to think of themselves as emotionally repressed, and extraordinary self-indulgence: "I want my Queen to grieve with me," as some woman said—as if you had the right to demand that people would grieve with you. That was beyond my capacity to understand what was going on.

Ivan Head The death of Diana was just one of those oddball things, a rare outburst of emotion, and it's inexplicable. The Canadian media made every bit as large a play about it, covered it as intensely, and as continuously: CBC had nothing else the night that the news broke. It was there, just as in America and everywhere in the world. It was a phenomenon.

Why? I don't know. I think in years to come there will be a more balanced—as it's starting to happen—account of Diana and the manipulation that she was able to employ in all of this. But it's all part of the soap opera that is the Royal Household.

Lady Longford I was surprised at the intensity, and the enormous number of people. Here that doesn't often happen—that the masses suddenly take things into their hands and express emotion.

But it was partly, I'm bound to say, that a lot of people who had never thought of her at all, never set eyes on her, just liked being part of the great mass emotional movement. People joined up—just like in the old days: when they saw a brass band marching through the street, they'd all join and march with them.

Lady Young I was astonished. There are a lot of women who feel themselves to be victims, and saw Diana as a victim and identified with her. Here was this emotional woman who loved cuddling people, in marked contrast to the rest of the Royal Family, and they identified with her.

And that's why there was this absolute outpouring and grief, very un-British, I thought. It partly is a generational thing.

She was a very controversial, very sad, character, in my opinion, really a tragic figure. And, of course, her death was an absolute tragedy at the age of thirty-six, and under those circumstances. And it was right that there should be national mourning and grief, that extraordinary outpouring by people.

Lord Powell I would not have expected it. That may say something about my own generation, or my own particular attitude.

I was sufficiently interested to go down on a couple of evenings to the area near Buckingham Palace just to walk through the crowd and get some direct sensation of what it was all about.

I remember being struck by one or two things. One is that there *wasn't* an air of great sadness about it all. I wouldn't say that it was a carnival atmosphere, but the people were milling around, talking a lot, more the atmosphere of a public event than of great national mourning.

Secondly, the crowd was very clearly composed of predominantly younger people, predominantly females, with a very high proportion of ethnic minorities. She was seen as a bit of a rebel, sort of a supporter of minority causes. There weren't many older people, or people like me, in business suits, standing around Buckingham Palace. I stuck out like a sore thumb.

Sir Oliver Wright I absolutely did not anticipate the extent of the public outpouring following Princess Diana's death. Of course, a beautiful, "wronged" young woman can be made into an attractive figure. But I was totally surprised at the extent of the mourning.

It has set a deplorable trend: just down the lane from our home, there was a motorcar crash. One of the car's occupants, a young person, was killed and another severely injured. At that corner, people started laying flowers. After a time, the flowers got very tatty indeed, because, unlike the flowers that were laid in Kensington Gardens, there weren't the tidying up squads that came when the flowers were dead.

I suppose you could say, without being cynical, that this is good for the flower-sellers. The whole reaction to Diana's death seems to me to be unseemly. Perhaps I haven't modernized myself enough.

Tim Heald What I found most upsetting, in a way, was the mood of hysteria, and that for the people to express unhappiness, grief, and sadness in the normal way was made very difficult—that if you weren't behaving in a very *un-British* sort of way—actually, in a fundamentally dishonest way—then you were branded as being heartless, and not caring. It was not a good moment.

I was up in London the night before her funeral. Oddly enough, I'd been to see that film about John Brown [*Mrs. Brown*, about Queen Victoria's relationship with her devoted Highland servant], with Judi Dench in it, and I came out of the cinema, which was somewhere around Leicester Square, at about nine o'clock at night, and I thought: I'll just walk the route down to the Abbey and see what's going on. There were people in sleeping bags, and I thought: Well, it's an unusual moment.

I can remember a bishop's appearing, and the anchorman [of a television crew interviewing the crowds] saying: "Bishop, this is a very sad day, and I assume that you knew the Princess well," and he saying: "Well, I never really met her ..." And gradually you realized that for the first two or three hours it seemed that there was not a single person who had any status at all talking about anything. And I was very surprised.

Then I got into Parliament Square and I was aware of two tall figures in dark suits with dog collars [clergymen], and people in sleeping bags, and they were saying: "Make way, make way." And there was another character, kneeling in the gutter, talking to these people in sleeping bags, and I thought: I *know* this preacher—there were no television cameras, no press, nothing to do with publicity at all. It was the Archbishop of Canterbury! I thought: I don't know what's going on; all I know is that it's very strange; I'm not happy with this. I'm going to go and have a drink!

Philip Ziegler The depth of the feeling staggered me. We live within three or four hundred yards of Kensington Palace and it impinged on us quite vigorously.

We had some Mexican friends to lunch a day or two afterwards, and we took them out to the park to take a look. And she [the woman guest in the luncheon party] looked around, and said, totally bemused: "I never, never knew the British could behave like Mexicans!"

I knew what she meant. But it was not something because of some mass hysteria whipped up by the media: the vast majority of these people were sedate, very middle-class and working-class people putting on their respectable clothes, clutching a bunch of flowers, bringing the kiddies out—genuinely upset and moved.

Sir Shridath Ramphal Everyone would have to say, if they were honest, that they were surprised by the immensity of it. I had certainly never witnessed, anywhere, an outpouring as great as that.

But I was not surprised that there *was* an outpouring because she had, through all she had done in only a couple of years, really won a lot of affection and esteem in people's hearts.

She had a kind of naturalness with the poor and sick that, I thought, was quite remarkable. I remember seeing a photograph of her with AIDS patients at a time when the world—all of us—were treating AIDS like the plague, and there was not an element of hesitancy about her touching them, and giving them comfort.

That transmitted itself: she was doing it so naturally. That was the great quality that made people liken her to Mother Teresa. She wasn't *acting*; she wasn't *straining*. And that touched people's hearts. And then, of course, it was the drama of the death.

Mohamed Al Fayed It was like a saint died. And it was just like a revolution: they came back; they put the flag up; then the government forced them to put her in Westminster Abbey.

The sadness and the grief was tremendous, not only for her, but also for Dodi. I have millions of letters; I have support from ninety percent of the people here, if you go out and take an opinion poll, people will support me.

Lord Glentoran I believe that was not really monarchy-related, that it was one hundred percent personal: Princess Diana had a serious cult of followers, and she had done it brilliantly, and she'd done a lot of wonderful things, and she was an astoundingly good-looking girl—she really was. I didn't meet her very often, but as her marriage was breaking up, she came up to meet us and she was still a staggeringly good-looking girl.

And the way she appeared, and the things that she did, and everything, she really had a massive following of people, like a huge star of some sort. And somehow, she had this sort of magic: she related to people, to everybody, all sorts of people.

Then there are others who simply thought she was a terrible bitch. There were plenty of them about, but they're very much in the minority.

Canon Paul Oestreicher "Queen of Hearts" was what most people called her. Yes, it became a kind of quasi-religious thing for people who weren't religious: they wanted very much a goddess—a secular goddess.

But remember this: fifty-five million people live in the United Kingdom. The number of people who publicly mourned, and cried, and went out into the streets were, at an optimistic level, a quarter their number.

Fifteen million people publicly grieving is a hell of a lot of people. But it would be quite wrong to say that the whole British nation were publicly grieving.

This is a misconception. A very, very large number were. But to draw the conclusion from that that the whole British nation was grieving was a grave journalistic error.

Lord Armstrong I remember going to look at some of the flowers outside St. James's Palace and being *astonished* to read some of the inscriptions: there were several to "Diana, Queen of Heaven," and "Regina Cielo"; in the Catholic Church, "Queen of Heaven"—"Regina Cielo"—is a title reserved for the Virgin Mary.

Another one I remember seeing was: "To Diana and Dodi, together in heaven." Well, that seemed to me an extraordinary reaction because the relationship with Dodi Fayed didn't seem to anybody to be a very attractive one.

I was surprised at the extent of the feeling about her, and I wondered whether it added something to the need that people have, to have a kind of figure like the Virgin Mary—a goddess figure —and that, in some curious way, she was the young and attractive goddess. The Virgin Mary would be the Christian thing; the goddess Diana, if you look at the

Romans—some romanticized female figure becomes an icon in religious terms. I don't believe it was very healthy.

Archdeacon George Austin It's hard to imagine anybody *less* like the Virgin Mary. I don't mean morally; I mean in other ways.

I don't believe any of us could understand the reaction, because it was over the top, almost like the veneration of a medieval saint, which she was not. It just spiraled out of control almost.

Bishop Hugh Montefiore It was pathological; some people thought it was nearly the end of the world. I'm sorry she died the way she did and, as I say, I was won over by her—there was a side of her that was deeply caring. It was sad that she died, but she died.

THE FUNERAL

Princess Diana's funeral, held in Westminster Abbey on September 6, 1997, was attended by two thousand mourners, including the Royal Family.

Earl Spencer, the Princess's brother, caused a furor in certain circles when in his eulogy he obliquely criticized the Palace for having stripped Diana of her title as a Royal Highness, and implied that the Spencers would assume a major role in the future guidance of Princes William and Harry.

* * *

Philip Ziegler You could only compare her funeral with those of Elvis Presley and Rudolph Valentino: she had that sort of immediate, pit-of-the-stomach appeal. She was devastating: on the odd occasions I met her, I couldn't take my eyes off her. I thought she was mesmerizing, charming.

She was a *star*; she really did have radiant star quality, and she used the media with skill, which no other member of the Royal Family has got within striking distance of doing. She invited me to lunch a couple of times at Kensington Palace, and I ended up totally supporting her.

Alfonso I didn't work the day of the funeral; I watched it all on T.V. If it had been the Queen, or Prince Charles, I would have gone to work.

Lord Healey I went to the service and it was quite remarkable: grown men embracing one another in tears. It was quite extraordinary, really.

Earl Spencer's speech was seen as that [as being divisive and a message to the Queen], and intended as such. But I believe it was rather unfair. I mean, the plain fact is that she was too dazzling to be the wife of a future Monarch, in a way, and, inevitably, people compared her with Charles, to his disadvantage, which wasn't really fair: he's a completely different type of personality.

Fr. Michael Seed The Earl Spencer actually, in the presence of the entire Royal Family and millions of viewers, criticized the Queen and the Royal Family for removing her title. It was incredible. You'd have had your head chopped off in the old days! But it just shows that he not only had the freedom to say this, but that he got away with it! And a lot of people applauded him.

Michael Whitlam I didn't know him at all, so I didn't know what to expect from him. I was a bit surprised, taken aback, by what he said. But I think his genuine wish that the boys would be brought up more in their mother's way of doing things was genuine.

It didn't hit me at the time what a powerful speech he had made until we heard the ripple of the applause outside the Abbey. And being almost as far away from the door as you can get, I was among the last to hear it.

It was only in the discussions afterward that I began to think about it. But at the time, I could resonate with what he was saying, in that she was a very caring mother—she cared enormously for her two boys and she hated being away from them when she was traveling, and she would have done a lot for them.

I believe what Earl Spencer was saying was that here are two young men who have lost their mother, and she had something special, and she would have given them something special, and that he would do his best to be able to make sure that they don't lose that.

Tim Heald Spencer's speech, which seemed so wonderful to a lot of people at the time—everybody loved him—now seems not just vacuous, but actually positively dishonest: if he really believed in doing the best thing for the boys, that was the most divisive thing he could possibly say at that particular occasion.

Sir Bernard Ingham The Spencers are a pretty curious lot. Although Princess Diana's two sisters seem to be very substantial people, her brother seems to be an absolute, total menace—really a very, very curious and undistinguished character.

This is true of all families; there are always black sheep—people who do worse than better. Half of them [the Spencers] have done badly; Princess Diana and her brother. The other two seem to be very substantial people.

Alfonso Earl Spencer is a nice guy. I have friends who drive him; he is very generous, very polite. He loved his sister and when he saw her mentally tortured, obviously, he wasn't going to like it, so there was a reason for his anger.

Michael Whitlam I refused to do any interviews that day, and we walked together from the Abbey to my office on Hyde Park Corner—it takes about twenty minutes—and I've never known London like it: it was just eerie—an eerie silence that we walked through—people sobbing, and traffic hardly moving. It was an afternoon I don't think I'll ever, ever forget.

WAS THE MONARCHY TOTTERING IN THE WAKE OF THE PRINCESS'S DEATH?

Lord McNally Obviously Charles couldn't handle the Diana phenomenon, and neither could the Queen. I don't believe that they ever came to terms with the fact that Diana had this enormous rapport with the British people, and that's why they so grotesquely misjudged her death, which they did: if ever the monarchy wobbled, it was in those forty-eight hours when they were stuck up in Balmoral, when the country wanted the Queen in London—and *grieving*.

We will never know quite what messages were passed [to the Queen], But she did come down and made that broadcast. But before that ... It's rather pathetic when you find that Charles resented Diana. But, of course, Britain is clearly divided into pro-Diana and anti-Diana. There's no rationale to this.

Canon Paul Oestreicher There was no real danger of the monarchy being toppled on that occasion. That was a fantasy, partly a journalistic manipulation.

The way they represented the Queen's coolness did shock many people. But nobody was in a position to say that it shocked the majority of the people, who, I don't think were particularly concerned about how the Queen reacted.

They didn't do anything outrageous; they just behaved in their normal, reserved manner. If they cried, they cried privately. It's not part of the British upper-class tradition to express your emotions in public. It's not English. It's not done. And all that royalty did was to behave like they normally behave.

A LESSENING OF FEELING FOR PRINCESS DIANA AND NEWLY FOUND ESTEEM FOR PRINCE CHARLES

Philip Ziegler When Charles Spencer made that speech, or sermon, or whatever you would call it [during Princess Diana's funeral], and the applause started outside, I believe that was a manifestation of: We're on Diana's side.

Since then, people have thought a lot about it and discovered, certainly, more about Princess Diana, and discovered that nothing was black and white with her and the Prince of Wales: in no way was he the horror she invented for the media wars; and in no way was she the Joan of Arc who she had managed to induce people to think that she was.

And on the whole, people will still, I believe, look back on her death as being a tragedy, but the mood of months of the excitement and resentment of the Royal Family is totally behind us—for certain.[4]

Sir Rex Hunt What a marvelous story for the press! It was ideal for the tabloid press: the beautiful Princess just finding happiness and crashing in the car—a fairy story with a grim end.

I felt sorry for the boys, but Diana, I believe, asked for a lot of that: she should never have gone on television if she'd really felt that the children mattered most. They should have. She couldn't possibly have gone on television. And she said that both her boys had been listening. It must have been terrible. If she really had put the boys' interests first, rather than her own, trying to get revenge for what the Prince of Wales had said on his program, she should not have done it.

I'm not excusing her behavior in any way, but I don't think he's behaved well, at all. But Diana being whiter than white?

Bishop Hugh Montefiore He who had been vastly unpopular when his wife was alive is now becoming vastly popular within a couple of years of her death. It's extraordinary, the volatility of public opinion.

For some reason, the media have decided to boost Prince Charles. But there is also a feeling, now that some of the truth about Diana is coming out, that he was as much sinned against as sinning.

And the realization of the quite wonderful work he has done: the Prince's Trust, which is generally not known as it should have been, has done more for the young, unemployed in this country than any government, or any other group of people. And the number of causes he's championed is really splendid—and this is beginning to percolate.

CHAPTER 26

Lords Reform and Scottish Devolution

O N NOVEMBER 24, 1998, the queen, in her annual Queen's Speech on the State Opening of Parliament, gave voice to the position of the government of Prime Minister Tony Blair, when she stated: "A Bill will be introduced to remove the right of hereditary peers to sit and vote in the House of Lords. It will be the first stage in a process of reform to make the House of Lords more democratic and representative."

The Blair government's effort was hardly the first of its kind as there have been movements in the past, most notably in 1890 and 1911, to reform the House of Lords.

* * *

Lord Thurlow We all accept that ever since 1911, it's been a ruling principle that the House of Lords should be rationalized by a differently composed kind of advisory legislative chamber.

And there is quite a strong sense amongst most of the hereditary peers active in the House of Lords that it would have been better not to have made any change in the present working arrangements of the House until it had been settled what was going to happen in the long run.

Sir Adam Ridley Reflecting on 1911, my great-grandfather, Mr. Asquith[1] was the prime minister at that time. The stages went progressively: you had, first of all, the early stages of welfare reform, which was seen as incredibly subversive by the center and the right—the right-wing Conservatives. And that was what inspired the peers to start shaking down the vaunted political government.

In today's circumstances, we have accidents of timing, but I don't think there is anyone getting up and saying: "The House of Lords haven't tried to provide the proper powers."

Therefore, there is absolutely no reason why it should be this year, or next year, or another time. If someone says: "We've certainly got to get on and reform the House of Lords," you'd say: "No. You can take your time. You've had seven or eight hundred years like this; you can carry on for a little while and do it right."

* * *

As the Queen entered the chamber for the 1998 Queen's Speech, events of the day must have weighed greatly on her mind. As journalist Jonathan Freedland, writing the following day in the *Guardian*, put it: "The irony of the event was exquisite, the person who sits at the very pinnacle of heredity forced to proclaim the execution of a caste whose defining principle is the same as her own."

As the Queen proceeded to the Throne from which she would make the Queen's Speech, she stared straight ahead, her demeanor somber, in contrast to that of the Duke of Edinburgh, who looked all about him with a slightly bemused expression.

* * *

Peter Jay If you put that Crown on your head, you would be like that. Quite seriously, it is immensely heavy, and it is not all that stably fixed on your head—it is like these women walking with jars of water on their heads; they walk absolutely straight, don't they? That's why she walks like that. She *can't* look around; it would fall off her head if she did—and that would create a great fuss!

The Duke of Edinburgh has not got that thing on his head, and he's free to look around. I would expect anybody in that situation to look around; it is a dazzling spectacle.

* * *

In 1998, there was a change in procedure attendant to the Queen's Speech, a lessening of the ceremony of the day.

* * *

Duke of Norfolk I am in command, in the name of the Queen, of the Opening of Parliament.

The Queen tried to modernize it and have her less important. One of the things she said was that the Lord Chancellor need not walk back-wards after he delivered the speech to her.

Well, the present Lord Chancellor said: "Fine, I'll turn round and walk down the steps." And I said: "Now, look here, I'm going to walk backwards in the procession in front of her." I thought: bloody hell, she's the *Queen*. She said: "Miles, if you want, you needn't." I said: "Ma'am, I'm going to."

Lord Cholmondeley There is a feeling of carrying on a tradition, and the weight of many generations looking down on you. It is quite an awe-inspiring day and ceremony to take part in.

It's quite exciting the first time one does it, as well. You're obviously very careful to do everything right—not just right, but absolutely *on time*. Everything has to be *to the minute*. When it says on the timetable: "The Crown will arrive at eleven fifty-seven," it's eleven fifty-seven, not eleven fifty-six or eleven fifty-eight. So everybody is watching the clock; it's one of the few occasions when timing is so precise.

And it's quite a moment when you see the Crown being carried up the stairs and it coming into view from the chamber, waiting there to receive it, coming on its cushion and borne up. The Crown on its cushion is quite something to behold.

The Queen's professionalism is extraordinary—it's almost effortless. But she knows exactly when things should happen, and her speech is always perfectly prepared and delivered.

She only has a moment to herself in the robing room, getting ready, when the robe and the train is put on, and then the trumpets sound and the ceremony starts. And it's impressive to watch her.

THE REMOVAL OF MOST OF THE HEREDITARY PEERS
FROM THE HOUSE OF LORDS

The reconstitution of the then-758-member House of Lords ended eight hundred years of parliamentary tradition when the House of Lords Act of 1999 was put forward in March 1999, in the name of "the Queen's most Excellent Majesty," in which was stated the intention to: "End member-ship in the House of Lords by virtue of a hereditary peerage; to make related provision about disqualifications for voting at elections to, and for membership of, the House of Commons; and for connected purposes."

A great debate ensued as to who would replace the hereditaries and how they were to be chosen. On May 11, 1999, on the fourth day of a line-for-line examination of the House of Lords Bill in the Upper Chamber, the peers voted a compromise deal put forward by Lord Weatherill and known as the "Weatherill Amendment."

Under the terms of the amendment, ninety-two hereditary peers would remain in the House of Lords for a time, thus ensuring continuity prior to the creation of a new second chamber.

Seventy-five hereditaries, one tenth of the total number of hereditary peers, would remain in the Upper Chamber, following election by their respective parties. In addition, fifteen places would be reserved for deputy speakers and committee chairs, as well for the Earl Marshal, the Duke of Norfolk, and the Lord Great Chamberlain, the Marquess of Cholmondeley.

On Thursday, November 11, 1999, the Bill was voted and most of the hereditary peers completed their last day of work in the House of Lords. After adjourning for forty minutes to obtain the Royal Assent, the parliamentary session formally came to an end.

The Bill's passage paved the way for Prime Minister Tony Blair to press on with the second stage of his modernization agenda.

* * *

Lord Weatherill I was responsible for brokering the Weatherill Amendment. It was only then that I discovered that the hereditary peers referred to life peers as "day boys," as opposed to "boarders"—day boys are not quite the same; our parents couldn't afford to send us to boarding schools.

Raymond G. H. Seitz There is generally agreement in this country that the House of Lords is an anomaly and that it doesn't fit very comfortably within the democratic structures. There is a fondness for the tradition of it, but it's something that is rather difficult to justify.

It becomes more difficult to justify as the constitutional base of Britain shrinks, so that you have all the very elaborate titles of the hereditary aristocracy, and the paraphernalia of the Queen and the State Opening of Parliament, and all these other people around—which in almost any other country would be comedy. But the British carry it off with such self-confidence—and we all rather like it, and it's quite a show.

Still, the degree of change has been such that some of these things do seem anachronistic. And the challenge is then: how do you moderate the change so that you don't disturb too many things, so that you don't penalize people but, at the same time, move it along?

Duke of Norfolk Everybody realized we must really change this system, and they brought in life peers. And that was a very sensible thing to do because now you can be a peer for life, not just by inheritance.

They ought to have said to the present House of Lords: "We want to have a new House of Lords which say, will be half elected, half nominated by the prime minister, and maybe some hereditary peers." But it's all gone the wrong way round.

Bryan Forbes Not all the hereditary peers were idiots, or certifiably insane backwoodsmen, no more idiots than some of the life peers—a pretty motley group—and they made an absolute pig's porridge of doing that because they haven't actually put anything in its place; they've sort of botched it, and patched it up. That was a sort of spiteful thing: Get rid of the House of Lords!

They had eighteen years to prepare what they were going to do and they didn't know what they wanted to do—just get rid of them! Well, fine, but every democracy needs a second chamber because it's a safety valve and the standard of debate in the House of Lords was always superior to the House of Commons, and had some very good brains there. And they gave a lot of their time to it, and for very little money. So they did it out of a desire to serve, really.

Earl of Harewood Personally, I'm totally in favor of reform of the House of Lords: it's perfectly ridiculous to have people who may be either foolish, or uninterested.

But I believe there's an argument to have a representative group of ancient peers. The people who seem to do most of the work in the House of Lords are excellent, and are very bright, and clued up on the whole function of the second house.

IS THE REMOVAL OF MOST OF THE HEREDITARY PEERS A THREAT TO THE MONARCHY'S SURVIVAL?

Lady Mar Yes, very directly, because we're a part of the supporting mechanism for the monarchy, and if *we* go, then the next thing will be the monarchy. All these things are interdependent on each other; none of these institutions stands alone, and Parliament in this country is the House of Lords, the House of Commons, and the Queen.

Part of the importance of the House of Lords is the fact that you've got this continuity: you've got people who go on regardless of general elections; you've got people who have an eye to history, because we all know we've come from somewhere, and where our place in the House of Lords is in history; and we've also got an eye to the future because we've got our children and whoever is going to inherit in the future.

Margaret Ewing I don't think the Lords is necessarily associated in the minds of the Scottish people with the monarchy itself. I think it's associated with the imperial Establishment—using that word "imperial" because that's how I envisage it. I believe that the danger is more the concept of the Establishment rather than the monarchy itself.

Earl of Harewood The argument would be that the removal of any ancient traditional function makes any other ancient traditional function, like the monarchy, slightly less secure.

Lord McNally The hereditaries defend their position that they're part of a slippery slope, and it is true, in many ways, that the constitutional history of Britain has been a gradual move of power away from the Monarch, and then away from the [House of] Lords, through to the [House of] Commons.

The power of the House of Lords had been the landowners, and the greatest landowner of all was the King, or the Queen. As power changed from being based on property to democracy that has changed.

What we're dealing with at the moment is the last bit of unfinished business from 1911, which is to have two parliamentary chambers that have a kind of democratic legitimacy within a democracy. That is clearly separate from the role of a constitutional, but hereditary, monarchy.

People see benefits to a hereditary, constitutional monarchy, and will continue to do so as long as the monarchy in return accepts the terms of engagement, which are included with the job.

Lord Merlyn-Rees You could argue: once you've done it with the hereditary peers then you can do it for the monarchy. But in the monarchy, you got rid of King Edward VIII; they executed Charles I. We are given to not letting the Monarch succeed in the way that hereditary principle determines.

There are so many differences in the hereditary monarchy: the Tudors went out of the window when the Stuarts came in; the Stuarts were then taken over by the Hanoverians, a small German state, and eventually Queen Victoria took over the Throne. So if there is a decision taken to do away with the monarchy, it won't be on the grounds that we've done away with the hereditary peerage.

Lord Thurlow It is quite easy to say: "If you don't have the hereditary principle anywhere else, do you really want to keep it in the head of state?" It's sort of logical, and so you shall hear more of that as time goes on.

Sir Adam Ridley I get slightly spooked if I see the press beginning to articulate the possibility in such a manner as to make one suspect that a little ball is being rolled down the hill here.

I look on the whole thing with a bit of trepidation, actually. And I've always felt that all the obvious things that have been said about it—all the obvious criticisms—have been correct: it's very damaging, and very dangerous, to launch on a process whose ultimate destination hasn't been sketched out, let alone agreed.

Sir Bernard Ingham It's a perfectly reasonable interpretation: if you are seeking to kill the hereditary system for peers, then, by simple process of logic, you are sooner or later going to acquire the appetite to kill the hereditary monarchy. The Queen was probably rather disconcerted by the Labour peers saying: "Here, here."

It does raise serious questions about the logic of the Lords' reform, whether indeed it is a stalking horse—as it's often seen—or whether it is just a plain, straightforward spasm of the class war which will burn itself out after a time.

But the point is, it will have established a very considerable precedent. And, in the future, if you get a mildly revolutionary government, they will see the precedent as not having really been so broad, and they could act. We shall have to watch it. It is a very uncomfortable precedent.

Philip Ziegler I don't believe that the Queen sees it as being a cause for great distress. And certainly she doesn't feel in any way that it reflects on her position.

And if it does, I can't see, really, that the fact that they don't want hereditary legislators has got anything to do with whether the government does not want a constitutional, hereditary monarchy. I don't believe it personally weakens her position at all.

Sir Edward Ford It's difficult to say, really, whether it will have much effect. But, of course, an awful lot of our institutions are still dependent largely on a sort of survival of the feudal setup. A lot of peers would never have done what they have done, or done their public service, had they not been peers. They would have gone into the City, or become estate agents, or whatever. The fact of the peerage imposes obligations of a political nature on them, which they have accepted.

So it is a change in the structure of the state. If you take away the peers and their role as voters, and then merely make them like the French court, they've got no real status—nobody expects the Comte de Chambrun in France to do anything, except, possibly, live in an old castle.

It's rather a pity that you had this body of people who, on the whole, did feel that they had a public role to fulfill. And that is going to go. So they are losing something.

SCOTTISH DEVOLUTION

The emotion-charged issue of Scottish devolution has its roots in the Act of Union of 1707, in which England and Scotland agreed to a shared flag and Parliament, with Scotland retaining its own Church and legal system.

In 1885, the Scottish Office, a government ministry, was established in Edinburgh and the post of secretary for Scotland was created. And only three years later, in 1888, debate began in the House of Commons on its first motion proposing Home Rule for Scotland.

The move toward devolution accelerated in the twentieth century, with the founding in 1933 of the Scottish National Party (SNP), and the winning of its first two parliamentary seats in 1945.

Following the discovery of oil in 1969 off the Scottish coast, the SNP campaigned using the slogan: "It's Scotland's oil," and in 1973, a Royal Commission recommended devolution for Scotland and Wales.

More than two decades later, following the holding of a referendum, as well as Acts of Parliament, elections were held in 1999 for the establishment of a Scottish Parliament, which opened officially on July 1 of that year.

* * *

Sir Malcolm Rifkind We had the first debate over devolution back in the late 1970s. There was a referendum then. The Queen made quite an important intervention. She didn't take sides in the argument— you wouldn't expect her to—but she made a speech which was widely reported, saying: "I never forget that when I became Queen, I became Queen of the United Kingdom."

It was basically a speech saying that what shape the United Kingdom takes is for Parliament to decide, not for a constitutional Monarch to determine. But she was saying: "I believe in the United Kingdom and I hope people will continue to share that view." And it had quite an impact at the time. The Monarch was performing a proper constitutional Monarch's role: to advise, to encourage, to warn, and was doing it in a very acceptable way.

Inevitably, if you're going through an unprecedented period of constitutional change, I should imagine, not just the Queen, you're all slightly nervous as to what is going to be the consequence of a process.

So I have no doubt that the monarchy was concerned. But they have a particular opportunity to influence in a positive way these developments. In the case of Scotland and England, it was a King of Scotland who became King of England. Scotland was never conquered; it's not like Ireland, or Wales. It wasn't forcibly absorbed into England. It was a treaty of union between two Parliaments a hundred years after the Scottish King became King of England.

So that has given the Royal Family a particular acceptability in Scotland, because they are descended from the Stuart dynasty, which was itself a Scottish dynasty.

Margaret Ewing The Queen had her Silver Jubilee in 1977 and she addressed the plenary of all the Members of Parliament in Westminster Hall—and Westminster Hall is of course where Sir William Wallace, Braveheart,[2] was condemned, hanged, and drawn and quartered. And she sat there with all of the panoply of the Jubilee around her and said: "I will never forget that I was crowned Queen of the United Kingdom."

And that caused a huge reaction, and that was probably one of the first times where I actively questioned the monarchy because the monarchy is supposed to be separate from politics and her deliberate statement was made, which has undermined the cause of devolution at that particular stage in Scotland, and indeed in Wales. And that has been a significant factor in—not to say that I dislike her, but it certainly altered my constitutional vision of where the Royal Family should be.

Theoretically she said it for herself. But one wonders: Who were the advisers? Was she speaking for the government? Was it a deliberate undermining of the democratic political forces?

And one leader, from the Western Isles, one of the most mild-mannered, decent, lovely people that one could ever hope to meet in one's life, and I remember that day so well, was interviewed by the press and he said: "If I have to choose between the monarchy and an independent republic, I will choose the republic."

And this was not a man who was by any manner or means in the mode of a Ken Livingstone,[3] or anything like that; this was a man who was a staunch member of the Scottish Presbyterian Church. But it obviously struck something within him—and struck in many of us—and it didn't change the Party's policy, but it made us a lot more skeptical about whether the Queen was always going to be objective, as one would have expected.

Lady Young What is happening is terribly serious. We are witnessing the break-up of the United Kingdom. And although no one thinks that the Scots really want to go independent, we have created a situation in which we've stirred up Scottish nationalism.

The Scots have always made a major contribution to British life—one never thinks of people as being particularly Scottish. Now the English, who are eighty-five percent of the population, are going to be split up into regions. The outcome would be that the United Kingdom would be reduced practically to what it was a thousand years ago: just a number of small kingdoms.

Today the wheel will have turned full circle. It's a most dreadful prospect for the country. The British people haven't woken up to this. It's difficult enough to hold your own in the world as a small country, as we are, *united*. But to be weakened by being separated will mean a weakening of our voice, particularly in the world and, also, a new turning inward upon ourselves, an unhealthy thing to do.

The Scots now have seventy-one M.P.s sitting in Westminster, deciding what the English shall do. Whereas we, the English, have no influence on Scottish affairs. It's a recipe for disaster.

THE QUEEN OPENS PARLIAMENT IN PLAIN CLOTHES

When on July 1, 1999, the Queen opened Scotland's first Parliament in 292 years, in its temporary quarters in the Church of Scotland Assembly Hall, calling that occasion the dawn of "a new constitutional age," and carefully emphasizing Scotland's role within the United Kingdom, she did so in day dress, rather than the elaborate ceremonial robes she wears for the State Opening of Parliament at Westminster.

The Queen was addressed by the presiding officer, Lord [David] Steel, on that historic occasion as the "Queen of Scots," the first Monarch to be so addressed since 1707, when, in the pre-union style, the Scottish Sovereign had taken the title from the people and not the land.

* * *

Sir Malcolm Rifkind The Queen very rarely wears state robes. She wore them for her Coronation, and she wears them once a year, for the State Opening of Parliament.

It is a particularly sensitive question in Scotland because on her visit to Scotland in 1953, she wore ordinary day dress at a special ceremony in St. Giles Cathedral, and there was a lot of criticism at that time: when the Queen is in London she wears state robes; she comes to Edinburgh and she wears an ordinary dress. This is not showing suitable dignity.

When the ceremony was being prepared [for the July 1, 1999, Opening of the Scottish Parliament], the government decided they wanted it to be a modern ceremony, not too traditional, and they didn't want it just to be a copy of what happens in London. The Crown was not to be worn. So there was no controversy on this occasion that the Queen did not wear formal robes. She actually had on a very beautiful dress in the colors of the thistle—green and purple—and it was thought to be just right.

Margaret Ewing One of the things that was agreed was that the so-called National Anthem would not be played within the confines of the Scottish Parliament. It was a very clear decision by the elected members from all the parties that they should not be seen to have pomp and circumstance.

I think she performed extremely well. The beautiful part, because none of us were quite sure—we'd all been marched up and down and around, and we got to our seats and were waiting for the arrival of the Queen—so when she eventually arrived we didn't know what we were supposed to do because we didn't have clear instructions.

The worst moment was when this woman, the lady-in-waiting, stood, glittering, and dressed in all the livery, the strange garb that these people wear. It was a real kind of "Miss Jean Brodie" face.

And the doors opened, and the fanfare started, and we were all sitting there, waiting. And her face was like a picture, and it was incredible just watching her pass. The Queen, I think, was very determined to make it a very happy, family-type day.

Lord Younger The ceremonial side is understandable—and a bit tempo-rary: the Scots are not natural admirers of overblown pomp; the Scotsman rather tends to think of himself as good as anyone else.

Having said that, nobody likes ceremony really more than a Scot—the streets of Edinburgh were lined with Scots of all sorts; they *loved* it. But if you asked them, they would be rather sort of half-hearted about it.

I do think it's temporary because, in the first go at a Scottish Parliament, they were terribly anxious to express the fact that it was different, that it wasn't as pompous as what they would see the London events were: it had to be different.

But, I'm sure that they will tend from now on to want it to be more and more prestigious, and I expect that there will be more soldiers, and more Household Cavalry, and all that, in the years to come. It'll settle down.

Adm. Sir Henry Leach Whatever the advice may have been, I believe it was a great mistake that the Queen attended the opening of the Parliament in Edinburgh dressed in plain clothes. I believe she should have been in full fig [dazzling array].

I think this is a pity, it puts the unfortunate Queen in an almost impossible position because she's trying to be perceived as not totally on an enormously high pedestal, but approachable, and a normal human being, on the one hand, and yet on occasion—not all occasions, but occasions of great ceremony such as that, national ceremony—you've *got* to be on a pedestal, because that's what it's all about, otherwise you don't have a ceremony. And, therefore, you dress accordingly.

IS DEVOLUTION A THREAT TO THE MONARCHY?

Canon Paul Oestreicher I don't believe it is. It could have a potentially positive effect in that the Scots, who don't like the English but still like the Queen, and the Welsh, who don't like the English, still like the Queen.

In other words, if Britain becomes a federal state and is no longer a unitary state ruled from London—the Scots ruling themselves; and the Northern Irish ruling themselves; and the Welsh ruling themselves, with their own Parliaments—the Queen could be the symbolic tie among them all, because you need some things in common.

So if Britain became a federal monarchy, rather than a unitary monarchy, that would give the Royal Household a new function: to hold these nation-states together. They now all have their own Parliaments, but she is formally the head of all of those Parliaments.

Winston Churchill Mr. Blair disingenuously says that what he has put in place will keep the kingdom united. I fear that the opposite is the case.

Without being a United Kingdom there was no way that we could have stood up against Hitler; there was no way that we as a people could punch above our weight in NATO, in the councils of the world. If we had been divided, almost certainly we would have been invaded by Hitler.

And even though the Scots are only about 5.5 million, about ten percent of the United Kingdom population, they are, nonetheless, a very significant part: the prime minister's Scottish, the Chancellor of the Exchequer's Scottish, the Lord Chancellor's Scottish, Mr. Cook [Foreign Secretary] is Scottish.

And if there was one Englishman who was appointed to a position in Scotland, there would be an uproar. We accept it as completely natural that the Scots should come down here and kick us around.

It remains to be seen whether the United Kingdom can survive this process. I believe it would be tragic [if it didn't]. It really would be the end of what my grandfather called "our island story."

Lord Healey In a way it strengthens the monarchy because the monarchy will be a symbol of the unity of the state as a whole, and, therefore, a little bit more important. It becomes more important than the Parliament in Westminster then, as a symbol of the unity of the United Kingdom.

Lady Mar My ancestor was responsible for bribing the Scottish nobility, the lairds, into signing the Act of Union.

Margaret Thatcher said that Scotland was an accident, and that's been the attitude of the English government for a long time. Wait and see: they may be knocking on the door and saying: "Can we come back?" But I don't think so.

* * *

In a conversation with New York City's former mayor Michael Bloomberg, David Cameron said that the Queen had "purred" when she spoke to him following the no vote in the Scottish independence referendum in 2014. The Scottish National Party continues to push for a second referendum.

* * *

Lord Heseltine I can only assume that Her Majesty is the Queen of the *United* Kingdom and that she would be extremely upset that the historic achievement would be fractured, as would I.

Sir Bernard Ingham, interviewed 2021 Scottish nationalism is an unknown quantity as some people do not know what they stand for, other than their independence from the English, distinct from independence from the European Union. I just posed twenty questions on the issue in my *Yorkshire Post* column; the Scots want independence and yet subservience. How daft can you *get*?

I suppose that if the Scots vote for a referendum, so will the Welsh nationalists. But they have always been more pragmatic than the Scots. At least some of them are currently showing an interest in independence.

PART SIX

The Future of the Monarchy

CHAPTER 27

The Heir Apparent:
Who *Is* He?

ARCHDEACON GEORGE AUSTIN I've met him. He isn't easy to talk to. The difficulty is that one moment he's happy for you to talk to him as an equal. But if you forget for a moment that in his view you're not an equal, then you're out. There's a line. And you can never really assume anything.

He has the difficulty of his upbringing: he will tend to talk to courtiers because he knows how to, but he finds it difficult to talk to *us*.

Rabbi Sidney Brichto I have a very good relationship with him and I feel closer to him because he is younger. He's basically a decent fellow.

Those Camilla tapes are incredible. If he can be so desperately in love with Camilla, he's a human being. But it *is* hard to believe that this person could have expressed himself in such imagery [the Tampax quote]. Could he be the same person who could be haughty and aloof from the general community?

Stephen Day He *longs* to be useful: he's been given all these privileges; he sees people around him achieving great things.

I believe he feels an enormous sympathy for lack of privilege—a real sense of the thought that he's had all these advantages and he's been given wealth and, therefore, he should give something back to them, encourage them, help them—use the powers that he has of securing donations, mobilizing people, cheering them up.

In that world where he's going daily, he realized that there is this enormous voluntary sector of people who do things voluntarily, and the need to pat them on the back, and say: "Good on you."

Adnan Khashoggi Prince Charles sponsored a charity for the handicapped, and I contributed to it so I met him in Monte Carlo. He was very charming, and very funny. People say that he's stiff. That's not true. When you sit down with him, he's a very sweet man. I was teasing him at that time to marry [Princess] Caroline [of Monaco], because she wasn't married then.

There was depth, substance, and knowledge. He was a little bit quiet in a crowd, but he was very eloquent. And he has a sense of humor. It's not loud, but it's there.

Nelson Mandela I went to a suburb of London with Prince Charles where he has got some projects. He was so popular that people just brushed me aside in order to shake hands with him. And we were so overwhelmed that the police had to be called to rescue us from the crowd, and we had to go to a police station to get our people sorted out and come and escort us back to the center of London.

He is a man of the people and I think he will do very well. We saw the Spice Girls together: "Hello, Charles! Hello, Nelson!" And they started to do all sorts of things, and Charles didn't object at all. And later he said: "Well, these Spice Girls left us bruised!" He will make a good Monarch.

Imogen Campbell-Johnson He has a lovely sense of humor. When my eldest granddaughter, Vickie, [...] was first starting her architecture studies in 1992, in Rome, we were celebrating the bicentenary of Shelley's[1] birth, and Charles came to a great evening which was given at Catherine de Medici's childhood home twenty miles outside Rome. And I had the chance, just as Vickie was starting her university architecture studies, of presenting her to the Prince.

Then [...] at the European Academy here, Prince Charles was at an evening, and I was able to tell him that Vickie had passed her first-class honors, and also that she'd passed the state exam. And he laughed and said: "A *real* architect!"

Michael Deaver Prince Charles came to see the president in May 1981, after he was shot. Their meeting was in the Oval Office, and there were Filipino stewards, petty officers in the U.S. Navy, serving coffee or tea. Prince Charles asked for tea. But to my horror, they served him a cup with a tea bag in it. And he never touched it.

When we left and we were going back down the colonnade to go back to his car, I said: "I am terribly sorry about the tea bag; the steward is not used to brewing a pot of tea."

And he looked at me and said: "Oh, is *that* what that was?"

PRINCE CHARLES'S INTEREST IN ISSUES

Stephen Day He developed an intense interest in the Arab world and Islam. He came and stayed with me in Tunisia, where I did a deal with him: he was totally incognito. He walked around as a tourist, in an open-neck shirt, and painted; he walked through the Old City in the evening; he was never recognized by anybody.

[On a visit to the Middle East later on, during the Prince's marriage to Princess Diana] we left Muscat and we had to kill time before flying on to Qatar, so we stopped along the coast for an impromptu picnic and swim.

The Prince saw a fort in the distance, a couple of miles away, and said: "Let's go and have a walk along the beach and I will paint it." I knew that two people had been murdered along that coast a couple of years before, but I thought it was all right.

Six of us walked off—the Princess went back to *Britannia*—to this fort and saw that it was actually a small fishing village, with some trees, and all the old men were sitting around with their fishing boats. They couldn't see *Britannia*, which was around the corner.

We sort of came in off the moon, as we were speaking English, and we sat down, and I interpreted for them. They actually thought we were fishermen. They put up with us, and we drank coffee, and we had dates, and we chatted with them. And then he went off and painted—the painting he did is in one of his books.

It was a wonderful afternoon, an absolutely magnificent afternoon, because he saw original Arabia, absolutely untouched, exactly as it would have been a hundred, or two hundred years beforehand—how they sat around; how the headman orchestrated the discussion; the friendship with Britain.

The elders of the village could have been briefed by a great director because when he discovered we were British, he [the headman] said: "Ah, Britain, *you my man*"—just like that. He had no *idea* who we were—the Prince of Wales loved it.

That led on to a series of things because I was briefing him on how Saudi Arabia worked, and I said: "What you saw in that village is actually how the kingdom works: the elder sits there with his people ..."

There is what they call a *majlis*, which is a way they sit and conduct discussions after dinner, semi-formally. It is a very, very effective way of discussing and taking a decision: the aim is to tease out all the views, and the chairman, the boss, decides. It's not our way of doing it, but it works. I tried to explain to Prince Charles how it works.

In Bahrain, we got them to do one for him. And he was terribly pleased with that, and thought he'd do one at Buckingham Palace when he got back.

S. A. Pasha I was invited to a lecture he gave at Oxford University. I heard his speech and from that I gathered that the man has some close attachment to Islam.

It was a very historic speech. He said that Islam has contributed so much to Western civilization and that the presence of the Muslim community is a bridge of understanding between this country and the Muslim world. And then I met him also at the reception. He was very polite, very friendly, very forthcoming.

I've met him many times. He opened the mosque in Northolt. He wore a Muslim headgear. It looked very nice. The point is that this country has got now some very close relationships with Muslim countries, particularly the relationship with Saudi Arabia—they are very close. And it's not just emotional; it's economic links. There is a lot of benefit to this country by this close association with Muslim countries.

I invited him to our annual dinner to celebrate the birthday of our Holy Prophet, Mohammed. I said: "Why don't you come and be our chief guest?" And he replied: "*Inshalla*" [God willing]. I was very happy that he knows some Arabic words. He didn't come.

Lord Archer He's an eccentric man; it will serve him well with some people, and will be a detriment with others. He's immensely sincere, he's immensely decent. He's a good man, a kind man. He's a well-educated, well-informed man. And along with that come some interesting views, not fully understood by those even around him.

Winston Churchill He has his problems in his private life. Don't we all? But he is a wonderful human being. He isn't a bloated buffoon— somebody who just goes about his own pleasures; who doesn't care. He cares *deeply* and he does so much through his charities; there's hardly a strand of British public life that he is not involved with, whether it's the farming community, or the armed forces. And he's dived on submarines; he's parachuted with airborne forces; he's served in the Royal Navy; he's commanded his own ship.

He is to me a wholly admirable person. And of course there's nobody who is perfect, who satisfies everybody's requirements, and it's easy to snipe. But I think he will make a first-class Sovereign.

Lord Glentoran Charles has always been interested in architecture. And why shouldn't he be? He lives in some of the finest, lovely places, and spends a lot of time, and is very conscious of the environment in which he lives and he inherited.

I'm not sure that he's not on dangerous ground getting involved in [the argument over] genetically modified crops[2] because some say their argument is scientifically sound but others would say his is. He could end up with egg on his face if he starts to go too far down that route, and he needs to be advised.

Robert Davies A lot of these things are linked—organic farming, respect for land, the environment, sustainable communities and planning. In his view, they're all part of the same thing. It's an approach to life—sustainability, respect for others, respect for the spiritual side of life, the natural balance.

When he started off—he inherited a large estate through being the Duke of Cornwall—he decided that he would like to break from the past. He felt, eventually, that he ought to be committed to organic principles—he ought to put it into practice. But when he started, people said: "He must be completely dotty, with these ideas."

But now in this country, organic produce is at a premium; throughout Europe, organic produce is making more money than conventional produce. It has now been shown that more money has had to be spent on conventional farming.

The man who was considered to be slightly dotty and mad, and off-beam, and marginal, by the whole farming lobby, the government, and everyone, is now seen as being part of the mainstream. The fact is, he was just ahead of his time on this.

Everybody laughed when he came out with ideas about developing his own village, Poundbury [in Dorset]. Now the absolute mainstream in, certainly, British planning are adopting these ideas as their planning guidelines.

I remember the change. We worked with the Prince on that. And eventually the government adopted the basics of his thesis on urban villages as the basis for a new planning regime in 1994.

Lord Ouseley As early as the mid-1980s, the Prince of Wales was saying: "Why do I never see black faces among the guards at the Royal Household, or in the Household Cavalry?" He championed that cause.

When I arrived at the Commission for Racial Equality, we eventually met and the Prince of Wales expressed his concerns to officials in the armed services, and he pushed hard to get them to realize there was a problem, and that they had to do something, so I gained a better understanding of how the monarchy and those associated with it were making a contribution.

Brig. Johnny Rickett I know him well. Anybody who knows him would agree that he is actually a human, humble, understanding, interested in what you're doing-type person. He's done so much for the underprivileged, those who need help—the Prince's Trust sort of thing.

I know that he feels desperately frustrated. I believe, frankly, that he hasn't been able to have his way at things.

Michael Noakes This particular project that we're doing started because of Prince Charles. In the 1980s, he said one day: "In Victorian times, artists very often traveled round with the Royal Family. Would you find it useful to sit in when I'm doing something for the Duchy of Cornwall, or with my private secretary?"

And I did that a couple of times. And from that, really, grew the idea that we should do a year in his life. We contacted Vivien's agent and she was beginning to mention it to publishers, and it was all arranged.

And a single phone call came through from Edward Adeane, who at that time was his private secretary, aborting it without an explanation, very apologetic: "I'm very sorry, I'm afraid I've got to say that we can't go ahead." I did meet him at some function and he said: "I'm sorry about that." But, again, there was no explanation.

Our later realization was that when this young woman joined him as his wife, he didn't keep her informed, and I believe that when it came to this book that we were going to do with him, she said: "You didn't ask me; I don't want these people hanging around. No!" So it lay dormant for a long time.

Lord Carrington To me, he's just a boy. If you look at what is possible for a member of the Royal Family, particularly for the heir to the Throne, there are certain things he *can't* do: he can't get mixed up in politics— King Edward got mixed up in politics and got into terrible trouble in the very short time he was King.

Prince Charles has occupied himself in architecture and organic farming. If you take his architectural views—I don't happen to agree— the fact is that he's done a great service; people look at things in a way that has made them more aware of their surroundings, because he said that.

Nobody automatically inherits respect; you do it by earning it, as the Queen has done. He has, like his mother, duty and obligation.

Donald Macdonald As a Canadian in Britain who was observing this, whoever counseled Prince Charles to pick up certain issues and speak as an authority on them did him a disservice because eventually he puts himself up against professionals on these issues—architecture, for example.

He was present at the ceremonial opening of a very tall building in Canary Wharf and he offered the opinion to the group standing around that, of course, his preference was for three-story buildings from the age of Queen Anne.

And the architect turned half away from him and made the aside: "How fortunate that His Royal Highness wasn't responsible for anything when the great English cathedrals were being constructed."

He obviously got advice to do this. I believe it's a mistake: leave the business of pros to pros, and don't appear to be criticizing them because, while people can't correct or contradict him, on the other hand, if he's plainly wrong, we'll know that and it doesn't win him respect. You don't have to take him seriously.

They are put on a very difficult tightrope because, on the one hand, they've all got to maintain their balance as they go across on that particular rope, but also, people are suggesting: you've got to do some interesting and different things while you're up there.

And the trouble is, if you start doing juggling acts and so on, you're going to lose your balance on the rope itself. So I believe that to espouse some controversial issues, to put him in a position where he has to take a stand on all of them, is unfair.

Michael Noakes You must feel that your best years are beginning to slip by, and that you could do things. I remember him saying once, during a sitting: "Why do people think that of me? I didn't ask for this." He was good natured about it, but he gets sick of people implying that he was loony.

Sir Kenneth Bloomfield His involvement in work for younger people, like the Prince's Trust, is extraordinary.

I was the chairman of an organization called Children in Need. The BBC raises and distributes through a big, televised appeal something like £20 million a year. I had been invited to dinner at Highgrove because we had given money to, amongst others, the Prince's Trust.

Most of the other people were big businessmen who'd contributed lots of money. What was fascinating was that the exception to this was a young girl from Liverpool, who had been assisted by the trust to set herself up, ultimately, in business as a photographer.

His ability to show empathy for people like that is greatly underestimated and really quite remarkable. I would have no doubt that he cares a lot about people and he really does care, some would say, almost too much.

Sir Bernard Ingham Prince Charles is a thinking person's monarchy link, if you like: he is interested in ideas; he's interested in tradition, which is best expressed through his approach to architecture and the rural society. He's a thinker—although a lot of people decry his intelligence, but they would, wouldn't they?

Thank God we've got somebody concerned up there, because they don't exactly *have* to be concerned, do they? I mean, they love shooting; they can go shooting.

* * *

During a visit of the Chinese president Jiang Zemin to London, in the fall of 1999, Prince Charles demonstrated his displeasure with the Chinese regime by refusing to attend a dinner hosted by the president in honor of the Queen.

* * *

Fr. Michael Seed Prince Charles refuses to meet him and chooses to meet the Dalai Lama, which I think is splendid. Prince Charles by doing that insulted the prime minister and the Queen!

Robert Lacey It was constitutionally mistaken on his part to do that. But I also believe that it was another well-understood custom in this area of the constitution that the heir to the Throne has a little more latitude because the day will come when he, or she, will have no latitude at all.

But it's an issue one can debate about Prince Charles: he strikes these attitudes on such matters as genetically modified food, and modern architecture, and that sort of thing, and it gains him some personal popularity, but it's a very double-edged sword. And it's a reminder of the paradox that these people are human at the end of the day.

GIVEN HIS OUTSPOKENNESS, WOULD HE BE
FRUSTRATED AS KING?

Brig. Johnny Rickett It would certainly confine him. But they are moving forward now. We're in an open age, with instant communications. And because he's obviously made so many of his views well-known, I'm quite certain that he would stick to them. But I would think he'd probably have to button up a bit.

Lady Pamela Hicks My husband[3] hated the word "compromise" because to any creative person "compromise" is a wicked word. But to the average person going on with life, comprise is the stuff of life, isn't it?

And I suppose Prince Charles as King will bring a lot of his enthusiasm and new ideas. He will, eventually, when it becomes his responsibility, probably bring a lot of fresh air to it. But at the same time, he inevitably will realize that in his position—and I'm sure he realizes now—if he were Sovereign, he would not be free to speak in ways that his government would not be comfortable with.

Lord Armstrong I'm sure that he would be the first to agree that if and when he becomes the King, he will have to act constitutionally; he will have to act on the advice of his ministers. And I have no doubt he would be very willing to accept that.

But until that time—unless and until he becomes the King—he is a degree freer to take an interest, to express an interest, to express opinions on these subjects. And more power to him.

I dare say there will be differences in the way he talks to people. But I don't know that he would do it in his own style, in his own way. But I'm sure that he would be no less conscious of his duties—his constitutional role and duty.

I believe that when he turned out to deliver the King's Speech, he'd be wearing his crown, his robe, and all that stuff. And he would deliver the speech with the same poker-faced immobility with which the Queen does it now.

Ian Adams I suspect he may be a more talkative Monarch than we've had before, and be prepared to speak out on various things. He's got a good precedent in Prince Albert, who was in a much more difficult position because he was only the consort and not King, but who, nevertheless, really succeeded in imposing his views in a great many useful ways.

I rather suspect that Prince Charles might actually find his *métier* in something of the same sort that Albert did.

Robert Lacey I don't think the monarchy will evolve. It's clearly understood—not least by Prince Charles himself—that when he becomes King all this will end. And just as, as Prince of Wales, he does not have sight of all sorts of state documents, that means he feels himself freer to behave in this sort of way.

It is said to be a certain source of grievance to Prince Charles that his mother doesn't give him more access to state documents, and things like that.

Therefore, maybe he feels consciously, or subconsciously, that if he's not going to be trusted with the state documents, why should he have to toe the constitutional line? But I have no doubt that he well understands that when he becomes King he has to absolutely toe the line.

These people are puppets—sacred puppets—and that means by definition that the strings are pulled by the people ultimately. I always say that the crucial date in the history of the modern Royal Family was 1649, when, of course, we cut off the head of Charles I and we then invited his son back on our own terms.

Sir Kenneth Bloomfield [...] He's a person of great merit. And I like the fact that he has passionate interests of his own. Now, he has to be careful about those because there's a line over which royals shouldn't tread in our country, lest they step on the toes of government.

Sir Malcolm Rifkind I believe we're incredibly fortunate to have him as Prince of Wales. Some people take a different view on that, but I've got to know him reasonably well over the years.

When it comes to playing the role of Sovereign, there may be aspects of his personality which may prove controversial. But I believe he has total commitment to the interests of the country; he has no desire to interfere in party politics; he will scrupulously observe the role of the Sovereign; he will introduce some modern elements to the monarchy so that it will be a bit easier for him than for the Queen.

I would expect the Queen to progressively hand over her functions to the Prince of Wales. She would remain Queen; he would remain Prince of Wales. But on a day-to-day basis, he would do most of the things that she currently does. In terms of dealing with all the state papers, going on state visits, traveling round the country, doing hundreds of functions, the Prince of Wales will do all that. But he won't become King till she dies.

Lord McNally If Charles proves as idiosyncratic a Monarch as he does as a Prince, he would have difficulties.

The Queen, constitutionally, has set the ground rules for a modern monarchy. And they are very limited, indeed; no government would welcome an opinionated and an initiative-taking King Charles; he would very quickly, regardless of the government's political complexion, run into trouble if he started to press his own agenda—whether it be on the environment, or social issues, or anything else. That's not the job of the Monarch.

There is certainly the job description, and a responsibility to advise the prime minister of the day from the experience that comes with the job. But it's not to go public, and the Queen has been extremely successful in keeping her views to herself, both domestically and in the Commonwealth, and playing very strictly to the rules.

For the institution to survive, that's exactly what Charles would have to do: constitutionally, he has to stick to the rules; and behaviorally, he mustn't flaunt the privilege that, obviously, comes with the job.

* * *

ON HER MAJESTY'S PASSING, WHAT WILL
CAMILLA'S ROLE BE?

On April 9, 2005, Prince Charles married his long-time companion Camilla Parker Bowles in a civil ceremony taking place at Windsor Guildhall. In an eerie coincidence, Prince Philip would die on that day sixteen years later. While the nuptials had been scheduled to occur on April 8, they were put forward one day to enable the Prince to represent the Queen at the funeral of Pope John Paul II.

Her Majesty was not present at the ceremony but attended the official blessing at St. George's Chapel offered by the Archbishop of Canterbury, Dr. Rowan Williams, and hosted a reception where, in an allusion to the Grand National horse race, she commented: "They have overcome Becher's Brook and The Chair and all kinds of terrible obstacles. They have come through and I'm very proud and wish them well. My son is home and dry with the woman he loves."

Camilla, who in deference to the late Princess Diana has eschewed the title "Princess of Wales" although eligible to do so, will likely become known as Princess rather than Queen Consort upon her husband's accession to the Throne.

* * *

Lord King; interviewed here 2021 There are some in the Commonwealth who are upset with Charles's being divorced. The Queen, too, was upset, speaking at the time of the year of the break-up of Charles and Diana's marriage as her *"annus horribilis."*

Camilla's role is as it has been ever since she married Prince Charles: she has done extremely well and is a source of great support to him. Obviously, there are going to be issues, but at this moment, we are on a steadier path with William and Catherine; they represent a very good standard of family life.

Lord Butler She might be called "The Queen Consort" but it has not been decided what formal title she will be given. She is performing skillfully and modestly, and is a moral supporter of her husband.

DOES CHARLES REALLY WANT TO BE KING?

Philip Ziegler Poor chap. I think he asks himself the same question. He knows perfectly well that once he is Monarch he will not be able to tease architects, or make remarks about organic vegetables, or air all his various hobby horses.

I believe that he regrets this because he has a lot of fun as Prince of Wales, in spite of the obvious difficulties and pains of the situation. And I believe he feels he is performing as a kind of licensed gadfly. I believe he's performing quite a useful role.

People who say that he is fretting impatiently have got it completely wrong: it's the last thing he wants to do. I believe he'd be delighted if the Queen were to last another fifteen years [so far she has lasted another twenty-two]. That would leave him freed up to pursue his own interests.

I think he will regret very much giving them up. But I think he will: he is a man of great responsibility, and I believe he will, regretfully, follow sort of like Henry V—put Falstaff to one side and concentrate on the boring business of opening Parliament, and that sort of thing.

[...]

Robert Davies He doesn't have any choice in the matter. He accepts the position. And whatever circumstances bring, he will rise to it.

I have no evidence that he sits around thinking: I'm looking forward to it. Nor would I have any sense that he sits around thinking: Goodness me, that will restrict my movement. He lives his life in the way that he gets fulfillment in what he's doing.

Sir Peter Estlin Prince Charles is already indicating that there will be changes during his reign.

While he is outspoken about architecture and the environment, his opinions humanize the heir apparent.

One might argue that while Charles has been ahead of his time, if you examine previous eras, there have been significant periods of upheaval not specifically due to the monarchy.

Lady Featherstone I do not think that he will go wild as he has become more circumspect the older he has become.

Lord Howard Prince Charles will not want to change the fact that he will be Head of the Church of England although he has always taken an interest in the work of the Council of Christians and Jews, of which I am a member, and in Islam.

Lady Featherstone Prince Charles is very supportive of our Jewish community.

He even has his own kippah, or yarmulka, with the royal feathers on it and he visited my reform synagogue during the celebration of our 175th anniversary, which was a great occasion; we had a Thursday morning Torah reading for him.

Lord Desai Having observed Prince Charles four or five times, I believe he is very serious but, in my view, will not have a gravitas as his reign will not be one of seventy years.

Lady Greenfield There could, to a certain extent, be changes for Charles as he will have his own style. He knows that he will be king and that he will be moving into a different world.

I have only met with Charles once or twice and have seen him at work, supporting women in science.

It is good that he clearly cares about the environment, which he has been saying for a long time, way before doing so was fashionable. I believe that his interest would be more in ecology and climate change than in the hard sciences.

But as he does not have the people's affection nor do the people have empathy with him as they do with his mother, it will be different for *King Charles*.

Lord Blunkett Speaking obviously at quite a distance, it is not the case that one must have no views—one would well die of boredom if one had ideas and was not interested in what was going on.

Two members of the Royal Family, Prince Charles and Prince Edward's wife, Sophie, the Duchess of Wessex, have shown a great interest in education, a subject of great interest to me, she quietly doing a lot of good, while Charles actually does the most, holding seminars and trying to engage people in debate, such as at sessions he set up at his country estate at Highgrove, almost mischievously trying to get participants to air their views.

Lord Butler Charles has mellowed—in some respects, he is like his father, the late Duke of Edinburgh, who also had strong opinions but restricted them to matters not coming into conflict with the elected government's. Taking advice given by the elected government, *King Charles* would always be expected to put his own interests second.

As for his having stated his intention to be "defender of faiths," he was seeking to emphasize that he would be the Monarch of a multireligious society despite his formal position in relation to the Church of England as Defender of *the* Faith.

Donald McKinnon While Charles has had his ups and downs as Prince of Wales, I believe he will be a better king as he will have guidance from his senior officials and will also have witnessed how his mother operated, and how that made her very popular.

On the other hand, however, he is also *his father's* son.

Lord King; interviewed 2021 Having been the Prince of Wales for fifty years, the heir apparent has had great preparation, including taking on increasing responsibilities, such as accompanying Her Majesty to the Opening of Parliament, whereas Prince Philip used to be beside her, traveling, and greeting many visitors, including presidents and prime ministers.

On becoming King, Charles will carry on much as he has been doing. Having had the freedom as Prince of Wales to express his own opinions, he will obviously not become a Trappist monk. But, of course, he will not be critical of his government, although he will maintain his views, on climate change, for example.

That is a slight worry due to his so-called black spider letters (handwritten and so-called as his penmanship is spidery in nature). He has been writing to the prime minister and politicians, and people were taken aback that a person from the Royal Family should so express his views. This issue is important for the Royal Family as they are "The Dignified" and the government is "The Efficient." The two must be complementary but *separate*; you must have a neutral body that rises above individual actions and arguments. Otherwise, you might as well just have a president.

Lord Steel I do not believe that Her Majesty will resign but will turn more and more things over to Charles. I believe that she meant the vow made when in South Africa as a girl that her life, whether long or short, would be dedicated to her duty. But I do believe that she will slow down just due to her age.

Lord Butler He certainly will not have as long a reign as his mother is having, so he won't be setting a record in that respect. It is rather sad for him in many ways as he will only succeed to the Crown when at a very advanced age.

BEYOND CHARLES: IS PRINCE WILLIAM THE HOPE FOR THE MONARCHY?

Robert Lacey It was commonly feared during the breakdown of the marriage of Charles and Diana that these traumatic events would erode William's stability in all sorts of ways. And, to date, it looks as if the reverse is the case—that it's hardened him, toughened him, that he's capable of taking a detached view of his mother without downgrading in any sense his love and affection for her memory.

It's pretty well established that on the first anniversary of her death, it was William—he was then sixteen years old—who personally insisted on a statement being issued, in the name of himself and Harry after the anniversary, thanking people for their mourning and their shared sympathy, but saying it was now time to move on, and to look forward.[4]

There was no sense in which that could have come from Charles; it must have come from William. And we can see his mother in this; we can see his mother in his very strong feelings about the press, and not being afraid to speak his mind.

He was the person who was the one to tell us as a nation to move on, and he's the one who is perfectly happy for his father to move on in the changed circumstances.

Sir Kenneth Bloomfield If, unhappily, something were to happen to the Queen, I've no doubt that the constitution would take its course, and Charles would be proclaimed King from St. James's Palace, and the whole thing would roll ahead: he would be invested with the kind of magic and authority of the position. And he would have the chance to show, perhaps even more clearly, the sort of person he is.

Here is a man who actually does want to do good things in the country. And I can't see him actually being willing to step aside; I'd be amazed if he were. His whole life has been an apprenticeship to do this—imagine being an apprentice all those years, all those decades, and then saying: "Well, perhaps I shouldn't do the job at all." I can't see any good reason why he should say that.

And also, frankly, to plunge a very young man, which almost certainly William would be, into these terribly burdensome responsibilities, I'd say: "For goodness sake, let the young guy enjoy life before they put all these fetters on him."

Sir Bernard Ingham, interviewed 2021 Prince Charles has had the longest apprenticeship to accession of any heir. While I believe that he is an alarmist regarding the environment, we ought to be pleased that an heir to the Throne *does* actually take life seriously.

Prince Charles's stepping down in favor of William—this notion is part of some people's antipathy toward the heir—would neither do the monarchy *nor William* any good, whatsoever.

Lord Steel The idea that Charles will be a stopgap King is not fair at all, because he is a very serious, committed person.

Although sometimes ridiculed as being a bit odd, I do not think he is. I have always liked him and believe he is very straightforward despite having a bad press heretofore.

In a recent interview with the BBC, the Prince made it quite clear that his role as King will be quite different from that as Prince of Wales—that he could say things in that position that he will not be able to as King.

CHAPTER 28

Queen Elizabeth II's Legacy and the Future of the Monarchy

FEBRUARY 6, 1992, the fortieth anniversary of the accession of Elizabeth II to the Throne, was not celebrated as had been the Queen's Silver Jubilee in 1977. By November of that year, the Queen, looking and sounding exhausted as she addressed an anniversary gathering at London's Guildhall, in a rare departure from her usual formality, confided that: "1992 is not a year on which I shall look back with undiluted pleasure. In the words of one of my more sympathetic correspondents, it has turned out to be an *annus horribilis*."

The year had begun badly for the monarchy with the publication in January of photographs of the Duchess of York on holiday with Steve Wyatt, a wealthy American, to be followed in August by even more shocking photographs of the Princess with another American, her toe-kissing "financial adviser" John Bryan. Then in February Princess Diana was photographed alone at the Taj Mahal during a visit with Prince Charles to India, emphasizing the Waleses' marital problems.

In June, Princess Diana upped the ante in advertising the failure of her relationship with the heir apparent with the serialization by the *Sunday Times* of Andrew Morton's *Diana: Her True Story*, revealing such details as having thrown herself down a staircase at Sandringham in 1981, while pregnant, and having slashed her wrists in desperate bids for attention from her husband.

Following the media feeding frenzy that had begun with *Diana: Her True Story*, another newspaper, the *Sun*, released the "Squidgygate" tape, in which Princess Diana was openly critical of the Royal Family. That was followed in November by the release of the "Camillagate" tape, in which the heir apparent yearned to be a Tampax inside his married lover's body.

The Queen herself came under siege, when in August it was reported that she was considering paying income tax in the future and was attacked for creating a smokescreen to obscure the marital problems of her two elder sons, when in reality the subject had been under discussion for some time.

Then, on November 20, a fire broke out in the private chapel of Windsor Castle, heavily damaging the state dining room, as well as three drawing rooms, and causing several sections of the Castle's roof to collapse.

The Queen, Prince Andrew reported from the scene of the still-smoldering fire, was "shocked and devastated," as she observed the firefighting efforts to save the Castle.

Emotions aroused over the fire would give way to a firestorm, however, when it was announced by Heritage Secretary Peter Brooke that, as the Castle had not been insured, the government would pay for its repair at an estimated cost of between £20 million and £40 million.

* * *

Claire Rayner Some idiotic Tory politician said on television: "Well, of course the nation will pay for the rebuilding of Windsor." And *I* said: "No we bloody well won't!" I would have gone to the gallows to fight that. Why the hell should we have to pay when people are sleeping on the streets? And that reaction went right across the country.

Raymond G. H. Seitz The government got way out of hand. This didn't go down well, and they picked up on that very quickly at the Palace, and that then led to the question of the Queen making a contribution.

So they've been aware that they're a little out of sync, and that adjustments have to be made. But there are two things: they recognize that the monarchy has gone on for hundreds and hundreds of years, and you don't adjust it to public opinion.

That's a very tough decision to hold in this world, when public opinion appears to guide everything, whether it's our politics in Washington, or in London. You don't want to respond to a fad; there's great resistance to that.

Sir Edward Ford This was the fortieth year [of the Queen's reign] and I simply wrote an ordinary letter, in my own hand, to Robert Fellowes, the Queen's private secretary, saying how sorry I was that the year had turned out to be an *annus horribilis*.

Well, he was taken by this in some way and showed it to the Queen, who said: "I'll use that in my speech at the Guildhall." But she hadn't asked for it. Nor had I indeed any thought of trying to provide material for what she should say. In any case, I had no right to do so. But she just took it up.

Lady Young She had a very bad cold when she was speaking; she looked unwell. She is a human being. She undoubtedly suffered. I can't believe for one moment that she would be other than unhappy—for her poor grandchildren, apart from anything else.

Bishop Michael Mann There was a sense of: What should I have done? What haven't I done? There was a sense of anguish. But much more a sense of disappointment, and compassion. She's not the sort of person who's going to say: "I told you so." She's the sort of person who's going to say: "Now how do we make this a better situation than it is at the minute?"

* * *

According to a MORI poll of 1,004 adults taken in July 2000, the British Royal Family was more popular then than at any time in the preceding decade.

Among the poll's conclusions were that seventy-one percent of respondents approved of the way the Queen performs her duties, fifty-five percent thought the Royal Family to be out of touch with British life, and sixty-four percent did not wish the family to receive as much money as it does.

The July poll was conducted in the wake of cabinet secretary Mo Mowlam's suggestion in June 2000 that the Royal Family should move out of Buckingham Palace.

In a series of polls taken in June 2000, prior to Mowlam's statement, with the highest support for the monarchy found in the fifty-five and older age group, eighty-nine percent of respondents wanted to retain the monarchy; seventy-two percent predicted that the monarchy would still exist thirty to forty years hence; and sixty-four percent were against the Queen's abdication.

And according to a poll commissioned by the *Mail* on July 2, 2000, 75 percent of respondents supported the Royal Family's remaining in the Palace, downgrading their approval rating of Mowlam from sixty percent to forty-nine percent.

There was obviously relief at the Palace as Prince Andrew, in a rare interview with the BBC, said of the respondents: "That's very kind of them. It's extremely good news."

* * *

Lady Mar You've got a whole lot of people at the moment—and I'm certainly one of them—who regard the monarchy as something that will hold us together. So, obviously, I am not in the minority of people who will say: "Get rid of the monarchy! They really don't serve any purpose."

Lord Glentoran There is a much higher regard for *this* Monarch than for the rest of the Royal Family.

We're very conservative as a nation—not in the political sense—and there is still a tremendous sense of pride and comfort going from the sovereignty situation, and that is supported by the fact of the honors—the various orders, the MBEs, and the OBEs—people just *love* that, down the line.

There are people all over the place who have done great work. When they get an honor of some sort, all their friends and family are really thrilled. In fact, everybody wants to go to Buckingham Place to see the Queen because she's still there.

Claire Rayner I find it anachronistic that we should have anything like an inherited head of state. It seems to me ludicrous that you should be able to *inherit* a job. We have so many things in this country that are wrong that flow because we have an hereditary monarchy: we have an unelected Upper House [of Parliament] which includes the bishops, because we have an established religion in this country, which is anathema to me. But you can't get rid of the House of Lords until you get rid of the hereditary monarchy.

Thomas Keneally I was visiting an English friend, a judge of the Queen's Bench, for the wedding of his daughter and I had a driver coming to pick me up from the publishers in London and we were all eating the leftovers in the living room on a Sunday, when he turned up.

I made the terrible mistake of bringing him into the living room—you wouldn't [have a problem with this] in Sydney because a man who owns his own limo is someone to be reckoned—he has that wonderful thing most writers don't have, cash flow.

But my friend intercepted him and said: "Is anything a problem?" And I could then see that the driver was embarrassed too. He had said: "Are you sure?" But I thought he meant: Are you sure there's enough food? I didn't think he meant: Are you sure I'm to go in here?

And I said: "I thought we all might be able to have a sandwich before driving back to London ..." And my friend said: "Ah, yes. Certainly. Come with me." And he took him right through, by a back way, to the kitchen, and sat him down, and told cook to look after him.

If he'd had that done to me, I would say: "Shove your sandwich up your ass." And most Australians would have. But it was quite normal for an English driver to accept such leavings at the table.

That stuff appalls me. And one of the functions of the Queen is to represent a pyramid of privilege in the United Kingdom. It's a pyramid of privilege which still bedevils the United Kingdom and it is a structure which should be removed for the good of the society.

IS THE MONARCHY AN ECONOMIC ASSET TO THE UNITED KINGDOM?

Sir Michael Oswald Their role as patrons of the [equine] sport is very important and has had an enormous effect on it. [...]

Robert Davies Clearly their presence in visiting things around the world does create good will: it creates good will for Britain; it creates good will for people who are able to use channels of good will for Britain.

The Prince of Wales's visit to a particular place has triggered off things for good, but I don't think it has been particularly good for Britain, or for goods. I'm sure that for Burberry raincoats—he opened their shop in Boston in 1986—that was helpful. But there's a limit: he wasn't willing to be shown with a coat, or wearing it. It was much more down-key.

What the Prince of Wales, in particular, brings is a sense of balancing the social dimension with the economic: he has gone on record as saying that a headlong dash for growth in the world won't bring us quality of life; you've got to be sensitive to the impact on things like society and culture.

Lord Archer It's important because of tourism, and because of the deals we can achieve by inviting people to Buckingham Palace for tea, who are more excited by that than by being invited to the Elysée Palace. And Buckingham Palace would have a greater aura than the White House, which is trampled over by people every day as part of their democracy.

Claire Rayner No intelligent tourist actually thinks they are going to *meet* the royals: John Doe, in Duluth, doesn't say: "Let's go to London and see the Queen." They might say: "Let's go to London and see the palaces, the Tower, the history." The European palace that gets the most visitors per annum is Versailles, and *they* haven't had a Royal Family for many generations.

Margaret Ewing I must admit coming past Buckingham Palace regularly on the way to work I am very conscious of a huge amount of tourists.

But then if you go to Moscow you'll see people taking photographs of where the Tsar and the Tsarina lived because it's just that it's interesting, architecturally, to have been there.

Lord Rees I wouldn't like to put the case for it purely on economic grounds: it's the core of our public life. Their value to business is one of the pluses. But a lot of republican compatriots would, no doubt, dwell on the expense of the monarchy.

Sir Adam Ridley The benefit of things royal is very substantial. And I can't see that the relatively tiny sums which the Queen enjoys in the Civil List [now the Sovereign Grant] amount to more than a drop in the ocean.

And if it is seen as an investment, it's a phenomenally *good* investment. And it's seen as a reward for hard work and benefit. I personally think it's a very inadequate reward.

Peter Jay The monarchy is not about the economy. I don't believe that the monarchy has more than the incidental impact. That's not what it's for, and that's not what it ought to be for.

While, no doubt, it can re-enforce—and does re-enforce—particular trade missions, and trade events, and some business may be done on the back of this, as a percentage of the total trade, or the GNP, it's not important.

IS THE ROYAL FAMILY HELPFUL TO CHARITABLE CAUSES?

Lord Ouseley I was surprised and pleased to learn of my knighthood. Yet I wasn't certain that I wanted to accept it because I didn't know how some people would react.

When I mentioned the possibility of receiving a knighthood to people I wanted to sound out—on a hypothetical basis—they were very keen that I should take it. Indeed, when the official announcement was made, it was amazing how many people in my local community began to knock on my door and ask my help for their organizations. That is exactly what some people had said to me when I raised the issue, that is: "We want to make use of it."

I suddenly realized, as never before, how status-conscious Britain is—I was getting calls from people I had been trying to meet with for months. The important thing to me was that the use of my name was bringing benefit to the community.

My understanding of the role of the monarchy became clearer as I grew older. Largely through the Prince of Wales—I chair one of the committees of the Prince's Trust and am involved with his aspirations—I've become more involved in interacting with bits of the monarchy because of some of the high-profile activities I've been involved in and seeing the way in which they have interacted within the charitable world in which I am also engaged.

I have seen how they help raise the profile of charities, and how they help raise funds, so I have a better appreciation of some of the things they do which often go unheralded.

Lord Blunkett Because I cannot see, I have, obviously, been involved for many years with the Royal National Institute for the Blind. The royals have been very helpful and involved regarding learning disabilities which in the past was neglected, like cerebral palsy.

Michael Whitlam There are three types of charities. Those which have a royal charter, like the Royal National Institute for the Deaf, are enabled to have certain privileges.

It's nice to have the royal charter; from a marketing point of view it gives credibility to the organization, which a lot of charities don't have.

The second group of charities are those that have members of the Royal Family as patrons or presidents. From my experience of the last twenty-five years or so—and all the charity directors I know—we all want, and find having a royal patron very helpful.

DIMINISHED RESPECT FOR THE MONARCH
AND THE MONARCHY

Lady Mar We all used to stand up for the National Anthem; I can remember standing up in my sitting room when I had the wireless on! When it came on the radio, you stood up, regardless! But not anymore. The American president receives more respect for the American National Anthem.

For an example of what has happened to our National Anthem, there was an event in Edinburgh, and they had a brass band, and it sounded awful. The Queen had not been told about the brass band beforehand and you could see on her face that it was appalling.

Lord Powell I can't think of any other country where they play the National Anthem in the cinema. I don't expect them to play "The Star-Spangled Banner" anytime I go to a cinema in the United States.

Bishop Michael Mann Just now I went to the Post Office to get some stamps and there was a lady there who had just bought some stamps, and she said to her husband: "Oh, I've stuck the Queen's head on upside down. Do you think that matters?" He said: "No. Go ahead and put it in [the post box]." Well, when I was a boy, that *would* have mattered.

Lord Rees There certainly is a degree of less respect, but generally it's that the tone of life, regrettably—deference and formal good manners—has been on the decline for a few decades.

It hasn't gone completely though. When I'm in London I go to the morning service at the Guards Chapel. At the service, you will always have one of the bands of one of the Guards regiments. And there you would find the picket officer, the duty officer, if not in full dress, at least in a scarlet tunic and that kind of thing. And we always finished the service with "God Save the Queen."

Archdeacon George Austin Prince Charles goes to visit a factory and they let him play with a machine and they're asked afterwards: "How did he do?" They say: "Oh, wonderfully; he would have made a good mechanic." It's absolute nonsense! But they've lived with that all their lives—that they're wonderful—and it's not surprising that they think they are. And the deference must have an effect on them.

I believe people are very much less [deferential] now [...] Some of the royals would be offended, but I believe they will have to accept it.

There was a story in the newspaper the other day about one of the minor duchesses, the Duchess of Gloucester. She came down early one day and passed a maid who was holding a pile of clean linen and the maid said: "Good morning, Your Highness," and she said: "Haven't you forgotten something?" And the maid said: "I'm sorry, I don't think so." And the Duchess said: "You forgot to curtsy." If it had been me I'd have thrown the lot across the floor. It's the age we live in. Why should we treat them like that?

THE MYSTERY OF THE MONARCHY VERSUS
MORE ACCESSIBILITY

Raymond G. H. Seitz There was recognition that there needed to be adjustment, that it should be gradual. It was given tremendous impetus by the breakdown of the second generation, and the role of the press, and the sense that everything was just going wrong. A lot of ridicule and, of course, this poisonous thing between Charles and Diana—all that stuff just going on and on.

That tended to crystalize a lot of the opinion, which I don't think was hostile to the Queen. But there was the feeling—very much stimulated by the media as well—that this is a cold institution.

Lord McNally It's difficult to know whether the monarchy's attempt to popularize itself has taken the magic off, or that the magic was going anyway and it just needed a different response.

Charles, Anne, Andrew, and Edward were the first generation of royals that had to grow up under an intense, and irreverent, media spotlight [...] But at a time when the country was becoming more meritocratic, there was less support for what was clearly a privileged elite, living a very privileged life—and, therefore, not a lot of sympathy.

Some of the attempts to popularize royalty—and what some people think of as a landmark—was *It's a Knockout*, which lost the magic. I believe that people still want a certain dignity from their royalty; they don't want them as a kind of cabaret act.

That, of course, is the great success of the Queen, amidst all the turbulence that has been going on around her. It's been said that if the Windsors lived on a council estate, they would have been treated as a dysfunctional family and have a host of social workers supporting them.

But despite the fact that you could list the problems of the children, and the peccadilloes of the husband, the Queen has sailed through it with still a very high esteem for her.

Canon Paul Oestreicher I made only one contribution to an attempt to change the monarchy: I wrote to the Queen's private secretary—you don't write to the Queen; you write to her private secretary; this is part of the mystique—and I said:

> In this country sixty-five institutions carry the title "Her Majesty's Prison." In these institutions, a large number of people work, and a large number of people are held captive. As you enter each prison, there is a large notice which says: "Her Majesty's Prison …"
>
> These prisoners are all doing their time in "Her Majesty's Prisons." What is publicly known at the moment is that the staffs of these prisons are deeply demoralized because their pay is bad; their conditions of work are not good; there are not enough prisons—they're all overcrowded; it is making for bad treatment of prisoners; and it has demoralized the staff to a considerable extent.
>
> Would it not help the morale of prison service people, and also the dignity of those who are imprisoned, if from time to time, Your Majesty worshipped God, together with prisoners and prison staff, in a prison chapel?

I made the suggestion about two or three years ago [in 1996 or 1997]. She has never done it. I got a very polite letter from her private secretary saying this was a very good suggestion, which was being taken very seriously, that it would be discussed at all sorts of levels.

* * *

Since then, in 2014, the Queen has visited Crumlin Road Gaol in Belfast. Prince Charles, Princess Anne and the Duchess of Cambridge have also made visits to Her Majesty's Prisons.

* * *

Sir Adam Ridley In the early days of really ruthless television interviewing, people were beginning to think: You've got to show that Mr. X is a man of the people—that he can peel a potato, or take the kids to school.

It culminated, I remember, in a very extreme way, when Mrs. Thatcher was just about to be elected and she was interviewed with her apron on, working in the kitchen, for heaven's sake!

This is absolutely nutty. It is *insane*! You're appealing in entirely the wrong way. Happily, it was not a sustained part of the projection of her image.

But analogous things that have happened since made me realize more and more that if you wish to create an image, you must preserve a lot of mystique.

Lord Powell We don't want bicycling monarchs here, as we have on the continent: I never want to see the Queen peddle a bicycle around the Mall; I wouldn't like to see the Queen washing up; and I would not like to see the Queen going out to the launderette. That would be absurd; that would rob the institution of its value.

Much depends on presenting a certain mystique. I myself dislike anything that seems to make the monarchy trendy, or going too far towards putting it in the hands of spin doctors and other people who want to give it a popular tinge. That doesn't mean that I am against any modernization of the monarchy. It does mean not going into any "cool Britannia" antics, which some people favor. The Queen has to be somewhat on a pedestal, otherwise the institution doesn't work.

Bishop Michael Mann I personally put a question mark as to whether it has been wise to be so available and open to the public as the Royal Family has become.

Maybe it has been inevitable and couldn't have been stopped. But it's a bit like worship in the Church of England: the powers that be have been so concerned with becoming relevant—opening things so that they could be understood—that I really begin to ponder if we haven't replaced "God All Mighty" with "God All Matey."

There is an essential part of spiritual worship and an essential part of the monarchy that is a sense of awe and a sense of mystery. And if you reduce the monarchy to "the kitchen sink," then eventually you're going to destroy it.

Sir Edward Ford It would be much better if the monarchy still remained rather mysterious. All the time that I was there we were not trying, particularly, to promote the Monarch as a person. We were trying, in arranging what she did in her speeches and in her visits, to bring her more closely to the people.

Charles said that somebody invented the "walkabout." Well, actually it was going on all the time; it wasn't an invention. It was the thing that we were constantly arranging in the course of visits to small, provincial places in this country, and going and having tea in somebody's cottage.

You don't need spin doctors for that. Nowadays, having a person there to promote the thing makes it almost a little bit artificial, to my mind. It was taking place quietly, and I think you can overdo it. You don't want to get into a position where any accident that happens, the Queen has got to be there the next day with flowers, and so on.

It sounds rather rude to say, but I have a feeling it's going to burden the future monarchy an awful lot if gestures are without spontaneousness, almost forced. You don't want a puppet Monarch; the whole thing is that their public actions should be spontaneous. That's what I'm frightened of with the spin doctors—that they will make these things become too routine, and too common.

Raymond G. H. Seitz I happened to be sitting next to the Queen the day before she opened her web site, at a dinner, and she was very tickled by this; she thought it was the equivalent maybe of when her grandmother had first driven a car—a little wild, a little racy, a little unmonarchical, but sort of fun, too. Again, with that little bit of humor you see in her from time to time.

Michael Parker We'd come from the Navy, with the very latest of equipment all around us, and used to it. We set up Clarence House for their home [in 1947] and we put everything we could think of in that, and we were going on merrily until the King died.

Then we moved to the Palace, which was like going into an antique shop, you know. But the media have made much of this point, rather too much. We didn't go through the whole place and rip it apart.

What we did do was put in those things that would be constructive and useful. For example, if the King, or the Queen, wanted to see someone, she'd ring them up, or send a footman to go and get them. He'd have to go all the way there, upstairs and round about, find out what it was, go back and do it.

We thought: well why not just press a button and talk to the person in question? And the Princess was very keen about those sorts of things, too. But she was of another generation.

I put in an answering machine in my office the year the King died—it was the first answering machine in the United Kingdom, really. It nearly sent the bureaucrats nuts. I had some incredibly funny reactions to the answering machine. Being an Australian, coming into this atmosphere,

I nearly killed myself laughing. The girls would say: "Quick, come listen to *this*."

Lady Mar That mystery was destroyed when the television came in the 1960s. The mystery is gone. You need something you're not quite sure about. Once you know exactly how something works, you don't have respect for it.

It can't come back. Is it a loss? Yes.

Lady Greenfield It is said that when the Queen decided in the late 1960s to allow a documentary firm to film the Royal family, that letting light into their mystique was a mistake. There would no longer be the magic surrounding the monarchy.

As for giving interviews, the Queen has a right *not* to do so as the mystique of the royals is in our not knowing them as individuals, to understand what they do, what they represent, but to know them not as individuals but as *symbols*.

Sir Bernard Ingham, interviewed 2021 I do not believe that the Queen's job has changed all that much, nor do I think that the attitude of most people toward the monarchy has changed today.

I do become a bit worried, however, concerning the sheer hypocrisy of those who are against Prince Charles because he married Camilla. Bearing in mind the divorce rate in Britain today, this is disgraceful!

Lord Steel The monarchy has on the whole moved with developments, basically and socially, here in the United Kingdom. Despite her age, the Queen accepts that things change and adapts very easily.

Lord Desai Her Majesty has obviously adapted to the modern media and has done so beautifully. As English monarchs go, you would have to search far and wide for a better one. Everything has changed during her lifetime and she has coped with dignity, and that is quite remarkable.

Sir Bernard Ingham, interviewed 2021 Frankly, I do not go along with all this nonsense. I have nothing to do with Netflix—lots of my generation don't either—and I believe that we pay too much attention to the idiots of the world, those who spend their time blasting off, quite often libelously, on the Internet rather than simply getting on with life and doing good.

And I do not watch *The Crown* as I don't believe that it adds much to our human knowledge, but adds to the sum total of distortion about the monarchy.

Lord Blunkett This institution has survived in Britain because it is seen as an established part of the constitution, avoiding the necessity of having an elected president and thus being above the political fray.

There is a very great tension in many respects in the policy agenda as opposed to the personalities of what is now referred to as "The Royal Family" and they have managed to walk that tightrope of the twenty-four hour a day, seven days a week news cycle, but with great difficulty.

Lady Greenfield People respect Her Majesty because she shows great determination and resilience, being a survivor of all sorts of horrors, from the war to her sister's causing a public outcry over her love affair with Peter Townsend to some of her children being divorced, and, of course, the death of the Princess of Wales.

Within three days of her husband's death, she was resuming her duties again, including, amazingly, being publicly vaccinated [against COVID-19] to persuade others to do so.

Lord Cholmondeley; interviewed 2021 Given Prince Philip's not being well when he came out of hospital, the Queen had actually prepared for this moment.

Having said when she would return to her duties, she would do exactly that, and pretty quickly, including the Opening of Parliament, accompanied by Prince Charles.

Her Majesty has a very strong spirit.

Lord Desai While the Royals tried to be as equal as possible, they are *not* equal and that is why we are all wanting to meet them; it is like fans meeting a *star*. And they are trying to put us at ease, saying: "It doesn't matter; we are ordinary people who just happen to be the Monarch."

Lord Cholmondeley It is good that for the monarchy to be more accessible—to be open and available, to appear in different ways, as Her Majesty does, appearing on television, but not too much.

Lord Butler It is a remarkable achievement that Her Majesty can be approachable and pleasant but always maintain her dignity.

The Crown is now having to adapt to a changing world and while some will say that the institution of the monarchy is *still* out of touch, they are adapting to modern circumstances, and that is a remarkable achievement.

There is a paradox, however, in that while the British public is proud that the Royal Family do ceremonial events so well, of which Prince Philip's funeral is a wonderful example, at the same time, they don't wish to see money wasted on what they would describe as "extravagances."

This is a very difficult balance for the Royal Family to maintain, one that Charles, as King, will want to maintain.

THE TROUBLE WITH HARRY

On May 19, 2018, Prince Harry and the American actress Meghan Markle, who had met on a blind date two years previously, married at St. George's Chapel, Windsor. During a controversial 2021 television interview with Oprah Winfrey, however, the couple revealed that they had been married three days earlier by the Archbishop of Canterbury in the garden of their residence.

Upon their marriage they were titled Their Royal Highnesses, The Duke and Duchess of Sussex. Less than two years later Harry and Meghan announced their plan to step down as senior members of the Royal Family, dividing their time between the United Kingdom and North America, with the aim of becoming financially independent.

Prince Harry did not remain in the United Kingdom for the Monarch's ninety-fifth birthday on April 21, 2021.

Now the parents of Archibald Harrison Mountbatten-Windsor and Lilibet Diana, they have apparently achieved their goal after establishing a multimedia production company. While it is difficult to fully comprehend the reasons for Harry and Meghan's decision, they did discuss in their Oprah interview Harry's tense relationship with Prince Charles as well as Meghan's unease over perceived racial animosity within royal circles.

Although Harry and Meghan retain their respective titles of Duke and Duchess, they will no longer be allowed to be designated as Royal Highnesses. In addition, they have relinquished their honorary military appointments and royal patronages.

* * *

Patrick Jephson An interview with Oprah is purpose enough in itself and it is where the line between entertainment and royalty gets blurred that problems arise. A screen actress having an interview with Oprah is no big deal; a Prince who is sixth in line to the British Throne is no big deal!

One wonders: What are Harry and Meghan going to do next?

Baroness Rabbi Neuberger It is not considered a good thing in this country to go on Oprah and do as you like—not *at all*! The British "stiff upper lip" exists for a reason!

I believe that the Royal Family is absolutely getting a bad rap from Meghan and Harry as its senior members work extremely hard.

Lord Heseltine I believe that in a short time the Harry/Meghan interview in the U.S. will pass almost unnoticed.

While it is a real event, those anticipating long-term damage to Her Majesty and the monarchy do not really understand the strength surrounding the Queen and the institution, that it is something that one witnesses and feels.

Lord Blunkett There was no evidence produced that there could have been any kind of conversation that was misinterpreted.

Lady Greenfield Harry and Meghan complained when terrible things had happened to others. You do not complain; you just make *do*. That Oprah interview was such a horror!

Bishop Nicholas Baines I would be careful about making such a judgment as Harry has a lot of support here because of having witnessed what happened to his mother and being that young boy walking behind his mother's coffin in public and now, as an ex-serviceman having drawn attention to the impact of mental health, telling it as it is.

A member of my staff who thinks that Meghan was trouble—that she stole Harry! That is an insult to him, as well as to Meghan. I believe that he was quite restrained, given some of the rhetoric of sheer racism abounding in this country, and he won't get protection from the media.

Lord Blunkett It is an age issue in Britain: if you talk with older people, they are overwhelmingly in favor of the Queen and very skeptical about why Meghan and Harry should not have *quietly* reached an agreement that they would step out, but without any public controversy; but when you speak with younger people, they are much more sympathetic with Meghan and Harry.

My own view is that there was some bad advice given by those surrounding the Royal Family in terms of when to respond and when *not* to, and my heart mostly goes out to the Queen in terms of thinking: Couldn't we just settle this thing quietly? Couldn't people just get on with their lives? If they don't want to be part of the Establishment, that is fine.

Lady Greenfield Historically, the Queen's role is not about airing one's laundry in public. Never once has she complained and that is why she is so respected.

That is why it is so upsetting for Prince Harry and Meghan Markle to talk as they did. This was not the time, when she had just lost her husband of many years, to bother the Queen with this problem.

There was, apparently, a meeting between Prince Harry, Prince William, and their father at the time of Prince Philip's funeral. We do not know what they said, nor should we *want* to know.

It must have been very upsetting to the Queen that during the Oprah interview, Prince Harry started talking about his relationship with his father, about his not taking his calls. This is not really *our* affair. After all, we are not the Kardashians; this is not something everybody has a front seat to.

The fact that more than two million viewers worldwide watched Prince Philip's funeral than did the Oprah interview says *a lot*.

Sir Bernard Ingham, interviewed 2021 I believe that Harry's motivation in going public was to earn money.

Quite frankly, the Royal family has two problems; they are called the Duke of York [for his purported tie to the late Jeffrey Epstein] and Prince Harry, both of whom are lacking in any judgment. This is a problem not only for the Royal Family, but for the United Kingdom.

As for the monarchy's being racist, this is one of the most idiotic assumptions ever made, bearing in mind that the Queen is head of the Commonwealth of fifty-three nations, comprised of people of all races, creeds, and colors, it is just daft that that somebody would wonder: What will the color of Harry and Meghan's child be? For heaven's sake!

Lord Desai This recent problem has, unfortunately, given the impression that the Royals are all racists. But I came to Britain in 1965 at the age of twenty-five and was well received.

Lord Steel While Prince Harry is the only member of the Royal Family whom I have never met, I can understand why he and his wife decided to set up on their own. While I believe theirs was a rash, perhaps even inconsiderate, decision, I wish them well.

Sir Peter Estlin I believe that the media will become bored with Harry and Meghan over time and that they will live as they wish to.

Lord Butler Prince Harry has chosen to live a different life, to step back from royal duties, and a lot of people have great compassion for him. I certainly have.

Sir David Haslam It is obvious that Prince Harry's comments about living in a "fishbowl" are bringing back memories of those dreadful photographs at the age of twelve walking behind his mother's coffin.

PRINCE WILLIAM AND THE DUCHESS OF CAMBRIDGE'S IMPORTANCE FOR THE MONARCHY'S FUTURE

Prince William, second in line to the British Throne, and Kate Middleton met in 2001 while studying art history at Scotland's St. Andrews University. As William would later recall: "When I first met Kate, I knew there was something special about her. I knew there was possibly something I wanted to explore there."

The couple married at Westminster Abbey on April 29, 2011, in the presence of 2,000 invited guests, including David Beckham and Elton John. The service was conducted by the dean of Westminster, the Very Reverend Dr. John Hall, and the marriage solemnized by Dr. Rowan Williams, the Archbishop of Canterbury.

In his wedding address, the Right Reverend Dr. Richard Chartres, the Bishop of London, advised the couple: "Be who God meant you to be and you will set the world on fire." Following the ceremony, Kate continued a tradition begun in 1923 by Lady Elizabeth Bowes-Lyon, who on her wedding to the then Duke of York placed her bouquet on the Abbey's tomb of the Unknown Soldier.

William and Kate are parents to Prince George, Princess Charlotte, and Prince Louis, third, fourth, and fifth, respectively, in the line of succession.

On the couple's eighth anniversary, the Queen, who has the sole authority to bestow honors of the Royal Victorian Order, created Kate a Dame Grand Cross of the order.

When, upon his father's accession, William becomes Prince of Wales, it is expected that Kate, now the Duchess of Cambridge, will in honor of Princess Diana assume the title of Princess of Wales.

* * *

Lady Greenfield Although Charles will take over on the Queen's passing, William is very important to the Royals and everybody looks to him, Kate, and their three children.

Currently, during the COVID crisis, William and Kate are through their zoom calls trying hard to identify with the public and have been very valuable in boosting morale.

Lady Featherstone He and Kate seem to be very modern and handling things very well.

While I am not really a monarchist, myself—I believe that it is a symbol of privilege—the monarchy does bring in a lot of money and I do not believe that this country will change.

I do believe that William and Kate will modernize the institution enough to find a new way and be less separate from their people.

WILL THE MONARCHY SURVIVE AFTER THE QUEEN'S DEATH?

Sir Bernard Ingham, interviewed 2021 Of course it will!

We are fortunate in having a Queen and if you seriously think that Great Britain would welcome *President* Tony Blair, Jeremy Corbyn, or David Cameron, of course they wouldn't!

And, of course, our monarchy is steeped in history, which is more than can be said of most republics.

I do not think, even with our preoccupation with the social media, that we do not give enough credit to the common sense of ordinary people, who want the monarchy to remain.

There *are* idiots, of course, but the majority would want to maintain the stability we have known for a long time.

Andrew Burnham I am not a born royalist in that I have a Catholic background with roots in Ireland, and my family was not staunchly monarchist.

I have always understood what the monarchy means to the British people, however. On becoming a Member of Parliament, I represented a formerly very working class, yet very traditional, mining area, thus I was aware of how much the people there support the Royal Family.

I developed strong respect for this and, therefore, in my dealings with the royals, I would represent the views of my constituency.

Secondly, as a minister I would be in contact with individual members of the Royal Family in ways I had never thought I would. This says something about their reach and in these fractious, polarizing times they are important as a uniting force for the nation and are still of value to people from all walks of life, thus I cannot foresee a day when Buckingham Palace will become something other than a royal residence. That will never happen in *my* lifetime.

HER MAJESTY, QUEEN ELIZABETH II'S LEGACY

On February 6, 2022, the Queen will become the first British Monarch to serve for seventy years. In celebration of this remarkable milestone, a year-long series of events will be conducted in the United Kingdom and in the Commonwealth nations. The main focus of the Queen's Platinum Jubilee will occur during the period June 2–5, featuring a birthday parade, a service of thanksgiving at St. Paul's Cathedral, the lighting of beacons in the United Kingdom as well as in Commonwealth capitals, street fairs uniting citizens in hundreds of communities, and a live concert from Buckingham Palace that will be broadcast throughout the world.

* * *

Canon Paul Oestreicher She is the most constitutionally perfect person you could imagine. She is just absolutely made for the office: she doesn't try to interfere; she is a symbolic figure; she obviously enjoys being Queen—she was brought up to it; she's deeply in the tradition; everybody respects her.

So as long as she's around, the monarchy is going to survive. Beyond that, it's a wide open question.

Lord Archer The monarchy is very solid. William is immensely popular. If he weren't, it could be a different situation. Charles is more popular than he was a year ago, and will become King, there is no question about that. And William will become King. [...]

The Queen will never stand down; it's not even worthy of discussion. The Queen is the Monarch; when she dies, we will have a new Monarch. End of discussion!

She will live to one hundred. Charles will naturally succeed, even if he is King for only ten minutes, unless the world changes completely, which it might in ten years. But as we stand here [in 1998], Charles will be King.

Lady Greenfield More than anybody else, she has put her duty absolutely before all else, having done so in extreme situations and, for this reason, she is respected by all.

Bishop Nicholas Baines She is the last vestige of honor, duty, service, and faithfulness in the face of the realities of today—our last link with the wartime generation and the British Empire.

Lord Cholmondeley A remarkable Queen, she has done so much for the Commonwealth.

I am sure that Prince Charles will be sustained by his memories of the activities Her Majesty took on.

Lord Blunkett She has sacrificed an enormous amount to maintain the Crown and its place in our constitutional monarchy.

Sir Bernard Ingham, interviewed 2021 If you want to define unparalleled devotion to duty, then you must look to Queen Elizabeth II. While you might say that she was born to it, the way she conducts herself is an inspiration to many. I believe that on becoming King, Prince Charles will have that sense of duty, as well.

Lord Butler Despite experiencing sadness at many points in her life, she soldiered on, with a sense of duty. People admire her for that, as I do.

Sir Peter Estlin A Monarch who has overseen a remarkable period in world history, she had the resilience to get back on her feet in a steadfast and constructive way.

Andrew Burnham In addition to her role in the Commonwealth, she had the capacity to hold together an at times fractious United Kingdom. Her life has been one of personal integrity beyond repute—truly remarkable in these days, when public figures are held to so much scrutiny.

Lady Featherstone There will be huge admiration for the fact that she adjusted her own desires in a life of serving her people, nation, and Commonwealth. She has done that really well.

Lord Steel After arriving in Nairobi [on Friday, February 1, 1953], Princess Elizabeth would visit the church of my father, the Very Reverend Dr. David Steel. A boy of fifteen at the time, I was present on that day; that was my first glimpse of Britain's future Monarch. [...] Her sense of duty had already been instilled and become very much a part of her own ethos.

Afterword

A S THE QUEEN approaches the seventieth anniversary of her accession to the Throne on February 6, 1952, following the sudden death of her beloved father, King George VI, she will likely look back with satisfaction upon her extraordinary tenure as Monarch, as well as anticipate the reigns of her son Charles, grandson William, and great-grandson George.

On the day that Princess Elizabeth became Queen, Great Britain continued to suffer the economic and societal aftershocks of world war. The nation was wracked by food and fuel shortages as well as labor unrest.

Further, the rapid breakdown of the colonial order following the war's end displaced thousands of citizens who had found both employment and status in bearing "the white man's burden."

Thus, it is not surprising that in the United Kingdom, as well as in the nascent Commonwealth of Nations, hope arose for a "New Elizabethan Age," one that during the attractive and youthful Monarch's reign would usher in prosperity while engendering renewed interest in, and allegiance to, a royal system often shrouded in a heretofore largely unfathomable mystique.

Thus, throughout her reign, the Queen has taken incremental steps in making the institution of the monarchy more publicly accessible. This process has in recent times been accelerated by advances in communication technology so that the royal website, along with social media, is supplementing personal appearance walkabouts and Her Majesty's annual Christmas broadcast.

And while the Queen, much to the consternation of a small army of royal media watchers, continues to decline interview requests, she has from time to time spoken out on specific events and topics, including televised statements concerning the death of Princess Diana and regarding the COVID pandemic.

This question arises: Will the copious personal diary she likely compiles one day become a posthumous memoir?

Surely, despite her constitutional limitation, as famously delineated by the journalist Walter Bagehot "to be consulted, to encourage and to warn," Queen Elizabeth has signaled opinions on specific subjects, as in her apparent opposition to Prime Minister Margaret Thatcher's views on South Africa's apartheid. Her views can also be detected regarding individuals she designates as Knights and Ladies of the Garter, and of the Thistle—honors solely in her province to bestow.

Many of the Queen's accomplishments are due to her more than seven-decades-long marriage to the late Prince Philip, a great-great-grandson of Queen Victoria. Queen Elizabeth's consort served with distinction as a combat officer during World War Two. As Duke of Edinburgh, he would be a full partner, joining with Her Majesty on state occasions, accompanying her on overseas travels, and maintaining his own schedule of events.

Having played a key role as the Queen's eyes and ears, a loyal confidant, and sounding board, while given to occasional episodes of boorish behavior, he will be remembered for his deep concern for young people, epitomized in his founding of an awards scheme that touched the lives of millions while demonstrating his humanity and vision.

The Queen, as the Earth's best known, and widely respected Monarch, has immense symbolic power. Nations within and outside the Commonwealth vie for her presence while presidents, prime ministers, and other notables from all walks of life treasure invitations to Buckingham Palace or other royal residences, delighting in the opportunity to bask in her celebrity.

That Her Majesty's life is one of immense privilege cannot be denied. As the Monarch, living and working in her palaces, she is surrounded by a retinue of senior advisers, personal aides, and retainers—Buckingham Palace has many hundreds of employees—all facilitating her personal and royal responsibilities. The Queen is wealthy, although her personal assets, estimated at $500 million, are dwarfed by those of an ever-increasing number of billionaires, numbering one hundred and seventy-one in the United Kingdom.

Those seeking an end to the monarchial system often cite its cost; others argue that the institution, as a result of tourism, trade promotion, and contributions to the media industry resulting from coverage of the Royal Family, brings hundreds of millions of pounds into the economies of Britain and the Commonwealth nations.

At this time, as Prince Charles is the Crown's most well-prepared heir in modern history, the future of the monarchy appears to be secure. The Prince will inherit an institution molded by the Queen's devotion to duty, an attribute that has enabled the monarchy to remain relevant and relatively unscathed.

One can only imagine what it must be like for Elizabeth II to summon the discipline required to peruse red boxes of official papers, meet with members of her government, as well as receive diplomats and other representatives of foreign nations, and host or attend a seemingly endless round of meetings and functions, all the while knowing that to each individual she must act the *Queen*, with all this entails, even her attire being scrutinized by a media only too eager to record any royal missteps.

At the same time, Her Majesty's personal life is complicated by the divorces—once anathema—of three of her children. In August 2021, a civil action against Prince Andrew was initiated in New York under that state's Child Victims Act by a woman claiming that he had engaged in sexual relations with her when she was age seventeen.

The Queen would endure additional anguish when Harry and Meghan, having left the United Kingdom (and its hostile press) to live in the United States, participated in that televised interview with Oprah Winfrey, criticizing members of the Royal Family, including Prince Charles, and leveling charges of racism against unnamed Palace insiders.

Harry, who as a result of the births of William's three children has dropped to ninth in the order of succession, making his accession to the Throne highly unlikely, can choose to be a long-term irritant, marring the reigns of both his father and brother. Or he and Meghan may settle into what, at least in the fiscal sense, will be hugely successful lives. Their choice is unknowable at this moment in time.

As King, Charles will bear the burden of succeeding Britain's longest-reigning Monarch, one widely admired for bridging the ever-widening gap between tradition and modernity.

Although he has enjoyed the opportunity of witnessing the manner in which his mother exercises her prerogatives, Charles will likely carve out new potentially controversial paths, having already signaled his interest in paring down the number of senior royals. And, as a Prince of Wales who communicates directly, at times forcefully, with the nation's political class, he may break new ground in how the monarchy interfaces with elected leadership.

While he surely knows how he will act, questions arise as to whether he will have the popular and institutional support necessary to implement change. His recent decision to retain the title "Defender of the Faith," as opposed to his earlier determination to be defender of *faiths*, suggests either his willingness to compromise or cautiousness born of experience as he moves toward occupying the Throne.

Now, at the age of seventy-five, seven years shy of the actuarial lifespan of a British male, his rule may be transitional, although the longevity of his maternal grandmother, as well as of his parents, suggests the possibility of a decades-long turn as Monarch.

However long Charles occupies the Throne, the future will belong to William.

Now forty years of age, he has observed the way in which his grandparents, Queen Elizabeth and the late Philip, conducted themselves.

Further, he will have the advantage of witnessing his father as Monarch. In the coming years, William, and Kate, the Duchess of Cambridge, both popular with the British public, will strengthen their royal profile in preparation for becoming King and Queen. Their accession will bring renewed luster to the institution, particularly if Charles's reign is marked by a pattern of eccentricity and controversy.

Whatever the future holds, history will record with great approbation that for at least seventy years Elizabeth Alexandra Mary Windsor played the cards dealt her with remarkably consistent devotion to the monarchy.

In so doing, she garnered the respect of not only the peoples of the United Kingdom and Commonwealth but of citizens of other nations who value stability and tradition while being open to positive societal change.

In a unique manner, these words of the British National Anthem are indeed fitting:

"Long to reign over us,
God save the Queen."

References

Chapter 1

1. An heiress—or heir—presumptive is the next in line to the Throne whose claim could be defeated by someone with a superior claim. At the time of her father's accession in 1936, the ten-year-old Princess Elizabeth became the heiress presumptive. Had a boy been born to King George VI and the then-Queen Elizabeth, however, that child, being the male heir, would have had the superior claim as heir apparent.

2. Successor in 1953 to Sir Alan Lascelles, who resigned his post as private secretary to the Queen following her Coronation.

3. George, Duke of Kent, Queen Mary and King George V's fourth son, was killed on August 24, 1942, at the age of thirty-nine, in a plane crash while en route to Iceland. His death, however, was not due to enemy action.

4. Known for the dignified tone of his voice.

5. Arundel Castle, the Norfolk family seat.

6. Canon Oestreicher was born in Germany in 1931. His family fled Nazi Germany in 1939, finding refuge in Dunedin, New Zealand. Canon Oestreicher joined the Anglican Church while living in New Zealand. He is now a Quaker.

7. King George VI had an almost life-long stammer, which he learned to control after undergoing treatment in the 1920s, when he was still the Duke of York, with an Australian speech therapist at the behest of the Duchess of York.

8. The King lay in state from February 11–15, 1952, and 305,806 mourners filed past his casket during that period.

9. As the supreme Allied commander during World War Two, General Eisenhower had become close to the Royal Family. He was elected president of the United States in November 1952.

10. In Queen Elizabeth's address to the opening session of the 1999 biennial CHOGM, held on November 12 in Durban, South Africa, she recalled that "it was in Kenya that word reached me of the death of my father, and of the responsibilities I then assumed as Queen and as head of the Commonwealth in 1952."

11. Once airborne again, the aircraft made numerous refueling stops, the onward journey from Entebbe taking twenty-four hours before the royal party finally landed at Heathrow.

Chapter 2

1. Stanley Baldwin (1867–1947).
2. Princess Adelaide of Saxe-Meiningen, who married the third son of King George III in 1818 after his long search for a wife. As William IV, he reigned from 1830–37.
3. George III is thought to have suffered from porphyria, an hereditary disorder.
4. Desmond Fitzgerald, who served as minister of external affairs of the Irish Free State (1922–27), and then as minister of defense (1927–32).
5. Mabel Fitzgerald, née McConnell.
6. The Earl of Harewood was sued for divorce in 1967 by his then-wife, the former Marion Stein. He later married Patricia Tuckwell, and Marion Stein married Jeremy Thorpe.
7. Diana Mitford was married to Sir Oswald Ernald Mosley, a British Fascist (1896–1980).
8. Ambassador Kaiser was a Rhodes Scholar at Oxford University during that period.
9. The large American management agency for the entertainment industry.
10. The night of November 9–10, 1938, when Nazi troops attacked Jewish communities throughout the Third Reich, murdering Jews, sending many of the survivors to concentration camps, and destroying synagogues and other Jewish community buildings, as well as Jewish-owned businesses and residences. The attack came to be known as Kristallnacht due to the masses of shattered glass resulting from the destruction.
11. Adolf Hitler's manifesto, written during his imprisonment following an attempted putsch at a Munich beer-hall on November 8, 1923, and published in 1925.
12. Princess Mary, the Princess Royal (1897–1965), the only daughter of King George V and Queen Mary.
13. Sir Harry Oakes, a Canadian millionaire whose fortune derived from gold mining. On July 8, 1943, his burned and beaten body was discovered in his home near Nassau. The Duke of Windsor attempted to embargo the news and then went over the heads of local law enforcement officials to invite an officer of the Miami, Florida, police force to fly to the Bahamas immediately to investigate the murder. In addition, the Duke assumed that the murder had been committed by Oakes's son-in-law, Alfred de Marigny, who had quarreled with Oakes and whom the Duke did not like. There was no evidence to support the Duke's belief and de Marigny was subsequently acquitted. The Duke of Windsor then avidly sought de Marigny's deportation, but he left the Bahamas of his own accord.
14. Governor-general of the Bahamas, 1968–72.

Chapter 3

1. On the evening of September 30, 1938, the British prime minister, Neville Chamberlain, landing in Britain at the Heston Aerodrome following the Munich talks, waved a piece of paper in the air and declared: "I believe it is peace for our time."
2. The Turkish peninsula between the Dardanelles and the Saros Gulf. Churchill was removed from his Admiralty position in May 1915, following the landing on the peninsula in late April of British, Australian, New Zealand, and French forces who sustained heavy casualties, being mowed down by enemy fire even as they emerged from their landing craft. On December 20 of that year, following months of fighting, with 25,000 dead, 76,000 wounded, and 13,000 missing in action, the British abandoned the Gallipoli campaign.
3. Scapa Flow, a sea basin in the Orkney Islands, located off northern Scotland.

Chapter 4

1. The Labour Party won 393 seats in Parliament, the Tory Party 213, the Liberal Party 12, and Independents 22.
2. Prince Philip was born in a royal residence on the Ionian isle of Corfu in June 1921. Within eighteen months, a Greek revolutionary court passed a death sentence on his father, Prince Andrew, and the family fled into exile.
3. Lord Louis Mountbatten, Prince Philip's uncle.
4. Lord Mountbatten's wife, the former Edwina Ashley, the daughter of Conservative M.P. Wilfred Ashley and the maternal granddaughter of Sir Ernest Cassel, a German-born Jewish banker who was a financial adviser to King Edward VII, died in February 1960.
5. Né Henry Stirling Nahun. Along with Cecil Beaton and Antony Armstrong-Jones, Baron was known as a "society photographer." The Thursday Club was a males-only eating and drinking club whose members often enjoyed racy stories and jokes.
6. Parliamentary under secretary of state, the War Office (1946–47).

Chapter 5

1. Prince Philip's Danish-derived family name was Schleswig-Holstein Sonderburg-Glucksburg.
2. Dowager Queen Mary died on March 24, 1953, at the age of eighty-six.
3. The recording of an intimate forty-minute conversation between Princess Diana and her friend James Gilbey on New Year's Eve 1989, which was made available to the British public by the *Sun* in 1992, the Queen's *annus horribilis*. The tape, allegedly recorded by a seventy-year-old retired bank manager, but likely the work of one with professional

taping equipment, was heard by more than 60,000 British people who paid a total of £100,000 to listen to the conversation.

4. Known also as a mouth organ.
5. Bishop Mann's son was killed while on active duty there.
6. The British impresario.
7. Baron Britten of Aldeburgh, 1913–76, composer of *Peter Grimes* (1945), *Billy Budd* (1951), *Death in Venice* (1973).
8. On the rainy, windy Coronation eve of Monday, June 1, 1953, as nearly half a million people already lined the Coronation procession route, news reached them that two climbers, New Zealander Edmund Hillary and Nepalese Sherpa Tenzing Norgay, members of a Commonwealth expedition, had reached the summit of Mount Everest, at five-and-a-half miles the highest peak in the world. There was an explosion of great rejoicing in the crowd. The excitement of the moment was captured by the *Daily Express* in a headline above a photograph of the crowd and a sketch of the Queen's Coronation robes: "All this and Everest too!"

Chapter 6

1. The Consort of Queen Juliana, one of Europe's so-called "bicycling monarchs" and, reportedly, one of the wealthiest monarchs in the world.
2. On his mother's side.
3. Julius Nyerere (1922–99) was prime minister of Tanganyika 1961–62; president 1963–4; and president of successor nation Tanzania 1964–85.
4. One-time London theatrical home of opera and ballet.
5. The young of the herring, or the sprat. A reference to the treatment of Larry Adler by the Un-American Activities Committee of the U.S. House of Representatives due to his left-wing political philosophy.
6. A remark made to some Western students encountered during a state visit to China in 1986.

Chapter 7

1. Mrs. Deaver.
2. *The Queen's Daily Life: An Artist's View* by Michael and Vivien Noakes (2000).
3. This requirement was done away with in November 1998, on the occasion of the Queen's Speech on the State Opening of Parliament. Some members of the House of Lords, however, observed the custom on that occasion, out of respect for the Queen.
4. In 1957, during President Eisenhower's state visit to Britain.
5. William Heseltine, private secretary.
6. President Nicolae Ceausescu (1918–89) was the General Secretary and President of Romania's Communist Party 1965 to 1989.
7. Forbes and his actress wife, Nanette Newman, met the Princess at the home of actor Peter Sellers.

8. English public (i.e., private) boys' school founded in memory of the Duke of Wellington.

9. An elegant San Francisco hotel noted for its old-world charm.

10. At a shipboard dinner in 1977, during the Silver Jubilee.

11. Commonwealth Heads of Government Meeting. South Africa left the Commonwealth in 1961 under Prime Minister Verwoerd to avoid being expelled due to its policy of apartheid and rejoined in 1994.

12. Daniel T. arap Moi, the president of Kenya.

13. The Progressive Conservative leader who became prime minister of Canada in 1984.

14. The Labor Party leader and prime minister of Australia.

15. Marcia Williams, although devoted to Prime Minister Harold Wilson, was widely disliked due to her overbearing manner and temper tantrums.

16. At a dinner during the Queens Silver Jubilee in 1977.

17. For U.S. President Reagan's state visit to Britain in 1982.

18. In 1977, during the Queen's Silver Jubilee.

19. Labour prime minister, 1976–79.

20. The farewell dinner for Prime Minister Wilson.

21. Leader of the Labour Party, 1980–83.

22. Satirical T.V. program among whose puppet caricatures the Royal Family were featured regularly.

Chapter 8

1. Victoria of Hesse (1863–1950), the daughter of Queen Victoria's second daughter, Princess Alice (1843–78), and Louis IV of Hesse (1837–92). Victoria of Hesse married Louis of Battenberg, First Marquess of Milford Haven (1854–1921). The Battenbergs' elder son, George, became the Second Marquess of Milford Haven, and their daughter, Alice, married Prince Andrew of Greece. Prince Philip is their son.

2. Weatherill & Sons, a tailoring establishment on Savile Row which specializes in military uniforms and is outfitter to the Royal Family.

3. The Declaration of Rights, 1689, which established William III and Mary II as joint sovereigns to replace the ousted Catholic James II, and forbade future monarchs to be or marry a Roman Catholic, a law which survives to this day.

4. The Rt. Hon. William Lyon Mackenzie King, of the Liberal Party, who served as prime minister of Canada for three terms: December 29, 1921—June 28, 1926; September 25, 1926—August 7, 1930; and October 23, 1935—November 15, 1948.

5. A county in northwest England, bordering on the Irish Sea.

6. British statesman (1836–1914) and the father of Sir Joseph Austen Chamberlain (1863–1937) and Arthur Neville Chamberlain, prime minister (1869–1940).

Chapter 9

1. Labour prime minister, 1924, 1929–31; and of coalition, 1931–35.
2. Following his trial and conviction for treason, the King was executed on January 30, 1649, on a block set up just outside a window of the northern annex of the Banqueting Hall of Whitehall Palace. The King's execution followed many years of struggle for power between himself and Parliament, which led to a seven-year civil war.
3. The public executioner was a man named Brandon.
4. 1826–77, author of standard reference work *English Constitution* (1867).
5. In 1977, during Mr. Jay's first audience with the Queen on being appointed ambassador of the Court of St. James's to the United States.
6. Value Added Tax.

Chapter 10

1. The White House was burned to a shell by the British in August 1814, during the War of 1812. As the fire spread through the building, the first lady, Dolley Madison, remained behind in order to rescue national treasures, including Gilbert Stuart's portrait of George Washington.
2. Harold Wilson served as prime minister twice, from 1964–70 and 1974–76, when he retired.
3. James Callaghan succeeded Harold Wilson as prime minister, serving from 1976–79.
4. Later Sir Alec Douglas-Home.
5. Baron Donahue, head of Harold Wilson's policy unit, 1974–76.
6. In Ben Pimlott's book *The Queen: A Biography of Queen Elizabeth II* (1996), the Queen is reported, on page 430, as having told Noakes on March 16, 1976, that she wasn't surprised at Wilson's resignation, saying: "I expected he'd go at about this point."
7. A symbolic distribution of charity by the Queen on Maundy Thursday, the day before Good Friday.
8. Published on July 20, 1986.

Chapter 11

1. James VI of Scotland, I of England, who reigned in England from 1603 to 1625.
2. Henry VIII (1509–47) was named "Defender of the Faith" by Pope Leo X for writing a book against Martin Luther.
3. In 2018, the Office for National Statistics said that, out of a total population of over 65 million, there are 3,372,966 Muslims, 336,965 Jews and 1,021,449 Hindus in the U.K. All denominations of Christians count for 33,111,246, and 23,725,080 have no faith. https://www.ons.gov.uk/aboutus/transparencyandgovernance/freedomofinformationfoi/muslimpopulationintheuk/

4. Lady Longford and her husband were practicing Catholics.
5. The government removed James II and invited William of Orange and Mary to assume the Throne.

Chapter 12

1. (1904–97), Communist leader of the People's Republic of China (1977–97).
2. During her 1991 state visit to the United States.

Chapter 13

1. The Picts originated in what is today Scotland. King Bridei, who lived in the sixth century (d. 584), was converted to Christianity by St. Columba, a missionary from central Ireland. St. Columba's biographer, Adomnan, would in the seventh century recount the missionary's observations about King Bridei's court.
2. In Northamptonshire.
3. In the late 1990s the Noakeses undertook a book, a year in the Queen's life, consisting of paintings made by Mr. Noakes as he followed the Queen in her pursuits, with text by Dr. Noakes.

Chapter 14

1. Caroline Alpass, who married Jeremy Thorpe in May 1968, was killed in a car crash in June 1970. The Thorpes had one son, Rupert, born in 1968.
2. Sir Gordon Jewkes was accompanied on this visit by his wife.
3. The Queen's annual address upon the State Opening of Parliament.
4. William Davis, a Conservative.
5. The new prime minister, while described as kissing hands on appointment, does not do so in the Palace ceremony, but later, in council.
6. Civil or political power, as distinguished from spiritual or ecclesiastical authority.
7. The ambassador was critically wounded by a terrorist in early June 1982, just days before Israel's invasion of South Lebanon in its Peace for the Galilee operation.
8. Lester Bowles Pearson was also a recipient of the Nobel Peace Prize, which he was awarded in 1957 while serving as Canada's minister for external affairs, for his work on behalf of the United Nations in resolving the 1956 Arab–Israeli War.
9. In 1976, during that year's Commonwealth Games.
10. In reference to the satirical Victorian operettas of W. S. Gilbert and Arthur Sullivan.
11. Prime Minister Macmillan's principal private secretary.

Chapter 15

1. Formerly known as Ellice Islands, and comprised of islands in the western Pacific, north of Fiji, Tuvalu as of the 1990s had a population of 10,000. In 2019 the population was estimated at 11,655 (https://data.worldbank.org/). Tuvalu became an independent member of the Commonwealth in 1978. The population of India was estimated at 1.366 billion in 2019 (https://data.worldbank.org/).
2. Mohandas Karamchand Gandhi. Born in 1869, the Indian nationalist leader known for his pacifist approach to independence was assassinated in 1948 by a Hindu extremist.
3. Jawaharlal Nehru (1889–1964) served as India's prime minister from 1947 to 1964. His daughter, Indira Gandhi—no relation to Mohandas Gandhi—born in 1917, would serve as prime minister for two terms, 1966–77 and 1980–84. She was assassinated in 1984, while still in office. Her son, Rajiv Gandhi, who succeeded her as prime minister, was assassinated in 1989.
4. (1876–1948), the Muslim political figure who served as Pakistan's first governor-general from 1947 until his death from cancer.
5. Nepalese soldiers in the British Army.
6. Baron General Hastings Lionel Ismay, 1887–1965.
7. Muhammad Ayub Khan (1907–74), president of Pakistan, 1958–69.
8. Jan Christiaan Smuts (1870–1950), South African field marshal; prime minister 1919–24 and 1939–48.
9. Daniel Francois Malan (1874–1959), editor; South African prime minister 1948–54.
10. Julius Kambarage Nyerere (1922–99), president of Tanganyika, 1962–64; and following the union of Tanganyika and Zanzibar, president of the Republic of Tanzania, 1964–85.
11. (1924–2021), president of Zambia, 1964–91.
12. (1923–2015), prime minister of Singapore, 1959–90.
13. (1898–1997), president of Malawi, 1966–94.
14. Antigua and Barbuda, Australia, the Bahamas, Barbados, Belize, Canada, Grenada, Jamaica, New Zealand, Papua New Guinea, St. Christopher-Nevis, St. Lucia, St. Vincent and the Grenadines, the Solomon Islands, and Tuvalu.
15. Rhodesia's white racist Unilateral Declaration of Independence in 1965 caused years of conflict within the Commonwealth.

Chapter 16

1. An apparent exception was the Queen's state visit to Mozambique in November 1999, immediately following the fiftieth Anniversary CHOGM, held November 12–14, 1999, in Durban, South Africa. At

that time, Mozambique's president Joaquim A. Chissano, the leader of FRELIMO [Frente de Libertacao de Mozambique], was running for re-election to his third term in office. On the Queen's arrival at Maputo Airport on November 15, 1999, the crowd greeting Her Majesty was packed with FRELIMO supporters clad in Party tee-shirts and carrying banners. Adherents of the opposition RENAMO [Resistencia Nacional de Mocambique] Party were nowhere to be seen.

2. A large, international Jewish fraternal organization.

3. (1841–1919), a Liberal, and the first French-speaking Canadian to become prime minister.

4. References, respectively, to the noun used collectively when speaking of Oxford and Cambridge universities, and to the British custom of having an elevated table in the dining hall of a college for use by the master and fellows of the college, as well as distinguished guests.

5. The Liberal Party leader in Quebec, elected premier there in 1960.

Chapter 17

1. Sir Robert Gordon Menzies, PC, CH, QC (1894–1978), who as the holder of that office from December 19, 1949, to January 26, 1966, was Australia's longest-serving prime minister. Warden of the Cinque Ports is an honorary post previously held by Sir Winston Churchill and subsequently by the Queen Mother.

2. Edward Gough Whitlam, QC, had become prime minister on May 12, 1972.

3. John Malcolm Fraser, PC, CH, AC, who was named prime minister on November 11, 1975, and was later elected in his own right, serving until November 3, 1983.

4. *Matters for Judgement: An Autobiography* (1979).

5. The first of thirteen visits through to April 2000.

6. Originally denoting an institution of Talmudic learning, but now more broadly defined as an Orthodox Jewish rabbinical seminary, or a Jewish day school providing both secular and religious instruction.

7. Australian journalist and statesman Herbert Vere Evatt (1894–1965).

8. Prime minister of Australia 1941–45, John Curtin (1885–1945).

9. John Paul Keating, prime minister of Australia, December 1991– November 1996.

10. John Howard, who assumed the office in November 1996.

11. The Australians' own, affectionate, nickname for themselves.

12. The governor-general's residence.

Chapter 18

1. Kwame Nkrumah (1909–72), prime minister of Ghana, 1957–60; president, 1960–66.

2. Ian Smith (1919–2007) as prime minister of Rhodesia issued a Unilateral

Declaration of Independence in 1965. He was able to maintain white minority rule until the election in 1979 of a black prime minister, Bishop Abel Muzorewa.

3. His premiership only lasted a few months. In 1980 Robert Mugabe (1924–2019) was swept to power and was prime minister of Zimbabwe 1980–1987 and president 1987–2017.

4. A leader of South Africa's notoriously racist Nationalist Party, who served as his nation's president from 1958–66.

5. The Labour Party leader.

6. Frente de Libertacao de Mozambique, the party of liberation from the then-ruling Portuguese.

7. The Queen did, however, meet privately later in the day with the leader of the opposition.

8. A Psion 7 Series mobile computer to the president, and an oval carriage clock from Garrards, an upscale London establishment, to Mrs. Chissano.

Chapter 19

1. Yitzhak Shamir, the prime minister of Israel during the period under discussion, had led the Stern Gang, a pre-State underground movement for independence from the United Kingdom—a fact still very much in the historical consciousness of many people in Britain.

Chapter 20

1. Jack Lynch, the taoiseach [prime minister], had been on holiday in Portugal at the time of Lord Mountbatten's assassination.

Chapter 21

1. On June 3 and 4, 1989, soldiers of the People's Liberation Army attacked pro-democracy demonstrators, many of them students, who had gathered in Beijing's Tiananmen Square.

Chapter 22

1. General Leopoldo Galtieri, president of Argentina 1981–82.

2. Captain Hector Bonzo. Of the believed total of the *General Belgrano*'s 1,042 crewmen, 368 died when the 13,645-ton ship was sunk on May 2, 1982. The *General Belgrano*, formerly the American World War II cruiser the *Phoenix*, had been at Pearl Harbor when the Japanese attacked on December 7, 1941, and was sold to Argentina in 1951.

3. The inhabitants of the 2,900 square miles of islands lying westernmost off the coast of Scotland, in the North Atlantic.

Chapter 23

1. Muggeridge suggested that many Britons "feel that another photograph of the Royal Family will be more than they can bear."
2. A reference to the more informal behavior of the Scandinavian and Dutch royal families.
3. Then the Queen's press secretary, Heseltine had been assistant press secretary under Commander Richard Colville since 1965 and assumed the post on Colville's resignation in early 1968.
4. Jonathan Dimbleby, *The Prince of Wales: A Biography* (1994).
5. Blake Publishing, Ltd., United Kingdom, 1999.

Chapter 24

1. Diana's grandmother, as well as five other female members of the Spencer family, had served the Queen Mother, and Earl Spencer had served as equerry to both King George VI and the present Queen.
2. When asked in that interview whether he was "in love," the Prince surprised some romantics when he said he supposed he was, "whatever in love means."
3. Ceaucescu (1918–89) was president of Romania from 1974 until December 25, 1989, when he and his wife were killed while prisoners of representatives of a new government that had deposed him.
4. In the fall of 1994, journalist and broadcaster Jonathan Dimbleby, author of *The Prince of Wales*, conducted a prepublication interview with the Prince on ITV, in which the Prince acknowledged his adultery with Camilla Parker Bowles.

Chapter 25

1. In which he referred to "the people's Princess."
2. *Grace*, G.P. Putnam's Sons, New York, 1994.
3. Which Mohamed Al Fayed now owns and has restored to its former grandeur. Dodi Fayed is reported to have taken Princess Diana to see the house while the couple were in Paris.
4. In a poll taken in August 1998, less than ten percent of the British population planned to personally commemorate the first anniversary of Princess Diana's death; less than half of the respondents agreed with the statement: "Diana was a woman with unique qualities, a true People's Princess"; and fifty-eight percent of those polled answered affirmatively when asked: "Is the Royal Family more in tune with the national mood?"

Chapter 26

1. Herbert Henry Asquith [1852–1928], the First Earl of Oxford and Asquith, introduced the Parliament Act, which abolished the Lords'

power to reject financial legislation and only permitted them to delay other legislation for three sessions,

2. The Scottish patriot (circa 1270–1305).
3. Labour M.P. and first elected mayor of London, in 2000, known for his radical left politics.

Chapter 27

1. The English poet Percy Bysshe Shelley (1792–1822), who died in Italy.
2. The Duke of Edinburgh and Princess Anne had taken issue publicly with Prince Charles's view on organic farming.
3. David Hicks, the interior decorator, known for his colorful designs.
4. On turning eighteen, Prince William paid tribute to his mother by incorporating a small red escallop shell from the Spencer coat-of-arms into his own, new coat-of-arms.

List of Interviewees

The page number in brackets after each name locates the biographical note; this is followed by the venue and date of the interview.

Ian Adams [10], London, October 18, 1999
Larry Adler [39], London, October 18, 1999
Sir Emeka Anyaoku [105], London, July 9, 1998
Lord Archer [99], London, July 7, 1998
Lord Armstrong [13], London, December 1, 1998
Archdeacon George Austin [12], York, July 7, 1999
Yehuda Avner [49], Jerusalem, December 20, 1998
Bishop Nicholas Baines [131], United Kingdom by Zoom, April 29, 2021
S. N. Bharadwaj [223], London, February 22, 2000
Sir Kenneth Bloomfield [12], Belfast, July 1, 1999
Lord Blunkett [121], United Kingdom by telephone, April 7, 2021
Rabbi Sidney Brichto [221], London, July 9, 1998
Andrew Burnham [102], United Kingdom by telephone, July 8, 2021
Lord Butler [98], United Kingdom by telephone, April 30, 2021
Imogen Campbell-Johnson [28], London, October 18, 1999
Lord Carrington [110], London, July 9, 1998
Anson Chan [122], Hong Kong, May 12, 2000
Lord Cholmondeley [102], London, May 20, 2000, and United Kingdom by telephone, June 2, 2021
Jean Chrétien [117], Canada by telephone, March 23, 2021
Winston Churchill [72], London, May 16, 2000
Elizabeth Ward Collins [283], London, February 25, 2000
Sir Zelman Cowen [150], Melbourne, May 5, 2000
Conor Cruise O'Brien [156], Dublin, December 9, 1999
Cardinal Cahal Daly [155], Belfast, June 30, 1999
Robert Davies [419], London, October 19, 1999
Stephen Day [55], London, December 9, 1998
Michael Deaver [105], Washington, D.C., September 16, 1999
Lord Desai [125], India by telephone, April 29, 2021
John Dixon [371], Belfast, July 1, 1999

Sir Edward du Cann [105], London, July 7, 1998

Anthony Eggleton [302], Canberra, May 3, 2000

John Eisenhower [37], Trappe, Maryland, September 1, 1999

Sir Peter Estlin [113], United Kingdom by telephone, May 27, 2021

Margaret Ewing [144], London, February 29, 2000

Mohamed Al Fayed [430], London, February 24, 2000

Lady Featherstone [101], United Kingdom by telephone, May 8, 2021

Lord Fitt [364], London, July 12, 1999

Garret Fitzgerald [26], Dublin, October 8, 1999

Bryan Forbes [69], London, May 17, 2000

Sir Edward Ford [5], London, October 22, 1999

Lord Glentoran [123], London, May 18, 2000

Gen. Andrew Goodpaster [14], Washington, August 18, 1999

Lady Greenfield [83], United Kingdom by Zoom, April 20, 2021

John Grigg [99], London, July 9, 1998

Joe Haines [92], Tunbridge, November 30, 1998

Earl of Harewood [16], London, July 5, 1999

Sir David Haslam [132], United Kingdom by telephone, June 1, 2021

Bob Hawke [301], Sydney, May 4, 2000

Ivan Head [96], Toronto, January 11, 2000

Tim Heald [11], London, December 10, 1998

Lord Healey [11], London, March 23, 1999

Lord Heseltine [130], United Kingdom by telephone, March 8, 2021

Lady Pamela Hicks [4], London, February 26, 2000

Lord Howard [97], United Kingdom by telephone, December 15, 2020

Lord Howe [100], London, December 9, 1998

Sir Rex Hunt [43], Sunningdale, March 24, 1999

Sir Bernard Ingham [52], London, November 26, 1998, and July 6, 1999, and United Kingdom by telephone, April 8, 2021

Peter Jay [22], Woodstock, Oxfordshire, December 4, 1998

Patrick Jephson [132], United States by telephone, May 12, 2021

Sir Gordon Jewkes [13], London, December 10, 1998

Philip Kaiser [33], Washington, September 15, 1999

Thomas Keneally [150], New York, April 19, 2000

Adnan Khashoggi [94], Cannes, July 19, 1999

Lord King [170], London, October 21, 1999, and United Kingdom by telephone, April 19, 2021

Robert Lacey [8], London, February 27, 2000

Adm. Sir Henry Leach [14], Wonston, Hampshire, July 11, 1999

Lady Longford [9], London, July 6, 1999

Lord Longford [147], London, February 23, 2000

Donald Macdonald [95], Toronto, January 11, 2000

Stuart Macintyre [149], Melbourne, May 8, 2000

Nelson Mandela [124], Johannesburg, November 17, 1999

Bishop Michael Mann [75], Eastington, Gloucestershire, July 6, 1998

Lady Mar [190], March 30, 1999

Sir Donald McKinnon [96], New Zealand by telephone, July 4, 2021

Lord McNally [82], London, December 11, 1998

Lord Merlyn-Rees [49], London, July 6, 1999

Bishop Hugh Montefiore [34], London, December 1, 1998

Eric Moonman [32], London, March 30, 1999

Baroness (Rabbi) Neuberger [98], United Kingdom by telephone, June 7, 2021

Michael Noakes [106], London, February 21, 2000

Vivien Noakes [10], London, February 21, 2000

Duke of Norfolk [30], London, July 7, 1999

Canon Paul Oestreicher [9], Coventry, July 9, 1999

Lady Angela Oswald [8], Norfolk, May 22, 2000

Sir Michael Oswald [10], Norfolk, May 22, 2000

Lord Ouseley [148], London, May 18, 2000

Rev. Ian Paisley [135], Belfast, October 7, 1999

Sir Michael Palliser [39], London, November 27, 1998

Michael Parker [3], Melbourne, May 5, 2000

S. A. Pasha [160], London, October 20, 1999

Geoffrey Pearson [108], Ottawa, January 26, 2000

Earl of Perth [26], London, July 14, 1999

Ben Pimlott [167], London, December 11, 1998

Lord Powell [64], London, July 7, 1998

Sir Shridath Ramphal [9], London, March 26, 1999

Claire Rayner [51], London, July 10, 1998

Lord Rees [70], London, July 5, 1999

Brig. Johnny Rickett [82], London, February 24, 2000

Sir Adam Ridley [78], London, March 30, 1999

Sir Malcolm Rifkind [78], London, July 13, 1999

Gordon Robertson [158], Ottawa, January 25, 2000

Harry Robinson [344], Canberra, May 2, 2000

Sir David Scott [18], London, March 29, 1999

Fr. Michael Seed [119], London, February 28, 2000

Hugh Segal [100], Montreal, January 27, 2000

Raymond G. H. Seitz [170], London, November 24, 1998

Sir Harold Smedley [269], Ferring, West Sussex, April 1, 1999
Sir David Smith [242], Canberra, May 2, 2000
Lord Steel [97], United Kingdom by Zoom, May 4, 2021
Jeremy Thorpe [26], London, March 29, 1999
Lord Thurlow [18], London, March 25, 1999
Lord Weatherill [146], London, February 22, 2000
Michael Whitlam [144], London, February 29, 2000
Adm. Sir Sandy Woodward [14], Twickenham, southwest London, February 21, 2000
Neville Wran [10], Sydney, May 4, 2000
Sir Oliver Wright [105], London, July 9, 1998
Lord Wright [11], London, March 31, 1999
Lady Young [4], London, July 8, 1999
Lord Younger [67], London, July 12, 1999
Philip Ziegler [11], London, March 25, 1999

And also

Alfonso, a limousine driver, enroute to Eastington, July 6, 1998
Taxi drivers, Belfast, June 30 to July 3, 1999

Abbreviations of Titles

AC	Companion of the Order of Australia
AK	Knight of the Order of Australia
AM	Member of the Order of Australia
AO	Office of the Order of Australia
Bt	Baronet
CB	Companion of the Order of Bath
CBE	Commander of the Order of the British Empire
CC	Companion of the Order of Canada
CD	Canadian Forces' Decoration
CFR	Commander of the Order of the Federal Republic
CH	Companion of Honour
CI	Imperial Order of the Crown of India
CM	Member of the Order of Canada
CMG	Companion of the Order of St. Michael and St. George
CNZM	Companion of the New Zealand Order of Merit
CON	Commander of the Order of the Niger
CVO	Commander of the Royal Victorian Order
DBE	Dame Commander of the Order of the British Empire
DL	Deputy Lieutenant
DSC	Distinguished Service Cross
FAHA	Australian Academy of the Humanities
FASSA	Academy of the Social Societies in Australia
FBA	Fellow of the British Academy
FRCP	Fellow of the Royal College of Physicians
FRCGP	Fellow of the Royal College of General Practitioners
FRS	Fellow of the Royal Society
FRSA	Fellow of the Royal Society of Arts
FRSC	Fellow of the Royal Society of Canada
FRSL	Fellow of the Royal Society of Literature
GBE	Knight/Dame Grand Cross of the British Empire
GBM	Grand Bauhinia Medal
GCB	Knight/Dame Grand Cross of the Order of Bath
GCMG	Knight/Dame Grand Cross of the Order of St. Michael and St. George

GCVO	Knight/Dame Grand Cross of the Royal Victorian Order
KB	Knight Commander of the Order of Bath
KBE	Knight Commander of the Order of the British Empire
KCB	Knight Commander of the Order of the Bath
KCVO	Knight Commander of the Royal Victorian Order
KG	Knight of the Garter
KSJT	Member of the Order of St. John
KT	Knight of the Thistle
LG	Lady of the Garter
LT	Lady of the Thistle
LVO	Lieutenant of the Royal Victorian Order
MBE	Member of the Order of the British Empire
MC	Military Cross, Missionaries of Charity
M.P.	Member of Parliament
MVO	Member of the Royal Victorian Order
OBE	Officer of the Order of the British Empire
OC	Officer of the Order of Canada
OCC	Member of the Order of the Caribbean Community
OE	Member of the Order of Excellence of Guyana
OM	Member of the Commonwealth Order of Merit
ONZ	Member of the Order of New Zealand
OOnt	Order of Ontario
PC	Privy Counselor
PPROI	Past President Royal Institute of Portrait Painters
RP	Member, Royal Society of Portrait Painters

Bibliographical Note

Our research was facilitated particularly by the following books and reference works:

Allison, Ronald, and Ridell, Sarah (editors), *The Royal Encyclopedia*, Macmillan Press, London, 1991.

Andersen, Christopher, *The Day Diana Died*, William Morrow and Company, New York, 1998.

Bradford, Sarah, *Elizabeth*, Riverhead Books, New York, 1966.

Campbell-Johnson, Alan, *Mission with Mountbatten*, New Age International Ltd., India, 1994.

Cannon, John, and Griffiths, Ralph, *The Oxford Illustrated History of the British Monarchy*, Oxford University Press, New York, 1988.

Coogan, Tim Pat, *The Troubles: Ireland's Ordeal 1966–96 and the Search for Peace*, Roberts Rinehart Publishers, Boulder, Colorado, 1997.

Dimbleby, Jonathan, *The Prince of Wales*, William Morrow and Company, New York, 1994.

Du Cann, Edward, *Two Lives*, Images Publishing, 1995.

Haines, Joe, *The Politics of Power*, Jonathan Cape, London, 1977.

Howe, Geoffrey, *Conflict of Loyalty*, Pan Books, London, 1995.

Judd, Denis, *Empire*, Basic Books, New York, 1996.

Keneally, Thomas, *The Great Shame and the Triumph of the Irish in the English-Speaking World*, Nan Talese, Doubleday, New York, 1999.

Lacey, Robert, *Majesty: Elizabeth II and the House of Windsor*, Harcourt Brace Jovanovich, New York, 1977.

Longford, Elizabeth, *Elizabeth R*, Weidenfeld & Nicolson, London, 1983.

Marshall, P. J. (editor), *The Cambridge Illustrated History of the British Empire*, Cambridge University Press, Cambridge, England, 1996.

Mercer, Derek (editor-in-chief), *Chronicle of the 20th Century*, Dorling Kindersley, London, 1995.

Middlebrook, Martin, *The Falklands War, 1982*, Penguin Books, London, 1987.

Pimlott, Ben, *The Queen*, Wiley and Sons, New York, 1997; and *Harold Wilson*, HarperCollins, London, 1993.

Seitz, Raymond, *Over Here*, Weidenfeld & Nicolson, London, 1998.

Thatcher, Margaret, *The Downing Street Years: 1979–90*, HarperPerennial, New York, 1993.

Williamson, David, *Brewer's British Royalty*, Cassell, London, 1996.

Whitaker's Concise Almanack, The Stationery Office, London, 1999, 2000.

Zeigler, Philip, *King Edward VIII*, Alfred Knopf, New York, 1991; and *Mountbatten*, Harper and Row, New York, 1986.

Photograph Permissions

Page 8

Top: PA Images / Alamy Stock Photo; middle: PA Images / Alamy Stock Photo; bottom: Keystone Press / Alamy Stock Photo.

Page 9

Top: Keystone Press / Alamy Stock Photo; middle: Trinity Mirror / Mirrorpix / Alamy Stock Photo; bottom: Everett Collection Inc / Alamy Stock Photo.

Page 10

Top: PA Images / Alamy Stock Photo; middle: PA Images / Alamy Stock Photo; bottom: Trinity Mirror / Mirrorpix / Alamy Stock Photo.

Page 11

Top: PA Images / Alamy Stock Photo; middle: PA Images / Alamy Stock Photo; bottom: Trinity Mirror / Mirrorpix / Alamy Stock Photo.

Page 12

Top: Trinity Mirror / Mirrorpix / Alamy Stock Photo; middle: REUTERS / Alamy Stock Photo; bottom: PA Images / Alamy Stock Photo.

Page 13

Top: Trinity Mirror / Mirrorpix / Alamy Stock Photo; middle: Trinity Mirror / Mirrorpix / Alamy Stock Photo; bottom: Trinity Mirror / Mirrorpix / Alamy Stock Photo.

Page 14

Top left: REUTERS / Alamy Stock Photo; top right: Independent / Alamy Stock Photo; bottom left: PA Images / Alamy Stock Photo; bottom right: PA Images / Alamy Stock Photo.

Page 15

Top: Raymond Tang / Alamy Stock Photo; middle: Tribune Content Agency LLC / Alamy Stock; bottom: PA Images / Alamy Stock Photo.

Page 16

PA Images / Alamy Stock Photo.

Acknowledgments

Queen Elizabeth II: The Oral History could not have been written without the participation of our interviewees, all of whom received us with unfailing courtesy, responded during interviews with candor, shared with us their personal recollections, and enlightened us through their wealth of knowledge of British history and constitutional issues.

We would like to express particular appreciation to the authors Tim Heald, Robert Lacey, Lady Longford, Ben Pimlott, and Philip Ziegler for graciously agreeing to be interviewed and for sharing insights gleaned from years of experience in writing about the Royal Family.

We also thank author Tom Keneally, and Harry Robinson, an old friend from his days in New York, for their valuable insights on Australia's people and politics.

In addition, we deeply appreciate the efforts on our behalf during the early stage of our work of Edward du Cann; Bernard Ingham; Charles Powell; and Oliver Wright; and in the U.S. Edwin Meese III and our friend Robert Shaheen.

While we did not seek official sanction from Buckingham Palace, the Queen's press secretary Geoffrey Crawford LVO and his associate Penny Russell-Smith LVO were at all stages of our project both encouraging and helpful, offering suggestions and assistance in arranging specific interviews.

In Britain, we were helped particularly by Peter Bursey of the Foreign and Commonwealth Office; Kaye Whitman and Cheryl Doral of the Commonwealth Secretariat; Patsy Robertson, who provided insight on Commonwealth leaders; and by Ginette Haiat and her very able staff. In New York, Janet Bacon gave us access to the British Information Services Library.

In Africa we were assisted by Charles Manning; by the press relations staff of the South African Foreign Ministry, including Thabang Chilone and his colleagues Mac and Sputnik; by Rusty Evans; and by Andrew Bowes, press and public affairs officer for the British High Commission in Maputo.

We also want to thank Salvador Adriano of the Embassy of Mozambique in Washington, D.C., who briefed us prior to our departure for Africa and provided press liaison for us during the Queen's visit to Maputo.

And how can we adequately express our appreciation to our agent and friend Aaron Priest and his helpful staff?

We also deeply appreciate the constant support and steadfast friendship of Abner Stein, our initial British agent, who believed in our project from its inception. We would like to express appreciation to Andrew Lownie, our agent for this edition.

Stephen Rubin, president and publisher of Doubleday Broadway, offered us an opportunity we could not refuse: to explore the feasibility of undertaking this challenge.

And we have been most fortunate in having marvelous editors: in New York, Eric Major, whose professional expertise, knowledge of the United Kingdom, friendly spirit, and enthusiasm made working on this project a special pleasure. And Margaret Body in Britain, whose knowledge of things royal is truly amazing, and who took on the formidable challenge of pruning our manuscript, as well as copy editing the text.

For the Hutchinson edition, it was a pleasure to work and become acquainted with the late Paul Sidey, whose enthusiasm for this book and determination to extend its reach to a larger readership buoyed our spirits anew.

We appreciate the vision of Hannah MacDonald, who developed the concept for this new edition and offered her enthusiastic support. Our sincere thanks go to Charlotte Cole, September Publishing's managing editor, for navigating the complexities involved in this updated work. We would also like to thank Kurtis Hetherington, Sue Amaradivakara, Ed Pickford, as well as Turnaround.

Lastly, we pay tribute to our remarkable children and their partners, Jeremy Benjamin and Silvanne Helle, Lori Sterling, Robin Strober, and Michelle Meyers, and to our loving grandchildren Ran and Eyal Benjamin and Marley and Kai Sterling, as well as to Dr. Mortimer Civan, the husband of our late sister Judith.